GOLDEN SHEAVES

GATHERED FROM THE FIELDS OF ANCIENT AND MODERN

LITERATURE.

A MISCELLANY OF

CHOICE READING

FOR THE ENTERTAINMENT OF THE OLD AND THE YOUNG

IN HOURS THAT ARE LONELY AND WEARY.

SELECTED AND ARRANGED

BY

H. A. CLEVELAND.

ZEIGLER, McCURDY & CO.,
PHILADELPHIA, PA.; CINCINNATI, OHIO;
CHICAGO, ILL.; ST. LOUIS, MO.

CONTENTS.

PREFACE.

THE author of this volume does not consider himself alone responsible for its existence. He had long thought, however, that such a work if judiciously compiled would fill a vacant place in our general literature, and had collected some materials with that object remotely in view. But his thought might never, and certainly would not so soon, have ripened, had not his enterprising publishers, several months ago, put in his hands a volume of "*Gathered Treasures*"—a book long since out of print, and although containing many beautiful gems, yet somewhat ancient in its general contents—and urged him to make it the basis of a new compilation which should be comprehensive in subject, just in sentiment, beautiful in expression, and while not ignoring the claims of antiquity, duly respectful of the interests of the present. They argued that while books of every sort were already numerous and rapidly increasing, many of them were costly, and some very excellent ones so rare, as to be found only in the great libraries; that many persons, as the young, the busy, and the aged, who have neither the time nor the patience necessary for the perusal of continuous or bulky volumes, would read short stories and elegant extracts with eagerness; that these would gladly improve the opportunity such a compilation affords, for obtaining some acquaintance with works not in their possession, and thus entertain themselves in a way beneficial to head and heart.

The author, yielding to the solicitation thus earnestly stated, has prepared this volume to meet the wants that seemed important and pressing, and in so doing has contented himself with simply binding under these green bands the selected products of some of the most eminent writers.

And now if "*Golden Sheaves*" shall carry one happier feeling, or purer thought, or higher aspiration, into a home dark with care, and to a heart weary with toil, or sad with loneliness, the desire of the gleaner will have been answered, while the kindness of those who have permitted him to wander through their richly laden fields and reap what they had sown, will be as nobly rewarded as it is hereby gratefully acknowledged.

H. A. C.

Philadelphia,
February 20*th*, 1869.

GOLDEN SHEAVES.

MORAL TALES AND SKETCHES.

YOUTH, BOOKS, LABOR, AGE.

For the most part, we studious men do not very clearly comprehend people who are simply practical; when called upon to classify them, we always start from our own individuality; we imagine that every one ought to resemble ourselves; we estimate the intelligence of our cook by his style of penmanship.

It is very rare that men are able to escape from the thraldom of their individual predilections, so as to throw themselves into the midst of the world of realities, and estimate individuals according to their aptitude for satisfying those realities. We all resemble M. Vestris more or less, who was astonished to hear that one of his old pupils, whom he could never teach to dance the gavotte, had become a great statesman. It seems as if each of us were inclined to set up his own habits and occupations as the standard measure of human capacity; hence the indignation which we see manifested when one of your vulgar practical men acquires fortune or influence. With what profound contempt we point the finger at such upstarts of action! what protestations there are against the state of society, when the grocer at the corner grows wealthy more surely and more rapidly than the artist, the professor, or the author! As if society lived only upon books, problems, or statues, and had not above all things need of the journeymen of life!—as if the most favored by nature ought also to be the most favored by man, and to find themselves fortunate here below, as kings are powerful "by the grace of God!"

How is it we do not perceive that this world is a vast machine produced by a superhuman hand, which has given to each part a duty and not a privilege? Wherefore should the proud wheels, which serve to regulate the motion, cast reproaches at the thousand steel cranks destined to receive it, or at the bronze which adorns them, and the oil which facilitates their efforts?

My daughter wrote to me lately that, as an opportunity offered, she should not wait for the holidays to send Blanche and Henry to me; but as it depended upon the person who was to take charge of them, she could not name beforehand the exact day of their arrival.

This morning I heard all of a sudden in the hall the fresh voices of two children; the door opened, and a little girl advanced, smiling, with a boy about a year younger than herself peeping from behind her; I divined at once who they were; my heart beat faster, but I waited in expectation.

The little girl came towards me somewhat timidly, and said: "Here we are, grandpapa!"

I opened my arms, and both the children ran forward to embrace me.

Their conductor stood in the hall where he could observe our affectionate greetings. At length he determined on entering, when he gave me the best account of them both, and after the warmest expression of thanks on my part, he retired.

Well, at last, then, I behold them, these dear blossoms from a stalk almost dried up. There they stand before me in all the verdure of their spring growth; I hold Blanche on my right side, Henry on my left, and press them thus against my bosom, with their sweet faces turned towards me, and their breath fanning my cheeks.

I scan their features in order to discover that family likeness which is, as it were, the everlasting re-birth of the old who die, in the young who survive. Both of them, no doubt, very soon felt how dear they were to me, for they grew familiar at once. Blanche leaned her curly head on my shoulder, whilst Henry played with the seals of my watch; then they began to chatter away freely. In one hour I had read through those young hearts where there was nothing for concealment.

Blanche, who is the elder, already assumes the character of protectress and counsellor; she admonishes Henry, she aids and excuses him. The sister from afar plays the part of mother. Henry, more ardent, rushes forward at a venture on every new path, but returns at the voice of Blanche; cries out to her, "I am here, fear nothing!" and starts off again. The boy is striving to become the man.

Our renewed acquaintance being thus made, I presented them both to Mr. Baptiste, who saluted them with his customary formal bow; I explained that he would treat them just as they treated him, and Mr. Baptiste confirmed my words. The two children looked at his grave face with some wonderment, and hardly knew if they ought to feel afraid or the reverse; but habit will set all right; the birds soon grow bold enough to build their nests in the sombrest trees. . . .

I was sure of it; Blanche, Henry, and Mr. Baptiste live very comfortably together, although a little ceremoniously. Father Labat relates that, in his time, when the Spanish soldiers relieved guard, they bowed to each other before exchanging the password, and asked most politely after each others' welfare. I am witness every morning to a similar spectacle, when for the first time the children and Mr. Baptiste encounter each other.

After all, I like these acts of politeness, even when carried to excess; they habituate us to respect others, and to maintain dominion over ourselves. It is said that politeness is the make-pretence for real kindness of heart, in which case rudeness must be the make-pretence for aversion; now, mask for mask, I prefer that which smiles on me to that which inspires disgust. There is, besides, something more in politeness than the mere appearance; it is, as its name indicates, a certain *polish* in our habits and manners, thanks to which the spring-wheels of life meet together without abrasion.

So everything goes on at home wonderfully well; no quarrels, no complaints. The house has resumed its former bustle; here on the chimney-piece is some crochet work just begun; the piano is again heard; the merry laughter of children has interrupted the staid silence of old age and the widower's home; I hear little feet running about the empty and long deserted rooms, and I repeat half aloud the sweet lines of a poet whom I have the happiness to understand, although he lived before my era:

> "Preserve me, Lord, preserve my kindred and my friends,
> And even those whose bitter hatred condescends
> To mock at my distress.
> From ever seeing, Lord, the summer without flowers,
> The cage without a bird, the hives all empty in the bowers,
> The home no children bless!"

Twenty times a day Blanche or Henry just opens the door of the little room which I occupy, peeps in, and says, softly

"Are you busy, grandpapa?"

I turn toward them with a smile, and beckon them in. One of the advantages at my time of life, as I have already explained, is that I am always at leisure to give audience to joy. Blanche, after kissing me, remains most frequently leaning against my shoulder without speaking; it is evident that she has come simply to be near me—not to be alone—to feel herself beloved; whereas Henry stands forward and questions me; he, for his part, begins to observe and wishes to acquire information. I yield, and reply to his questions, I return his sister's caresses, I am all things to them both, without objection, and without reserve. My tenderness is restrained by no scruples, for I have not, in their case, as formerly with my own son and daughter, the responsibility of their education. Withdrawn from action, the grandfather has not time left to undertake such duties: he is in the vacation of life, and has the privilege of asking children only for their smiles and their kisses. Let others, in their turn, watch over the class with eye severe, he resembles henceforth only the ancient tree, which yields a grateful shade for the hours of recreation.

Sweet and tender privilege! Old age thus relieves us of a weight of responsibility. Whilst others, with the balance of justice in their hands, estimate the quality of action and redress wrongs, we, elevated into the serene sphere which separates the two worlds, join the rank of those princes to whom a constitutional fiction has left only the prerogative of mercy; we reign, but we do not govern.

Henry did not wish entirely to suspend his course of study; he works daily for some hours, and one of these mornings he brought me the Eclogues of Virgil, begging me to translate for him two lines which he could not understand.

My explanation no doubt satisfied him, for he shortly returned with the history of Justinian, and then with one of Cicero's essays. Insensibly our consultations merged into a veritable course of instruction, and now for three days past I have become an improvised teacher, turning over once more the leaves of my schoolday authors.

I can hardly describe the effect they have had upon me! My memory rushes back across their metaphors and their trains of thought, like a wanderer returning again to his native place after an absence of half a century. I recollect myself by degrees; a thousand images return; I hear again the tones once so familiar. The history of my childhood rises up, chapter by chapter, between the pages of these old volumes. I see myself again at the farther end of the dark schoolroom, with its wooden benches, and tables smeared with ink. I hear the monotonous voice of our schoolmaster in his college gown, as he murmurs from behind the shadow of his desk. Two long lines of pupils stand there, ranged against the wall; I recognize their features one after the other, and my thoughts involuntary follow them into the busy world beyond, where I rapidly survey their histories, now, alas! for the most part brought to a close.

But there is one face, above all the rest, especially impressed upon my mind, which this volume of Eclogues has recalled. In turning over the last pages, I caught sight, on the pasteboard cover, of a name almost obliterated. It is that of my first schoolboy companion, of that schoolmate with whom one shares everything—hopes, blows, jealousies, and pots of preserve. Cherished for his sake, and transferred successively from my son to my grandson, this book seems brought back before my eyes, to reproach me with my long forgetfulness of its first master.

I fancy, indeed, that I see him again crossing our playground for the first time, led by his mother—a poor woman with pale face and stooping shoulders, clad in widow's mourning. Although he was even then tall, he held her band from the still remaining habit of infancy, and we, who had interrupted our games to look at the "new boy," exchanged derisive smiles. Observing the care bestowed, down to the minutest details, on the dress of our new schoolfellow, the elegance of his manner, and the solicitude visible in every movement of his mother, who seemed to guard him as a treasure, the scapegrace of our division cried out, "Oh, here comes the Dauphin!"* and he was never known amongst us by any other name afterwards.

But the spirit of raillery which had thus maliciously christened him, after the manner of the wicked fairies in the story-book, was destined to fail like them. The natural goodness of the lad vanquished his evil god-mother; the nickname intended to make him ridiculous, clung to him indeed, but harmlessly, and his gentleness ended in drawing from the sarcasm its sting.

Poor Dauphin! how well he knew how to atone to us for his respect towards his masters, by complaisance towards his schoolfellows. When at times the recollection of his mother came upon him too forcibly, and he went down to walk by himself in the shadow of the high wall which enclosed our grounds, how at the first summons he dried his moistened cheek; how he ran up, smiling and eager, to join in the first game proposed!

But then what attention he displayed at the class when the tutor spoke! What devoton to study! There was not a single slip of memory, not a single case of negligence, not a solitary lie! At the end of each half year he carried off all the prizes, and none of us thought of envying him, so well he seemed to have deserved them; we said: "They are for the Dauphin;" as we might have said: "The rivers are for the ocean."

He himself displayed neither ambition nor vanity, but the desire only of gratifying his mother; it was she alone whom they virtually crowned on his brow. Every year she was present at the distribution of prizes, dressed in the same mourning habits. She and her son had become the greatest objects of interest and pride on these occasions; the school, in fact, had adopted them both. When the celebration was over, the Dauphin left us, loaded with books and chaplets, and sustaining on

* The title of the heir-apparent to the French throne under the monarchy.

one arm the widow trembling with happiness: every eye followed them; we loved them for so loving each other.

Six years passed thus; the end of the last term approached, and at the same time the period of our separation. My schoolmate never spoke of it, but he redoubled his efforts; it was evident that he wished his leaving school might be for his mother the end of all her trials. To accomplish his purpose, it was necessary that he should pass with sufficient distinction to ensure a career being at once opened to him; hopes of this had already been held out, and in order to merit it, he no longer joined us during the hours of recreation; he prolonged his studies into the middle of the night, he resumed them with the first rays of the sun.

One day, however, he did not come down-stairs. We went to inquire for him. He was not able to leave his bed, where he lay suffering from an attack of fever. Our doctor had already paid his morning visit, and he was not again sent for that day; we waited in the hope that a little repose would be all that was necessary for the invalid; but by the evening his cheeks were deep scarlet, his breath burning hot, and his eyes sparkling; the next day he no longer recognized us.

Every care was now lavished on him, but in vain. The delirium of the Dauphin only increased; he fancied himself before his tutors, and repeated aloud the recent lessons he had learned. At certain moments his memory failed him, when his features would contract, his hand press convulsively against his forehead, his eyes assume a fixed and agonized expression of doubt; then by an effort of will which seemed to survive in him, he recovered the lost thread, and began his interrupted recitations once more.

At other times he fancied himself to be undergoing some important examination which was to decide his fate: he replied to imaginary questions, and translated aloud the required passages, commenting on them with painful hesitation. His schoolfellows came one after the other to his bedside, and retired, bowing their heads, and with troubled hearts; all hope was evidently gone.

I had obtained leave not to quit my companion's side, and watched the rapid progress of that delirious attack. Soon his vital powers declined, and the sufferer lay still; he repeated now indistinctly and with enfeebled voice some lines of Virgil, whose writings he was particularly fond of. It appeared to me as if all the rest—poets, orators, historians—had deserted the dying boy, and the peasant of Mantua alone remained, breathing into his ear some melodious fragments of his verse, like a mother singing her child to sleep. In the ebb and flow of the wandering thoughts which passed through his agonized brain, each muttered line seemed an allusion, or a passing souvenir,

Sometimes a sweet scene of his childhood welled up in that final dream, and he repeated quite low:

> Alter ab undecimo tam me jam ceperat annus,
> Jam fragiles potuam a terrâ contingere ramos.*

Then a tenderer recollection succeeded, a gentle face passed vaguely before his half-closed eyes, his lips just gave trembling utterance to the well-known line:

> Incipe parve puer, risu cognoscere matrem.†

And as I bent over him in the effort gently to impose silence, he resumed in a louder tone:

> Cantantes licet usque (minus via lædat) eamus.‡

But almost immediately afterwards seized with sudden weakness, he re-closed his heavy eyelids, and his voice died away, whispering the poet's farewell:

> Surgamus; solet esse gravis contantibus umbra.§

These were the last words I could distinguish. The sufferer relapsed afterwards into that convulsive drowsiness which precedes the final separation; another night passed, but the following morning his breathing insensibly grew fainter and fainter, and when the doctor came, all was over.

The entire college followed the corpse to its final abode. It was the first time I had seen any one put into the earth whose hands I had clasped—whom I had known full of life like myself. The smallest details are still present to my mind. The day was bright and cold; the fields recently ploughed, and streaked with snow, had the appearance of an immense black pall fringed with white tassels; the priests walked in front chanting the funeral service; between each verse there was a pause, and then the only sounds heard were those made by our footsteps on the frozen snow. At length we reached the cemetery. The coffin was laid beside the grave, and whilst the gravediggers consulted together in a low voice, there was rather a long interval in the service. I looked into the dark pit where the companion of my studies and my sports was about to disappear; a little bird suffering from the cold chirped plaintively a few yards off on the leafless branch of a weeping willow. As far as my eyes wandered I could see only graves half buried under the snow, or leaning crosses from which icicles hung down like falling tears; until then I had remained firm; but that mingling of cold, sorrow, and death, made me shudder; I felt my heart swell, and hurried back to join the ranks behind. The noise of the coffin, as it struck the sides of the grave in its descent, made me return in spite of myself; I heard the earth rattling down,

* I was just entering my twelfth year, and was able now to reach with my fingers the fragile branches.

† Begin, little one, to recognize thy mother with a smile.

‡ Let us go forward singing; songs shorten the way.

§ Let us arise; the mists are fatal to those who sing.

and saw the bearers draw out the ropes which creaked under the weight of the coffin; then the priests raised their voices again, the last benediction was spoken over the departed, and the gravediggers began to shovel in the earth upon the coffin, whilst we passed round the opening one after the other.

At the moment of my reaching the grave-side, one end of the coffin only was visible; it seemed to me, on looking down into the grave, as if the dead had made an effort within the oaken envelope to rise from his funeral bed. I gave a start, and in the agitation my foot stumbled; I should have fallen into the pit, still only partly filled up, but for an arm which held me back. It was that of our excellent master.

"Take care!" said he, with mournful tenderness; "one is enough, and more than we can spare!"

Then, turning towards the coffin, which had now nearly disappeared, he slowly uncovered his gray head, and addressed to him whom we were never to see again, in the language he knew so well, the exclamation of the gladiators in the imperial Circus:

Morituri te salutant.*

The following days were full of sadness. When the Dauphin was with us, few thought about him; but now he had disappeared, all eyes seemed to seek his form. His single unoccupied seat attracted more attention, than all the other seats with their occupants put together.

I especially could not reconcile myself to his absence—it took very many days to accomplish that; at last, Time performed his usual office. Nearly a month had passed; a new comer occupied the place of the departed, we had all resumed our usual habits, when one day, during our play-hour which followed dinner, a few words passed rapidly from the nearest boy to his next companion, and pronounced only in a whisper, startled us like a sudden cry:

"The mother of the Dauphin! The mother of the Dauphin!"

All our games were stopped, and every eye was turned in the same direction. The widow crossed our playground, clad as usual in mourning, but paler and more bent down. Behind her walked the college porter carrying all her son's relics: his books, his violin, and some portfolios filled with his manuscripts. The poor woman turned round each moment to look at her mournful treasures, afraid less she might still lose them. As she passed near us she paused, her eyes wandered down our ranks as if hoping to discover some more vivid traces of her son; she seemed to look for what could best recall him to her, to seek in the spots where he was accustomed to wander, those amongst us who were his favorites.

At one moment I thought she was about to speak to us, sac

* Those about to die, salute thee!

had made a step towards the group where I was standing, but the effort was doubtless too great; she turned away suddenly, drew down her black veil, and rapidly crossed the court.

We followed her with our eyes until she was lost in the distance, then looked at each other, and separated without saying a word.

Alas! a few years before we had all seen her cross the same spot, holding in her hand the boy whom she had only weaned from her bosom, to nourish with her tenderness; we had seen her return on six anniversaries to rejoice in his triumph. Too confiding mother, she had lavished on the college the fruit of her sufferings and watchings, her past sacrifices and her future hopes, and the college gave her back only a few books without a master, and the inscription on a tomb.

This incident, which recurred to me on taking up the familiar volume of Virgil, and turning over its leaves with my grandson, led me to reflect on my own history. I thought that I, too, might have died just when the difficulties of early study had terminated, and the period of action was about to commence. Poets, no doubt, might have envied my falling thus asleep in the morning of life, with my hands full of flowers, and revelling in all the illusions of youth; sweet and attractive end! But I, O my God! who have ever regarded Thy creation with love, I give Thee thanks for having prolonged my life to derive enjoyment from it. Let others be enamored of death, I bless Thee for length of life. I bless Thee also that Thou hast enabled me equally to experience the enchantments of youth, the throes of temptation, and the calm joy of victory in the fulfilment of duty. To die at the commencement of existence is to stop at the very threshold of our journey with pilgrim-staff in hand. Others pass onward with songs; they talk of mighty rivers, of marvellous cities, of smiling countries before them, but as for us, a fatal hand draws us back; a voice says to us: "These thou shalt never see." I myself, however, have seen them; I have perused all the stanzas of that epic poem of which so many others know but the preface; I have followed my course here below even to the goal, forcing myself to brave in turn the rain and the sunshine, and not to forget my life's purpose when enjoying grateful shelter; so that I repeat sometimes to myself with humble satisfaction, the verses of a modern poet on the destiny of man:

Possessor of a field he holds no lease,
Weary, though strong from healthful plough and flail,
The peasant seeks his cottage in the vale;
When night descends he falls asleep in peace.

Let us, too, ponder on the day's decline,
Thy laborers, O God! sent here below
To reap the harvest difficult and slow
Which the soul yields—to be accounted thine.

Let us plough deep into the ungrateful soil;
Sow seed that richly shall repay our toil;
 Far from the honest grain cast forth the thorn.
O, fellow-workers! while day yet remains
Let us fulfil our task so full of pains,
 That we may sweetly sleep until the eternal morn.*

But is it true that the task is so full of pain? Does the laborer of whom the poet speaks, really find in his work only weariness and vexation of spirit? Has he not also the freshness of the dawn, the repose at noontide beneath his fruit-trees, the bread doubly enjoyed by the hedge-side in presence of his ripening harvest, and at the hour of his return home the women's songs mingled with the laughter of children? If his home is to-day lonely like mine, the recollections of youth may still dwell there—smiling sylphs, who in invisible circles sing around his hearth. No! no! God has not made life too burdensome for us to support; there is enough of gladness bestowed to lighten its duties; hence, when we shall appear before Him, let us not imagine that it will suffice to answer, like the man who, when asked what he had been doing during the great Revolution, replied, "Nothing; I have lived."—*Emile Souvestre.*

THE TOOLS GREAT MEN WORK WITH.

It is not tools that make the workmen, but the trained skill and perseverance of the man himself. Indeed it is proverbial that the bad workman never yet had a good tool. Some one asked Opie by what wonderful process he mixed his colors. "I mix them with my brains, sir," was his reply. It is the same with every workman who would excel. Ferguson made marvellous things—such as his wooden clock, that accurately measured the hours—by means of a common penknife, a tool in everybody's hand, but then everybody is not a Ferguson. A pan of water and two thermometers were the tools by which Dr. Black discovered latent heat; and a prism, a lens, and sheet of pasteboard, enabled Newton to unfold the composition of light and the origin of color. An eminent foreign *savant* once called upon Dr. Wollaston, and requested to be shown over his laboratories, in which science had been enriched by so many important discoveries, when the doctor took him into a study, and, pointing to an old tea-tray on the table, containing a few watch glasses, test-papers, a small balance, and a blow-pipe, said, "There is all the laboratory I have!" Stothard learnt the art of combining colors by closely studying butterflies' wings; he

* From a volume of Sonnets by Boulay-Paty, which received a prize from the French Academy.

would often say that no one knew what he owed to these tiny insects. A burnt stick and a barn-door served Wilkie in lieu of pencil and canvas. Bewick first practised drawing on the cottage-walls of his native village, which he covered with his sketches in chalk; and Benjamin West made his first brushes out of the cat's tail. Ferguson laid himself down in the fields at night in a blanket, and made a map of the heavenly bodies, by means of a thread with small beads on it, stretched between his eye and the stars. Franklin first robbed the thunder-cloud of its lightning by means of a kite made with two cross-sticks and a silk handkerchief. Watt made his first model of the condensing steam-engine out of an old anatomist's syringe used to inject the arteries previous to dissection. Gifford worked his first problem in mathematics, when a cobbler's apprentice, upon small scraps of leather, which he beat smooth for the purpose, while Rittenhouse, the astronomer, first calculated eclipses on his plow-handle.—*Smiles' Self Help.*

LIVE NOT TO YOURSELF.

BY REV. J. TODD.

On the frail little stem in the garden hangs the opening rose. Go ask why it hangs there. "I hang here," says the beautiful flower, "to sweeten the air which man breathes, to open my beauties, to kindle emotion in his eyes, to show him the hand of his God, who penciled each leaf and laid them thus on my bosom. And whether you find me here to greet him every morning, or whether you find me on the lone mountain side, with the bare possibility that he will throw me one passing glance, my end is the same. I live not to myself."

Beside yon highway stands an aged tree, solitary and alone. You see no living thing near it, and you say surely that must stand for itself alone. "No," says the tree, "God never made me for a purpose so small. For more than a hundred years I have stood here. In summer I have spread out my arms and sheltered the panting flocks which hastened to my shade. In my bosom I have protected and concealed the brood of young birds, as they lay and rocked in their nest in the storm. I have more than once received in my body the lightning's bolt, which had else destroyed the traveler; the acorns which I have matured from year to year, have been carried far and near, and groves of forest trees can claim me as their parent. I have lived for the eagle, which has perched upon my top; for the humming bird, that has paused and refreshed its giddy wing ere it danced away again like a blossom of the air; for insects that have found a home within the folds of my bark; and when I stand no longer, I shall fall by the hand of man, and shall go to strengthen the ship which makes him lord of the ocean, and to his dwelling to warm his hearth and cheer his home. I live not to myself."

On yonder mountain see comes down the silver brook, in the distance resembling a ribbon of silver, running and leaping as it dashes joyously and fearlessly down. Go ask the leaper what it is doing. "I was born," says the brook, "high up the mountain; but there I could do no good: so I hurried down, running where I can, and leaping where I must; but hastening down to water the sweet valley—where the lark may sing on my margin, and where I may drive the mill for the accommodation of man, and then widen into a great river, and bear up his steamboats and shipping, and finally plunge into the ocean, to rise again in mist, and perhaps come back again in the clouds to my own native mountain, and live my first life over again. Not a drop of water comes down my channel, in whose face you may not read, 'None of us liveth to himself.'"

Speak now to that solitary star that hangs in the far verge of heaven, and ask the bright sparkler what it is doing there. Its voice comes down the path of life, and cries: "I am a mighty world. I was stationed here at the creation. I was among the morning stars that sung together, and among the sons of God that shouted for joy at the creation of the earth. Aye, aye, I was there—

'When the radiant morn of creation broke,
And the world in the smile of God awoke,
And the empty realms of darkness and death
Were moved through their depths by his mighty breath,
And the orbs of beauty and spheres of flame
From the void of abyss by myriads came,
In the joy of youth, as they darted away
Through the widening waste of space to play,
Their silver voices in chorus rung,
And this was the song that the bright ones sung.'"

And thus God has written upon the flower that sweetens the air, upon the breeze that rocks the flower upon its stem, upon the raindrops that swell the mighty river, upon the dew-drop that refreshes the smallest sprig of moss that rears its head in the desert, upon the ocean that rocks every swimmer in its channel, upon every penciled shell that sleeps in the caverns of the deep, as well as upon the mighty sun which warms and cheers the millions of creatures that live in his light—upon all has he written, "None of us liveth to himself."

And if you will read this lesson in characters still more distinct and striking, you will go to the garden of Gethsemane, and hear the Redeemer in prayer, while the angel of God strengthens him. You will read it on the hill of Calvary, where a voice that might be the concentrated voice of God, proclaims that the highest, noblest deed which the Infinite can do is to do good to others,—live not to himself.

THE TEMPEST.

BY GEORGE D. PRENTICE.

I WAS never a man of feeble courage. There are few scenes either of human or elemental strife upon which I have not looked with a brow of daring. I have stood in the front of the battle when swords were gleaming and circling around me like fiery serpents of the air—I have sat on the mountain pinnacle, when the whirlwind was rending its oaks from their rocky cliffs, and scattering them piece-meal to the clouds—I have seen these things with a swelling soul, that knew not, that recked no danger; but there is something in the thunder's voice that makes me tremble like a child. I have tried to overcome the unmanly weakness—I have called pride to my aid—I have sought for moral courage in the lessons of philosophy—but it avails me nothing—at the first low moaning of the distant cloud, my heart shrinks, quivers, gasps, and dies within me.

My involuntary dread of thunder had its origin in an incident, that occurred when I was a boy of ten years. I had a little cousin—a girl of the same age with myself, who had been the constant companion of my childhood. Strange, that after the lapse of so many years, that countenance should be so familiar to me. I can see the bright, young creature—her large eyes flashing like a beautiful gem, her free locks streaming as in joy upon the rising gale, and her cheeks glowing like rubies through a wreath of transparent snow. Her voice had the melody and joyousness of a bird's, and when she bounded over the wooded hill or the fresh green valley, shouting a glad answer to every voice of nature, and clapping her little hands in the very ecstacy of young existence, she looked as if breaking away like a freed nightingale from the earth, and going off where all things are beautiful and happy like her.

It was a morning in the middle of August. The little girl had been passing some days at my father's house, and she was now to return home. Her path lay across the fields, and I gladly became the companion of her walk. I never knew a summer morning more beautiful and still. Only one little cloud was visible, and that seemed as pure, and white, and peaceful, as if it had been the incense smoke of some burning censor of the skies. The leaves hung silent in the woods, the waters in the bay had forgotten their undulations, the flowers were bending their heads as if dreaming of the rainbow and dew, and the whole atmosphere was of such a soft and luxurious sweetness that it seemed a cloud of roses, scattered down by the hands of Peri, from the afar-off gardens of Paradise. The green earth and the blue sea lay abroad in their boundlessness, and the peaceful sky bent over and blessed them. The little creature at my side was in a delirium of happiness, and her clear, sweet voice came ringing upon the air as often as she heard the tones of a favorite bird, or found some strange and lovely flower in her frolic wanderings.

The unbroken and almost supernatural tranquility of the day continued until near noon. Then for the first time the indications of an approaching tempest were manifest. Over the summit of a mountain at the distance of about a mile, the folds of a dark cloud became suddenly visible, and at the same instant, a hollow roar came down upon the winds, as if it had been the sound of waves in a rocky cavern. The cloud rolled out like a banner folded upon the air, but still the atmosphere was as calm, and the leaves as motionless as before, and there was not even a quiver upon the sleeping waters to tell of the coming hurricane.

To escape the tempest was impossible. As the only resort, we fled to an oak that stood at the foot of a tall and rugged precipice. Here we remained and gazed almost breathlessly upon the clouds marshalling themselves like bloody giants in the sky. The thunder was not frequent, but every burst was so fearful that the young creature who stood by me shut her eyes convulsively, clung with desperate strength to my arm, and shrieked as if her very heart would break.

A few minutes and the storm was upon us. During the height of its fury, the little girl lifted her finger towards the precipice that towered above us. I looked up, and the next moment the clouds opened, the rocks tottered to their foundations, a roar like the groan of the universe filled the air, and I felt myself blinded, and thrown I knew not whither. How long I remained insensible I cannot tell, but, when consciousness returned, the violence of the tempest was abating, the roar of the winds was dying in the tree tops, and the deep tones of the thunder-cloud came in fainter murmurs from the eastern hills.

I arose and looked tremblingly and almost deliriously around. She was there—the dear idol of my infant love—stretched out on the green earth. After a moment of irresolution, I went up and looked upon her. The handkerchief upon her neck was slightly rent, and a single dark spot upon her bosom told where the pathway of her death had been. At first I clasped her to my breast with a cry of agony, and then laid her down, and gazed upon her face almost with a feeling of calmness. Her bright, disheveled ringlets, clustered sweetly around her brow, the look of terror had faded from her lips, and infant smiles were pictured beautifully there; the red-rose tinge upon her cheeks was lovely as in life, and as I pressed it to my own, the fountains of tears were opened, and I wept as if my heart were waters. I have but a dim recollection of what followed—I only know that I remained weeping and motionless till the coming of twilight, and I was then taken tenderly by the hand and led away where I saw the countenance of parents and sister.

Many years have gone by on the wings of light and shadow, but the scenes I have portrayed still come over me, at times, with a terrible distinctness. The oak yet stands at the base of the precipice, but its limbs are black and dead, and the hollow trunk, looking upwards to the sky, as "if calling to the clouds for drink," is an emblem of rapid and noiseless decay. A year ago I visited the spot, and the thoughts of by-gone years came mournfully back to me—thoughts of the little innocent being who fell by my side like some beautiful tree of spring, rent up by the whirlwind in the midst of its blossoming. But I remembered—and oh! there was joy in the memory!—that she had gone where no lightnings slumber in the folds of the rainbow-cloud, and where the sunlit waters are broken only by the storm-breath of Omnipotence.

My readers will understand why I shrink in terror from the sound of thunder. Even the consciousness of security is no relief to me—my fears have assumed the nature of an instinct, and seem indeed a part of my existence.

BATTLE OF BUNKER HILL.

BY J. FENIMORE COOPER.

The whole scene now lay before them. Nearly in their front was the village of Charlestown, with its deserted streets, and silent roofs, looking like a place of the dead; or, if the signs of life were visible within its open avenues, 'twas merely some figure moving swiftly in the solitude, like one who hastened to quit the devoted spot. On the opposite point of the south-eastern face of the peninsula, and at the distance of a thousand yards, the ground was already covered by masses of human beings, in scarlet, with their arms glittering in a noon-day sun. Between the two, though in the more immediate vicinity of the silent town, the rounded ridge, already described, rose abruptly from a flat that was bounded by the water, until, having attained an elevation of some fifty or sixty feet, it swelled gradually to the little crest, where was planted the humble object that had occasioned all this commotion. The meadows, on the right, were still peaceful and smiling, as in the most quiet days of the province, though the excited fancy of Lionel imagined that a sullen stillness lingered about the neglected kilns in their front, and over the whole landscape, that was in gloomy consonance with the approaching scene. Far on the left, across the waters of the Charles, the American camp had poured forth its thousands to the hills; and the whole population of the country, for many miles inland, had gathered to a point, to witness a struggle charged with the fate of their nation. Beacon Hill rose from out the appalling silence of the town of Boston, like a pyramid of living faces, with every eye fixed on the fatal point; and men hung along the yards of the shipping, or were suspended on cornices, cupolas, and steeples, in thoughtless security, while every other sense was lost in the absorbing interest of the sight. The vessels of war had hauled deep into the rivers, or, more properly, those narrow arms of the sea, which formed the peninsula, and sent their iron missiles with unwearied industry across the low passage, which alone opened the means of communication between the self-devoted yeomen on the hill and their distant countrymen. While battalion landed after battalion on the point, cannon-balls from the battery of Copp's, and the vessels of war, were glancing up the natural glacis that surrounded the redoubt, burying themselves in its earthen parapet, or plunging with violence into the deserted sides of the loftier hight which lay a few hundred yards in its rear; and the black and smoking bombs appeared to hover about the spot, as if pausing to select the places in which to plant their deadly combustibles.

Notwithstanding these appalling preparations, and ceaseless annoyances, throughout that long and anxious morning, the stout husbandmen on the hill had never ceased their steady efforts to maintain, to the uttermost extremity, the post they had so daringly assumed. In vain the English exhausted every means to disturb their stubborn foes; the pick, the shovel and the spade continued to perform their offices, and mound rose after mound, amidst the din and danger of the cannonade, steadily, and as well as if the fanciful conceits of Job Pray embraced their real objects, and the laborers were employed in the peaceful pursuits of their ordinary lives. This firmness, however, was not like the proud front which high training can impart to the most common mind; for, ignorant of the glare of military show; in the simple and rude vestments of their calling; armed with such weapons as they had seized from the hooks above their own mantels; and without even a banner to wave its cheering folds above their heads, they stood, sustained only by the righteousness of their cause, and those deep moral principles, which they had received from their fathers, and which they intended this day should show were to be transmitted untarnished to their children. It was afterwards known, that they endured their labors and their dangers even in want of that sustenance, which is so essential to support animal spirits in moments of calmness and ease; while their enemies, on the point, awaiting the arrival of their latest bands, were securely devouring a meal, which, to hundreds amongst them, proved to be their last. The fatal instant now seemed approaching. A general movement was seen among the battalions of the British, who began to spread along the shore, under cover of the brow of the hill—the lingering boats having arrived with the rear of their detachments—and officers hurried from regiment to regiment with the final mandates of their chief. At this moment a body of Americans appeared on the crown of Bunker Hill, and, descending swiftly by the road, disappeared in the meadows to the left of their own redoubt. This band was followed by others, who, like themselves, had broken through the dangers of the narrow pass, by braving the fire of the shipping, and who also hurried to join their comrades on the lowland. The British general determined at once to anticipate the arrival of further reinforcements, and gave forth the long-expected order to prepare for the attack.

The Americans had made a show, in the course of that fearful morning, of returning the fire of their enemies, by throwing a few shot from their light field-pieces, as if in mockery of the tremendous cannonade, which they sustained. But as the moment of severest trial approached, the same awful stillness, which had settled upon the deserted streets of Charlestown, hovered around the redoubt. On the meadows, to its left, the recently arrived bands hastily threw the rails of two fences into one, and covering the whole with the mown grass that surrounded them, they posted themselves along the frail defence, which answered no better purpose than to conceal their weakness from their adversaries. Behind this characteristic rampart, several bodies of husbandmen, from the neighboring provinces of New Hampshire and Connecticut, lay on their arms, in sullen expectation. Their line extended from the shore to the base of the ridge, where it terminated several hundred feet behind the works; leaving a wide opening, in a diagonal direction, between the fence and an earthen breastwork, which ran a short distance down the declivity of the hill, from the north-eastern angle of the redoubt. A few hundred yards in the rear of this rude disposition, the naked crest of Bunker Hill rose unoccupied and undefended; and the streams of the Charles and Mystic, sweeping around its base, approached so near each other as to blend the sounds of their rippling. It was across this low and narrow isthmus, that the royal frigates poured a stream of fire, that never ceased, while around it hovered the numerous parties of undisciplined Americans, hesitating to attempt the dangerous passage.

In this manner Gage had, in a great degree, surrounded the devoted peninsula with his power; and the bold men, who had so daringly planted themselves under the muzzles of his cannon, were left, as already stated, unsupported, without nourishment, and with weapons from their own gunhooks, singly to maintain the honor of their nation. Including men of all ages and conditions, there might have been two thousand of them; but, as the day advanced, small bodies of their countrymen, taking counsel of their feelings, and animated by the example of the old partisan of the woods, who crossed and recrossed the neck, loudly scoffing at the danger, broke through the fire of the shipping in time to join in the closing and bloody business of the hour.

On the other hand, Howe led more than an equal number of the chosen troops of his prince; and as boats continued to ply between the two peninsulas throughout the afternoon, the relative disparity continued undiminished to the end of the struggle. It was at this point in our narrative that, deeming himself sufficiently strong to force the defences of his despised foes, the arrangements immediately preparatory to such an undertaking were made in full view of the excited spectators. Notwithstanding the security with which the English general marshalled his warriors, he felt that the approaching contest would be a battle of no common incidents. The eyes of tens of thousands were fastened on his movements, and the occasion demanded the richest display of the pageantry of war.

The troops formed with beautiful accuracy, and the columns moved steadily along the shore, and took their assigned stations under cover of the brow of the eminence. Their force was in some measure divided; one moiety attempting the toilsome ascent of the hill, and the other moving along the beach, or in the orchards of the more level ground, toward the husbandmen on the meadows. The latter soon disappeared behind some fruit-trees and the brick-kilns just mentioned. The advance of the royal columns up the ascent was slow and measured, giving time to their field-guns to add their efforts to the uproar of the cannonade, which broke out with new fury as the battalions prepared to march. When each column arrived at the allotted point, it spread the gallant array of its glittering warriors under a bright sun.

"It is a glorious spectacle," murmured the graceful chieftain by the side of Lionel, keenly alive to all the poetry of his alluring profession; "how exceeding soldier-like! and with what accuracy his 'first-arm ascends the hill,' towards his enemy!"

The intensity of his feelings prevented Major Lincoln from replying, and the other soon forgot that he had spoken, in the overwhelming anxiety of the moment. The advance of the British line, so beautiful and slow, resembled rather the ordered steadiness of a drill, than an approach to a deadly struggle. Their standards fluttered proudly above them; and there were moments when the wild music of their bands was heard rising on the air, and tempering the rude sounds of the artillery. The young and thoughtless in their ranks turned their faces backward, and smiled exultingly, as they beheld steeples, roofs, masts, and hights, teeming with their thousands of eyes, bent on the show of their bright array. As the British lines moved in open view of the little redoubt, and began slowly to gather around its different faces, gun after gun became silent, and the curious artillerist, or tried seaman, lay extended on his heated piece, gazing in mute wonder at the spectacle. There was just then a minute when the roar of the cannonade seemed passing away like the rumbling of distant thunder.

"They will not fight, Lincoln," said the animated leader at the side of Lionel—"the military front of Howe has chilled the hearts of the knaves, and our victory will be bloodless!"

"We shall see, sir—we shall see!"

These words were barely uttered, when platoon after platoon, among the British, delivered its fire, the blaze of musketry flashing swiftly around the brow of the hill, and was immediately followed by heavy volleys that ascended from the orchard. Still no answering sound was heard from the Americans, and the royal troops were soon lost to the eye, as they slowly marched into the white cloud which their own fire had alone created.

"They are cowed, by heavens!—the dogs are cowed!" once more cried the gay companion of Lionel, "and Howe is within two hundred feet of them unharmed!"

At that instant a sheet of flame glanced through the smoke, like lightning playing in a cloud, while at one report a thousand muskets were added to the uproar. It was not altogether fancy, which led Lionel to imagine that he saw the smoky canopy of the hill to wave, as if the trained warriors it enveloped faltered before this close and appalling discharge; but, in another instant, the stimulating war-cry, and the loud shouts of the combatants, were born across the strait to his ears, even amid the horrid din of the combat. Ten breathless minutes flew by like a moment of time, and the bewildered spectators on Copp's were still gazing intently on the scene, when a voice was raised among them, shouting—

"Hurrah! let the rake-hellies go up to Breed's; the people will teach 'em the law!"

"Throw the rebel scoundrel from the hill! Blow him from the muzzle of a gun!" cried twenty soldiers in a breath.

"Hold!" exclaimed Lionel—"'tis a simpleton, an idiot, a fool!"

But the angry and savage murmurs as quickly subsided, and were lost in other feelings, as the bright red lines of the royal troops were seen issuing from the smoke, waving and recoiling before the still vivid fire of their enemies.

"Ha!" said Burgoyne—"'tis some feint to draw the rebels from their hold!"

"'Tis a palpable and disgraceful retreat!" muttered the stern warrior nigh him, whose truer eye detected at a glance the discomfiture of the assailants. "'Tis another base retreat before the rebels!"

"Hurrah!" shouted the reckless changeling again; "there come the reg'lars out of the orchard too!—see the grannies skulking behind the kilns! Let them go on to Breed's: the people will teach 'em the law!"

No cry of vengeance preceded the act this time, but fifty of the soldiery rushed, as by a common impulse, on their prey. Lionel had not time to utter a word of remonstrance, before Job appeared in the air, borne on the uplifted arms of a dozen men, and at the next instant he was seen rolling down the steep declivity, with a velocity that carried him to the water's edge. Springing to his feet, the undaunted changeling once more waved his hat in triumph, and shouted forth again his offensive challenge. Then turning, he launched his canoe from its hiding-place among the adjacent lumber, amid a shower of stones, and glided across the strait; his little bark escaping unnoticed in the crowd of boats that were rowing in all directions. But his progress was watched by the uneasy eye of Lionel, who saw him land and disappear, with hasty steps, in the silent streets of the town.

While this trifling by-play was enacting, the great drama of the day was not at a stand. The smoky veil, which clung around the brow of the eminence, was lifted by the air, and sailed heavily away to the south-west, leaving the scene of the bloody struggle again open to the view. Lionel witnessed the grave and meaning glances which the two lieutenants of the king exchanged as they simultaneously turned their glasses from the fatal spot, and, taking the one proffered by Burgoyne, he read their explanation in the numbers of the dead that lay profusely scattered in front of the redoubt. At this instant, an officer from the field held an earnest communication with the two leaders; when, having delivered his orders, he hastened back to his boat, like one who felt himself employed in matters of life and death.

"It shall be done, sir," repeated Clinton, as the other departed, his own honest brow sternly knit under high martial excitement. "The artillery have their orders, and the work will be accomplished without delay."

"This, Major Lincoln!" cried his more sophisticated companion, "this is one of the trying duties of the soldier! To fight, to bleed, or even to die, for his prince, is his happy privilege; but it is sometimes his unfortunate lot to become the instrument of vengeance."

Lionel waited but a moment for an explanation—the flaming balls were soon seen taking their wide circuit in the air, and carrying their desolation among the close and inflammable roofs of the opposite town. In a very few minutes, a dense, black smoke arose from the deserted buildings, and forked flames played actively along the heated shingles, as though rioting in their unmolested possession of the place. He regarded the gathering destruction in painful silence; and, on bending his looks towards his companions, he fancied, notwithstanding the language of the other, that he read the deepest regret in the averted eye of him, who had so unhesitatingly uttered the fatal mandate to destroy.

In scenes like these we are attempting to describe, hours appear to be minutes, and time flies as imperceptibly as life slides from beneath the feet of age. The disordered ranks of the British had been arrested at the base of the hill, and were again forming under the eyes of their leaders, with admirable discipline, and extraordinary care. Fresh battalions, from Boston, marched with high military pride into the line, and every thing betokened that a second assault was at hand. When the moment of stupid amazement, which succeeded the retreat of the royal troops, had passed, the troops and batteries poured out their wrath with tenfold fury on their enemies. Shot were incessantly glancing up the gentle acclivity, madly ploughing across its grassy surface, while black and threatening shells appeared to hover above the work, like the monsters of the air, about to stoop upon their prey.

Still all lay quiet and immoveable within the low mounds of earth, as if none there had a stake in the issue of the bloody day. For a few moments only, the tall figure of an aged man was seen slowly moving along the summit of the ramparts calmly regarding the dispositions of the English general in the more distant part of his line, and, after exchanging a few words with a gentleman, who joined him in his dangerous look-out, they disappeared together behind the grassy banks. Lionel soon detected the name of Prescott of Pepperel, passing through the crowd in low murmurs, and his glass did not deceive him when he thought, in the smaller of the two, he had himself described the graceful person of the unknown leader of the "caucus."

All eyes were now watching the advance of the battalions, which once more drew nigh the point of contest. The heads of the columns were already in view of their enemies, when a man was seen swiftly ascending the hill from the burning town: he paused amid the peril, on the natural glacis, and swung his hat triumphantly, and Lionel even fancied he heard the exulting cry, as he recognized the ungainly form of the simpleton, before it plunged into the work.

The right of the British once more disappeared in the orchard, and the columns in front of the redoubt again opened with all the imposing exactness of their high discipline. Their arms were already glittering in a line with the green faces of the mound, and Lionel heard the experienced warrior at his side murmuring to himself—

"Let him hold his fire, and he will go in at the point of the bayonet!"

But the trial was too great for even the practiced courage of the royal troops. Volley succeeded volley, and in a few moments they had again curtained their ranks behind the misty screen produced by their own fire. Then came the terrible flash from the redoubt, and the eddying volumes from the adverse hosts rolled into one cloud, enveloping the combatants in its folds, as if to conceal their bloody work from the spectators. Twenty times, in the short space of as many minutes, Major Lincoln fancied he heard the incessant roll of the American musketry die away before the heavy and regular volleys of the troops; and then he thought the sounds of the latter grew more faint, and were given at longer intervals.

The result, however, was soon known. The heavy bank of smoke which now even clung along the ground, was broken in fifty places; and the disordered masses of the British were seen driven before their deliberate foes in wild confusion. The flashing swords of the officers in vain attempted to arrest the torrent, nor did the flight cease, with many of the regiments, until they had even reached their boats. At this moment a hum was heard in Boston, like the sudden rush of wind, and men gazed in each other's faces with undisguised amazement. Here and there a low sound of exultation escaped some unguarded lip, and many an eye gleamed with a triumph that could nc longer be suppressed. Until this moment the feelings of Lionel had vacillated between the pride of country and his military spirit; but losing all other feelings in the latter sensation, he now looked fiercely about him, as if he would seek the man who dare exult in the repulse of his comrades. The poetic chieftain was still at his side, biting his nether lip in vexation; but his more tried companion had suddenly disappeared. Another quick glance fell upon his missing form in the act of entering a boat at the foot of the hill. Quicker than thought, Lionel was on the shore, crying, as he flew to the water's edge—

"Hold! for God's sake, hold! remember the 47th is in the field, and that I am its major!"

"Receive him," said Clinton, with that grim satisfaction, with which men acknowledge a valued friend in moments of great trial; "and then row for your lives, or, what is of more value, for the honor of the British name."

The brain of Lionel whirled as the boat shot along its watery bed, but, before it had gained the middle of the stream, he had time to consider the whole of the appalling scene. The fire had spread from house to house, and the whole village of Charlestown, with its four hundred buildings, was just bursting into flames. The air seemed filled with whistling balls, as they hurtled above his head, and the black sides of the vessels of war were vomiting their sheets of flame with unwearied industry. Amid this tumult, the English general and his companions sprung to land. The former rushed into the disordered ranks, and by his presence and voice recalled the men of one regiment to their duty. But long and loud appeals to their spirit and their ancient fame were necessary to restore a moiety of their former confidence to men, who had been thus rudely repulsed, and who now looked along their thinned and exhausted ranks, missing in many instances, more than half the well-known countenances of their fellows. In the midst of the faltering troops stood their stern and unbending chief; but of all those gay and gallant youths, who followed in his train as he had departed from Province-House that morning, not one remained, but in his blood. He alone seemed undisturbed in that disordered crowd; and his mandates went forth as usual, calm and determined. At length the panic, in some degree, subsided, and order was once more restored, as the high-spirited and mortified gentlemen of the detachment regained their lost authority.

The leaders consulted together, apart, and the dispositions were immediately renewed for the assault. Military show was no longer affected, but the soldiers laid down all the useless implements of their trade, and many even cast aside their outer garments, under the warmth of a broiling sun, added to the heat of the conflagration, which began to diffuse itself along the extremity of the peninsula. Fresh companies were placed in the columns, and most of the troops were withdrawn from the meadows, leaving merely a few skirmishers to amuse the Americans who lay behind the fence. When each disposition was completed, the final signal was given to advance.

Lionel had taken post in his regiment, but, marching on the skirt of the column, he commanded a view of most of the scene of battle. In his front moved a battalion, reduced to a handful of men in the previous assaults. Behind these came a party of the marine guards, from the shipping, led by their own veteran major; and next followed the dejected Nesbitt and his corps, amongst whom Lionel looked in vain for the features of the good-natured Polwarth. Similar columns marched on their right and left, encircling three sides of the redoubt by their battalions.

A few minutes brought him in full view of that humble and unfinished mound of earth, for the possession of which so much blood had that day been spilt in vain. It lay, as before, still as if none breathed within its bosom, though a terrific row of dark tubes were arrayed along its top, following the movements of the approaching columns, as the eyes of the imaginary charmers of our own wilderness are said to watch their victims. As the uproar of the artillery again grew fainter, the crash of falling streets, and the appalling sounds of the conflagration, on their left, became more audible. Immense volumes of black smoke issued from the smouldering ruins, and bellying outward, fold beyond fold, it overhung the work in a hideous cloud, casting its gloomy shadow across the place of blood.

A strong column was now seen ascending, as if from out the burning town, and the advance of the whole became quick and spirited. A low call ran through the platoons, to note the naked weapons of their adversaries, and it was followed by the cry of, "To the bayonet! to the bayonet!"

"Hurrah! for the Royal Irish!" shouted M'Fuse, at the head of the dark column from the conflagration.

"Hurrah!" echoed a well known voice from the silent mound; "let them come on to Breed's; the people will teach 'em the law!"

Men think at such moments with the rapidity of lightning, and Lionel had even fancied his comrades in possession of the work, when the terrible stream of fire flashed in the faces of the men in front.

"Push on with the ——th," cried the veteran major of marines—"push on, or the 18th will get the honor of the day!"

"We can not," murmured the soldiers of the ——th; "their fire is too heavy!"

"Then break, and let the marines pass through you!"

The feeble battalion melted away, and the warriors of the deep, trained to conflicts of hand to hand, sprang forward, with a loud shout, in their places. The Americans, exhausted of their ammunition, now sunk sullenly back, a few hurling stones at their foes, in desperate indignation. The cannon of the British had been brought to enfilade their short breast-work, which was no longer tenable; and, as the columns approached closer to the low rampart, it became a mutual protection to the adverse parties.

"Hurrah for the Royal Irish!" again shouted M'Fuse, rushing up the trifling ascent, which was but of little more than his own hight.

"Hurrah!" repeated Pitcairn, waving his sword on another angle of the work—"the day's our own!"

One more sheet of flame issued out of the bosom of the work, and all those brave men, who had emulated the examples of their officers, were swept away as though a whirlwind had passed along. The grenadier gave his war-cry once more, before he pitched headlong among his enemies; while Pitcairn fell back into the arms of his own child. The cry of "Forward, 47th," rung through their ranks, and in their turn this veteran battalion gallantly mounted the ramparts. In the shallow ditch Lionel passed the expiring marine, and caught the dying and despairing look from his eyes, and in another instant he formed himself in the presence of his foes. As company followed company into the defenceless redoubt, the Americans sullenly retired by its rear, keeping the bayonets of the soldiers at bay with clubbed muskets and sinewy arms. When the whole issued upon the open ground, the husbandmen received a close and fatal fire from the battalions, which were now gathering around them on three sides. A scene of wild and savage confusion then succeeded to the order of the fight, and many fatal blows were given and taken, the melee rendering the use of fire-arms nearly impossible for several minutes.

Lionel continued in advance, pressing on the footsteps of the retiring foe, stepping over many a lifeless body in his difficult progress. Notwithstanding the hurry, and vast disorder of the fray, his eye fell on the form of the graceful stranger, stretched lifeless on the parched grass, which had greedily drank his blood. Amid the ferocious cries, and fiercer passions of the moment, the young man paused, and glanced his eyes around him, with an expression that said, he thought the work of death should cease. At this instant the trappings of his attire caught the glaring eye-balls of a dying yeoman, who exerted his wasting strength to sacrifice one more worthy victim to the manes of his countrymen. The whole of the tumultuous scene vanished from the senses of Lionel at the flash of the musket of this man, and he sunk beneath the feet of the combatants, insensible of further triumph, and of every danger.

The fall of a single officer, in such a contest, was a circumstance not to be regarded; and regiments passed over him, without a single man stooping to inquire into his fate. When the Americans had disengaged themselves from the troops, they descended into the little hollow between the two hills, swiftly, and like a disordered crowd, bearing off most of their wounded, and leaving but few prisoners in the hands of their foes. The formation of the ground favored their retreat, as hundreds of bullets whistled harmlessly above their heads; and by the time they gained the acclivity of Bunker, distance was added to their security. Finding the field lost, the men at the fence broke away in a body from their position, and abandoned the meadows; the whole moving in confused masses behind the crest of the adjacent hight. The shouting soldiery followed in their footsteps, pouring in fruitless and distant volleys; but, on the summit of Bunker, their tired platoons were halted, and they beheld the throng move fearlessly through the tremendous fire that enfiladed the low pass, as little injured as though most of them bore charmed lives.

The day was now drawing to a close. With the disappearance of their enemies, the ships and batteries ceased their cannonade; and, presently, not a musket was heard in that place, where so fierce a contest had so long raged. The troops commenced fortifying the outward eminence, on which they rested, in order to maintain their barren conquest; and nothing further remained for the achievement of the royal lieutenants, but to go and mourn over their victory.

THE SEA AND ITS DANGERS.

BY J. BROOKWELL PEAT.

THERE are perils on the deep, occurrences of a fearful kind, the relation of which stirs up the heart's blood, and sends it hurriedly through the system. It was the lot of the writer to be made personally acquainted with one of this character. In the month of ———, he sailed in the G—— D——, from the port of New Orleans, bound for Liverpool, and laden with cotton. We were towed to the Balize by the steamer Persian, and then, in order to insure the success of our vessel over the bar, that forms at the outlet of the Father of Waters, we engaged the assistance of another powerful steamer, the Phœnix; but yet, for awhile, our course was impeded, and but for the determination of the captain, and a somewhat dangerous application of steam, we should have remained there until released by an increased depth of water. At last, passing the bar with a leap, in company with other two vessels, and with a fine, favorable breeze, we merrily bounded away for the white cliffs of Old England.

The commencement of our voyage was very favorable; and we pleasantly passed our time in conversation, reading, fishing, and other amusements. With rapture I gazed upon the sea, and with enthusiasm I watched its towering billows. To me things, of but small consideration to the sailor, afforded a great degree of interest. And when the flying-fish would leap from its marine abode, and skim with its white-tipped wing the bosom of the wave to escape the pursuit of some hungry dolphin; and the porpoise would come madly leaping and gamboling through the briny depths, according to the sailors, a sure indication of squally weather, and at which we would occasionally launch the harpoon; and the grampus heave his huge carcass in his change of latitude;—I enjoyed it with feelings which, to be understood, must be experienced on that waste of waters. Night after night, with none, save the watch on deck, have I gazed on the beauties of the heavens—nowhere seen so beautiful as on the wide, wide main—and the phosphorescent appearance of the sea, with its white-capped waves lit up with ten thousand times ten thousand beams of flashing light, and at our noble vessel ploughing her onward march amid the myriad scintillations that danced around her bow, and sparkled in her foaming wake.

The sea, the sea! O the deep, blue sea! the "ever bounding, ever free!" Who dare say, Canute-like, "thus far shalt thou come, and no farther; and here shall thy proud waves be stayed?" It laughs at the impotent limits set to its power, mocks the puny efforts of man to confine it within boundaries, sports with the vessels that furrow its bosom, and sends them, riven and shattered, down to the depths of its hidden caverns, to perish there forever. To behold the grandeur of the ocean, and to witness the unlimited power of its billows, you should ride on it when the tempest rages; when the storm-god, unchaining the rude winds, sends them moaning, howling, and blustering across the broad Atlantic; when, gathering the sleeping waters into hills and mountain-hights, he rolls them onward and upward, until the tall, towering mass is curled and twined into foamy wreaths of spray. A terrific grandeur reigns around: the clouds lower above your head, burdened with fury, and death rides triumphant on the wings of the rushing wind. Destruction apparently awaits you in the deep-opening waters, sighs your requiem in the shrouds, and screams your welcome in the loud and pitiless blast.

It is in such scenes as these, that the power and sublimity of the ocean is manifest, presenting a scene of majestic grandeur that leaves the beholder humbled, subdued, and abashed. But whether in a storm, in a frail and feeble bark, where, as far as the eye can throw its vision, the mighty expanse of water is agitated by the fury of the storm—exhibiting a continued succession of yeasty waves, swelling in apparent hight, until the farthest foam-capped billow seems to lash the very heavens; or whether the sea presents a smooth and beautifully-polished surface, a mirror of tranquility and repose, on whose bosom the sunbeams brightly play or moonbeams dance, and the stars reflect their beauty and luster;—you cannot but admire the magnificent scenery, and adore the Hand that, in the greatness of its power, sustains the mighty depths. Kingdoms and empires have passed away, many of the proudest monuments erected by art and science, have crumbled into ruins, and the mighty, and the brave, and the beautiful of past ages slumber in the silence of the grave; but, Ocean!

"Time writes no wrinkles on thy azure brow
Such as creation's dawn beheld, thou rollest now!"

And until yonder sun shall be extinguished, and the moon and the stars hide themselves in the light of eternity, the loud anthems of thy voice shall continue to swell, and roll in tones of sweetest note, that shall "please the ear of God!"

* * * * * * * *

Our voyage, like voyages generally, was mingled with the varied changes of the sea—calms, storms, and gales. The latter our vessel outrode most gallantly, mounting each crested billow as gracefully as the bird whose home is on the sea, whose cradle is the deep. It may be termed superstition, but previous to the night of the 15th of

——, in latitude ——, a dark cloud of some impending calamity rested heavily on my mind, and my spirits were unusually depressed. The weather, during the week, had been cloudy and stormy, and the night was remarkably dark. I had retired to my berth earlier than usual, taking the precaution, as formerly, to place my clothes in a position ready to be obtained in case of an emergency, at the same time lying down in a part of my habit, when I was overcome by "slumber's potent charm." In this state I remained until two o'clock in the morning, when I was suddenly aroused by the cry and hurrying footsteps of the watch. To spring from my berth, and to rush on deck, was but the work of a moment; when I immediately ascertained the fearful cause of alarm. The darkness of the night had prevented our look-out from observing a large bark, the J—— H——, from New-Brunswick, laden with timber, running across the pathway of our vessel, until too near to avoid collision. Aboard our vessel, all was hurry, confusion, and terror; and our bell now startled the midnight air with its loud peal of alarm. Up rushed the watch of the lower deck, and the few passengers we had on board, many in the same condition in which they had retired to rest, with terror and dismay on their countenances. Now was heard, above the din of the tempest, the loud shouts of the crew, and the hoarse trumpet of the bark, warning us, for Heaven's sake, to keep off, and not to run them down. Then many a stout heart beat with a palsy ing chill, and many a blooming cheek turned pale.

With deep anxiety I waited the fate of the two unfortunate vessels, and endeavored to compose my mind to a sleep in the ocean's grave. One moment I had for reflection; and O, what thoughts crowded upon the memory, and excited my imagination! I thought of the home of my youth, with all its dearly cherished scenes, from which I had been absent so many years, and to see which I had had so many ardent longings of spirit; then of the home of my adoption and choice, with its many social enjoyments and endeared friends; and then the great, the unknown future, spread out before my mind with its deep and hidden mysteries and glorious assurances. 'Twas terrible to think of going down to the ocean's depths under such circumstances, the tale of our melancholy fate probably never entering the ear of the world. But a consoling refuge was there; and I cast myself on the mercy of Him, whose voice once hushed the wild ragings of Galilee, and tremblingly awaited the issue.

All that could be done, for the safety of the vessel, was done with energy and dispatch; and the orders given by the officers were promptly executed by the crew. The helm was put "hard down," and our alliards let go, to break the force of the collision. But all too late: and the bows of the vessels came together with a tremendous crash. All was now confusion and terror; and the harsh voice of the trumpet, and the shoutings, supplications, warnings, and threatenings of the crews, and the flappings of the loosened sails, mingled with the loud bellowings of the storm. Crash, crash! went our bowsprit and foreguards; and the vessels becoming entangled in the rigging, lashed their timbered sides together, like two infuriated demons, apparently determined on each other's destruction. At length the strong rigging gave way, and becoming disentangled, we passed along-side of each other, with a harsh, grating sound, tearing in the contest our main-mast and main-top-sail, and losing our bowsprit, with its attendant boom and sails, and a part of our larboard quarter. The well was immediately sounded, and some idea of our carpenter's excitement may be formed, when he reported seven feet of water, when there were only six inches. Immediately both vessels tacked, which nearly resulted in another collision. As the brig glided past, her captain beseeched us not to abandon them, as they were in a sinking condition. He was told to drive before the wind, and in the morning we ascertained that she had lost an anchor, sprung her foremast, and sustained other serious injuries, resulting in a very bad leak. She had then several feet of water in the hold, but being a timber vessel, the captain had resolved to remain aboard, and trust to his cargo.

O how we welcomed the smiles of the sun in the morning, who had kept his face hid for several days past: the wind, too, dying away, resulted in a calm, which enabled us to rig a jury-bowsprit, repair damages, and stay by the bark three days, when, providentially, a favorable breeze sprung up, and then, with anxious solicitation for her welfare, we left her to her fate.

Two or three days after, the coast of the Emerald Isle loomed up in the distance. Here, to our great joy, we entered upon beautiful and exciting scenes. The channel was studded with the white sails of numerous vessels and fishing boats, and the coast presented many a splendid mansion and lighthouse glittering in the beams of a summer's sun, green slopes and fields of golden corn, ready for the reaper's sickle, and to repay the toils of the liberal husbandman; and in the distance, mountains reared their lofty summits, capped by the clouds of heaven.

FIRMNESS OF RELIGIOUS PRINCIPLE.

ANONYMOUS.

Frank Edwards, a young married man, employed as a machinist in an English manufactory, was converted. His conversion was deep and genuine; it reached both heart and life. The change was complete, and from being notoriously trifling and thoughtless, he became a proverb for cheerful gravity and serious deportment.

Very delightful was the first experience of that young man. A good workman, he enjoyed constant employment, with wages sufficient to procure the comforts of life. He had a thrifty wife, who was led to Jesus by his own influence. Their cottage was the house of prayer. Religion, plenty, health, and contentment, dwelt with them; probably there was not another home in England more pleasant than that of this young, pious mechanic.

But piety is not an effectual shield to defend from trouble. It supports—gloriously supports the sufferer—but his path to heaven is appointed to lead through "*much tribulation.*" As in our nature, the storm-cloud gathers in the horizon, while the sun shines with splendor in the heavens, so in the kingdom of grace, while the child of God rejoices in ease and prosperity, and ascends the summit of Pisgah, he may rest assured that events are in preparation, which may hurl him down to the vale of Baca—to the place of weeping and lamentation.

It was thus with Frank Edwards and his happy family. In the midst of prosperity, adversity looked in at their cottage door; poverty sat down at their table. Let us trace the cause of their trouble.

One day the machinery of the manufactory broke, and its operations were stopped. All hands were set to repairing it with the utmost haste. The week was closing, and the work was unfinished. On Saturday morning, the overseer entered and said to the men, "You must work all day to-morrow."

Frank instantly remembered the fourth commandment. He resolved to keep it, because he felt that his duty to God required him, under all circumstances, to refrain from labor on the Sabbath day. Offering an inward prayer to God, he respectfully addressed the overseer:

"Sir, to-morrow is Sunday."

"I know it, but our mill must be repaired."

"Will you excuse me, sir, from working on the Sabbath?"

"No, Frank, I can't excuse any one. The company will give you double wages, and you must work."

"I am sorry, sir, but I can not work to-morrow."

"Why not, Mr. Edwards; you know our necessities, and we offer you a fair remuneration?"

"Sir, it will be a sin against God, and no necessity is strong enough—no price high enough, to induce me to offend my Maker any more."

"I am not here to argue the morality of the question, Frank; you must either work to-morrow, or be discharged."

"I can not hesitate, sir, a moment; I have resolved to please God. Cost what earthly price it may, I will keep his commandments."

"Then, Mr. Edwards, if you will step into the counting-room, I will pay you what the company owes you, and you will then leave our establishment."

To say that Frank's heart did not shrink from this trial, would be to deny his humanity; but his faith came to his help. Casting himself upon God, he gathered up his tools, and entered the counting-room.

The overseer was extremely unwilling to part with Frank, for he was a superior workman, and since his conversion, had been the most trusty man in the employment of the company. He therefore addressed him very kindly, while handing him his wages: "Mr Edwards, had you not better reconsider your resolution? Remember, work is scarce, we pay you high wages, and it is not often we require you to labor on the Sabbath."

"Sir," replied Frank, "my mind is fixed; I will not work on Sundays, if I have to starve to death."

"Very well, sir," was the cool answer of the overseer; who, not being a Christian, could not appreciate the noble heroism of Frank's reply.

On reaching his humble cottage, the mechanic could not forbear a sigh, as the thought flitted across his mind, that possibly he might soon lose his home-comforts. But that sigh was momentary; he remembered the promise of God, and grew calmly peaceful. Entering his house, he said to his wife, "Mary, I am discharged!"

"Discharged, Frank! What has happened! O what will become of us! Tell me, why you are discharged?"

"Be calm, Mary! God will provide! I left the shop because I would not break the Sabbath. They wanted me to work to-morrow, and because I refused, they discharged me."

Mary was silent. She looked doubtful, as if not quite sure that her husband was right. Her faith was not so strong as Frank's, nor was her character so decided. In her heart she thought, as thousands of fearful disciples would, under similar circumstances, that her husband had gone too far; but although she said nothing, Frank read her thoughts, and grieved over her want of faith.

Sweet was the hour of family prayer to Frank that evening; sweeter still was the secret devotion of the closet, and he never closed his eyes with more heavenly calmness of spirit, than when he sunk to sleep on that eventful evening.

The following week brought Frank's character to a severer test. All his friends condemned him; even some members of his church said they thought he had gone beyond the strict requirement of his duty. "It was well," they said, "to keep the Sabbath; but then, a man like Frank Edwards ought to look to the wants of his family, and not strain at a gnat, and perhaps be compelled to go to the workhouse."

This was dastardly language for Christians; but there are always too many of this class of irresolute, sight-walking disciples. Frank met them on all sides, and found himself without sympathy. A few noble, enlightened Christians, however, admired and encouraged him Frank held to his purpose with the spirit worthy of a martyr.

The cloud grew darker. Through the influence of his former employers, who were vexed because he left them, the other corporations refused to employ him. Winter came on with its frosts and storms. His little stock of savings gradually disappeared. Poverty stared them in the face; Frank's watch, Mary's silver spoons, their best furniture, went to the auction shop. They had to leave their pleasant cottage, and one little garret held the little afflicted family, and the slender remains of their cottage furniture.

Did Frank regret his devotion to God? No! he rejoiced in it. He had obeyed God, he said, and God would take care of him. Light would break out of darkness; all would be well. So spoke his unyielding faith; his fixed heart doubted not. The blacker the cloud, the more piercing grew the eye of his triumphing faith. With his Mary the case was different. Her faith was weak, and, pressing her babes to her bosom, she often wept, and bent before the sweeping storm.

The winter passed away, and Frank was still in the fiery furnace, rejoicing, however, amidst the flames. Some friends offered him the means of emigrating to the United States. Here was a light gleam. He rejoiced in it, and prepared to quit a place which refused him bread because he feared God.

Behold him! that martyr-mechanic, on board the emigrant-ship. Her white sails catch the favoring beeze, and with a soul full of hope, Frank looked toward this western world. A short, pleasant passage, brought them to one of our Atlantic cities.

Here he soon found that his faith had not been misplaced. The first week of his arrival saw him not merely employed, but filling the station of foreman in the establishment of some extensive machinists.

Prosperity now smiled on Frank, and Mary once more rejoiced in the possession of home comforts. They lived in a style far better and more comfortable than when in their English cottage. "Mary," Frank would often ask, pointing to their charming little parlor, "is it not best to obey God?"

Mary could only reply to this question with smiles and tears; for every thing around them said, "*Blessed is that man that maketh the Lord his trust, and respecteth not the proud; surely he shall not be moved forever.*"

But Frank's trials were not over. A similar claim for Sabbath labor was made upon him in his new situation. An engine for a railroad or steamboat was broken, and must be repaired. "You will keep your men employed through to-morrow, Mr. Edwards; so that the engine may be finished on Monday morning," said the chief overseer.

"I cannot do it, sir; I cannot break the Lord's day. I will work until midnight on Saturday, and begin directly after midnight on Monday morning; God's holy time I will not touch."

"That won't do, Mr. Edwards, you must work your men through the Sabbath, or the owners will dismiss you."

"Be it so, sir!" replied Frank. "I crossed the Atlantic because I would not work on Sabbath; I will not do it here."

Monday came, the work was unfinished. Frank expected his discharge. While at work, a gentleman inquired of him: "I wish you to go with me to ——, to take charge of my establishment; will you go?"

"I don't know," replied Frank. "If, as I expect, my present employers dismiss me, I will go; if they do not, I have no wish to leave."

"This is settled. They intend to dismiss you, and I know the reason; I honor you for it, and wish you to enter my establishment."

Here again our mechanic saw the hand of God. His decision had again brought him into trial, and God had come to his aid. The new situation for which he had just engaged was worth much more than the one he was to leave. God had kept his promise.

UNDER THE ICE.

THE ALPINE HUNTER'S MIRACULOUS ESCAPE.

THERE was no braver guide, or more skilful hunter, that ever sat foot upon the Matterhorn, or crawled over the dangerous glaciers of Monte Rosa, than Ulric Peterson. He was a man of immense strength and great daring; and had often tracked the wilderness of snow when those who followed the same calling willingly remained in their cottages, in the well-protected villages. He laughed at his companions, when they talked of danger; and made light of the fears of his good wife, when she trembled at the howling of the fierce winds, or the avalanche of snow, that now and then swept down, with irresistible force, upon the little chalets. With well-spiked shoes, a stout alpenstock, confidence in himself, and a firm and fervent trust in God, he avowed that a man was as safe upon the topmost cliffs of the cloud-pierced Matterhorn, as in the brook threaded valley of Tourmanches. But the timid heart of womanhood could not look upon the matter in the same light, although her trust in the good Lord was equally strong; and so, when she saw him take down his trusty rifle, powder-horn, and heavily shod iron staff, one morning, she clung to him, and begged that he would not go upon the mountains. "There is every sign of a storm," she said. "You know how terrible they are. We have food enough in the cottage. Do stay at home with the little ones."

"That would I, wife," was the reply "if I had not seen an ibex as I was coming home yesterday evening. He was a stout old fellow, with huge horns; and I fancied he was almost laughing at me as I crept around the cliff upon which he was standing.

"But, Ulric, think of the storm that is certainly coming."

"I have been in many a one, and care nothing for them. I

love the free whistling of the wind upon the mountain tops, and the whirling of the feathery snow. So, good wife, get me something to eat. I must be off before the day dawns."

With a heavy sigh, the woman did as he had requested, and with his fond kiss still lingering upon her lips, she saw him climb the mountain side, until a turn in the path hid him from her view. Then she sunk upon her knees, by the bedside of her still slumbering children, and committed him into the keeping of that God who had thus far preserved him in the midst of every danger. Meantime, Ulric hastened onward with a light foot. It was still dark in the valley; but far above him he could see the white peak glittering in the dim light of the morning, and the fast paling stars. Higher and higher he climbed, and soon the sun arose, shedding its rays of rosy gold upon the icy piles and making them flash as if builded of myriad diamonds. To a stranger it would have been a dazzling sight; to the brave hunter it had lost something of its charm by familiarity, and he pressed onward and upward. The road grew rough and difficult. He was obliged to pick his way, to clamber up steep crags; but at last he reached the edge of a large glacier. He sat down and rested for a little time, satisfied his hunger, examined his shoes and the point of his alpenstock, and again set bravely forth, leaping the yawning chasms, and guarding against the treacherous cracks.

A wall of polished ice arose before him, and he knew that he would have to scale it, before he could get within shot of the coveted game. With great difficulty it was accomplished; and finding the tracks of the ibex, he followed them, until suddenly turning a ragged point, he found himself within easy shot, and in an instant the report of his rifle had awakened the echoes of the mountains. With the "thud" of the bullet the beast sprang forward, but its tail was dropped, its head hanging heavily down, its gait slow and step uncertain. He knew that the whizzing lead had reached its mark; that the animal would soon die; and he paused to reload his rifle before he followed him. "I will surprise my good wife," he thought, "by returning sooner than she expected, and I will have a hearty laugh at the cowards who dared not venture from their snug cottages, for fear of a storm."

With a smile upon his lips, he hastened to where the ibex was lying, and raised it in his arms. Then, with a cry of horror, he felt his footing give way—and hunter and game were swallowed up in a crevasse of almost unfathomable depth The thin covering of ice had been sufficiently strong to bear the weight of the beast; but that of Ulric added had shivered it as if it had been an egg-shell.

Down, down. Hunter and ibex, through the debris of snow and ice, lying there for a thousand years. He fancied that the bottom would never be reached. The most profound darkness enveloped him; his hands could clutch nothing but dampness —but chilling flakes.

Fortunately the carcass of the beast was beneath him. Yet, for all that safeguard, he lay for a long time insensible. When consciousness returned, another day had dawned, and its golden glories had found their way even to the bottom of the yawning grave in which he was lying. He thought upon the utter helplessness of his situation—that he must perish from cold and hunger—of the lingering tortures he would be forced to endure, before death came to put an end to his misery, and every nerve in his body quivered with horror. He looked around to see if there was not some possible chance of escape. On either side smooth ice walls arose, emitting a bluish steel glitter. He felt that he was buried alive! "O, God! Why was I not instantly killed?" he exclaimed, in the agony of despair, and then, as better thoughts swayed him, he thanked the Almighty, with whom nothing is impossible, for his safety thus far, and prayed to Him for guidance and deliverance.

His next thought was of his gun. When it was found that he did not return, his neighbors would certainly search for him, and by firing the gun he could attract their attention. Vain hope! Search as he would he could find nothing of it. Even if he had discovered it, it would have been useless, for his powder-horn was gone as well. Over and over he turned the snow—down deep he dug into it, until his hands burned like fire, and great drops of perspiration rolled from his forehead—until his arms grew stiff and sore, and he was forced to give up the useless labor from sheer exhaustion. With his back against the frozen prison walls, he looked aloft, and saw the great vulture, sailing upon its immense and tireless wings, around the mouth of the chasm, and the strong man shuddered, as he shook his fist defiantly, and murmured, with his hoarse voice, "Your time has not come yet!" He thought also of his happy home, and of his dear wife and children, and then, naturally, for he was faint and hungry, he thought of the food his wife had prepared for him. Having eaten of the bread and goats-milk-cheese, and drank of the little bottle of wine (which, strange to say, had remained unbroken), he reasoned that it would be cowardly to lie down and die, without an effort, and he remembered the goodness of God, and once more fervently implored His help. Then a bold idea came to him. Why might he not cut his way through the solid ice! He had a hatchet, such as his class never travel without. Ah! but he was forgetful that the walls might be hundreds of feet thick, that they were of excessive hardness and would soon render blunt both hatchet and knife. The bright hope that had been born within him was darkened by no such shadow. For the time being he knew that he was safe, he was accustomed to the cold, was warmly clad, could use the skin of the ibex, in case of need, and its flesh would drive away the wolves of starvation for many a day. A brief rest and he began the task, and toiled faithfully until darkness forced him to stop. A night of uneasy rest, a breakfast of the raw flesh of the ibex, and he resumed his labors. Another day of toil, and he again stretched himself upon the skin of the beast, wrapping it around him as much as was possible, and slept long and heavily, although there had been a sudden fall in the temperature, and it was now excessively cold.

For four days he toiled thus, his only food the raw and frozen flesh of the ibex; for four nights he slept within the hole he had cut away in the thick ice walls, closing up the entrance, and thus obtaining partial shelter from the chilling blasts, and once he heard the firing of guns, and his heart beat wildly within him. He dropped his dulled hatchet, crawled to the centre of the chasm, and shouted with all his remaining strength—shouted until his strained voice was reduced to the very ghost of a hoarse whisper. He knew that his friends were in search of him; imagined that he could hear his name called; could do nothing to attract their attention; and, as the firing grew fainter and farther and farther away, he flung himself down, weeping and wringing his hands. The last plank to which he had clung had been shivered. His neighbors and friends had come, and gone. They would never search that part of the mountain again. None would ever know of his fate. He was buried in an icy tomb, until the last trump should sound, and hot flashes of flame dissolve the frost-work around him.

With his mind trembling upon the verge of madness, overpowered by sorrow, crushed by bitter agony, he fell back insensible, and lay, for a long time, upon the cold, damp snow, that soon must be his winding sheet. The black vulture flapped its wings above him, and he knew nothing of it. But, after some hours, the hunter's consciousness returned, though he was far too much crushed, in body and soul, to resume his labors. He crept into the little cavern he had excavated (would it not be to him a tomb?) and gave passionate vent to his grief. For many weary hours nothing passed his lips, and with aching head, and fevered brain, with trembling limbs, and convulsive sobs, he prayed for deliverance, if by no other hand, at least the skeleton one of death.

It was rayless, sunless, starless, darkness, in the ice cavern, when the springs of his life again became capable of action; he was ravenously hungry, and arose to satisfy his hunger with a portion of the ibex he had left remaining outside in the chasm. He felt around, but could discover no outlet. Had he been frozen in—shut out from God's blessed sunshine forever? Nothing but smooth ice met his burning and blistered fingers.

Then, after an hour's search, he found a soft spot, and instantly solved the mystery, he knew there must have been a heavy fall of snow in the night, and that it had drifted into, and blocked up the opening; and with the strength of despair, he soon dug through. It was still snowing heavily; the flakes fell like great feathers around; and he drew the remnant of the carcass of the ibex into the cave, and made another rude meal. And thus refreshed, a new hope was born within him; and again the ice walls resounded with the blows of his little hatchet. But it was slow work, and much of the time was taken up in clearing the chips from the little grotto.

A week passed—a week of the most severe toil and terrible anxiety—and yet, he was not disheartened. His trust in God had returned; and love for his wife and dependent children kept alive his often sinking heart. He was yet in hopes of reaching the upper air, of seeing his dear ones again. But even as he was thinking thus, with something of his old time cheerfulness, a new anxiety took possession of and nearly overpowered him. The carcass of the ibex, that had been the innocent cause of all his troubles, was picked almost to the bones.

With dire starvation staring him in the face, he bowed his head and wept like a child. Starvation, that is dreadful, even in thought! Starvation, that has in it more of horror than a thousand other deaths! He could almost see it silently approaching, and for a time despair alone had possession of him. Then his trust in the Supreme Being returned, and he committed himself unto His holy keeping. "Heavenly Father!" he murmured, from between his parched and blackened lips, "it is Thy hand that has sustained me so far—has saved me from all danger. Thou givest food to the young ravens, and markest even the fall of the tiny sparrow. None but Thou can hear or help. Hear my prayer! Save me, O God! Save me!"

Something of sweet consolation came with the utterance of the words, and he laid down to sleep more tranquilly than he had done for many previous nights. Yet, it was only to be awakened by a new fear. It needed no seer to tell him that the fohn, or hot south wind, was sweeping over the glaciers, and snow fields of the high Alps; and that the rain was falling in torrents, and the enormous blocks of ice melting, as by the touch of fire. The cavern he had dug with infinite labor was almost breast-deep with water, and it was rushing in with all the swiftness of a mountain torrent. Instantly he was wet to the skin, and stood almost paralyzed with terror. Then he breasted his way out into the chasm, but it was only to return again as quickly as possible. Never cataract raged more fiercely than the surging water there. Cutting little niches in the ice-wall, he climbed beyond the reach of the water, and tremblingly awaited his fate. The waves rose rapidly, higher and higher.

He had climbed until his head rested against the top of the little cave—he could go no further. And yet, the waves rolled upward around him. They reached his waist—surged higher to his breast—crept to his throat, and despite all his efforts, began to trickle into his mouth. In another moment he would be strangled by them; his hold would be torn away, and his body dashed hither and thither against the sharp points of the ice. "O God! Save me! Save me!" burst from him in the terrible agony of the instant, the moment of time that lay between him and death.

A noise like thunder—a shivering crash—resounded through the chasm. It appeared as if the very foundations of the world were tottering beneath him. Now, indeed, he felt that his end had come. No! Terror was instantly changed to rapture. The water rushed out of the cavern with the most amazing velocity; he could descend and stand upon the bottom without fear. How this had been accomplished, he was forced to wait until the morning light to determine; and, with the first beams, he saw a great fissure had been opened, through which the imprisoned waters had found their way to the valley below. This unlooked for preservation again inspired him with confidence—rendered more firm his trust in God. Through that tunnel he saw a way to freedom. It was small, to be sure, but he could enlarge it, and he worked diligently, until his strength utterly failed. The ibex was entirely devoured. He had split the bones and sucked out the marrow; had gnawed them over and over again, to appease his hunger. For two days he had not tasted a morsel of food. The hatchet slipped from his hand when he endeavored to strike a blow, and he was forced to abandon the undertaking. There was nothing left him now but to die.

Another day passed, and no help came. He lay crouched in a corner wishing that the end would come, and that swiftly. His eyes were already filmed and his heart beat faintly. Then a strange noise aroused him. He looked aloft and saw a chamois vainly striving to defend itself from the attack of two old vultures, that were striking at it with wing and beak. It was an unequal contest, and, at length, the animal, driven to desperation, attempted to leap the broad chasm. The effort was a noble one, but it failed of success. The chamois missed its footing, and fell, bruised and helpless, at the very feet of the starving man. In an instant his knife was plunged into its throat; and the warm blood was drained by his eager lips. This gave him new life, and he renewed his labor. It was almost an herculean task. More than once he fell fainting beside it. But hope was very strong within him. Still, he would have utterly failed had not Heaven assisted him.

Again, the fohn was busy at its work of destruction; again, the windows of heaven were opened; and the "rains descended, and the floods came," and accomplished more in a single night than his hands could have done in months. With the morning light, he crawled through the now large tunnel; but, when he reached the out end, found, to his horror, that he was on the top of a mighty precipice. His blood boiled; his brain seemed on fire; his heart beat as if it would break through ribs and flesh. He was, if possible, more desperately imprisoned than before. How was he to get down? Through his bewildered mind suddenly flashed the thought of the skins of the ibex and the chamois, and he was not long in making a rope of them. He then cut a deep hole in the ice, drove down his alpenstock, fastened one end to it, and swinging himself off, reached the bottom in safety.

With a cry of joy and a prayer of thankfulness, he hastened along the well-known path; and when the bell of the little chapel, that reared its gilded cross in the Matter Valley, was tolling for the evening prayers, he staggered like a drunken man into the very midst of the astonished worshippers, even as the voice of the good priest was repeating, "God is everywhere with me; and everywhere, even in the most threatening dangers, his voice speaks to me in tones of comfort, and says, 'Call upon me in the day of trouble, and I will deliver thee, and thou shalt glorify me!'"—staggering toward the altar to kneel beside it, he fell fainting into the arms of his wife, who again nursed him to health, strength, and manhood.—*Translated from the German.*

SPLENDID MISERY; OR, HUMBLE HAPPINESS.

Of sixty-seven royal and imperial Queens of France, only thirteen have died without leaving their histories a record of misery or sin. Eleven were divorced, two executed, nine died young, seven were soon widowed, three cruelly treated, three exiled. The poisoned, and broken-hearted, make up the rest. The pillow of royalty is, indeed, filled with thorns; and though crowns may look very bright, they feel very cold, heavy, and hard.

The same principle applies to all happiness that is expected to flow from mere position or circumstances. Joy is an attribute of mind, not matter. Relations of matter are not requisite to its highest exercise. He whose soul is right, has a higher blessedness in the worst material surroundings, than he whose soul is wrong and material surroundings the best. Scourged Paul, and Silas, sang praises in their dungeons, while their imprisoners "feared" for the consequences of their deed. Daniel had angel company in the lion's den. Darius passed the night in fasting, and cried with a lamentable voice in the morning.

The desire to reinforce inward joy by pleasant outward relations, is certainly right. But it should always be regarded as mere reinforcement, and never as the main body. They are subordinate, and should be so regarded. The chief anxiety should be in reference to the chief occasion of joy. Erring in this regard, men look to their material resources for their principal comfort—labor most assiduously for their increase—mourn most inconsolably for their loss. They, indeed, gather scanty harvests from the carefully-cultured surface, but they neglect exhaustless gold beds below. They, indeed, gain an occasional joy from their store's increase, partially counterbalancing the constant fear, and frequent realization of loss, but always losing that contented mind which is a continual feast. They, indeed, get joys through the senses, which are few, very limited in range, easily and frequently cloyed into nausea—as sensitive to pangs as joys—but, all the while, fountains of infinite blessedness within them are utterly sealed.

But he who takes his motto, "My mind to me a kingdom is," leads a different, higher life. He looks over its provinces and departments; he stations motives and officers to control the wrong; he sets agents to encourage and develop the right. He makes conquests in the realms of knowledge. No power can re-conquer those possessions. They are forever his. He develops the ample resources of suavity, which is equivalent to a treaty of peace with surrounding nations. He soothes and eradicates the nettles of irritability, which is the conquest of internal traitors and disturbers of peace at home. He wakens feelings which are equal to the invention and use of the magnetic telegraph in his dominions. This kingdom he knows to be an everlasting kingdom, and every development is of imperishable worth.

But this constant hankering after style—exquisite conformity to fashion—and straining after the next peg in the social ladder—degrades all man's best powers, changes his relations, subordinates him to fleeting customs, and makes him a mere clothes-horse for the support and display of garments. This is splendid misery. An apprentice lately rose to be chief master. By the contemplation of grand plans, by association with men of thought, he rose with his position, and he is now master of his sphere. Not so his wife. Studious of the conventionalities of her new position, she imitates those excesses of refined society which are more easily seen than the exquisite tone and harmony of cultured taste. Conscious of a lack of taste, she is the tormented and suspicious subject of her pensioned guides in this respect. Ambitious for the welfare of her daughters, she draws around her the dregs of the grade above her, rather than the best of that below; and rather than lead, where she might, she is content to follow where her not equal steps produce the lively sensations of a sneak. A man, poor in goods, but rich in mind, seeing her perpetual anxiety and torment, was led to say, "What a curse money may become." Had she but cultured her mind, rose with her circumstances, been mistress of them, developed solid worth, rather than polished the outside glitter—been twice as mindful of doing good and being good, half as mindful of worldly position—her splendid misery might have been unspeakable profit and joy.

The discords, the straining after effect—and the deep, hollow tones, indicative of emptiness in our lives—often result from starting on a wrong key-note. Fairly pitched, some tunes will almost sing themselves; wrongly started, it is torture to sing, and agony to hear them. Start a life on the key of self. It is too low. Every note has a hollow emptiness. It takes all our breath, leaves utter exhaustion. The key-note of love is the only one consonant with existing laws of harmony. Key the soul up to the standard pitch, and with all the harmonies of God pealing round you, the psalm of life, gliding into these harmonies, shall most resoundingly sing itself. Love, shown in service, was the key-note of the life of Jesus, and must be of all his followers who would know His joy and peace.

Does it seem like lowly life? It is the highest. Even the Son of man came not to be ministered unto, but to minister. He might have eclipsed the glory of royalty, might have continually shone with that brightness that made Peter, James, and John afraid—might have been preceded, followed, and flanked by legions of angels. But, for the subjugation of earth and hell at once, he chose the mightier agencies of humility and suffering. Not the guest of kings, he served those too poor to give him house or food. In his own life, he gives a ground for his exhortations to that content, which is consistent with the widest ambition. The world's content is a euphemism for stupidity. But while Christ's apostle learns to be content in whatsoever state of temporal things he is, his ambition leaps towards the highest goal. He fights a good fight, wins an everlasting crown. His strife is toward humility and service; for, by self-abasement, comes divine exaltation.

Toil is often deemed degrading. So it is, if the object is self. But, where toil is for wife, children, and, reaching beyond these, which are a part of self, for the Scripture neighbor, it becomes God's service, and however menial, is as honorable as the work of angels. How self-denial would elevate the life of the grovelling worldling! How personal charity would glorify his scarcely valued gains! How active, practical benevolence, would dissipate that *ennui* that disgusts! More real, upspringing joy sings and laughs in the heart of an humble Christian worker, than ever visits the soul of the trifling or anxious millionaire.

God has inseparably linked righteousness and loving service with profit and joy. True, they bring persecutions. But the promise is, of a hundred-fold of blessing here—designedly and indubitably surpassing persecutions—while, in the world to come, the life has fulness of joy. Even so surely, wickedness, or selfishness—which if the same thing—brings misery and harm. True, the misery may be splendid, but it is no less misery.

In man's central being, lie his powers of enjoyment or suffer ing. These are most sensitive to, and most deeply moved by spiritual and mental influences. These influences, in full play, so affect his powers of appreciation, that the influences of material things are not regarded. Newton, buried in thought, forgets to eat; and Moses, communing with God, fasts forty days. Here, then, is the real field for culture, the true source of profit and joy.

While recognizing the supremacy of these chief incitants, we may reasonably use the prayer of Agar in reference to subordinate ones, "Give me neither poverty nor riches."—*Bishop Thomson.*

HOITY TOITY.

Hoity Toity wears a fool's cap, but Hoity Toity is no fool. Hoity Toity has a grim gray beard, but Hoity Toity is as young as ever he was, and there isn't a kinder heart than the one that beats like a little bird's under his little jerkin. Some people think Hoity Toity a fool because he does queer things sometimes; but they are foolish people themselves, who won't wait and watch until he has finished. And some people say that Hoity Toity has been laid up with the rheumatism for many a year; but they won't take the trouble to look for him, or they might soon see him slipping in and out of the hedges like a little wren, whenever they took a walk. And some people say that Hoity Toity is a spiteful little toad. I'll tell you how that is. Hoity Toity has a stick with two horns, which he calls Easum and Stoppum; for though he looks very grave sometimes, he is almost always a very merry little fellow in his heart. And this is the way he uses his stick. One day he saw a little boy trying to learn his Latin grammar. He was in the second declension, and had shut his book, and was saying over *Dominus;* but he couldn't remember how the accusative ended. "No, I won't look—I'll go over it again," said the little boy. "N. *hic* Dominus—G. *hujus* Domini—D. *huic* Domino—A. *hunc* Domin—e, is it? no, that's the vocative—well, I'll go over it again. Father told me not to look if I could help it, and I haven't half tried yet."

"Oh, you're plainly a case for Eas-*um*," said Hoity Toity,

and he said *um* quite loud, whilst he gave the little boy a dig in the ribs with Easum.

The little boy burst out laughing, though he didn't know what had tickled him. "Yes, that's it," he cried—"A. *hunc* Domin-*um*. I wonder what brought it into my head all of a sudden."

Another time Hoity Toity saw another little boy. This little boy was a big bully, and he was going to thrash a little boy ever so much smaller than he was, little as he was; but Hoity Toity tripped him up with Stoppum, and when he got on his legs again, though he felt inclined at first to give the little boy a worse drubbing than he had meant to give before, he somehow grew ashamed of himself by the time he had brushed the dust off his knees, and he didn't.

"But that's no reason why people should call Hoity Toity a spiteful little toad." True, O King Solomon! But Hoity Toity is a very plucky little fellow, and when he sees grown-up people going to do what they would be sorry for afterwards, he hooks Stoppum round their instep, and brings them down on their noses, just as he would you or any other little boy. A good many of the grown-up people get very savage, and call Hoity Toity a spiteful little toad, (and so do a good many of you youngsters, too,) and they *will* do, after all, what they wanted to do. When they turn obstinate, Hoity Toity lets them have their way. He doesn't crow over them when they come to grief, but he can't help showing them his two horned stick. "There," he says, as he turns it about, looking as sad as a good little creature like Hoity Toity can, "you might have had this"—pointing to Easum—"but you would have this"—pointing to Stoppum—"and, after all, it has done you no good. But you've a chance yet, if you've only got eyes to see it."

Hoity Toity is a music and dancing master, and he teaches deportment too, but not like Mr. Turveydrop. He never professes anything: he does it. He taught the birds and the brooks to sing, and the leaves and the lambs to dance, and the wind to play the harp, and the sea to play the organ; and if we were to copy his manners, we should be the politest people in the world. And yet, for all that, Hoity Toity is to be found in some strange places, and he has some strange servants, and some of his dearest friends are most unfashionable people.

I was in a wood one day, lying in the deep green fern, just as if I had been floating in the trough of the deep green sea. Little wild-flowers trembled outside the fern here and there like foam-bells on a wave, and I was thinking how pretty they were, and wondering why there should be so many of them where scarcely any one ever came. But Hoity Toity loves bees, and butterflies, and birds, and living things of all kinds; and so he gives them pretty drinking-cups, and variegated lamps, and carpets softer and more splendid than a treble-piled Persian. We are apt to fancy that we are Hoity Toity's pets; but, perhaps, that is only our conceit: though he is so very, very kind to us, when we will let him be, that it is not wonderful that we should fancy so. Still there are millions, billions, trillions, quadrillions, quintillions of living things in the world besides the little thousand-millions of men and women, boys and girls, and babies. If we were to have a universal-suffrage election to choose a king for the whole earth, we should not be able to carry our candidate, for all the other things would vote for Hoity Toity, and I am afraid that a good many of us would be silly enough to vote for somebody else. Not that it would matter to Hoity Toity. He is king already without our votes—though, of course, he would like all his subjects to acknowledge him. He would be able to cut off Stoppum then, and use his stick for a sceptre. It would look more like a crook, you say, with only one horn on it? Well, a crook would just suit Hoity Toity's taste. Talking about crooks, though, my wits have gone wool-gathering. Where was I? Oh, yes, lying in the woods, looking at the pretty flowers. I saw something there that didn't seem so pretty—a big whitey-brown mushroom, that looked like a surly fairy's gig-umbrella. It was speckled on the top like a plum-pudding, but if I had eaten it, I should never have tasted a mince-pie again. It was a poisonous fungus—and yet there, at the very root, sat Hoity Toity, looking quite at home. Presently a lean little lizard—like a fairy crocodile—writhed over the mushroom, and put down his head, and looked at Hoity Toity with his bright little beads of eyes, just as Carlo looks at you with his big brown ones, and licked Hoity Toity's face with his lithe leathery little tongue, just as Carlo gives yours a moist rasp with his pink nutmeg-grater. Hoity Toity whispered something to the little lizard, and away he went, flicking Hoity Toity on the nose with the lanky tail he whisked about like a whiplash. I couldn't help thinking that the lizard might both have come to Hoity Toity, and have left him, in a more respectful manner; but Hoity Toity didn't seem to mind a bit. He knew that the lizard was only in a hurry to learn what he had to do, and then in as great a hurry to be off to do it. As soon as the lizard was gone, a staghorn beetle came crawling over the grass, crooking out his legs like a Life Guardsman walking up and down at the Horse-Guards. Hoity Toity didn't hurry him, but waited patiently till he had crept up to Hoity Toity's ear, and didn't flinch when the beetle laid hold of the lobe with his horns. Hoity Toity whispered something to the beetle too; and then the beetle seemed to remember that he had wings as well as legs. He lifted up his wing-cases, as hard as nut-shells, and shook out the crumpled gauze underneath like a little boy fussing over a crushed kite; and as soon as he could get under way, away he went, booming in a blind hurry. He hadn't gone far before he ran foul of a beech-tree, and down he tumbled like a beech-nut. More haste, less speed, you know, sometimes. Hoity Toity gave a funny little smile when he saw the beetle tumble down, and yet he looked rather anxious till he saw the beetle get up again, and go booming on once more—but not blowing his own trumpet quite so loud, and making bends instead of driving stem-on into beech-trees. The beetle, you see, had learnt from experience the impenetrability of matter. I am sorry to say, though, that he forgot his lesson nine or ten times before he got to the cobbler's. Hoity Toity began to finger his stick; but at last the beetle was out of the wood, with nothing but the cobbler's window-panes between him and the cobbler. Then Hoity Toity sat down again, and looked rather sadly at one little leaf left at the end of a long branch.

"Ah, I'll see to my poor shepherd myself," he said. "My little lizard must have got to my poor tailor by this time, and honest friend beetle can't well go wrong now." But Hoity Toity saw me looking at him as if I thought him a very fine little fellow, and Hoity Toity can't bear to be praised by those who do nothing but praise him, and he hates to be idle. He has got a notion, indeed, that if he were to cease to work he would cease to be, and the round world would shrivel up like a pricked bladder. So off went Hoity Toity like a lamplighter. No lamplighter, though, can trot as fast as Hoity Toity, or make such bright lights leap out in such dark corners. He uses his two-horned stick as the lamplighter uses his wand. Easum is the kindler, and Stoppum is the extinguisher; for Hoity Toity is obliged to put out lights sometimes—the very lights that he has lighted. The people who are left in the dark can't make it out at first; but, as they feel about in the dark, they often lay hold of the thing Hoity Toity wanted them to lay hold of, but they have never laid hold of before, though Hoity Toity lighted their lamp just to show them the way to it.

When Hoity Toity was gone, I looked at the big whitey-brown mushroom, and it seemed ever so much prettier than it did before, for Hoity Toity, who is always doing something, even when he seems quite idle, had cut his name on the stalk.

And then I went to see the tailor. It was easy to find him out, for there was only one tailor in those parts, and his name was Zephaniah Shears. It was a sunny afternoon, and the little lizard was basking on Zephaniah's threshold, looking up now and then with his shy bright little eyes, as if he was saying to himself, "It might do you some good if you'd take some notice of me; but I'm in no hurry: take your time, take your time, brother Zeph." It was no wonder that the little lizard looked at the tailor as if he thought him a big brother, for Zephaniah looked just like a big lizard in man's clothes, he was so long and lean. Zephaniah was saying to *himself*, "I wish I knew the wood where the guineas grow like wild apricots, for I've got no money. But that's silly talk. I must work for my wages. And what work have I got to do? Just two jobs. Here's Farmer Stubbs' velveteen breeches to seat; and that won't bring me in much, big as he be. And here's the old scarecrow coat I got to make into a jacket for Widow Wasp's little boy; and that won't bring me in anything. Not even thanks; she'll say I've boggled it because she is a lone, lorn woman. Well, I think I shall do the breeches first. Old Zeph must look after himself. There's nobody else to look after him." But just then Zeph looked up and saw the lizard, and he felt ashamed. "Yes, there is," he said, contradicting himself as gruffly as if somebody else had spoken. "There's the same to look after me as looks after that little thing, and I'll do the jacket first. Farmer Stubbs has plenty more breeches, but little Bob Wasp has only got his shirt to cover his back, and that's like a colander. I'm glad I found this old thing in the ditch, for I couldn't have afforded to buy cloth for the little chap. Ragged as it is, it ain't rotten, and I'll see if I can't make him look as spruce as a little squire. One of these days I may stumble on a trowser-piece for him. I can make him a waistcoat out of the cuttings of this, for poor little Bob ain't very broad in the chest."

And so Zephaniah spread the old coat on his board, and took out his chalk, and put his head on one side, and made his marks as knowingly as a writing-master flourishing a ciphering-book, and then he got his shears and began to cut. "Why, what's this?" he cried, presently, as he picked something out of the fusty old lining. "Well, I'm blest if it ain't a five-pound note! And if I haven't been and gone and cut it in two! Ah, I see what that means,—the widow must go halves." And, without waiting to put on his hat, Zephaniah rushed over the green as fast as his long legs would carry him—they looked as long and as lean as a shadow's legs—to Widow Wasp's cottage; and the lizard went back to report progress to Hoity Toity.

The cobbler lived close by the tailor, and *his* name was Benjamin Bradawl. He was thicker in the body than Zephaniah, and thicker in the head too. He was a very obstinate old fellow, was Benjie. Staring through his great horn spectacles, he looked as wise as a beetle. Benjie was the only thing like a beetle in his shop when I peeped in. The staghorn was still blundering about somewhere on the road. Perhaps Hoity Toity sends his swiftest messengers to those who are readiest to receive them. Benjie was holding up an old boot that sadly wanted soling, and upper-leathering too, for that matter. Benjie had not made the boot, and so he was growling over it scornfully.

"Just like all them town-made things," he said; "might as well wear wet brown paper. I don't know how I'm to mend the thing. Who's to know where to begin and when to leave off? Folks ought to be ashamed to go shod like that. It ain't respectable. Why didn't your father pitch it to the pigs?"

"Please, sir, he hain't got any pigs to pitch it to; and if he had, he couldn't afford to pitch away his boots," answered the little boy to whom Benjie spoke. "Father's stopping at home till you've done it, and if it ain't done the first thing in the morning, he'll lose his place, for he won't be able to take round the letters."

"That ain't true," said Benjie.

"Please, sir, I wouldn't tell a lie," said the little boy.

"Don't you tell me no more of them," said Benjie. "You and your father is both a bad lot. So you be off." And Benjie threw the old boot out of doors. The little boy ran to pick it up, looking very sad. Just after he had got outside, there came a great thud against the window.

"What do you mean by throwing stones at my window, you wicious young warmint?" shouted Benjie. And he rushed out, and was going to box the little boy's ears, when again he heard a *thud, thud, thud*, like the tap of a drum, on his window-pane. Benjie stared through his horn spectacles as if he was frightened. Whilst he was staring, something came against his spectacles with such a bang that it almost broke one of the glasses. He clapped up his hand to his eye, and when he had opened it, he called out, "Blowed if it ain't a beetle,"—and he was so much astonished to find that *he* could make a mistake, that the beetle flew away before he could kill it. Perhaps he wouldn't have killed it, though. At any rate, he gave the little boy a penny to buy marbles, and picked up the boot, and took it back, and waxed his thread, and began to work away for the poor postman just as if he had been the Squire. Hoity Toity, you see, had sent Staghorn to teach Beetle Benjie not to be quite so sure that he was always right and everybody else always wrong. Hoity Toity teaches all kinds of scholars all kinds of lessons, and sometimes he engages very funny ushers.

It was getting evening now, and when I had crossed the green I went along a lane, and so got on to a common. There I met a beautiful grand lady, with a little portfolio in her hand. The lady had lost her way, and she asked me if I could tell her which turning she must take. "I have been sketching," she said; "and it seems just as if some one had been drawing me on by making pretty pictures for me to copy. Sometimes a branch was lifted up for me to see the blue hills in the distance, and sometimes a brier-spray was bent down into a fairy-bridge with two butterflies fluttering over it, sometimes one thing and sometimes another, until I quite forgot myself. I haven't the least idea where I am. I was never here before." It was that sly little Hoity Toity who had been making pictures to lure the beautiful grand lady on. He wanted to please her, for one thing, because she was good as well as beautiful; but he wanted her, too, to meet somebody else he loved. Sly little Hoity Toity! Presently the lady said, "Oh, look at that lonely little cottage—yonder where the rough hillside comes down into the common—doesn't it look beautiful in the red sunset? I must get a sketch of that before the sun goes down." Whilst the lady was scratching away with her pencil, and scribbling down the names of all kinds of colors here, there, and everywhere, that she might know how to paint her picture next day, the cottage-door opened, and a man came out. He had to pass us; but he did not see us until he was close upon us, because we were in a sandy little hollow with furze-bushes round it. He was a great manly shepherd, but he walked as slowly as an old man. As he came nearer we saw that he was carrying a white lamb.

The lamb seemed to like to be carried, and was snuggling in his arms and looking up in his face like a little child; but he was looking down at it, oh! so sadly, and when he came quite close, we saw that the great manly fellow was crying.

"What is the matter, my poor man?" said the beautiful grand lady.

He looked ashamed at first at having been caught crying, but then he told the lady that he had lost all his sheep except this little lamb, and now he was obliged to sell it, though it was so fond of him, and was his little Bessy's pet, and she had no mother, or brother, or sister, poor lonely little lass.

"I put off bringing it away till she was asleep," said the shepherd; "and now I feel as if I could hardly drag my feet along. Seems as if I was cheating both the little lambs."

"Take Bessy back her little lamb," said the beautiful grand lady. "Here is some money for to-night, and come over to Bountiful Hall to-morrow. I will make inquiries about you, and if I find you are as honest as you look, you shall be my shepherd. I've hundreds of sheep, you know."

So *that* was the little game Hoity Toity had been playing with the beautiful grand lady who went out sketching and lost her way.

Besides what I saw, Hoity Toity did scores of kind things that I didn't see that afternoon; and he went on doing them when the sun went down, and the moon and the stars came up, and the larks began to sing, and the sun looked out from the east once more, as fresh as if he had been sound asleep all night instead of shining thousands of miles away. Hoity Toity is like the sun; he never goes to sleep, and he never gets tired.

"But how can he do so much, if he is so little?"—Oh, he makes himself little that he may get close to the little things he has to look after.—*Charles Camden.*

COAL AND SUNBEAMS.

WHAT the climate of the globe was at the time that coal-plants grew, may be found out from the fact that ferns and club-mosses thrive best, at the present day, in moist sheltered islands. Some think that the presence of tree-ferns shows a tropical warmth; but in New Zealand, where they still occur, the climate is very much like our own, and tree-ferns are found even at a height of upwards of a thousand feet, beside the end of glaciers, waving their green feathery fronds over the never-melting ice. Ferns and club-mosses can therefore endure a wide range of temperature, so that their occurrence is no proof of a particular climate. In all probability, however, the climate of the coal period was warmer, moister, and more uniform than now obtains; and the huge size of the coal-plants, and the vast quantity of coal which they formed, seem to prove that the atmosphere was highly charged with that carbonic acid gas which plants take in and work into all their structures. The sameness of the climate is shown by the general character of the coal-plants being the same over every portion of the earth's surface, the same kinds being found in the most distant countries.

How coal was formed from these plants is very difficult indeed to tell, because there is no process precisely of the same nature now going on anywhere. Most men of science believe that the plants have been swept down from the places where they grew, by rivers or currents, and left in basins and firths of the sea, or in fresh-water lakes. Sand and mud were heaped in alternate layers over them there, and thus formed the different strata of coal and sandstone which we now find in a coal-basin. We can trace the gradual change between perfect wood and perfect coal in such situations, from the blackened tree-trunks of our peat-bogs, through the *lignites* or brown coal, up through bituminous coal, to the true coals which we burn in our grates. After a long interment of the heaped-up plants beneath the water, gradually undergoing there the chemical changes necessary to convert them into the mineral condition, subterranean fires at last elevated the beds of coal above the waters, nearer the surface of the earth. Were it not for this the coal would have been buried far beyond the reach of man. Molten matter ran through the coal basin in different directions, like the lava that flows down the sides of Vesuvius, and this hardened into what is called trap-rocks. By these fiery eruptions of trap, the seams of coal were broken up and divided into parts that are easily worked, and the coal itself was brought from the profound depths within reach of man. We find many wonderful proofs of God's wisdom and care for man, in thus preparing and arranging the coal beds. Had they been formed on the surface, exposed to the air, they would have crumbled away into dross, but the precious treasure was safely hid deep down in the earth, under beds of rocks, and yet not so deep as to be beyond the industry of man to get it by digging. It was not covered with hard rocks like granite and quartz, which it would be very difficult to blast and penetrate; but with limestone, sandstone, shale, and clay ironstone, which can be easily pierced, and yet afford a sufficiently safe roof for the mine, and which are very valuable in themselves for man's uses.

A lump of coal, it is often said, is made up of sunbeams. We could believe this more readily of the diamond, which is just a crystal of coal, for it is so bright and sparkling, and makes brilliant sunshine in a shady place. But even the dull, black coal has been formed of the sunshine of long forgotten summers. Every sunbeam that fell upon the club-mosses and ferns of the old coal forests, enabled them to withdraw the minute unseen carbon from the air, and form out of it their own solid tissue. They thus caged and imprisoned the floating light itself, and wrought its bright threads in their loom, into the beautiful patterns of stem and leaf, which they showed. To form one of the little rings of wood in the trunk of one of the old pines took the sunshine of a long summer, falling upon all its thousand leaves; and who can tell how much sunshine has been worked up in all the stores of coal that lie concealed under our feet? This prisoned sunshine we set free whenever we kindle a fire of coals. When the sun ceases to shine upon us in these cold, misty, wintry days, we draw upon the sunshine of a million years ago, to drive away the frost and make us comfortable. The source of all labor is the sun; and we get the benefit of his labor when we burn the coal or the wood, in which he has condensed and preserved it. No ray of sunlight has ever been wasted or thrown away. It is because Nature has been so thrifty in her household ways, that we are enabled to be so prodigal of our resources to day, spending upwards of one hundred millions of tons of coal every year, and with that vast consumption of sun-labor producing all the varied and extraordinary work that we do under the sun.

Why is a lump of coal black if it is composed of sunbeams, which every one knows contains all the colors of the rainbow? Why is it black if it is made up of the green stems and branches and leaves of plants? It is because its particles are so formed and arranged, as to take in all the light that falls upon it without giving back any portion. A white object reflects all the light, and a black object absorbs all the light. What becomes, then, of the colors which the black coal has withdrawn from the sunshine? Are they lost? No! nothing in this world is lost. Every thing is accounted for. When anything has served its purpose in one form, it seems to vanish althogeter, but it reappears in another form, and in it works anew. There is everywhere change, but not loss. A growing plant absorbs some of the colors of the sunbeams that nourish it, and reflects others in its prevailing hues—yellow or blue or red or purple. But the colors that it absorbs are not lost; they generally reappear in some other or after part of the plant. So the colors of the sunshine that are absorbed in the black coal come out in the colored flames of the blazing fire. The red and yellow flame, over which you warm your hands, is just the flower into which the sunshine, concealed and stored up in the coal for ages, has blossomed. But more than this, the lost colors of the rainbow in coal are brought out still more strikingly by our modern manufacturers. Every one has heard of and most persons have seen what are called the coal-tar colors. Richest and brightest hues of blue and green, and mauve and magenta, and rose and yellow, are obtained from tar, and tar is obtained from coal. It would take me too long to describe the process, but it is very curious, and is one of the many triumphs of this extraordinary age.

Were I disposed to draw a moral from my little paper, I could show that there are hidden beauties in everything and every one, however ugly and unpromising, which it would be well worth our while to find and bring out. But I shall merely throw out this as a hint, and simply ask those who have accompanied me thus far without sleepy eyes and yawns as round as O's, if it is not true what I have said, that there are wonders in the fire, stranger than in any fairy story, stranger than any faces, and castles, and pictures that the young fancy sees in its glowing heat, in the twilight hours—wonders, the half of which has not been told them?—*Hugh Macmillan.*

CATHERINE OF RUSSIA.

ANONYMOUS.

THE day had closed, and the snow fell heavily, as the pastor Skovronski, returning from a visit to his sister, who lived a short distance from Marienburg, reached the skirt of the wood surrounding the town. The cries of a child attracting his attention, he stopped his horse; but the noise of the wind rushing through the trees could alone be heard, and he proceeded on his way, believing that he must have been mistaken. Suddenly the horse stood still, and no urging or soothing on the part of the pastor, could induce him to proceed. Supposing it was some obstacle hidden by the darkness of the night, he dismounted, and tried to force the animal forward; but his efforts were unavailing. He then perceived a slight elevation in the snow, at the horse's feet, and, stooping down, found it to be a half-frozen child wrapped in linen. Taking it in his arms, he found that it was still alive. This accounted for the cries which he had just heard. He anxiously endeavored, despite the darkness of the night, to discover those who, from misery or other causes, had thus abandoned their offspring in a desert place, covered with snow; but neither seeing nor hearing any one, the venerable pastor exclaimed in a loud voice, "If you who have deserted this child can now hear me, go in peace. In the name of the Great Being whom I serve, I promise that henceforth this child shall be my care."

Remounting his horse, with the child wrapped in his cloak before him, he quickened his pace, and soon arrived at his humble dwelling, though much later than usual.

"Mercy on me, Monsieur Skovronski, what could have delayed you until this hour?" said an old woman, as she advanced to hold the bridle while he alighted. "I have been imagining all kinds of misfortunes—that your sister Alexina was ill, that Biaska had fallen lame, or that you had been attacked by the Cossacks."

"Take this infant, Frederika," said the pastor, interrupting the old servant, and placing the child in her arms.

Surprise rendered her mute for an instant; but, like a torrent which had overflowed its banks, her words soon found utterance, and she exclaimed with volubility, "An infant, monsieur—an infant! And where have you found it? What are we to do with an infant in this place? Who is to take care of it? Who is to nurse it?"

"You, Frederika," quietly replied the old man, as he followed her into the house.

"What a beautiful little girl, monsieur! It can scarcely be a year old. See, as she opens her large black eyes, with what astonishment she looks around her."

The old pastor smiled, and placing some more logs on the hearth, and looking after the comfort of his little charge, he commenced his frugal supper, during which he recounted to the old woman the manner in which he had discovered the infant.

"How strange, monsieur, that Biaska should have refused to advance, is it not?"

"Horses have a noble instinct," replied the pastor; "they may throw down a man or a child while running, but will never pass over a body, dead or alive, lying in their path."

"And when you called out to know if any one was at hand, did you see anybody?"

"No one."

"Even her dress tells nothing. It is fine, but bears no mark by which she might be known. What shall we call her, monsieur?"

"Give me the calender, Frederika. This is St. Catherine's day, the 25th of November. We shall call her Catherine."

The old woman retired with the child, and soon after the venerable pastor sought his pillow, and enjoyed the sleep of a man conscious of having performed his duty.

Early the next morning, it was known to all in Marienburg that their pastor had found the child in the snow, and that he had adopted it. The previous night, a peasant, living in a cottage at the edge of the wood, had been awoke by the noise of a heavy body falling against his door, accompanied by groans, but the fearful and stupid man did not go to see what it was. On getting up next morning, he found a soldier dead outside his threshold. The pastor, hoping to discover some clue as to the history of his protegee, visited the cabin where the soldier lay, but could gain no information concerning him: and the only document which was found about his person was part of a letter, in which some vague allusion was made to "the children." The conjecture of the worthy Skovronski was, that the soldier had been overcome by the severity of the cold, and must have laid the child down, hoping by some violent exercise to warm his freezing limbs. But under that inclement sky, death comes on the snow-storm, and will not be dallied with. The pastor gave orders for the decent interment of the stranger, and carefully preserved the fragment of the letter, unsatisfactory though it was, and breaking off just where the words "children, dear children," occurred. He hoped, that slight as the clue was, it might help at some future time to identify the child. From that time forward, however, he treated her with the kindness and affection of a parent; and so endeared to him did the little Catherine become, by her docility and sweet temper, that perhaps, as years passed on, he ceased to regret that the inquiries he made, whenever opportunity offered, failed to draw forth any information as to who the dead soldier could have been, or who his helpless charge. Nor is there much wonder at this, for war was ravaging the country, and the circumstance of an obscure individual of the army being missing, when hundreds and thousands were dying around them, was one little likely to attract attention.

Years passed away, and Catherine, grown a tall, beautiful girl, assisted Frederika in the management of the household affairs. At night she always sang cheerful songs for her adopted father with a very sweet voice; and nothing was found to disturb the smoothness of her happy disposition, unless indeed we except two or three occasions on which her father—so she always called him—was visited by attacks of illness which seemed to threaten his life. Then indeed her young heart was rent with sorrow. It was on these trying occasions that, prompted by her deep affection, and perhaps instructed by the experienced Frederika, she acquired a skill as a nurse which was surprising in a mere child—a skill which, under the influence of another strong affection, and a remarkable destiny, proved in after-years of singular account. Strange it is to think of, and yet most true, that in reality there is not an action of our lives which is unimportant, or may not in its consequences influence our future.

One day, when Catherine was about thirteen years of age, the old pastor appeared restless after reading some letters which had been brought that morning; and calling Catherine, he said, "My dear child, my sister Alexina is old. She is often ill, and I should wish to have you near her for a short time."

"If such is your wish, my father, I shall go. I love your sister, for she is yours; but I confess I should prefer remaining with you."

"You shall return in a few days, Catherine, when I shall go for you myself—myself, Catherine—understand me, only myself."

"Be it so, my benefactor:" and, with the natural gaiety of youth, she hastened to prepare for her departure.

The pastor accompanied her until they arrived at the place where, as an infant, he had found her. It was summer, and the green grass had replaced the snow which at that time covered the ground. Catherine knelt.

"Give me your blessing here, father," said she in a voice of emotion. "It was here that, thirteen years ago, you first heard my feeble cries. God hears this day the prayers I offer for your happiness, and will listen to me as you then listened, and repay you for all that you have since done for me, and prolong your days to give happiness to all those that surround you."

The old man's agitation was extreme, as laying his trembling hands on the beautiful girl's head, he exclaimed, "Go in peace, my daughter. God is our master, and we must submit to whatever He wills. We cannot foresee in what manner He thinks right to dispose of his creatures. Whatever may happen, be assured that my sister will continue my work of charity and love. Go; and if Heaven wills that we shall not meet again, remember the last words of your poor old pastor, who, knowing his intellect inadequate to the training of thine, was content to model thy heart after his own. Be always good and obedient—be submissive, Catherine; and in whatever position it may be your fortune to be placed, always remember that thou once wert but a poor deserted infant, who in a few hours must have perished, had not God sent one of his humble servants to your assistance. Rise, my daughter; go in peace; always act rightly, speak truth, and do your duty, happen what may."

Raising the young girl from her knees, he kissed her forehead, and they separated.

"Catherine! Catherine! why do you remain at the door instead of assisting me in laying by these clothes, or spinning the rest of the flax? Do you think that my brother has sent you to me to do nothing but to fold your arms and amuse yourself? Do you hear me, Catherine?"

The person who spoke was the old pastor's aged sister, who resided a few miles from Marienburg, in Livonia. The usually joyous countenance of the young girl whom she addressed bespoke intense anxiety.

"Oh, Madame Alexina, do you not hear the roaring of the cannon?" asked she, still remaining at the door.

"It is perhaps thunder, or some public rejoicing, Catherine. What day of the month is this?"

"The 20th of August, 1702, Madame Alexina."

"No, it is not the king's birth-day. Are you sure that it was cannon, Catherine?"

"Yesterday morning," said Catherine, half speaking to herself, and as if trying to recall something to her memory, "the pastor Skovronski, after his usual visits to his friends, called me to his side. He had an air of anxiety and trouble. 'My child,' said he, 'we are at length going to part. My sister is in need of you. You will not leave her until I go for you *myself*—myself, Catherine.' I was struck by his repeating *myself;* and not answering him, he continued, 'God is our master.' When anything weighed on his mind, that was his expression. And then he made me depart so quickly, too, without allowing me to speak to any one. And he appeared so agitated when he placed his hand on my head to bless me. Oh, I have seen him for the last time! Child that I am to have left him. Again the cannon—again!"

Carried away by her feelings, she wept unrestrainedly.

"Mercy on me! weeping! You, too, who are ever laughing," cried the old lady with surprise. "Do you weep because my brother appeared a little agitated, and his hand trembled! It was because he loves you, and looks upon you as a daughter."

"But why did he send me to you?"

"I am old—I am in need of you."

"He is also old; he, too, is in need of me."

"You love my brother better than you love me, Catherine. That is wrong," said the old Livonian, in a half-reproachful voice. "That is wrong," she repeated.

"Pardon me, madame, but it is true," replied Catherine, innocently; "and is it not right and natural? He who saved me, when an infant, from being frozen to death, and ever since has been to me as a father. Oh, I love the pastor of Marienburg as I should have loved my own father, if God had been pleased that I should have known one—as I would have loved a mother. I would freely give my life to save his. But do you not again hear the cannon?"

At this moment a horse stopped at the door of the cottage, and a young man, travel-stained, hastily dismounted. "The Russians are at Marienburg!" exclaimed he, rushing into the apartment. "I have escaped with difficulty to bring this letter from your brother, who has given his horse to expedite me."

"What of the pastor Skovronski?" asked Catherine hurriedly.

"Oh, how happy you ought to be, mademoiselle," said the messenger, "to have neither father, nor mother, nor family."

"You think so, Paul?" replied Catherine with a look of scorn which she did not attempt to conceal.

"Yes, mademoiselle; for you are not obliged to break your heart by leaving them."

"And wherefore do you leave them?"

"They besought me on my knees to do so, and now I tremble for them."

"Persons do not tremble for those whom they may defend," replied Catherine. "But tell me, what has occurred at Marienburg?"

"Why, mademoiselle, do you hear the cannon? General Scheremetief, with his army, is bombarding Marienburg. Oh, it is a cruel sight to behold!"

"My benefactor, my father!" cried Catherine, sobbing.

"Thy benefactor, thy father," said Madame Alexina, having finished the perusal of the letter, "conjures thee by all that is sacred not to leave me. He thinks it is his duty to remain with those intrusted to his care, and asks for our prayers for his safety; and if God wills that his life should be the sacrifice, he leaves thee all he possesses."

"Madame Alexina," said Catherine, taking her hand and raising it to her lips respectfully, "you have a heart—you are good, and you will understand me. I return to Marienburg! In this I must be disobedient."

"But you have not heard what Paul has said—that the Russians are already in the town," replied Alexina, endeavoring to hold her hand.

"I'll go to find my benefactor."

"But by this time, mademoiselle," observed Paul, "all the inhabitants are either dead or taken prisoners."

"I shall then die with them, or be a prisoner," cried Catherine, raising her head, and speaking in a tone of determination. Slipping her hand from that of the old Livonian, she suddenly sprang on the horse which Paul had left at the door, and before either he or the old lady could recover from their surprise, she had disappeared.

The evening was closing as a horse, covered with foam, reached the border of the wood lying nearest to the gates of Marienburg. At the moment it emerged from the shade of the trees, a man suddenly seized the bridle.

"Where are you going?" demanded he of the rider, in a peremptory tone.

"What is that to you?" was the reply, in an equally peremptory voice.

Astonished by this boldness, the stranger's arm was raised to inflict summary punishment; but on perceiving that it was a girl who spoke, he desisted, and repeated, though in a milder tone, "Where are you going?"

"What is that to you?" again repeated the young girl. "I am in haste, and I pray you to let me pass."

"You of course are not aware, then, that the town is in the hands of the Russians?" said the man, still retaining the bridle.

"Well, what then?" interrupted Catherine, for it was indeed she who spoke.

"That all the inhabitants are prisoners; and if you pursue your route, you will also be taken."

"Thank you for your advice; but know in your turn, monsieur, that he whom I look up to as a father is in the town, and I am determined to share his fate, whatever it may be."

"But if he is a prisoner?"

"I will be a prisoner too."

"But if he is dead?"

This supposition rendered Catherine mute; but recovering her courage and self-possession, she said with sweetness, "I have told you, monsieur, that I should like to share his fate."

"Go, then, and God preserve you," answered the man, letting go the bridle of the horse, which started off at once at full gallop.

She had not gone many paces when a loud "Who goes there?" was heard, and Catherine not answering, a ball whistled by her so close as to tear the sleeve of her dress. She immediately drew up the horse.

"Well, when I reply to you ''Tis I!' will you be much the wiser?" cried she.

She was immediately surrounded by a number of rough and barbarous-looking men.

"Dismount, my pretty girl, and follow us," said one who, from the tone he assumed, appeared to be their officer.

But Catherine, perceiving amongst the men him whom she had met at the border of the forest, and whom she immediately recognised by his noble and majestic bearing, contrasting so favorably with the rude men by whom he was surrounded, said, addressing him, "Monsieur, I pray you to speak to these men to let me go: you know that I am but a poor child; incapable of doing harm."

"I have told you what would happen if you pursued your route," replied the young unknown: then turning to the Cossack officer, he added, "Do your duty!"

"Your name?" asked the soldier of the young girl.

"Catherine," replied she quickly. "I am the adopted child of the pastor Skovronski. I left yesterday morning by his wish—I return to-day by my own. Let me pass, I pray you."

The officer exchanged a glance with the stranger to whom she had first appealed, and then replied, "Thou art a Livonian. Livonia belongs this day to our czar, Peter I. of Russia—you are therefore a prisoner. Come, dismount, if you do not wish me to assist you, and follow us to prison."

"Touch me not!" said Catherine, her beautiful dark eyes flashing with a look beyond her years. Leaping from her horse, she added, "I did not return to Marienburg solely to be made a prisoner, but to find my adopted father. Conduct me then to him—in his house—in a dungeon—no matter where, so that I may be with him."

"It is not for prisoners to dictate their orders," replied the officer, amused by the boldness of the young girl.

Catherine reflected a moment, and then asked, "Who is your chief—your general?"

"General Scheremetief," said the stranger, advancing, having hitherto kept aloof, though listening with attention to the altercation between Catherine and the Cossack officer.

"I wish, then, to speak to the general."

Receiving a sign from the unknown, the Cossack ordered her to follow him, and marched in the direction of the town. As Catherine stopped at the gates while the officer was making inquiries as to where the general was to be found, an old woman perceiving her, uttered a cry of despair.

"Oh, my dear child, you will see your protector no more! My poor master!" said she, sobbing; "he is dead on the field of battle. I saw him fall, struck by a Russian bullet, at the moment that he was binding up the wounds of a poor Livonian. He is dead—my poor master!"

Catherine, pale and trembling, asked, "What do you say, Frederika?"

"Truth, my dear child, truth!—as will be found on looking for him among the dead."

"And have you, then, left him there without help—without prayers?" asked Catherine quickly.

"What could we do, mademoiselle? The bullets whistled about our ears, killing all they reached."

The Cossack officer said that the general was near them, and bade her follow him. She rather went before than came after him. On entering the tent, the first person she saw was the young unknown; but, without taking further notice of him, seeing that he was not the chief, she threw herself at the feet of the great general whose name had been echoed far and near.

"A grace, general! for pity's sake, a grace!" said she, raising her hands in the attitude of supplication.

"What does this child want?" demanded the general, turning to the officer who had conducted her to his presence.

"She requests to speak to you, general."

"It is true," replied Catherine. "I believed my protector—my father—to be a prisoner, and wished to share his prison; but I have since learned that he is among the dead. The favor I ask is, to be allowed to seek for his body, that it may be buried in the manner it deserves. Oh, if you had known how good he was—the poor pastor Skovronski!"

The tone of her voice was so peculiar, and her countenance so commanding, yet so ingenuous, that the general, moved at the sight of her youth and courage, said, "The camp is situated outside the walls; if I grant your request, what guarantee shall I have that you will not try to escape?"

"My word!" replied Catherine innocently.

"Go, then," said the general, beckoning her to rise; "but remember that you belong to me when you return."

The first person Catherine encountered on leaving the tent was old Frederika, the pastor's servant. "Come," said she, taking her hand; "come, show me the place where you saw him fall."

"Think not of such a thing, Catherine. Would you go among the dead at this hour?"

"Remain, Frederika, if you have any fear. I shall go alone; he may be yet alive."

"Let us go, then," said the old woman; "it shall not be said that a child had more humanity than I had."

The night was dark, and it was with difficulty they could see their way. When they got outside the town, they came upon a field covered with the bodies of men and horses, while the cries that arose told that many were still alive. The young girl was seized with horror, and stopped. "Oh, my God, guide me!" she exclaimed, and again advanced. Suddenly she heard footsteps following. "Who are you?" she cried, turning to some person, whom the darkness prevented her from distinguishing, adding, "You are, no doubt, like us, an unfortunate. You seek perhaps some friend—a brother. I seek my father, and perhaps he is dead! Oh! why have I come without a light, as if I could distinguish my benefactor in this terrible darkness. Heaven guide me!"

"Wait for me; I shall soon return," said the person who had followed them.

He soon appeared, carrying a lantern, and Catherine recognized the stranger whom she had first met in the wood. The light discovered to the young girl the earth covered with the dead and dying; but overcoming her repugnance to such a scene, she diligently pursued her search, Frederika being unable to recollect the spot where she had seen her master fall. The stranger followed in silence. Each moment the agitation of the young girl increased, and the sickening sights around her, joined to the fruitless search, overcame her fortitude, and sinking on the ground, she covered her face with her hands, and wept violently.

"Catherine," said the unknown, "you have undertaken a task too much for your age and strength; leave the search to me, and at daybreak, when the dead are separated from the wounded, I shall myself seek him with the assistance of some of the inhabitants of the town, who will be able to recognize their pastor, and perhaps he may not be amongst the dead."

"What I have commenced I shall finish," said Catherine; "but you, monsieur, whom do you seek?"

"Hear me, Catherine," replied the stranger. "I am but a soldier, and perhaps may have the courage of a soldier; but, on my word, your's astonishes me. You are not formed to be a slave, though a general may be your master. You are now beyond the camp: no person has seen you. Fly! If you want money, here it is."

"'Tis Heaven that has sent you," exclaimed the old woman, taking the purse from his hand. "Catherine, do not refuse such goodness: let us fly."

"Fly? when I have given my word not to do so. Do you consider that as nothing, monsieur?" said the girl, in surprise.

"No—when given by a man," replied the soldier. "But it is of little consequence when broken by such as you—a girl without name, without birth. Think well of what you must endure if you return: the hopes of your youth changed into misery, and you yourself become a slave. I conjure you to fly."

But Catherine, firm to her purpose, replied, "I am ignorant for what God has destined me. I am aware that I am but a child, unknown, and without name; but ought the obscurity of my birth to authorize me in doing a wrong action? If I was a princess, I should keep my promise. Perhaps I have the heart of a princess. Monsieur, I shall keep my word." Then rising and turning to Frederika, she added, "Come, Frederika, let us continue our search; I feel myself stronger now."

At this moment a stifled groan was heard a short distance from where they stood. "Hush!" whispered Catherine, listening with breathless anxiety. The groan was repeated, and, like a young fawn, she sprang to the spot whence it proceeded, and throwing herself on her knees by the side of an old man stretched on the ground, she exclaimed, "Frederika, the light! It is he! Quick! quick! Oh, my father, my benefactor, speak to me! It is your child, your little Catherine, who calls."

Frederika held the light to the countenance of the old man, while Catherine, with an address and attention far beyond her years, endeavored to find the wound from which the pastor was suffering. As she raised his arm to extricate him from the bodies lying around, he uttered a cry of pain, at the same time opening his eyes. "Where am I?" asked he. Recognizing Catherine and Frederika, but not knowing the young soldier, he repeated, "Where am I?"

"With your friends," replied Catherine, kissing his forehead; "with your little Catherine. Oh rise, my father, and accompany us."

"Here, old man, take some of this *eau de vie*," said the soldier, placing a gourd to the lips of the pastor; "it will strengthen you."

The pastor obeyed; and, reanimated by the welcome draught, he endeavored to rise. Catherine having taken his arm, he again exclaimed, as if in pain; adding, in a gentle voice, "My arm is broken."

"Oh! what shall we do?" cried Catherine.

"Do not move, old man," said the soldier; "I shall return to Marienburg, and send two comrades to carry you to your home: I shall also send a surgeon, who will set your arm to rights. Adieu, Catherine," added he, retiring, "follow my advice—profit by your present liberty, and fly."

They had not to wait long for the promised assistance. Three men advanced, two of them carrying a litter, on which they laid the wounded pastor, and carefully conveyed him home, Catherine never leaving his side.

"It was God who inspired me," said she: "one would almost say that he took me by the hand, and led me to the border of the forest, that I might become a prisoner."

"You are a prisoner, then, my poor child?" said the old man with emotion.

"Yes, my father; and what I at first looked on as a misfortune, has proved a blessing. If I had not been taken prisoner, I should not have been carried before the general, and would have missed seeing Frederika, who told me of your death; and had I not seen her, I should never have thought of seeking for you on the field of battle. Do you not think, then, that God led me by the hand to where I found you?"

Catherine ceased speaking as the litter entered the interior of the parsonage. The pastor was removed to his bed, and the operation of setting his broken arm being quickly performed by the surgeon who had accompanied them, he and the two soldiers retired. After offering up a prayer, the old man sank into slumber, and the females watched by his bedside the remainder of the night.

When day appeared, Catherine sought her own little chamber; and, having changed her dress, and fastened her long black hair in a knot under her bonnet, she descended to the room of the pastor, who had just awoke.

"My dear benefactor," said she, kneeling by his bedside, "bless your poor Catherine, who is obliged to leave you for ever."

"What do you say, child?" asked the old man, astonished at her words, and seeing the tears which fell from the young Livonian.

"Yesterday, my father, I was taken prisoner, and now belong to the Russian general. He permitted me to seek for you, on giving my promise that I should return."

"Is it not foolish for her to do so, monsieur?" asked Frederika, overcome at the idea of losing her dearly-loved child. "I am now old, and want help; and who can assist me like Catherine? Who will sing for you the songs to which you have so often listened? Who will give you an arm to lean on when you walk, and amuse you as she could? No, Catherine, you must not leave us for an unhappy promise given at hazard—forced from you. You know it was forced from you. If it had been given freely, I should be the first to say go."

The pastor and Catherine listened without interruption to the old woman. Skovronski first spoke—"You have promised the general that you would return, my child?"

"Yes, my father," answered Catherine, sobbing; "and is it kind of Frederika to try to dissuade me from my resolution, by thus bringing to my memory all the happiness that I have enjoyed, and which I am about to lose forever?"

"Go, my child; go, my dear Catherine," said the old man in a solemn voice; "do your duty, and God will bless you."

The pastor laid his hand on her head, and, as the poor girl sobbed, without having the power to rise from her knees, he added, in a tone of affection—"A promise given should never be broken, my child: the day advances—go, and may your heavenly Father watch over you."

Catherine arose, and kissing the lips of the old man, exclaimed, "Adieu, my father! adieu, Frederika!" and left the house precipitately.

As Catherine entered the tent of the general, she was met by the young soldier who had accompanied her in the previous night's search, and who started on seeing her. She had dried her tears, and, with a calm countenance, presented herself before the general, who was engaged giving audience, and listening to the prayers of some of the inhabitants of Marienburg.

"Is this you, little one?" said he, perceiving Catherine. "I feared that I should not have seen you again."

"I gave you my word," was the brief reply of Catherine.

The general smiled. "You are young and intelligent, and seem to be good-humoured: you ought to make a good servant. Let me see how you prepare a breakfast for me."

Catherine retired without speaking, and shortly returned to the tent, bearing a tray with the required *dejeuner*.

The general and the young unknown were the only occupants, but without remarking the familiarity which existed between him who was the leader of a great army, and one who, to judge by his dress, appeared but a simple soldier, Catherine arranged the table for the pair.

"Some wine, my child," said the soldier, holding towards her his glass to be filled, and added, "How old are you?"

"Thirteen years," answered Catherine.

"With a heart of thirty! Why, general, if you had seen her last night searching amongst the dead for the body of her benefactor, pale and trembling, but full of courage, you would have admired her as I did. You had then no fear of the dead, my child?"

Catherine blushed as she replied, "I had no thought of fear; I thought but of finding my benefactor, the poor pastor Skovronski."

"As a servant to a pastor, she ought to be familiar with the dead," said the general. "It is not the first time you have seen them?"

"I have not seen many," replied Catherine.

"Why should she be afraid?" said the soldier; "if she had to seek her benefactor in the midst of guns and swords, it might be different. I should like to see her in the centre of a battle with that little resolute face of hers."

"You have seen the effect produced on me by the bullets of your sentries," said Catherine, smiling.

"It is unquestionably true, general; she appeared to care as little for them as I should myself. This child will be a noble-hearted woman. Scheremetief, will you sell your prisoner?"

"And what will you do with her?" asked the general, studiously avoiding to give a title to his guest.

"Make her my wife, the wife of a soldier! She is born for it!"

Well, what say you, my child?" added he, turning to Catherine, who seemed bewildered.

"I say—I say," replied she, hesitating, "that my choice is not difficult; I would rather be the wife of a soldier than the slave of a general."

"Bravo, Catherine; and from this moment you belong to me!"

"But——" said the general.

"I know what you would say, general," hastily interrupted the stranger; "you know I never do anything like anybody else. This young girl pleases me: she is courageous and gay, and her temper ought to be sweet and equal. We shall see if she does not prove sensible enough for a wife. It is decided: I shall make her my wife. Put down that tray, Catherine: put off your apron, and follow me. Henceforward, if you serve anybody, it shall be a husband."

The soldier rose from the table, and beckoning to Catherine to follow him, he left the tent. "Do you know who I am, Catherine?" said he as they walked along.

"No; but you said that you wished to be my husband."

"Very well; but do you know my rank in the army?"

"It does not signify," said Catherine; "you cannot suppose that I am proud myself—a child without family, without name."

"Just so, my little one. You are content, then, to link your destiny with mine?" said the soldier, taking the hand of the young Livonian.

"Yes," replied Catherine, "for you have the air of a brave man; and I like you because you have been kind to me, poor child that I am."

"You are not sorry, then, that I am nothing but a poor soldier?"

"Too happy, provided that you permit me to follow you, and never leave you."

The soldier stopped before a tent more elevated than the rest. "This is the tent of the Czar," said he; "remain where you are. It is right that I should ask his permission to marry you."

Catherine had waited but a few minutes, when a young officer advancing, said, "Mademoiselle, the Czar Peter wishes to see you."

She followed, and on entering the tent, saw a large number of officers standing, in the centre of whom was seated a man of about thirty years of age, whom she immediately recognized as her late companion. "Where, then, is the Czar?" asked Catherine, turning towards the young officer.

"There!" said he, pointing to the soldier who was seated.

"There! That is my husband!"

"He is thy husband and the Czar likewise, Catherine," said the emperor of Russia, for it was he; and added, "How astonished you appear. Does the news grieve you? Does my title prevent you from loving me?"

"I loved you as a soldier," said she; "I will love you as an emperor." And Peter I., Czar of Russia, taking the hand of the young orphan, presented her to his officers as the future empress of Russia

It will readily be believed that Catherine did not forget the pastor Skovronski. True, he must still lose the society of his dear child: but what a difference between yielding her up to be the wife of a prince, from knowing that she was the servant of the conqueror—a slave! But, alas! he was not long spared to regret her absence. He never thoroughly recovered from the wounds he had received; and his sister, and the faithful Frederika, both nearly as old as himself, soon followed him to the grave. Catherine had no one in the world to divide her affection from her husband.

After their marriage, the Czar placed her in a private dwelling in Moscow, where he paid her frequent visits, and often came to transact public business with his officers. It was in this modest retreat that her two children were born; Anne in 1708, and Elizabeth in 1709. When Peter made war on the Turks in 1711, he had a wish that his wife should accompany him; and during this campaign she distinguished herself in a manner too remarkable, and too honorable to herself, for us to pass it over.

From the skill in military tactics of Peter the Great and his generals, and also from the admirable discipline of his troops, a body of eight thousand Russians had sustained the attack of a hundred and fifty thousand Turks. The loss and suffering on each side had been great, yet it could not be said that either party had gained the victory. The Russians, however, were in circumstances of peculiar distress. They were surrounded by an immense body of their foes, and thus shut out, not only from every means of procuring provisions, but even from approaching the river Pruth, which was close at hand, and on which they depended for a supply of water. Thirst and starvation were more dreadful to encounter than Turkish swords; and it seemed that, after all, they would become the slaves of the Mahommedans.

All the memoirs of the time agree that the Czar, divided within himself what steps to take—if he could indeed any way avoid the impending destruction for himself, his wife, and his army—retired to his tent oppressed with grief, having given positive orders that he should not be disturbed—his proud spirit naturally disliking a witness to the distraction of his mind. But notwithstanding his command, Catherine felt that, as his wife, her place was at his side, and accordingly she forced her way to him. She found him suffering from one of those epileptic fits to which at all times he was subject, and which she had on former occasions often alleviated by her presence of mind and watchful attention. The convulsions were unusually violent, aggravated no doubt by the anguish of his mind; and probably, when Peter recovered, he felt that, under Providence, he owed his life to Catherine's resolution.

She had come, however, as a counsellor; and a wife who, like her, had faced death in its most frightful shapes, and exposed herself to every danger, like the meanest soldier, had a right to be heard. She showed admirable sense and penetration of mind, by pointing out to her husband that the enemy had themselves suffered so much, and were doubtless so impressed with the daring of the Russians, and perhaps even ignorant of their desperate condition, that there was every probability they would listen to overtures for a truce. It is really surprising that no one else seemed to have thought of this project: but the instances in Catherine's life were very numerous in which she evinced great superiority of mind to those about her—a superiority which her husband seemed to have recognized when he first saw her at Marienburg, and so quickly determined to make her the sharer of his throne.

Catherine was well aware that it had been a custom for ages throughout the East, when any people applied for an audience of the sovereign, or his representative, to approach with a present. Accordingly, she mustered the few jewels she had brought with her on this military expedition, in which neither magnificence nor luxury was admitted, and to these she added two black foxes' skins, and whatever money she could collect—the latter being designed for a present to the kiaia, an officer under the grand vizier. She then made choice of a Russian officer, on whose fidelity and intelligence she could rely, who, accompanied by two servants, carried the presents to the grand vizier, and delivered the money into the kiaia's own hand. The Turks agreed to the truce, and the Russians were saved. So sensible was Peter of the services rendered by his wife on this occasion, that, though naturally averse to displays of magnificence, looking upon regal shows as money idly spent, he caused her to be solemnly crowned as a commemoration of the event; and in the declaration which he issued, we find these words—"She has been of the greatest assistance to us in all our dangers, and particularly in the battle of Pruth."

The fragment of a letter which had been found on the dead soldier when Catherine was an infant, had been carefully preserved by her; but she had long given up all expectation of discovering her kindred. A romantic incident, however, brought to light the meaning of the word "children." An envoy from a foreign court to Peter the Great being on his return home through Courland, put up at an inn, where he heard the voice of some person in distress, whom the people of the house were treating in an insulting manner. He heard the stranger make answer, in a tone of resentment, that they would not use him thus if he could once get speech of the Czar, at whose court he had more influence than they imagined. On this the envoy had the curiosity to ask the man some questions, and from the answers he let fall, and on examination of his countenance, he thought he traced in him some resemblance to the Empress Catherine. Soon afterwards he was writing to one of his friends at St. Petersburgh, and could not forbear relating the adventure. This letter by some accident reached the hands of the Czar, who immediately sent an order to the governor of Riga, to endeavor to find out the person who was mentioned. The governor took such prompt measures, that he soon discovered the stranger, who proved to be the son of a Lithuanian gentleman who had been killed in the wars of Poland, leaving two young children, a boy and a girl, then in the cradle.

Peter certainly spoke the truth, when he said he never did anything like other people; for the manner in which he sent for the stranger, whom he suspected to be a relative of his wife, and wished to welcome, was to cause him to be arrested on the charge of some pretended crime, and brought as a prisoner to his court; though orders to his guards were privately given to treat him well.

On questioning him, the Czar was so persuaded that he was Catherine's brother, that he called him toward him, saying, "Come hither and kiss the hand of the Empress, and embrace your sister." It is said that Catherine fainted with surprise, and that, when she came to herself, the Czar exclaimed, "This is but natural; and if your brother has merit, we will make something of him; if he has not, we must leave him as he is." A speech very characteristic of Peter the Great. It is to be supposed that he had some merit, since we find he was created a count, and married to a lady of quality. The adventures of his childhood and youth are not recorded; but whatever guardians he had found, must have known who he was, or he could not have suspected that the orphan whom all the world knew Peter had married, was his sister. Peter the Great died in 1725, and left to Catherine the title of Empress, which she sustained with dignity; and after reigning two years and some months, expired on the 27th of May, 1727, at the age of thirty-eight.

THE BLIND PREACHER.

BY WM. WIRT.

It was one Sunday, as I traveled through the county of Orange, that my eye was caught by a cluster of horses tied near a ruinous, old, wooden house in the forest, not far from the road-side. Having frequently seen such objects before, in traveling through these States, I had no difficulty in understanding that this was a place of religious worship.

Devotion alone should have stopped me, to join in the duties of the congregation; but I must confess, that curiosity to hear the preacher of such a wilderness, was not the least of my motives. On entering, I was struck with his preternatural appearance. He was a tall and very spare old man; his head, which was covered with a white linen cap, his shriveled hands, and his voice, were all shaking under the influence of a palsy; and a few moments ascertained to me that he was perfectly blind.

The first emotions that touched my breast were those of mingled pity and veneration. But how soon were all my feelings changed! The lips of Plato were never more worthy of a prognostic swarm of bees, than were the lips of this holy man! It was a day of the administration of the sacrament; and his subject was, of course, the passion of our Savior. I had heard the subject handled a thousand times: I had thought it exhausted long ago. Little did I suppose that in the wild woods of America, I was to meet with a man, whose eloquence would give to this topic a new and more sublime pathos, than I had ever before witnessed.

As he descended from the pulpit to distribute the mystic symbols, there was a peculiar, a more than human solemnity in his air and manner, which made my blood run cold, and my whole frame shiver.

He then drew a picture of the sufferings of our Savior; his trial before Pilate; his ascent up Calvary; his crucifixion; and his death. I knew the whole history; but never until then had I heard the circumstances so selected, so arranged, so colored! It was all new; and I seemed to have heard it for the first time in my life. His enunciation was so deliberate, that his voice trembled on every syllable; and every heart in the assembly trembled in unison. His peculiar phrases had that force of description, that the original scene appeared to be at that moment acting before our eyes. We saw the very faces of the Jews; the staring, frightful distortions of malice and rage. We saw the buffet: my soul kindled with a flame of indignation; and my hands were involuntarily and convulsively clinched.

But when he came to touch on the patience, the forgiving meekness of our Savior; when he drew, to the life, his blessed eyes streaming in tears to heaven; his voice breathing to God a soft and gentle prayer of pardon on his enemies, "Father, forgive them, for they know not what they do,"—the voice of the preacher, which had all along faltered, grew fainter and fainter, until, his utterance being entirely obstructed by the force of his feelings, he raised his handkerchief to his eyes, and burst into a loud and irrepressible flood of grief. The effect is inconceivable. The whole house resounded with the mingled groans, and sobs, and shrieks of the congregation.

It was sometime before the tumult had subsided, so far as to permit him to proceed. Indeed, judging by the usual, but fallacious standard of my own weakness, I began to be very uneasy for the situation of the preacher. For I could not conceive how he would be able to let his audience down from the hight to which he had wound them, without impairing the solemnity and dignity of his subject, or perhaps shocking them by the abruptness of the fall. But—no: the descent was as beautiful and sublime as the elevation had been rapid and enthusiastic.

The first sentence, with which he broke the awful silence, was a quotation from Rousseau: "Socrates died like a philosopher, but Jesus Christ like a God!"

I despair of giving you any idea of the effect produced by this short sentence, unless you could perfectly conceive the whole manner of the man, as well as the peculiar crisis in the discourse. Never before did I completely understand what Demosthenes meant by laying such stress on delivery. You are to bring before you the venerable figure of the preacher ; his blindness, constantly recalling to your recollection old Homer, Ossian, and Milton, and associating with his performance the melancholy grandeur of their geniuses ; you are to imagine that you hear his slow, solemn, well-accented enunciation, and his voice of affecting, trembling melody ; you are to remember the pitch of passion and enthusiasm, to which the congregation were raised; and then the few moments of portentous, death-like silence, which reigned throughout the house: the preacher, removing his white handkerchief from his aged face, (even yet wet from the recent torrent of his tears,) and slowly stretching forth the palsied hand which holds it, begins the sentence, "Socrates died like a philosopher"—then, pausing, raising his other hand, pressing them both, clasped together, with warmth and energy, to his breast, lifting his "sightless balls" to heaven, and pouring his whole soul into his tremulous voice—"but Jesus Christ—like a God!" If he had been indeed and in truth an angel of light, the effect could scarcely have been more divine. Whatever I had been able to conceive of the sublimity of Massillon or the force of Bourdeloue, had fallen far short of the power which I felt from the delivery of this simple sentence.

If this description gives you the impression, that this incomparable minister had anything of shallow, theatrical trick in his manner, it does him great injustice. I have never seen, in any other orator, such a union of simplicity and majesty. He had not a gesture, an attitude, or an accent, to which he does not seem forced by the sentiment he is expressing. His mind is too serious, too earnest, too solicitous, and, at the same time, too dignified, to stoop to artifice. Although as far removed from ostentation as a man can be, yet it is clear, from the train, the style and substance of his thoughts, that he is not only a very polite scholar, but a man of extensive and profound erudition. I was forcibly struck with a short, yet beautiful character, which he drew of your learned and amiable countryman, Sir Robert Boyle: he spoke of him, as if "his noble mind had, even before death, divested herself of all influence from his frail tabernacle of flesh;" and called him, in his peculiarly emphatic and impressive manner, "a pure intelligence: a link between men and angels."

This man has been before my imagination almost ever since. A thousand times, as I rode along, I dropped the reins of my bridle, stretched forth my hand, and tried to imitate his quotation from Rousseau; a thousand times I abandoned the attempt in despair, and felt persuaded, that his peculiar manner and power arose from an energy of soul, which nature could give, but which no human being could justly copy. As I recall, at this moment, several of his awfully striking attitudes, the chilling tide, with which my blood begins to pour along my arteries, reminds me of the emotions produced by the first sight of Gray's introductory picture of his Bard.

DESTRUCTION OF A FAMILY OF THE PILGRIMS BY THE SAVAGES.

BY MISS SEDGWICK.

All was joy in Mrs. Fletcher's dwelling. "My dear mother," said Everell, "it is now quite time to look out for father and Hope Leslie. I have turned the hour-glass three times since dinner, and counted all the sands, I think. Let us all go on the front portico, where we can catch the first glimpse of them, as they come past the elm trees Here, Oneco," he continued, as he saw assent in his mother's smile, "help me out with mother's rocking chair: rather rough rocking,"—he added, as he adjusted the rockers lengthwise with the logs that served for the flooring,—"but mother won't mind trifles just now. Ah! blessed babe, brother," he continued, taking in his arms the beautiful infant, "you shall come, too, even though you cheat me out of my birthright, and get the first embrace from father." Thus saying, he placed the laughing infant in his go-cart, beside his mother. He then aided his little sisters in their arrangement of the playthings they had brought forth to welcome and astonish Hope; and finally he made an elevated position for Faith Leslie, where she might, he said, as she ought, catch the very first glimpse at her sister.

"Thank, thank you, Everell," said the little, girl, as she mounted her pinnacle: "if you knew Hope, you would want to see her first, too; every body loves Hope. We shall always have pleasant times when Hope gets here."

It was one of the most beautiful afternoons at the close of the month of May. The lagging Spring had at last come forth in all her power; "her work of gladness" was finished, and forests, fields and meadows were bright with renovated life. The full Connecticut swept triumphantly on, as if still exulting in its release from the fetters of winter. Every gushing rill had the spring-note of joy. The meadows were, for the first time, enriched with patches of English grain, which the new settlers had sown scantily, by way of experiment, prudently occupying the greatest portion of the rich mould with the native Indian corn. This product of our soil is beautiful in all its progress, from the moment when, as now it studded the meadow with hillocks, shooting its bright pointed spear from its mother earth, to its maturity, when the long golden ear bursts from the rustling leaf.

The grounds about Mrs. Fletcher's house had been prepared with the neatness of English taste; and a rich bed of clover, that overspread the lawn immediately before the portico, already rewarded the industry of the cultivators. Over this delicate carpet, the domestic fowls, the first civilized inhabitants of the country of their tribe, were now treading, picking their food here and there like dainty little epicures.

The scene had also its minstrels; the birds, those ministers and worshippers of nature, were on the wing, filling the air with melody, while, like diligent little housewives, they ransacked the forest and field for materials for their house-keeping.

A mother, encircled by healthful, sporting children, is always a beautiful spectacle—a spectacle that appeals to nature in every human breast. Mrs. Fletcher, in obedience to matrimonial duty, or, it may be, from some lingering of female vanity, had on this occasion attired herself with extraordinary care. What woman does not wish to look handsome in the eyes of her husband!

"Mother," said Everell, putting aside the exquisitely fine lace that shaded her cheek, "I do not believe you looked more beautiful than you do to-day, when, as I have heard, they called you 'the rose of the wilderness.' Our little Mary's cheek is as round and as bright as a peach, but it is not so handsome as yours, mother. Your heart has sent this color here," he continued, kissing her tenderly; "it seems to have come forth to tell us that our father is near."

"It would shame me, Everell," replied his mother, embracing him with a feeling that the proudest drawing-room belle might have envied, "to take such flattery from any lips, but thine." "Oh, do not call it flattery, mother—look, Magawisca—for Heaven's sake cheer up—look, would you know mother's eye? just turn it, mother, one minute from the road—and her pale cheek too—with this rich color on it?"

"Alas! alas!" replied Magawisca, glancing her eyes at Mrs. Fletcher, and then, as if heart-struck, withdrawing them, "how soon the flush of the setting sun fades from the evening cloud!"

"Oh, Magawisca!" said Everell, impatiently, "why are you so dismal? your voice is too sweet for a bird of ill-omen. I shall begin to think as Jennet says—though Jennet is no text-book for me—I shall begin to think old Nelema has really bewitched you." "You call me a bird of ill-omen," replied Magawisca, half proud, half sorrowful, "and you call the owl a bird of ill-omen, but we hold him sacred; he is our sentinel, and, when danger is near, he cries, 'Awake! awake!'"

"Magawisca, you are positively unkind. Jeremiah's lamentations on a holyday would not be more out of time than your croaking is now. The very skies, earth, and air, seem to partake of our joy at father's return, and you only make a discord. Do you think, if your father was near, I would not share your joy?"

Tears fell fast from Magawisca's eyes, but she made no reply, and Mrs. Fletcher, observing and compassionating her emotion, and thinking it probably arose from comparing her orphan state to that of the merry children about her, called her, and said, "Magawisca, you are neither a stranger nor a servant; will you not share our joy? do you not love us?"

"Love you!" she exclaimed, clasping her hands, "love you! I would give my life for you."

"We do not ask your life, my good girl," replied Mrs. Fletcher, kindly smiling on her, "but a light heart, and a cheerful look. A sad countenance doth not become this joyful hour. Go and help Oneco; he is quite out of breath blowing those soap-bubbles for the children." Oneco smiled, and shook his head, and continued to send off one after another of the prismatic globes, and, as they rose and floated on the air, and brightened with the many-colored ray, the little girls clapped their hands, and the baby stretched his to grasp the brilliant vapor. "Oh!" said Magawisca, impetuously, covering her eyes, "I do not like to see anything so beautiful pass so quickly away."

Scarcely had she uttered these words, when suddenly, as if the earth had opened on them, three Indian warriors darted from the forest, and pealed on the air their horrible yells.

"My father! my father!" burst from the lips of Magawisca and Oneco. Faith Leslie sprang towards the Indian boy, and clung fast to him, and the children clustered about their mother; she instinctively caught her infant, and held it close within her arms, as if their ineffectual shelter were a rampart.

Magawisca uttered a cry of agony, and, springing forward with her arms uplifted, as if deprecating his approach, she sunk down at her father's feet, and, clasping her hands, "Save them!—save them!" she cried; "the mother—the children—oh! they are all good: take vengeance on your enemies, but spare, spare our friends! our benefactors! I bleed when they are struck; oh! command them to stop!" she screamed, looking to the companions of her father, who, unchecked by her cries, were pressing on to their deadly work.

Mononotto was silent and motionless: his eye glanced wildly from Magawisca to Oneco. Magawisca replied to the glance of fire: "Yes, they have sheltered us—they have spread the wing of love over us—save them—save them—oh! it will be too late," she cried, springing from her father, whose silence and fixedness showed that, if his better nature rebelled against the work of revenge, there was no relenting of purpose. Magawisca darted before the Indian, who was advancing towards Mrs. Fletcher with an uplifted hatchet. "You shall hew me to pieces ere you touch her," she said, and planted herself as a shield before her benefactress. The warrior's obdurate heart, untouched by the sight of the helpless mother and her little ones, was thrilled by the courage of the heroic girl: he paused, and grimly smiled on her, when his companion, crying, "Hasten! the dogs will be on us!" leveled a deadly blow at Mrs. Fletcher; but his uplifted arm was penetrated by a musket shot, and the hatchet fell harmless to the floor.

"Courage, mother!" cried Everell, reloading the piece; but neither courage nor celerity could avail: the second Indian sprang upon him, threw him on the floor, wrested his musket from him, and, brandishing his tomahawk over his head, he would have aimed the fatal stroke, when a cry from Mononotto arrested his arm.

Everell extricated himself from his grasp, and, a ray of hope flashing into his mind, he seized a bugle-horn, which hung beside the door, and winded it. This was the conventional signal of alarm, and he sent forth a blast long and loud—a death-cry.

Mrs. Grafton and her attendants were just mounting their horses to return home. Digby listened for a moment: then, exclaiming, "It comes from our master's dwelling! ride for your life, Hutton!" He tossed away a bandbox that encumbered him, and spurred his horse to its utmost speed.

The alarm was spread through the village, and, in a brief space, Mr. Pynchon, with six armed men, was pressing toward the fatal scene. In the mean time the tragedy was proceeding at Bethel. Mrs. Fletcher's senses had been stunned with terror. She had neither spoken nor moved after she grasped her infant. Everell's gallant interposition restored a momentary consciousness; she screamed to him, "Fly, Everell, my son, fly; for your father's sake, fly!"

"Never!" he replied, springing to his mother's side.

The savages, always rapid in their movements, were now aware that their safety depended on despatch. "Finish your work, warriors!" cried Mononotto. Obedient to the command, and infuriated by his bleeding wound, the Indian, who, on receiving the shot, had staggered back and leaned against the wall, now sprang forward, and tore the infant from its mother's breast. She shrieked, and in that shriek passed the agony of death. She was unconscious that her son, putting forth a strength beyond nature, for a moment kept the Indian at bay; she neither saw nor felt the knife struck at her own heart. She felt not the arms of her defenders, Everell and Magawisca, as they met around her neck. She fainted and fell to the floor, dragging her impotent protectors with her.

The savage, in his struggle with Everell, had tossed the infant boy to the ground: he fell, quite unharmed, on the turf at Mononotto's feet; there, raising his head, and looking up into the chieftain's face, he probably perceived a gleam of mercy; for, with the quick instinct of infancy, that with unerring sagacity directs its appeal, he clasped the naked leg of the savage with one arm, and stretched the other towards him with a piteous supplication, that no words could have expressed.

Mononotto's heart melted within him: he stooped to raise the sweet suppliant, when one of the Mohawks fiercely seized him, tossed him wildly round his head, and dashed him on the door-stone. But the silent prayer, perhaps the celestial inspiration of the innocent creature, was not lost. "We have had blood enough," cried Mononotto; "you have well avenged me, brothers."

Then, looking at Oneco, who had remained in one corner of the portico, clasping Faith Leslie in his arms, he commanded him to follow him with the child. Everell was torn from the lifeless bodies of his mother and sisters, and dragged into the forest. Magawisca uttered one cry of agony and despair, as she looked for the last time on the bloody scene, and then followed her father.

As they passed the boundary of the cleared ground, Mononotto tore from Oneco his English dress, and, casting it from him, "Thus perish," he said, every mark of the captivity of my children. Thou shalt return to our forests," he continued, wrapping a skin around him, "with the badge of thy people." * * * * *

We hope our readers will not think we have wantonly sported with their feelings, by drawing a picture of calamity that only exists in the fictitious tale. No—such events as we have feebly related were common in our early annals, and attended by horrors that it would be impossible for the imagination to exaggerate. Not only families, but villages, were cut off by the most dreaded of all foes—the ruthless, vengeful savage.

In the quiet possession of the blessings transmitted, we are, perhaps, in danger of forgetting or undervaluing the sufferings by which they were obtained. We forget that the noble pilgrims lived and endured for us; that, when they came to the wilderness, they said truly, though it may be, somewhat quaintly, that they turned their backs on Egypt. They did virtually renounce all dependence on earthly support; they left the land of their birth, of their homes, of their fathers' sepulchres; they sacrificed ease and preferment, and all the delights of sense—and for what?—to open for themselves an earthly paradise?—to dress their bowers of pleasure, and rejoice with their wives and children? No!—they came not for themselves; they lived not to themselves. An exiled and suffering people, they came forth in the dignity of the chosen servants of the Lord, to open the forests to the sunbeam, and to the light of the Sun of righteousness; to restore man, man, oppressed and trampled on by his fellow, to religious and civil liberty, and equal rights; to replace the creatures of God on their natural level; to bring down the hills, and make smooth the rough places, which the pride and cruelty of man had wrought on the fair creation of the Father of all.

What was their reward? Fortune?—distinctions?—the sweet charities of home? No—but their feet were planted on the mount of vision, and they saw, with sublime joy, a multitude of people where the solitary savage roamed the forest; the forest vanished, and pleasant villages and busy cities appeared; the tangled foot-path expanded to the thronged highway; the consecrated church was planted on the rock of heathen sacrifice.

And, that we might realize this vision,—enter into this promised land of faith,—they endured hardship, and braved death, deeming, as said one of their company, that "he is not worthy to live at all, who, for fear of danger or death, shunneth his country's service or his own honor—since death is inevitable, and the fame of virtue immortal."

If these were the fervors of enthusiasm, it was an enthusiasm kindled and fed by the holy flame that glows on the altar of God; an enthusiasm that never abates, but gathers life and strength as the immortal soul expands in the image of its Creator.

THE BURNING PRAIRIE.

BY GEO. D. PRENTICE.

The fires alway run before the wind, with an advanced tongue or fork, and two receding flanks; and in a tight wind so rapidly do the dancing, curling, careering flames leap from point to point of the dry grass, that it is sometimes difficult for the swiftest horsemen to escape. The sight, especially in the night, is beautiful, and at times grand beyond description. But after awhile we become familiarized to it, and look upon it without emotion; as all of us learn to do upon the glorious sun, the most splendid object in nature.

At the time I refer to, I had been two or three days' drive to the town of C———, with my horse and buggy, and was on my return home. All day I had noticed signs indicating a fire on the prairie—masses of smoke in the distance, lying like white clouds upon the horizon, and a hazy, oppressive atmosphere—but these gave me no trouble, so long as they were far away; and busy with my own thoughts for hours, I would pay no attention to them whatever. At length, after one of those periods of abstraction, I observed, with some apprehension, that the conflagration was drawing nearer, and had actually worked around in my rear, until it had crossed the path by which I had traveled; that all behind me was fast becoming a smoking sea of fire; and, for the first time, thought of danger, that I might be overtaken or possibly surrounded, occurred to me.

My horse was a powerful one, but not very fleet, nor yet fresh, but without the loss of a moment I applied the whip, and quitting my direct route bore to the left, because that placed me more squarely before my enemy. Soon the tongue of fire, the advance-guard of my terrible foe, became distinctly visible on my right, at about two miles distance, as near as I could judge, stretching on with a speed that was really frightful. I knew the struggle was to be with that, and pushing my horse to the utmost, kept my eye fixed upon it, like the wily racer, intent on measuring the power of his antagonist before the final effort. For a few minutes the result was in doubt, but not long. Sinews of flesh were no match for the wing of the wind, which bore on that fleet and terrific column of fire, and I became satisfied that it was outstripping me, and almost with a feeling of indifference; for I thought, for the moment, that my last hope was gone, and was bracing my heart and nerves for the final event of life.

It was now twilight, and as the day departed, and the shadows of night fell around, the cordon of fire seemed to magnify its splendors and its terrors, and, like a vast serpent, to extend itself behind and on both sides, and to be enclosing up its folds to encircle me. I was no stranger on that part of the prairie; its general localities, though one portion is very much like another, were familiar to me; and in recalling them to mind, I recollected a little ragged mound or hill, some twenty or thirty feet in hight, and was satisfied that I was at no great distance from it. With my hopes revived a little, I taxed my sight to the utmost on every swell of ground that I passed, and at length detected the faint outline of the eminence, in advance. But the fire was making for it too, and the subtle, lapping tongue on my right, now quite ahead of me already, seemed almost between us, and prepared with a single leap to cross my path and secure its victim. Still, with my almost exhausted horse, I pressed on, with an energy and despair so mighty, as almost of themselves to wreck the powers of life. I have not recovered from the effects of the mental struggle to this day—but, as you have no doubt already concluded, the mound saved me. In the race for life, I was obliged, as it were, to place myself side-by-side with that giant and awful sword of flame, and for the last half mile, the contest was doubtful, hopeless, dreadful. But God nerved my horse with an unnatural strength, as it seemed to me, and guarded his footsteps so that every effort told; and at last I dashed up the bare side of the mound, where there was no fit substance for the devouring element to follow, and was safe.

The flame swept by with a dull, heavy roar, and a hot, sweltering, suffocating breath, burning with an intensity and grandeur which realized to the imagination my ideas of the final catastrophe of nature, encircled and passed the little eminence on which I stood, and stretched off in two long lines as far as the eye could reach. I fell upon my knees, and since that terrible night, I trust I have been a more thoughtful and a more thankful man.

"I HAVE SEEN AN END OF ALL PERFECTION."

BY MRS. SIGOURNEY.

I HAVE seen a man in the glory of his days and the pride of his strength. He was built like the tall cedar that lifts its head above the forest trees; like the strong oak that strikes its root deeply into the earth. He feared no danger; he felt no sickness; he wondered that any should groan or sigh at pain. His mind was vigorous, like his body: he was perplexed at no intricacy; he was daunted at no difficulty; into hidden things he searched, and what was crooked he made plain. He went forth fearlessly upon the face of the mighty deep; he surveyed the nations of the earth; he measured the distance of the stars, and called them by their names; he gloried in the extent of his knowledge, in the vigor of his understanding, and strove to search even into what the Almighty had concealed. And when I looked on him I said, "What a piece of work is man! how noble in reason! how infinite in faculties! in form and moving how express and admirable! in action how like an angel! in apprehension how like a God!"

I returned—his look was no more lofty, nor his step proud; his broken frame was like some ruined tower; his hairs were white and scattered; and his eye gazed vacantly upon what was passing around him. The vigor of his intellect was wasted, and of all that he had gained by study, nothing remained. He feared when there was no danger, and when there was no sorrow he wept. His memory was decayed and treacherous, and showed him only broken images of the glory that was departed. His house was to him like a strange land, and his friends were counted as his enemies; and he thought himself strong and healthful while his foot tottered on the verge of the grave. He said of his son, "He is my brother;" of his daughter, "I know her not;" and he inquired what was his own name. And one who supported his last steps, and ministered to his many wants, said to me, as I looked on the melancholy scene, "Let thine heart receive instruction, for thou hast seen an end of all earthly perfection."

I have seen a beautiful female treading the first stages of youth, and entering joyfully into the pleasures of life. The glance of her eye was variable and sweet, and on her cheek trembled something like the first blush of the morning; her lips moved, and there was harmony; and when she floated in the dance, her light form, like the aspen, seemed to move with every breeze. I returned, but she was not in the dance; I sought her in the gay circle of her companions, but I found her not. Her eye sparkled not there—the music of her voice was silent—she rejoiced on earth no more. I saw a train, sable and slow-paced, who bore sadly to an opened grave what once was animated and beautiful. They paused as they approached, and a voice broke the awful silence: "Mingle ashes with ashes, and dust with its original dust. To the earth, whence it was taken, consign we the body of our sister." They covered her with the damp soil and the cold clods of the valley; and the worms crowded into her silent abode. Yet one sad mourner lingered, to cast himself upon the grave; and as he wept he said, "There is no beauty, or grace, or loveliness, that continueth in man; for this is the end of all his glory and perfection."

I have seen an infant with a fair brow, and a frame like polished ivory. Its limbs were pliant in its sports; it rejoiced, and again it wept; but whether its glowing cheek dimpled with smiles, or its blue eye was brilliant with tears, still I said to my heart, "It is beautiful." It was like the first pure blossom, which some cherished plant has shot forth, whose cup is filled with a dew-drop, and whose head reclines upon its parent stem.

I again saw this child when the lamp of reason first dawned in its mind. Its soul was gentle and peaceful; its eye sparkled with joy, as it looked round on this good and pleasant world. It ran swiftly in the ways of knowledge; it bowed its ear to instruction; it stood like a lamb before its teachers. It was not proud, or envious, or stubborn; and it had never heard of the vices and vanities of the world. And when I looked upon it, I rembered that our Savior had said, "Except ye become as little children, ye cannot enter into the kingdom of heaven."

But the scene was changed, and I saw a man whom the world called honorable, and many waited for his smile. They pointed out the fields that were his, and talked of the silver and gold that he had gathered; they admired the stateliness of his domes, and extolled the honor of his family. And his heart answered secretly, "By my wisdom have I gotten all this;" so he returned no thanks to God, neither did he fear or serve him. And as I passed along, I heard the complaints of laborers who had reaped down his fields, and the cries of the poor, whose covering he had taken away; but the sound of feasting and revelry was in his apartments, and the unfed beggar came tottering from his door. But he considered not that the cries of the oppressed were continually entering into the ears of the Most High. And when I knew that this man was once the teachable child that I had loved, the beautiful infant that I had gazed upon with delight, I said in my bitterness, "I have seen an end of all perfection;" and I laid my mouth in the dust.

THE TWINS.

During the period of the war of the revolution, there resided, in the western part of Massachusetts, a farmer by the name of Stedman. He was a man of substance, descended from a very respectable English family, well educated, distinguished for great firmness of character in general, and alike remarkable for inflexible integrity and steadfast loyalty to his king. Such was the reputation he sustained, that, even when the most violent antipathies against royalism swayed the community, it was still admitted on all hands, that farmer Stedman, though a tory, was honest in his opinions, and firmly believed them to be right.

The period came when Burgoyne was advancing from the north. It was a time of great anxiety with both the friends and foes of the revolution, and one which called forth their highest exertions. The patriotic militia flocked to the standard of Gates and Stark, while many of the tories resorted to the quarters of Burgoyne and Baum.

Among the latter was Stedman. He had no sooner decided it to be his duty, than he took a kind farewell of his wife, a woman of uncommon beauty, gave his children, a twin boy and girl, a long embrace, then mounted his horse and departed. He joined himself to the unfortunate expedition of Baum, and was taken, with other prisoners of war, by the victorious Stark.

He made no attempt to conceal his name or character, which were both soon discovered, and he was accordingly committed to prison as a traitor. The gaol, in which he was confined, was in the western part of Massachusetts, and nearly in a ruinous condition. The farmer was one night waked from his sleep by several persons in his room: "Come," said they, "you can now regain your liberty; we have made a breach in the prison, through which you can escape." To their astonishment, Stedman utterly refused to leave his prison. In vain they expostulated with him; in vain they represented to him that life was at stake. His reply was, that he was a true man, and a servant of king George, and he would not creep out of a hole at night, and sneak away from the rebels, to save his neck from the gallows. Finding it altogether fruitless to attempt to move him, his friends left him, with some expressions of spleen.

The time at length arrived for the trial of the prisoner. The distance to the place where the court was sitting was about sixty miles. Stedman remarked to the sheriff, when he came to attend him, that it would save some expense and inconvenience, if he could be permitted to go alone, and on foot. "And suppose," said the sheriff, "that you should prefer your safety to your honor, and leave me to seek you in the British camp?" "I had thought," said the farmer, reddening with indignation, "that I was speaking to one who knew me." "I do know you, indeed," said the sheriff; "I spoke but in jest; you shall have your way. Go, and on the third day I shall expect to see you at S——." * * * * The farmer departed, and at the appointed time he placed himself in the hands of the sheriff.

I was now engaged as his counsel. Stedman insisted, before the court, upon telling his whole story; and, when I would have taken advantage of some technical points, he sharply rebuked me, and told me that he had not employed me to prevaricate, but only to assist him in telling the truth. I had never seen such a display of simple integrity. It was affecting to witness his love of holy, unvarnished truth, elevating him above every other consideration, and presiding in his breast as a sentiment even superior to the love of life. I saw the tears more than once springing to the eyes of his judges; never before, or since, have I felt such an interest in a client. I plead for him as I would have plead for my own life. I drew tears, but I could not sway the judgment of stern men, controlled rather by a sense of duty than the compassionate promptings of humanity. Stedman was condemned. I told him there was a chance of pardon, if he would ask for it. I drew up a petition, and requested him to sign it; but he refused. "I have done," said he, "what I thought my duty. I can ask pardon of my God, and my king; but it would be hypocrisy to ask forgiveness of these men, for an action which I should repeat, were I placed, again in similar circumstances. No! ask me not to sign that petition. If what you call the cause of American freedom requires the blood of an honest man for a conscientious discharge of what he deemed his duty, let me be its victim. Go to my judges, and tell them that I place not my fears nor my hopes in them." It was in vain that I pressed the subject; and I went away in despair.

In returning to my house, I accidentally called on an acquaintance, a young man of brilliant genius, the subject of a passionate predilection for painting. This led him frequently to take excursions into the country, for the purpose of sketching such objects and scenes as were interesting to him. From one of these rambles he had just returned. I found him sitting at his easel, giving the last touches to the picture which attracted your attention. He asked my opinion of it. "It is a fine picture," said I; "is it a fancy piece, or are they portraits?" "They are portraits," said he; "and, save perhaps a little embellishment, they are, I think, striking portraits of the wife and children of your unfortunate client, Stedman. In the course of my rambles, I chanced to call at his house in H——. I never saw a more beautiful group. The mother is one of a thousand; and the twins are a pair of cherubs." "Tell me," said I, laying my hand on the picture, "tell me, are they true and faithful portraits of the wife and children of Stedman?" My earnestness made my friend stare. He assured me that, so far as he could be permitted to judge of his own productions, they were striking representations. I asked no further questions; I seized the picture, and hurried with it to the prison where my client was confined. I found him sitting, his face covered with his hands, and apparently wrung by keen emotion. I placed the picture in such a situation that he could not fail to see it. I laid the petition on the little table by his side, and left the room.

In half an hour I returned. The farmer grasped my hand, while tears stole down his cheeks; his eye glanced first upon the picture, and then to the petition. He said nothing, but handed the latter to me. I took it, and left the apartment. He had put his name to it. The petition was granted, and Stedman was set at liberty.—*Token.*

THE LONE INDIAN.

BY MISS FRANCIS.

For many a returning autumn, a lone Indian was seen standing at the consecrated spot we have mentioned; but, just thirty years after the death of Soonseetah, he was noticed for the last time. His step was then firm, and his figure erect, though he seemed old and way-worn. Age had not dimmed the fire of his eye, but an expression of deep melancholy had settled on his wrinkled brow. It was Powontonamo—he who had once been the Eagle of the Mohawks! He came to lie down and die beneath the broad oak, which shadowed the grave of Sunny-eye. Alas, the white man's axe had been there! The tree he had planted was dead; and the vine, which had leaped so vigorously from branch to branch, now, yellow and withering, was falling to the ground. A deep groan burst from the soul of the savage. For thirty wearisome years, he had watched that oak, with its twining tendrils. They were the only things left in the wide world for him to love, and they were gone! He looked abroad. The hunting land of his tribe was changed, like its chieftain. No light canoe now shot down the river, like a bird upon the wing. The laden boat of the white man alone broke its smooth surface. The Englishman's road wound like a serpent around the banks of the Mohawk; and iron hoofs had so beaten down the war path, that a hawk's eye could not discover an Indian track. The last wigwam was destroyed; and the sun looked boldly down upon spots he had visited only by stealth, during thousands and thousands of moons. The few remaining trees, clothed in the fantastic mourning of autumn; the long line of heavy clouds, melting away before the coming sun; and the distant mountain, seen through the blue mist of departing twilight, alone remained as he had seen them in his boyhood. All things spoke a sad language to the heart of the desolate Indian. "Yes," said he, the young oak and the vine are like the Eagle and the Sunny-eye. They are cut down, torn and trampled on. The leaves are falling, and the clouds are scattering, like my people. I wish I could once more see the trees standing thick, as they did when my mother held me to her bosom, and sung the warlike deeds of the Mohawks."

A mingled expression of grief and anger passed over his face, as he watched a loaded boat in its passage across the stream. "The white man carries food to his wife and children, and he finds them in his home," said he. "Where is the squaw and the pappoose of the red man? They are here!" As he spoke, he fixed his eye thoughtfully upon the grave. After a gloomy silence, he again looked round upon the fair scene, with a wandering and troubled gaze. "The pale face may like it," murmured he; "but an Indian cannot die here in peace." So saying, he broke his bow-string, snapped his arrows, threw them on the burial-place of his fathers, and departed forever.

BURNING OF THE RICHMOND THEATRE—1811.

The house was fuller than on any night of the season. The play was over, and the first act of the pantomime had passed. The second and last had begun. All was yet gayety, all so far had been pleasure, curiosity was yet alive, and further gratification anticipated—the orchestra sent forth its sounds of harmony and joy—when the audience perceived some confusion on the stage, and presently a shower of sparks falling from above. Some were startled, others thought it was a scenic exhibition. A performer on the stage received a portion of the burning materials from on high, and it was perceived that others were tearing down the scenery. Some one cried out from the stage that there was no danger. Immediately after, Hopkins Robinson came forward and cried out, "the house is on fire!" pointing to the ceiling where the flames were progressing like wildfire. In a moment all was appalling horror and distress. Robinson handed several persons from the boxes to the stage, as a ready way for their escape. The cry of "Fire! Fire!" ran through the house, mingled with the wailings of females and children. The general rush was to gain the lobbies. It appears from the following description of the house, and the scene that ensued, that this was the cause of the great loss of life.

The general entrance to the pit and boxes was through a door not more than large enough to admit three persons abreast. This outer entrance was within a trifling distance of the pit door, and gave an easy escape to those in that part of the house. But to attain the boxes from the street, it was necessary to descend into a long passage, and ascend again by an angular staircase. The gallery had a distinct entrance, and its occupants escaped. The suffering and death fell on the occupants of the boxes, who, panic struck, did not see that the pit was immediately left vacant, but pressed on to the crowded and tortuous way by which they had entered. The pit door was so near the general entrance, that those who occupied that portion of the house, gained the street with ease. A gentleman who escaped from the pit among the last, saw it empty, and when in the street, looked back again upon the general entrance to the pit and boxes, and the door had not yet been reached by those from the lobbies. A gentleman and lady were saved by being thrown accidentally into the pit; and most of those who perished would have escaped if they had leaped from the boxes, and sought that avenue to the street. But all darted to the lobbies. The stairs were blocked up. All was enveloped in hot, scorching smoke and flame. The lights were extinguished by the black and smothering vapor, and the shrieks of despair were appalling. Happy for a moment were those who gained a window, and inhaled the air of heaven. Those who had issued to the street cried to the sufferers to the windows to leap down, and stretched out their arms to save them. Some were seen struggling to gain the apertures to inhale the fresh air. Men, women, and children, precipitated themselves from the first and second stories. Some escaped unhurt—others were killed or mangled by the fall. Some with their clothes on fire, shrieking, leaped from the windows to gain a short reprieve and die in agonies.

"Who can picture," says a correspondent of the Mirror, "the distress of those, who, unable to gain the windows, or afraid to leap from them, were pent up in the long, narrow passages." The cries of those who reached the upper windows are described as heart-sickening. Many who found their way to the street, were so scorched or burnt as to die in consequence, and some were crushed to death under foot after reaching the outer door.

Add to this mass of suffering, the feelings of those who knew that they had relatives or friends who had gone to the house that night. Such rushed half frantic to the spot with the crowds of citizens from all quarters—while the tolling of bells sounded the knell of death to the heart of the father or mother, whose child had been permitted to visit the theatre on that night of horror.

"As my father was leading me home," said Mr. Henry Placide, "we saw Mr. Greene, exhausted by previous exertion, leaning on the fence, and looking at the scene of ruin. For all was now one black mass of smoking destruction. 'Thank God,' ejaculated Greene, 'thank God, I prohibited Nancy from coming to the house to-night! She is safe!'"

Nancy was his only daughter, just springing into womanhood, still at the boarding-school of Mrs. Gibson; and as beautiful and lovely a girl as imagination can picture.

Mrs. Gibson and the boarders had made up a party for the theatre that evening, and Nancy Greene asked her father's permission to accompany them. He refused—but unfortunately added his reason —"the house will be crowded, and you will occupy a seat that would otherwise be paid for." On these words hung the fate of youth, innocence, and beauty. "I will pay for your ticket," said the kind instructress, "we will not leave you behind." The teacher and the pupil were buried in the ruins on which the father gazed, and over which he returned thanks for the safety of his child. He went home and learned the truth.

An instance of the escape of a family is given. The husband, with three children, were in the second boxes; his wife, with a female friend, were in another part of the house. The wife gained a window —leaped out and escaped unhurt. Her friend followed and was killed. The father clasped his two helpless little girls to his breast, and left a boy of twelve years of age to follow; the boy was forced from the father, ran to a window, sprang out, and was safe. The parent, with his precious charge, followed the stairway, pressed upon by those behind him, and those who mounted on the heads and shoulders of the crowd before them: he became unconscious, but was still borne along; he was taken up, carried to his bed, and opened his eyes to see all his family safe.

On the contrary, Lieutenant Gibbon, of the Navy, as exemplary in private life, as heroic in the service of his country, and on the brink of a union with Miss Conyers, the pride of Richmond for every accomplishment and virtue, was swept into eternity, while exerting himself to do all that man should do in such trying circumstances. He was with his mother at the theatre, and carried her to a place of safety—then rushed back to save her in whose fate his own was bound up; he caught her in his arms, had borne her partly down the staircase, when the steps gave way, and a body of flame swept them to eternity.

Friday, the 27th of September, 1811, was a day of mourning to Richmond. The banks and stores were closed. A law was passed prohibiting amusements of every kind for four months. A day was set apart for humiliation and prayer. A monument was resolved on, to be erected to the memory of the dead and the event.

A law passed to prohibit amusements of any kind for *four months!* Would it not have better comported with the deep scene of wretchedness which pervaded that city, not to have prohibited all kinds of amusements for four months—but to have banished the theatre forever

---

THE BROTHERS' QUARREL.

Of the divided affections too often observed among brothers, a most remarkable instance happened a few years ago, in the family of a gentleman of the north of Scotland. George and William Sterling were the only sons of the gentleman alluded to, and they had grown to manhood in the exercise of that mutual friendship, which is so delightful to observe in relations in that degree of consanguinity. I was not aware that there was anything remarkable in their characters: they were simply, two respectable young men, of good education; and while the elder was reared to the enjoyment of a competent fortune, the younger soon attained such a degree of distinction at the bar, as rendered his fate little less enviable.

On the death of their mother, which took place when they were between twenty and thirty years of age, some dispute arose, respecting a legacy, the distinction of which had not been expressed in terms sufficiently clear, and which, after a brief suit at law was determined in favor of the elder brother. At first, it was resolved by the two brothers that this plea should be amicably conducted, merely for the purpose of deciding an uncertain matter; but some circumstances unexpectedly occured, which, acting upon the inflammable nature of the elder, and not being met by a proper spirit by the younger brother, speedily produced a decided alienation between them. Each retired suddenly into the fortress of his own pride; nor were their father's entreaties and good offices, or their common recollection of twenty affectionate and happy years, of the least avail, in bringing them once more together.

They did not meet again for ten years: it was at their father's funeral. The old gentleman had died in the presence of his oldest son only, reiterating with his latest breath those injunctions so often before employed in vain, that his two sons might be restored to brotherly friendship, an object, he said, which engrossed his thoughts so much in life, that he felt as if he could not rest in peace in his grave unless it were accomplished. The two brothers met, but without taking the least notice of each other, when respectively mounting their carriages, in order to follow the corpse of their father to the family burying-ground in Aberdeen. Their hearts were still filled with fierce and indignant feelings toward each other, though it is not improbable that the elder had been somewhat touched, almost imperceptibly to himself, by the dying entreaties of his father. The procession, consisting of a hearse and the carriages of the two brothers, set out on its long and dreary journey, which was rendered additionally melancholy by the gloom of a December day.

It was originally designed that there should be no stoppage, except to exchange horses, till they reached their destination ; but this arrangement was destined to be strangely disconcerted. A fall of snow which had begun only that morning in the low country, was found, when they reached the hilly region, to have been of two days' continuance; and it was with the greatest difficulty that they reached a lonely inn, about half way to the capitol, beyond which it was declared by the postillions, there was no possibility of proceeding that day. This humble place of entertainment was accustomed to lodge only such guests as carriers, and as it was partly occupied, on the present occasion, by various wayfarers, the host, with all anxiety to accommodate such distinguished guests as those who had just arrived, found he could not by any means offer them more than two rooms. It was his expectation, that, while one of these was devoted, as decency required, to the reception of the corpse, the other would serve for the two mourners, and he accordingly proposed to make up an additional bed in the room, which he had marked as that which should receive his living guests. What was his astonishment, and what was the astonishment of all the inmates of the house, when he was informed by a servant that one of the gentlemen would sleep in one of the rooms, while the other had no objection to that in which he had placed the corpse! It was not, however, for him to make any resistance to such an arrangement, and he accordingly caused the rooms to be prepared as befitted the tastes of his guests.

It must communicate a strange feeling to know that two brothers, men of cultivated understandings, and each respected in his sphere for public and private worth—actually carried this dreadful arrangement into effect, in order to avoid what they must have contemplated as a more painful thing—the spending of a single night in each other's company. It was the younger who proposed, as a solution of the dilemma, in which he found they were placed, to take up his quarters in the same chamber with the corpse ; unpardonable as the elder was for his share of the dissension, it was but justice to him to state that he could not, after the dying request of his father, have encountered the sensations which might be expected to arise in so dreadful a situation.

During the evening, as the storm prevented them from going out of doors, each kept his own room, and was severally served with the refreshments, which he required. Night came and each went to rest. Morning returned, and still the storm was unabated. It was therefore necessary to spend another day in the same extraordinary circumstances. Slowly, slowly waned the hours of the twilight day; and still the snow continued to fall in its broad and lazy flakes, seeming to the two brothers, as each surveyed it listlessly from his window, the very personification of monotony. As the rooms were close to each other, and only divided by a thin partition, through which there was a door of communication, each of the unhappy gentlemen could over-hear everything that his neighbor did, almost to his very breathing. It at length became the amusement of each, unknown to his fellow, to watch the proceedings of the other—to note every footfall, to register every sigh. George in particular, became interested in spite of himself, in the situation of his brother, which, in consideration of what he had heard from the lips of his dying father, bore to him an aspect more repulsive and painful than perhaps to the actual sufferer.

At length, when after a weary day, the time of rest again drew nigh, and the house became more than usually still, he heard a groan—a groan partly suppressed, but still bearing distinctly the impress of unutterable anguish—proceed from his brother's room. He listened more intently, and in a few minutes he could make out that the living tenant of the death-chamber was prostrated beside the coffin, weeping—bitterly weeping—but still making every effort to bury the expression of his grief in his own bosom. It may easily be imagined that such sounds, coming upon a heart which had been insensibly undergoing a softening process during the whole day, must have had the best effect. Still the rancor of ten years was not to be got over by tears shed under such circumstances. He softly stole, however, to the door, and watched with the most intense anxiety, every respiration and movements of his afflicted brother. After waiting a few minutes, he distinctly heard William breathe forth the words, "Oh, mother!" and that in a tone which referred so pointedly to the source of their unhappy quarrel, that he could no longer entertain a doubt as to the nature of his brother's present reflections. A thousand tender associations were awakened by that endeared word; he reverted to their early days, when they had no contentions, but for her affections, no rivalry, but for the kind bounty, which she was always ready to bestow upon each alike. Human nature could hold no longer, and he gently tapped at the door which had hitherto kept them apart: "William," he said, "may I come in?" The voice of affection could not be mistaken. William opened the door in an instant, and, as if he had guessed intuitively the disposition of his brother, rushed into his arms.

The next day saw the two brothers amicably proceeding in one vehicle to the family burying-place, where, in the grave of their father, they inhumed every bitter feeling they had ever entertained against each other; and at present, taught by the sufferings they endured in their period of alienation, there is no pair of friends who take such pains to cherish each other's affections, or to avoid all means of converting them into gall.

AN HONEST LAWYER'S FEE.

It is now five years since the widow Stiles called on me, one morning before breakfast, and asked me to recommend her to some lawyer, as she thought her friend Stubbs was less correct than he might be. I asked her to step into the parlor, and went myself to my breakfast, and to my wife, whose advice I always asked on such points. We had known Mrs. Jared Stiles many years. Her husband was a great land-owner in a goodly town of the western country, and with a distinguished love that deserved some better aim, ever pressed it on his helpmate, as the first rule of life, to get all she could, and keep all she got. He died, and Mrs. Stiles became more religious and alms-giving, but also more and more fond of wealth, and sensible of the admirable advice which her husband had given her.

I stated the fact to my wife, and awaited her opinion.

"Well, William," she said, after drinking a cup of coffee on my story, "I fear the old lady has some money-getting claim in view; you know she has of late given all her affections to the getting of more wealth. I would therefore recommend her to the most honest and conscientious lawyer in town, and not to the most acute and thorough one. She relies on your judgment; use it; not for her *seeming*, but her *real* good."

I counted my legal acquaintance over—twice over—before I hit on one answering the terms, "honest and conscientious," in the sense in which I knew Ellen used them. At length I found him, and taking my hat, walked with the widow to his office.

We found Mr. Sawyer at his desk; he arose and gave us chairs, and awaited Mrs. Stiles' statement. But before I go on in this point, let me say a few words of this phenomenon—this man with his head under his left-arm, close to his heart—this honest lawyer, in the broadest, highest sense of the term. He was a man of thirty-five; he had studied law because he liked the study, and began to practice because he had to get a living; and now he continued in the profession, in spite of bad opponents, and bad courts, because he thought he had done, and might yet do much good by his labors; not only by saving the innocent and needy from the strong and cruel; but preventing strife, putting a stop to half-knavish practices, and dissuading men and women from unjust suits, and passion-rousing quarrels. Mr. Sawyer thought it not only proper for him to refuse acting for those whose claims he thought dishonest, but he counted it also a duty and privilege, nay, a mere charity, to strive to persuade them to forget such claims. He sought fame and extensive practice as means whereby to exert a *moral* influence over the community. He thought a lawyer bound to serve, not a client only, but God and his country; and looked on him, who for gain would prosecute a suit which he thought unfair, as a traitor to his country and his religion, in act, whatever he might be in intention. In short, as Bill Blunt once said, "Sawyer was such a fool as to think it an attorney's business to help the parson make men good Christians."

And now we shall let Mrs. Stiles state her business. It seems that her husband had sold and conveyed several lots, which her father had left in trust for her, and in such a form that she, meaning to release her fee in the lots, had in term, merely released right of dower. These lots she understood she could get back.

"Did you receive the money for them?" said Mr. Sawyer.

"Certainly, sir."

"Was it a fair, full price for the land?"

"It was all we asked, sir."

"Did you sign the deed willingly?"

"Of course; do you think Jared would have driven me to do it?"

"Did you mean to convey a full title in fee, Mrs. Stiles?"

"Beyond doubt; but as we didn't, they tell me the land never passed."

"Suppose, Mrs. Stiles, the money had been paid before you had drawn the deed, should you have thought it honest, after getting the money to refuse to give the deed?"

"Why, lawyer, that would have been thieving right down."

"Well, Mrs. Stiles, you have not yet given the deed—shall I draw one for you to sign?"

"Why, bless your soul, Sawyer, that is the deed you hold in your hand."

"Mrs. Stiles, if you had given the man, when he paid you money for the lots, a sheet of blank paper, and he had not looked at it, would that have been a deed?"

"Of course not."

"But you meant to give a full title in fee?"

"Yes."

"Well, this is not such a title any more than a sheet of blank paper; you have not yet given the deed. Shall I draw a quit-claim deed for you to sign?"

Mrs. Stiles looked at me, and looked at the window; looked very much puzzled, and somewhat abashed. At last she said: "But don't the law say the land's mine, 'squire?"

"We can't tell that," said Mr. Sawyer, "till the case is tried. First, let us get things straight, and have the bargain complete; and then, if you please, we will go to law about it."

The widow was fairly caught in a corner. At length, with a gasp, she asked how much he would ask for a quit-claim deed; this charge, the attorney told her, the other party would willingly pay, he had no doubt, and taking down a blank proceeded to fill it. Before we left, the bargain was complete; the deed was signed, witnessed, and acknowledged.

"And pray," said the widow, as we walked home, "what sort of a lawyer do you call that man? I verily believe he has cheated me out of all them lots! I have a great mind to go back and tear that deed all to flinders."

I assured her that not only was it too late, but that she had done the proper thing under the circumstances, and advised her in future to employ no one but Mr. Sawyer. Much to my surprise, she took my advice, and thenceforth that gentleman was her solicitor and counselor.

Last week the widow Stiles died, leaving me her executor. After the funeral we opened her will, and found it, to our astonishment, in her own hand-writing:

"Know ye all," it began, "that whereas I'm going to give something to my attorney. I write this myself; that is, I, Jane, relict of Jared Stiles, being of sound mind and body,—Know all men, that whereas said attorney, to wit, videlicet: James Sawyer, of this said town that I'm of, namely, the town of Jackson, whereas I say, first led me to see the folly of giving my old age to the heaping up of filthy lucre, and caused me to turn aside from a course that was, as I have seen, wholly wrong, for which be he blessed in this life and forever. Therefore, know ye, that as a small token of respect and love, for said attorney, to wit, namely James Sawyer, who has of late, been unfortunate, and much distressed in worldly matters, I do hereby, by these presents, give, bequeath, will, transfer, make over, and pass unto the aforesaid Sawyer, every cent I've got in the world; goods, chattels, land, money, books, dress and jewels, for his and his heirs' good; leaving it to him to give to my several friends such articles as are marked with their names.

Witness my hand and seal, November 20th, 1836.

JANE STILES."

Knowing, as I did, Mr. Sawyer's troubles in these hard times, I shook his hand most joyfully.

"It is a fee, my friend, said he, "that I must thank you for."

"She must leave fifty thousand dollars," I replied.

"I was thinking," answered he, "not of the money, but the change of life and heart; *that* is the fee I prize."

PERILOUS INCIDENT ON A CANADIAN RIVER.*

A young man and his sister have kept this ferry several years, during which they have performed many acts of heroic benevolence, and have rescued numbers of their fellow-creatures from a watery grave. One of these had so much of perilous adventure in it, that I shall make no apology for giving some account of it, the more especially as I was myself one of the trembling and anxious spectators of the whole scene.

A raft of timber on its way down the river to the nearest port, was dashed to pieces by the violence of the rapids. There was the usual number of men upon it, all of whom, except two, were fortunate enough to get upon a few logs, which kept together, and were comparatively safe, while their two comrades, were helplessly contending with the tumbling waves, almost within reach of them, but without their being able to afford them the slightest assistance. After a minute or two, and when one more would have been their last, a long oar or sweep, belonging to the wretched raft, came sweeping by.

They instantly seized it, and held on till they were carried down more than a mile, loudly calling for help as they went along; but what aid could we render them ? No craft, none, at least, which were on the banks of the river, could live in such a boiling torrent as that; for it was during one of the high spring freshets. But the ferryman was of a different opinion, and could not brook the thought of their dying before his eyes without his ever making a single effort to save them. "How could I stand idly looking on," said he to me afterward, "with a tough ash oar in my hand, and a tight little craft at my feet, and hear their cries for help, and see them drowned?" He determined, at all risks, to try to rescue them from the fate which seemed to us inevitable. He could not, however, go alone, and there was not another man on that side of the river within half a mile of him. His sister knew this, and courageously, like another Grace Darling, proposed, at once, to accompany him in his perilous adventure.

From being so often on the water with her brother, she knew well how to handle an oar. Often, indeed, without him she had paddled a passenger across the ferry in her little canoe. He accepted her proposal, and we had the satisfaction of seeing the light punt put off from the shore opposite to that from which we were idly and uselessly looking on, and go gallantly over the surging torrent toward the sinking men. We feared, however, that it would not be in time to save them, as their cries for help grew fainter and fainter, till each one, we thought, would have been their last. We saw that the oar,

*From Memoirs of a Church Missionary in Canada.

with the drowning men clinging to it, was rapidly floating down the middle of the stream, which, in this particular locality, is more than a quarter of a mile in breadth, and would inevitably, in two or three minutes more, be in the white water among the breakers, when their fate must be sealed, and the boat, if it followed, dashed to pieces among the rocks. This was the principal point of danger, and they had to run down within a most fearful proximity of it, to cross the course down which the drowning men were drifting, and as they did so, to seize hold of them without losing their own headway; for there was not time for that. They succeeded in shooting athwart the current, rapid as it was, just below the men. With breathless and painful anxiety we saw them execute this dangerous manœuver. We saw the ferryman lean over the side of the boat for a moment, as it passed them, while his sister backed water with her oar.

"They were saved!" some one said, close behind me, in a whisper so deep and earnest that I started, and turned to look at the speaker; when another, who heard him, exclaimed, "No, no! they are gone! they are lost! the boat has left them!" And sure enough, it had. But in an instant afterward, just as we thought they were about to be driven into the fatal breakers, they turned, to our inexpressible delight, as if drawn by some invisible power (the rope the ferryman had attached to the oar, was indeed invisible to us,) and followed the boat.

The ferryman and his sister had yet to pull a fearful distance for the time they had to do it in, to get out of that part of the current leading to the breakers; and they accomplished it. The man had the bow oar, and we could see the tough ash bend like a willow-wand as he stretched out to keep the head of the boat partially up the stream. His sister, too, "kept her own," and the little punt shot out rapidly into the comparatively quiet stream, beyond the influence of the fearful current, which was rapidly driving them upon the breakers. When this was accomplished, our fears for the noble-hearted brother and sister were at an end, and we took a long breath; it was indeed a relief to do so. Still we continued to watch their further proceedings with the deepest interest.

The moment they got into a less rapid current, which, they knew, led into comparatively still water, they ceased rowing, and allowed the punt to float down with it. The young ferryman now drew up the sweep alongside, and succeeded in getting the two unfortunate men into his boat. While he was doing this, his sister went aft, and used her oar as a rudder to steer the boat. At the foot of the current, which they soon afterward reached, there was no further danger. But we watched them still; and we saw them row ashore, on their own side of the river. One of the poor fellows was so much exhausted, that the ferryman had to carry him on his back to the nearest house, where he soon recovered.

Twelve months after this took place, I had the satisfaction of presenting to this worthy ferryman, in the presence of above five hundred men, a beautiful silver medallion, sent out to me by the Royal Humane Society, to which I had transmitted an account of the occurrence. Nor was the heroine of my story forgotten. A similar medallion was given to him for his sister. She could not, with propriety, be present herself, as it was the annual muster-day of the militia in that locality.

EXTRICATION OF A FRIGATE FROM THE SHOALS.

BY J. FENIMORE COOPER.

The extraordinary activity of Griffith, which communicated itself with promptitude to the whole crew, was produced by a sudden alteration in the weather. In place of the well-defined streak along the horizon, that has been already described, an immense body of misty light appeared to be moving in, with rapidity, from the ocean, while a distinct but distant roaring announced the sure approach of the tempest that had so long troubled the waters. Even Griffith, while thundering his orders through the trumpet, and urging the men, by his cries, to expedition, would pause, for instants, to cast anxious glances in the direction of the coming storm, and the faces of the sailors who lay on the yards were turned, instinctively, towards the same quarter of the heavens, while they knotted the reef-points, or passed the gaskets, that were to confine the unruly canvas to the prescribed limits.

The pilot alone, in that confused and busy throng, where voice rose above voice, and cry echoed cry, in quick succession, appeared as if he held no interest in the important stake. With his eyes steadily fixed on the approaching mist, and his arms folded together, in composure, he stood calmly awaiting the result.

The ship had fallen off, with her broadside to the sea, and was become unmanageable, and the sails were already brought into the folds necessary to her security, when the quick and heavy fluttering of canvas was thrown across the water, with all the gloomy and chilling sensations that such sounds produce, where darkness and danger unite to appall the seaman.

"The schooner has it!" cried Griffith; "Barnstable has held on, like himself, to the last moment—God send that the squall leave him cloth enough to keep him from the shore!"

"His sails are easily handled," the commander observed, "and she must be over the principal danger. We are falling off before it, Mr. Gray; shall we try a cast of the lead?"

The pilot turned from his contemplative posture, and moved slowly across the deck, before he returned any reply to this question—like a man who not only felt that everything depended on himself, but that he was equal to the emergency.

"'Tis unnecessary," he at length said; "'t would be certain destruction to be taken aback, and it is difficult to say, within several points, how the wind may strike us."

"'T is difficult no longer," cried Griffith; "for here it comes, and in right earnest!"

The rushing sounds of the wind were now, indeed, heard at hand, and the words were hardly passed the lips of the young lieutenant, before the vessel bowed down heavily to one side, and then, as she began to move through the water, rose again majestically to her upright position, as if saluting, like a courteous champion, the powerful antagonist with which she was about to contend. Not another minute elapsed, before the ship was throwing the waters aside, with a lively progress, and, obedient to her helm, was brought as near to the desired course, as the direction of the wind would allow. The hurry and bustle on the yards gradually subsided, and the men slowly descended to the deck, all straining their eyes to pierce the gloom in which they were enveloped, and some shaking their heads in melancholy doubt, afraid to express the apprehensions they really entertained. All on board anxiously waited for the fury of the gale; for there were none so ignorant or inexperienced in that gallant frigate, as not to know, that they, as yet, only felt the infant efforts of the wind. Each moment, however, it increased in power, though so gradual was the alteration, that the relieved mariners began to believe that all their gloomy forebodings were not to be realized. During this short interval of uncertainty, no other sounds were heard than the whistling of the breeze, as it passed quickly through the mass of rigging that belonged to the vessel, and the dashing of the spray, that began to fly from her bows, like the foam of a cataract.

"It blows fresh," cried Griffith, who was the first to speak in that moment of doubt and anxiety; "but it is no more than a cap-full of wind, after all. Give us elbow-room, and the right canvas, Mr. Pilot, and I'll handle the ship like a gentleman's yacht, in this breeze."

"Will she stay, think ye, under this sail?" said the low voice of the stranger.

"She will do all that man, in reason, can ask of wood and iron," returned the lieutenant; "but the vessel don't float the ocean that will tack under double-reefed topsails alone, against a heavy sea. Help her with the courses, pilot, and you'll see her come round like a dancing-master."

"Let us feel the strength of the gale first," returned the man who was called Mr. Gray, moving from the side of Griffith to the weather gang-way of the vessel, where he stood in silence, looking ahead of the ship, with an air of singular coolness and abstraction.

All the lanterns had been extinguished on the deck of the frigate, when her anchor was secured, and as the first mist of the gale had passed over, it was succeeded by a faint light, that was a good deal aided by the glittering foam of the waters, which now broke in white curls around the vessel, in every direction. The land could be faintly discerned, rising, like a heavy bank of black fog, above the margin of the waters, and was only distinguishable from the heavens, by its deeper gloom and obscurity. The last rope was coiled, and deposited in its proper place, by the seamen, and for several minutes the stillness of death pervaded the crowded decks. It was evident to every one, that their ship was dashing at a prodigious rate through the waves; and, as she was approaching, with such velocity, the quarter of the bay where the shoals and dangers were known to be situated, nothing but the habits of the most exact discipline could suppress the uneasiness of the officers and men within their own bosoms. At length the voice of Captain Munson was heard, calling to the pilot.

"Shall I send a hand into the chains, Mr. Gray," he said, "and try our water?"

* * * * * * * * * * * * *

"Tack your ship, sir, tack your ship; I would see how she works, before we reach the point, where she *must* behave well, or we perish."

Griffith gazed after him in wonder, while the pilot slowly paced the quarter-deck, and then, rousing from his trance, gave forth the cheering order that called each man to his station, to perform the desired evolution. The confident assurances which the young officer had given to the pilot, respecting the qualities of his vessel, and his own ability to manage her, were fully realized by the result. The helm was no sooner put a-lee, than the huge ship bore up gallantly against the wind, and, dashing directly through the waves, threw the foam high into the air, as she looked boldly into the very eye of the wind, and then, yielding gracefully to its power, she fell off on the other tack, with her head pointed from those dangerous shoals that she had so recently approached with such terrifying velocity. The heavy yards swung round, as if they had been vanes to indicate the currents of the air, and in a few moments the frigate again moved, with stately progress, through the water, leaving the rocks and shoals behind her on one side of the bay, but advancing towards those that offered equal danger on the other.

During this time, the sea was becoming more agitated, and the violence of the wind was gradually increasing. The latter no longer whistled amid the cordage of the vessel, but it seemed to howl, surlily, as it passed the complicated machinery that the frigate obtruded on its path. An endless succession of white surges rose above the heavy billows, and the very air was glittering with the light that was disengaged from the ocean. The ship yielded, each moment, more and more before the storm, and, in less than half an hour from the time that she had lifted her anchor, she was driven along, with tremendous fury, by the full power of a gale of wind. Still, the hardy and experienced mariners, who directed her movements, held her to the course that was necessary to their preservation, and still Griffith gave forth, when directed by their unknown pilot, those orders that turned her in the narrow channel where safety was, alone, to be found.

So far, the performance of his duty appeared easy to the stranger, and he gave the required directions in those still, calm tones, that formed so remarkable a contrast to the responsibility of his situation. But when the land was becoming dim, in distance as well as darkness, and the agitated sea was only to be discovered as it swept by them in foam, he broke in upon the monotonous roaring of the tempest, with the sounds of his voice, seeming to shake off his apathy, and rouse himself to the occasion.

"Now is the time to watch her closely, Mr. Griffith," he cried; "here we get the true and the real danger. Place the best quarter-master of your ship in those chains, and let an officer stand by him, and see that he gives us the right water."

"I will take the office on myself," said the captain; "pass a light into the weather main-chains."

"Stand by your braces!" exclaimed the pilot, with startling quickness. "Heave away that lead!"

These preparations taught the crew to expect the crisis, and every officer and man stood in fearful silence, at his assigned station, awaiting the issue of the trial. Even the quarter-master at the cun gave out his orders to the men at the wheel in deeper and hoarser tones than usual, as if anxious not to disturb the quiet and order of the vessel.

While this deep expectation pervaded the frigate, the piercing cry of the leadsman, as he called, "By the mark seven!" rose above the tempest, crossed over the decks, and appeared to pass away to leeward, borne on the blast, like the warnings of some water spirit.

"'Tis well," returned the pilot, calmly; "try it again."

The short pause was succeeded by another cry, "and a half-five!"

"She shoals! she shoals!" exclaimed Griffith; "keep her a good full."

"Ay! you must hold the vessel in command, now," said the pilot, with those cool tones that are most appalling in critical moments, because they seem to denote most preparation and care.

The third call of "By the deep four!" was followed by a prompt direction from the stranger to tack.

Griffith seemed to emulate the coolness of the pilot, in issuing the necessary orders to execute this manœuvre.

The vessel rose slowly from the inclined position into which she had been forced by the tempest, and the sails were shaking violently, as if to release themselves from their confinement, while the ship stemmed the billows, when the well-known voice of the sailing-master was heard shouting from the forecastle—

"Breakers! breakers, dead ahead!"

This appalling sound seemed yet to be lingering about the ship, when a second voice cried—

"Breakers on our lee-bow!"

"We are in a bight of the shoals, Mr. Gray," said the commander. "She loses her way; perhaps an anchor might hold her."

"Clear away that best-bower!" shouted Griffith through his trumpet.

"Hold on!" cried the pilot, in a voice that reached the very hearts of all who heard him; "hold on every thing."

The young man turned fiercely to the daring stranger, who thus defied the discipline of his vessel, and at once demanded,

"Who is it that dares to countermand my orders?—is it not enough that you run the ship into danger, but you must interfere to keep her there! If another word—"

"Peace, Mr. Griffith," interrupted the captain, bending from the rigging, his gray locks blowing about in the wind, and adding a look of wildness to the haggard care that he exhibited by the light of his lantern; "yield the trumpet to Mr. Gray; he alone can save us."

Griffith threw his speaking trumpet on the deck, and, as he walked proudly away, muttered in bitterness of feeling,

"Then all is lost, indeed, and, among the rest, the foolish hopes with which I visited this coast."

There was, however, no time for reply; the ship had been rapidly running into the wind, and, as the efforts of the crew were paralyzed by the contradictory orders they had heard, she gradually lost her way, and, in a few seconds, all her sails were taken aback.

Before the crew understood their situation, the pilot had applied the trumpet to his mouth, and, in a voice that rose above the tempest, he thundered forth his orders. Each command was given distinctly, and with a precision that showed him to be master of his profession. The helm was kept fast, the head yards swung up heavily against the wind, and the vessel was soon whirling round on her heel, with a retrograde movement.

Griffith was too much of a seaman, not to perceive that the pilot had seized, with a perception almost intuitive, the only method that promised to extricate the vessel from her situation. He was young, impetuous, and proud; but he was also generous. Forgetting his resentment and his mortification, he rushed forward among the men, and, by his presence and example, added certainty to the experiment. The ship fell off slowly before the gale, and bowed her yards nearly to the water, as she felt the blast pouring its fury on her broadside, while the surly waves beat violently against her stern, as if in reproach at departing from her usual manner of moving.

The voice of the pilot, however, was still heard, steady and calm, and yet so clear and high as to reach every ear; and the obedient seamen whirled the yards at his bidding, in despite of the tempest, as if they handled the toys of their childhood. When the ship had fallen off dead before the wind, her head sails were shaken, her after yards trimmed, and her helm shifted, before she had time to run upon the danger that had threatened, as well to leeward as to windward. The beautiful fabric, obedient to her government, threw her bows up gracefully towards the wind again, and, as her sails were trimmed, moved out from amongst the dangerous shoals, in which she had been embayed, as steadily and swiftly as she had approached them.

A moment of breathless astonishment succeeded the accomplishment of this nice manœuvre, but there was no time for the usual expressions of surprise. The stranger still held the trumpet, and continued to lift his voice amid the howlings of the blast, whenever prudence or skill directed any change in the management of the ship. For an hour longer, there was a fearful struggle for their preservation, the channel becoming, at each step, more complicated, and the shoals thickening around the mariners, on every side. The lead was cast rapidly, and the quick eye of the pilot seemed to pierce the darkness, with a keenness of vision that exceeded human power. It was apparent to all in the vessel, that they were under the guidance of one who understood the navigation thoroughly, and their exertions kept pace with their reviving confidence. Again and again the frigate appeared to be rushing blindly on shoals, where the sea was covered with foam, and where destruction would have been as sudden as it was certain, when the clear voice of the stranger was heard warning them of the danger, and inciting them to their duty. The vessel was implicitly yielded to his government, and during those anxious moments, when she was dashing the waters aside, throwing the spray over her enormous yards, each ear would listen eagerly for those sounds that had obtained a command over the crew, that can only be acquired, under such circumstances, by great steadiness and consummate skill. The ship was recovering from the inaction of changing her course, in one of those critical tacks that she had made so often, when the pilot, for the first time, addressed the commander of the frigate, who still continued to superintend the all-important duty of the leadsman.

"Now is the pinch," he said, "and if the ship behaves well, we are safe—but if otherwise, all we have yet done will be useless."

The veteran seaman whom he addressed left the chains, at this portentous notice, and, calling to his first lieutenant, required of the stranger an explanation of his warning.

"See you yon light on the southern headland ?" returned the pilot; "you may know it from the star near it by its sinking, at times, in the ocean. Now observe the hummoc, a little north of it, looking like a shadow in the horizon—'tis a hill far inland. If we keep that light open from the hill, we shall do well—but if not, we surely go to pieces."

"Let us tack again!" exclaimed the lieutenant.

The pilot shook his head, as he replied—

"There is no more tacking or box-hauling to be done to-night.

We have barely room to pass out of the shoals on this course, and if we can weather the 'Devil's-Grip,' we clear their outermost point—but if not, as I said before, there is but an alternative."

"If we had beaten out the way we entered," exclaimed Griffith, "we should have done well."

"Say, also, if the tide would have let us do so," returned the pilot, calmly. "Gentlemen, we must be prompt; we have but a mile to go, and the ship appears to fly. That topsail is not enough to keep her up to the wind; we want both jib and mainsail."

"'T is a perilous thing to loosen canvas in such a tempest!" observed the doubtful captain.

"It must be done," returned the collected stranger; "we perish, without it—see! the light already touches the edge of the hummoc; the sea casts us to leeward!"

"It shall be done!" cried Griffith, seizing the trumpet from the hand of the pilot.

The orders of the lieutenant were executed almost as soon as issued, and, every thing being ready, the enormous folds of the mainsail were trusted, loose, to the blast. There was an instant when the result was doubtful; the tremendous threshing of the heavy sails, seeming to bid defiance to all restraint, shaking the ship to her centre; but art and strength prevailed, and gradually the canvas was distended, and, bellying as it filled, was drawn down to its usual place, by the power of a hundred men. The vessel yielded to this immense additional force, and bowed before it, like a reed bending to a breeze. But the success of the measure was announced by a joyful cry from the stranger, that seemed to burst from his inmost soul.

"She feels it! she springs her luff! observe," he said, "the light opens from the hummoc already; if she will only bear her canvas, we shall go clear!"

A report, like that of a cannon, interrupted his exclamation, and something resembling a white cloud was seen drifting before the wind from the head of the ship, till it was driven into the gloom, far to leeward.

"'T is the jib, blown from the bolt-ropes," said the commander of the frigate. "This is no time to spread light duck—but the mainsail may stand it yet."

"The sail would laugh at a tornado," returned the lieutenant; "but that mast springs like a piece of steel."

"Silence all!" cried the pilot. "Now, gentlemen, we shall soon know our fate. Let her luff—luff you can!"

This warning effectually closed all discourse, and the hardy mariners, knowing that they had already done all in the power of man to ensure their safety, stood in breathless anxiety, awaiting the result. At a short distance ahead of them, the whole ocean was white with foam, and the waves, instead of rolling on, in regular succession, appeared to be tossing about in mad gambols. A single streak of dark billows, not half a cable's length in width, could be discerned running into this chaos of water; but it was soon lost to the eye, amid the confusion of the disturbed element. Along this narrow path the vessel moved more heavily than before, being brought so near the wind as to keep her sails touching. The pilot silently proceeded to the wheel, and, with his own hands, he undertook the steerage of the ship. No noise proceeded from the frigate to interrupt the horrid tumult of the ocean, and she entered the channel among the breakers, with the silence of a desperate calmness. Twenty times, as the foam rolled away to leeward, the crew were on the eve of uttering their joy, as they supposed the vessel past the danger; but breaker after breaker would still rise before them, following each other into the general mass, to check their exultation. Occasionally, the fluttering of the sails would be heard; and, when the looks of the startled seamen were turned to the wheel, they beheld the stranger grasping its spokes, with his quick eye glancing from the water to the canvas. At length the ship reached a point, where she appeared to be rushing directly into the jaws of destruction, when, suddenly, her course was changed, and her head receded rapidly from the wind. At the same moment, the voice of the pilot was heard, shouting,

"Square away the yards!—in mainsail!"

A general burst from the crew echoed, "Square away the yards!" and, quick as thought, the frigate was seen gliding along the channel, before the wind. The eye had hardly time to dwell on the foam, which seemed like clouds driving in the heavens, and directly the gallant vessel issued from her perils, and rose and fell on the heavy waves of the open sea.

EXPLOSION OF THE STEAMER MOZELLE

A THRILLING SKETCH.*

"Captain of the Mozelle, sir?"

"Yes."

"Up for Cairo and New Orleans, I see."

"Just so."

"When do you leave?"

"At three, this afternoon."

"Please book my name for Cairo."

"Be aboard before three or you will be left."

"I will," said I, though I knew it would be a wonderful thing, if a boat should leave at its advertised time.

The Mozelle was a new, excellent, and fast boat; she had never

* This sketch of the terrible explosion of this unfortunate steamboat, nearly opposite Cincinnati, in 1838, is by an eye-witness, and copied from Arthur's Home Gazette.

made a trip, but her commander intended on this day to show her off to the best advantage.

Before three o'clock I went on board; she was thronged with passengers, many of them the elite of the city, all in good humor, anticipating a delightful voyage in this palace of the waters.

At Fulton, a small village about two miles up the river, were a large number of emigrants—Germans I believe—consisting of men, women, and children, who were to be taken aboard the Mozelle at that place.

An hour was spent in taking aboard the emigrants and their heavy luggage. Many an eye then brightened with hope as it rested on the noble craft, which they thought, would so soon bring them to the promised land. Not a tear of regret was shed on leaving a strange shore, where no sympathizing friends stood to wave them an adieu. Alas! that there was so soon cause for a thousand eyes to weep.

"Cast off there!" shouted the captain, on the hurricane deck.

"Ay, ay, sir."

"Draw in the plank."

Right gallantly did she walk the water, her sharp-cutting bow dividing the stream so smoothly as scarce to cause a sparkle of foam on her breast; but a highway of milk-white foam issued from beneath her rushing keel, marking her course to the destined landing, while her roaring steam-pipes hardly drowned the deafening shouts of the excited and admiring spectators.

"Captain, we ought to blow off steam, the boilers are very hot and the gauge indicates extraordinary pressure," said the engineer, as he came upon the hurricane deck, and stood near the captain, by the wheel-house.

"I told you, sir, to blow off no steam while we lay here; enough, sir, go below."

"But, sir, ——" said the engineer.

"I swear, sir, that I'll not blow off steam, and *I'll blow her to* —— rather than fail going past the city faster than any other boat that ever floated these waters. To your duty, sir."

The engineer reluctantly obeyed. Myself and several others heard the blasphemy, and were shocked beyond measure. There was a whispering among the passengers, and many, myself among the number, ordered our baggage ashore, and left the boat, fearing the consequences of remaining. We had barely time to leave, ere the plank was drawn aboard.

Majestically she swings around her breast to the current, proudly the captain stands on the dizzy edge of the hurricane deck, enjoying the admiration of the spectators. One revolution of her paddles, and then, O, horrors! an explosion of sound, as if the whole "artillery of heaven" shook the air, mingled with the noise of a thousand crashing oaks. A breathless moment of silence, and then shrieks upon shrieks, groans upon groans, wailing and yells of despair, pierced the horror-struck ear. Riveted with terror to the spot, around us fell in fearful and sickening showers, fragments of human flesh, parts of arms, legs, headless trunks, and ghastly faces; bits of furniture and the wreck covered the shore.

All about the ill-fated boat, living and dead, dotted the surface of the river, most of them to sink forever.

The shattered hull floated down stream a few rods, and sank close to the city water-works. Terrible was the scene! And O! what thoughts must have fired the brain of more than a hundred human beings, blinded by steam, still crowded in the crazy hull, as the rushing waters through her shattered sides reached higher and higher, till their gurgling throats were silenced in the deep!

She sank to the depth of her cabin floor. Boats, planks, and every other available means were put in requisition to reach the wreck, and save the life that yet might be. Few were saved; some in the cabin were rescued, also some who were thrown into the river by the concussion, but none of the multitude that crowded the steerage ever looked on the scene of the disaster again. All that afternoon, and for several succeeding days, men fished for the dead, through holes cut in the cabin floor. Hardly a soul of that unfortunate band of emigrants, was left to mourn the sad catastrophe, or weep over the mangled dead. A little boy, belonging to them, stood wet and trembling on the river's brink, from which he had just been rescued. I spoke to him kindly, but he only answered with a wild and vacant stare, and pointing to the wreck upon which he was gazing, gave an unearthly shrick, threw his arms aloft, and sprung into the boiling flood beyond the reach of human help.

The ill-fated commander was found, shockingly disfigured, a few days after, on the Kentucky shore. Engineers, firemen, pilot, and clerk, ended their life's voyage here.

More than one hundred and seventy-five human beings were thus sacrificed on the altar of Pride.

Unhappy man! thou didst keep thine oath but too faithfully. The force of the explosion was terrible—the six boilers of the boat were burst into a thousand fragments, and cast at a great distance, wounding some of the spectators on the landing, and in the street above. The body of a man was blown high in the air, and coming down head foremost, burst through the roof of a brick house, and there hung, part of the body on the roof, and part on the inside. A small hatchet, too, was cast with such violence as to enter the window of a house, penetrate the partition, and pass through another window on the opposite side of the house, into a back yard, where it was found.

O! how wretched the scene in that little village of Fulton! scarcely a house but contained the wounded and dying; crowds of eager eyes were about every door, and peering in at every window; some from idle curiosity, others, perchance, seeking some friend or relative who had been on the wreck.

The noise of the explosion was heard in the heart of the city, and as soon as the awful explanation was given, thousands rushed to the spot. Many of the beautiful and brave, the dearest ornaments of the Queen City, were numbered among the victims. Wildly throbbed the hearts of fathers and wives, as they approached with swift and trembling steps the wretched scene, eager to learn the fate of those they loved. But who shall paint the agony of those doomed to behold the mutilated and scarcely recognizable dead or living remains of him they sought, or the despair of those who had found them? But let us draw the veil.

'Tis the Sabbath; a pall of mourning hangs over the afflicted city; crape rustles at the entrance of many a pleasant home, whose doors and windows, notwithstanding the summer's heat, are solemnly closed, the picture of desolation.

Subdued and plaintive musical notes tremble on the air, and the silent streets echo to the tread of a solemn death-train. Forty hearses and other vehicles, shrouded in black, bear the remains of the human sacrifice. Thousands of the citizens follow reverently and silently the gloomy pageant, to the last resting-place of man. Ah, no! for the death-wail is yet to be borne to distant lands, causing fresh hearts to bleed, and woe to hang her darksome drapery around many a broken hearth circle.

COMPULSORY SOLITUDE.

August 9th.—Still suffering from the fatigue of my visit to Félicité yesterday, but attracted by the freshness of the air, I determined to start this morning and take Roger by surprise, at his own house; after having scarcely accomplished a third of the walk, however, I was compelled to retrace my steps, and only succeeded in reaching home by resting several times on the way.

For some time past now, I have felt an extreme weariness on each occasion after walking out, but I have persisted in attributing it to a momentary derangement of the system. I am at length, however, forced to acknowledge that my strength is failing, and that walking will soon become impossible for me altogether. At the first thought of this, I must confess, that the anticipation of an indefinitely prolonged imprisonment, the prospect of remaining eternally confined to my own room, greatly affected me. I began to think with pain and regret on the public walk shaded by trees, where every day my favorite seat awaited me. It seemed to me that the sight of the accustomed spots, the gossips, not perhaps appealing much to the affections, or higher feelings, but easy and familiar, with one's companions in age and leisure—who from morning to night, form under the same lime-trees a permanent group, constantly being renewed —I felt as if all this were indispensable to my existence; and I could not help bitterly accusing old age, which seemed about to reduce me to the loneliness of isolation and abandonment.

But how is this? I have never spent my hours more agreeably, or more profitably, than during the past day.

Hardly had I reclined motionless for a few minutes in my arm-chair before a light, as it were, diffused itself over my dejected soul; my spirits, for the moment depressed, became gradually raised by an inner and spontaneous power. I began to contemplate the objects that surround me, and with which I am henceforth to live on almost exclusive terms of intimacy, with a more attentive, more sympathetic eye; and lo! every thing has become clothed with a fresh aspect, and with a charm previously unsuspected. The sun's rays, which entered my room by the open window and illuminated the carpet with a golden border, struck me as having a brilliancy and a glory that I had never remarked before. A pot of mignonette stands upon my desk, on which formerly, before going out, or on my return, I hardly bestowed a passing glance, now I take a singular pleasure in examining it; I look with admiration, almost gratitude, towards this little homely flower, which exhales its perfumed breath around me, with such generous profusion, with such untiring energy.

Hence I perceive that it is from lack of perception and good will, that we do not derive more enjoyment from the many precious objects spread around us. If we thought only of gathering up those scattered particles, as the diamond-cutter his diamond dust; to sum up all the blessings which enrich our original poverty, we should find an abundant supply of subjects to gladden us and to engage our love. Inattention, indifference to others, and apathy, divide betwixt them the dominion over our minds: as they have not the stout appearance of the active vices, these defects escape our moral vigilance, and exert their pernicious influence in secret. They are enemies on whom I shall henceforth keep a vigilant eye; and shall strive to conquer, now that age, having deprived me of external resources, leaves me more exposed to their subtle attacks.

But it is my books above all else, which have suddenly grown dearer to me; books, which a short time ago were no more to me than so many volumes, ornaments, pieces of furniture even, have become, as it were, endowed with life; the spirit enshrined within their pages has come forth to meet my own; I have found in them inquirers who have communicated to me their thoughts; friends who have taken possession of me, and introduced me into the inner circle of their lives. Incomparable society, ever ready to receive me; inexhaustible friendship, which will never fail me, which waits only for my own invitation to afford me sympathy and delight.

With Plato behold me transported to Athens, listening in the shade of a marble portico, raised on elegant columns—to which the sun of Greece has given the polish and amber tint of ivory—to one of those inimitable conversations, where Socrates, by the spell of his eloquence, strives to inspire his disciples with his own sublime and radiant wisdom. I recline at one of those banquets, where the grave philosopher disdains not to mingle with frivolous youth, well knowing that the charm of his voice will soon make the revellers forget their cups. I see Alcibiades himself, who enters just now with a supercilious smile on his lips, and his head crowned with violets, lend by degrees a more willing ear; at first attracted, then subjugated, he listens in silence. Shame, and soon respect, depict themselves on his now serious countenance, tears of enthusiasm glisten in his eyes, and, snatching off his crown of flowers, he places it on the brow of the master, whom he declares to be inspired by the gods!

Then Virgil takes possession of my thoughts, and conducts me through his magic landscapes; I wander with him on the lonely shore, where the stork pursues her staid and solitary course beneath a sky charged with storm-clouds; I penetrate some ancient forest, where the crowded oaks intermingle their dark shadows; I smell in the heavy air the dank and baneful odors of the marshes; I hear re-echoed beneath leafy domes the wild bird's shrill cry. Soon, however, brighter scenes invite and attract me; vast landscapes spread themselves out beneath the fruitful rays of the sun: here I behold yellow plains, where the ripe grain undulates with every breeze, there prairies, with herds grazing beside the river as it flows between its low lying banks; pale green willows and shrubs, all glowing with their purple berries, separate the various orchards, where the husbandman is singing while he prunes his trees. The bees hum in the blue expanse; and, mingled with the lowing of cattle, I hear the champing of horses in their stables.

From the depths of nature, Plutarch wins me back to the ranks of humanity; guided by him, I pass in review, one after the other, the heroes whom he has assembled in his writings as in a glorious Pantheon; less ready, indeed, to linger near those famous conquerors, who derived nearly all their prestige from the workings of ambition and pride; but delighted to attach myself to the plain citizens who, though of obscure birth, and uncertain of future fame, devoted their lives to the good of their country, and to the triumph of virtue. I love to follow across the steaming furrow, step by step, the humble plough with which hands so recently victorious, do not disdain to be occupied; I sit down at the domestic hearth, closed, like a sanctuary, against commotion without, and sacred to the household gods, where the Roman wife guards her virtues, where the child grows up between tenderness and discipline, where the energies of the soul are braced by labor and abstinence. Insipid, classical trivialities only! exclaim those who listen but with the ear, who in words perceive only sounds, and grow angry at unsensational monotony; but endless subjects for thought, and sources of refined pleasure, to those who read with the soul, and who, in the personages of history, recognize men and cherish brothers.

The scene changes. St. Augustin and the "Imitation of Christ" transport me into a new world, the sun of Athens and of Rome is eclipsed: a mystic light, more brilliant, and yet softer, spreads over the earth; the Parthenon and the Capitol are lost in haze, and give place to the spires of monasteries, and the towers of cathedrals. I love to take refuge, far from battle-fields and the clashing of swords and spears, under the domes of these peaceful retreats; to listen to the despairing avowals, and groans of the human conscience suddenly aroused from its long sleep; and at the same time to hear those sublime chants, those fervent hymns, which celebrate a hope and a joy hitherto unknown in this world. Marvellous power of mind! From a corner of my chamber—from the arm-chair which I occupy—I can traverse the immense abysses of the past. I am present at the foundation of cities, the birth and growth of empires; I accompany various races as they wander over the earth, establish themselves and found nations; I take note of that perpetual movement of humanity, as it seeks its level on the globe which has been given to it for an inheritance. Or, fatigued with these generalities, I repose in the tent of the patriarch Abraham, or beneath the oak of St. Louis. From the tribune of Cicero I pass to the pulpit of Bossuet; distances are nothing to me; I traverse them by an instantaneous bound, whether those of space or time. From the east I hasten to the west, from the early days of the world I pass on to the hour which has just struck; wherever an attractive spectacle summons me, I am there in spirit; or a noble action or an elevated conversation invites me, I am present to applaud or take part. Magnificent empire of memory! vast power and inexhaustible activity of thought! . . . I cease to be troubled now at my solitude and forced inaction.—*Emile Souvestre.*

AUNT KINDLY.

BY THEODORE PARKER, FROM HIS SERMON ON "OLD AGE."

MISS KINDLY is aunt to every body, and has been for so long a time, that none remember to the contrary. The little children love her; and she helped their grandmothers to ridal ornaments threescore years ago. Nay, this boy's grandfather found that the way to college lay through her pocket. Generations, not her own, rise up and call her blessed. To this man's father

her patient toil gave the first start in life. When that great fortune was a seed, it was she who carried it in her hand. That wide river of reputation ran out of the cup which her bounty filled. Now she is old, very old. The little children who cling about her, with open mouth and great round eyes, wonder that any body should ever be so old; or ask themselves whether Aunt Kindly ever had a mother to kiss her mouth. To them she is coeval with the sun, and, like that, an institution of the country. At Christmas they think she is the wife of St. Nicholas himself, such an advent is there of blessings from her hand.

Her hands are thin, her voice is feeble, her back is bent, and she walks with a staff, which is the best limb of the three. She wears a cap of antique pattern, yet of her own nice make. She has great round spectacles, and holds her book away off the other side of the candle, when she reads. For more than sixty years she has been a special providence to the family. How she used to go forth, the very charity of God, to heal and soothe and bless! How industrious are her hands! How thoughtful and witty that fertile mind! Her heart has gathered power to love in all the eighty-six years of her toilsome life. When the birth-angel came to a related house, she was there to be the mother's mother; aye, mother also to the new-born baby's soul. And when the wings of death flapped in the street and shook a neighbor's door, she smoothed the pillow for the fainting head; she soothed and cheered the spirit of the waiting man, opening the curtains of heaven that he might look through and see the welcoming face of the dear Infinite Mother; nay, she put the wings of her own strong, experienced piety under him, and sought to bear him up.

Now, these things are passed by. No, they are not passed by; for they are in the memory of the dear God, and every good deed she has done is treasured in her own heart. The bulb shuts up the summer in its breast, which in winter will come out a fragrant hyacinth. Stratum after stratum, her good works are laid up, imperishable, in the geology of her character.

It is near noon, now, and she is alone. She has been thoughtful all day, talking inwardly to herself. The family notice it, but say nothing. In her chamber, she takes a little casket from her private drawer, and from thence a book, gilt-edged and clasped; but the clasp is worn, the gilding is old, the binding faded by long use. Her hands tremble as she opens it. First she reads her own name, on the fly leaf; only her Christian name, "Agnes," and the date. Sixty-eight years ago this day, that name was written there, in a clear, youthful, clerkly hand, with a little tremble in it, as if the heart beat over quick. It is very well worn, that dear old Bible. It opens of its own accord, at the fourteenth chapter of St. John. There is a little folded paper there; it touches the first verse and the twenty-seventh. She *sees* neither; she reads both out of her *soul.* "Let not your heart be troubled; ye believe in God, believe also in me." "Peace I leave with you. My peace I give unto you. Not as the world giveth, give I unto you." She opens the paper. There is a little brown dust in it, the remnant of a flower. She takes the precious relic in her hand, made cold by emotion. She drops a tear on it, and the dust is transfigured before her eyes: it is a red rose of the spring, not quite half blown, dewy fresh. She is old no longer. She is not Aunt Kindly now; she is sweet Agnes, as the maiden of eighteen was, eight and sixty years ago, one day in May, when all nature was woosome and winning, and every flower-bell rung in the marriage of the year. Her lover had just put that red rose of the spring into her hand, and the good God put another on her cheek, not quite half blown, dewy fresh. The young man's arm is around her; her brown curls fall on his shoulders; she feels his breath on her face, his cheek on hers; their lips join, and like two morning dew-drops in that rose their two loves rush into one.

But the youth must wander away to a far land. She bids him take her Bible. They will think of each other as they look at the North Star. He saw the North Star hang over the turrets of many a foreign town. His soul went to God;—there is as straight a road thither from India as from any other spot. His Bible came back to her; the Divine love in it, without the human lover; the leaf turned down at the blessed words of St. John, first and twenty-seventh verse of the fourteenth chapter. She put the rose there to mark the spot; what marks the thought holds now the symbol of their youthful love. To-day, her soul is with him; her maiden soul with his angel-soul; and one day the two, like two dew-drops, will rush into one immortal wedlock, and the old age of earth shall become eternal youth in the kingdom of heaven.

THE HUMANITY-GOD.

BY ERNEST NAVILLE.

If the Humanity-God is always right, it must be that two contradictory propositions can be true at the same time, since contradictions abound in the history of human thoughts. If two contradictory propositions can be true, there is no more truth. What then is our reason, of which truth is the object? We are seized with giddiness. Might not everything in the world be illusion? and myself—? Listen to a voice which reaches us, across the ages, from the countries crowned by the Himalayas. "Nothing exists. . . . By the study of first principles, one acquires this knowledge, absolute, incontestable, comprehensible to the intelligence alone; I neither am, nor does anything which is mine, nor do I myself, exist." What is there beneath these strange lines? The feeling of giddiness, which seeks to steady itself by language. Here is now the modern echo of these ancient words. One of those writers who accept all, in the hope of understanding all, describes himself as having come at last to be aware that he is "only one of the most fugitive illusions in the bosom of the infinite illusion." One of his colleagues expresses himself on this subject as follows: "Is this the last word of all?—And why not?—The illusion which knows itself—is it in fact an illusion? Does it not in some sort triumph over itself? Does it not attain to *the sovereign reality*, that of the thought which thinks itself, that of the dream which knows itself a dream, that *of nothingness, which ceases to be so*, in order to recognize itself and to assert itself?" We are gone back to ancient India. You will remark here three stages of thought. The fugitive illusion is man. The infinite illusion is the universe. The universal principle of the appearances which compose the universe is nothingness. Here is the explanation of the universe! Nothingness takes life; nothingness takes life only to know itself to be nothingness, and the nothingness which says to itself, "I am nothingness," is the reason of existence of all that is. I said just now that the sun was declining to the horizon. Now the last glimmer of twilight has disappeared; night has closed in —a dark and starless night. Yes, Sirs, but there is never on the earth a night so dark as to warrant us in despairing of the return of the dawn. If the modern mind is such as it is described to us, it has lost all the rays of light; but the sun is not dead.

The doctrine of non-existence and of illusion is entirely incomprehensible, in the sense in which to comprehend signifies to have a clear idea, and one capable of being directly apprehended. But, if one follows the chain of ideas as logically unrolled, in the way that a mathematician follows the transformations of an algebraical formula, without considering its real contents, it is easy to account for the origin of this theory. If the human mind has no rule superior to itself, if it is the absolute mind, God, all its thoughts are equally true, since we cannot point out error without having recourse to a rule of truth. If all doctrines are equally true, propositions, directly and absolutely contradictory, are equally true. If all is true, there is no truth; for truth is not conceived except in opposition to at least possible error. If there is no truth, the human reason, which seeks truth by a natural impulse belonging to its very essence, as the magnetized needle seeks the pole—reason, I say, is a chimera. The truth which reason seeks is an exact relation of human thought to the reality of the world. If the search for this relation is chimerical, the two terms, mind, and the world, may be illusions. A fugitive illusion in presence of an infinite illusion: there is all. You see that these thoughts hang together with rigorous precision. The darkness is becoming visible to us, or, in other words, we are acquiring a perfect understanding of the origin and developments of the absurdity. Put God aside, the law of our will, the warrant of our thought; deify human nature; and a fatal current will run you aground twice over—on the shores of moral absurdity, and on those of intellectual absurdity. These sad shipwrecks are set before our eyes in striking examples; it has been easy to indicate their cause.

The consideration of the beautiful would give occasion to analogous observations. The human mind becoming the object of our adoration, we must give up judging it in every particular, and suppress the rules of the ideal in art, as those of morals in the conduct, and truth in the intellect. We must form a system of æsthetics which accepts all, and finds equally legitimate whatever affords recreation to the Humanity-God, in the great variety of its tastes. Then high aspirations are extinguished, the beautiful gives place to the agreeable; and since the ugly and misshapen please a vicious taste, room must be made for the ugly in the Pantheon of beauty. Art despoiled of its crown becomes the sad, and often the ignoble slave of the tastes and caprices of the public. I do not insist further. The pretension of the worshippers of humanity is to make their conscience wide enough to accept all, and to have their intellect broad enough to understand all. They explain all, except these three small particulars—the conscience, the heart, and the reason. Goodness and truth avenge themselves in the end, for the long contempt cast upon them; and the first punishment those suffer who accept all, in the hope of understanding all, is no longer to understand what constitutes the life of humanity.

Let us not be setting up altars to the human mind; for an adulterous incense stupefies it, and ends by destroying it. Before they deified man, the pagans at least transfigured him by placing him on Olympus. At this day, it is humanity as it is upon earth that is proposed to our adoration, humanity with its profound miseries and its fearful defilements. They seek to throw a veil over the mad audacity of this attempt, by telling us of the progress which is to bring about, by little and little, the realization of our divinity. But, alas! our history is long already, and no reasonable induction justifies the vague hopes of heated imaginations. Great progress is being effected, but none which gives any promise that the profound needs of our nature can ever be satisfied in this life. Charity has appeared on the earth; but there are still poor amongst us, and it seems that there always will be. A breath of justice and humanity has penetrated social institutions; still politics have not become the domain of perfect truth and of absolute justice, and there seems small likelihood that they ever will. Industry has given birth to marvels; we devour space in these days, but we shall never go so fast that suffering and death will not succeed in overtaking us. The great sources of grief are not dried up;

the song of our poets causes still the chords of sorrow to vibrate as in the days of yore. Progress is being accomplished, sure witness of a beneficent Hand which is guiding humanity in its destinies; but everything tells us that the soil of our planet will be always steeped in tears, that the atmosphere which envelops us will always resound with the vibrations of sorrow. Far as our view can stretch itself, we foresee a suffering humanity, which will not be able to find peace, joy, and hope, except in the expectation of new heavens and a new earth, wherein dwelleth righteousness.

If there be no God above humanity, no eternity above time, no divine world higher than our present place of sojourn; if our profoundest desires are to be forever deceived; if the cries we raise to heaven are never to be heard; if all our hope is a future in which we shall be no more; if humanity as we know it is the perfection of the universe; if all this is so, then indeed the answer to the universal enigma is illusion and falsehood. Then, before the monster of destiny, which brings us into being only to destroy us, which creates in our breast the desire of happiness only to deride our miseries; in view of that starry vault which speaks to us of the infinite, while yet there is no infinite; in presence of that lying nature which adorns itself with a thousand symbols of immortality, while yet there is no immortality; in presence of all these deceptions, man may be allowed to curse the day of his birth, or to abandon himself to the intoxication of thoughtless pleasure. But, a secret instinct tells us that wretchedness is a disorder, and thoughtless pleasure a degradation. Let us have confidence in this deep utterance of our nature. Good, truth, beauty, descend as rays of streaming light into the shadows of our existence; let us follow them with the eye of faith to the divine focus from whence they proceed. All is fleeting, all is disappearing incessantly beneath our steps; but our soul is not staggered at this swift lapse of all things, only because she carries in herself the pledges of a changeless eternity. "The ephemeral spectator of an eternal spectacle, man raises for a moment his eyes to heaven, and closes them again forever; but during the fleeting instant which is granted to him, from all points of the sky, and from the bounds of the universe, sets forth from every world a consoling ray and strikes his upward gaze, announcing to him that between that measureless space and himself there exists a close relation, and that he is allied to eternity."

And are these sublime *presentiments* only dreams after all? Dreams! Know you not that our dreams create nothing, and that they are never anything else than confused reminiscences and fantastic combinations of the realities of our waking consciousness? What then is that mysterious waking during which we have seen the eternal, the infinite, the perfection of goodness, the fulness of joy, all those sublime images which come to haunt our spirit during the dream of life? Recollections of our origin! foreshadowings of our destinies! While then all below is transitory, and is escaping from us in a ceaseless flight, let us abandon ourselves without fear to these instincts of the soul.

ESCAPE OF HARVEY BIRCH AND CAPTAIN WHARTON.

BY J. FENIMORE COOPER.

The road which it was necessary for the pedler and the English captain to travel, in order to reach the shelter of the hills, lay, for a half-mile, in full view from the door of the building, that had so recently been the prison of the latter; running for the whole distance over the rich plain, that spreads to the very foot of the mountains, which here rise in a nearly perpendicular ascent from their bases; it then turned short to the right, and was obliged to follow the windings of nature, as it won its way into the bosom of the Highlands.

To preserve the supposed difference in their stations, Harvey rode a short distance ahead of his companion, and maintained the sober, dignified pace that was suited to his assumed character. On their right, the regiment of foot, that we have already mentioned, lay in tents; and the sentinels, who guarded their encampment, were to be seen moving, with measured tread, under the skirts of the hills themselves. The first impulse of Henry was, certainly, to urge the beast he rode to his greatest speed at once, and, by a coup-de-main, not only to accomplish his escape, but relieve himself from the torturing suspense of his situation. But the forward movement that the youth made for this purpose was instantly checked by the pedler.

"Hold up!" he cried, dexterously reining his own horse across the path of the other; would you ruin us both? Fall into the place of a black following his master. Did you not see their blooded chargers, all saddled and bridled, standing in the sun before the house? How long do you think that miserable Dutch horse you are on would hold his speed, if pursued by the Virginians? Every foot that we can gain without giving the alarm, counts us a day in our lives. Ride steadily after me, and on no account look back. They are as subtle as foxes, ay, and as ravenous for blood as wolves."

Henry reluctantly restrained his impatience, and followed the direction of the pedler. His imagination, however, continually alarmed him with the fancied sounds of pursuit; though Birch, who occasionally looked back under the pretence of addressing his companion, assured him that all continued quiet and peaceful.

"But," said Henry, "it will not be possible for Cæsar to remain ong undiscovered: had we not better put our horses to the gallop?"

and, by the time they can reflect on the cause of our flight, we can reach the corner of the woods."

"Ah! you little know them, Captain Wharton," returned the pedler; "there is a sergeant at this moment looking after us, as if he thought all was not right; the keen-eyed fellow watches me like a tiger laying in wait for his leap; when I stood on the horse-block, he half suspected something was wrong; nay, check your beast; we must let the animals walk a little, for he is laying his hand on the pommel of his saddle; if he mounts now, we are gone. The foot soldiers could reach us with their muskets."

"What does he do?" asked Henry, reining his horse to a walk, but, at the same time, pressing his heels into the animal's sides, to be in readiness for a spring.

"He turns from his charger, and looks the other way. Now, trot on gently; not so fast, not so fast; observe the sentinel in the field a little ahead of us; he eyes us keenly."

"Never mind the footman," said Henry, impatiently; "he can do nothing but shoot us; whereas these dragoons may make me a captive again. Surely, Harvey, there are horsemen moving down the road behind us. Do you see nothing particular?"

"Humph!" ejaculated the pedler; "there is something particular, indeed, to be seen behind the thicket on your left; turn your head a little, and you may see and profit by it too."

Henry eagerly seized his permission to look aside, and his blood curdled to the heart as he observed they were passing a gallows, that had unquestionably been erected for his own execution. He turned his face from the sight in undisguised horror.

"There is a warning to be prudent in that bit of wood," said the pedler, in that sententious manner that he often adopted.

"It is a terrific sight indeed!" cried Henry, for a moment veiling his face with his hands, as if to drive a vision from before him.

The pedler moved his body partly around, and spoke with energetic but gloomy bitterness—"and yet, Captain Wharton, you see it when the setting sun shines full upon you; the air you breathe is clear, and fresh from the hills before you. Every step that you take leaves that hated gallows behind; and every dark hollow, and every shapeless rock in the mountains offers you a hiding-place from the vengeance of your enemies. But I have seen the gibbet raised, when no place of refuge offered. Twice have I been buried in dungeons, where, fettered and in chains, I have passed nights in torture, looking forward to the morning's dawn that was to light me to a death of infamy. The sweat has started from my limbs that seemed already drained of their moisture, and if I ventured to the hole that admitted air through grates of iron, to look out upon the smiles of nature, which God has bestowed for the meanest of his creatures, the gibbet has glared before my eyes, like an evil conscience, harrowing the soul of a dying man. Four times have I been in their power, besides this last; but—twice—twice did I think that my hour had come. It is hard to die at the best, Captain Wharton; but to spend your last moments alone and unpitied, to know that none near you so much as think of the fate that is to you the closing of all that is earthly; to think that in a few hours you are to be led from the gloom—which, as you dwell on what follows, becomes dear to you—to the face of day, and there to meet all eyes upon you, as if you were a wild beast; and to lose sight of every thing amidst the jeers and scoffs of your fellow-creatures;—that, Captain Wharton, that indeed is to die."

Henry listened in amazement, as his companion uttered this speech with a vehemence altogether new to him; both seemed to have forgotten their danger and their disguises, as he cried—

"What! were you ever so near death as that?"

"Have I not been the hunted beast of these hills for three years past?" resumed Harvey; "and once they even led me to the foot of the gallows itself, and I escaped only by an alarm from the royal troops. Had they been a quarter of an hour later, I must have died. There was I placed, in the midst of unfeeling men, and gaping women and children, as a monster to be cursed. When I would pray to God, my ears were insulted with the history of my crimes; and when, in all that multitude, I looked around for a single face that showed me any pity, I could find none—no, not even one—all cursed me as a wretch who would sell his country for gold. The sun was brighter to my eyes than common—but then it was the last time I should see it. The fields were gay and pleasant, and every thing seemed as if this world was a kind of heaven. Oh! how sweet life was to me at that moment! 'Twas a dreadful hour, Captain Wharton, and such as you have never known. You have friends to feel for you; but I had none but a father to mourn my loss when he might hear of it; there was no pity, no consolation near to soothe my anguish. Every thing seemed to have deserted me,—I even thought that He had forgotten that I lived."

"What! did you feel that God had forsaken you, Harvey?" cried the youth, with a strong sympathy.

"God never forsakes his servants," returned Birch, with reverence, and exhibiting naturally a devotion that hitherto he had only assumed.

"And who did you mean by He?"

The pedler raised himself in his saddle to the stiff and upright posture that was suited to the outward appearance. The look of fire, that, for a short time, glowed upon his countenance, disappeared in the solemn lines of unbending, self-abasement, and, speaking as if addressing a negro, he replied—

"In heaven, there is no distinction of color, my brother; therefore you have a precious charge within you, that you must hereafter render an account of,"—dropping his voice; "this is the last sentinel near the road; look not back, as you value your life."

Henry remembered his situation, and instantly assumed again the humble demeanor of his adopted character. The unaccountable energy of the pedler's manner was soon forgotten in the sense of his own immediate danger; and with the recollection of his critical situation returned all the uneasiness that he had momentarily forgotten.

"What see you, Harvey?" he cried, observing the pedler to gaze towards the building they had left, with ominous interest; "what see you at the house?"

"That which bodes no good to us," returned the pretended priest. "Throw aside the mask and wig—you will need all your senses without much delay—throw them in the road: there are none before us that I dread, but there are those, behind us, who will give us a fearful race."

"Nay, then," cried the captain, casting the implements of his disguise into the highway, "let us improve our time to the utmost; we want a full quarter to the turn; why not push for it at once?"

"Be cool—they are in alarm, but they will not mount without an officer, unless they see us fly—now he comes—he moves to the stables—trot briskly—a dozen are in their saddles, but the officer stops to tighten his girths—they hope to steal a march upon us—he is mounted—now ride, Captain Wharton, for your life, and keep at my heels. If you quit me you will be lost."

A second request was unnecessary. The instant that Harvey put his horse to his speed, Captain Wharton was at his heels, urging the miserable animal that he rode to the utmost. Birch had selected the beast on which he rode, and, although vastly inferior to the high-fed and blooded chargers of the dragoons, still it was much superior to the little pony that had been thought good enough to carry Cæsar Thompson on an errand. A very few jumps convinced the captain that his companion was fast leaving him, and a fearful glance that he threw behind informed the fugitive that his enemies were as speedily approaching. With that abandonment that makes misery doubly grievous, when it is to be supported alone, Henry called aloud to the pedler not to desert him. Harvey instantly drew up, and suffered his companion to run along-side of his own horse. The cocked hat and wig of the pedler fell from his head the moment that his steed began to move briskly, and this development of their disguise, as it might be termed, was witnessed by the dragoons, who announced their observation by a boisterous shout, that seemed to be uttered in the very ears of the fugitives—so loud was the cry, and so short the distance between them.

"Had we not better leave our horses," said Henry, "and make for the hills across the fields on our left?—the fence will stop our pursuers."

"That way lies the gallows," returned the pedler—"these fellows go three feet to our two, and would mind them fences no more than we do these ruts; but it is a short quarter to the turn, and there are two roads behind the wood. They may stand to choose until they can take the track, and we shall gain a little upon them there."

"But this miserable horse is blown already," cried Henry, urging his beast with the end of his bridle, at the same time that Harvey aided his efforts by applying the lash of a heavy riding-whip that he carried; "he will never stand it for half a mile further."

"A quarter will do—a quarter will do," said the pedler; "a single quarter will save us, if you follow my directions."

Somewhat cheered by the cool and confident manner of his companion, Henry continued silently urging his horse forward. A few moments brought them to the desired turn, and, as they doubled round a point of low under-brush, the fugitives caught a glimpse of their pursuers scattered along the highway. Mason and the sergeant, being better mounted than the rest of the party, were much nearer to their heels than even the pedler thought could be possible.

At the foot of the hills, and for some distance up the dark valley that wound among the mountains, a thick underwood of saplings had been suffered to shoot up, when the heavier growth was felled for the sake of fuel. At the sight of this cover, Henry again urged the pedler to dismount, and to plunge into the woods; but his request was promptly refused. The two roads before mentioned met at a very sharp angle, at a short distance from the turn, and both were circuitous, so that but little of either could be seen at a time. The pedler took the one which led to the left, but held it only a moment, for, on reaching a partial opening in the thicket, he darted across the right-hand path, and led the way up a steep ascent, which lay directly before them. This manœuver saved them. On reaching the fork, the dragoons followed the track, and passed the spot where the fugitives had crossed to the other road, before they missed the marks of the footsteps. Their loud cries were heard by Henry and the pedler, as their wearied and breathless animals toiled up the hill, ordering their comrades in the rear to ride in the right direction. The captain again proposed to leave their horses and dash into the thicket.

"Not yet—not yet," said Birch in a low voice; "the road falls from the top of this hill as steep as it rises—first let us gain the top." While speaking they reached the desired summit, and both threw themselves from their horses. Henry plunged into the thick underwood, which covered the side of the mountain for some distance above them. Harvey stopped to give each of their beasts a few severe blows of his whip, that drove them headlong down the path on the other side of the eminence, and then followed his example.

The pedler entered the thicket with a little caution, and avoided, as much as possible, rustling or breaking the branches in his way. There was but time only to shelter his person from view, when a dragoon led up the ascent, and, on reaching the hight, he cried aloud—

"I saw one of their horses turning the hill this minute."

"Drive on—spur forward, my lads," shouted Mason; "give the Englishman quarter, but cut down the pedler, and make an end of him."

Henry felt his companion gripe his arm hard, as he listened, in a great tremor to this cry, which was followed by the passage of a dozen horsemen, with a vigor and speed that showed too plainly how little security their over-tired steeds could have afforded them.

"Now," said the pedler, rising from his cover to reconnoitre, and standing for a moment in suspense, "all that we gain is clear gain; for, as we go up, they go down. Let us be stirring."

"But will they not follow us, and surround this mountain?" said Henry, rising, and imitating the labored but rapid progress of his companion; "remember they have foot as well as horse, and at any rate we shall starve in the hills."

"Fear nothing, Captain Wharton," returned the pedler, with confidence; "this is not the mountain that I would be on, but necessity has made me a dexterous pilot among these hills. I will lead you where no man will dare to follow. See, the sun is already setting behind the tops of the western mountains, and it will be two hours to the rising of the moon. Who, think you, will follow us far, on a November night, among these rocks and precipices?"

"But, listen!" exclaimed Henry; "the dragoons are shouting to each other—they miss us already."

"Come to the point of this rock, and you may see them," said Harvey, composedly setting himself down to rest. "Nay, they can see us—notice, they are pointing up with their fingers. There! one has fired his pistol, but the distance is too great for even a musket to carry upward."

"They will pursue us," cried the impatient Henry; "let us be moving"

"They will not think of such a thing," returned the pedler, picking the chickerberries that grew on the thin soil where he sat," and very deliberately chewing them, leaves and all, to refresh his mouth. "What progress could they make here, in their boots and spurs, with their long swords, or even pistols? No, no—they may go back and turn out the foot; but the horse pass through these defiles, when they can keep the saddle with fear and trembling. Come, follow me, Captain Wharton; we have a troublesome march before us, but I will bring you where none will think of venturing this night."

So saying, they both arose, and were soon hid from view amongst the rocks and caverns of the mountain.

THE KIDNAPPED BOY.

A SHORT time ago a respectably-dressed man walked into a working-jeweler's shop. He was about the middle age, of dark, or rather sun-burnt complexion, of easy manners, and of a gentlemanly appearance. The proprietor of the shop was engaged in transacting business with an elderly lady, who was attired in mourning; she had called respecting some repairs to be done to her watch, which was on the counter, and the subject of conversation between her and the jeweler. The strange gentleman, too well-mannered to interrupt the business, amused himself by examining several articles in the shop; but the master, after requesting the lady to excuse his leaving her for a moment, accosted the stranger, and inquired his pleasure. The stranger then drew from his bosom, suspended from his neck by a black ribbon, a small pocket-case, which he opened, and took therefrom, an ancient-looking crimson-velvet cushion; this cushion might have formed a model for Cupid's heart; it was, moreover, encased in silver filigree-work, which traced the outlines of several similarly-shaped hearts, and many other devices. On presenting the cushion to the jeweler, the stranger observed, that although the article appeared a trifle, its value to him was above price, and that, as it had sustained a slight injury, he was anxious to have it carefully repaired. The lady in black had not seen the face of the stranger, but when the jeweler left her to wait upon him, she occupied herself with looking at the *bijouterie* in a glass-case on the counter. While the gentleman was addressing the jeweler, he held out the cushion in his fingers, and as he was about to pass it from his hand, the lady turned round, and instantly fixed her eyes upon the cushion; she seized the gentleman's arm, her whole frame trembling from agitation; she uttered a shriek, and then fell lifeless into the arms of the stranger. She was immediately removed into an adjoining parlor, and in a short time, kindness had successfully applied the required restoratives. Now followed exclamations, and questions, and explanations, in rapid succession. In a word, a mother had found a long-lost son! The tale is brief.

Some five-and-thirty years ago, a gentleman and lady, with two children, a boy and girl, took up their residence in a small village in Monmouthshire; the spot was one of those delightful ones for which this country is justly celebrated; the varieties of hill and dale, wood and water, were here beheld in prospects that combined the soft with the picturesque, and were never gazed upon but with pleasurable emotion. The income of this couple was not large, but ample for the exigencies of comfort and even elegance, though inadequate to an ostentatious style of living. The gentleman had a share in a mercantile house in London, in which concern he was a sleeping partner; this establishment was the destination he intended for his son. He had also some property in the funds, with which he purposed portioning off his daughter. After he had thus provided for his children, he would still have sufficiency to insure to himself and wife, ease and comfort in their old age. The daughter was now seven years of age, the son five, and the parents were at that time of life when an increase of family is not common. Both boy and girl were educated by the father, whose chief pursuits were of a literary cast. It was usual for the youngsters to have a holiday once a week, when they either went to spend the day at the house of a neighbor, who had a family of two boys, and a girl of a similar age, or their playmates came and spent the day with them at their father's house. It happened on one occasion, the boy made one of those weekly visits alone, his sister having, from some cause or other, been detained at home. It was in the month of September, and the boy left his friend's house at the close of as fine an autumnal evening as ever glowed in the western heavens, and beautified the face of the earth. But the quiet loveliness of the scene was a faithless harbinger to the parents of the boy, for it betokened, not the sweet serenity of a contented mind, but the wild fitfulness of despair—they never saw their boy again! Diligent inquiries in every corner of the county, the searching of woods, the dragging of ponds and a river, rewards for restoration, and prosecution for detention: in fine, all that parental love could devise—and what will it not devise in so hapless an emergency?—was put into action; but, alas! without success.

Year rolled after year, but no tidings of the lost child ever reached the ears of the fond and mourning parents. The father was observed always to carry about him an air of abstraction, that made him appear solitary in the midst of a crowd, and he never looked upon a child but his eyes were seen reading the lineaments of its face. Ten years after the fatal event, he witnessed the death of his daughter, who died by the hand of that fell destroyer of youth and beauty—pulmonary consumption. This second shock he survived but a few years; but he left behind him a wife who had developed all those virtues of her sex which enable a woman, albeit of keener sensibilities, to comfort and help the husband in the hour of sorrow and of sickness. She survived him, and bore her bereavements with the meekness of a Christian, and the gentleness of a woman; she never afterwards appeared but in the sable habiliments of grief, and thus her outward person harmonized with her sorrowing heart. She lived in close retirement, and seldom went beyond the boundaries of her wonted walks, for they wooed her into a musing recollection of the infant days of her children. Her distant friends urged her to forsake Monmouthshire forever, for their hopes were, that a total change of scene would produce a change of habits, and a more lively enjoyment of life. But no: she loved to linger on the spot sanctified by her endearments as a wife and mother, and she fondly indulged a hope that her boy lived, and would some day be restored to her longing arms. Her hope was attached to the heart by one of those imperceptible threads which the mind almost unconsciously weaves when surrounded by despair; for if that thread were visible, it would appear frail indeed, and quite unable to sustain the slightest shock; nevertheless, its texture is of that elastic tenacity which, while it yields to the severest strain, never breaks, but recovers its wonted position, and retains its firm hold on the heart, until death severs the cord that life could not break.

But the boy, now the man—hear his own tale. He has a dim recollection of the events of his childhood. He well remembers the evening when he was returning home from his playmates; he remembers walking along with a man, and a woman in a red cloak, and that when he cried, he was threatened to have his head cut off if he did not keep silent and go along quietly, as he would not be hurt, for he was being taken to see his papa and mamma, who had gone out visiting, and had sent the man and woman for him. Some such narrative is vividly impressed on his remembrance, and has ever been floating in his mind. He also remembers residing for several months in a large seaport town, but was never allowed to go out from the little house where he lived, except at night, and then only in company with the man or woman: he recollects very well the person who saw him frequently in that house, because he was very kind to him, and at length took him on board a ship. The first town he remembers abroad was Kingston in Jamaica, where, he believes, he remained about nine years with the person who took him out. This individual was the owner of a large store, and the lad was employed in its business. During this time his education was not totally neglected, as his patron took some pleasure in improving his reading and writing.

Having frequently expressed a desire for the sea service, our young hero was bound apprentice to a merchant captain, whose vessel traded between the West India Islands and the ports of the United States and South America. In this vessel he remained eight years, and had become so far a favorite of the captain, that the last year he kept his accounts, acted in some manner as his secretary, and was rapidly advancing in his affections, when death broke the connexion. The captain died in New York. He now thought of visiting England, but not with any special intention of seeking his parents, as he had been assured by the person who took him to Jamaica that he was an orphan, but had been taken care of in early infancy by the benevolence of a lady and gentleman, and that he had been sent to sea to get a livelihood as he best could. However, as he could not readily obtain a suitable situation on board a British vessel, for which, moreover, he was not very anxious, as the times had been, and were likely to continue, very troublous, he succeeded in getting into a merchant's office in New York, where he began at a very subordinate post. Being of temperate and persevering habits, he became in five years a corresponding clerk. He was rising high in the scale of advancement, when one of his brother clerks married a daughter of the merchant, and was immediately taken into partnership. His elevation caused the new partner to assume consequential airs, which discomfited the peace of the establishment, and ended in our hero's separation from the house. He afterward filled another responsible situation in New York, when, after two years' service, he accepted a lucrative offer to superintend a merchant's office in New Orleans, and subsequently he became a partner in the concern, and accumulated a moderate fortune. For these last ten years he had had a growing desire to visit England, and at length he resolved on its gratification. About three months ago he landed in Liverpool; and after sojourning in that town and

London some six weeks, he visited Bristol. From the appearance of some of the public buildings in Bristol, particularly the Exchange, he was convinced that Bristol was the port whence he sailed from England. After spending a fortnight at Clifton, he determined on returning to Liverpool, through South Wales, by way of Monmouthshire; and it was in this county that accident threw him in the path of his mother. The recognition has been described; but the history of the means, namely, the cushion, remains to be told.

When the hapless boy was kidnapped from his home, he had the cushion-case in his pocket; he knew it was dearly prized by his mother, and he had often heard her say it had been given to her by his grandmother. In the silver filigree-work that enclosed the cushion, was traced in a circle the Christian name of his grandmother, and the words, "Keep this in remembrance of me." The boy managed to preserve the cushion, and as he grew to manhood, his affection for the relic became stronger. This little memento of the days of his childhood perhaps served to fix the remembrance of them more firmly in his mind. Of late years he wore it in his bosom, suspended from his neck by a black ribbon. On ascending the steps of the far-famed Wind Cliff, his foot slipped, he fell against one of the stone steps, and damaged the filigree that encased the cushion.

On his arrival at the first town in his route, he hastened to the shop of a working-jeweler. The reader already knows the sequel; his mother cast her eyes upon the relic, read her mother's name, and the never-forgotten words, "Keep this in remembrance of me." She felt as none but mothers can feel, but as no mortal can describe; and the evening of her old age will be smoothed by the affectionate attentions of a beloved but long-lost son.

JERRY GUTTRIDGE.

A TALE OF THE EARLY AMERICAN SETTLEMENTS.

"WHAT shall we have for dinner, Mr. Guttridge?" said the wife of Jerry Guttridge in a sad, desponding tone, as her husband came into the log hovel from a neighboring grog-shop about twelve o'clock on a hot July day.

"Oh, pick up something," said Jerry; "and I wish you would be spry and get it ready, for I'm hungry now, and I want to go back to the shop; for Sam Willard and Seth Harmon are coming over by-an'-by to swap horses, and they'll want me to ride 'em. Come, stir round: I can't wait."

"We haven't got any thing at all in the house to eat," said Mrs. Guttridge. "What shall I get?"

"Well, *cook* something," said Jerry; "no matter what it is."

"But, Mr. Guttridge, we haven't got the least thing in the house to cook."

"Well, well, pick up *something*," said Jerry rather snappishly, "for I'm in a hurry."

"I can't make victuals out of nothing," said the wife: "if you'll only bring any thing in the world into the house to cook, I'll cook it. But I tell you we haven't got a mouthful of meat in the house, nor a mouthful of bread, nor a speck of meal; and the last potatoes we had in the house we ate for breakfast; and you know we didn't have more than half enough for breakfast neither."

"Well, what have you been doing all this forenoon," said Jerry, "that you haven't picked up something? Why didn't you go over to Mr. Whitman's and borrow some meal?"

"Because," said Mrs. Guttridge, "we've borrowed meal there three times that isn't returned yet; and I was ashamed to go again till that was paid. And besides, the baby 's cried so, I've had to 'tend him the whole forenoon, and couldn't go out."

"Then you a'n't a-goin' to give us any dinner, are you?" said Jerry with a reproachful tone and look. "I pity the man that has a helpless, shiftless wife; he has a hard row to hoe. What's become of that fish I brought in yesterday?"

"Why, Mr. Guttridge," said his wife with tears in her eyes, "you and the children ate that fish for your supper last night. I never tasted a morsel of it, and haven't tasted any thing but potatoes these two days; and I'm so faint now, I can hardly stand."

"Always a-grumblin'," said Jerry; "I can't never come into the house but what I must hear a fuss about something or other. What's this boy snivelling about?" he continued, turning to little Bobby, his oldest boy—a little ragged, dirty-faced, sickly-looking thing, about six years' old—at the same time giving the child a box on the ear, which laid him at his length on the floor. "Now get up!" said Jerry, "or I'll learn you to be crying about all day for nothing."

The tears rolled afresh down the cheeks of Mrs. Guttridge; she sighed heavily as she raised the child from the floor, and seated him on a bench on the opposite side of the room.

"What is Bob crying about?" said Jerry fretfully.

"Why, Mr. Guttridge," said his wife, sinking upon the bench beside her little boy, and wiping his tears with her apron, "the poor child has been crying for a piece of bread these two hours. He's ate nothin' to-day but one potato, and I s'pose the poor thing is half-starved."

At this moment their neighbor, Mr. Nat. Frier, a substantial farmer, a worthy man, made his appearance at the door, and as it was wide open, he walked in and took a seat. He knew the destitute condition of Guttridge's family, and had often relieved their distresses. His visit at the present time was partly an errand of charity; for, being in want of some extra labor in his haying-field that afternoon, and knowing that Jerry was doing nothing, while his family was starving, he thought he would endeavor to get him to work for him, and pay him in provisions.

Jerry seated himself rather sullenly on a broken-backed chair, the only sound one in the house being occupied by Mr. Frier, toward whom he cast sundry gruff looks and surly glances. The truth was, Jerry had not received the visits of his neighbors of late years with a very gracious welcome. He regarded them rather as spies, who came to search out the nakedness of the land, than as neighborly visitors calling to exchange friendly salutations. He said not a word; and the first address of Mr. Frier was to little Bobby.

"What's the matter with little Bobby?" said he in a gentle tone; "come, my little fellow, come here and tell me what's the matter."

"Go, run, Bobby; go and see Mr. Frier," said the mother, slightly pushing him forward with her hand.

The boy, with one finger in his mouth, and the tears still rolling over his dirty face, edged along sideways up to Mr. Frier, who took him in his lap, and asked him again what was the matter.

"I want a piece of bread!" said Bobby.

"And wont your mother give you some?" said Mr. Frier tenderly.

"She han't got none," replied Bobby; "nor 'taters too." Mrs. Guttridge's tears told the rest of the story. The worthy farmer knew they were entirely out of provisions again, and he forbore to ask any further questions, but told Bobby if he would go over to his house he would give him something to eat. Then turning to Jerry, said he, "Neighbor Guttridge, I've got four tons of hay down, that needs to go in this afternoon, for it looks as if we should have rain to-morrow, and I've come over to see if I can get you to go and help me. If you'll go this afternoon and assist me to get it in, I'll give you a bushel of meal, or a half-bushel of meal and a bushel of potatoes, and two pounds of pork."

"I can't go," said Jerry; "I've got something else to do."

"Oh, well," said Mr. Frier, if you've got any thing else to do that will be more profitable, I'm glad of it, for there's enough hands that I can get; only I thought you might like to go, bein' you was scant of provisions."

"Do, pray go, Mr. Guttridge!" said his wife with a beseeching look; "for you are only going over to the shop to ride them horses, and that wont do no good; you'll only spend all the afternoon for nothing, and then we shall have to go to bed without our supper again. Do, pray go, Mr. Guttridge; do!"

"I wish you would hold your everlasting clack!" said Jerry; "you are always full of complainings. It's got to be a fine time of day if the women are a-goin' to rule the roast. I *shall* go over and ride them horses, and it's no business to you nor nobody else; and if you're too lazy to get your own supper, you may go without it; that's all I've got to say."

With that he aimed for the door, when Mr. Frier addressed him as follows:—"Now I must say, neighbor Guttridge, if you are going to spend the afternoon over at the shop, to ride horses for them jockeys and leave your family without provisions, when you have a good chance to 'arn enough this afternoon to last them nigh about a week, I must say, neighbor Guttridge, that I think you are not in the way of your duty."

Upon this Jerry whirled round, and looked Mr. Frier full in the face, and grinning horribly, he said, "You old, meddling vagabond! who made *you* a master over me, to be telling me what's my duty? You had better go home and take care of your own children, and let your neighbors' alone!"

Mr. Frier sat and looked Jerry calmly in the face without uttering a syllable; while he, having blown his blast, marched out of doors, and steered directly for the grog-shop, leaving his wife to "pick up something" if she could, to keep herself and children from absolute starvation.

Mr. Frier was a benevolent man, and a Christian, and in the true spirit of Christianity he always sought to relieve distress wherever he found it. He was endowed, too, with a good share of plain, common sense, and knew something of human nature; and as he was well aware that Mrs. Guttridge really loved her husband, notwithstanding his idle habits and cold, brutal, treatment to his family, he forbore to remark upon the scene which had just passed; but telling the afflicted woman he would send her something to eat, he took little Bobby by the hand and led him home. A plate of victuals was set before the child, who devoured it with a greediness that was piteous to behold.

"Poor cre'tur!" said Mrs. Frier; "why, he's half-starved! Betsy, bring him a dish of bread and milk; that will sit the best on his poor, empty, starved stomach."

Betsy ran and brought the bowl of milk, and little Bobby's hand soon began to move from the dish to his mouth with a motion as steady and rapid as the pendulum of a clock. The whole family stood and looked on with pity and surprise until he had finished his meal, or rather until he had eaten as much as they dared allow him to eat at once; for although he had devoured a large plate of meat and vegetables, and two dishes of bread and milk, his appetite seemed as ravenous as when he first began.

While Bobby had been eating, Mr. Frier had been relating to his family the events which had occurred at Guttridge's house, and the starving condition of the inmates; and it was at once agreed that something should be sent over immediately; for they all said, "Mrs. Guttridge was a clever woman, and it was a shame that she should be left to suffer so."

Accordingly a basket was filled with bread, a jug of milk, and some meat and vegetables, ready cooked, which had been left from their dinner; and Betsy ran and brought a pie, made from their last year's pumpkins, and asked her mother if she might not put that in, "so that the poor starving cre'turs might have a little taste of something that was good?"

"Yes," said her mother, "and put in a bit of cheese with it. I don't think we shall be any the poorer for it; for 'he that giveth to the poor lendeth to the Lord.'"

"Yes, yes," said Mr. Frier; "and I guess you may as well put in a little dried pumpkin; she can stew it up for the little ones, and it'll be good for 'em. We've got a plenty of green stuff a-growin' to last till pumpkins come again." So a quantity of dried pumpkins was also packed into the basket, and the pie laid on the top, and George was despatched, in company with little Bobby, to carry it over.

Mr. Frier's benevolent feelings had become highly excited. He forgot his four tons of hay, and sat down to consult with his wife about what could be done for the Guttridge family. Something must be done soon; he was not able to support them all the time; and if they were left alone much longer they would starve. He told his wife he "had a good mind to go and enter a complaint ag'in' Jerry, for a lazy, idle person, that didn't provide for his family. The court sits at Saco to-morrow; and don't you think, wife, I had better go and do it?"

His wife thought he had better go over first and talk with Mrs. Guttridge about it; and if she was willing, he had better do it. Mr. Frier said "he could go over and talk with her, but he didn't think it would be of the least use, for she loved Jerry, ugly as he was, and he did n't believe she would be willing to have him punished by the court."

However, after due consultation, he concluded to go over and have a talk with Mrs. Guttridge about the matter. Accordingly, he took his hat and walked over. He found the door open, as usual, and walked in without ceremony. Here he beheld the whole family, including Jerry himself, seated at their little pine-table, doing ample justice to the basket of provisions which he had just before sent them. He observed the pie had been cut into two pieces, and one half of it, and he thought rather the largest half, was laid on Jerry's plate, the rest being cut up into small bits, and divided among the children. Mrs. Guttridge had reserved none to herself, except a small spoonful of the soft part, with which she was trying to feed the baby. The other eatables seemed to be distributed very much in the same proportion.

Mr. Frier was a cool, considerate man, whose passions were always under the most perfect control; but he always confessed, for years afterward, "that for a minute or two he thought he felt a little something like anger rising up in his stomach!"

He sat and looked on until they had finished their meal, and Jerry had eaten bread and meat and vegetables enough for two common men's dinners, and swallowed his half of the pie, and a large slice of cheese, by way of dessert; and then rose, took his hat, and without saying a word, marched deliberately out of the house, directing his course again to the grog-shop.

Mr. Frier now broached the subject of his visit to Mrs. Guttridge.

He told her the neighbors could not afford to support her family much longer, and unless her husband went to work, he didn't see but they would have to starve.

Mrs. Guttridge began to cry. She said "she did n't know what they should do: she had talked as long as talking would do any good, but somehow, Mr. Guttridge didn't seem to love to work. She believed it wasn't his natur' to work."

"Well, Mrs. Guttridge, do you believe the scriptures?" said Mr. Frier, solemnly.

"I'm sure I do," said Mrs. Guttridge; "I believe all there is in the Bible."

"And don't you know," said Mr. Frier, "the Bible says, 'He that will not work, neither shall he eat?'"

"I know there's something in the Bible like that," said Mrs. Guttridge, with a very serious look.

Mr. Frier now represented to Mrs. Guttridge the impropriety of her husband's behavior—cruel towards her and her family, and unjust towards her neighbors. In short, though somewhat against her will, he reconciled her to a plan he had in view for bringing Jerry to his senses; namely, that of suing him before the court.

Mr. Frier returned home, but the afternoon was so far spent, that he postponed his visit to the court till next morning. Accordingly, next day, as soon as breakfast was over, he wended his way to court, to appear before the grand jury.

"Well, Mr. Frier, what do *you* want?" asked the foreman, as the complainant entered the room.

"I come to complain of Jerry Guttridge to the grand jury," replied Mr. Frier, taking off his hat.

"Why, what has Jerry Guttridge done?" said the foreman. "I didn't think he had life enough to do any thing worth complaining of to the grand jury."

"It's because he *hasn't* got life enough to do any thing," said Mr. Frier, "that I've come to complain of him. The fact is, Mr. Foreman, he's a lazy, idle fellow, and wont work, nor provide nothing for his family to eat; and they've been half-starving this long time; and the neighbors have had to keep sending in something all the time to keep them alive."

"But," said the foreman, "Jerry's a peaceable kind of a chap, Mr Frier; has any body ever talked to him about it in a neighborly way, and advised him to do differently? And may-be he has no chance to work where he could get any thing for it?"

"I'm sorry to say," replied Mr. Frier, "that he's been talked to a good deal, and it don't do no good; and I tried hard to get him to work for me yesterday afternoon, and offered to give him victuals enough to last his family almost a week; but I couldn't get him to; and he went off to the grog-shop to see some jockeys swap horses. And when I told him calmly I didn't think he was in the way of his duty, he flew in a passion, and called me an old meddling vagabond!"

"Abominable!" exclaimed one of the jury. "Who ever heard of such outrageous conduct?"

"What a wretch!" exclaimed another.

"Well," said the foreman, "there is no more to be said. Jerry certainly deserves to be indicted, if any body in this world ever did."

Accordingly the indictment was drawn up, a warrant was issued, and the next day Jerry was brought before the court to answer to the charges preferred against him. Mrs. Sally Guttridge and Mr. Nat. Frier were summoned as witnesses. When the honorable court was ready to hear the case, the clerk called Jerry Guttridge, and bade him hearken to an indictment found against him by the grand inquest for the district of Maine, now sitting at Saco, in the words following; namely:—"We present Jerry Guttridge for an idle person, and not providing for his family; and giving reproachful language to Mr. Nat. Frier, when he reproved him for his idleness."

"Jerry Guttridge, what say you to this indictment? Are you guilty thereof, or not guilty?"

"Not guilty," said Jerry; "and here's my wife can tell you the same any day. Sally, haven't I always provided for my family?"

"Why, yes," said Mrs. Guttridge; "I don't know but you have as well as——"

"Stop, stop!" said the judge, looking down over the top of his spectacles at the witness; "stop, Mrs. Guttridge; you must not answer questions until you have been sworn."

The court then directed the clerk to swear the witnesses; whereupon he called Nat. Frier and Sally Guttridge to step forward and hold up their right-hands. Mr. Frier advanced with a ready, honest air, and held up his hand. Mrs. Guttridge lingered a little behind; but when at last she faltered along, with feeble and hesitating step, and held up her thin, trembling hand, and raised her pale blue eyes, half swimming in tears, towards the court, and exhibited her care-worn features, which, though sun-burnt, were pale and sickly, the judge had in his own mind more than half decided the case against Jerry. The witnesses having been sworn, Mrs. Guttridge was called to the stand.

"Now, Mrs. Guttridge," said the judge, "you are not obliged to testify against your husband any thing more than you choose; your testimony must be voluntary. The court will ask you questions touching the case, and you can answer them or not, as you may think best. And in the first place, I will ask you whether your husband neglects to provide for the necessary wants of his family; and whether you do, or do not, have comfortable food and clothing for yourself and children?"

"Well, we go pretty hungry a good deal of the time," said Mrs. Guttridge, trembling; "but I don't know but Mr. Guttridge does the best he can about it. There don't seem to be any victuals that he can get a good deal of the time."

"Well, is he, or is he not, in the habit of spending his time idly, when he might be at work, and earning something for his family to live upon ?"

"Why, as to that," replied the witness, "Mr. Guttridge don't work much; but I don't know as he can help it: it doesn't seem to be his natur' to work. Somehow he don't seem to be made like other folks; for if he tries ever so much, he can't never work but a few minutes at a time: the natur' don't seem to be in him."

"Well, well," said the judge, casting a dignified and judicial glance at the culprit, who stood with mouth wide open and eyes fixed on the court with an intentness that showed he began to take some interest in the matter—"well, well, perhaps the court will be able to *put* the natur' in him."

Mrs. Guttridge was directed to step aside, and Mr. Nat. Frier was called to the stand. His testimony was very much to the point—clear and conclusive. But as the reader is already in possession of the substance of it, it is unnecessary to recapitulate it. Suffice it to say, that the judge retained a dignified self-possession, and settling back in his chair, said the case was clearly made out; Jerry Guttridge was unquestionably guilty of the charges preferred against him.

The court, out of delicacy towards the feelings of his wife, refrained from pronouncing sentence until she had retired, which she did on an intimation being given her that the case was closed, and she could return home. Jerry was then called, and ordered to hearken to his sentence, as the court had recorded it.

Jerry stood up and faced the court with fixed eyes and gaping mouth, and the clerk repeated as follows: "Jerry Guttridge! you having been found guilty of being an idle and lazy person, and not providing for your family, and giving reproachful language to Mr. Nat. Frier, when he reproved you for your idleness, the court orders that you receive twenty smart lashes with the cat-o'-nine tails upon your naked back, and that this sentence be executed forthwith by the constables, at the whipping-post in the yard adjoining the court-house."

Jerry dropped his head, and his face assumed divers deep colors, sometimes red, and sometimes shading upon the blue. He tried to glance round upon the assembled multitude, but his look was very sheepish; and, unable to stand the gaze of the hundreds of eyes that were turned upon him, he settled back on a bench, leant his head on his hand, and looked steadily upon the floor. The constables having been directed by the court to proceed forthwith to execute the sentence, they led him out into the yard, put his arms round the whipping-post, and tied his hands together. He submitted without resistance; but when they commenced tying his hands round the post, he began to cry and beg, and promise better fashions, if they would only let him go this time. But the constables told him it was too late now; the sentence of the court had been passed, and the punishment must be inflicted. The whole throng of spectators had issued from the court-house, and stood round in a large ring, to see the sentence enforced. The judge himself had stepped to a side window, which commanded a view of the yard, and stood peering solemnly through his spectacles, to see that the ceremony was duly performed. All things being in readiness, the stoutest constable took the cat-o'-nine tails and brought them heavily across the naked back of the victim. At every blow, Jerry jumped and screamed, so that he might have been heard well-nigh a mile. When the twenty blows were counted, and the ceremony was ended, he was loosed from his confinement, and told that he might go. He put on his garments with a sullen but subdued air, and without stopping to pay his respects to the court, or even to bid any one good-by, he made for home as fast as he could.

Mrs. Guttridge met him at the door with a kind and piteous look, and asked him if they had hurt him. He made no reply, but pushed along into the house. There he found the table set, and well supplied for dinner; for Mrs. Guttridge, partly through the kindness of Mr. Frier, and partly from her own exertions, had managed to "pick up something," that served to make quite a comfortable meal. Jerry ate his dinner in silence, but his wife thought he manifested more tenderness and less selfishness than she had known him to exhibit for years; for instead of appropriating the most and the best of the food to himself, he several times placed fair proportions of it upon the plates of his wife and each of the children.

The next morning, before the sun had dried the dew from the grass, whoever passed the haying field of Mr. Nat. Frier, might have beheld Jerry Guttridge busily at work, shaking out the wet hay to the sun; and for a month afterward, the passer-by might have seen him, every day, early and late, in that and the adjoining fields, a perfect pattern of industry.

A change soon became perceptible in the condition and circumstances of his family. His house began to wear more of an air of comfort outside and in. His wife improved in health and spirits; and little Bobby became a fat, hearty boy, and grew like a pumpkin. And years afterward, Mrs. Guttridge was heard to say, that "somehow, ever since that trial, Mr. Guttridge's nature seemed to be entirely changed!"—*Knickerbocker*.

ABBY'S YEAR IN LOWELL.

I.

"Mr. Atkins, I say! Husband, why can't you speak? Do you hear what Abby says?"

"Any thing worth hearing?" was the responsive question of Mr. Atkins; and he laid down the New Hampshire Patriot, and peered over his spectacles with a look which seemed to say, that an event so uncommon deserved particular attention.

"Why, she says that she means to go to Lowell and work in the factory."

"Well, wife, let her go;" and Mr. Atkins took up the Patriot again.

"But I do not see how I can spare her; the spring cleaning is not done, nor the soap made, nor the boys' summer-clothes; and you say that you intend to board your own 'men-folks,' and keep two more cows than you did last year; and Charley can scarcely go alone. I do not see how I can get along without her."

"But you say she does not assist you any about the house."

"Well, husband, she *might*."

"Yes, she might do a great many things which she does not think of doing; and as I do not see that she means to be useful here, we will let her go to the factory."

"Father! are you in earnest? May I go to Lowell?" said Abby; and she raised her bright, black eyes to her father's with a look of exquisite delight.

"Yes, Abby, if you will promise me one thing; and that is, that you will stay a whole year without visiting us, excepting in case of sickness, and that you will stay but one year."

"I will promise any thing, father, if you will only let me go; for I thought you would say that I had better stay at home and pick rocks, and weed the garden, and drop corn, and rake hay; and I do not want to do such work any longer. May I go with the Slater girls next Tuesday, for that is the day they have set for their return?"

"Yes, Abby, if you will remember that you are to stay a year, and only one year."

Abby retired to rest that night with a heart fluttering with pleasure; for ever since the visit of the Slater girls, with new silk dresses, and Navarino bonnets trimmed with flowers, and lace veils, and gauze handkerchiefs, her head had been filled with visions of fine clothes; and she thought if she could only go where she could dress like them, she should be completely happy. She was naturally very fond of dress, and often, while a little girl, had she sat on the grass-bank by the roadside watching the stage which went daily by her father's retired dwelling; and when she saw the gay ribbons and smart shawls, which passed like a bright phantom before her wondering eyes, she had thought that, when older, she, too, would have such things; and she looked forward to womanhood, as to a state in which the chief pleasure must exist in wearing fine clothes. But as years passed over her, she became aware that this was a source from which she could never derive any enjoyment whilst she remained at home; for her father was neither able nor willing to gratify her in this respect, and she had begun to fear that she must always wear the same brown cambric bonnet, and that the same calico gown would always be her "go-to-meeting dress." And now what a bright picture had been formed by her ardent and uncultivated imagination! Yes, she would go to Lowell, and earn all that she possibly could, and spend those earnings in beautiful attire; she would have silk dresses—one of grass green, and another of cherry red, and another upon the color of which she would decide when she purchased it; and she would have a new Navarino bonnet, far more beautiful than Judith Slater's; and when at last she fell asleep, it was to dream of satin and lace, and her glowing fancy reveled all night in a vast and beautiful collection of milliners' finery.

But very different were the dreams of Abby's mother; and when she awoke the next morning, her first words to her husband were, "Mr. Atkins, were you serious last night, when you told Abby that she might go to Lowell? I thought at first that you were vexed because I interrupted you, and said it to stop the conversation."

"Yes, wife, I was serious, and you did not interrupt me, for I had been listening to all that you and Abby were saying. She is a wild, thoughtless girl, and I hardly know what it is best to do with her; but perhaps it will be as well to try an experiment, and let her think and act a little while for herself. I expect that she will spend all her earnings in fine clothes; but after she has done so, she may see the folly of it; at all events, she will be rather more likely to understand the value of money when she has been obliged to work for it. After she has had her own way for one year, she may possibly be willing to return home and become a little more steady, and be willing to devote her active energies (for she is a very capable girl,) to household duties, for hitherto, her services have been principally out of doors, where she is now too old to work. I am also willing that she should see a little of the world, and what is going on in it; and I hope that if she receives no benefit, she will at least return to us uninjured."

"Oh, husband, I have many fears for her," was the reply of Mrs. Atkins, "she is so very giddy and thoughtless; and the Slater girls are as hair-brained as herself, and will lead her on in all sorts of folly. I wish you would tell her that she must stay at home."

"I have made a promise," said Mr. Atkins, "and I will keep it; and Abby, I trust, will keep hers."

Abby flew round in high spirits to make the necessary preparations for her departure, and her mother assisted her with a heavy heart.

II.

The evening before she left home, her father called her to him, and fixing upon her a calm, earnest, and almost mournful look, he said, "Abby, do you ever think?" Abby was subdued and almost awed by her father's look and manner. There was something unusual in it—something in his expression which was unexpected in him, bu which reminded her of her teacher's look at the Sabbath school, when he was endeavoring to impress upon her mind some serious truth.

"Yes, father," she at length replied, "I have thought a great deal lately about going to Lowell."

"But I do not believe, my child, that you have had one serious reflection upon the subject, and I fear that I have done wrong in consenting to let you go from home. If I were too poor to maintain you here, and had no employment about which you could make yourself useful, I should feel no self-reproach, and would let you go trusting all might yet be well; but now I have done what I may at some that future time severely repent of; and, Abby, if you do not wish to make me wretched, you will return to us a better, milder, and more thoughtful girl."

That night Abby reflected more seriously than she had ever done in her life before. Her father's words, rendered more impressive by the look and tone with which they were delivered, had sunk into her heart as words of his had never done before. She had been surprised at his ready acquiescence in her wishes, but it had now a new meaning. She felt that she was about to be abandoned to herself, because her parents despaired of being able to do any thing for her; they thought her too wild, reckless, and untameable to be softened by aught but the stern lessons of experience. I will surprise them, said she to herself; I will show them that I have some reflection; and after I come home, my father shall never ask me if I *think*. Yes, I know what their fears are, and I will let them see that I can take care of myself, and as good care as they have ever taken of me. I know that I have not done as well as I might have done; but I will begin *now*, and when I return, they shall see that I am a better, milder, and more thoughtful girl. And the money which I intended to spend in fine dress shall be put into the bank; I will save it all, and my father shall see that I can earn money, and take care of it too. Oh how different I will be from what they think I am; and how very glad it will make my father and mother to see that I am not so very bad after all!

New feelings and new ideas had begotten new resolutions, and Abby's dreams that night were of smiles from her mother, and words from her father, such as she had never received nor deserved.

When she bade them farewell the next morning, she said nothing of the change which had taken place in her views and feelings, for she felt a slight degree of self-distrust in her own firmness of purpose.

Abby's self-distrust was commendable and auspicious; but she had a very prominent development in that part of the head where phrenologists locate the organ of firmness; and when she had once determined upon a thing, she usually went through with it. She had now resolved to pursue a course entirely different from that which was expected of her, and as different from the one she had first marked out for herself. This was more difficult, on account of her strong propensity for dress, a love of which was freely gratified by her companions. But when Judith Slater pressed her to purchase this beautiful piece of silk, or that splendid piece of muslin, her constant reply was, "No, I have determined not to buy any such things, and I will keep my resolution."

Before she came to Lowell, she wondered in her simplicity, how people could live where there were so many stores, and not spend all their money; and it now required all her firmness to resist being overcome by the tempting display of beauties which met her eyes whenever she promenaded the illuminated streets. It was hard to walk by the milliners' shops with an unwavering step; and when she came to the confectionaries, she could not help stopping. But she did not yield to the temptation; she did not spend her money in them. When she saw fine strawberries, she said to herself, "I can gather them in our own pasture next year;" when she looked upon the nice peaches, cherries, and plums, which stood in tempting array behind their crystal barriers, she said again, "I will do without them *this* summer;" and when apples, pears, and nuts were offered to her for sale, she thought that she would eat none of them till she went home. But she felt that the only safe place for her earnings was the savings' bank, and there they were regularly deposited, that it might be out of her power to indulge in momentary whims. She gratified no feeling but a newly-awakened desire for mental improvement, and spent her leisure hours in reading useful books.

Abby's year was one of perpetual self-contest and self-denial; but it was by no means one of unmitigated misery. The ruling desire of years was not to be conquered by the resolution of a moment; but when the contest was over, there was for her the triumph of victory. If the battle was sometimes desperate, there was so much more merit in being conqueror. One Sabbath was spent in tears, because Judith Slater did not wish her to attend their meeting with such a dowdy bonnet; and another fellow-boarder thought her gown must have been made in "the year one." The color mounted to her cheeks, and the lightning flashed from her eyes, when asked if she had "*just come down*;" and she felt as though she should be glad to be away from them all, when she heard their sly innuendos about "bush-whackers." Still she remained unshaken. It is but for a year, said she to herself, and the time and money that my father thought I should spend in folly shall be devoted to a better purpose.

III.

At the close of a pleasant April day, Mr. Atkins sat at his kitchen fireside, with Charley upon his knee. "Wife," said he to Mrs. Atkins, who was busily preparing the evening meal, "is it not a year since Abby left home?"

"Why, husband, let me think: I always clean up the house thoroughly just before fast-day, and I had not done it when Abby went away. I remember speaking to her about it, and telling her that it was wrong to leave me at such a busy time; and she said, 'Mother, I will be at home to do it all next year.' Yes, it is a year, and I should not be surprised if she should come this week."

"Perhaps she will not come at all," said Mr. Atkins, with a gloomy look; "she has written us but few letters, and they have been very short and unsatisfactory. I suppose she has sense enough to know that no news is better than bad news; and having nothing pleasant to tell about herself, she thinks she will tell us nothing at all. But if I ever get her home again, I will keep her here. I assure you her first year in Lowell shall also be her last."

"Husband, I told you my fears, and if you had set up your authority, Abby would have been obliged to stay at home; but perhaps she is doing pretty well. You know she is not accustomed to writing, and that may account for the few and short letters we have received; but they have all, even the shortest, contained the assurance that she would be at home at the close of the year."

"Pa, the stage has stopped here," said little Charley, and he bounded from his father's knee. The next moment the room rang with the shout of "Abby has come! Abby has come!" In a few moments more she was in the midst of the joyful throng. Her father pressed her hand in silence, and tears gushed from her mother's eyes. Her brothers and sisters were clamorous with delight, all but little Charley, to whom Abby was a stranger, and who repelled with terror all her overtures for a better acquaintance. Her parents gazed upon her with speechless pleasure, for they felt that a change for the better had taken place in their once wayward girl. Yes, there she stood before them, a little taller and a little thinner, and, when the flush of emotion had faded away, perhaps a little paler; but the eyes were bright in their joyous radiance, and the smile of health and innocence was playing around the rosy lips. She carefully laid aside her new straw-bonnet, with its plain trimming of light-blue ribbon, and her dark merino dress showed to the best advantage her neat symmetrical form. There was more delicacy of personal appearance than when she left them, and also more softness of manner; for constant collision with so many young females had worn off the little asperities which had marked her conduct while at home.

"Well, Abby, how many silk gowns have you got?" said her father, as she opened a large new trunk.

"Not *one*, father," said she, and she fixed her dark eyes upon him with an expression that told all. "But here are some little books for the children, and a new calico dress for mother; and here is a nice black silk handkerchief for you to wear around your neck on Sundays. Accept it, dear father, for it is your daughter's first gift."

"You had better have bought me a pair of spectacles, for I am sure I cannot see any thing." There were tears in the rough farmer's eyes, but he tried to laugh and joke, that they might not be perceived. "But what did you do with all your money?"

"I thought I had better leave it there," said Abby, and she placed her bank-book in her father's hand. Mr. Atkins looked a moment, and the forced smile faded away. The surprise had been too great, and tears fell thick and fast from the father's eyes.

"It is but a little," said Abby.

"But it was all you could save," replied her father, "and I am proud of you, Abby; yes, proud that I am the father of such a girl. It is not this paltry sum which pleases me so much, but the prudence, self-command, and real affection for us which you have displayed. But was it not sometimes hard to resist temptation?"

"Yes, father, *you* can never know how hard; but it was the thought of *this* night which sustained me through it all. I knew how you would smile, and what my mother would say and feel; and though there have been moments, yes, hours, that have seen me wretched enough, yet this one evening will repay for all. There is but one thing now to mar my happiness, and that is the thought that this little fellow has quite forgotten me," and she drew Charley to her side. But the new picture-book had already effected wonders, and in a few moments he was in her lap, with his arms around her neck, and his mother could not persuade him to retire that night until he had given "Sister Abby" a hundred kisses.

"Father," said Abby, as she arose to retire when the tall clock struck eleven, "may I not some time go back to Lowell? I should like to add a little to the sum in the bank, and I should be glad of *one* silk gown."

"Yes, Abby, you may do any thing you wish. I shall never again be afraid to let you spend a year in Lowell. You have shown yourself to be possessed of a virtue, without which no one can expect to gain either respect or confidence—SELF-DENIAL."—*Lowell Offering.*

JAMES WALLACE.

"How far is it from here to the sun, Jim?" asked Harman Lee of his father's apprentice, James Wallace, in a tone of light raillery, intending by the question to elicit some reply that would exhibit the boy's ignorance.

James Wallace, a boy of fourteen, turned his bright intelligent eyes upon the son of his master, and after regarding him for a moment, he replied, "I don't know, Harman. How far is it?"

There was something so honest and earnest in the tone of the boy, that much as Harman had felt disposed at first to sport with his ignorance, he could not refrain from giving him a true answer. Still, his contempt for the ignorant apprentice was not to be concealed, and he replied, "Ninety-five millions of miles, you ignoramus!" James did not retort, but repeating over in his mind the distance named, fixed it indelibly upon his memory.

On the same evening, after he had finished his day's work, he obtained a small text-book on astronomy, which belonged to Harman Lee, and went up into his garret with a candle, and there, alone, attempted to dive into the mysteries of that sublime science. As he read, the earnestness of his attention fixed nearly every fact upon his mind. So intent was he, that he perceived not the flight of time, and was only called back to a consciousness of where he was by the sudden sinking of the wick of his candle into the melted mass of tallow that had filled the cup of his candlestick. In another moment he was in total darkness. The cry of the watchman had told him that the hours had flown, until it was past ten o'clock.

Slowly undressing himself in his dark chamber, his mind recurring with a strong interest to what he had been reading, he lay down upon his hard bed, and gave full play to his thoughts. Hour after hour passed away, but he could not sleep, so absorbed was he in reviewing the new and wonderful things he had read. At last wearied nature gave way, and he fell into a slumber filled with dreams of planets, moons, comets, and fixed stars.

The next morning the apprentice boy resumed his place at the work-bench with a new feeling; and with this feeling was mingled one of regret, that he could not go to school as did his master's son.

"But I can study at night while he is asleep," he said to himself.

Just then Harman Lee came into the shop, and approaching James, said, for the purpose of teasing him, "How big round is the earth, Jim?"

"Twenty-five thousand miles," was the unhesitating answer.

Harman looked surprised for a moment, and then responded, with a sneer—for he was not a kind-hearted boy, but, on the contrary, very selfish, and disposed to injure rather than do good to others—"Oh dear! How wonderfully wise you are! And no doubt you can tell how many moons Jupiter has? Come, let's hear."

"Jupiter has four moons," James answered, with something of exultation in his tone.

"And no doubt you can tell how many rings it has?"

"Jupiter has no rings. Saturn has rings, and Jupiter belts," James replied in a decisive tone.

For a moment or two Harman was silent with surprise and mortification, to think that his father's apprentice, whom he esteemed so far below him, should be possessed of knowledge equal to his, and on the points in reference to which he had chosen to question him; and that he should be able to convict him of an error into which he had purposely fallen. "I should like to know how long it is since you became so wonderfully wise," Harman at length said with a sneer.

"Not very long," James replied calmly. "I have been reading one of your books on astronomy."

"Well you're not going to have my books, mister, I can tell you!

Anyhow, I should like to know what business you have to touch one of them! Let me catch you at it again, and see if I don't cuff you soundly. You'd better, a great deal, be minding your work."

"But I didn't neglect my work, Harman; I read at night after I was done with my work; and I didn't hurt your book."

"I don't care if you didn't hurt it. You're not going to have my books, I can tell you. So do you just let them alone."

Poor James's heart sank in his bosom at this unexpected obstacle so suddenly thrown in his way. He had no money of his own to buy, and knew of no one from whom he could borrow the book that had all at once become necessary to his happiness. "Do, Harman," he said appealingly, "lend me the book; I will take good care of it."

"No I wont: and don't you dare to touch it," was the angry reply.

James Wallace knew well enough the selfish disposition of his master's son, older than he two or three years, to be convinced that there was now but little hope of his having the use of his books, except by stealth; and from that his natural, open and honest principles revolted. All day he thought earnestly over the means whereby he should be able to obtain a book on astronomy, to quench the ardent thirst that he had created in his mind. And night came without any satisfactory answer being obtained to his earnest inquiries of his own thoughts.

He was learning the trade of a blind-maker. Having been already an apprentice for two years, and being industrious and intelligent, he had acquired a readiness with tools and much skill in some parts of his trade. While sitting alone after he had finished his work for the day, his mind searching about for some means whereby he could get books, it occurred to him that he might, by working in the evening, earn some money, and with it buy such as he wanted. But in what manner to obtain work he knew not. It finally occurred to him that, in passing a house near the shop, he frequently observed a pair of window-blinds with faded hangings and soiled colors. "Perhaps," said he to himself, "if I could do it cheap, they would let me paint and put new hangings to their blinds."

The thought was scarcely suggested, when he was on his feet moving towards the street. In a few minutes he stood knocking at the door of the house, which was soon opened. "Well, my little man, what do you want?" was the kind salutation of the individual who answered the call.

James felt confused, and stammered out, "The hangings of your blinds are a good deal faded."

"That's a very true remark, my little man," was the reply made in an encouraging tone.

"And they very much want painting."

"Also very true," said the man, with a good-humored smile; for he felt amused with the boy's earnest manner and novelty of speech.

"Wouldn't you like to have them painted, and new hangings put to them?" pursued James.

"I don't know. It would certainly improve them much."

"Oh yes, sir; they would look just like new. And if you will let me do them, I will fix them up nice for you, cheap."

"Will you indeed? But what is your name, and where do you live?"

"My name is James Wallace, and I live with Mr. Lee, the blind-maker."

"Do you indeed? Well, how much will you charge for painting them and putting on new hangings?"

"I will do it for two dollars, sir. The hangings and tassels will cost me three-quarters of a dollar, and the paint and varnish a quarter more. And it will take two or three evenings, besides getting up very early in the morning to work for Mr. Lee, so that I may paint and varnish them when the sun shines."

"But will Mr. Lee let you do this?"

"I don't know, sir; but I will ask him."

"Very well, my little man. If Mr. Lee does not object, I am willing."

James ran back to the house, and found Mr. Lee standing at the door. Much to his delight his request was granted. Four days from that he possessed a book of his own, and had half a dollar with which to buy some other volume, when he should have thoroughly mastered the contents of that. Every night found him poring over this book; and as soon as it was light enough in the morning to see, he was up and reading.

Of course there was much in it that he could not understand, and many terms the meaning of which was hidden from him. To help him in this difficulty, he purchased with his remaining half dollar, at a second-hand book-stall, a dictionary. By the aid of this he acquired the information he sought much more rapidly. But the more he read, the broader the unexplored expanse of knowledge appeared to open before him. He did not, however, give way to feelings of discouragement, but steadily devoted every evening, and an hour every morning, to study; while all the day his mind was pondering over the things he had read, as his hands were diligently employed in the labor assigned him.

It occurred just at this time that a number of benevolent individuals established, in the town where James lived, one of those excellent institutions, an Apprentices' Library. To this he at once applied, and obtained the books he needed. And thus—none dreaming of his devotion to the acquirement of knowledge—did this poor apprentice boy lay the foundation of future eminence and usefulness. We cannot trace his course, step by step, through a long series of seven years, though it would afford many lessons of perseverance and triumph over almost insurmountable difficulties. But at twenty-one he was master of his trade; and what was more, had laid up a vast amount of general and scientific information. He was well read in history; had studied thoroughly the science of astronomy, for which he ever retained a lively affection; was familiar with mathematical principles, and could readily solve the most difficult geometrical and algebraic problems; his geographical knowledge was minute; and to this he added tolerably correct information in regard to the manners and customs of different nations. To natural history he had also given much attention. But with all his varied acquirements, James Wallace felt, on attaining the age of manhood, that he knew comparatively but little.

Let us now turn for a few moments to mark the progress of the young student in one of the best seminaries in his native city, and afterwards at college. Like too many tradesmen whose honest industry and steady perseverance have gained them a competence, Mr. Lee felt indisposed to give his son a trade, or to subject him to the same restraints and discipline in youth to which he had been subjected. He felt ambitious for him, and determined to educate him for one of the learned professions. To this end he sent him to school early, and provided for him the best instruction.

The idea that he was to be a lawyer or a doctor, soon took possession of the mind of Harman, and this caused him to feel contempt for other boys who were merely designed for trades or storekeeping. Like too many others, he had no love for learning, nor any right appreciation of its legitimate uses. To be a lawyer he thought would be much more honorable than to be a mere mechanic; and for this reason alone, as far as he had any thoughts on the subject, did he desire to be a lawyer. As for James Wallace, he, as the poor illiterate apprentice of his father, was most heartily despised, and never treated by Harman with the smallest degree of kind consideration.

At the age of eighteen, he was sent away to one of the eastern universities, and there remained—except during the semi-annual vacations—until he was twenty years of age, when he graduated, and came home with the honorary title of A.B. At this time James Wallace was between seventeen and eighteen years of age, somewhat rough in appearance, but with a sound mind in a sound body—although each day he regularly toiled at the work-bench, and as regularly returned to his books when evening released him from labor, and was up at the peep of dawn, to lay the first offerings of his mind upon the shrine of learning. But all this devotion to the acquirement of knowledge won for him no sympathy, no honorable estimation from his master's son. He despised these patient persevering efforts as much as he despised his condition as an apprentice to a trade. But it was not many years before others began to perceive the contrast between them, although on the very day that James completed his term of apprenticeship, Harman was admitted to the bar.

The one completed his education—as far as general knowledge and a rigid discipline of the mind was concerned—when he left college. The other became more really the student when the broader and brighter light of rationality shone clearly on his pathway, as he passed the threshold of manhood. James still continued to work at his trade, but not for so many hours each day as while he was an apprentice. He was a good and fast workman, and could readily earn all that he required for his support in six or eight hours of every twenty-four. Eight hours were regularly devoted to study. From some cause, he determined he would make law his profession. To the acquirement of a knowledge of legal matters, therefore, he bent all the energies of a well disciplined, active, and comprehensive mind. Two years passed away in an untiring devotion to the studies he had assigned himself, and he then made application for admission to the bar.

[Young Wallace passed his examinations with some applause, and the first case on which he was employed chanced to be one of great difficulty, which required all his skill. The lawyer on the opposite side was Harman Lee, who entertained for his father's old apprentice the most profound contempt.]

The cause came on within a week, for all parties interested in the result, were anxious for it to come to trial, and therefore no legal obstacles were thrown in the way.

There was a profound silence, and a marked attention and interest when the young stranger arose in the court-room to open the case. A smile of contempt, as he did so, curled the lip of Harman Lee, but Wallace saw it not. The prominent points of the case were presented in plain but concise language to the court; and a few remarks bearing upon the merits being made, the young lawyer took his seat, and gave room for the defense.

Instantly Harman Lee was on his feet, and began referring to the points presented by his "very learned brother" in a flippant, contemptuous manner. There were those present who marked the light that kindled in the eye of Wallace, and the flash that passed over his countenance, at the first contemptuous word and tone that were uttered by his antagonist at the bar. These soon gave place to attention, and an air of conscious power. Once on his feet, with so flimsy a position to tear into tatters as that which his "learned brother" had presented, Lee seemed never to grow tired of the tearing process. Nearly an hour had passed away, when he resumed his seat with a look of exultation, which was followed by a pitying and contemptuous smile as Wallace again slowly rose.

Ten minutes, however, had not passed when that smile had changed to a look of surprise, mortification, and alarm, all blended into a single expression. The young lawyer's maiden speech showed him to be a man, of calm, deep, systematic thought—well skilled in points of law and in authorities; and, more than all, a lawyer of practical and comprehensive views. When he sat down, no important point in the case had been left untouched, and none that had been touched required further elucidation.

Lee followed briefly, in a vain attempt to torture his language and break down his positions. But he felt that he was contending with weapons whose edges were turned at every blow. When he took his seat again, Wallace merely remarked that he was prepared, without further argument, to submit the case to the court.

The case was accordingly submitted, and a decision unhesitatingly made in favor of the plaintiffs, or Wallace's clients.

From that hour James Wallace took his true position. The despised apprentice became the able and profound lawyer, and was esteemed for real talent and real moral worth, which, when combined, ever place their possessor in his true position.

Ten years from that day Wallace was elevated to the bench, while Lee, a second-rate lawyer, never rose above that position.

In the histories of these two persons is seen the difference between simply receiving an education, as it is called, and being self-educated. This fact every student, and every humble apprentice with limited advantages, should bear in mind. It should infuse new life into the studies of the one, and inspire the other with a determination to imbue his mind with knowledge. The education that a boy receives at colleges and seminaries does not make him a learned man. He only acquires there the rudiments of knowledge. Beyond these he must go. He must continue *even after* a student, or others will leave him in the rear—others of humbler means and fewer opportunities; the apprentice of the handicraftsman, for instance, whose few hours of devotion to study, from a genuine love of learning, have given him a taste and a habit that remain with him in all after-time.

THE WIDOW'S SON.

BY MRS. STONE.

"Come, Susan, do not take on so; it is true the death of your husband is a sad loss; still it is your duty to submit."

"I know that," said Susan to her visitor; "I know that; but it *is* main hard." And the new-made widow wrung her hands, and wept in the extremity of grief. Just then a gentlemen entered the cottage.

"I'm glad you're come, sir, for Susan's in a sad way; mayhap you can make her hear reason."

"She must have time, poor woman; she must have time. Don't bother her, Betty; let her weep; it will do her good."

So saying, the gentleman, who was Mr. Fenton, the master of the free grammar-school, sat down, took the widow's only child, a boy of about four years, between his knees, and began to talk to the visitor on indifferent topics.

By degrees the paroxysm of the poor woman's grief subsided; though she still wept, her tears fell calmly, and she was able to look about her, and to pay some attention to the conversation of those who were around.

Mr. Fenton, though he appeared to take no notice, had observed her from time to time, quietly waiting till she would be in a state to "hear reason," as her friend Betty termed it, before he addressed her; and when he did so, to Betty's great surprise, it was to talk hopefully of the future, not to lament over the past.

"What a fine boy Tommy is grown," said he, stroking the boy's head; "how old is he now?"

"I am five years old," said Tommy, quite manfully.

"Five years! why, you're growing quite a man. What do you mean to do with him, Susan?"

"I know not, sir; he's owre young yet for aught. He's a good child, but a sore burden for a lone woman to have to keep."

"A sore burden! not at all, if you train him up well, and make him useful. He might do something now."

"No, no; he's owre young yet for aught but play."

"My good woman, the plays children find for themselves are far harder and more toilsome than any work I would put him to. The habit, the early habit of industry and usefulness, is what you must try to give your child; and that habit alone is the best fortune he can have. But, as I said, he is not too young even now to achieve something useful, as well as to gain a habit of industry. He can pick up stones, I warrant."

"Yes, to be sure," said the widow.

"Yes, and I'll be bound he could weed out the groundsel and chickweed in a garden bed, if he were kindly and plainly shown which they are."

"Yes, he's a sharp boy, and minds what's said to him."

"Sharp and attentive, and five years old! oh, never tell me he can do nothing. I hear you begin your charring again on Monday, and Mrs. Fenton says, that now the school's so full, she can find you almost constant employment at our house. Now, Susan, listen to me. Bring your boy with you; I have a small field I want cleared of stones, and I have some rough but very easy and light work in my garden. I will take care that the child is properly set agoing. Thus he will be out of harm's way; he will be acquiring a habit of industry, besides learning his letters; and he will be even earning a trifle towards his own support. You will mind what I say?"

"I will, sir, and I offer you many, many thanks."

The good effect of this judicious kindness on the poor woman was immediate; for the remainder of the funeral week, instead of being passed in vain tears and lamentations, was busily occupied in mending up Tommy's clothes, that he might "go decent o' Monday."

Monday came, and Tommy was duly initiated into the mystery not merely of filling a little basket with stones, and emptying it again (for in that he was, like the rest of the world of children, a tolerable proficient), but he was taught always to empty the basket at one spot, so as to make a heap; and he directly felt a laudable pride in the size of his heap, and worked manfully.

It was no very long time before Tommy became really useful, for he was docile, and attentive, and industrious. The schoolmaster—whose servant, before her marriage, Susan had been, and who respected her for her strict integrity and steady industry—kept, amid his own important avocations, an observant eye on her boy, and took care that some sort of work, suited to his age, should always be found for him. In due time Tommy was elevated to the post of errand-boy and shoe-cleaner to the school, and there was now no need to seek out for work for him; his own vocation brought him abundance; but the principle of industry was already securely inculcated: the boy never shirked his work.

It was about this time that Mr. Fenton frequently observed Tom and his own son, who was a year or two younger, in earnest conference, apart from the other boys. Their usual rendezvous was the steps of a dry-well in the playground. One day he came upon them quite unexpectedly, and both boys started, whilst his own endeavored to huddle something into his pocket.

"What is that you are hiding, Harry?" said Mr. Fenton. "Give it to me."

"Please, father, it's only this," said the boy, holding out a tattered horn-book.

"Why do you hide this, Harry? What are you doing with it?"

"Only teaching Tom to read, father."

"Which is creditable both to you and him. You need not be ashamed of it, either of you. So, you wish to learn to read, Tom?"

"I would give all I have in the world to learn, sir."

"Well, my boy," said Mr. Fenton, smiling, "it shall not cost you so much as that; nevertheless you must pay for it."

Tom stared at the idea of *his* paying, and so did Harry.

"What I mean is this, Tom: you are hired here to perform certain duties—you are paid for them—and I must have none of them omitted, or even neglected. But, *by working a little harder*, you may contrive to have a spare hour in the afternoon, and that hour you may spend in the schoolroom. This extra work, Tom, this coming an hour earlier in the morning, or working in your dinner hour—for one or the other you must do—this is the way in which you must pay for your learning. And as you grow older, you will find that nothing great or important can be achieved without self-denial and exertion; you must begin to practise both *now*, even to learn to read."

A proud day it was for Tom Multon, and for his happy mother, when, with newly-washed hands, and a face as shining as soap and water could make it, he made his first appearance in the schoolroom as a *scholar*. He blushed scarlet, and felt painfully confused as he glanced timidly round, and saw the jeering and quizzical looks that were cast on him; but Harry Fenton smiled kindly on him, and the usher, who had been previously instructed by Mr. Fenton, called him to a form near himself, and immediately set him to work.

From this day Tom never once missed his afternoon attendance at school; his time of entering became earlier and earlier, till at last he habitually came in almost as soon as the bell rang. Mr. Fenton at first made some remark, as, "Are you not too early, Tom?" but the invariable answer was, "I've done my work, sir, every bit of it;" and as the answer was always true, as nothing of his regular employment was ever neglected, the schoolmaster ceased to notice the matter.

He could not shut his eyes, however, to the extraordinary progress Tom made in his schooling. The usher, who began to take quite a pride in the boy, frequently called his attention to the fact, and begged him to enlarge the circumscribed plan which he had laid down for his learning. For a long time Mr. Fenton refused to do this. He was afraid of entailing misery on the boy, by giving him tastes beyond what his station in life would permit him to gratify. His mother was earning her bread by the sorest drudgery; the boy had no prospect but of doing the same; and he thought that, by enabling him to read English, to write a little, and cast common accounts, he was giving him learning sufficient to make him respectable in his own station of life, and even to elevate him moderately above it. He was not proof, however, against the repeated hints of his usher, the solicitations of his own son, and more especially the patient perseverance of the boy himself, when he found that he had absolutely, against orders, been secretly toiling at the Latin grammar. Moreover, he began to feel that, possessing, from his own position, every facility to help Tom forward, he might himself be doing wrong to repress, determinately, the evidently strong bent of his disposition. The boy was quiet and docile, perseveringly *industrious* in all he had to do, but above all, *fond of his book.*

So, having at length made up his own mind, the schoolmaster betook himself to the widow, to induce her to dispense with the present profit of her son's labor, and to let him give himself entirely to the school. She remonstrated sorely: "she saw no good so much learning would do him; she was a lone widow; she had nobody to work for her; and she could not afford to keep a great boy like him in idleness."

The schoolmaster urged her to try, for her boy's sake, for his future good; and at length, but not without considerable difficulty, he obtained her consent, promising that she should be at no expense about books, and that he would endeavor to help her in the matter of clothes.

These latter stipulations Mr. Fenton managed in a peculiar way; for, with a heart open as the day to charity, he had not a purse wherewithal to second his wishes.

"I have a great favor to beg of you, Mr. Courtney," said he to a gentleman who had come to take his son home for the holidays.

"Pray, name it, Mr. Fenton; I shall feel much pleasure in obliging you, if it be in my power."

"It is quite so; easily so. I have a *protege,* a poor lad, humble and industrious, but with such an irrepressible love of books that it is useless to attempt to curb it. I am willing to give him the run of the school; his mother, a hard-working woman, consents to give up his time; but we are at a loss for clothes and books. Your son is about a year older, and my petition to you is, that I may have Master Edward's cast-off suit, at the end of each half-year, for poor Tom Multon."

"Oh, willingly—most willingly."

"And perhaps I may be permitted to take Master Edward's school classics as he relinquishes them: truth compels me to say, they will hardly grace your library shelves after they have done duty here."

There is hardly need to add, that ready permission was granted, and, moreover, that a lasting interest in his fortunes was thus awakened for Tom in Mr. Courtney's breast. Similar applications were made, as they became requisite, by Mr. Fenton to other parents, and with the like success. Thus was the errand-boy provided regularly and permanently with clothes, with books, and placed in the path of scholarship. And he became a scholar; not a great, not a shining one, but a safe, a sure, a correct one. He was always assiduous, always attentive, always industrious. If he made no great or sudden steps forward, he never retrograded; and thus gradually and surely winning his onward way, he was fully qualified in a few years to succeed, in the post of usher, the young man who had so kindly and cordially co-operated with Mr. Fenton in his education. And it may be doubtful whether Tom Multon himself, now called Mr. Thomas, was more proud of his advancement than was his ever kind patron, Mr. Fenton, or his fast friend, Harry Fenton, who was now bound for the university.

But there was yet another who, silent, unobserved, unsuspected, watched Tom Multon's progress with a far deeper interest than either his patron, his school-friend, or even she who watched his cradle, and fostered him with a mother's love. This was a young girl of domestic habits and retired manners, gentle and unobtrusive, who had been nurtured from infancy in the house which now, since he assumed the duties of usher, was also his home. Rose Fenton was an orphan, but not a destitute one, for her good uncle and guardian had taken care that the little patrimony bequeathed to her should not diminish in his hands. She was kind and good-tempered, a clever housewife for her years, obliging to those about her, and very good to her poor neighbors. Her uncle used to say jokingly, but most kindly, that she was "cut out for a parson's wife;" but at present all Rose's hopes and wishes seemed to be centered in the home of her childhood. But ere long they began to stray, and it could not escape the notice of so observant a person as Mr. Fenton, that a warm and mutual attachment was ripening between his usher and his niece.

At first it sorely grieved and perplexed him; for he felt, naturally enough, the inequality of their stations; for though bred up in a homely and domestic way, Rose Fenton had a right to look to a much higher marriage than one with the child of charity, the son of his charwoman, Susan. But when, again, he reflected on the youth's course of conduct even from his cradle until now; his unvarying integrity, industry, and docility; his good temper, his kind disposition, and the advance in station which his own unwearied perseverance had already achieved—he thought perhaps he might rather congratulate his niece than otherwise. He determined to let matters take their course.

But whatever hopes Thomas Multon might secretly cherish, he was too prudent as yet to give any expression to them. True, he had made his way wonderfully; but he felt he had yet much to achieve ere he dared to whisper his hopes to Miss Fenton, or seek the approbation of her uncle. His mother was yet drudging as a servant; she, who had for years deprived herself of every superfluity, in order to procure him the necessaries of life whilst he was a school-boy—a mere burden on her hands. His first object must be to place her above want. He had, from the moment he received a fixed allowance as assistant teacher, set aside a part of it for her; but she, with the energy which had characterized her, placed it, with her other little savings, to accumulate. "She did not need to rest yet," she said. Nevertheless, her son hoped to see her rest before long.

So some years passed away, whilst he continued patiently toiling through his duties as usher, but devoting, unremittingly, his private hours to study, with a view to qualify himself for the function of a clergyman. Mr. Fenton would fain have dissuaded him from the last step, as he saw little prospect of advancement for him; but in this one instance Multon's wishes were too powerful to be persuaded away. Ordination at that time, and in that district, was easily obtained, without those fitting and decent preliminaries which are now indispensable; and being fortunate enough, through Mr. Fenton's influence, to obtain a nomination to an adjoining curacy, the duties of which would not interfere with those of the school, he was ordained by the bishop of the diocese. And this great point being achieved, our errand-boy, now the Rev. Thomas Multon, asked and obtained Mr. Fenton's consent to a union with Rose, so soon as he should have obtained the means to support her in respectability and comfort.

These came suddenly, as good fortune generally does, and from an unlooked-for quarter. On entering the little parlor one day at tea-time, a few months after his ordination, Mr. Multon was surprised to find an elderly gentleman whom he did not know, and a young man in a military undress, whom he was some time in recognizing as Edward Courtney, the youth to whose library and wardrobe he nad himself been indebted for several years. The gentleman had been making a tour in the northern counties, and at the earnest desire of the younger one, had turned aside to visit his old schoolfellow. His greeting to Mr. Multon was frank and cordial; that of the old gentleman was kind and even respectful, for Mr. Fenton had been preparing the way for his young friend's appearance.

No allusion whatever was made to his circumstances that night; but a few weeks afterwards, a letter arrived from the elder Mr. Courtney to Mr. Multon, presenting him the rectory of Northerton, in ———, worth £200 a-year, with a commodious parsonage house. And thus was the poor widow's son rewarded for his perseverance in well-doing.

A few years ago, a friend paid me a morning visit, bringing with her a young lady of most prepossessing appearance, and of gentle manners and speech; and who, I was informed, was Rose Multon, the daughter of the rector of Northerton—one of six children, united and affectionate, and as much respected as their parents.

"And what of old Susan," inquired I, "as her old acquaintance here still call her?"

"Old Mrs. Multon," replied my friend, "lives happily in a small cottage near her son, which, partly from her own former savings, and partly from his liberality, she is able to keep in very comfortable order. I hear but of one dissatisfaction in the family."

"What is that?"

"It is the rector himself, who complains that his children have quite superseded him in his mother's good graces, and that he really often fancies that she does not think half so much of him now, as she did when he was an ERRAND-BOY."

SURPRISE AND DESTRUCTION OF THE PEQUOD INDIANS.

BY MISS SEDGWICK.

MAGAWISCA paused a few moments, sighed deeply, and then began the recital of the last acts in the tragedy of her people, the principal circumstances of which are detailed in the chronicles of the times, by the witnesses of the bloody scenes. "You know," she said, "our fortress-homes were on the level summit of a hill. Thence we could see, as far as the eye could stretch, our hunting-grounds, and our gardens, which lay beneath us on the borders of a stream that glided around our hill, and so near to it, that in the still nights we could hear its gentle voice. Our fort and wigwams were encompassed with a palisade, formed of young trees, and branches interwoven and sharply pointed. No enemy's foot had ever approached this nest, which the eagles of the tribe had built for their mates and their young. Sassacus and my father were both away on that dreadful night. They had called a council of our chiefs, and old men; our young men had been out in their canoes, and, when they returned, they had danced and feasted, and were now in deep sleep. My mother was in her hut with her children, not sleeping, for my brother Samoset had lingered behind his companions, and had not yet returned from the water-sport. The warning spirit, that ever keeps its station at a mother's pillow, whispered that some evil was near; and my mother, bidding me lie still with the little ones, went forth in quest of my brother.

"All the servants of the Great Spirit spoke to my mother's ear and eye of danger and death. The moon, as she sunk behind the hills, appeared a ball of fire: strange lights darted through the air; to my mother's eye they seemed fiery arrows; to her ear the air was filled with death-sighs.

"She had passed the palisade, and was descending the hill, when she met old Cushmakin. 'Do you know aught of my boy?' she asked.

"'Your boy is safe, and sleeps with his companions; he returned by the Sassafras knoll; that way can only be trodden by the strong-limbed and light-footed.'

"'My boy is safe,' said my mother; 'then tell me, for thou art wise, and canst see quite through the dark future, tell me, what evil is coming to our tribe?' She then described the omens she had seen. 'I know not,' said Cushmakin; 'of late darkness hath spread over my soul, and all is black there, as before those eyes, that the arrows of death hath pierced; but tell me, Monoco, what see you now in the fields of heaven?'

"'Oh, now,' said my mother, 'I see nothing but the blue depths and the watching stars. The spirits of the air hath ceased their moaning, and steal over my cheek like an infant's breath. The water-spirits are rising, and will soon spread their soft wings around the nest of our tribe.'

"'The boy sleeps safely,' muttered the old man, 'and I have listened to the idle fear of a doating mother.'

"'I come not of a fearful race,' said my mother.

"'Nay, that I did not mean,' replied Cushmakin; 'but the panther watching her young is fearful as a doe.' The night was far spent, and my mother bade him go home with her, for our powwows have always a mat in the wigwam of their chief. 'Nay,' he said, 'the day is near, and I am always abroad at the rising of the sun.' It seemed that the first warm touch of the sun opened the eye of the old man's soul, and he saw again the flushed hills, and the shaded valleys, the sparkling waters, the green maize, and the gray old rocks of our home. They were just passing the little gate of the palisade, when the old man's dog sprang from him with a fearful bark. A rushing sound was heard. 'Owanox! Owanox! (the English! the English!') cried Cushmakin. My mother joined her voice to his, and in an instant the cry of alarm spread through the wigwams. The enemy were indeed upon us. They had surrounded the palisade, and opened their fire."

"Was it so sudden? Did they so rush on sleeping women and children?" asked Everell, who was unconsciously lending all his interest to the party of the narrator.

"Even so; they were guided to us by the traitor Wequash; he, from whose bloody hand my mother had shielded the captive English maidens—he who had eaten from my father's dish, and slept on his mat. They were flanked by the cowardly Narragansetts, who shrunk from the sight of our tribe—who were pale as white men at the thought of Sassacus, and so feared him that, when his name was spoken, they were like an unstrung bow, and they said, 'He is all one God—no man can kill him.' These cowardly allies waited for the prey they dared not attack."

"Then," said Everell, "as I have heard, our people had all the honor of the fight?"

"Honor! was it, Everell?—ye shall hear. Our warriors rushed forth to meet the foe; they surrounded the huts of their mothers, wives, sisters, children; they fought as if each man had a hundred lives, and would give each and all to redeem their homes. Oh! the dreadful fray even now rings in my ears! Those fearful guns, that we had never heard before—the shouts of your people—our own battle-yell—the piteous cries of the little children—the groans of our mothers—and, oh! worse, worse than all—the silence of those that could not speak. The English fell back; they were driven to the palisade, some beyond it, when their leader gave the cry to fire our huts, and led the way to my mother's. Samoset, the noble boy, defended the entrance with a princelike courage, till they struck him down; prostate and bleeding, he again bent his bow, and had taken deadly aim at the English leader, when a sabre-blow severed his bowstring. Then was taken from our hearth-stone, where the English had been so often warmed and cherished, the brand to consume our dwellings. They were covered with mats, and burnt like dried straw. The enemy retreated without the palisade. In vain did our warriors fight for a path by which we might escape from the consuming fire; they were beaten back; the fierce element gained on us; the Narragansetts pressed on the English, howling like wolves for their prey. Some of our people threw themselves into the midst of the crackling flames, and their courageous souls parted with one shout of triumph; others mounted the palisade, but they were shot, and dropped like a flock of birds smitten by the hunter's arrows. Thus did the strangers destroy, in our own homes, hundreds of our tribe."

"And how did you escape in that dreadful hour, Magawisca? You were not then taken prisoner?"

"No; there was a rock at one extremity of our hut, and beneath it a cavity, into which my mother crept, with Oneco, myself, and the two little ones that afterwards perished. Our simple habitations were soon consumed; we heard the foe retiring, and, when the last sound had died away, we came forth to a sight that made us lament to be among the living. The sun was scarce an hour from his rising, and yet in this brief space, our homes had vanished. The bodies of our people were strewn about the smouldering ruins ; and all around the palisade lay the strong and valiant warriors—cold—silent—powerless as the unformed clay."

Magawisca paused ; she was overcome with the recollection of this scene of desolation. She looked upward with an intent gaze, as if she held communion with an invisible being. "Spirit of my mother!" burst from her lips; "oh! that I could follow thee to that blessed land, where I should no more dread the war-cry, nor the death-knife." Everell dashed the gathering tears from his eyes, and Magawisca proceeded in her narrative.

"While we all stood silent and motionless, we heard footsteps and cheerful voices. They came from my father and Sassacus, and their band, returning from the friendly council. They approached on the side of the hill that was covered with a thicket of oaks, and their ruined homes at once burst upon their view. Oh! what horrid sounds then pealed on the air! shouts of wailing and cries of vengeance. Every eye was turned with suspicion and hatred on my father. *He* had been the friend of the English ; *he* had counselled peace and alliance with them ; *he* had protected their traders, delivered the captives taken from them, and restored them to their people : now his wife and children alone were living, and they called him traitor. I heard an angry murmur, and many hands were lifted to strike the death-blow. He moved not. 'Nay, nay,' cried Sassacus, beating them off. 'Touch him not; his soul is bright as the sun ; sooner shall you darken that, than find treason in his breast. If he hath shown the dove's heart to the English, when he believed them friends, he will show himself the fierce eagle, now he knows them enemies. Touch him not, warriors ; remember my blood runneth in his veins.'

"From that moment my father was a changed man. He neither spoke nor looked at his wife, or children ; but placing himself at the head of one band of the young men, he shouted his war-cry, and then silently pursued the enemy. Sassacus went forth to assemble the tribe, and we followed my mother to one of our villages."

"You did not tell me, Magawisca," said Everell, "how Samoset perished : was he consumed in the flames, or shot from the palisade?"

"Neither—neither. He was reserved to whet my father's revenge to a still keener edge. He had forced a passage through the English, and, hastily collecting a few warriors, they pursued the enemy, sprung upon them from a covert, and did so annoy them that the English turned, and gave them battle. All fled save my brother, and him they took prisoner. They told him they would spare his life if he would guide them to our strong holds. He refused. He had lived but sixteen summers ; he loved the light of the sun even as we love it ; his manly spirit was tamed by wounds and weariness ; his limbs were like a bending reed, and his heart beat like a woman's ; but the fire of his soul burnt clear. Again they pressed him with offers of life and reward; he faithfully refused, and with one sabre-stroke they severed his head from his body."

Magawisca paused. She looked at Everell, and said with a bitter smile, "You English tell us, Everell, that the book of your law is better than that written on our hearts, for, ye say, it teaches mercy, compassion, forgiveness—if ye had such a law, and believed it, would ye thus have treated a captive boy?"

Magawisca's reflecting mind suggested the most serious obstacle to the progress of the Christian religion, in all ages and under all circumstances; the contrariety between its divine principles and the conduct of its professors; which, instead of always being a medium for the light that emanates from our holy law, is too often the darkest cloud that obstructs the passage of its rays to the hearts of heathen men. Everell had been carefully instructed in the principles of his religion, and he felt Magawisca's relation to be an awkward comment on them, and her inquiry natural; but, though he knew not what answer to make, he was sure there must be a good one, and, mentally resolving to refer the case to his mother, he begged Magawisca to proceed with her narrative.

"The fragments of our broken tribe," she said, "were collected, and some other small dependant tribes persuaded to join us. We were obliged to flee from the open grounds, and shelter ourselves in a dismal swamp. The English surrounded us; they sent in to us a messenger, and offered life and pardon to all who had not shed the blood of Englishmen. Our allies listened, and fled from us, as frightened birds fly from a falling tree. My father looked upon his warriors: they answered that look with their battle-shout. 'Tell your people,' said my father to the messenger, 'that we have shed and drank English blood, and that we will take nothing from them but death.' The messenger departed, and again returned with offers of pardon, if we would come forth, and lay our arrows and our tomahawks at the feet of the English. 'What say you, warriors!' cried my father; 'shall we take *pardon* from those who have burned your wives and children, and given your homes to the beasts of prey?—who have robbed you of your hunting-grounds, and driven your canoes from their waters?' A hundred arrows were pointed to the messenger. 'Enough—you have your answer,' said my father; and the messenger returned to announce the fate we had chosen."

"Where was Sassacus? Had he abandoned his people?" asked Everell.

"Abandoned them! No—his life was in theirs; but, accustomed to attack and victory, he could not bear to be thus driven like a fox to his hole. His soul was sick within him, and he was silent, and left all to my father. All day we heard the strokes of the English axes felling the trees that defended us, and, when night came, they had approached so near, that we could see the glimmering of their watch-lights through the branches of the trees. All night they were pouring in their bullets, alike on warriors, women, and children. Old Cushmakin was lying at my mother's feet, when he received a death-wound. Gasping for breath, he called on Sassacus and my father: Stay not here,' he said; 'look not on your wives and children, but burst your prison bound; sound through the nations the cry of revenge! Linked together, ye shall drive the English into the sea. I speak the word of the Great Spirit—obey it!' While he was yet speaking, he stiffened in death. 'Obey him, warriors,' cried my mother; 'see,' she said, pointing to the mist that was now wrapping tself around the wood like a thick curtain, 'see, our friends have come from the spirit-land to shelter you. Nay look not on us; our hearts have been tender in the wigwam, but we can die before our enemies without a groan. Go forth and avenge us.'

"'Have we come to the counsel of old men and old women!' said Sassacus, in the bitterness of his spirit.

"'When women put down their womanish thoughts and counsel like men, they should be obeyed,' said my father. 'Follow me, warriors.'

"They burst through the enclosure. We saw nothing more, but we heard the shout from the foe, as they issued from the wood—the momentary fierce encounter and the cry, 'They have escaped!' Then it was that my mother, who had listened with breathless silence, threw herself down on the mossy stones, and, laying her hot cheek to mine, 'Oh, my children, my children!' she said, 'would that I could die for you! But fear not death; the blood of a hundred chieftains, that never knew fear, runneth in your veins. Hark! the enemy comes nearer and nearer. Now lift up your heads, my children, and show them that even the weak ones of our tribe are strong in soul.'

"We rose from the ground—all about sat women and children in family clusters, awaiting unmoved their fate. The English had penetrated the forest-screen, and were already on the rising ground, where we had been intrenched. Death was dealt freely. None resisted—not a movement was made—not a voice lifted—not a sound escaped, save the wailings of the dying children.

"One of your soldiers knew my mother, and a command was given that her life and that of her children should be spared. A guard was stationed round us.

"You know that, after our tribe was thus cut off, we were taken, with a few other captives, to Boston. Some were sent to the Islands of the Sun, to bend their free limbs to bondage, like your beasts of burden. There are among your people those who have not put out the light of the Great Spirit; they can remember a kindness, albeit done by an Indian; and when it was known to your sachems that the wife of Mononotto, once the protector and friend of your people, was a prisoner, they treated her with honor and gentleness. But her people were extinguished—her husband driven to distant forests—forced on earth to the misery of wicked souls—to wander without a home; her children were captives—and her heart was broken."

LIVES AND INCIDENTS OF EMINENT MEN.

EMINENT ASTRONOMERS.*

COPERNICUS.

Nicolas Copernicus was born February 19, 1743, at Thorn, on the Vistula—a place now included in the dominions of the king of Prussia. The father of Copernicus was a native of Westphalia, a part of Germany: he had chanced to settle at Thorn, as a surgeon, about ten years before the birth of his son. Young Copernicus was educated for the profession of medicine at the university of Cracow; but his favorite studies were mathematics, perspective, astronomy, and painting. At an early age, inspired by an eager wish to distinguish himself in astronomy, he proceeded to Italy and studied that science at the university at Bologna. It is supposed that a discovery of his teacher, Dominic Maria, respecting the changing of the axis of the earth, was what first awakened his mind to the errors of the planetary system then taught. From Bologna he proceeded to Rome, where for some time he taught mathematics with great success—pursuing all the while, as far as circumstances would permit, his astronomical observations.

When he afterwards returned to his native country, his maternal uncle, the bishop of Ermeland, appointed him a canon in the cathedral of Frauenburg, and at the same time he was nominated by the inhabitants of his native town to be archdeacon in one of their churches. He then resolved to devote his life to three objects—the performance of his clerical duties, gratuitous medical attendance on the poor, and the pursuit of his favorite studies. His residence was established in one of the houses belonging to the canons of Frauenburg, on the brow of a hight, near the cathedral, where astronomical observations could

* It is not designed to enter extensively upon the department of Biography, but to sketch the lives of a few individuals who have become distinguished, and so illustrate the pursuits of knowledge under difficulties, and stimulate attempts at mental and moral excellence by showing that to those who earnestly apply themselves to the acquisition of knowledge, difficulties, though formidable, are nevertheless surmountable—Ed.

be conducted under very favorable circumstances ; and in its walls are still to be seen the openings which he made in order to observe the passage of stars across the meridian. It is supposed to have been about the year 1507, that he first became convinced of the superiority of the planetary theory of Pythagoras. He determined, however, to be very cautious in adopting, and still more cautious in announcing, an opinion so much at variance with the ordinary ideas of mankind. Mathematical instruments were in that age very rude, and the telescope had not been invented. The only implements which Copernicus had for making observations were two, coarsely framed of fir-wood, with measures marked by lines of ink. Thus provided, he devoted himself for several years to the inquiries necessary for proving his theory; and at length, about the year 1530, he had completed a work, in which the whole system was expounded—namely, the immobility of the sun in the centre of the planetary system; while its apparent motion, and the alternations of day and night, were to be attributed to the annual and diurnal movements of the earth. The real distances of the planets, and the declination of the pole of the earth were also explained.

The doctrines of Copernicus were already known to a considerable number of learned and comparatively enlightened persons, who received them with due respect; and it is creditable to the Romish church, that several of its dignitaries were among the number. But the bulk of mankind, including their religious teachers, were then comparatively ignorant, and accordingly prejudiced; and however firm the conviction of the astronomer as to the truth of his theory, he yet hesitated to make it public, dreading the opposition it would have to encounter—seeing that it opposed the inveterate prejudices of the learned, and the illusory testimony of the senses. In reasoning, they acted under the guidance of rules which made it scarcely possible for them to ascertain truth, or to acknowledge it when it was presented to them in the clearest light. If any thing had been said in former times by a person whose memory they respected, they would not willingly listen to any thing which contradicted, or seemed to contradict it. They walked, in short, by authority, and not by the dictates of reflection; and the consequence was, that every new truth which experience or the inquiries of the best minds brought forth, had to contend with the less worthy notions which had come down from earlier and darker ages. Amongst the opinions received by them, was that which represented the earth as the immovable centre of the universe. It was sanctioned by the greatest men of ancient times; it had long been taught; it was conformable to the common appearances of things; and various passages in the scriptures were believed to assert it, though in reality those passages only do not contradict (and this probably for wise purposes,) the ordinary ideas of mankind respecting the stability of the earth. Copernicus only acted, therefore, with necessary caution, when he hesitated to publish the work which had cost him the labor of so many years.

Rheticus, one of the friends to whom he had communicated his theory, at length, in 1540, ventured to give an outline of it to the world in a small pamphlet, which he published without his name. As this excited no disapprobation, the same person reprinted it next year with his name. In both publications the doctrines were ascribed openly to Nicolas Copernicus. About the same time, a learned man, Erasmus Reinhold, in a work which he published, spoke of the new doctrines with the greatest respect, and styled their author a second Ptolemy; for it often happens that the greatest compliment that can be paid to the discoverer of truth, is to mention him in the same breath with some founder of error. Copernicus now allowed himself to be persuaded by his friends to publish his work; and it was accordingly put to press at Nuremberg, under the care of some learned persons of that city. But he was now an old man, and it was not his lot to live to see the book published. As soon as it was printed, a copy of it was sent to him by his friend Rheticus, but it only reached him, May 23, 1543, a few hours before he expired. He appeared to be scarcely conscious of the object to which so many years of his life had been devoted. But his mission was accomplished. Committed to the perpetuating operations of the infant printing-press, all danger was over of losing the germ of those great and fertile truths which in our days render astronomy the most perfect of sciences.

The theory of Copernicus was thus brought before the world; but, whether from the death of the philosopher, or because little disturbance of popular notions was anticipated from so learned a work, or from whatever other circumstances, it was visited with no marks of reprobation from any quarter at the time. In proportion, however, as it became known, so did its opponents increase. Those were the days when the fagot and stake made short work with those who presumed to strike out a course of thinking for themselves; and though the author of the system, and its immediate adopters, passed unmolested, yet during the century which ensued were its followers and supporters persecuted with all the zeal and cruelty that bigotry and ignorant prejudice could devise. Truth, however, is imperishable; and, though repressed and retarded for a season, is ever sure to take its right place among the established beliefs of mankind. And thus it has been with the Copernican theory, whose importance to the progress of accurate science we cannot in reality over estimate. To form any thing like an adequate idea of the value of its author's services to the cause of science, we must place ourselves back in the times and circumstances which saw their birth. Then, it must be remembered, the want of telescopes rendered all appearances in the sky much more difficult of explanation than they would have been a century later. The accumulated errors and superstitions of fourteen centuries were not to be easily shaken and removed; neither were the prejudices and dogmas of the learned to be disturbed with impunity. What might have been astronomical science, was, even in the writings of the fathers, little better than a mass of absurd and subtle disquisitions on the substance of the heavens and the heavenly bodies. All these Copernicus had to surmount; and the elaboration of his theory presents an ever-memorable example of the power of patient and earnest thought in the investigation of a complicated subject, and acuteness of discrimination between the true and the fallacious.

GALILEO.

The Copernican theory, which Tycho had labored in vain to supersede, was next received and supported by an Italian philosopher, whose name and history are inseparably interwoven with the progress of astronomy. That illustrious individual, Galileo Galilei, usually known by his Christian name, was born at Pisa, in 1564. His father, a Tuscan nobleman of small fortune, caused him to be educated for the profession of medicine at the university of his native city. While studying there, he became deeply sensible of the absurdities of the philosophy of Aristotle, as it had then come to be taught, and he became its declared enemy. That spirit of observation for which he was so distinguished was early developed. When only nineteen years old, the swinging of a lamp suspended from the ceiling of the cathedral in Pisa, led him to investigate the laws of the oscillation of the pendulum, which he was the first to employ as a measurer of time. He left it incomplete, however, and it was brought to perfection by his son, Vincenzo, and particularly by Huygens, the latter of whom must be regarded as the true inventor of the pendulum. About this period Galileo devoted himself exclusively to mathematics and natural science, and in 1586 was led to the invention of the hydrostatic balance. In 1589, his distinction in the exact sciences gained for him the chair of mathematics in his native university, where, immediately on his installation, he began to assert the laws of nature against a perverted philosophy. In the presence of numerous spectators, he performed a series of experiments in the tower of the cathedral, to show that weight has no influence on the velocity of falling bodies. By this means he excited the opposition of the adherents of Aristotle to such a degree, that, after two years, he was forced to resign his professorship. Driven from Pisa, he retired into private life; but his genius being appreciated in another part of Italy, he was, in 1592, appointed professor of mathematics at Padua. He lectured here with unparalleled success. Scholars from the most distant regions of Europe crowded round him. He delivered his lectures in the Italian language instead of Latin, which was considered a daring innovation.

During eighteen years which he spent at Padua, he made many discoveries in natural philosophy, which he introduced into his lectures, without regard to their inconsistency with the doctrines previously taught. Among these may be mentioned his discovery of the rate of descent in falling bodies; certain improvements on the thermometer; some interesting observations on the magnet; and a number of experiments relative to the floating and sinking of solid bodies in water. In 1609, hearing that one Jansen, a Dutchman, had made an instrument by which distant objects were made to appear near, Galileo, whose mind was prepared for the discovery, instantly conceived on what principle it was constructed, and, without losing a day, he fashioned a similar instrument with many improvements: such was the origin of the telescope, the most interesting of all instruments connected with science.

Turning his optical tube towards the heavens, Galileo perceived the moon to be a body of uneven surface, the elevations of which he computed by their shadows; and the sun to be occasionally spotted; and from the regular advance from east to west of these spots, he inferred the rotation of the sun, and the inclination of its axis to the plane of the ecliptic. From a particular nebula, which his rude instrument enabled him to resolve into individual stars, he even conjectured, what Lord Rosse has but recently proved, that the whole Milky Way was but a vast assemblage of stars and systems. He discovered that the planet Venus waxed and waned like the moon, that Saturn had something like wings by its sides (afterwards found to be a ring), and that Jupiter was surrounded by four satellites. It is now altogether impossible to imagine the wonder and delight with which these discoveries must have filled the mind of a philosopher like Galileo, who had perhaps long surmised that all was not as it seemed in the heavens, but despaired of ever being able to penetrate the mystery. In the year 1611, while entering upon his investigations, he was induced, by the invitation of his prince, the Grand Duke of Tuscany, to return to Pisa, and resume the chair of mathematics there, with a large salary. It was consequently at that city that he first gave his discoveries to the world. That persecution which had only been suspended by accident in the case of Copernicus, now fell with full weight on the head of the Italian philosopher. Having openly declared, in a work which he published, that his discoveries proved the truth of the Copernican theory, he was denounced by the elergy as an heretic, and obliged, in 1615, to proceed to Rome, and appear before the court of Inquisition, who obliged him to promise that he would never more broach such dangerous doctrines. It has been stated, but is not quite certain, that he was on this occasion imprisoned by the Inquisition for five months, and that he would have suffered still more severely if the Grand Duke had not interceded for him.

For several years he observed the silence enjoined upon him, but continued to pursue the study of the true theory of the heavens. Panting to make known to the world a complete account of the system of Copernicus, yet dreading the prejudices of his enemies, he fell upon the expedient of writing a work, in which, without giving his own opinion, he introduces three persons in a dialogue, of whom the first defends the Copernican system, the second the Ptolemæan (or that of Aristotle,) and the third weighs the reasons of both in such a way, that the subject seems problematical, though it is impossible to mistake the preponderance of arguments in favor of Copernicus. With this great work, which is still held in reverence, Galileo went to Rome in 1630, in the sixty-sixth year of his age, and by an extraordinary stretch of favor, received permission to print it. Scarcely had it appeared at Rome and Florence, when it was attacked by the disciples of Aristotle, and most violently of all by the teacher of philosophy at Pisa. A congregation of cardinals, monks, and mathematicians, was appointed to examine his work, which they unhesitatingly condemned as highly dangerous, and summoned him before the tribunal of the Inquisition. This blow fell heavily on the head of Galileo, now an old man, and left defenceless by the death of his friend and patron, Cosmo II. He was compelled to go to Rome in the winter of 1633, and was immediately immured in a cell in one of the prisons of the Inquisition. There he remained for several months, when, being brought before an assembly of his judges, he was condemned to renounce, kneeling before them, with his hand upon the gospels, what were called the "sinful and detestable errors and heresies" which he had maintained. The firmness of Galileo gave way at this critical moment of his life: he pronounced the recantation. But at the moment he rose, indignant at having sworn in violation of his conviction, he exclaimed, stamping his foot, "*E pur si muove!*"—("It still moves!") Upon this dreadful relapse into heresy, he was sentenced to imprisonment in the Inquisition for life, and every week for three years was to repeat the seven penitential psalms; his "Dialogues" were also prohibited, and his system utterly condemned. Although Galileo was in this manner sentenced to confinement, it appeared to those who judged him that he would not be able, from his age, to endure such a severe punishment, and they mercifully banished him to a particular spot near Florence.

Here Galileo lived for several years, employing his time in the study of mechanics and other branches of natural philosophy. The results are found in two important works on the laws of motion, the foundation of the present system of physics and astronomy. At the same time he tried to make use of Jupiter's satellites for the calculation of longitudes; and though he brought nothing to perfection in this branch, he was the first who reflected systematically on such a method of fixing geographical longitudes. He was at this time afflicted with a disease in his eyes, one of which was wholly blind, and the other almost useless, when, in 1637, he discovered the libration of the moon. Blindness, deafness, want of sleep, and pain in his limbs, united to imbitter his declining years; still his mind was active. "In my darkness," he writes in the year 1638, "I muse now upon this object of nature, and now upon that, and find it impossible to soothe my restless head, however much I wish it. This perpetual action of mind deprives me almost wholly ot sleep." In this condition, and affected by a slowly-consuming fever, he expired in January, 1642, in the seventy-eighth year of his age. His relics were deposited in the church of Santa Croce, at Florence, where posterity did justice to his memory by erecting a splendid monument in 1737.

Galileo is represented by his biographers as of diminutive stature, but strong and healthy, of agreeable countenance, and lively conversation and manner. He preferred living in the country, where his relaxations consisted in the cultivation of his garden, and in the company and conversation of his friends. He loved music, drawing and poetry; and is said to have been so fond of Aristo, that he knew the whole of the "Orlando" by heart. He had few books: "The best book," he said, "is nature." A complete edition of his works, in thirteen volumes, appeared at Milan in 1803, the style of which is natural and fluent, so elegant and pure, that it has been held up by competent judges as a model of classical Italian. "Altogether," says Professor Playfair, "Galileo is one of those to whom human knowledge is under the greatest obligation. His discoveries in the theory of motion, in the laws of the descent of heavy bodies, and in the motion of projectiles, laid the foundation of all the great improvements which have since been made by the application of mathematics to natural philosophy. If to these we add the invention of the telescope, the discoveries made by that instrument, the confirmation of the Copernican system which these discoveries afforded, and lastly, the wit and argument with which he combated and exposed the prejudice and presumption of the schools, we must admit that the history of human knowledge contains few greater names than that of Galileo."

NEWTON.

THE year in which Galileo died, was that in which ISAAC NEWTON was born. This eminent individual, who was destined to establish the truth of the discoveries of his illustrious predecessors, Copernicus and Galileo, was born on the 25th of December, 1642, at Coltersworth, in Lincolnshire, where his father cultivated his own moderate paternal property. After receiving the rudiments of education, under the superintendence of his mother, he was sent, at the age of twelve, to the grammar-school at Grantham, where the bias of his early genius was shown by a skill in mechanical contrivances which excited no small admiration. Whilst other boys were at play, his leisure hours were employed in forming working models of mills and machinery; he constructed a water clock from an old box, which had an index moved by a piece of wood sinking as the drops fell from the bottom, and a regular dial-plate to indicate the hours.

On his removal from school, it was intended that he should follow the profession of a farmer, but his utter unfitness for the laborious toils of such a life, was soon manifested. He was frequently found reading under a tree when he should have been inspecting cattle, or superintending laborers; and when he was sent to dispose of farming produce at Grantham market, he was occupied in solving mathematical problems in a garret or hay-loft, whilst the business was transacted by an old servant who had accompanied him to town. These strong indications of the bias of his disposition were not neglected by his anxious mother. She sent him again for a few months to school, and on the 5th of June, 1660, he was admitted a student of Trinity College, Cambridge.

The combination of industry and talents, with an amiable disposition and unassuming manners, naturally attracted the notice of his tutors, and the friendship of his admiring companions; amongst these was Isaac Barrow, afterwards justly celebrated as a preacher and a mathematician. Saunderson's Logic, Kepler's Optics, and the Arithmetic of Infinites by Wallis, were the books first studied by Newton at Cambridge. He read the Geometry of Descartes diligently, and looked into the subject of judicial astrology, which then engaged some attention. He read little of Euclid, and is said to have regretted, in a subsequent part of his life, that he had not studied the old mathematicians more deeply.

The attention of Newton, while at Cambridge, was attracted to a branch of natural philosophy, hitherto little understood, namely, light. It was the opinion of the celebrated philosopher Descartes, that light is caused by a certain motion or undulation of a very thin elastic medium, which he supposed pervaded space. Newton overturned this theory. Taking a piece of glass with angular sides, called a prism, he caused the sun to shine upon it through a small hole in the shutter of a darkened apartment. By this experiment he found that the light, in passing through the glass, was so refracted or broken, as to exhibit on the wall an image of seven different tints or colors; and after varying his experiments in a most ingenious way, he established the very interesting facts, that light is composed of rays resoluble into particles, that every ray of white light consists of three primary and differently-colored rays, (red, yellow, and blue,) each of which three is more or less refrangible than the other. This remarkable discovery laid the foundation of the science of optics.

In 1665, the students of the university of Cambridge were suddenly dispersed by the breaking out of a pestilential disorder in the place. Newton retired for safety to his paternal estate; and though he lost for a time the advantages of public libraries and literary conversation, he rendered the years of his retreat a memorable era in his own existence, and in the history of science, by another of his great discoveries—that of the theory of gravitation, or the tendency of bodies towards the centre of our globe. One day, while sitting in his garden, he happened to see an apple fall from a tree, and immediately began to consider the general laws which must regulate all falling bodies. Resuming the subject afterwards, he found that the same cause which made the apple fall to the ground, retained the moon and planets in their orbits, and regulated, with a simplicity and power truly wonderful, the motions of all the heavenly bodies. In this manner was discovered the principle of gravitation, by a knowledge of which the science of astronomy is rendered comparatively perfect.

On his return to Cambridge in 1667, he was elected Fellow of Trinity College; and two years afterwards, he was appointed professor of mathematics in the place of his friend Dr. Barrow, who resigned. His great discoveries in the science of optics formed for some time the principal subject of his lectures, and his new theory of light and colors was explained, with a clearness arising from perfect knowledge, to the satisfaction of a crowded and admiring audience. He was elected a Fellow of the Royal Society in 1671, and is reputed to have been compelled to apply for a dispensation from the usual payment of one shilling weekly, which is contributed by each member towards the expenses. He had at this period of his life no income except what he derived from his college and his professorship, the produce of his estate being absorbed in supporting his mother and her family. His personal wishes were so moderate, that he never could regret the want of money, except inasmuch as it limited his purchases of books and scientific instruments, and restricted his power of relieving the distresses of others. About the year 1683, he composed his great work, *The Principia*, or *Mathematical Principles of Natural Philosophy*. In 1688, the memorable year of the Revolution, he was chosen to represent the university in parliament, and the honor thus conferred on him was repeated in 1701. His great merit at last attracted the notice of those who had it in their power to bestow substantial rewards, and he was appointed warden of the Mint, an office for which his patient and accurate investigations singularly fitted him, and which he held with general approbation till his death. Honors and emoluments at last flowed upon him. Leibnitz, having felt envious of the discoveries of Newton, tried to revenge himself by transmitting a problem, which he thought would show his superiority, by baffling the skill of the English mathematician. It was received by Newton in the evening, after his usual day's labor at the Mint, and he solved it before he retired to rest. After this there was no further attempt made to traduce his fame. In 1705 he received the honor of knighthood from Queen Anne.

Newton's benevolence of disposition led him to perform all the minor duties of social life with great exactness. He paid and received frequent visits; he assumed no superiority in his conversation; he was candid, cheerful, and affable; his society was therefore much sought, and he submitted to intrusions on his valuable time without a murmur; but by early rising, and by a methodical distribution of his hours, he found leisure to study and compose, and every moment which he could command, he passed with a pen in his hand and a book before him. He was generous and charitable—one of his maxims being, *that those who gave nothing before death, never, in fact, gave at all.* His wonderful faculties were very little impaired, even in extreme old age; and his cheerful disposition, combined with temperance and a constitution naturally sound, preserved him from the usual infirmities of life. He was of middle size, with a figure inclining to plumpness; his eyes were animated, piercing, and intelligent; the general expression of his countenance was full of life and kindness; his sight was preserved to the last; and his hair in the decline of his days was white as snow. The severe trial of bodily suffering was reserved for the last stage of his existence, and he supported it with characteristic resignation. On the 20th of March, 1727, he expired at the advanced age of eighty-four years.

The character of Newton cannot be delineated and discussed like that of ordinary men: it is so beautiful, that the biographer dwells upon it with delight, and the inquiry, by what means he attained an undisputed superiority over his fellow-creatures, must be both interesting and useful. Newton was endowed with talents of the highest order; but those who are less eminently gifted, may study his life with advantage, and derive instruction from every part of his career. With a power of intellect almost divine, he demonstrated the motions of the planets, the orbits of the comets, and the cause of the tides of ocean; he investigated, with complete success, the properties of light and colors, which no man before had even suspected; he was the diligent, sagacious, and faithful interpreter of nature, while his researches all tended to illustrate the power, wisdom, and goodness of the Creator. Notwithstanding, also, his reach of understanding and knowledge, his modesty was such, that he thought nothing of his own acquirements; and he left behind him the celebrated saying, "that he appeared to himself as only a child picking up pebbles from the shore, while the great ocean of truth lay unexplored before him."

FERGUSON.

James Ferguson, the ingenious experimental philosoper, mechanist, and astronomer, was born in 1710, a few miles from Keith, a village in Banffshire, in the north of Scotland. His parents were of the poorest order, but honest and religious, and, by toilsome labor in the cultivation of a few rented acres, contrived to rear to manhood a large family of children. Of the manner in which James acquired the rudiments of education, and how he struggled to rise from obscurity to distinction, we have a most interesting account in a memoir by himself, which we cannot do better than quote in an abridged form.

After mentioning how he learned to read with a very scanty aid from an old woman and his father, and that little more than three months' tuition at the grammar-school of Keith was all the education he ever received, he thus proceeds: "My taste for mechanics was soon developed; but as my father could not afford to maintain me while I was in pursuit only of these matters, and as I was rather too young and weak for hard labor, he put me out to a neighbor to keep sheep, which I continued to do for some years; and in that time I began to study the stars in the night. In the daytime I amused myself by making models of mills, spinning-wheels, and such other things as I happened to see. I then went to serve a considerable farmer in the neighborhood, whose name was James Glasham. I found him very kind and indulgent; but he soon observed, that in the evenings, when my work was over, I went into a field with a blanket about me, lay down on my back, and stretched a thread with small beads upon it, at arm's length, between my eye and the stars, sliding the beads upon it till they hid such and such stars from my eye, in order to take their apparent distances from one-another; and then, laying the thread down on a paper, I marked the stars thereon by the beads, according to their respective positions, having a candle by me. My master at first laughed at me; but when I explained my meaning to him he encouraged me to go on; and, that I might make fair copies in the daytime of what I had done in the night, he often worked for me himself. I shall always have a respect for the memory of that man.

"I soon after was introduced by a schoolmaster, whom I knew, to a Mr. Cantley, an ingenious man, who acted as butler to Thomas Grant, Esq., of Achoynaney, and from whom I received some instruction, particularly in decimal arithmetic, algebra, and the first elements of geometry. He also made me a present of 'Gordon's Geographical Grammar,' which at that time was to me a great treasure. There is no figure of a globe in it, although it contains a tolerable description of the globes, and their use. From this description I made a globe in three weeks at my father's, having turned the ball thereof out of a piece of wood, which ball I covered with paper, and delineated a map of the world upon it, made the meridian ring and horizon of wood, covered them with paper, and graduated them; and I was happy to find that by my globe, which was the first I ever saw, I could solve the problems. But this was not likely to afford me bread; and I could not think of staying with my father, who I knew full well could not maintain me in that way, as it could be of no service to him; and he had, without my assistance, hands sufficient for all his work."

Thinking it would be a very easy matter to attend a mill, and that he would have plenty of leisure for study, poor Ferguson next engaged himself to a miller; but the fellow turned out to be a harsh, ignorant drunkard, who required every moment of the boy's time, starving and ill-using him besides, so that at the end of a year he had to betake himself to the roof of his father. He next hired himself to a farmer; but here, again, he was worked beyond the strength of his naturally delicate constitution: illness ensued, and he had again to seek the paternal refuge. "In order to amuse myself in this low state I made a wooden clock, the frame of which was also of wood; and it kept time pretty well. The bell on which the hammer struck the hours was the neck of a broken bottle. Having then no idea how any timekeeper could go but by a weight and a line, I wondered how a watch could go in all positions, and was sorry that

I had never thought of asking Mr. Cantley, who could very easily have informed me. But happening one day to see a gentleman ride by my father's house, which was close by a public road, I asked him what o'clock it then was; he looked at his watch, and told me. As he did that with so much good-nature, I begged of him to show me the inside of his watch; and though he was an entire stranger, he immediately opened the watch, and put it into my hands. I saw the spring-box with part of the chain round it, and asked him what it was that made the box turn round; he told me that it was turned round by a steel spring within it. Having then never seen any other spring than that of my father's gun-lock, I asked how a spring within a box could turn the box so often round as to wind all the chain upon it. He answered that the spring was long and thin, that one end of it was fastened to the axis of the box, and the other end to the inside of the box; that the axis was fixed, and the box was loose upon it. I told him I did not yet thoroughly understand the matter. 'Well, my lad,' says he, 'take a long thin piece of whalebone, hold one end of it fast between your finger and thumb, and wind it round your finger, it will then endeavor to unwind itself; and if you fix the other end of it to the inside of a small hoop, and leave it to itself, it will turn the hoop round and round, and wind up a thread tied to the outside of the hoop.' I thanked the gentleman, and told him I understood the thing very well. I then tried to make a watch with wooden wheels, and made the spring of whalebone; but found that I could not make the watch go when the balance was put on, because the teeth of the wheels were rather too weak to bear the force of a spring sufficient to move the balance, although the wheels would run fast enough when the balance was taken off. I enclosed the whole in a wooden case very little bigger than a breakfast tea-cup; but a clumsy neighbor one day looking at my watch, happened to let it fall, and turning hastily about to pick it up, set his foot upon it, and crushed it all to pieces; which so provoked my father, that he was almost ready to beat the man, and discouraged me so much, that I never attempted to make such another machine again, especially as I was thoroughly convinced that I could never make one that would be of any real use."

He now turned his attention to the repairing and cleaning of clocks, and in this way managed for some time to make a livelihood. While traveling the country for this purpose, he happened to attract the notice of Sir James Dunbar of Durn, who bestowed on him the warmest patronage, and requested him to make his mansion his home. While there, geometry, mechanics, and astronomy, alternately engaged him. "Two large globular stones stood on the top of his gate; on one of them I painted with oil colors a map of the terrestrial globe, and on the other a map of the celestial, from a planisphere of the stars which I copied on paper from a celestial globe belonging to a neighboring gentleman. The poles of the painted globe stood toward the poles of the heavens; on each the twenty-four hours were placed around the equinoctial, so as to show the time of the day when the sun shone out, by the boundary where the half of the globe, at any time enlightened by the sun was parted from the other half in the shade; the enlightened parts of the terrestrial globe answering to the like enlightened parts of the earth at all times; so that, whenever the sun shone on the globe, one might see to what places the sun was then rising, to what places it was setting, and all the places where it was then day or night throughout the earth."

While enjoying the hospitality of Durn, he was introduced to Lady Dipple, Sir James's sister, who also extended to him the warmest patronage. This lady, seeing his taste for design, employed him in drawing patterns for needlework on gowns, aprons, &c., recommended his work to her acquaintances, and in a short while created, as it were, a flourishing domestic trade for the young philosopher. On removing to Edinburgh, she advised Ferguson to accompany her household, in which he would have the benefit of another year's hospitality, assured that, in the more extensive field of the metropolis, he would have a much better opportunity of rising into notice. Thither he accordingly went; was introduced into new families of distinction; drew and designed for fancy needlework; and latterly turned his attention to miniature painting, in which he so far excelled, that for six-and-twenty years after, it was the business to which he trusted for a maintenance. But while engaged in painting, and enjoying the estimation of those who had been his patrons, "I somehow or other took a violent inclination to study anatomy, surgery, and physic, all from reading of books and conversing with gentlemen on these subjects, which for that time put all thoughts of astronomy out of my mind; and I had no inclination to become acquainted with any one there who taught either mathematics or astronomy, for nothing would serve me but to be a doctor.

"At the end of the second year I left Edinburgh, and went to see my father, thinking myself tolerably well qualified to be a physician in that part of the country, and I carried a good deal of medicines, plasters, &c., thither; but, to my mortification, I soon found that all my medical theories and study were of little use in practice. And then, finding that very few paid me for the medicines they had, and that I was far from being so successful as I could wish, I quite left off that business, and began to think of taking to the more sure one of drawing pictures again. For this purpose I went to Inverness, where I had eight months' business. When I was there I began to think of astronomy again, and was heartily sorry for having quite neglected it at Edinburgh, where I might have improved my knowledge by conversing with those who were very able to assist me."

Having spent some time in astronomical pursuits at Inverness, Ferguson returned to Edinburgh, where he made himself known to Mr. Maclaurin, professor of mathematics, by whom he was kindly patronized, and instructed on points wherein he was deficient. Being greatly delighted with the orrery of the professor, he set about constructing one after a somewhat different principle, and succeeded so well in the undertaking, that his patron not only commended it to the young men attending his class, but desired the constructor to read them a lecture on it. This so far encouraged the young philosopher, that he instantly set about the construction of another more complex, and of higher finish. This was purchased by Sir Dudley Rider when Ferguson first went to London; and he mentions in his memoir, that altogether eight orreries were constructed chiefly by his own hand, and that in no two of them was the wheelwork alike. We now follow him to London, whither he went in May, 1743.

"I had a letter of recommendation from Mr. Baron Eldin at Edinburgh to the Right Hon. Stephen Poyntz, Esq., at St. James's, who had been preceptor to his Royal Highness the late Duke of Cumberland, and was well known to be possessed of all the good qualities that can adorn a human mind. To me his goodness was really beyond my power of expression; and I had not been a month in London, till he informed me that he had written to an eminent professor of mathematics to take me into his house, and give me board and lodging, with all proper instructions to qualify me for teaching a mathematical school he (Mr. Poyntz) had in view for me, and would get me settled in it. This I should have liked very well, especially as I began to be tired of drawing pictures; in which, I confess, I never strove to excel, because my mind was still pursuing things more agreeable. He soon after told me he had just received an answer from the mathematical master, desiring I might be sent immediately to him. On hearing this, I told Mr. Poyntz that I did not know how to maintain my wife during the time I must be under the master's tuition. 'What!' says he, 'are you a married man?' I told him I had been so ever since May, in the year 1739. He said he was sorry for it, because it quite defeated his scheme, as the master of the school he had in view for me must be a bachelor.

"He then asked me what business I intended to follow. I answered that I knew of none besides that of drawing pictures. On this he desired me to draw the pictures of his lady and children, that he might show them, in order to recommend me to others; and told me that when I was out of business, I should come to him, and he would find me as much as he could—and I soon found as much as I could execute; but he died in a few years after, to my inexpressible grief.

"Soon afterwards it appeared to me, that although the moon goes round the earth, and that the sun is far on the outside of the moon's orbit, yet the moon's motion must be in a line—that is, always concave towards the sun; and upon making a delineation representing her absolute path in the heavens, I found it to be really so. I then made a simple machine for delineating both her path and the earth's on a long paper laid on the floor. I carried the machine and delineation to the late Martin Felkes, Esq., president of the Royal Society, on a Thursday afternoon. He expressed great satisfaction at seeing it, as it was a new discovery; and took me that evening with him to the Royal Society, where I showed the delineation, and the method of doing it.

"In the year 1747, I published a dissertation on the phenomena of the harvest moon, with the description of a new orrery, in which there are only four wheels. But having never had grammatical education, nor time to study the rules of just composition, I acknowledge that I was afraid to put it to the press; and for the same cause I ought to have the same fears still. But having the pleasure to find that this my first work was not ill received, I was emboldened to go on in publishing my 'Astronomy,' 'Mechanical Lectures,' 'Tables and Tracts relative to several Arts and Sciences,' 'The Young Gentleman and Lady's Astronomy,' a small treatise on 'Electricity,' and 'Select Mechanical Exercises.'

"In the year 1748, I ventured to read lectures on the eclipse of the sun that fell on the 14th of July in that year. Afterwards I began to read astronomical lectures on an orrery which I made, and of which the figures of all the wheelwork are contained in the sixth and seventh plates of 'Mechanical Exercises.' I next began to make an apparatus for lectures on mechanics, and gradually increased the apparatus for other parts of experimental philosophy, buying from others what I could not make for myself. I then entirely left off drawing pictures, and employed myself in the much pleasanter business of reading lectures on mechanics, hydrostatics, hydraulics, pneumatics, electricity, and astronomy; in all which my encouragement has been greater than I could have expected."

To this narrative we shall add the few particulars which are necessary to complete the view of Ferguson's life and character. It was through the zeal of George III. in behalf of science, that Ferguson was honored with the royal bounty of £50 a-year. His majesty had attended some of the lectures of the ingenious astronomer, and often, after his accession, sent for him to converse upon scientific topics. He had the extraordinary honor of being elected a member of the Royal Society, without paying the initiatory or the annual fees, which were dispensed with in his case, from a supposition of his being too poor to pay them without inconvenience. To the astonishment of all who knew him, it was discovered, after his death, that he was possessed of considerable wealth—about £6000. "Ferguson," says Charles Hutton in his *Mathematical Dictionary*, "must be allowed to have been a very uncommon genius, especially in mechanical contrivances and inventions, for he constructed many machines himself in a very neat manner. He had also a good taste in astronomy, as well as in natural and experimental philosophy, and was possessed of a happy manner of explaining himself in a clear, easy, and familiar way. His general mathematical knowledge, however, was little or nothing. Of algebra he understood little more than the notation; and he has often told me, that he could never demonstrate one proposition in Euclid's Elements; his constant method being to satisfy himself as to the truth of any problem with a measurement by scale and compasses." He was a man of a very clear judgment in every thing that he professed, and of unwearied application to study: benevolent, meek, and innocent in his manners as a child: humble, courteous, and communicative: instead of pedantry, philosophy seemed to produce in him only diffidence and urbanity. After a long and useful life, worn out with study, age, and infirmities, he died November 16, 1776.

SIR WILLIAM JONES.

The extraordinary industry and ability displayed in the acquisition of languages by the subject of the present memoir, affords one of the best examples of what persevering diligence may usefully accomplish. William Jones was born in London, September 20, 1746. He lost his father when only three years of age, and the care of his education fell on his mother, a lady of uncommon endowments. While yet in infancy, he was a miracle of industry, and showed how strongly he was inspired with the love of knowledge. It is related of him that, when he was only three or four years of age, if he applied to his mother for information upon any subject, her constant answer to him was, "Read, and you will know." He thus acquired a passion for books, which only grew in strength with increasing years. At the close of his seventh year, he was placed at the school at Harrow, and in 1764, he entered University College, Oxford. Unlike the majority of youths at these educational establishments, young Jones devoted his whole mind to his studies, his voluntary exertions always exceeding in amount his prescribed task. Such was his activity at school, that one of his masters was wont to say of him, "that if he were left naked and friendless on Salisbury Plain, he would, nevertheless, find the road to fame and riches." At this time he was frequently in the habit of devoting whole nights to study, when he would generally take coffee or tea to ward off sleep—a practice, however, which was any thing but commendable. He had already, merely to divert his leisure hours, commenced the study of the law; and it is mentioned that he would often amuse and surprise his mother's legal acquaintance by putting cases to them from an abridgment of "Coke's Institutes," which he had read and mastered.

The leaning of Jones's genius seems to have been towards the study of languages. It may be very frequently remarked, that individuals who possess the knack of acquiring languages, seldom have a genius for any thing else; but such does not appear to have been the case with respect to Jones, whose intellect grasped at several of the most important departments of human knowledge and polite learning. While at Oxford, he became desirous of studying the Oriental languages, and he supported a native of Aleppo, at his own expense, to instruct him in the pronunciation of the Arabic tongue. The Greek and Latin languages he was already master of. During the college vacations, he embraced the opportunity of learning riding and fencing, and to read all the best authors in Italian, Spanish, Portuguese, and French. To these accomplishments he found leisure to add dancing, the use of the broadsword, music, and the art of playing on the Welsh harp, the instrument of the country of his forefathers.

While engaged in these various studies, he did not allow himself to rest in the pursuit of the object he had in view—namely, a fellowship, in order to spare his mother the expense of his education. Not succeeding to his wish in obtaining this object of his ambition, he accepted, in 1765, the office of tutor to Lord Althorp, afterwards Earl Spencer; and, sometime afterwards, he obtained a fellowship also. He availed himself of a residence at the German Spa, with his pupil, in 1767, to acquire the German language, and on his return translated into French a Persian life of Nadir Shah, brought over in manuscript by the king of Denmark, at the request of the under-secretary of the Duke of Grafton. Another tour to the continent with his pupil and family followed, which occupied his time until 1770, when his tutorship ceasing, he entered himself as a law student in the Temple. He did not, however, wholly sacrifice literature to his professional pursuits; but on the appearance of the life and works of Zoroaster, by Anquetil du Perron, he vindicated the university of Oxford, which had been attacked by that writer, in an able pamphlet in the French language, which he wrote with great elegance. He also published, in 1772, a small collection of poems, chiefly from the poets of Asia, and was the same year elected a fellow of the Royal Society. In 1774, appeared his work "De Poesi Asiatica," containing commentaries on Asiatic poetry in general, with metrical specimens in Latin and English. He was soon after called to the bar, and, in 1776, made a commissioner of bankrupts. About this time his correspondence with his pupil evinced the manly spirit of constitutional freedom by which he was actuated; and to his feelings on the American contest he gave vent in a spirited Latin "Ode to Liberty." In 1778, appeared his translation of the "Orations of Isæus," with a prefatory discourse, notes, and commentary, which, for elegance of style and profound critical and historical research, excited much admiration.

In the meantime he rapidly advanced in professional reputation, although his opinion of the American contest stood in the way of his progress to legal honors. The tumults of 1780, induced him to write a pamphlet on the "Legal Mode of Suppressing Riots;" and in the following winter he completed a translation from the Arabic of seven poems of the highest repute. He also wrote the much-admired ode, commencing "What constitutes a state?" These pursuits did not prevent a professional "Essay on the Law of Bailments." He distinguished himself, in 1782, among the friends to a reform in parliament, and also became a member of the Society for Constitutional

Information. The same year he drew up a "Dialogue between a Farmer and a Country Gentleman on the Principles of Government;" for the publication of which the dean of St. Asaph, afterwards his brother-in-law, had a bill of indictment preferred against him for sedition. Upon this event he sent a letter to Lord Kenyon, the chief-justice of Chester, owning himself the author, and defending his positions. On the accession of the Shelbourne administration, through the influence of Lord Ashburton, he obtained, what had long been the object of his ambition, the appointment of judge in the Supreme Court of Judicature, Bengal, to which he was nominated in March 1783, and knighted.

Jones (now Sir William,) arrived at Calcutta in September, 1783. Here a new and extensive field of action opened to him. While filling the office of judge in the Supreme Court of Bengal, and loaded with professional duties of the most laborious nature, he contrived to do more than ever in the study of general literature and philosophy. He had scarcely arrived in the country, when he exerted himself to establish a society in Calcutta on the model of the Royal Society of London, of which he officiated as president as long as he lived, enriching its transactions every year with the most elaborate and valuble disquisitions in every department of Oriental philology and antiquities.

Almost his only time for study now was during the vacation of the courts; and here is the account, as found among his papers, of how he was accustomed to spend his day during the long vacation in 1785. In the morning, after writing one letter, he read several chapters of the Bible, and then studied Sanscrit grammar and Hindoo law; the afternoon was given to the geography of India, and the evening to Roman history; when the day was closed by a few games at chess, and the reading of a portion of Ariosto.

Already, however, his health was beginning to break down under the climate, and his eyes had become so weak, that he had been obliged to discontinue writing by candle-light. But nothing could prevent him from pursuing the studies he loved, while any strength remained to him. Even while confined by illness to his couch, he taught himself botany; and it was during a tour he was advised to take for the recovery of his health, that he wrote his learned "Treatise on the Gods of Greece, Italy, and India," as if he had actually so disciplined his mind, that it adopted labor like this almost for a relaxation.

His health, after a time, was partially restored; and we find him again devoting himself both to his professional duties and his private studies with more zeal and assiduity than ever. When business required his attendance daily in Calcutta, he resided at a country-house on the banks of the Ganges, about five miles from the city. "To this spot he returned every evening after sunset, and in the morning rose so early, as to reach his apartments in town, by walking, at the first appearance of dawn. The intervening period of each morning, until the opening of court, was regularly allotted and applied to distinct studies." At this time his hour of rising used to be between three and four.

During the vacation of the court he was equally occupied. Writing from Crishna, his vacation residence, in 1787, he says: "We are in love with this pastoral cottage; but though these three months are called a vacation, yet I have no vacant hours. It rarely happens that favorite studies are closely connected with the strict discharge of our duty, as mine happily are: even in this cottage I am assisting the court by studying Arabic and Sanscrit, and have now rendered it an impossibility for the Mohammedan or Hindoo lawyers to impose upon us with erroneous opinions." It was these constant exertions, in truth, that gave its chief enjoyment to his life. In connection with this pursuit, he employed his active mind in planning the compilation of a complete digest of the Hindoo and Mohammedan laws, with a view to the better administration of justice among the natives. This work he did not live to finish, but its subsequent accomplishment was entirely owing to his recommendation and primary labors. His object, in this instance, was to secure a due attention to the rights of the natives; and he showed himself equally jealous of those of the British inhabitants, by opposing an attempt to supersede the trial by jury.

In 1789 he gave to the world the translation of an Indian drama, entitled "Sacontala, or the Fatal Ring." His translation of the Ordinances of Menu, the famous Hindoo lawgiver, appeared early in 1794, and is very interesting to the student of ancient manners and opinions. This eminent and admirable man, however, at last fell a sacrifice to an undue zeal in the discharge of his duty and his pursuits in literature. In April, 1794, he was seized at Calcutta with an inflammation of the liver, which terminated his life on the 27th of the same month, in the forty-eighth year of his age.

It was by a persevering observance to a few simple maxims that Sir William Jones was principally enabled to accomplish what he did. One of these was, never to neglect an opportunity of improvement: another was, that whatever had been attained by others, was attainable by him, and that therefore the real or supposed difficulties of any pursuit formed no reason why he should not engage in it, and with perfect confidence of success. "It was also," says his biographer, Lord Teignmouth, "a fixed principle with him, from which he never voluntarily deviated, not to be deterred by any difficulties which were surmountable, from prosecuting to a successful termination what he had once deliberately undertaken. But what appears to me," adds his lordship, "more particularly to have enabled him to employ his talents so much to his own and the public advantage, was the regular allotment of his time to particular occupations, and a scrupulous adherence to the distribution which he had fixed; hence all his studies were pursued without interruption or confusion."

Few men have died more regretted, or whose loss to the world of letters was more deeply felt, than Sir William Jones, who, as a linguist, has scarcely ever been surpassed. His acquaintance with the history, philosophy, laws, religion, science, and manners of nations, was most extensive and profound. As a poet, too, he would probably have risen to great eminence, if his ardor to transplant foreign beauties, and his professional and multifarious pursuits, had allowed him to cultivate his own invention with sufficient intensity. His private character was estimable in the domestic relations, and he was equally liberal and spirited in public life.

The memory of Sir William Jones received many testimonies of respect both in England and India. The directors of the East India Company voted him a monument in St. Paul's Cathedral, and a statue in Bengal; but the most effecual monument of his fame was raised by his widow, who published a splendid edition of his works, in six volumes quarto, 1799, and also, at her own expense, placed a fine marble statue of him, executed by Flaxman, in the antechamber of University College, Oxford

ANECDOTES OF THE EARLY PAINTERS.

CIMABUE AND GIOTTO.

Cimabue was born at Florence in 1240, and while still a child, manifested a taste for drawing. Happening to see the works of some Greek painters, he was affected by an extraordinary desire to study under them; his wishes were agreed to; and so diligently did he pursue his profession, that he soon excelled his masters. From his performances a school of art sprung up in Florence, which thus took the lead in the revival of taste. Cimabue lived to the age of sixty, and died in 1300. A notice of Cimabue interestingly leads to the history of his successor.

In the year 1276, about forty miles from Florence, in the town of Vespignano, there lived a poor laboring man named Bondone. This man had a son whom he brought up in the ignorance usual to the lowly condition of a peasant boy. But the extraordinary powers of the child, uncultivated as they necessarily were, and his surprising quickness of perception and never-failing vivacity, made him the delight of his father, and of the unsophisticated people among whom he lived. At the age of ten, his father intrusted him with the care of a flock. Now the happy little shepherd-boy strolled at his will over meadow and plain with his woolly charge, and amused himself with lying on the grass and sketching, as fancy led him, the surrounding objects on broad flat stones, sand, or soft earth. His sole pencils were a hard stick or a sharp piece of stone; his chief models were his flock, which he used to copy as they gathered around him in various attitudes.

One day as the shepherd-boy lay in the midst of his flock, earnestly sketching something on a stone, there came by a traveler. Struck with the boy's deep attention to his work, and the unconscious grace of his attitude, the stranger stopped, and went to look at his work. It was a sketch of a sheep, drawn with such freedom and truth of nature, that the traveler beheld it with astonishment.

"Whose son are you?" cried he with eagerness.

The startled boy looked up in the face of his questioner. "My father is Bondone the laborer, and I am his little Giotto, so please the signor," said he.

"Well, then, little Giotto, should you like to come and live with me, and learn how to draw and paint sheep like this, and horses, and even men?"

The child's eyes flashed with delight. "I will go with you anywhere to learn that. But," he added, as a sudden reflection made him change color, "I must first go and ask my father; I can do nothing without his leave."

"That is quite right, my boy, and so we will go to him together," said the stranger. It was the painter Cimabue.

Great was the wonder of old Bondone at such a sudden proposal; but he perceived his son's wish, though Giotto was fearful of expressing it, and consented. He accompanied his boy to Florence, and there left his little Giotto under the painter's care.

His pupil's progress surpassed Cimabue's expectations. In delineating nature Giotto soon went beyond his master, to whom a good deal of the formality of modern Greek art, which he had been the first to cast aside, still clung. One morning the artist came into his studio, and looking at a half-finished head, saw a fly resting on the nose. Cimabue tried to brush it off, when he discovered that it was only painted.

"Who has done this?" cried he, half angry and half delighted.

Giotto crept trembling from a corner, and confessed his fault. But he met with praise instead of reproof from his master, who loved art too well to be indignant at his pupil's talent, even though the frolic were directed against himself.

As Giotto grew older, his fame spread far and wide. Pope Benedict IX. sent messengers to him one day; they entered the artist's studio, and informed him of the pope's request, that he should send a design for an intended church; for Giotto, like most of the artists of those early times, was an architect as well as a painter. He took a sheet of paper, fixed his elbow at his side to keep his hand steady, and drew instantly a perfect circle.

"Tell his holiness that this is my design," said he; and with all their remonstrances, Giotto refused to give any other. Pope Benedict was a learned man; he saw that Giotto had given the best instance of perfection in his art; sent for him to Rome, and honored and rewarded him. "Round as Giotto's O," became an Italian proverb. Giotto, as these stories testify, was a pleasant and humorous man.

The talents of Giotto won him the patronage of the great of his country He visited in succession Padua, Verona, and Ferrara. At the latter city he remained some time, painting for the Prince of Este. While there, Dante heard of Giotto, and invited him to Ravenna. the present abode of the exiled Florentine poet. There also he painted many of his works, and formed a strong friendship with the great Dante. The poor shepherd-boy of Vespignano was now in the hight of his fame. Admitted into the society of the Italian nobles, enjoying the friendship of the talented men of his age—Dante, Boccaccio, and Petrarch—and admired by all, his was indeed an enviable position. And he was a good man, as well as great, loved by all his friends; and as his biographer Vasari says, "a good Christian, as well as an excellent painter." He died at Milan in the year 1336, and was followed to the grave by the sorrow of his friends, his obsequies receiving those public honors which he so well merited.

MICHAEL-ANGELO BUONAROTTI.

On the 6th of March, 1474, at the Castle Caprese, in Tuscany, was born the child who was afterwards to become so renowned. Michael-Angelo was noble by birth ; his father was descended from the Counts of Canosa. Probably his wealth did not equal his patrician ancestry, for the proud nobleman sent his son to a grammar-school at Florence. A public school is no unusual place for genius to develop itself, and here it was that Michael-Angelo's soon shone forth. His facility in sketching—a talent always appreciated by schoolboys—made him popular among his young companions; they encouraged him, and their praises fostered the love of art in his bosom. This passion for drawing, however, was pursued in secret; for his father used all his efforts to discourage the boy, thinking, poor man! in his foolish pride, that it would disgrace the noble House of Canosa to produce an artist! He did not know that, but for that great artist, his ancient house would have been forgotten; and that now Michael-Angelo is remembered for his genius, not for his nobility.

The first story of the boy's progress in art is told of him in his thirteenth year. He borrowed a picture from a friend, and copied it with such exactitude, that it could hardly be distinguished from the original. A plan for a boyish deception came into his head: he confided the secret to one of his playfellows, and the two boys, with grave faces and many thanks, brought to the lender, not his own picture, but Michael's copy. He, worthy soul, discovered not the cheat put upon him, and was restoring with perfect composure the fac-simile to the place of the original, when Michael's playfellow could resist his mirth no longer, and his irrepressible laughter revealed the jest. This story became known; his undoubted success encouraged the boy, and to his father's horror, he declared his first resolution to be an artist.

Most likely the incident of the borrowed picture influenced greatly Michael's future life; for in his fourteenth year we find him a pupil of Domenico Ghirlandajo, one of the best painters of the day, and who had studied under Giotto. Doubtless it was only after many struggles with his prejudiced father that Michael-Angelo obtained this favor; but when gained, he profited by it in proportion to the difficulty with which he had secured it. When fifteen, he one day saw a figure on his master's easel, drawn in a style which he considered far from perfect He made outlines of the incorrect portions of the drawing on its margin. These outlines were far superior to the picture itself; and his own consciousness of this, and a mean jealousy unworthy of the noble art he followed, made Ghirlandajo ever after strive to depress and injure the bold and talented boy who had dared thus openly to compete with his master.

Michael-Angelo remained with Ghirlandajo only three years, during which time his improvement was owing to his own exertions, and not to his jealous master, who scarcely ever condescended to give him the least instruction. But perseverance often fully atones for the want of imparted knowledge; and so it was with Michael. Before he left the studio of Ghirlandajo, he had availed himself of permission given to the pupils of Ghirlandajo, by Lorenzo de Medici, to study in an academy which that wise and generous nobleman had instituted for the advancement of sculpture. Here Michael still continued to improve himself, and attracted the attention of Lorenzo the Magnificent by his beautiful drawings. The academy was held, like those early ones of ancient Athens, in a garden. This garden Lorenzo supplied with beautiful sculpture, chiefly ancient—for the moderns were very far from perfection until Da Vinci's time—and hither the good nobleman often walked among the objects of his taste and delight, supplied by his own munificent hand, or amused himself in watching the progress of the young artists whom he had invited to study in his grounds, with a kindly liberality which now, alas! exists only in name.

In this garden of art the young Michael-Angelo one day saw a fellow-student modeling in clay—a branch of instruction then very uncommon. He felt a wish to do the same, and attempted an imitation, which Lorenzo, who happened to pass by, praised with such warmth, that the young artist determined to try his skill in marble. He begged a piece of broken marble and a tool from some workmen, who were employed in ornamenting the palace, and cheerfully and eagerly set to work. He chose as his model a mask of a "Laughing Faun," which was lying in the garden, much mutilated by time. But Michael remedied all these defects in his copy, and likewise added some improvements from his own powers of invention. The mask was nearly finished, when, a few days after, Lorenzo again visited his garden.

"This is wonderful in a youth like you," cried the delighted nobleman. He examined the work, compared it with the original, and praised the several additions which Michael's genius had prompted.

"But," said this acute patron and lover of art, with a good-humored smile, "there is one thing I do not quite approve, though it is but a slight fault in so good a work—you have restored all the old man's teeth; whereas, you know, a person of that age has generally some wanting."

The young man acquiesced in this sensible remark; and when Lorenzo had departed, he broke a tooth from the upper jaw of the mask, and drilled a hole in the gum, to show that it had decayed and fallen out in course of nature. On Lorenzo's next visit, he was so delighted with the ingenious way in which Michael-Angelo had followed up his patron's hint, that he gave the young artist an apartment in his house; made him a guest at his table; introduced him to the noble, wealthy, and learned that thronged the palace of the greatest of the Medici; and, in short, adopted him as his own son.

When only seventeen, Michael-Angelo executed for Lorenzo a basso-relievo in bronze; the subject was the "Battle of Centaurs." When very old, the great painter once came to see this work of his early youth, and was heard to say that he regretted that he had not entirely devoted himself to sculpture. His next work was a "Sleeping Cupid." The wise of that age thought it impossible for modern art to produce any thing equal to the antique; and they were not far wrong, for Michael-Angelo had not then arisen. So the dealer who purchased his Cupid had the cunning adroitness to stain it in imitation of the defacements of time, and bury it in a vineyard. He afterwards pretended to discover it by accident, and sold it as an antique statue to Cardinal San Giorgio. The praise it obtained induced him to reveal the secret; the deceived public generously forgave the trick, and the artist was invited to Rome, where Pope Julius II. commissioned him to erect a mausoleum. Michael's design was magnificent. When he showed it to the pope, his holiness inquired the cost of such a splendid work. Michael answered that it would amount to a hundred thousand crowns; and the pope liberally gave him permission to expend twice that sum. The mausoleum was commenced: Pope Julius was so delighted with it, that he had a covered way from his palace erected, that he might visit the artist at his work *incognito*. This was too great a favor not to excite the envy of a court. Ill words and unkind slanders were spoken of Michael. They reached the pope's ear, as it was intended, and he visited Buonarotti no more. Michael came to the Vatican, which had been at all times open to him, but it was not so now. A groom of the chamber stopped his entrance.

"Do you know to whom you speak?" asked the indignant painter.

"Perfectly well," said the man; "and I only do my duty in obeying the orders my master has given."

"Then tell the pope," replied Michael, "if he wants me, he may come and seek me elsewhere himself."

The insulted artist returned immediately to his house, ordered his servants to sell his furniture, and follow him to Florence; and left Rome that very night. Great was the pope's consternation. Couriers were immediately sent after Michael. But it was too late; he had already passed the boundary of the pope's jurisdiction, and force was of no avail. The Courier's reached Florence, and delivered the pope's letter. Michael's answer was this: "I have been expelled from the antechamber of your holiness without meriting disgrace; therefore I have left Rome to preserve my reputation. I will not return, as your holiness commands. If I have been deemed worthless one day, how can I be valued the next, except by a caprice alike discreditable to the one who shows it, and the one towards whom it is shown."

Julius next wrote to the government of Florence, using these conciliatory words: "We know the humor of men like Michael-Angelo. If he will return, we promise that none shall offend him or interfere with him, and he shall be reinstated in our apostolic grace." But Michael was inflexible. Again and again the pope wrote, and still this proud and high-spirited man refused to heed him. At last the chief-magistrate of Florence became alarmed. He sent for the artist, and said, "You have treated the pope as the king of France himself would not have dared. We cannot bring him to war against the state on your account; therefore you must obey his will." The magistrate promised, also, if Michael feared for his personal safety, to send him as ambassador to Rome, in which case his person would be inviolable. At last Michael relented, and met the pope at Bologna. Julius glanced at him with displeasure, and did not for some time deign to speak. At last he said, "Instead of your coming to us, you seem to have expected that we should wait upon you."

Michael answered with a slight apology for his conduct, which, however, was so haughtily expressed, that a prelate, who had introduced him, thought it necessary to observe, "One must needs make allowance for such men, who are ignorant of every thing except their art."

Wise and generous, too, was the pope's indignant reply to this speech. He turned to the prelate: "Foolish man! it is thou who hast vilified Michael-Angelo; I have not. He is a man of genius, and thou an ignorant fellow. Depart from my sight this moment." And the contemner of art was forcibly driven from the room.

Michael-Angelo's first commission after this, was a statue of Pope Julius. It was the work of sixteen months, and worthy of Michael's genius. But its fame was short: in a popular riot this statue was thrown down, dragged through the streets, and broken to pieces, in contempt of the pontiff whom it represented. The head alone was preserved by the Duke of Ferrara. After Michael had completed this statue, he returned to Rome, and again set to work on the mausoleum. But Julius had changed his mind, and determined to build the Sistine Chapel, to the memory of his uncle, Sixtus VI. This chapel Michael was to adorn with fresco paintings. His first attempt showed how universal were his powers of mind. He began to paint the ceiling; but the only scaffolding which the architect Bramante could contrive, was suspended by ropes passed through holes in the roof. Michael-Angelo asked how he was to paint a ceiling thus pierced with holes. Bramante could arrange no other plan; and Buonarotti invented some machinery so complete, that the carpenter who made it under his direction, realized a large fortune, through Michael's generosity in allowing him to profit by the invention.

In twenty months the frescos were completed, to the delighted wonder of his friends, and the envy of his enemies; all being the work of Michael-Angelo's own hand, unassisted by any one. The pope had almost daily climbed to the top of the platform to watch the artist's progress; and by his persuasions, Michael took down the scaffolding almost before the frescos were finished. Crowds of the learned rushed to the building to see this wonderful work. But when the pope had gratified his impatience by viewing the painted ceiling from below, he began to wish for more ornaments on the drapery of some figures—more gilding and show. But Michael's reproof was not long wanting.

"I have painted," said he, "men who were poor, nor wished for riches—holy men, to whom gold was an object of contempt. I will add nothing."

The Sistine Chapel was publicly opened on All-Saint's Day, 1512. From that time to the present, Michael-Angelo's frescos have been acknowledged the most glorious triumph of art in any age. They consist of a series of colossal paintings descriptive of the progress of the Christian religion, from the creation of the world until the last judgment of all men. To particularize them is impossible; and their praise has been a universal theme. Most of them are painted on the arched ceiling; and it is said that many figures were executed by the artist lying on his back on a heap of cushions; this being the only position in which he could reach them.

Three months after the completion of the Sistine Chapel, Pope Julius died. Leo X., who succeeded him, was by no means a warm friend to Michael-Angelo. But his fame was now too well established to suffer from this lack of favor. He was now growing old; but his energies and talents were unwearied. Beside that of the Sistine, another chapel was erected called the Paoline. For this he painted two pictures—the "Conversion of St. Paul," and the "Crucifixion of St. Peter." At the age of seventy-two, he was nominated architect of St. Peter's. This magnificent building, the grandest temple in Christendom, was the design and erection of Michael-Angelo. It was the work of many years and many struggles. The artist had to contend with the poverty and illiberality of his patrons; and once they endeavored to displace him. He had, in their opinions, not given light enough to the church in one portion of it.

"Three more windows will be placed there?" said Michael-Angelo.

"You never told us of that before?" replied a cardinal.

"Nor will I be accountable to you for declaring all that I do, or intend to do," cried the high-spirited painter. "It is yours to provide money and keep off thieves: to build St. Peter's is mine!"

This independent speech won him the favor of the then pope, Julius III. From this time he placed unlimited confidence and regard in the artist, often saying that should Michael-Angelo die before himself, his body should be embalmed, and kept in the palace, that his mortal form should endure as long as his works. But Julius died in 1555; and his successor, Paul IV., insulted the painter by wishing to *reform* the "Last Judgment" in the Sistine. Michael sent this message in answer:—"If his holiness will undertake to reform mankind, I will engage that my picture shall reform itself."

This pope plunged Rome into war and bloodshed. Michael-Angelo, then eighty-two years of age, took refuge in a monastery until these perilous times were over. It was with regret that he left this quiet abode to enter again on the turmoil of the world. He lived until the age of eighty-nine, and then died peaceably and calmly, uttering his last will in these words: "My soul I resign to God, my body to the earth, my worldly goods to my next of kin."

Michael-Angelo's countenance was like his mind—full of noble grandeur. Straight Greek features, a high and rather projecting forehead, with clustering hair and beard, gave his portrait a character of sublimity which is like his works. These works were the grandest in conception and execution that mortal man could do—not beautiful but sublime. It is often a reproach to a great man that his life is far inferior to his works; but Michael-Angelo was in every way a noble and good man, not winning, but austere in his virtue and simplicity of character at an age when the contrary was most in fashion. He was never married, and used to say that his works were his children, who must bear his name to posterity. He lived in study and seclusion, never ceasing to seek after knowledge throughout his long life. In his old age, he was found one day by Cardinal Sarnite walking alone in the ruins of the Coliseum. The cardinal expressed surprise. "I go yet to school," said Michael, "that I may continue to learn."

This great artist's soul was full of high principle: he scorned every thing mean and dishonorable. His disposition was generous, and many a kindness did he show to inferior artists, and others who needed it. Sometimes his gifts were munificent. To his old servant Urbino he gave two thousand crowns: a donation in those days considered worthy of a monarch. This man died when Michael was eighty-two, and his aged master remained with him day and night in his last illness, and afterwards wrote this of him: "Urbino's death has been a heavy loss to me, yet also an impressive lesson of the grace of God; for it has shown me that he who in his lifetime comforted me in the enjoyment of life, dying, has taught me how to die, not with reluctance, but even with a desire for death."

His poems were numerous, and all breathe the spirit of purest Christianity. The sternness of his character won little affection from his cotemporaries, yet none ever breathed a word against him. The fame of Michael-Angelo's works will live forever, and with that his memory as a truly great and virtuous man.

WILLIAM GIFFORD.

William Gifford was born in 1755, at Ashburton, in Devonshire, England, and for several years led the miserable kind of life which is common among the children of a drunken and reckless father. This worthless man died when only forty years of age, leaving his wife with two children, the youngest little more than eight months old, and no available means for their support. In about a year afterwards his wife followed, and thus was William, at the age of thirteen, and his infant brother, thrown upon the world in an utterly destitute condition.

The parish workhouse now received the younger of the orphans, and William was taken home to the house of a person named Carlile, his godfather—who, whatever might have been his kindness in this respect, had at least taken care of his own interests, by seizing on every article left by the widow Gifford, on pretence of repaying himself for money which he had advanced to her in her greatest necessities. The only benefit derived by William from this removal, was a little education, Carlile sending him to school, where he acquired the elements of instruction. His chief proficiency, as he tells us, was in arithmetic; but he was not suffered to make much progress in his studies, for, grudging the expense, his patron took him from school, with the object of making him a plowboy. To the plow he would accordingly have gone, but for a weakness in his chest, the result of an accident some years before. It was now proposed to send him to a storehouse in Newfoundland; but the person who was to be benefitted by his services declared him to be too small, and this plan was also dropped. "My godfather," says William, "had now humbler views for me, and I had little heart to resist any thing. He proposed to send me on board one of the Torbay fishing-boats. I ventured, however, to remonstrate against this, and the matter was compromised by my consenting to go on board a coaster. A coaster was speedily found for me at Brixham, and thither I went when little more than thirteen."

In this vessel he remained for nearly a twelvemonth. "It will be easily conceived," he remarks, "that my life was a life of hardship. I was not only 'a ship-boy on the high and giddy mast,' but also in the cabin, where every menial office fell to my lot; yet if I was restless and discontented, I can safely say it was not so much on account of this, as of my being precluded from all possibility of reading; as my master did not possess, nor do I recollect seeing during the whole time of my abode with him, a single book of any description except the 'Coasting Pilot.'"

While in this humble situation, however, and seeming to himself almost an outcast from the world, he was not altogether forgotten. He had broken off all connexion with Ashburton, where his godfather lived; but "the women of Brixham," says he, "who traveled to Ashburton twice a-week with fish, and who had known my parents, did not see me without kind concern running about the beach in a ragged jacket and trousers." They often mentioned him to their acquaintances at Ashburton; and the tale excited so much commiseration in the place, that his godfather at last found himself obliged to send for him home. At this time he wanted some months of fourteen. He proceeds with his own story as follows:

"After the holidays, I returned to my darling pursuit—arithmetic. My progress was now so rapid, that in a few months I was at the head of the school, and qualified to assist my master (Mr. E. Furlong,) on any extraordinary emergency. As he usually gave me a trifle on these occasions, it raised a thought in me that, by engaging with him as a regular assistant, and undertaking the instruction of a few evening scholars, I might, with a little additional aid, be enabled to support myself. God knows my ideas of support at this time were of no very extravagant nature. I had, besides, another object in view. Mr. Hugh Smerdon (my first master,) was now grown old and infirm; it seemed unlikely that he should hold out above three or four years; and I fondly flattered myself that, notwithstanding my youth, I might possibly be appointed to succeed him. I was in my fifteenth year when I built these castles. A storm, however, was collecting, which unexpectedly burst upon me, and swept them all away.

"On mentioning my little plan to Carlile, he treated it with the utmost contempt; and told me, in his turn, that as I had learned enough, and more than enough, at school, he must be considered as having fairly discharged his duty (so indeed he had;) he added that he had been negotiating with his cousin, a shoemaker of some respectability, who had liberally agreed to take me, without a fee, as an apprentice. I was so shocked at this intelligence, that I did not remonstrate, but went in sullenness and silence to my new master, to whom I was soon after bound, till I should attain the age of twenty-one.

"At this time I possessed but one book in the world: it was a treatise on algebra, given to me by a young woman, who had found it in a lodging-house. I considered it as a treasure; but it was a treasure locked up; for it supposed the reader to be well acquainted with simple equations, and I knew nothing of the matter. My master's son had purchased Fenning's Introduction: this was precisely what I wanted; but he carefully concealed it from me, and I was indebted to chance alone for stumbling upon his hiding-place. I sat up for the greatest part of several nights successively, and, before he suspected that his treatise was discovered, had completely mastered it. I could now enter upon my own, and that carried me pretty far into the science. This was not done without difficulty. I had not a farthing on earth, nor a friend to give me one; pen, ink, and paper, therefore, were for the most part as completely out of my reach as a crown and sceptre. There was, indeed, a resource; but the utmost caution and secrecy were necessary in applying to it. I beat out pieces of leather as smooth as possible, and wrote my problems on them with a blunted awl; for the rest my memory was tenacious, and I could multiply and divide by it to a great extent."

Persevering under these untoward difficulties, he at length obtained some alleviation of his poverty. Having attempted to write some verses, his productions were received with applause, and sometimes, he adds, "with favors more substantial: little collections were now and then made, and I have received sixpence in an evening. To one who had long lived in the absolute want of money, such a resource seemed a Peruvian mine. I furnished myself by degrees with paper, &c., and, what was of more importance, with books of geometry, and of the higher branches of algebra, which I cautiously concealed. Poetry, even at this time, was no amusement of mine—it was subservient to other purposes; and I only had recourse to it when I wanted money for my mathematical pursuits."

Gifford's master having capriciously put a stop to these literary recreations, and taken away all his books and papers, he was greatly mortified, if not reduced to a state of despair. "I look back," he says, "on that part of my life which immediately followed this event with little satisfaction: it was a period of gloom and savage unsociability. By degrees I sunk into a kind of corporeal torpor; or, if roused into activity by the spirit of youth, wasted the exertion in splenetic and vexatious tricks, which alienated the few acquaintances which compassion had yet left me."

Fortunately, this despondency in time gave way to a natural buoyancy of his disposition; some evidences of kindly feeling from those around him, tended a good deal to mitigate his recklessness; and especially as the term of his apprenticeship drew toward a close, his former aspirations and hopes began to return to him. Working with renewed diligence at his craft, he, at the end of six years, came under the notice of Mr. William Cookesly, and, struck with his talents, this benevolent person resolved on rescuing him from obscurity. "The plan," says Gifford, "that occurred to him, was naturally that which had so often suggested itself to me. There were, indeed, several obstacles to be overcome. My handwriting was bad, and my language very incorrect; but nothing could slacken the zeal of this excellent man. He procured a few of my poor attempts at rhyme, dispersed them amongst his friends and acquaintance, and when my name was become somewhat familiar to them, set on foot a subscription for my relief. I still preserve the original paper; its title was not very magnificent, though it exceeded the most sanguine wishes of my heart. It ran thus:—'A subscription for purchasing the remainder of the time of William Gifford, and for enabling him to improve himself in writing and English grammar.' Few contributed more than five shillings, and none went beyond ten and sixpence; enough, however, was collected to free me from my apprenticeship, and to maintain me for a few months, during which I assiduously attended the Rev. Thomas Smerdon."

Pleased with the advances he made in this short period, it was agreed to maintain him at school for an entire year. "Such liberality," says Gifford, "was not lost upon me: I grew anxious to make the best return in my power, and I redoubled my diligence. Now that I am sunk into indolence, I look back with some degree of skepticism to the exertions of that period." In two years and two months from what he calls the day of his emancipation, he was pronounced by his master to be fit for the university; and a small office having been obtained for him, by Mr. Cookesly's exertions, at Oxford, he was entered of Exeter College; that gentleman undertaking to provide the additional means necessary to enable him to live till he should take his degree. Mr. Gifford's first patron died before his protege had time to fulfil the good man's fond anticipations of his future celebrity; but he afterward found, in Lord Grosvenor, another much more able, though it was impossible that any other could have shown more zeal, to advance his interests.

Gifford was now on the way to fame, and he may be said to have ever afterward enjoyed a prosperous career. On the commencement of the Quarterly Review, in 1809, he was appointed editor of that periodical, and under his management it attained a distinguished success. After a useful literary career, Mr. Gifford died in London, on the 31st of December, 1826, in the seventy-first year of his age. Reversing the Latin proverb, it might be justly observed, that in him *a shoemaker happily went beyond his last.*

HENRY CLAY.

Henry Clay was born April 12th, 1777, in Hanover county, Virginia. His father was a Baptist clergyman of small means, who died when his son was only five years of age. He was one of a large family of children, who were left under the care of their mother—a firm-minded and truly excellent woman. Henry's early advantages consisted in the privileges of attending a common country Virginia school; and such were the circumstances of the widow, that thus early, he was obliged to contribute to the support of the family. His work was generally on the farm. At fourteen years of age he was placed in a small retail shop in Richmond, Virginia. The next year he entered the office of Mr. Tinsley, clerk of the High Court of Chancery, where, among other valuable acquaintances, he attracted the notice and acquired the friendship of the distinguished and beloved Chancellor Wythe—one of the venerable signers of the Declaration of Independence. With him the poor orphan found a patron and a home. Under the direction of his great benefactor, and for the purpose of studying his profession, he entered the law office of Robert Brook, attorney-general of the state. In 1797 he removed to Lexington, Kentucky, where, before he commenced the practice of the law, he devoted some months to severe study. Such were the youthful trials of this great man. The foundation of his long, eminent, patriotic and glorious career was thus, not family, nor wealth, nor titles, but talents, industry, integrity, and worth.

Our space will not permit a full detail of a progress, alike honorable to a people who saw and appreciated his value as a man, and to the patriot who devoted himself zealously to the public service. This commenced in 1797, when he took part in the debates relating to the call of a Convention, to form a constitution for Kentucky, and in 1798, when he zealously entered the field against the celebrated alien and sedition laws. As soon as he was eligible, he was elected to the Legislature of Kentucky. He was a leading member until 1806, when he was sent to the Senate of the United States, to fill the place occasioned by the resignation of General Adir. This, however, was only a fraction of a term; and at the close of the session, Mr. Clay was again chosen to a seat in the Legislature. He was Speaker several years. In 1809 he was a second time elected to the United States Senate, and to fill a fractional part of a term. This expired in 1811, when he was elected a member of the House of Representatives. On the first ballot he was elected Speaker, which office he filled with distinguished ability. It is no more than justice to remark, that thus far Mr. Clay had proved himself equal, and more than equal, to every place which he had been called upon to fill. Indeed, he was a member of the Republican party, and so signal had been his eloquence, his patriotism, his influence, and his efficiency, as to have attracted the eyes of the nation. He nobly sustained the administration of Mr. Madison and the war of 1812. After the conclusion of the treaty of Ghent, Mr. Clay, with Mr. Adams and Mr. Gallatin, went to London, where a Commercial Convention between this country and Great Britain was concluded. Mr. Clay was again elected to the House of Representatives in 1815, and again made Speaker. Subsequently, after two years' absence from Congress, he was re-elected in 1823, and again made the Speaker, which place he filled until 1825, when he was appointed Secretary of State, by John Quincy Adams. He was Speaker of the House from 1811 to 1825, with the exception of two years, during which time he voluntarily retired from Congress. He continued in the office of Secretary of State until 1829. Two years later, in December, 1831, he was again elected to the Senate of the United States, and continued a member of that body until March 31st, 1842, when he resigned. Mr. Clay lived in elegant retirement at Ashland, until he was again (1849) elected to the Senate. And here, after a brilliant parliamentary career, he closed his life, as his friend John Quincy Adams did, with his harness on—still serving the country, for whose welfare his heart so ferventlv beat. He died on the 29th of June, 1852.

BARON ROTHSCHILD.

SOME CURIOUS STORIES.

A PARIS correspondent writes as follows of Baron Rothschild: Apart from politics the talk is still (1869) about Baron Rothschild. His life and character furnish ample material, and most persons have their little nut to crack at the expense of *le grand baron*. As Albert Wolff remarks, there are two men in one envelope; the Baron snatching up money with voluptuous greed, and then the Baron dealing it out to the poor with careful but generous prodigality. The "lender to kings" was "fierce in business. He never could be put out by the most unforseen circumstances. Once a visitor was ushered in the presence of M. D. Rothschild, to cash a draft on a foreign bank. The Baron asked his Secretary, in German, what was the charge for exchange. Being promptly informed that it was one per cent., he as quickly told his customer that he would charge him two per cent. It so happened, however that the stranger understood German perfectly. He smartly objected, therefore, to an exaction of one hundred per cent. profit, besides the customary gain. Preserving the greatest coolness, the Baron remarked: "Ah! you understand German! Well, since you are a friend, I will do it for one and a half per cent.

The Rothschilds, when they correspond with each other, frequently write in Hebrew. One day a spectator on the Bourse, well versed in the Hebrew tongue, chanced to stand behind the chair of the Baron while he was writing, looking over his shoulders he saw that the letter contained some details about a great operation to be done with the Northern Railway shares. With the prompt eagerness of a true business man, he determined not to lose the advantages that should accrue from such precious information. Our speculator rushed to the Stock Exchange, sold everything he had, and then invested in the Northern Railway shares. His horror can barely be depicted when next day, instead of a rise, there was a terrible fall. Of course the speculator was completely ruined. In his despair he called on M. de Rothschild, who was much surprised that so prudent a man had come to grief. As the baron inquired most kindly after him, he made bold to confess his indiscretion. "So you read from over my shoulders, did you?" replied M. de Rothschild, "But how is it you did not surmise that a man like myself had prepared for all? What I write to my brother has no meaning unless it is accompanied with certain mysterious signs at the bottom of the letter. I need not relate my business to every one—a letter can be lost. Thus, in this special case, when I said to my brother, '*Buy!*' it meant exactly that he was to *sell*. I am sure I am very sorry for you." And then the Baron indulged in a hearty laugh. The poor speculator felt himself about to collapse, when the great banker continued, "Ah! well, my good fellow, since, without knowing it, I have ruined you, I must pull you out of the mud." The very same day Baron Rothschild paid the debts of the unfortunate speculator.

In bodily exertion Baron Rothschild did not fail. After the battle of Waterloo he was about the first person who crossed the channel to England. The storm raging at that period rendered the journey too hazardous for the ordinary passenger ships. The Baron, however, hired a fishing smack, and thanks to its tub-shape, and the roughness, he crossed in safety, arriving in time to speculate on the London Exchange. When the Duke of Berry was assassinated at the opera, M. de Rothschild was dangerously ill through a fall from his horse. He nevertheless leaped out of bed, and clinging to the bell to call his servants, fell, rope in hand, as he cried, with almost dying accents, "The keys of my desk; you must go quick to the Bourse, the Duke of Berry assassinated, to sell! to sell!" This effort nearly cost him his life. The Baron is reproached for the haughtiness of his tone towards the persons he employed; still, he could single out those of great merit. Among these may be specially mentioned M. Benari: "This boy (he would say, with certain pride) is the first accountant in Europe—except *me*." M. Benari rose rapidly, and is now the partner of one of the most important banking-houses in Paris. The originality of Baron Rothschild's pocket purse gave rise to much merriment. It opened with a wonderful key, hung to the Baron's watch chain, and when it *was* opened, it frequently happened that there was no money in it.

VICTOR COUSIN.

Victor Cousin, the great philosopher of France, since Descartes, and the man who has done more than any other of the age, to promote knowledge in his native country, is dead. Although he outlived the study of metaphysics, which even in Germany has yielded to the positive and to exact science, he did not outlive his great reputation, nor the results of his masterly activity.

The deceased was born in Paris, November 28th, 1792. His father was a clockmaker, a disciple of Rousseau, and a revolutionist. The first public school which he attended was the Charlemagne Lyceum, in which he distinguished himself by industry, and gained many prizes. Excelling in scholarship, art, and music, he determined to devote himself to literature, and his name was, in 1810, placed first on the list of pupils admitted into the newly-appointed Normal School. He became assistant Greek professor in 1812, and at the same time taught philosophy in the Napoleon Lyceum. Laromigniére, "the most graceful of the disciples of Condillac," himself the most logical and elegant of Locke's followers, led Cousin at first into materialism. But there was a current setting against this in the spirit of the age, socially, and in every direction. Catholics, sentimentalists, in essays and poets, romantic artists, and all were working against it, and at last Royer Collard, one of those men who achieve great results without gaining permanent popularity, made the first step towards the New Philosophy by teaching Dugald Stewart and other Scotch philosophers. From Collard, Maine de Biran and Reid, the step for Cousin was easy to Kant and Fichte. As a teacher he became popular. The young men who attended his lectures were taken captive by his rare combination of profound thought and glowing eloquence. He spoke under the inspiration of ideas which seemed to have gained possession of his soul. No teacher of philosophy before him had shown an equal power in representing metaphysical abstractions, in such animated and graphic sketches. After a course of travels in Germany, in 1817 and 1818, and Italy, which he had undertaken for philosophical purposes, on his return to France, in 1820, he found a change in the views of the government; he was suspected of liberal sentiments in politics; his lectures at the University were suspended, and he remained in disgrace for several years. During this interval, though deprived of all public employment, and destitute of fortune, he did not abate his devotion to philosophy, and his writings at this period served to increase his reputation and to promote the interests of his favorite study. In 1824, while travelling in Germany, he was arrested at Dresden, and conducted to Berlin, where he was detained in prison for several months. This was at the instigation of the Jesuits, who had become his enemies, on account of his attachment to a liberal policy, and who accused him of having engaged in a plot against the German governments. The affair, however, terminated to his honor, and to the shame of his persecutors. He displayed throughout the whole process a firmness and moderation which gained for him the highest esteem of the Prussian government, and, indeed, of all the enlightened men of Germany. At this time he was visited in prison by Hagel, where he also became acquainted with Schleiermacher and Schelling. Returning to Paris, he published, in 1826, the first series of his *Fragments*

Philosophiques, and in 1827 he was restored to his chair of philosophy in the Sorbonne, with Guizot and Villemain for colleagues. This triumvirate drew to the University an immense number of students. Having gone over so many systems, and broken his way through from materialism to the new philosophy, and naturally been led by Schelling to the congenial Neo-Platonic masters, Cousin boldly revived the eclectic or selective philosophy of Ammonius Saccas of the second century, in an eclecticism of his own, which met with great success. After the revolution of 1850 he might easily have entered the path of political distinction, and been honored with public office, like his colleagues, Guizot, and Villemain, and his friend Thiers, but he declared that he would remain faithful to philosophy. "Politics," said he at that time, "are an episode with me; but the foundation of my life belongs to philosophy." He was placed at the head of the Normal School, which he re-established and re-organized, and from 1830 to 1840 he published several of the most important works, which he contributed to the development of philosophy in the nineteenth century. For the last fifteen years he devoted his studies mainly to the social and intellectual condition of France, during the seventeenth century, and published several historical and biographical monographs in illustration of the subject. His labors in the cause of popular education have given a great impulse to the progress of intellectual culture, and many of his suggestions have been adopted in the best schools of this country. The philosophy of Cousin was essentially a protest against the materialistic schools of the eighteenth century, embodying, in a broad, catholic system, the conclusions of the highest speculative thought of the present age, although his method was original, and deeply stamped with his own powerful individuality. It aimed to reconcile the results of positive science with the fruits of spiritual intuition; and while accepting, to the full extent, the deductions of experience, to place on a deep foundation the universal primitive beliefs of humanity. His examination of the philosophical system of Locke is a masterpiece of analysis and reasoning. Such a lucid exposition of the first principles on which religion and morality, and the noblest hopes of man essentially depend, has been presented by no modern writer; and this production alone establishes his position on the same level with his illustrious countrymen, Descartes and Malebranche. The principal philosophical works of Cousin have been translated into English by several American scholars.

It can readily be understood that as Cousin taught that we should be each our own philosopher, conditioning only that we should read over all that had been written, and master as much as we could, he had an immense effect—firstly, in encouraging the boldest thought and most daring speculation, and secondly, in encouraging scholarship. Under the influence of the eclectic philosophy, scholarship at Paris took new life. Not only were translations made of every branch of German literature, but of every other literature, European or Oriental, making true in detail what he himself taught effectively, that his philosophy was not an *absolute* one, but one to be judged by its effects and results.

LONGFELLOW.

All that Longfellow has written is characterized by child-like simplicity, blended with deep philosophy, all the more deep because it is unconscious and unlabored. It never suggests to us any tedious research or academic lore. The robe and cap of the professor never mingle with the bright creations of his fancy. There is no odor of midnight oil in the verses which sparkle on his page like dew-drops, which a rose shakes off. No aching-head and toil-worn brain have throbbed over the sweet nature pictures of Evangeline; and not from dusty libraries or anti-quarian meditations has Hyperion borrowed its rare beauty and freshness. His poems are life sketches, photographs of each passing mood that visited the poet's mind, and being, as all real art is, true to life, we cannot but appreciate them; something within us responds to their truth. The vivid words of the poet have drawn from their hiding places thoughts which, but for them, would have remained forever concealed. There can be no more powerful witness to a poet's truth than that quick and certain transmission, as it were, of his own mind to ours. His words may at first appear strange, but hardly have we read them, when we perceive that they are the subtile interpreters of our own thoughts. The poet does not give us new ideas, he only gives form and distinctness and reality to those which already vaguely existed within us, but of whose existence we were unconscious, not having the power to express them to ourselves in language.

Longfellow is, *par excellence*, the poet of Nature. He is the organist of her great cathedral, he is the translator of her hidden language into the speech of daily life, he is the white-robed priest of her leafy altars. To him there is a deep meaning in the flowers, and a mystic language in the forest. For him the winds and leaves have a voice, and give him eloquent teachings. The treasury of his mind has gathered its stores from many lands, but amid the wild, beautiful scenery of his own vast land has he learned a wisdom which only its hoary forests and primeval plains can teach. He has dived deep down into the German philosophy, and gathered from it all that its murky depths can yield. There was a charm to him, passing sweet, in the land where Schiller sung, where Goethe wove his glittering webs of moonshine, where Hoffman dreamed strange dreams and penned stranger stories, and beneath whose sunny sky the genial, warm-hearted Richter, "Jean Paul, the only one," lived and wrote and died. There was a spell for him in its crumbling cathedrals, with their traditions reaching far back into olden times, and its ivy-bound fortresses with their

"Tales that had the rime of age,
And chronicles of eld."

Spain too, the land of chivalry and romance, lent him its legends of stately heroism, and Switzerland, the land of freedom, gave vigor and true-heartedness to his song. But in his own land, where the voices of the past are yet unheard, where the utterances of ancient bard or seer are unknown, in the page of whose history no world-thrilling name is yet embalmed, where no hoary cathedrals rise to tell of monkish times, and no ruined castles whisper tales of violence and oppression and wrong, in his own land he has listened to the voice of Nature. In her green moss-garlanded solitudes she has placed in his hand the key which unlocks her hidden treasures, and reveals the hieroglyphics in her vast picture-book. And in all that he has thought and written there is the impress of this companionship.—*Edenglen Magazine.*

CHARACTER OF WASHINGTON.

There has scarcely appeared a really great man, whose character has been more admired in his lifetime, or less correctly understood by his admirers. When it is comprehended, it is no easy task to delineate its excellencies in such a manner as to give to the portrait both interest and resemblance; for it requires thought and study to understand the true ground of the superiority of his character over many others, whom he resembled in the principles of action, and even in the manner of acting. But perhaps he excels all the great men that ever lived, in the steadiness of his adherence to his maxims of life, and in the uniformity of all his conduct to the same maxims. These maxims, though wise, were yet not so remarkable for their wisdom, as for their authority over his life; for, if there were any errors in his judgment, (and he discovered as few as any man,) we know of no blemishes in his virtue. He was the patriot without reproach; he loved his country well enough to hold his success in serving it, an ample recompense. Thus far self-love and love of country coincided; but when his country needed sacrifices that no other man could, or perhaps would, be willing to make, he did not even hesitate. This was virtue in its most exalted character. More than once he put his fame at hazard, when he had reason to think it would be sacrificed, at least in this age. Two instances cannot be denied; when the army was disbanded, and again, when he stood, like Leonidas at the pass of Thermopylæ, to defend our independence against France.

It is, indeed, almost as difficult to draw his character, as the portrait of Virtue. The reasons are similar: our ideas of moral excellence are obscure, because they are complex, and we are obliged to resort to illustrations. Washington's example is the happiest to show what virtue is; and to delineate his character, we naturally expatiate on the beauty of virtue; much must be felt, and much imagined. His pre-eminence is not so much to be seen in the display of any one virtue, as in the possession of them all, and in the practice of the most difficult. Hereafter, therefore, his character must be studied before it will be striking; and then it will be admitted as a model, a precious one to a free republic.

It is no less difficult to speak of his talents. They were adapted to lead, without dazzling mankind; and to draw forth and employ the talents of others, without being misled by them. In this he was certainly superior, that he neither mistook nor misapplied his own. His great modesty and reserve would have concealed them, if great occasions had not called them forth; and then, as he never spoke from the affectation to shine, nor acted from any sinister motives, it is from their effects only, that we are to judge of their greatness and extent. In public trusts, where men, acting conspicuously, are cautious, and in those private concerns where few conceal or resist their weaknesses, Washington was uniformly great, pursuing right conduct from right maxims. His talents were such as assist a sound judgment, and ripen with it. His prudence was consummate, and seemed to take the direction of his powers and passions; for, as a soldier, he was more solicitous to avoid mistakes that might be fatal, than to perform exploits that are brilliant; and, as a statesman, to adhere to just principles, however old, than to pursue novelties; and therefore, in both characters, his qualities were singularly adapted to the interest, and were tried in the greatest perils of the country. His habits of inquiry were so far remarkable, that he was never satisfied with investigating, nor desisted from it, so long as he had less than all the light that he could obtain upon a subject, and then he made his decision without bias.

This command over the partialities that so generally stop men short, or turn them aside in their pursuit of truth, is one of the chief causes of his unvaried course of right conduct in so many difficult scenes, where every human actor must be presumed to err. If he had strong passions, he had learned to subdue them, and to be moderate and mild If he had weaknesses, he concealed them, which is rare, and excluded them from the government of his temper and conduct, which is still more rare. If he loved fame, he never made improper compliances for what is called popularity. The fame he enjoyed, is of the kind that will last forever; yet it was rather the effect, than the motive of his conduct. Some future Plutarch will search for a parallel to his character. Epaminondas is perhaps the brightest name of all antiquity. Our Washington resembled him in the purity and ardor of his patriotism; and like him he first exalted the glory of his country. There, it is to be hoped, the parallel ends; for Thebes fell with Epaminondas. But such comparisons cannot be pursued far without departing from the similitude. For we shall find it as difficult to compare great men as great rivers. Some we admire for the length and rapidity of their current, and the grandeur of their cataracts; others for the majestic silence and fullness of their streams: we cannot bring them together to measure the difference of their waters. The unambitious life of Washington, declining fame, yet courted by it, seemed, like the Ohio, to choose its long way through solitudes, diffusing fertility; or, like his own Potomac, widening and deepening his channel as he approaches the sea, and displaying most the usefulness and serenity of his greatness toward the end of his course. Such a citizen would do honor to any country. The constant affection and veneration of his country will show that it was worthy of such a citizen.

However his military fame may excite the wonder of mankind, it is chiefly by his civil magistracy, that his example will instruct them. Great generals have arisen in all ages of the world, and perhaps most in those of despotism and darkness. In times of violence and convulsion, they rise, by the force of the whirlwind, high enough to ride in it, and direct the storm. Like meteors, they glare on the black clouds with a splendor, that, while it dazzles and terrifies, makes nothing visible but the darkness. The fame of heroes is indeed growing vulgar; they multiply in every long war; they stand in history, and thicken in their ranks, almost as undistinguished as their own soldiers.

But such a chief magistrate as Washington appears, like the pole star in a clear sky, to direct the skillful statesman. His presidency will form an epoch, and be distinguished as the age of Washington. Already it assumes its high place in the political region. Like the Milky Way, it whitens along its allotted portion of the hemisphere. The latest generations of men will survey, through the telescope of history, the space where so many virtues blend their rays, and delight to separate them into groups and distinct virtues. As the best illustration of them, the living monument to which the first of patriots would have chosen to consign his fame, it is my earnest prayer to Heaven, that our country may subsist, even to that late day, in the plenitude of its liberty and happiness, and mingle its mild glory with Washington's.—Ames.

INTEGRITY OF WASHINGTON.

During the administration of Washington, as President of the United States, an application was made to him by a gentleman for a lucrative and highly responsible office within his gift. The application was made with more confidence of success, from the fact, that this gentleman had been the friend and companion of the General throughout the whole course of the Revolutionary war, during which he had received, on various occasions, indubitable marks of his kindness and partiality. He had become, in the estimation, if not of himself, of his friends, in a degree necessary to the happiness of Washington, and had therefore, in their opinion, only to apply for the office, to receive it. It was a boon, which, while it would ensure competency and ease to a friend, would bring that friend into frequent intercourse with his patron, and former associate in arms.

For the same office, however, there was a competitor; but as he was decidedly hostile to the politics of Washington, and had made himself conspicuous among the opposers of his administration, no serious apprehensions were felt from this quarter. Towards such a man—a well known political enemy—Washington surely could feel under no obligations, and was not likely to prefer such an one to a personal friend and favorite. Every one acquainted with the pretensions of the two applicants, was at no loss to judge as to the President's decision, and the concurrent opinion was in favor of the friend, and against his competitor.

Judge, then, the general surprise, when it was announced that the political opponent of Washington was appointed to the office, and the former associate of the General in the toils and deprivations of the camp, was left destitute and dejected.

When his decision was known, a mutual friend, who interested himself in the affair, ventured to remonstrate with the President on the injustice of his appointment. "My friend," replied this illustrious man, "I receive with a cordial welcome; he is welcome to my house, and welcome to my heart; but with all his good qualities, he is not a man of business. His opponent, with all his political hostility to me, is a man of business. My private feelings have nothing to do in the case! I am not George Washington, but President of the United States. As George Washington, I would do this man any kindness in my power; but as President of the United States, I can do nothing."

Who can read this incident in the life of this distinguished man, and not admire his integrity? The temptation to hazard the public good for the benefit and gratification of a friend—must have been powerful. Some might have persuaded themselves that the public weal would not suffer; at least, they would have been willing to make the experiment. But Washington seems to have proceeded in this instance, and in what similar instance did he not proceed, upon just and conscientious principles? His friend, with all his estimable qualities, had no business tact; his enemy was a gentleman of strong integrity, promptitude, and fidelity in business, and every quality, which, if called into exercise, would render service to the state. The decision of Washington, therefore, was, just, honorable, and patriotic.

But whence this admirable, I may say almost singular integrity? Was Washington an exception to the infirmities of our nature? Or was his piety of a higher order, and more efficient in its influence? The first is inadmissible—the latter, improbable. But the true explanation of his sterling integrity is to be found, I think, in that *happy and efficient maternal influence*, which it is well known, was exercised upon him in his early days. On the death of his father, which occurred when he was only ten years old, the charge of his education devolved upon his mother. All accounts concur in the admission that she was an extraordinary woman—possessing not only rare intellectual endowments, but those moral qualities which give elevation, worth, and dignity to the soul. These lessons she was particularly anxious to engraft upon the heart of a beloved son, and with what success, the history of his life displays.

The particular process by which she accomplished so happy a design, it is not in my power at this time to describe; but a story occurs to my recollection, which may serve to show the adroit and admirable manner in which she proceeded on a certain occasion.

In the ample pasture belonging to her plantation, was a colt, which, on account of his beauty and high promise, she valued very much. Although of sufficient age to be used, it had never been mounted.; no one seemed disposed to attempt to break its wild and vicious spirit. One day, George proposed to some of his companions to assist him at a future time to secure the colt, until he could mount, and he would curb his proud spirit. Accordingly, soon after sunrise, one morning, the youthful band assembled, and having drove the animal into an enclosure, succeeded, with no small difficulty however, in bridling him. In a moment, George sprung upon his back, and the next moment the surprised, wild, maddened creature bounded forth into the open field—rearing, running, plunging; but George grinding his teeth and clinching fast the bridle and the mane, held his seat firmly, as much determined to subdue, as the colt was determined not to be subdued. The struggle was mutually desperate; and as the companions of George looked on, their terror and amazement increased with every passing moment. At length, the colt obtained the advantage, and bounding forward with the speed of an arrow, made a misstep, and in his fall broke a blood-vessel, and died on the spot.

George came down unhurt, but when he beheld the gasping of the noble animal, and thought of his mother's regard for it, he was troubled. His companions hurried to the spot, and joining in the regrets of George, anxiously inquired, "what will your mother say—who can tell her?"

At this moment they were summoned to breakfast. When seated at the table, Mrs. Washington said, "well, young gentleman, have you seen my fine sorrel colt in your ramble this morning?" The question was natural—but what a question it was! No answer was returned—and it was repeated. Upon this, George, with perfect frankness, replied, "Mother, your sorrel colt is dead." This was followed by an exact account of the whole affair. As the youthful and agitated narrator passed along in his story, a flush of displeasure was seen rising upon her cheek; but it soon passed away, and she kindly and calmly said, "while I regret the loss of my favorite, *I rejoice in my son, who always speaks the truth.*"

I scarcely know in what terms to express my admiration of the woman, or of the manner in which she treated this delicate and difficult case. George was greatly in fault, and her rebuke was appropriate and commensurate;—he frankly confessed the whole wrong, and she expressed her high sense of his regard to truth. That speech, short as it was, I dare say, told upon his heart—drew his mother nearer to his bosom, and taught him more effectually and more lastingly the importance and value of truth and integrity, than a volume of lecturing would have done.

It was by such means that this part of the character of Washington was formed. Under the tutelage of such a mother, the foundation of a character was laid, which was the admiration of the generation that was contemporary with him; which has lost nothing of its glory to the present time—and will lose nothing, as long as his memory shall last.

BENJAMIN FRANKLIN.

Dr. Franklin, the great American philosopher, was born at Boston, in the year 1707, and was placed at a very early age under one of his brothers, who was a printer, in which art he made rapid progress, and contracted an attachment for the press, which continued as long as he lived. Scarcely emerged from infancy, Franklin was a philosopher without being conscious of it; and by the continual exercise of his genius, prepared himself for those great discoveries in science which have since associated his name with that of Newton, and for those political reflections which have placed him by the side of a Solon and a Lycurgus. He died April 17, 1790. As an author he never wrote a work of any length. His political works consist of letters or short tracts; but all of them, even those of humor, bear the marks of his observing genius and mild philosophy. He wrote many for that rank of people who have no opportunity for study, and whom it is yet of so much consequence to instruct; and he was well skilled in reducing useful truths to maxims easily retained, and sometimes to proverbs, or little tales, the simple and natural graces of which acquire a new value when associated with the name of their author. In short, the whole life of Franklin, his meditations and his labors, have all been directed to public utility; but the grand object that he had always in view, did not shut his heart against private friendship: he loved his family, his friends, and was extremely beneficent. In society he was sententious, but not fluent; a listener rather than a talker; an informing rather than a pleasing companion: impatient of interruption, he often mentioned the custom of the Indians, who always remain silent some time before they give an answer to a question which they have heard attentively; unlike some of the politest societies in Europe, where a sentence can scarcely be finished without interruption. In the midst of his greatest occupations for the liberty of his country, he had some physical experiment near him in his closet; and the sciences, which he had rather discovered than studied, afforded him a continual source of pleasure. He made various bequests and donations to cities, public bodies, and individuals, and requested that the following epitaph, which he had composed for himself some years before, might be inscribed on his tombstone:

"The body of
BENJAMIN FRANKLIN, Printer,
(like the cover of an old book,
its contents torn out,
and stript of its lettering and gilding,)
lies here food for worms,
yet the work itself shall not be lost,
but will (as he believed) appear once more
in a new
and more beautiful edition,
corrected and amended
by
THE AUTHOR."

We cannot do better than close this history of the man to whom "antiquity would have raised altars to his vast and mighty genius, who, for the advantage of human kind, embracing earth and heaven in his ideas, could tame the rage of thunder and of despotism," with an account of his first appearance in Philadelphia, written by himself, and his grand electrical experiment, written by Stuber:

FRANKLIN'S FIRST ENTRANCE INTO PHILADELPHIA.

I HAVE entered into the particulars of my voyage, and shall, in like manner, describe my first entrance into this city, that you may be able to compare beginnings so little auspicious with the figure I have since made.

On my arrival at Philadelphia, I was in my working dress, my best clothes being to come by sea. I was covered with dirt; my pockets were filled with shirts and stockings; I was unacquainted with a single soul in the place, and knew not where to seek a lodging. Fatigued with walking, rowing, and having passed the night without sleep, I was extremely hungry, and all my money consisted of a Dutch dollar, and about a shilling's worth of coppers, which I gave to the boatmen for my passage. As I had assisted them in rowing, they refused it at first; but I insisted on their taking it. A man is sometimes more generous when he has little than when he has much money; probably because, in the first case, he is desirous of concealing his poverty.

I walked towards the top of the street, looking eagerly on both sides, till I came to Market Street, where I met with a child with a loaf of bread. Often had I made my dinner on dry bread. I inquired where he had bought it, and went straight to the baker's shop, which he pointed out to me. I asked for some biscuits, expecting to find such as we had at Boston: but they made, it seems, none of that sort at Philadelphia. I then asked for a threepenny loaf. They made no loaves of that price. Finding myself ignorant of the prices, as well as of the different kinds of bread, I desired him to let me have threepenny-worth of bread of some kind or other. He gave me three large rolls. I was surprised at receiving so much: I took them, however, and, having no room in my pockets, I walked on with a roll under each arm, eating a third. In this manner I went through Market Street to Fourth Street, and passed the house of Mr. Read, the father of my future wife. She was standing at the door, observed me, and thought, with reason, that I made a very singular and grotesque appearance.

I then turned the corner, and went through Chestnut Street, eating my roll all the way; and, having made this round, I found myself again on Market Street wharf, near the boat in which I arrived. I stepped into it to take a draught of the river water; and, finding myself satisfied with my first roll, I gave the other two to a woman and her child, who had come down with us in the boat, and was waiting to continue her journey. Thus refreshed, I regained the street, which was now full of well-dressed people, all going the same way. I joined them, and was thus led to a large Quakers' meeting-house near the market-place. I sat down with the rest, and, after looking round me for some time, hearing nothing said, and being drowsy from my last night's labor and want of rest, I fell into a sound sleep. In this state I continued till the assembly dispersed, when one of the congregation had the goodness to wake me. This was consequently the first house I entered, or in which I slept, at Philadelphia.

FRANKLIN'S GRAND ELECTRICAL EXPERIMENT.

In the year 1749, he first suggested his idea of explaining the phenomena of thunder-gusts, and of the aurora borealis, upon electrical principles. He points out many particulars in which lightning and electricity agree ; and he adduces many facts, and reasonings from facts, in support of his positions. In the same year he conceived the astonishingly bold and grand idea of ascertaining the truth of his doctrine, by actually drawing down the lightning, by means of sharp-pointed iron rods raised into the region of the clouds. Even in this uncertain state, his passion to be useful to mankind displays itself in a powerful manner. Admitting the identity of electricity and lightning, and knowing the power of points in repelling bodies charged with electricity, and in conducting their fire silently and imperceptibly, he suggested the idea of securing houses, ships, &c., from being damaged by lightning, by erecting pointed rods, that should rise some feet above the most elevated part, and descend some feet into the ground or the water. The effect of these, he concluded, would be either to prevent a stroke by repelling the cloud beyond the striking distance, or by drawing off the electrical fire which it contained; or, if they could not effect this, they would at least conduct the electric matter to the earth, without any injury to the building.

It was not until the summer of 1752, that he was enabled to complete his grand and unparalleled discovery by experiment. The plan which he had originally proposed, was, to erect on some high tower, or other elevated place, a sentry-box, from which should rise a pointed iron rod, insulated by being fixed in a cake of resin. Electrified clouds, passing over this, would, he conceived, impart to it a portion of their electricity, which would be rendered evident to the senses by sparks being emitted, when a key, the knuckle, or other conductor, was presented to it. Philadelphia, at this time, afforded no opportunity of trying an experiment of this kind. While Franklin was waiting for the erection of a spire, it occurred to him that he might have more ready access to the region of clouds by means of a common kite. He prepared one by fastening two cross sticks to a silk handkerchief, which would not suffer so much from the rain as paper. To the upright stick was affixed an iron point. The string was as usual, of hemp, except the lower part, which was silk. Where the hempen string terminated, a key was fastened. With this apparatus, on the appearance of a thunder-gust approaching, he went out into the commons, accompanied by his son, to whom alone he communicated his intentions, well knowing the ridicule, which, too generally for the interest of science, awaits unsuccessful experiments in philosophy. He placed himself under a shade, to avoid the rain—his kite was raised—a thunder-cloud passed over it—no sign of electricity appeared. He almost despaired of success, when suddenly he observed the loose fibres of his string to move towards an erect position. He now presented his knuckle to the key, and received a strong spark. How exquisite must his sensations have been at this moment! On this experiment depended the fate of his theory. If he succeeded, his name would rank high among those who had improved science; if he failed, he must inevitably be subjected to the derision of mankind, or, what is worse, their pity, as a well-meaning man, but a weak, silly projector. The anxiety with which he looked for the result of his experiment, may be easily conceived. Doubts and despair had begun to prevail, when the fact was ascertained in so clear a manner, that even the most incredulous could no longer withhold their assent. Repeated sparks were drawn from the key, a phial was charged, a shock given, and all the experiments made which are usually performed with electricity.

* * * * * * * *

By these experiments Franklin's theory was established in the most convincing manner. When the truth of it could no longer be doubted, envy and vanity endeavored to detract from its merit. That an American, an inhabitant of the obscure city of Philadelphia, the name of which was hardly known, should be able to make discoveries, and to frame theories, which had escaped the notice of the enlightened philosophers of Europe, was too mortifying to be admitted. He must certainly have taken the idea from some one else. An American, a being of an inferior order, make discoveries! — Impossible. It was said that the Abbe Nollet, 1748, had suggested the idea of the similarity of lightning and electricity in his *Lecons de Physique*. It is true that the abbe mentions the idea, but he throws it out as a bare conjecture, and proposes no mode of ascertaining the truth of it. He himself acknowledges, that Franklin first entertained the bold thought of bringing lightning from the heavens, by means of pointed rods fixed in the air. The similarity of lightning and electricity is so strong, that we need not be surprised at notice being taken of it, as soon as electrical phenomena became familiar. We find it mentioned by Dr. Wall and Mr. Grey, while the science was in its infancy. But the honor of forming a regular theory of thunder-gusts, of suggesting a mode of determining the truth of it by experiments, and of putting these experiments in practice, and thus establishing the theory upon a firm and solid basis, is incontestably due to Franklin.

THE SETTLEMENT OF PLYMOUTH.

Our fathers came hither to a land from which they were never to return. Hither they had brought, and here they were to fix their hopes, their attachments, and their objects. Some natural tears they shed, as they left the pleasant abodes of their fathers, and some emotions they suppressed when the white cliffs of their native country, now seen for the last time, grew dim to their sight. They were acting, however, upon a resolution not to be changed. With whatever stifled regrets, with whatever occasional hesitation, with whatever appalling apprehensions, which must sometimes arise with force to shake the firmest purpose, they had yet committed themselves to Heaven and the elements; and a thousand leagues of water soon interposed to separate them forever from the region which gave them birth. A new existence awaited them here; and when they saw these shores, rough, cold, barbarous, and barren as they then were, they beheld their country. That mixed and strong feeling, which we call love of country, and which is in general never extinguished in the heart of man, grasped and embraced its proper object here. Whatever constitutes *country*, except the earth and the sun, all the moral causes of affection and attachment which operate upon the heart, they had brought with them to their new abode. Here were now their families and friends, their homes, and their property. Before they reached the shore, they had established the elements of a social system, and at a much earlier period had settled their forms of religious worship. At the moment of their landing, therefore, they possessed institutions of government, and institutions of religion; and friends and families, and social and religious institutions, established by consent, founded on choice and preference, how nearly do these fill up our whole idea of country! The morning that beamed on the first night of their repose saw the Pilgrims already established in their country. There were political institutions, and civil liberty, and religious worship. Poetry has fancied nothing in the wanderings of heroes so distinct and characteristic. Here was man indeed unprotected, and unprovided for, on the shore of a rude and fearful wilderness; but it was politic, intelligent, and educated man. Every thing was civilized but the physical world. Institutions, containing in substance all that ages had done for human government, were established in a forest. Cultivated mind was to act on uncultivated nature; and, more than all, a government and a country were to commence with the very first foundations laid under the divine light of the Christian religion. Happy auspices of a happy futurity! Who would wish that his country's existence had otherwise begun? Who would desire the power of going back to the ages of fable? Who would wish for an origin obscured in the darkness of antiquity? Who would wish for other emblazoning of his country's heraldry, or other ornaments of her genealogy, than to be able to say that her first existence was with intelligence; her first breath the inspirations of liberty; her first principle the truth of divine religion?—Webster.

SUPPOSED SPEECH OF JOHN ADAMS IN FAVOR OF THE DECLARATION OF INDEPENDENCE.

Sink or swim, live or die, survive or perish, I give my hand and my heart to this vote. It is true, indeed, that in the beginning we aimed not at independence. But there's a divinity which shapes our ends. The injustice of England has driven us to arms; and, blinded to her own interest for our good, she has obstinately persisted, till independence is now within our grasp. We have but to reach forth to it, and it is ours.

Why then should we defer the declaration? Is any man so weak as now to hope for a reconciliation with England, which shall leave either safety to the country and its liberties, or safety to his own life and his own honor? Are not you, sir, who sit in that chair, is not he, our venerable colleague near you, are you not both already the proscribed and predestined objects of punishment and of vengeance? Cut off from all hope of royal clemency, what are you, what can you be, while the power of England remains, but outlaws?

If we postpone independence, do we mean to carry on, or to give up the war? Do we mean to submit to the measures of parliament, Boston port bill, and all? Do we mean to submit, and consent that we ourselves shall be ground to powder, and our country and its rights trodden down in the dust? I know we do not mean to submit. We never shall submit.

Do we intend to violate that most solemn obligation ever entered into by men, that plighting, before God, of our sacred honor to Washington, when putting him forth to incur the dangers of war, as well as the political hazards of the times, we promised to adhere to him, in every extremity, with our fortunes and our lives? I know there is not a man here, who would not rather see a general conflagration sweep over the land, or an earthquake sink it, than one jot or tittle of that plighted faith fall to the ground.

For myself, having, twelve months ago, in this place, moved you that General Washington be appointed commander of the forces, raised or to be raised, for defence of American liberty, may my right hand forget her cunning, and my tongue cleave to the roof of my mouth, if I hesitate or waver in the support I give him. The war, then, must go on. We must fight it through. And if the war must go on, why put off longer the declaration of independence? That measure will strengthen us. It will give us character abroad.

The nations will then treat with us, which they never can do while we acknowledge ourselves subjects, in arms against our sovereign. Nay, I maintain that England, herself, will sooner treat for peace with us on the footing of independence, than consent, by repealing her acts, to acknowledge that her whole conduct toward us has been a course of injustice and oppression. Her pride will be less wounded by submitting to that course of things which now predestinates our independence, than by yielding the points in controversy to her rebellious subjects. The former she would regard as the result of fortune; the latter she would feel as her own deep disgrace. Why then, why then, sir, do we not as soon as possible change this from a civil to a national war? And since we must fight it through, why not put ourselves in a state to enjoy all the benefits of victory, if we gain the victory?

If we fail, it can be no worse for us. But we shall not fail. The cause will raise up armies; the cause will create navies. The people, the people, if we are true to them, will carry us, and will carry themselves, gloriously, through this struggle. I care not how fickle other people have been found. I know the people of these colonies, and I know that resistance to British aggression is deep and settled in their hearts and cannot be eradicated. Every colony, indeed, has expressed its willingness to follow, if we but take the lead. Sir, the declaration will inspire the people with increased courage. Instead of a long and bloody war for restoration of privileges, for redress of grievances, for chartered immunities, held under a British king, set before them the glorious object of entire independence, and it will breathe into them anew the breath of life.

Read this declaration at the head of the army; every sword will be drawn from its scabbard, and the solemn vow uttered to maintain it, or to perish on the bed of honor. Publish it from the pulpit; religion will approve it, and the love of religious liberty will cling round it, resolved to stand with it, or fall with it. Send it to the public halls; proclaim it there; let them hear it, who heard the first roar of the enemy's cannon; let them see it, who saw their brothers and their sons fall on the field of Bunker hill, and in the streets of Lexington and Concord, and the very walls will cry out in its support.

Sir, I know the uncertainty of human affairs, but I see, I see clearly through this day's business. You and I, indeed, may rue it. We may not live to the time when this declaration shall be made good. We may die; die, colonists; die, slaves; die, it may be, ignominiously and on the scaffold. Be it so. If it be the pleasure of Heaven that my country shall require the poor offering of my life, the victim shall be ready, at the appointed hour of sacrifice, come when that hour may. But while I do live, let me have a country, or at least the hope of a country, and that a free country.

But whatever may be our fate, be assured, be assured, that this declaration will stand. It may cost treasure, and it may cost blood; but it will stand, and it will richly compensate for both. Through the thick gloom of the present, I see the brightness of the future, as the sun in heaven. We shall make this a glorious, an immortal day. When we are in our graves, our children will honor it. They will celebrate it, with thanksgiving, with festivity, with bonfires, and illuminations. On its annual return they will shed tears, copious, gushing tears, not of subjection and slavery, not of agony and distress, but of exultation, of gratitude, and of joy.

Sir, before God, I believe the hour is come. My judgment approves this measure, and my whole heart is in it. All that I have, and all that I am, and all that I hope, in this life, I am now ready here to stake upon it; and I leave off as I begun, that live or die, survive or perish, I am for the declaration. It is my living sentiment, and by the blessing of God it shall be my dying sentiment: independence *now;* and INDEPENDENCE FOR EVER! WEBSTER.

WILLIAM ELLERY CHANNING, D.D.

BY GEORGE BANCROFT.

WITH powers of such astonishing brilliancy as those which Channing possessed, united with his determined purpose of never allowing himself to be blinded to the abstract right by the fact of the existing law, it is not wonderful that his career should, by many, have been contemplated with appprehension and even with dread. For who could say to what revolutions the manly assertion of natural right might conduct? Who could set a limit to the purposes of reform, when it demanded immediately the application of absolute truth? But death annihilates that alarm. The fear of sudden change by his agency, vanishes; and, from the recesses of conscience, immortal witnesses rise up to confirm his thrilling oracles. Prejudice before might confine his influence; by death prejudice is annihilated, and the echoes of his eloquence are heard beyond its former bounds; as the fragrance of precious perfumes, when the vase that held them is broken, diffuses itself abroad without limits.

And yet, while we lift up our own minds to receive the sublime lessons which he uttered, if we look back upon his life, we shall find his love of reform balanced by a love of order, and the expansive energies of his benevolence restrained by a spirit of conservatism. He was not the mariner who eagerly lifts the anchor, spreads all his canvas, and embarks on the ocean of experiment; he resembled rather the seer, who stands on the high cliff along the shore, and gazes to see what wind is rising, and gives his prayers, and his counsels and benedictions to the more adventurous, who set sail. And sometimes he would call back the enterprising reformer; nor would he attempt progress by methods of disorder and riot, or even of party organization; he would rather postpone the establishment of a right than seek to assert it by bloodshed and violence; like the Jewish mother who submitted to be withheld from her offspring for a season, through fear lest, otherwise, her child should be rent in twain.

And yet this abhorence of violence hardly partook of timidity, certainly did not spring from a deficiency of decision. Did you consider his delicate organization, his light and frail frame, his sensitiveness to agreeable impressions, the exquisite culture of his taste, you might apprehend a want of firmness; but it was not so. He towered above the mediocrity of society, like the delicate and airy shafts of Melrose Abbey, of which the foliaged tracery seems woven of osier wreaths, and yet, as if changed by a fairy's spell, proves to be of stone. Like them his purposes were durable, unyielding, and aspiring to the skies. This firmness rested in an entire faith in moral power to renovate the race. Not the organized union of men, not temperance societies, not abolition societies, not conventions; MORAL POWER was to him the Egeria that dictated, the energy that accomplished reform. Hence, while he objected to associations, he was ever ready to advocate the great moral purposes for which men come together. Was he not among the first to rebuke the international selfishness that has so long held the commerce of the world in bonds? Was he not among the first to raise his voice against the criminality of war, the opprobrium of humanity? Who like him gathered the crowd to recognize the great lesson of temperance, carrying restoration to the desponding and feeble of will? Who like him asserted the moral dignity of man, irrespective of wealth and rank? Indeed, one could hardly hear him on any public occasion, or even in private, but the great truth of man's equality, as a consequence of his divine birth, struggled for utterance. He knew that man was made in the image of God; that the gift of reason opened to him the path to the knowledge of creation, and to mastery over its powers. Having the highest reverence for genius, he yet acknowledged the image of the divine original in every human being. Hence Channing became the advocate of equality; recognized the power of the people as the great result of the modern centuries; and, knowing well that labor is the lot of man, that every mechanic art must be exercised, every service in life fulfilled, he sought to dignify labor and exalt its character; not to lift the laborer out of his class, but to elevate that class into the highest regions of moral culture and enjoyment. And his efforts were in part, at least, rewarded. His words reached those for whose benefit they were spoken; and at his funeral, next to the fortitude with which his immediate friends had learned from him to bear affliction, the most touching spectacle was to see the laborers gathering near the aisles to pay one last tribute of gratitude to the remains of their counsellor

Nor could the clear mind of Channing turn from following his convictions to their results, with all the power of dialectics that gained its warmth from benevolence, its energy from moral conviction. Now that he is in his grave, now that the most timid can no longer fear from his influence divisions in church or in society, let us honor his memory by owning, that, in his main doctrine, he was in the right. His declaration respecting slavery was not an accidental phenomenon in his career; it lay at the very heart and core of his whole system of theology. His was a spirit that in its rapt trances sought intimate communion with the Divine; yet, shrinking alike from the terror of fixed decrees and the fatalism of Pantheism, binding alike destiny and chance to the footstool of God's throne, he was from the first an advocate for the free agency of man. This was his whole theory; this animated his life; this alone led him into the fields of controversy; and in the full maturity of years, with that faith, and with the deep reverence for the Deity, which contemplates him always, and sees him everywhere, he could not but rush to the conclusion that slavery is a wrong; a crime against humanity as well as a crime against God.

It was by degrees, after a struggle of years, that he burst the limits of social and sectarian narrowness, and rising ever higher and higher, became the advocate of universal truths and the champion of humanity. Not a city, not a faction, the mystic voice of the universe inspired him; as I have seen an Æolian harp placed at first where it failed to respond to the air, then lifted from bough to bough, higher and still higher, till at last it reached a point, where the winds of heaven breathed through it freely, and called forth music that seemed to descend from above.

WILLIAM TELL.

Surrounded by some of the most powerful nations of Europe, Switzerland, a comparatively small country, has for ages maintained a singular degree of freedom and independence, and been distinguished for the civil liberty which its people generally enjoy. For these enviable distinctions, it is allowed to have been greatly indebted to its physical character. Composed of ranges of lofty mountains, extensive lakes, almost inapproachable valleys, craggy steeps and passes, which may be easily defended, it has afforded a ready retreat against oppression, and its inhabitants have at various times defeated the largest armies brought by neighboring powers for their subjugation. How this intrepid people originally gained their liberty, forms an exceedingly interesting page in European history.

About six hundred years ago, a large portion of Switzerland belonged to the German empire; but this was little more than a nominal subjection to a supreme authority. Socially, it consisted of districts which were for the greater part the hereditary possessions of dukes, counts, and other nobles, who viewed the people on their properties as little better than serfs, and made free with their lives, their industry, and their chattels. In some instances, certain cities had formed alliances for mutual protection against the rapacity of these persons, and demolished many castles from which they exercised their oppression upon the peaceful husbandmen and merchants.

Things were in this state, when, in 1273, Rodolphe of Hapsburg, one of the most powerful of the noble proprietors, was chosen Emperor of Germany, an event which added greatly to his means of oppressing his Swiss vassals. Rodolphe, however, was a humane master, and did not abuse his power. Albert, his son, who succeeded to the imperial dynasty in 1298, was a person of a different character. He was a grasping prince, eager to extend his family possessions, and, by a most unjustifiable stretch of ambition, wished to unite certain free Swiss towns, with their surrounding districts, called the Waldstatte, or Forest-towns, with his hereditary estates, proposing to them at the same time to renounce their connexion with the German empire, and to submit themselves to him as Duke of Austria. They rejected his advances, and hence commenced the first of the memorable struggles for civil liberty in Switzerland.

Proud of his great rank, uniting, as he did, in his own person, the dignities of the house of Austria and the imperial throne, Albert was indignant at the refusal by which his propositions were followed, and forthwith resolved to hold no measured terms with what he deemed a set of rude peasants. His first impulse was to decide the question by the sword; but the result of any sudden attack was doubtful, and he finally resolved to proceed cautiously in his movements. Disguising his intentions, therefore, he confined himself, in the first instance, to introducing as governor Hermann Gessler of Brunegg, along with small parties of Austrian soldiers, after which his design of subjugating the district became too manifest to its unhappy inhabitants.

Once firmly established, Gessler, who was a fit instrument for the purposes of a tyrant, assumed an insolent bearing, and scrupled not to commit the most severe acts of oppression. The seat of his assumed authority was at Altorf, a small town near the head of the lake of Lucerne, on which the Waldstatte bordered, and surrounded by some of the most romantic scenery in Switzerland. Every great crisis in national disasters brings forth its great man; as Scotland, under the oppression of the Edwards, produced its William Wallace; as America its Washington, when its liberty was threatened; so did a part of Switzerland, under the vice-regal domination of Gessler, produce its WILLIAM TELL. Not much is really known of this patriot, but the little that has been wafted by history and tradition to our times is interesting, and possesses all the charm of poetry and romance.

William Tell, according to the best accounts, was born at Burglen, a secluded hamlet in the canton of Uri, near the lake of Lucerne, about the year 1275, and, like his forefathers, was the proprietor of a cottage, a few small fields, a vineyard, and an orchard. When William had reached the age of twenty, his father is said to have died, bequeathing to him these humble possessions, and earnestly requesting him, with his latest breath, to work diligently for his subsistence, and to die, should it be needed, in his country's service. These admonitions, addressed to a highly sensitive mind, were not disregarded.

Having consigned his father's body to the tomb, he gave himself up to the labors of the field, and by his assiduous industry, is said ever to have reaped a plentiful harvest.

Rising at dawn of day, he stood behind his rude plough, and left it only when darkness summoned both man and beast to repose. Endowed by nature with a lofty and energetic mind, Tell was distinguished also by great physical strength and manly beauty. He was taller by a head than most of his companions; he loved to climb the rugged rocks of his native mountains in pursuit of the chamois, and to steer his small boat across the lake in time of storm and of danger. The load of wood which he could bear upon his shoulders was prodigious, being, it is said, double that which any ordinary man could support.

In all out-door sports Tell likewise excelled. During holidays, when the young archers were trying their skill, according to ancient Swiss custom, Tell, who had no equal in the practice of the bow, was obliged to remain an idle spectator, in order to give others a chance for the prize. With such varied qualifications, and being also characterized by a courteous disposition, Tell was a general favorite among his countrymen, and an acceptable guest at every fireside. Meanwhile, in his humble home, he remained without a mate; and desirous of finding a partner who might grace his little domain, he fixed his attention on Emma, the daughter of Walter Furst, who was considered the best and fairest maiden of the whole canton of Uri. His advances being well received by both father and daughter, Tell in due time called Emma his wife, and henceforth his mountain home was the scene of happiness and contentment. The birth of a son, who was named Walter, in honor of his grandfather, added to the felicity of the pair. Until the age of six, Walter was left to his mother's care, but at that period the father undertook his education, carried him to the fields and pastures to instruct him in the works of nature, and spared no pains at home to cultivate and enlighten his mind. Other children subsequently added to the ties of family.

With other sources of happiness, Tell combined that of possessing a friend, who dwelt amid the rocky hights separating Uri from Underwald. Arnold Anderhalden of Melchthal was this associate. Although similar in many salient points of character, there was still an essential difference between the two men. Arnold of Melchthal, while he loved his country with an ardor equal to that of Tell, was capable of very great actions, without being prepared for much patient suffering or long endurance of wrong. Tell, whose temperament was more calm, and whose passions were more influenced by reason than impulse, only succeeded in restraining his friend's impulsive character by the stern force of example. Meantime the two friends passed their days in the enjoyment of one another's society, visiting at intervals each other's humble residence. Arnold had a daughter, Clair by name, and Walter, the son of Tell, learned as he grew up to love and cherish her. Thus, in simple and tranquil pleasures, in the industrious prosecution of their several occupations, these two families dwelt in tranquility and mutual happiness.

The introduction to power of Hermann Gessler broke in upon the joys of every citizen of Uri. Besides the allowance of the utmost license to his soldiers, the tolls were raised, the most slight and trivial offences punished by imprisonment and heavy fines, and the inhabitants treated with insolence and contempt. Gessler, passing on horseback before a house built by Stauffacher, in the village of Steinen, near Schwytz, cried, "What! shall it be borne that these contemptible peasants should build such an edifice as this? If *they* are to be thus lodged, what are we to do?" History records the indignant remonstrance of the wife of Stauffacher upon this occasion. "How long," exclaimed she, "shall we behold the oppressor triumphant, and the oppressed weep? How long shall the insolent stranger possess our lands, and bestow our inheritances upon his heirs? What avails it that our mountains and valleys are inhabited by men, if we, the mothers of Helvetia, are to suckle the children of slavery, and see our daughters swelling the train of our oppressors?" The energetic language of his wife was not thrown away upon Werner, but settled, and in due time brought forth fruit.

Meanwhile some of the instruments of oppression were punished when they were least prepared for retribution. As an example, we may instance the governor of Schwanau, a castle on the lake of Lowerz, who, having brought dishonor upon a family of distinction, perished by the hand of the eldest son. As a parallel instance, we may mention that a friend of Berenger of Landenberg, the young lord of Wolfenchiess, in Unterwalden, having seen the beautiful wife of Conrad of Baumgarten at Alzallen, and finding that her husband was absent, desired, in the most peremptory terms, that she should prepare him a bath; but the lady having called Conrad from the fields, and explained to him the repeated indignities to which she had been exposed, his resentment was so inflamed at the recital, that, rushing into the bath chamber, he sacrificed the young noble on the spot. In a state of society but just emerging from barbarism, and which as yet knew but little of law or justice, continual instances were of daily occurrence in which private individuals thus took the law into their own hands. The result, however chivalric the custom may look in the abstract, was most fearful and terrible, and is but one of the many proofs how great a blessing civilization has really been to mankind.

Tell foresaw, on the arrival of Gessler, many of the misfortunes which must inevitably follow his iron rule, and without explaining his views even to Arnold of Melchthal, without needlessly alarming his family, endeavoured to devise some means, not of bearing the yoke demurely, but of delivering his country from the galling oppression which Albert had brought upon it. The hero felt satisfied that the evil deeds of the governor would sooner or later bring just retribution upon him; for this, and many other reasons, therefore, despite his own secret wishes, when Arnold poured out his fiery wrath in the ear of his friend, he listened calmly, and, to avoid inflaming him more, avowed none of his own views or even feelings in return.

One evening, however, William Tell and his wife sat in the front of their cottage, watching their son amusing himself amid the flocks, when the former grew more thoughtful and sad than usual. Presently Tell spoke, and for the first time imparted to his wife some of his most secret designs. While the conversation was still proceeding, the parents saw their son rush towards them crying for help, and shouting the name of old Melchthal. As he spoke, Arnold's father appeared in view, led by Clair, and feeling his way with a stick. Tell and his wife hastened forward, and discovered, to their inconceivable horror, that their friend was blind, his eyes having been put out with hot irons. The hero of Burglen, burning with just indignation, called on the old man to explain the fearful sight, and also the cause of Arnold's absence. The unfortunate Melchthal seated himself, surrounded by his agonized friends, and immediately satisfied the impatient curiosity of Tell.

It appeared that that very morning the father, son, and granddaughter were in the fields loading a couple of oxen with produce for the market-town, when an Austrian soldier presented himself, and having examined the animals, which appeared to suit his fancy, ordered their owner to unyoke the beasts preparatory to his driving them off. Adding insolence to tyranny, he further remarked that such clodpoles might very well draw their own ploughs and carts. Arnold, furious at the man's daring impertinence, was only restrained by his father's earnest entreaties from sacrificing the robber on the spot; nothing, however, could prevent him from aiming a blow at him, which broke two of his fingers. The enraged soldier then retreated; but old Melchthal, who well knew the character of Gessler, immediately forced Arnold, much against his inclination, to go and conceal himself for some days in the Rhigi. This mountain rises in a somewhat isolated position—a rare circumstance with the Swiss Alps—and is one of the most conspicuous hills of Switzerland. In form a truncated cone, with its base watered by three lakes—Lucerne, Zug, and Zurich—this gigantic hill is pierced by deep caverns, of which two are famous—the Rruder-balm, and the hole of Kessis-Boden. Scarcely had Arnold departed in this direction, when a detachment of guards from Altorf surrounded their humble tenement, and dragging old Melchthal before Gessler, he ordered him to give up his son. Furious at the refusal which ensued, the tyrant commanded the old man's eyes to be put out, and then sent him forth blind to deplore his misfortunes.

Tell heard the story of Melchthal in silence, and when he had finished, inquired the exact place of his son's concealment. The father replied that it was in a particular cavern of Mount Rhigi, the desert rocks of which place were unknown to the emissaries of the governor, and there he had promised to remain until he received his parent's permission to come forth. This Tell requested might be granted immediately; and turning to his son, ordered him to start at once for Rhigi with a message to Arnold. Walter gladly obeyed, and providing himself with food, and receiving private instructions from his father, went on his journey under cover of the night.

Tell himself then threw around his own person a cloak of wolf-skin, seized his quiver full of sharp arrows, and taking his terrible bow, which few could bend, in hand, bade adieu to his wife for a few days, and took his departure in an opposite direction from that pursued by his son. It was quite dawn when Walter reached the Rhigi, and a slight column of blue smoke speedily directed him to the spot where Arnold lay concealed. The intrusion at first startled the fugitive; but recognizing Tell's son, he listened eagerly to his dismal story, the conclusion of which roused in him so much fury, that he would have rushed forth at once to have assassinated Gessler, had not Walter restrained him. Schooled by Tell, he informed him that his father was engaged in preparing vengeance for the tyrant's crime, being at that moment with Werner Stauffacher concerting proper measures of resistance. "Go," said my father, "and tell Arnold of this new villainy of the governor's, and say that it is not rage which can give us just revenge, but the utmost exertion of courage and prudence. I leave for Schwytz to bid Werner arm his canton; let Melchthal go to Stantz, and prepare the young men of Underwald for the outbreak; having done this, let him meet me, with Furst and Werner, in the field of Grutli."*

Arnold, scarcely taking time slightly to refresh himself with food, sent Walter on his homeward journey, while he started for Stantz. Walter, when alone, turned his steps towards Altorf, where, unfortunately, and unknown to himself, he came into the presence of Gessler, to whom he uttered somewhat hard things about the state of the country, being led to commit himself by the artful questions of the tyrant, who immediately ordered the lad into confinement, with strict injunctions to his guards to seize whomsoever should claim him.

Meanwhile certain doubts and fears, from he knew not what cause, arose in the mind of Gessler, and struck him with a presentiment that all was not right. He imagined that the people wore in their looks less abject submission to his authority; and the better to satisfy himself of the correctness or erroneousness of this view, he commanded Berenger to erect at dawn of day, in the market-place of Altorf, a pole, on the point of which he was to place the ducal cap of Austria. An order was further promulgated, to the effect that every one passing near, or within sight of it, should make obeisance, in proof of his homage and fealty to the duke.

Numerous soldiers under arms were directed to surround the place,

* A lonely, sequestered strip of meadow, called indifferently Rutli and Grutli, upon an angle of the lake of Lucerne, surrounded by thickets, at the foot of the rock of Seelisberg, and opposite the village of Brumen.

to keep the avenues, and compel the passers-by to bend with proper respect to the emblem of the governing power of the three cantons. Gessler likewise determined that, whoever should disobey the mandate, and pass the ducal badge without the requisite sign of honor, or who should exhibit by his bearing a feeling of independence, should be accused of disaffection, and be treated accordingly—a measure which promised both to discover the discontented, and furnish a sufficient ground for their punishment. Numerous detachments of troops, among whom money had been previously distributed, were then placed around to see that his commands were scrupulously obeyed. History scarcely records another instance of tyranny so galling and humiliating to the oppressed, and so insolent on the part of its author.

The proceedings of Tell in the interval were of the deepest concern to the country. Having arrived within the territory of Schwytz, and at the village of Steinen, he called at the house of Werner, and being admitted, threw at his feet a heavy bundle of lances, arrows, cross-bows, and swords. "Werner Stauffacher," cried Tell, "the time is come for action;" and without a moment's delay, he informed his friend of all that had passed, dwelling minutely on every detail; and when he had at length finished, the cautious Werner could restrain his wrath no longer, but exclaimed, clasping the hero's hand, "Friend, let us begin; I am ready." After further brief conference, they, by separate ways, carried round arms to their friends in the town and the neighboring villages. Many hours were thus consumed, and when the whole were at last distributed, they both returned to Stauffacher's house, snatched some slight refreshment, and then sped on their way to Grutli, accompanied by ten of their most tried adherents.

The lake of Lucerne was soon reached, and a boat procured. Werner, perceiving the water to be agitated by a furious tempest, inquired of Tell if his skill would enable him to struggle against the storm. "Arnold awaits us," cried William, "and the fate of our country depends upon this interview." With these words he leaped into the boat, Werner jumped after him, and the rest followed. Tell cast loose the agitated vessel, seized the tiller, and hoisting sail, the little craft flew along the waves.

Presently, it is said, the wind moderated, and ere they reached the opposite side, had ceased altogether—a phenomenon common in these mountain lakes. The boat was now made fast, and the conspirators hastened to the field of Grutli, where, at the mouth of a cavern of the same name. Arnold and Walter Furst awaited them, each with ten other companions. Tell allowed no considerations of natural feeling to silence the calls of duty, but at once came to the point. He first gave a brief sketch of the state of the country under the Austrian bailiffs, and having shown to the satisfaction of his companions the necessity for immediate and combined action, is related to have added—"We may have our plans frustrated by delay, and the time has come for action. I ask only a few days for preparation. Unterwalden and Schwytz are armed. Three hundred and fifty warriors are, I am assured, ready. I leave you to assign them a secluded valley as a place of rendezvous, which they may gain in small parties by different paths. I will return to Uri, and collect my contingent of a hundred men; Furst will aid me, and seek them in the Moderan and Urseren, even in the high hills whence flow the Aar, the Tessin, the Rhine, and the Rhone. I will remain in Altorf, and as soon as I receive tidings from Furst, will fire a huge pile of wood near my house. At this signal let all march to the rendezvous, and, when united, pour down upon Altorf, where I will then strive to arouse the people."

This plan of the campaign was, after some deliberation, agreed to; and it was further resolved unanimously, that, in the enterprise upon which they were now embarked, no one should be guided by his own private opinion, nor ever forsake his friends; that they should jointly live or die in defence of their common cause; that each should, in his own vicinity, promote the object in view, trusting that the whole nation would one day have cause to bless their friendly union; that the Count of Hapsburg should be deprived of none of his lands, vassals, or prerogatives; that the blood of his servants and bailiffs should not be spilt; but that the freedom which they had inherited from their fathers they were determined to assert, and to hand down to their children untainted and undiminished. Then Stauffacher, Furst, and Melchthal, and the other conspirators, stepped forward, and raising their hands, swore that they would die in defence of that freedom.

After this solemn oath, and after an agreement that New-Year's Day should be chosen for the outbreak, unless, in the meantime, a signal-fire should arouse the inhabitants on some sudden emergency, the heroes separated. Arnold returned to Stantz, Werner to Schwytz, while Tell and Furst took their way to Altorf. The sun already shone brightly as Tell entered the town, and he at once advanced into the public place, where the first object which caught his eye was a handsome cap, embroidered with gold, stuck upon the end of a long pole. Soldiers walked around it in respectful silence, and the people of Altorf, as they passed, bowed their heads profoundly to the symbol of power.

Tell was much surprised at this new and strange manifestation of servility, and leaning on his cross-bow, gazed contemptuously both on the people and the soldiers. Berenger, captain of the guard, at length observed this man, who alone, amid a cringing populace, carried his head erect. He went to him, and fiercely asked why he neglected to pay obedience to the orders of Hermann Gessler. Tell mildly replied that he was not aware of them, neither could he have thought that the intoxication of power could carry a man so far; though the cowardice of the people almost justified his conduct. This bold language somewhat surprised Berenger, who ordered Tell to be disarmed, and then, surrounded by guards, he was carried before the governor.

"Wherefore," demanded the incensed bailiff, "hast thou disobeyed my orders, and failed in thy respect to the emperor? Why hast thou dared to pass before the sacred badge of thy sovereign without the evidence of homage required of thee?"

"Verily," answered Tell with mock humility, "how this happened I know not; 'tis an accident, and no mark of contempt; suffer me, therefore, in thy clemency, to depart."

Gessler was both surprised and irritated at this reply, feeling assured that there was something beneath the tranquil and bitter smile of the prisoner which he could not fathom. Suddenly he was struck by the resemblance which existed between him and the boy Walter, whom he had met the previous day, and immediately ordered him to be brought forward. Gessler now inquired the prisoner's name, which he no sooner heard than he knew him to be the archer so much respected throughout the whole canton, and at once conceived the mode of punishment which he afterwards put in practice, and which was perhaps the most refined act of torture which man ever imagined. As soon as the youth arrived, the governor turned to Tell, and told him that he had heard of his extraordinary dexterity, and was accordingly determined to put it to the proof. "While beholding justice done, the people of Altorf shall also admire thy skill. Thy son shall be placed a hundred yards distant, with an apple on his head. If thou hast the good fortune to bear away the apple in triumph with one of thy arrows, I pardon both, and restore your liberty. If thou refusest this trial, thy son shall die before thine eyes."

Tell, horror-stricken, implored Gessler to spare him so cruel an experiment, though his son Walter encouraged his father to trust to his usual good fortune; and finding the governor inexorable, our hero accepted the trial. He was immediately conducted into the public place, where the required distance was measured by Berenger, a double row of soldiers shutting up three sides of the square. The people, awe-stricken and trembling, pressed behind. Walter stood with his back to a linden tree, patiently awaiting the exciting moment. Hermann Gessler, some distance behind, watched every motion. His cross-bow and one bolt were handed to Tell; he tried the point, broke the weapon, and demanded his quiver. It was brought to him, and emptied at his feet. William stooped down, and taking a long time to choose one, managed to hide a second in his girdle; the other he held in his hand, and proceeded to string his bow, while Berenger cleared away the remaining arrows.

After hesitating a long time—his whole soul beaming in his face, his paternal affection rendering him almost powerless—he at length roused himself—drew the bow—aimed—shot—and the apple, struck to the core, was carried away by the arrow!

The market-place of Altorf was filled by loud cries of admiration. Walter flew to embrace his father, who, overcome by the excess of his emotions, fell insensible to the ground, thus exposing the second arrow to view. Gessler stood over him, awaiting his recovery, which speedily taking place, Tell rose and turned away from the governor with horror, who, however, scarcely yet believing his senses, thus addressed him: "Incomparable archer, I will keep my promise; but," added he, "tell me, what needed you with that second arrow which you have, I see, secreted in your girdle? One was surely enough." Tell replied, with some slight evidence of embarrassment, "that it was customary among the bowmen of Uri to have always one arrow in reserve;" an explanation which only served to confirm the suspicions of Gessler. "Nay, nay," said he; "tell me thy real motive, and whatever it may have been, speak frankly, and thy life is spared." "The second shaft," replied Tell, "was to pierce thy heart, tyrant, if I had chanced to harm my son." At these words the terrified governor retired behind his guards, revoked his promise of pardon, commanding him further to be placed in irons, and to be reconducted to the fort. He was obeyed, and as slight murmurs rose amongst the people, double patrols of Austrian soldiers paraded the streets, and forced the citizens to retire to their houses. Walter, released, fled to join Arnold of Melchthal, according to a whispered order from his father."

Gessler, reflecting on the aspect of the people, and fearful that some plot was in progress, which his accidental shortness of provisions rendered more unfortunate, determined to rid his citadel of the object which might induce an attack. With these views he summoned Berenger, and addressed him in these words: "I am about to quit Altorf, and you shall command during my absence. I leave my brave soldiers, who will readily obey your voice; and, soon returning with supplies and reinforcements, we will crush this vile people, and punish them for their insolent murmurings. Prepare me a large boat, in which thirty men, picked from my guard, may depart with me. As soon as night draws in, you can load this audacious Tell with chains, and send him on board. I will myself take him where he may expiate his offences."

Tell was forthwith immediately conducted to Fluelen, the little port of Altorf, about a league distant, at the foot of Mount Rorstock. Gessler followed, and entered the bark which had been prepared with the utmost despatch, ordering the bow and quiver of the famous archer to be carefully put on board at the same time; with the intention, it is supposed, of either keeping them under safe custody, or hanging them up, according to religious custom, as an offering for his personal safety. Having started with the prisoner, under the safe conduct of his armed dependants, Gessler ordered them to row as far as Brunnen, a distance of three leagues and a half; intending, it is said, to land at that point, and, passing through the territory of

Schwytz, lodge the redoubted bowman in the dungeon of Kussnacht, there to undergo the rigor of his sentence.

The evening was fine and promising; the boat danced along the placid waters. The air was pure, the waves tranquil, the stars shone brightly in the sky. A light southern breeze aided the efforts of the oarsmen, and tempered the rigor of the cold, which night in that season rendered almost insupportable so near the glaciers. All appeared in Gessler's favor. The extent of the first section of the lake was soon passed, and the boat headed for Brunnen. Tell, meantime, loaded with irons, gazed with eager eye, shaded by melancholy, on the desert rocks of Grutli, where, the day before, he had planned with his friends the deliverance of his country. While painful thoughts crossed his mind, his looks were attracted to the neighborhood of Altorf by a dim light which burst forth near his own house. Presently this light increased, and before long, a tremendous blaze arose visible all over Uri. The heart of the prisoner beat joyously within him, for he felt that efforts were making to rescue him. Gessler and his satellites observed the flame, which in reality was a signal-fire to rouse the cantons; upon which, however, the Austrians gazed with indifference, supposing it some Swiss peasant's house accidentally on fire.

Suddenly, however, between Fluelen and Sissigen, when in deep water, intermingled with shoals, the south wind ceased to blow, and one of those storms which are common on the lake commenced. A north wind, occasionally shifting to the westward, burst upon them. The wind, which usually marked the approach of a dangerous tempest, raised the waves to a great hight, bore them one against another, and dashed them over the gunwale of the boat, which, giving way to the fury of the storm, turned and returned, and despite the efforts of the oarsmen, who were further damped by an unskillful pilot being at the helm, flew towards the shore, that, rocky and precipitous, menaced their lives: the wind, also, brought frost, snow, and clouds, which, obscuring the heavens, spread darkness over the water, and covered the hands and face of the rowers with sharp icicles. The soldiers, pale and horror-stricken, prayed for life; while Gessler, but ill prepared for death, was profuse in his offers of money and other rewards if they would rouse themselves to save him.

In this emergency the Austrian bailiff was reminded by one of his attendants that the prisoner Tell was no less skillful in the management of a boat than in the exercise of the bow. "And see, my lord," said one of the men, representing to Gessler the imminent peril they were all incurring—"all, even the pilot, are paralyzed with terror, and he is totally unfit to manage the helm. Why then not avail thyself, in desperate circumstances, of one who, though a prisoner, is robust, well-skilled in such stormy scenes, and who even now appears calm and collected? Gessler's fear of Tell induced him at first to hesitate; but the prayers of the soldiers becoming pressing, he addressed the prisoner, and told him that if he thought himself capable of promoting the general safety, he should be forthwith unbound. Tell, having replied that by the grace of God he could still save them, was instantly freed from his shackles, and placed at the helm, when the boat answering to a master's hand, kept its course steadily through the bellowing surge, as if conscious of the free spirit which had now taken the command.

Guiding the obedient tiller at his will, Tell pointed the head of the boat in the direction whence they came, which he knew to be the only safe course, and encouraging and cheering the rowers, made rapid and steady progress through the water. The darkness, which now wrapped them round, prevented Gessler from discovering that he had turned his back on his destination. Tell continued on his way nearly the whole night, the dying light of the signal-fire on the mountain serving as a beacon in enabling him to approach the shores of Schwytz, and to avoid the shoals.

Between Sissigen and Fluelen are two mountains, the greater and the lesser Achsenberg, whose sides, hemming in and rising perpendicularly from the bed of the lake, offered not a single platform where human foot could stand. When near this place, dawn broke in the eastern sky, and Gessler, the danger appearing to decrease, scowled upon William Tell in sullen silence. As the prow of the vessel was driven inland, Tell perceived a solitary table rock, and called to the rowers to redouble their efforts till they should have passed the precipice ahead, observing with ominous truth that it was the most dangerous point on the whole lake.

The soldiers here recognized their position, and pointed it out to Gessler, who, with angry voice, demanded of Tell what he meant by taking them back to Altorf. William, without answering him, turned the helm hard a-port, which brought the boat suddenly close upon the rock, seized his faithful bow, and with an effort which sent the unguided craft back into the lake, sprang lightly on shore, scaled the rocks, and took to the direction of Schwytz.

Having thus escaped the clutches of the governor, he made for the hights which border the main road between Art and Kussnacht, and choosing a small hollow in the road, hid himself under cover of the brush, intending to remain in ambush until such time as the bailiff should pass that way. It appears that the governor had the utmost difficulty to save himself and his attendants after this sudden disappearance of their pilot, but at length succeeded in effecting a safe landing at Brunnen. Here they provided themselves with horses, and proceeding in the direction above alluded to, advanced towards Kussnacht. In the spot still known as "the hollow way," and marked by a chapel, Tell overheard the threats pronounced against himself should he be once more caught, and, in default of his apprehension, vengeance was vowed against his family. Tell felt that the safety of himself and his wife and children, to say nothing of the duty he owed to his country, required the tyrant's death. He instantly, therefore, showed himself, and seizing an opportune moment, pierced Gessler to the heart with one of his arrows.

This bold deed accomplished, the excited hero, effecting his escape, made the best of his way to Art, and thence soon gained the village of Steinen, where he found Werner Stauffacher preparing to march. The news, however, which Tell brought, removed the necessity for further immediate action, and prompt measures were taken to arrest the progress of their allies. A joy, which deeply proved the wrongs of the people, spread over the whole land, and though they delayed to strike the blow for universal freedom from the Austrian yoke, the final decision of the conspirators was only the greater.

On the morning of New-Year's Day, 1308, the castle of Rossberg, in Obwalden, was adroitly taken possession of, and its keeper, Berenger of Landenberg, made prisoner, and compelled to promise that he never again would set foot within the territory of the three cantons; after which he was allowed to retire to Lucerne. Stauffacher, during the earlier hours of the same morning, at the head of the men of Schwytz, marched towards the lake Lowerz, and destroyed the fortress of Schwannau; while Tell and the men of Uri took possession of Altorf. On the following Sunday the deputies of Uri, Schwytz, and Unterwalden met and renewed that fraternal league which has endured even unto this day.

In 1315, Leopold, second son of Albert, determined to punish the confederate cantons for their revolt, and accordingly marched against them at the head of a considerable army, accompanied by a numerous retinue of nobles. Count Otho of Strassberg, one of his ablest generals, crossed the Bruning with a body of four thousand men, intending to attack Upper Unterwalden. The bailiffs of Willisau, of Wollhausen, and of Lucerne, meantime armed a fourth of that number to make a descent on the lower division of the same canton; while the emperor in person, at the head of his army of reserve, poured down from Egerson on Morgarten, in the country of Schwytz, ostentatiously displaying an extensive supply of rope wherewith to hang the chiefs of the rebels—a hasty reckoning of victory, which reminds us of similar conduct and similar results when Wallace repulsed the invaders of Scotland.

The confederates, in whose ranks were William Tell and Furst, in order to oppose this formidable invasion, occupied a position in the mountains, bordering on the convent of our Lady of the Hermits. Four hundred men of Uri, and three hundred of Unterwalden, had effected a junction with the warriors of Schwytz, who formed the principal numerical force of this little army. Fifty men, banished from this latter canton, offered themselves to combat beneath their native banner, intending to efface, by their valor and conduct, the remembrance of their past faults. Early on the morning of the 15th of November, 1315, some thousands of well-armed Austrian knights slowly ascended the hill on which the Swiss were posted, with the hope of dislodging them; the latter, however, advanced to meet their enemies, uttering the most terrific cries. The band of banished men, having precipitated huge stones and fragments of rocks from the hill-sides, and from overhanging cliffs, rushed from behind the sheltering influence of a thick fog, and threw the advancing host into confusion. The Austrians immediately broke their ranks, and presently a complete route, with terrible slaughter, ensued. The confederates marched boldly on, cheered by the voice and example of Henry of Ospenthal, and of the sons of old Redding of Biberegg.

The flower of the Austrian chivalry perished on the field of Morgarten, beneath the halberts, arrows, and iron-headed clubs of the shepherds. Leopold himself, though he succeeded in gaining the shattered remnant of his forces, had a narrow escape; while the Swiss, animated by victory, hastened to Unterwalden, where they defeated a body of Lucernois and Austrians. In this instance Count Otho had as narrow an escape as the emperor. After these two well-fought fields, the confederates hastened to renew their ancient alliance, which was solemnly sworn to in an assembly held at Brunnen on the 8th day of December.

All that remains to be told of the Swiss hero's life is the immemorial tradition, that Wilhelm Tell, the same who shot Gessler in 1307, assisted at a general meeting of the commune of Uri in 1337, and perished in 1350, by an inundation which destroyed the village of Burglen, his birth-place. According to Klingenberg's chronicle, however, written towards the close of the fourteenth century, when many of his contemporaries were still living, Wilhelmus Tellus of Uri, as he calls him, the liberator of his country, became, after the battle of Morgarten, administrator of the affairs of the church of Beringer, where he died in 1354.

Switzerland owes more to the archer of Burglen than, at a rough glance, she might be supposed to do. It was his bold and decisive act which first roused within its people that spirit of independence, before slumbering, and since so great in its results: Tell showed them, by his example, what courage and prudence could effect, and gave an impulse to his countrymen of which they have not failed to ke advantage.

ELOQUENCE AND HUMOR OF PATRICK HENRY.

Hook was a Scotchman, a man of wealth, and suspected of being unfriendly to the American cause. During the distresses of the American army, consequent on the joint invasion of Cornwallis and Phillips in 1781, a Mr. Venable, an army commissary, had taken two of Hook's steers for the use of the troops. The act had not been strictly legal; and, on the establishment of peace, Hook, on the advice of Mr. Cowan, a gentleman of some distinction in the law, thought proper to bring an action of trespass against Mr. Venable, in the district court of New London. Mr. Henry appeared for the defendant, and is said to have disported himself in this cause to the infinite enjoyment of his hearers, the unfortunate Hook always excepted. After Mr. Henry became animated in the cause, says a correspondent, he appeared to have complete control over the passions of his audience: at one time he excited their indignation against Hook; vengeance was visible in every countenance: again, when he chose to relax, and ridicule him, the whole audience was in a roar of laughter. He painted the distresses of the American Army, exposed, almost naked, to the rigors of a winter's sky, and marking the frozen ground over which they trod with the blood of their unshod feet. Where was the man, he said, who had an American heart in his bosom, who would not have thrown open his fields, his barns, his cellars, the doors of his house, the portals of his breast, to have received with open arms the meanest soldier in that little band of famished patriots? Where is the man? *There* he stands—but whether the heart of an American beats in his bosom, you, gentlemen, are to judge. He then carried the jury by the powers of his imagination to the plains around York, the surrender of which had followed shortly after the act complained of: he depicted the surrender in the most glowing and noble colors of his eloquence—the audience saw before their eyes the humiliation and dejection of the British as they marched out of their trenches—they saw the triumph which lighted up every patriot face, and heard the shouts of victory, and the cry of "Washington and liberty!" as it rung and echoed through the American ranks, and was reverberated from the hills and shores of the neighboring river—"but hark! what notes of discord are these, which disturb the general joy, and silence the acclamation of victory —they are the notes of John Hook, hoarsely bawling through the American camp, '*Beef! beef! beef!*'"

The whole audience were convulsed: a particular incident will give a better idea of the effect than any general description. The clerk of the court, unable to command himself, and unwilling to commit any breach of decorum in his place, rushed out of the court-house, and threw himself on the grass, in the most violent paroxysm of laughter, where he was rolling, when Hook, with very different feelings, came out for relief into the yard also. "Jemmy Steptoe," said he to the clerk, "what the devil ails ye, mon?" Mr. Steptoe was only able to say that *he could not help it*. "Never mind ye," said Hook; "wait till Billy Cowan gets up; he'll show him the la'!" Mr. Cowan, however, was so completely overwhelmed by the torrent which bore upon his client, that, when he rose to reply to Mr. Henry, he was scarcely able to make an intelligible or audible remark. The cause was decided almost by acclamation. The jury retired for form's sake, and instantly returned with a verdict for the defendant. Nor did the effect of Mr. Henry's speech stop here. The people were so highly excited by the tory audacity of such a suit, that Hook began to hear around him a cry more terrible than that of *beef*; it was the cry of *tar and feathers*; from the application of which, it is said, that nothing saved him but a precipitate flight and the speed of his horse.—WIRT.

TALLEYRAND AND ARNOLD.

THERE was a day when Talleyrand arrived in Havre, hot foot from Paris. It was in the darkest hour of the French Revolution. Pursued by the bloodhounds of the Reign of Terror, stripped of every wreck of property or power, Talleyrand secured a passage to America in a ship about to sail. He was going a beggar and a wanderer, to a strange land, to earn his bread by daily labor.

"Is there an American staying at your house?" he asked the landlord of his hotel. "I am bound to cross the water, and would like a letter to some person of influence in the New World."

The landlord hesitated a moment, and then said:

"There is a gentleman up stairs, either from America or Britain; whether an American or Englishman, I cannot tell."

He pointed the way, and Talleyrand—who in his life was bishop, prince, and prime-minister—ascended the stairs. A miserable suppliant, he stood before the stranger's door, knocked, and entered.

In the far corner of a dimly-lighted room, sat a gentleman of some fifty years, with his arms folded, and his head bowed on his breast. From a window directly opposite, a flood of light poured over his forehead. His eyes looking from beneath the downcast brows, gazed in Talleyrand's face with a peculiar and searching expression. His face was striking in its outline; the mouth and chin indicative of an iron will. His form, vigorous, even with the snows of fifty winters, was clad in dark, but rich and distinguished costume.

Talleyrand advanced: stated that as he was an American, he solicited his kind and feeling offices.

He poured forth his history in eloquent French and broken English. "I am a wanderer—an exile. I am forced to fly to the New World, without a friend or home. You are an American. Give me, then, I beseech you, a letter of yours, so that I may be able to earn my bread. I am willing to toil in any manner: the scenes of Paris have filled me with such horror, that a life of labor would be a paradise to a career of luxury in France. You will give me a letter to one of your friends. A gentleman like you has doubtless many friends."

The strange gentleman rose. With a look that Talleyrand never forgot, he retreated towards the door of the next chamber, his head downcast, and his eyes looking still from beneath his darkened brow. He spoke as he retreated: his voice was full of meaning.

"I am the only man born in the New World who can raise his hand to God and say—I have not a friend—not one in all America."

Talleyrand never forgot the overwhelming sadness of that look which accompanied these words."

"Who are you?" he cried, as the strange man retreated towards the next room. "Your name?"

"My name!"—with a smile that had more of mockery than joy in its conclusive expression—"my name is Benedict Arnold!"

He was gone. Talleyrand sank in a chair, gasping the words—

"Arnold the Traitor!"

Thus, you see, he wandered over the earth, another Cain, with a wanderer's mark upon his brow. Even in this secluded room at the Inn of Havre, his crimes found him out, and forced him to tell his name—that synonym of infamy.

The last twenty years of his life are covered with a cloud, from whose darkness but a few gleams of light flash out upon the page of history.

The manner of his death is not distinctly known. But we doubt not that he died utterly friendless—that his cold brow was not moistened by one farewell tear—that remorse pursued him to the grave, whispering "John Andre" in his ears; and the memory of his course of glory gnawed like a canker at his heart, murmuring forever, "True to your country, what might you have been, O Arnold, the Traitor!"

ANECDOTE OF JAMES OTIS.

Otis belonged to a club who met on evenings; of which club William Molineux was a member. Molineux had a petition before the legislature, which did not succeed to his wishes, and he became for several evenings sour, and wearied the company with his complaints of services, losses, sacrifices, &c., and said—"That a man who has behaved as I have should be treated as I am is intolerable!" Otis had said nothing; but the company were disgusted and out of patience, when Otis rose from his seat, and said—"Come, come, Will, quit this subject, and let us enjoy ourselves. I also have a list of grievances; will you hear it?" The club expected some fun, and all cried out, "Ay! ay! let us hear your list."

"Well, then, Will: in the first place, I resigned the office of advocate-general, which I held from the crown, that produced me—how much do you think?" "A great deal, no doubt," said Molineux. "Shall we say two hundred sterling a year?" "Ay, more, I believe," said Molineux. "Well, let it be two hundred; that, for ten years, is two thousand.

"In the next place, I have been obliged to relinquish the greatest part of my business at the bar. Will you set that at two hundred more?" "Oh! I believe it much more than that." "Well, let it be two hundred; this, for ten years, is two thousand more. You allow, then, I have lost four thousand pounds sterling," "Ay, and much more too," said Molineux.

"In the next place, I have lost an hundred friends; among whom were the men of the first rank, fortune and power in the province. At what price will you estimate them?" "At nothing," said Molineux; "you are better without them, than with them." A loud laugh. "Be it so," said Otis.

"In the next place, I have made a thousand enemies, among whom are the government of the province and the nation. What do you think of this item?" "That is as it may happen," said Molineux.

"In the next place, you know, I love pleasure; but I have renounced all amusement for ten years. What is that worth to a man of pleasure?" "No great matter," said Molineux; "you have made politics your amusement." A hearty laugh.

"In the next place, I have ruined as fine health, and as good a constitution of body, as nature ever gave to man." "This is melancholy indeed," said Molineux; "there is nothing to be said on that point."

"Once more," said Otis, holding his head down before Molineux; "look upon this head!" (where was a scar, in which a man might bury his finger;) "what do you think of this? and, what is worse, my friends think I have a monstrous crack in my skull."

This made all the company very grave, and look very solemn. But Otis, setting up a laugh, and with a gay countenance, said to Molineux—"Now, Willy, my advice to you is, to say no more about your grievances; for you and I had better put up our accounts of profit and loss in our pockets, and say no more about them, lest the world should laugh at us."

This whimsical dialogue put all the company, and Molineux himself, into good humor, and they passed the rest of the evening in joyous conviviality.—J. ADAMS.

INDIAN SPEECHES.

ELOQUENT SPEECH OF LOGAN, CHIEF OF THE MINGOES.

I MAY challenge the whole orations of Demosthenes and Cicero, and of any more eminent orator, if Europe has furnished more eminent, to produce a single passage superior to the speech of Logan, a Mingo chief, to Lord Dunmore, when governor of this state. And, as a testimony of their talents in this line, I beg leave to introduce it, first stating the incidents necessary for understanding it.

In the spring of the year 1774, a robbery was committed by some Indians on certain land adventurers on the river of Ohio. The whites in that quarter, according to their custom, undertook to punish this outrage in a summary way. Captain Michael Cresap and a certain Daniel Greathouse, leading on the parties, surprised, at different times, traveling and hunting parties of the Indians, having their women and children with them, and murdered many. Among these were unfortunately the family of Logan, a chief celebrated in peace and war, and long distinguished as the friend of the whites. This unworthy return provoked his vengeance. He accordingly signalized himself in the war which ensued. In the autumn of the same year a decisive battle was fought at the mouth of the Great Kanhaway, between the collected forces of the Shawanese, Mingoes and Delawares, and a detachment of the Virginia militia. The Indians were defeated, and sued for peace. Logan, however, disdained to be seen among the suppliants. But, lest the sincerity of a treaty should be distrusted, from which so distinguished a chief absented himself, he sent, by a messenger, the following speech to be delivered to Lord Dunmore.

"I appeal to any white man to say, if ever he entered Logan's cabin hungry, and he gave him not meat; if ever he came cold and naked, and clothed him not. During the course of the last long and bloody war, Logan remained idle in his cabin, an advocate for peace. Such was my love for the whites, that my countrymen pointed as they passed, and said, 'Logan is the friend of white men.' I had even thought to have lived with you, but for the injuries of one man. Colonel Cresap, the last spring, in cold blood, and unprovoked, murdered all the relations of Logan, not even sparing my women and children. There runs not a drop of my blood in the veins of any living creature. This called on me for revenge. I have sought it: I have killed many: I have fully glutted my vengeance. For my country, I rejoice at the beams of peace: but do not harbor a thought that mine is the joy of fear: Logan never felt fear: he will not turn on his heel to save his life. Who is there to mourn for Logan? Not one."—JEFFERSON.

SPEECH OF HO-NA-YU-WUS, OR FARMER'S BROTHER.

THE sachems, chiefs, and warriors of the Seneca nation to the sachems and chiefs assembled about the great council-fire of the state of New York.

Brothers: As you are once more assembled in council for the purpose of doing honor to yourselves and justice to your country, we, your brothers, the sachems, chiefs, and warriors of the Seneca nation, request you to open your ears, and give attention to our voice and wishes

Brothers—You will recollect the late contest between you and your father, the great king of England. This contest threw the inhabitants of this whole island into a great tumult and commotion, like a raging whirlwind, which tears up the trees, and tosses to and fro the leaves, so that no one knows from whence they come, or when they will fall.

Brothers—This whirlwind was so directed by the Great Spirit above, as to throw into our arms two of your infant children, Jasper Parrish and Horatio Jones. We adopted them into our families, and made them our children. We loved them and nourished them. They lived with us many years. At length the Great Spirit spoke to the whirlwind—and it was still. A clear and uninterrupted sky appeared. The path of peace was opened, and the chain of friendship was once more made bright. Then these, our adopted children, left us to seek their relations. We wished them to remain among us, and promised, if they would return and live in our country, to give each of them a seat of land for them and their children to sit down upon.

Brothers—They have returned, and have for several years past been serviceable to us as interpreters. We still feel our hearts beat with affection for them, and now wish to fulfill the promise we made them, and to reward them for their services. We have, therefore, made up our minds to give them a seat of two square miles of land lying on the outlet of Lake Erie, about three miles below Black Rock.

Brothers—We have now made known to you our minds. We expect and earnestly request, that you will permit our friends to receive this our gift, and will make the same good to them, according to the laws and customs of your nation.

Brothers—Why should you hesitate to make our minds easy with regard to this our request? To you it is but a little thing; and have you not complied with the request, and confirmed the gift, of our brothers the Oneidas, the Onondagas, and Cayugas, to their interpreters? and shall we ask, and not be heard?

Brothers—We send you this our speech, to which we expect your answer before the breaking up of your great council-fire.

SPEECH OVER THE GRAVE OF BLACK BUFFALOE, CHIEF OF THE TETON TRIBE OF INDIANS.

Do not grieve. Misfortune will happen to the wisest and best men. Death will come, and always comes out of season. It is the command of the Great Spirit, and all nations and people must obey. What has passed, and cannot be prevented, should not be grieved for. Be not discouraged or displeased, then, that, in visiting your father here, you have lost your chief. A misfortune of this kind may never again befall you; but this would have attended you, perhaps, at your own village. Five times have I visited this land, and never returned with sorrow or pain. Misfortunes do not flourish particularly in our path. They grow everywhere. What a misfortune for me, that I could not have died this day, instead of the chief that lies before us!

The trifling loss my nation would have sustained in my death, would have been doubly paid for by the honors of my burial. They would have wiped off every thing like regret. Instead of being covered with a cloud of sorrow, my warriors would have felt the sunshine of joy in their hearts. To me it would have been a most glorious occurrence. Hereafter, when I die at home, instead of a noble grave and a grand procession—the rolling music and the thundering cannon—with a flag waving at my head,—I shall be wrapt in a robe—an old robe perhaps—and hoisted on a slender scaffold to the whistling winds, soon to be blown to the earth—my flesh to be devoured by the wolves, and my bones rattled on the plain by the wild beasts.

Chief of the soldiers!—your labors have not been in vain. Your attention shall not be forgotten. My nation shall know the respect that is paid over the dead. When I return I will echo the sound of your guns.—BIG ELK MAHA CHIEF.

DEATH OF PLINY THE ELDER.

THE following celebrated letter was written by Pliny the younger to his friend Tacitus. We give it a place in the *Gathered Treasures* for its *classical* merit, as well as for recording the melancholy death of a noble Roman citizen, by the memorable eruption of Mount Vesuvius, in the 39th year of the Christian era. Pliny the elder was residing at Misenum, on the northern promontory of the Gulf of Naples, when the eruption occurred, and which overwhelmed the cities of Herculaneum and Pompeii, occasioning the death of thousands of the unfortunate inhabitants.

"Your request that I would send you an account of my uncle's death, in order to transmit a more exact relation of it to posterity, deserves my acknowledgments; for if this accident shall be celebrated by your pen, the glory of it, I am well assured, will be rendered forever illustrious; and, notwithstanding he perished by a misfortune, which, as it involved at the same time a most beautiful country in ruins, and destroyed so many populous cities, seems to promise him an everlasting remembrance; notwithstanding he has himself composed many and lasting works; yet I am persuaded the mentioning of him in your immortal writings will greatly contribute to eternise his name. Happy I esteem those to be whom Providence has distinguished with the abilities either of doing such actions as are worthy of being related, or of relating them in a manner worthy of being read; but doubly happy are they who are blessed with both these uncommon talents; in the number of which my uncle, as his own writings and your history will evidently prove, may justly be ranked. It is with extreme willingness, therefore, that I execute your commands;

and should indeed have claimed the task, if you had not enjoined it.

"My uncle was at the time with the fleet under his command at Misenum. On the 23rd of August, about one o'clock in the afternoon, my mother desired him to observe a cloud which appeared of a very unusual size and shape. He had just returned from taking the benefit of the sun,* and after bathing himself in cold water, and taking a slight repast, had retired to his study. He immediately arose and went out upon an eminence from which he might more distinctly view this very uncommon appearance. It was not at that distance discernible from what mountain this cloud issued, but it was found afterwards to ascend from Mount Vesuvius. I cannot give you a more exact description of its figure than by resembling it to that of a pine tree, for it shot up a great hight in the form of a trunk, which extended itself at the top into a sort of branches; occasioned, I imagine, either by a sudden gust of air that impelled it, the force of which decreased as it advanced upwards: or the cloud itself being pressed back again by its own weight, expanded in this manner. It appeared sometimes bright, and sometimes dark and spotted, as it was either more or less impregnated with earth and cinders. This extraordinary phenomenon excited my uncle's philosophical curiosity to take a nearer view of it. He ordered a light vessel to be got ready, and gave me the liberty, if I thought proper, to attend him. I rather chose to continue my studies; for, as it happened, he had given me an employment of that kind. As he was coming out of the house, he received a note from Rectina, the wife of Bassus, who was in the utmost alarm at the imminent danger which threatened her; for her villa being situated at the foot of Mount Vesuvius, there was no way to escape but by sea. She earnestly entreated him, therefore, to come to her assistance. He accordingly changed his first design, and what he began with a philosophical, he pursued with a heroical turn of mind. He ordered the galleys to put to sea, and went himself on board, with an intention of assisting not only Rectina, but several others; for the villas stand extremely thick upon the beautiful coast. When hastening to the place from which others fled with the utmost terror, he steered his direct course to the point of danger, and with so much calmness and presence of mind, as to be able to make and dictate his observations upon the motion and figure of that dreadful scene. He was now so nigh the mountain that the cinders, which grew thicker and hotter the nearer he approached, fell into the ships, together with pumice-stones, and black pieces of burning rock; they were likewise in danger not only of being aground by the sudden retreat of the sea, but also from the vast fragments which rolled down from the mountain, and obstructed all the shore. Here he stopped to consider whether he should return back again, to which the pilot advising him—'Fortune favors the brave,' said he; 'carry me to Pomponianus.'

"Pomponianus was then at Stabiæ, separated by a gulf which the sea, after several insensible windings, forms upon that shore. He had already sent his baggage on board; for though he was not at that time in actual danger, yet being within the view of it, and indeed extremely near if it should in the least increase, he was determined to put to sea as soon as the wind should change. It was favorable, however, for carrying my uncle to Pomponianus, whom he found in the greatest consternation. He embraced him with tenderness, encouraging and exhorting him to keep up his spirits; and the more to dissipate his fears, he ordered, with an air of unconcern, the baths to be got ready; when, after having bathed, he sat down to supper with great cheerfulness, or at least (what is equally heroic,) with all the appearance of it. In the meanwhile, the eruption from Mount Vesuvius flamed out in several places with much violence, which the darkness of the night contributed to render still more visible and dreadful. But my uncle, in order to soothe the apprehensions of his friend, assured him it was only the burning of the villages, which the country people had abandoned to the flames. After this he retired to rest, and it is most certain he was so little discomposed as to fall into a deep sleep; for, being pretty fat, and breathing hard, those who attended without actually heard him snore. The court which led to his apartment being now almost filled with stones and ashes, if he had continued there any time longer, it would have been impossible for him to have made his way out; it was thought proper, therefore, to awaken him. He got up, and went to Pomponianus and the rest of his company, who were not unconcerned enough to think of going to bed. They consulted together whether it would be most prudent to trust to the houses, which now shook from side to side with frequent and violent concussions, or fly to the open fields, where the calcined stones and cinders, though light indeed, yet fell in large showers, and threatened destruction. In this distress they resolved for the fields, as the less dangerous situation of the two; a resolution which, while the rest of the company were hurried into it by their fears, my uncle embraced upon cool and deliberate consideration.

"They went out then, having pillows tied upon their heads with napkins, and this was their whole defence against the storm of stones that fell round them. Though it was day everywhere else, with them it was darker than the most obscure night, excepting only what light proceeded from the fire and flames. They thought proper to go down further upon the shore, to observe if they might safely put out to sea; but they found the waves still run extremely high and boisterous. There my uncle having drunk a draught or two of cold water, threw himself down upon a cloth which was spread for him, when immediately the flames, and a strong smell of sulphur, which was the forerunner of them, dispersed the rest of the company, and obliged him to arise. He raised himself up with the assistance of two of his servants, and instantly fell down dead; suffocated, as I conjecture, by some gross and noxious vapor, having always had weak lungs, and frequently subjected to a difficulty of breathing. As soon as it was light again, which was not till the third day after this melancholy accident, his body was found entire, and without any marks of violence upon it, exactly in the same posture that he fell, and looking more like a man asleep than dead."

DEATH OF JOHN RANDOLPH.

JOHN RANDOLPH of Roanoke was near his end. Dr. —— was sitting by the table, and his man John sitting by the bed, in perfect silence, when he closed his eyes, and for a few moments seemed, by his hard breathing, to be asleep. But, as the sequel proved, it was the intense working of his mind. Opening his keen eyes upon the doctor, he said, sharply, "*remorse*"—soon afterward more emphatically, "REMORSE"—presently at the top of his strength, he cried out, "REMORSE!" He then added, "Let me see the word." The doctor, not comprehending his desire, made no reply. Randolph then said to him with great energy, "Let me see the word: show it me in a dictionary." The doctor looked round and told him he believed there was none in the room. "Write it then," said Randolph. The doctor perceiving one of Randolph's engraved cards lying on the table, wrote the word in pencil under the printed name, and handed it to Randolph. He seized it, and holding it up to his eyes with great earnestness, seemed much agitated. After a few seconds, he handed back the card, saying, "Write it on the other side." The doctor did so, in larger letters. He took it again, and after gazing upon it a few seconds, returned it, and said, "Lend John your pencil, and let him put a stroke under it." John took the pencil and did so, leaving it on the table. "Ah!" said the dying man, "*Remorse*, you don't know what it means! you don't know what it means!" But added presently, "I cast myself on the Lord Jesus Christ for mercy."

WASHINGTON'S DEB[illegible]

ONE Reuben Rouzy, of Virginia, owed [illegible] thousand pounds. While President of the United States, one of his agents brought an action for the money; judgment was obtained, and execution issued against the body of the defendant, who was taken to jail. He had a considerable landed estate, but this kind of property cannot be sold in Virginia for debts unless at the discretion of the person. He had a large family, and for the sake of his children preferred lying in jail to selling his land. A friend hinted to him that probably General Washington did not know any thing of the proceeding, and that it might be well to send him a petition, with a statement of the circumstances. He did so, and the very next post from Philadelphia, after the arrival of his petition in that city, brought him an order for his immediate release, together with a full discharge and a severe reprimand to the agent for having acted in such a manner. Poor Rouzy was, in consequence, restored to his family, who never laid down their heads at night without presenting prayers to Heaven for their "beloved Washington."

Providence smiled upon the labors of the grateful family, and in a few years Rouzy enjoyed the exquisite pleasure of being able to lay the one thousand pounds, with the interest, at the feet of this truly great man. Washington reminded him that the debt was discharged. Rouzy replied, the debt of his family to the father of their country and preserver of their parent could never be discharged; and the general, to avoid the pressing importunity of the grateful Virginian, who would not be denied, accepted the money, only, however, to divide it among Rouzy's children, which he immediately did.

CONFESSION OF ROUSSEAU.

I CONFESS that the majesty of the Scriptures astonishes me, that the sanctity of the Gospel speaks to my heart. View the books of the philosophers with all their pomp, what a littleness have they, when compared with this. Is it possible that a book, at once so sublime and simple, should be the work of men? Is it possible that he, whose history it records, should be himself a mere man? Is this the style of an enthusiast, or of an ambitious sectary? What sweetness, what purity in his manners! what affecting grace in his instructions! what elevation in his maxims! what profound wisdom in his discourses! what presence of mind, what delicacy, and what justness in his replies! what empire over his passions! Where is the man, where is the philosopher, who knows how to act, to suffer and die without weakness and without ostentation? When Plato paints his imaginary just man, covered with all the ignominy of guilt, and deserving all the honors of virtue, he paints Jesus Christ in every stroke of his pencil! Their semblance is so strong that all the fathers have perceived it, and it is not possible to mistake it. What prejudices, what blindness must they have, who draw a comparison between the son of Soproniscus and the son of Mary? What distance is there between the one and the other? As Socrates died without pain and disgrace, he found no difficulty in supporting his character to the end; and if this easy death had not shed lustre on his life, we might have doubted whether Socrates, with all his genius, was any thing but a sophist. They say that he invented morality. Others before him had practiced it; he only said what they had done, he only read lessons on their examples. Aristides was just, before Socrates explained the nature of justice. Leonidas had died for his country, before Socrates had made it the duty of men to love their country. Sparta had been temperate, before Socrates praised temperance. Greece had abounded in virtuous men, before he had defined virtue. But where could Jesus have taken among his countrymen that elevated and pure morality of which he himself furnished both the precept and the example? The most lofty wisdom was heard from the bosom of the most furious fanaticism, and the simplicity of the most heroic virtues honored the vilest of all people. The death of Socrates, divinely philosophizing with his friends, is the most gentle that one can desire; that of Jesus expiring in torments, injured, derided, reviled by a whole people, is the most horrible that one can fear. When Socrates takes the poisoned cup, he blesses him who presents it, and who at the same time weeps. Jesus, in the midst of a horrid punishment, prays for his enraged executioners. Yes, if the life and death of Socrates are those of a philosopher, the life and death of Jesus Christ are those of a God! Shall we say that the history of the Gospel is invented at pleasure? My friend, it is not thus that men invent; and the actions of Socrates, concerning which there are no doubts, are less attested than those of Jesus Christ. After all, this is shifting the difficulty instead of solving it; for it would be more conceivable that a number of men should forge this book in concert, than that one should furnish the subject of it. Jewish authors would never have devised such a manner and such morality, and the gospel characters of truth; so great, so striking, so perfectly inimitable, that its inventor would be still more astonished than its hero.

LUTHER SUMMONED TO WORMS.

When Luther was summoned to attend the diet at Worms, his friends, notwithstanding the safe-conduct granted to him by the emperor, Charles V., apprehending danger to his person, would have dissuaded him from going thither. Luther replied, "I am determined to enter the city in the name of the Lord Jesus Christ, though as many devils should oppose me as there are tiles upon all the houses at Worms." He was accompanied from Wirtemberg by some divines, and one hundred horse; but he took only eight horsemen into Worms. When he stept out of the carriage, he said, in the presence of a great number of persons, "God shall be on my side."

CROMWELL AND THE FLORENTINE MERCHANT.

Francis Frescobald, a Florentine merchant, descended of a noble family in Italy, had gained a plentiful fortune, of which he was liberal-handed to all in necessity; which being well known to others, though concealed by himself, a young stranger applied to him for charity. Signior Frescobald, seeing something in his countenance more than ordinary, overlooked his tattered clothes, and compassionating his circumstance, asked him what he was, and of what country. "I am," answered the young man, "a native of England; my name is Thomas Cromwell, and my father-in-law is a poor shire-man. I left my country to seek my fortune; came with the French army that were routed at Gatylion, where I was page to a footman, and carried his pike and burgonet after him." Frescobald commiserating his necessities, and having a particular respect for the English nation, clothed him genteelly, took him into his house till he had recovered strength by better diet, and, at his taking leave, mounted him on a good horse, with sixteen ducats of gold in his pockets. Cromwell expressed his thankfulness in a very sensible manner, and returned by land towards England; where, being arrived, he was preferred into the services of Cardinal Wolsey.

After the cardinal's death, he worked himself so effectually into the favor of King Henry VIII., that his majesty made him a baron, viscount, Earl of Essex, and, at last, lord chancellor of England. In the meantime, Signior Frescobald, by repeated losses at sea and land, was reduced to poverty; and, calling to mind, without ever thinking of Cromwell, that some English merchants were indebted to him in the sum of fifteen thousand ducats, he came to London to procure payment.

Traveling in pursuit of this affair, he fortunately met with the lord chancellor, as he was riding to court; who, thinking him to be the same gentleman that had done him such great kindness in Italy, immediately alighted, embraced him, and, with tears of joy, asked him if he was not Signior Francis Frescobald, a Florentine merchant. "Yes, sir," said he, "and your most humble servant." "My servant!" said the chancellor. "No; you are my special friend, that relieved me in my wants, laid the foundation of my greatness, and as such I received you; and since the affairs of my sovereign will not now permit a longer conference, I beg you will oblige me this day with your company at my house to dine with me."

Signior Frescobald was surprised and astonished with admiration who this great man should be, that acknowledged such obligations, and so passionately expressed a kindness for him; but, contemplating awhile his mien, his voice and carriage, he concluded it to be Cromwell, whom he had relieved at Florence; and, therefore, not a little overjoyed, went to his house. His lordship came soon after, and taking his friend by the hand, turned to the lord high admiral, and other noblemen in his company, saying, "Do not your lordships wonder that I am so glad to see this gentleman? This is he who first contributed to my advancement." He then told them the whole story, and holding him still by the hand, led him into the dining-room, and placed him next himself at table. The company being gone, the chancellor made use of this opportunity to know what affair had brought him into England. Frescobald, in a few words, gave him a true state of his circumstances; to which Cromwell replied, "I am sorry for your misfortunes, and I will make them as easy to you as I can; but, because men ought to be just before they are kind, it is fit I should repay the debt I owe you." Then leading him to his closet, he locked the door, and, opening a coffer, first took out sixteen ducats, delivering them to Frescobald, and said, "My friend, here is the money you lent me at Florence, with ten pieces you laid out for my apparel, and ten more you paid for my horse; but considering that you are a merchant, and might have made some advantage by this money in the way of trade, take these four bags, in every one of which are four hundred ducats, and enjoy them as free gifts of your friend." These the modesty of Frescobald would have refused, but the other forced them upon him. He next caused him to give him the names of all his debtors, and the sums they owed; which account he gave to one of his servants, with a charge to find out the men, and oblige them to pay him in fifteen days, under the penalty of his displeasure; and the servant so well discharged his duty, that in a short time the entire sum was paid. All this time, Signior Frescobald lodged in the chancellor's house, where he was entertained according to his merits, was repeatedly invited to continue in England, and an offer of the loan of sixty thousand ducats for four years, if he would trade here; but he desired to return to Florence, which he did, with extraordinary favors from Cromwell.

TRUE MORAL COURAGE.

The Rev. Mr. Fletcher had a wild and profligate nephew in the army, who had been dismissed from the Sardinian service, for very bad conduct. He had engaged in several duels, and had spent his money in vice and folly. The wicked youth waited one day on his eldest uncle, General De Gons; and presenting a loaded pistol, threatened to shoot him, unless he would that *moment* advance him five hundred crowns. The general, though a brave man, well knew what a desperate fellow he had to deal with, and gave a draft for the money, at the same time, speaking freely to him on his conduct. The young man departed in high spirits, with his ill-gotten money.

In the evening, passing the door of his younger uncle, Mr. Fletcher, he called on him, and began with informing him, what General De

Gons had done; and, as a proof, showed a draft under De Gons' own hand. Mr. Fletcher took the draft from his nephew, and looked at him with surprise. Then after some remarks putting it into his pocket, said, "It strikes me, young man, that you have possessed yourself of this note by some wrong method; and in conscience, I cannot return it, but with my brother's knowledge and approbation." The nephew's pistol was in a moment at his breast. "My life," replied Mr. Fletcher, with perfect calmness, "is secure in the protection of an Almighty power; nor will he suffer it to be the forfeit of my integrity, and your rashness." This firmness drew from the nephew the observation, "that his uncle De Gons, though an old soldier, was more afraid of death than his brother." "Afraid of death!" rejoined Mr. Fletcher, "do you think I have been twenty-five years a minister of the Lord of life, to be afraid of death now? No, sir, it is for *you* to be afraid of death. *You* are a gamester and a cheat; yet you call yourself a gentleman! *You* are the seducer of female innocence; and still say you are a gentleman! *You* are a duellist, and for this you style yourself a man of honor! Look there, sir," pointing to the heavens, "the broad eye of Heaven is fixed upon us. Tremble in the presence of your Maker, who can in a moment kill your body, and forever punish your soul in hell."

The unhappy young prodigal turned pale, and trembled, with fear and rage. He still threatened his uncle, with instant death. Mr. Fletcher, though thus threatened, gave no alarm, sought for no weapon, and attempted not to escape. He calmly conversed with his profligate relation; and, at length, perceiving him to be affected, addressed him in the kindest language, till he fairly disarmed and subdued him! He would not return his brother's draft; but engaged to procure for the young man some immediate relief. He then prayed with him; and after fulfilling his promise of assistance, parted with him, with much good advice on one side, and many fair promises on the other.

WESLEY'S CHARITY.

In the year —— the Rev. John Wesley received the following letter, in consequence of a recent resolution of the government, that circulars should be sent to all persons who were suspected of having plate, on which they had not paid duty:

"*Reverend Sir*,—As the commissioners cannot doubt that you have plate for which you have hitherto neglected to make an entry, they have directed me to send you a copy of the lords' order, and to inform you that they expect that you forthwith make the entry of all your plate, such an entry to bear date from the commencement of the plate duty, or from such time as you have owned, used, had, or kept any quantity of silver plate, chargeable by the act of parliament; as in default thereof, the board will be obliged to signify your refusal to their lordships.

"N. B. An immediate answer is desired."

Mr. Wesley replied as follows:

"Sir,—I have two silver tea-spoons at London, and two at Bristol: this is all the plate which I have at present; and I shall not buy any more while so many around me want bread.

I am, sir, your most humble servant,

JOHN WESLEY."

Perhaps there never was a more charitable man than Mr. Wesley. His liberality knew no bounds, but an empty pocket. He gave away not merely a certain part of his income, but all that he had: his own wants being provided for, he devoted all the rest to the necessities of others. He entered upon this good work at a very early period. We are told, that when he had thirty pounds a year, he lived on twenty-eight, and gave away forty shillings. The next year, receiving sixty pounds, he still lived on twenty-eight, and gave away two-and-thirty. The third year he received ninety pounds, and gave away sixty-two. The fourth year he received one hundred and twenty pounds. Still he lived on twenty-eight, and gave to the poor ninety-two. During the rest of his life he lived economically; and, in the course of fifty years, it has been supposed, he gave away more than thirty thousand pounds—over one hundred and thirty-eight thousand dollars.

WHITEFIELD'S PREACHING.

As a proof of the power of Mr. Whitefield's preaching, Mr. Newton mentioned, that an officer at Glasgow, who had heard him preach, laid a wager with another, that at a certain charity sermon, though he went with prejudice, he would be compelled to give something; the other to make sure that he would not, laid all the money out of his pockets; but, before he left the church, he was glad to borrow some, and lose his bet. Mr. Newton mentioned, as another striking example of Mr. Whitefield's persuasive oratory, his collecting at one sermon six hundred pounds for the inhabitants of an obscure village in Germany, that had been burned down. After sermon, Mr. Whitefield said, "We shall sing a hymn, during which those who do not choose to give their mite on this awful occasion, may sneak off." Not one moved; he got down from the pulpit, ordered all the doors to be shut but one, at which he held the plate himself, and collected the above large sum Mr. Newton related what he knew to be a fact, that at the time cf Whitefield's greatest persecution, when obliged to preach in the streets, in one week he received not fewer than a thousand letters from persons distressed in their consciences by the energy of his preaching.

ANOTHER.

An extraordinary attestation to the excellence of Mr. Whitefield, as a preacher, was furnished by Hume, the historian, well known for his infidelity. An intimate friend having asked him what he thought of Mr. Whitefield's preaching. "He is, sir," said Mr. Hume, "the most ingenious preacher I ever heard: it is worth while to go twenty miles to hear him." He then repeated the following passage, which occurred towards the close of the discourse he had been hearing: "After a solemn pause, Mr. Whitefield thus addressed his numerous audience:—'The attendant angel is just about to leave the threshold, and ascend to heaven. And shall he ascend, and not bear with him the news of one sinner, among all this multitude, reclaimed from the error of his ways?' To give the greater effect to this exclamation, he stamped with his foot, lifted up his eyes and hands to heaven, and with gushing tears, cried aloud, 'Stop, Gabriel! Stop, Gabriel! Stop, ere you enter the sacred portals, and yet carry with you the news of one sinner converted to God.' He then, in the most simple, but energetic language, described what he called a Saviour's dying love to sinful man, so that almost the whole assembly melted into tears. This address was accompanied with such animated, yet natural action, that it surpassed any thing I ever saw or heard in any other preacher."

Happy had it been for Mr. Hume, if, in addition to his admiration of the preacher, he had received the doctrine which he taught, and afforded an instance of that conversion to God which Mr. Whitefield so ardently longed for on behalf of his hearers.

EDWARD COLSTON, THE BRISTOL MERCHANT.

Edward Colston, at the age of forty years, became a very eminent East India merchant, prior to the incorporation of the East India Company, and had forty sail of ships of his own, with immense riches flowing in upon him. He still remained uniform in his charitable disposition, distributing many thousand pounds to various charities in and about London, besides private gifts in many parts of the kingdom. In the year 1708, he instituted a very magnificent school in St. Augustine's-back, in Bristol, which cost him £11,000 in the building, and endowed the same with between £1,700, and £1,800 per annum forever. He likewise gave £10 for apprenticeing every boy, and for twelve years after his death £10 to put them into business. It has been frequently reported that his private charities far exceeded those in public. "We have heard," says the British Journal," that one of his ships trading to the East Indies had been missing upwards of three years, and was supposed to be destroyed at sea, but at length she arrived, richly laden. When his principal clerk brought him the report of her arrival, and of the riches on board, he said, as she was totally given up for lost, he would by no means claim any right to her; therefore he ordered the ship and merchandise to be sold, and the produce thereof to be applied towards the relief of the needy, which directions were immediately carried into execution. Another singular instance of his tender consciousness for charity was at the age of forty, when he entertained some thoughts of changing his condition. He paid his addresses to a lady, but being very timorous lest he should be hindered in his pious and charitable designs, he was determined to make a Christian trial of her temper and disposition, and therefore one morning filled his pockets with gold and silver, in order that, if any object presented itself in the course of their tour over London bridge, he might satisfy his intentions. While they were walking near St. Magnus Church, a poor woman solicited for alms. He beheld the wretched object, put his hand in his pocket, and took out a handful of gold and silver, casting it into the poor woman's lap. The lady being greatly alarmed at such profuse generosity, colored prodigiously; so that, when they were gone a little further towards the bridge-foot, she turned to him, and said, "Sir, do you know what you did a few minutes ago?" "Madam," replied Mr. Colston, "I never let my right hand know what my left hand doeth." He then took his leave of her, and for this reason never married to the day of his death, although he lived to the age of eighty-five.

EARL FITZWILLIAM, AND THE HONEST FARMER.

A FARMER called on the Earl Fitzwilliam to represent to him that his crop of wheat had been seriously injured in a field adjoining a certain wood where his lordship's hounds had during the winter frequently met to hunt. He stated that the young wheat had been so cut up and destroyed that in some parts he could not hope for any produce. "Well, my friend," said his lordship, "I am aware that we have frequently met in that field, and that we have done considerable injury; and if you can procure an estimate of the loss you have sustained I will repay you." The farmer replied, that anticipating his lordship's consideration and kindness, he had requested a friend to assist him in estimating the damage, and they thought that as the crop seemed quite destroyed, fifty pounds would not more than repay him. The earl immediately gave him the money.

As the harvest, however, approached, the wheat grew, and in those parts of the field which were most trampled the corn was strongest and most luxuriant. The farmer went again to his lordship, and being introduced, said, "I am come, my lord, respecting the field of wheat adjoining such a wood." His lordship immediately recollected the circumstance. "Well, my friend, did not I allow you sufficient to remunerate you for your loss?" "Yes, my lord, I find that I have sustained no loss at all, for where the horses had most cut up the land the crop is most promising, and I have therefore brought the fifty pounds back again." "Ah!" exclaimed the venerable earl, "this is what I like; this is as it should be between man and man." He then entered into conversation with the farmer, asking him some questions about his family—how many children he had, &c. His lordship then went into another room, and returning, presented the farmer with a cheque for one hundred pounds, saying, "Take care of this, and when your eldest son is of age present it to him, and tell him the occasion that produced it." We know not which to admire most, the honesty of the farmer on the one hand, or on the other, the benevolence and the wisdom displayed by this illustrious man; for while doing a noble act of generosity, he was handing down a lesson of integrity to another generation.

ANOTHER BRUTUS

In the reign of Henry the Eighth, Fitz-Stephen, merchant, Mayor of Galway, sent his only son, as commander of a ship, to Spain, for a cargo of wine. The son kept the money for the purchase of the cargo; and the Spanish merchant, who supplied the wine, sent his nephew to receive the debt. To conceal his fraud, young Fitz-Stephen conceived the plan of murdering the Spaniard; a project, in which he brought the crew to combine. The Spaniard was seized in bed, thrown overboard, and the ship arrived in port.

Some time after, one of the sailors was taken ill, and, being at the point of death, confessed the horrid deed in which he had participated. The father, though struck with horror, shook off the parent, and said, "Justice should take its course." And, as mayor, he caused his son to be committed, with the rest of the crew, and the father, like Brutus, sat in judgment on his son, and with his own lips pronounced the sentence which left him childless!

FACTS AND COUNSELS.

DR. MURRAY'S HABITS OF STUDY.

THE late Dr. Murray, of Elizabeth, New Jersey, a few years since was at a clerical conference, where each minister told for the benefit of the others his own experience in the matter of composing sermons. The doctor said that he spent usually the entire mornings of five days, never less than four days, in the composition of a sermon, and that he was never without at least three finished sermons ahead. It is a recorded fact that after his death there were found in his desk no less than four finished sermons, fully written out, which had never been preached, besides a fifth sermon already on the stocks. I am informed that he has, at times, had as many as eight sermons ahead. The doctor, moreover, was abundant in other labors of the pen. He wrote several books. He wrote many popular lectures and addresses. He wrote almost every week an article for the *New York Observer*, filling from one to two columns of that paper. He was a frequent attendant upon ecclesiastical councils of various kinds, and upon literary festivals. Yet he never seemed to be in a hurry, never pressed for time. He had all the comfort of a gentleman of leisure. It was simply because he early formed, and ever adhered to, the habit of being beforehand with every engagement. I knew him well, and I had from his own lips the circumstances in which he began his ministerial career. Immediately after leaving the seminary he entered upon an important charge at Wilkesbarre, Pennsylvania. He told me that on his first Sabbath there he exhausted his entire stock in trade, so far as written sermons went. He had gone to the place with nothing prepared but his presbyterial trial pieces, and he had used those all up the first week of his ministry. On the Monday morning following, the first thing after breakfast, he went to his study and put his next sermon on the anvil, and hammered away at it the entire morning, and he continued thus to work at it every day, and to the exclusion of every other thing, until the sermon was completed. He settled this irrevocably and unchangeably as his method of procedure, and he kept it up through life. It was the same with every other professional engagement. He never allowed himself to drift along till near the time when any public duty was to be performed, and then turn in with frantic haste to make his preparations. He pursued no such spendthrift course as that, but, on the contrary, was always in ample time. He lived intellectually on the right side of his income. The consequence was he was never hurried, never anxious, never thrown out by unforseen accidents. The habit gave him a feeling of ease and independence that shone forth in his very face.—*John S. Hart, LL. D.*

WORKING UNDER DISADVANTAGES.

WHO shall reckon up the countless circumstances which lie like a depressing burden on the energies of men, and make them work at that disadvantage which we have thought of under the figure of *carrying weight in life?* There are men who carry weight in a damp, marshy neighborhood, who, amid bracing mountain air, might have done things which now they will never do. There are men who carry weight in an uncomfortable house: in smoky chimneys: in a study with a dismal look-out: in distance from a railway-station: in ten miles between them and a bookseller's shop. Give another hundred a year of income, and the poor struggling parson who preaches dull sermons will astonish you by the talent he will exhibit, when his mind is freed from the dismal, depressing influence of ceaseless scheming to keep the wolf from the door. Let the poor little sick child grow strong and well, and with how much better heart will its father face the work of life! Let the clergyman who preached, in a spiritless enough way, to a handful of uneducated rustics, be placed in a charge where weekly he has to address a large cultivated congregation; and with the new stimulus, latent powers may manifest themselves which no one fancied he possessed, and he may prove quite an eloquent and attractive preacher. A dull, quiet man, whom you esteemed as a blockhead, may suddenly be valued very differently when circumstances unexpectedly call out the solid qualities he possesses, unsuspected before. A man, devoid of brilliancy, may on occasion show that he possesses great good sense; or that he has the power of sticking to his task, in spite of discouragement. Let a man be placed where dogged perseverance will stand him in stead, and you may see what he can do when he has but a chance. The especial weight which has held some men back—the thing which kept them from doing great things and attaining great fame—has been just this: that they were not able to say or to write what they have thought and felt. And indeed a great poet is nothing more than the one man in a million who has the gift to express that which has been in the mind and heart of multitudes. If even the most commonplace of human beings could write all the poetry he has felt, he would produce something that would go straight to the hearts of many.—*Country Parson.*

FLORENCE NIGHTINGALE.

WE have been looking at a photograph of Florence Nightingale, taken for Queen Victoria. It was a gift of one queen to another. The recipient was the sovereign of Britain; the giver is the "queen of hearts" the world over—the most popular woman on the globe. Neither of these two foremost women of our time are beautiful according to an artist's canons. Victoria has grown stout, florid, and matronly. Her character has ripened, too, into nobleness. Dr. M'Leod, of Glasgow, one of her chaplains, spent a week with her at Balmoral, and after many free familiar conversations with her Majesty, expressed his surprise at her mental vigor and reach of thought. He said he always knew his Queen had a good heart; he did not know that she had so vigorous a mind.

Florence Nightingale is younger than her royal sister of Windsor Castle, having just completed her fortieth year. Judging from the photograph, she is slight in person, and has a quiet, kindly, old-maidish face. She is just such a woman as the Creator would make for such a mission of benevolence. She is no bewitching Hebe, stealing young officers' hearts by diamond eyes and cherry lips; nor is she a hard-featured "Sairey Gamp," with sleeves and dress tucked up, and going about her work with the rueful alacrity of an undertaker. Her face is a trifle sad, but beaming with benevolence. After all, as Mrs. Primrose says, "what is good-looking but *looking good?*"

Miss Nightingale is the founder of our modern sanitary system, and did more than any one else to put it on the basis of Christianity and practical common-sense. So sensible an enthusiast has scarcely ever been known. Of English ancestry, she was yet born under the sunny skies of Italy, and received her name of Florence from the beautiful city of her birth. Her father's name was Shore, but he adopted the name of his grand-uncle, Peter Nightingale, on inheriting his estates. Florence's grandfather, Hon. William Smith, was a co-worker with Wilberforce in Parliament in the abolition of West India slavery. Reared in wealth, with elegant mental culture, she evinced an early passion for caring for the sick, and her favorite books were those which treated of hospitals and institutions for the infirm. One of her earliest ideas was that Protestanism needed some counterpart to the "Sisters of Charity" in the Romish Church. Accordingly, she went as a pupil to Pastor Fliedner's "school of deaconesses" at Kaiserswerth, on the Rhine. In 1854 the sorrowful tidings of the sufferings and barbarities in the Crimean Hospitals reached England, and aroused the intensest feeling of the British nation. Mr. Sidney Herbert proposed to Miss Nightingale that she should go thither with a staff of nurses. She took forty-two ladies with her; fifty more soon followed, and of these, like many of our own heroines in hospital duty, a large portion belonged to the refined ranks of society.

With Florence Nightingale's beautiful work of philanthropy at Scutari all our readers are familiar. How she revolutionized the hospitals; how she brought order out of confusion, carelessness, and chaos; how she won the poor wounded soldiers' hearts that one of them said that he kissed her shadow as it fell across his pillow; and how she stood up for twenty hours each day with a kind word and a smile for every sufferer; all this the world knows by heart. Her love-labor of two busy years at Scutari cost her her own health; she came home a broken invalid, never to regain the bloom and vigor of her early days. The queen sent her an autograph letter of thanks, with a costly diamond; the soldiers offered to build her a monument, which she declined; and a quarter of a million dollars was raised to found an institution for training nurses under her direction.

Miss Nightingale's home is among the emerald hills and leafy lanes of Derbyshire. She has employed her leisure hours in writing the admirable "Notes on Nursing," a capital volume, that appeared three years ago. This work ought to be in the hands of every nurse in our national army. It would do us all good to read it, and to listen to such considerate hints as the following passage contains; for who of us is not sometimes called to the ministrations of the sick-room? In replying to the petulant charge that the sick or wounded might have "more self-control," good, gentle Florence says:

"Believe me, almost any sick person, who behaves decently well, exercises more self-control every moment of his day than you will ever know till you are sick yourself. Almost every step that crosses his room is painful to him; almost every thought that crosses his brain is painful to him; and if he can speak without being savage, and look without being unpleasant, he is exercising self-control.

"Suppose you have been up all night, and instead of being allowed to have your cup of tea, you were to be told that you ought to 'exercise self-control,' what should you say? Now the nerves of the sick are always in the state that yours are in after you have been up all night."—P. 35.

Miss Nightingale is deservedly severe on the evil practice of worrying the sick and wounded with needless calls and exacting talk. "I hope you are none the worse for my call," is the frequent apology of such do-no-good intruders. "No real patient," observes Miss Florence, "will ever say 'Yes, I am a great deal worse,' even though such untimely visits have sometimes been followed by a night of delirium."

A few months since Miss Nightingale addressed a letter to Lord Stanley on the sanitary condition of the army in India

In this letter she makes one most important declaration, which we commend to our American officers, and not to them only, but to the whole nation. She says, "The long cherished idea as to the necessity of ardent spirits for the British soldier is thoroughly exploded. A man who drinks tea or coffee will do more work than a dram-drinker, though considered sober." Well spoken, good angel Florence! we would go a long way to kiss the hand that wrote these few weighty words. Her testimony on such a point is worth the "deliverances" of a score of synods and conventions.

TRIUMPH OF ARNOLD AND WORDSWORTH.

REV. F. W. ROBERTSON, M.A.

It was my lot, during a short university career, to witness a transition and a reaction, or revulsion, of public feeling, with respect to two great men whom I have already mentioned and contrasted. The first of these was one who was every inch a man—Arnold of Rugby. You will all recollect, how in his earlier life, Arnold was covered with suspicion and obloquy; how the wise men of his day charged him with latitudinarianism, and I know not with how many other heresies. But the public opinion altered, and he came to Oxford, and read lectures on Modern History. Such a scene had not been witnessed in Oxford before. The lecture-room was too small; all adjourned to the Oxford theatre; and all that was most brilliant, all that was most wise and most distinguished, gathered together there. He walked up to the rostrum with a quiet step and manly dignity. Those who had loved him when all the world despised him, felt that, at last, the hour of their triumph had come. But there was something deeper than any personal triumph they could enjoy; and those who saw him then will not soon forget the lesson read to them by his calm, dignified, simple step—a lesson teaching them the utter worthlessness of unpopularity, or of poplarity, as a test of manhood's worth.

The second occasion was when, in the same theatre, Wordsworth came forward to receive his honorary degree. Scarcely had his name been pronounced, than from three thousand voices at once, there broke forth a burst of applause, echoed and taken up again and again, when it seemed about to die away, and that thrice repeated—a cry in which

"Old England's heart and voice unite,
Whether she hail the wine cup or the fight,
Or bid each hand be strong, or bid each heart be light."

There were young eyes there filled with an emotion of which they had no need to be ashamed; there were hearts beating with the proud feeling of triumph, that, at last, the world had recognized the merit of the man they had loved so long, and acknowledged as their teacher; and yet, when that noise was protracted, there came a reaction in their feelings, and they began to perceive that *that* was not, after all, the true reward and recompense for all that Wordsworth had done for England; it seemed as if all that noise was vulgarizing the poet; it seemed more natural and desirable, to think of him afar off in his simple dales and mountains, the high priest of Nature, weaving in honored poverty his songs to liberty and truth, than to see him there clad in a scarlet robe, and bespattered with applause. Two young men went home together, part of the way in silence, and one only gave expression to the feelings of the other when he quoted those well-known, trite, and often-quoted lines—lines full of deepest truth—

"The self-approving hour whole worlds outweighs
Of stupid starers and of loud huzzas;
And more true joy Marcellus exiled feels
Than Cæsar with a senate at his heels.'

JOHN WESLEY'S DREAM.

DEAN STANLEY.

"IN my Father's house are many mansions." We do not know whether "those that shall be saved will be few or many." It may be that those who are able to struggle through the straight gate will be very few. It may be that the good, and the true, and the just will be in a minority in the next life, as they usually are in this life. But whether few or many, the Bible reveals to us most clearly the truth which our carnal, narrow hearts are very unwilling to receive—namely, that amongst the good, whom we hope to meet in heaven, there will be every variety of character, taste, and disposition. There is not one "mansion" there, but "many; there is not one "gate" to heaven, but many—there are not gates only on the north, but "on the east, three gates; on the west, three gates; and on the south, three gates." From opposite quarters of the theological compass, from opposite quarters of the religious world, from opposite quarters of human life and character; through different expressions of their common faith and hope, through different modes of conversion, through different kinds of instruction and teaching, through different portions of the Holy Scriptures—will the weary travellers enter the Heavenly City, and meet each other, "not without surprise," on the shores of the same river of life. And on those shores they will find a tree bearing, not the same kind of fruit always and at all times, but "twelve manner of fruits," for every different turn of mind—for the patient sufferer, for the active servant, for the holy and humble philosopher, for the spirits of just men now at last made perfect; and "the leaves of the tree shall be for the healing," not of one single church or people only, not for the Scotchman or the Englishman only, but for the healing of the nations,"—the Frenchman, the German, the Italian, the Russian—for all those from whom, it may be, in this world its fruits have been farthest removed, but who, nevertheless, have "hungered and thirsted after righteousness," and who, therefore, "*shall be filled.*"

And here again, let me tell a third tale of the dark night, which shows how the light of the other world, in this its most evangelical aspect, dawned upon the soul of a great teacher amongst ourselves. It is said that John Wesley once, in the visions of the night, found himself, as he thought, at the gates of hell. He knocked, and asked who were within. "Are there any Roman Catholics here?" he asked. "Yes," was the answer, "a great many." "Any Church of England men?" "Yes, a great many." "Any Presbyterians?" "Yes, a great many." "Any Wesleyans?" "Yes, a great many." Disappointed and dismayed, especially at the last reply, he turned his steps upwards, and found himself at the gates of Paradise, and here he repeated the same questions. "Any Wesleyans here?" "No." "Any Presbyterians?" "No." "Any Church of England men?" "No." "Any Roman Catholics?" "No." "Whom have you then here?" he asked in astonishment. "We know nothing here," was the reply, "of any of those names that you have mentioned. The only name of which we know anything here is 'Christian;' we are all Christians here, and of these we have a great multitude which no man can number, of all nations, and kindreds, and peoples, and tongues."

Yes, we shall be obliged in heaven to meet with Christians, with good men, of very different opinions. Had we not better prepare for that meeting, by consenting to meet with them on earth? We shall be obliged there to make little of our differences, to put up with diversity of opinions, and ranks, and pursuits. Had we not better moderate our differences here, and bear and forbear with these diversities in this world? Is it not a waste of time to try to force all our fellow travellers through our own gate now, when we shall be obliged hereafter to welcome those who entered from the western gate, though we have entered from the eastern, and those who have entered from the southern gate, though we have entered from the northern?

How wide the gates of heaven stand open! how many different characters will be found amongst the elect.

DURATION OF LIFE.

MANY attempts have been made—all of which appear to me total failures—to make out the ratio of man's whole life to the portion required for reaching maturity to be the same as with other animals. So far as I can make out, the time for full growth in the other mammals, is one seventh of the natural term of existence, and in man one fourth at the very utmost. To take eighty as about man's natural term (when acute diseases and accidents do not intervene) is rather the outside; and the full growth of the bones is seldom complete before twenty, often not till later.

A horse that has not been worked when young, (which nineteen twentieths or more are,) and is complete at five, is not older at thirty-five than a man at eighty. A dog, which is complete at or before two years, will live (if allowed) to thirteen or fourteen. And I believe the like ratio will hold good with most of the mammals when fairly used, namely, one seventh of the life is taken up in reaching maturity. Man, therefore, ought by the same rule, to reach his regular term at one hundred and forty years—double the Psalmist's allowance. As for the physical cause of the long duration of life in the early ages of the world, I think the only plausible theory is that which attributes it to the use of the tree of life by our first parents, before they were expelled from Paradise, which was likely to have imparted to the constitution of their descendants a strength, which was slowly and gradually worn out in many generations.

With reference to the final cause—the purpose to be answered—great longevity was manifestly of great importance, with a view to the invention of the arts of life before writing was in use, that each man might have the benefit of his own very long experience.—*Archbishop Whately.*

MEN OF GENIUS.

Tasso's conversation was neither gay nor brilliant. Dante was either taciturn or satirical. Butler was either sullen or biting. Gray seldom talked or smiled. Hogarth and Swift were absent-minded in company. Milton was very unsociable and irritable, when pressed into conversation. Kirwan, though copious and eloquent in public addresses, was meagre and dull in colloquial discourses. Virgil was heavy in conversation. La Fontaine appeared heavy, coarse and stupid; he could not speak and describe what he had just seen; but then he was the model of poetry. Chaucer's silence was more agreeable than his conversation. Dryden's conversation was slow and dull, his humor saturnine and reserved. Cornelius in conversation was so insipid that he never failed in wearying; he did not even speak correctly that language of which he was such a master. Ben Johnson used to sit silent in company and suck his wine.

Southey was stiff, sedate, and wrapped up in asceticism. Addison was good company with his intimate friends, but in mixed company he preserved his dignity by a stiff and reserved silence. Fox in conversation never flagged; his animation and vivacity were inexhaustible. Dr. Bentley was loquacious, as was also Grotius. Goldsmith "wrote like an angel and talked like poor poll." Burke was entertaining, enthusiastic, and interesting in conversation. Curran was a convivial deity. Leigh Hunt was a pleasant stream in conversation. Carlyle doubts, objects, and constantly demurs.

WORK WITHOUT WEARINESS.

REV. WM. MORLEY PUNSHON.

ACTION is the destiny and the lot of man. All the conditions of his existence suppose his activity. It is so in his physical frame. The elastic foot is for speed; the firm, lithe limb, for endurance; the arm, at once supple and sinewy, for toil; the eye and the ear for their respective revelries of sight and sound. It is so in his mental constitution. By the active exercise of the powers with which God has endowed him, he can classify objects and understand truth. He has a memory by which he can inherit the past, a regal imagination by which he can colonize and almost enact the future. It is so in his moral nature. There is a power of perception within him to distinguish between right and wrong; an instinct of worship which, however he may brutalize, he cannot stifle; yearnings after a nobler life which neither can debauchery extinguish, nor murder wholly kill. Moreover, God has made the vigor of the faculties contingent upon their exercise. The muscle will shrink if it be never strung. The moveless arm will stiffen into hopeless catalepsy, while

> "The athlete, worsted in the Olympic games,
> Gains strength, at least, for life."

Man was not made simply to live, the mere passive recipient of external impressions, a lifeless harp upon which each fitful wind might play; he was made to act, to will, to influence, to become a power, to be the living centre of ever radiating impressions. His existence is not to be that of a zoophyte, the mere clinging of a helpless parasite to its guardian rock; it is to be a life, beautiful and holy, beating with quick pulses of activity, adventurous with an energy of which insensate matter knows not, and finding in the rapturous doing life's very soul of joy.

But though doing is a necessity of all, well-doing is not now natural to any. We have lost the inheritance of moral manhood.

A strange weakness has paralyzed the sources of our former power. Distrust and alienation are the mildest forms of feeling in which we naturally think upon God; and so thorough is the spiritual decrepitude, so great the stoop and ail of our moral nature, that we can hardly conceive of a time when it was erect and healthy, and are almost disposed to think upon Eden as some fable of the classic olden time, or ancient limner's dream.

While this is the actual condition of humanity, there is hope in its future destiny, and in its present experience too, because Christianity has revealed her glad tidings of great joy. By the death of Christ, the accepted substitute and propitiation, provision is made for the transformation of the nature, and by the shedding forth of the Holy Ghost, the application of that provision is secured to the believing soul. It is quite possible, therefore, that an entire counteraction should be set up against the depravity of the Fall; well-doing may become, as it once was, not a casual achievement, nor a momentary chivalry, but the rule of every day, the native and constant forthputting of the clean heart and of the right spirit.

It is possible that many who did well should grow weary in well-doing. The exhortation deprecates this. Weariness in well-doing! How readily it creeps even upon the most vigilant of us! Who has not felt its tendencies, and had to rise and shake himself, if, happily, the drowsiness might be removed from his soul? Weariness in well-doing! Under the dread spell of its inconstancy, fair plans have proved abortive, and generous youth have languished into premature age, and Christian consistency has come by a scar upon its beauty, and the edifice of Christian graces has been stayed in its erection, till the scoffing world, gazing from the unfinished masonry to the sluggard builder, says, "This man began to build, and was not able to finish."

The causes of this weariness are manifold, and we may each of us find them for ourselves if we study the Book that is within. Was it *sloth* that overcame us? Did we shrink from the effort of continued resistance to evil, and of perpetual watchfulness against our own insidious sin? Was it *self-complacency* that obtained possession of our hearts; that old serpent of vanity which whispered us into carnal security? Was it *anger* which seized us in its petulant grasp, because we were not appreciated by our fellows, and were mortified to find the hollow preference given to inferior men, because some coveted preeminence was denied us, and our efforts to do good were met only with prejudice or scorn? Was it *respectability* which waved us off from commoner fellowship, which bade us leave all personal toil to the hewers and drawers among the people, and which told us that we could condone for our forsaken labor by our willingness to direct and to subscribe? Was it the *spirit of indifference* which exhausted our energies? Had we entered upon a work too high for us, which demanded sacrifices that our heroism could not reach, and imposed restraints from which our passion fretted in rebellion? Ah! how many are there who thus rest in luxurious harbors until they lose their roll, or lull themselves into disastrous, and well nigh hopeless slumber, upon the world's enchanted ground.

But why weary in well-doing? The obligations which pressed upon us so forcibly in our early decision have not diminished in their importance or grandeur. The soul is worth as much. God's claims are as imperative. Eternity is as magnificent, and it is not farther off, but nearer. Heaven has not withered from its eternal spring. Hell is not less certain and real. There is no change, save only in ourselves. The motives remain with equal, nay, with greater constraint upon us, for there are fewer sands in our life-glass than when we first began. Oh, to cast off the weariness, and in recovered strength to go forth in the service of the Lord!

"Ye shall reap if ye faint not." The harvest is certain, and it is nearing. Every pulse approximates it. Every day is hastening its approach. Every Sabbath brings us nearer to the sound of the joy bells, which, to usher in the eternal Sabbath, are ringing as for a bridal. Why be weary *now!* Does the pilgrim halt when he is in sight of the shrine? Though the racer may be panting and breathless, surely he will press on when the goal of his wishes is before him. Courage, my flagging brother! The call is upon thee, hearken to it, and thine shall be the recompence of the reward.

THE GREAT MOUNTAINS.

JOHN RUSKIN, M.A.

THE mountains could not stand for a day unless they were formed of materials altogether different from those which constitute the lower hills and the surfaces of the valleys. A harder substance had to be prepared for every mountain chain, yet not so hard but that it might be capable of crumbling down into earth, fit to nourish the Alpine forest and the Alpine flower; not so hard but that, in the midst of the utmost majesty of its enthroned strength, there should be seen on it the seal of death, and the writing of the same sentence that had gone forth against the human frame, "Dust thou art, and unto dust thou shalt return." And with this perishable substance the most majestic forms were to be framed that were consistent with the safety of man; and the peak was to be lifted, and the cliff rent, as high and as steeply as possible, in order yet to permit the shepherd to feed his flocks upon the slope, and the cottage to nestle beneath their shadow.

And observe, two distinct ends were to be accomplished in the doing this. It was, indeed, absolutely necessary that such eminences should be created, in order to fit the earth in any wise for human habitation; for without mountains the air could not be purified, nor the flowing of the rivers sustained, and the earth must have become for the most part desert plain, or stagnant marsh. But the feeding of the rivers, and the purifying of the winds, are the least of the services appointed to the hills. To fill the thirst of the human heart for the beauty of God's working—to startle its lethargy with the deep and pure agitation of astonishment—are their higher missions. They are as a great and noble architecture; first, giving shelter, comfort and rest; and covered also with mighty sculpture and painted legend. It is impossible to examine in their connected system, the features of even the most ordinary mountain scenery, without concluding that it has been prepared in order to unite, as far as possible, and in the closest compass, every means of delighting and sanctifying the heart of man. "As far as *possible*," that is, as far as is consistent with the fulfilment of the sentence of condemnation on the whole earth. Death must be upon the hills, and the cruelty of the tempest smite them, and the briar and thorn spring up upon them; but they so smite, as to bring their rocks into the fairest forms, and so spring, as to make the very desert blossom as the rose. Even among our own hills of Scotland and Cumberland, though often too barren to be perfectly beautiful, and always too low to be perfectly sublime, it is strange how many deep sources of delight are gathered into the compass of their glens and vales; and how, down to the most secret cluster of their far-away flowers, and the idlest leap of their straying streamlets, the whole heart of Nature seems thirsting to give, and still to give, shedding forth her everlasting beneficence with a profusion so patient, so passionate, that our utmost observance and thankfulness are but, at least, neglect of her nobleness, and apathy to her love. But among the true mountains of the greater orders, the Divine purpose of appeal at once to all the faculties of the human spirit becomes still more manifest. Inferior hills ordinarily interrupt, in some degree, the richness of the valleys at their feet; the gray downs of southern England, and treeless coteaux of central France, and gray swells of Scottish moor, whatever peculiar charm they may possess in themselves, are at least destitute of those which belong to the woods and fields of the lowlands. But the great mountains *lift* the lowlands *on their sides*. Let the reader imagine, first, the appearance of the most varied plain of some richly cultivated country; let him imagine it dark with graceful woods, and soft with deepest pastures; let him fill the space of it, to the utmost horizon, with innumerable and changeful incidents of scenery and life; leading pleasant streamlets through its meadows, strewing clusters of cottages beside their banks, tracing sweet footpaths through its avenues, and animating its fields with happy flocks, and slow wandering spots of cattle; and when he has wearied himself with endless imagining, and left no space without some loveliness of its own, let him conceive all this great plain, with its infinite treasures of natural beauty and happy human life, gathered up in God's hand from one end of the horizon to the other, like a woven garment, and shaken into deep falling folds, as the robes droop from a king's shoulders; all its bright rivers leaping into cataracts along the hollows of its fall, and all its forests rearing themselves aslant against its slopes, as a rider rears himself back when his horse plunges; and all its villages nestling themselves into the new windings of its glens; and all its pastures thrown into steep waves of greensward, dashed with dew along the edges of their folds, and sweeping down into endless slopes, with a cloud here and there lying quietly, half on the grass, half in the air; and he will have as yet, in all this lifted world, only the foundation of one of the great Alps.

They seem to have been built for the human race, as at once their schools and cathedrals; full of treasures of illuminated manuscript for the scholar, kindly in simple lessons to the worker, quiet in pale cloisters for the thinker, glorious in holiness for the worshippers. And of these great cathedrals of the earth, with their gates of rock, pavements of cloud, choirs of stream and stone, altars of snow, and vaults of purple, traversed by the continual stars—of these, as we have seen, it was written, nor long ago, by one of the best of the poor human race for whom it was built, wondering in himself for whom their Creator *could* have made them, and thinking to have entirely discerned the Divine intent in them—"They are inhabited by the Beasts."

Mountains are, to the rest of the body of the earth, what violent muscular action is to the body of man. The muscles and tendons of its anatomy, are, in the mountains, brought out with fierce and convulsive energy, full of expression, passion, and strength; the plains and the lower hills are the repose and the effortless motion of the frame, when its muscles lie dormant and concealed beneath the lines of its beauty, yet ruling those lines in their every undulation. This, then, is the first grand principle of the truth of the earth. The spirit of the hills is action; that of the lowlands, repose; and between these there is to be found every variety of motion and of rest; from the inactive plain sleeping like the firmament, with cities for stars, to the fiery peaks, which, with heaving bosoms and exulting limbs, with the clouds drifting like hair from their bright foreheads, lift up their Titan hands to Heaven, saying, "I live forever!"

EVILS OF MENTAL PRECOCITY.

THE premature development of the mind and neglect of the body, have long been prominent evils in our educational system. It is often very pleasant to fond parents to see how bright, intelligent, and witty their children are; and they often find great satisfaction in showing to others the brilliancy and mental sprightliness of their precocious darlings. Such parents know not what they are doing. All the praise lavished by such parental folly, and fond aunts, and doting grandparents, and injudicious friends, tends to the serious injury and almost certain destruction of their children. Their keen flashes and sparkling witticisms are but the indications of an over-stretched mind and a neglected body. Our many systems of education thus destroy many children every year. This neglect of the physical, and stimulating the mental man, is the more to be deplored, from the fact that this early precocity is wholly unnecessary, because many of the best educated and most useful men the world has ever seen, were very dull pupils in early childhood. Andrew Fuller, Sir Walter Scott, and Daniel Webster, were very dull scholars when children; and yet who has ever done more in theological discussion than the former? Or who, in the whole world of intellect, than the second? Or who at the bar and in the Senate than the latter?—*How to Enjoy Life.*

READERS AND WRITERS.

READING without purpose is sauntering, not exercise. More is got from one book on which the thought settles for a definite end in knowledge, than from libraries skimmed over by a wandering eye. A cottage flower gives honey to the bee, a king's garden none to the butterfly. Youths who are destined for active careers, or ambitious of distinction in such forms of literature as require freshness of invention or originality of thought, should avoid the habit of intense study for many hours at a stretch. There is a point in all tensions of the intellect beyond which effort is only waste of strength. Fresh ideas do not readily spring up within a weary brain; and whatever exhausts the mind, not only enfeebles its power, but narrows its scope. We often see men who have over-read at college, entering upon life as languidly as if they were about to leave it. They have not the vigor to cope with their own generation; for their own generation is young, and they have wasted the nervous energy which supplies the sinews of war to youth in its contest for fame or fortune.

Study with regularity, at settled hours. Those in the forenoon are the best, if they can be secured. The man who has acquired the habit of study, though for only one hour every day in the year, and keeps to the one thing studied till it is mastered, will be startled to see the progress he has made at the end of a twelvemonth. He is seldom overworked who can contrive to be in advance of his work. If you have three weeks before you to learn something which a man of average quickness could learn in a week, learn it the first week and not the third. Business dispatched is business well done, but business hurried is business ill done. In learning what others have thought, it is well to keep in practice the power to think for one's self; when an author has added to your knowledge, pause and consider if you can add nothing to his. Be not contented to have learned a problem by heart; try and deduce from it a corollary not in the book. Spare no pains in collecting details before you generalize; but it is only when details are generalized that a truth is grasped. The tendency to generalize is universal with all men who achieve great success, whether in art, literature, or action. The habit of generalizing, though at first gained with care and caution, secures by practice, a comprehensiveness of judgment, and a promptitude of decision, which seems to the crowd like the intuitions of genius. And, indeed, nothing more distinguishes the man of genius from the mere man of talent, than the facility of generalizing the various details, each of which demands the aptitude of a special talent; but all of which can be only gathered into a single whole by the grasp of a mind which may have no special aptitude for any.—*Bulwer.*

THE AGONY OF DOUBT.

THERE is an infidelity with which no good man should have any sympathy. There are infidels who are such, knowing what they oppose. There are men who, in no mistake, know the difference between good and evil, and distinctly knowing it, choose the evil and reject the good. But there is a state *called* infidelity, which deserves compassion rather than indignation—the dreadful state of one who craves light and cannot find it. I do think the way we treat that state, is most unpardonably cruel. It is an awful moment when the soul begins to find that the props on which it has blindly rested so long, are, many of them, rotten, and begin to suspect them all; when it begins to feel the nothingness of many of the traditionary opinions which have been received with implicit confidence, and in that horrible insecurity begins also to doubt whether there be anything to believe at all. It is an awful hour—let him who has passed through it say how awful—when this life has lost its meaning, and seems shrivelled into a span; when the grave appears to be the end of all, human goodness nothing but a name, and the sky above this universe a dead expanse, black with the void from which God himself has disappeared. In that fearful loneliness of spirit, when those who should have been his friends and counsellors only frown upon his misgivings, and profanely bid him stifle doubts, which for aught he knows may arise from the fountain of truth itself; to extinguish, as a glare from hell, that which for aught he knows may be light from Heaven, and everything seems wrapped in hideous uncertainty, I know but one way in which a man may come forth from his agony scathless; it is by holding fast to those things which are certain still—the grand, simple landmarks of morality. In the darkest hour through which a human soul can pass, whatever else is doubtful, this at least is certain. If there be no God and no future state, yet, even then, it is better to be generous than selfish, better to be chaste than licentious, better to be true than false, better to be brave than to be a coward. Blessed beyond all earthly blessedness in the man who, in the tempestuous darkness of the soul, has dared to hold fast to these venerable landmarks. Thrice blessed is he, who, when all is drear and cheerless within and without, when his teachers terrify him, and his friends shrink from him, has obstinately clung to moral good. Thrice blessed, because *his* night shall pass into clear, bright day.

I appeal to the recollection of any man who has passed through that hour of agony, and stood upon the rock at last, the surges stilled below him, and the last cloud drifted from the sky above, with a faith, and hope, and trust, no longer traditional, but of his own, a trust which neither earth nor hell shall shake thenceforth forever. But it is not in this way generally that men act who are tempted by doubt. Generally, the step from doubt is a reckless plunge into sensuality. Then comes the darkening of the moral being; and then from uncertainty and skepticism it may be that the path lies unobstructed, sheer down into Atheism. But if there be one on earth who deserves compassion, it is the sincere, earnest, and—may I say it without risk of being misunderstood?—honest doubter. Let who will denounce him, I will not. I would stand by his side, and say, Courage, my brother! You are darkening your own soul; you are contradicting the meaning of your own existence. But God is your Father, and an Infinite Spirit seeks to mingle itself with yours.—*Rev. F. W. Robertson, A.M.*

SOWING WILD OATS.

THIS is very bad farming. We appeal to the most inveterate protectionist, the most distressed farmer that ever lived, the sturdiest stickler for ploughing as our fathers ploughed, and sowing as our fathers sowed, whether it would not be the very worst possible style of farming for a young farmer to sow wild oats all over his estate—to plant weeds and thistles in every field. Would it not be found that the wild oats would destroy the crops of grain ; that the weeds and thistles would overpower the grass, until the whole presented a wide and melancholy ruin, which long years and large capital could scarcely bring again into a profitable state? As in the physical, so in the moral world ; the seeds of vice once sown are difficult to eradicate, and the wilful cultivation of these in the human heart will produce a still wider ruin than the worst weeds which ever mocked the hopes of the husbandman.

An old French writer has said, that "Disgust stands *at* the door of all bad places." It may be so, but it is to be feared that we too often put her *behind* the door as we enter; and it is only when we could come out that we meet her face to face. We cover up her form with all kinds of disguises; we endeavor to cheat ourselves into the belief that disgust is not her real name, and that it is not the door of vice at which she stands sentinel; and as we pass her by, and enter, we console ourselves with the thought that we are only having a bit of a spree! that we are in for a lark! or at any rate, that we "*must* sow some of our wild oats." We are confident in ourselves, have great reliance on our own correct principles and right intentions, and delude ourselves into the belief that we are only gaining a little knowledge of the world, and showing ourselves to be youths of spirit. And a most miserable delusion this is—fostered and encouraged by the wretched fallacy we are illustrating; and by the pernicious habit of glossing over vile things with eulogistic names. We begin, perhaps, by sowing our seeds with a careful hand, scattering a few here and a few there, with long intervals between them; we are not alarmed by any very great expenditure of seed; we hardly fancy that the correct principles on which we rely are disturbed or shocked by these slight deviations from the strict rule of right; we still keep in the common routine of our duties, while we are imperceptibly being led into temptations that, by degrees, cause us to scatter the seeds more thickly, and with fewer intervals between them. And we go on "sowing the wild oats" until the days of our youth are passed, and when a miserable and premature old age draws on, we find that the tillage is not yet complete; it is only when infirmities have rendered it impossible to pursue our former course, that the seed-time is over; and the harvest comes upon us at once in the shape of pains and penalties grievous to bear. We forsake not the sowing until the power to sow is departed. We forsake not the sin until the sin forsakes us.

CULTIVATE GOOD MANNERS.

Deem it not below the dignity of the occasion, that I urge upon you the duty of cultivating good manners. Young men often make a serious mistake on this point. They think, if they only have the substance, the form is of little moment. If they acquire learning and professional skill, that is all they need. They can work their way through by main force. It is a mistake. A man *may* have such extraordinary force of character and talents as to compel the path of promotion to open before him. But promotion so gained, is gained at entirely too great a sacrifice. It is gained in spite of a very heavy drawback. The same amount of intellectual force, combined with suitable manners and address, would have accomplished three times the result. A surgeon may remove a limb with the dull heavy cleaver of the butcher. But he would hardly be thought to be wise in preferring such an instrument to the keen, well-tempered blade suited to his profession. By the use of a sort of brute force, you may undoubtedly make a certain amount of impression. But if you would cut deeply, or use your force wisely, look well to your manner. Its power in human affairs is almost unbounded. Who that has ever been brought into contact with a highly educated Quaker, such for instance as the late Joseph John Gurney, but has felt the controlling sway of beautiful manners? It was difficult in the presence of that man to say what it was that affected you so powerfully. Other men have had a smile equally benignant, a voice equally melodious, a gait and motion equally graceful, a goodness of heart, a sweetness of disposition, a gentleness and openness of speech equally inspiring confidence. It was somehow the infinite delicacy with which, whatever there is to charm in voice or word or look or gesture, was in him so finely tempered together that you felt as if mingling with a being of a superior nature, and yet felt quite as much at your ease as if talking with those of common clay. It was real Christian goodness of heart speaking out through the whole man. The very hem of his garment seemed to speak. To analyze the manner of such a man and detect its hidden mystery, is like attempting to analyze a delicate perfume. The most etherial of its occult essences are sure to escape you. You only know in such a case that there is true Christian charity at the bottom, that there is varied knowledge and intellectual power, and that every adventitious advantage of person and dress is used to give whatever is said or done its very highest and happiest effect. Such a manner is the fruit of long-continued and most assiduous cultivation. It is indeed to some extent a gift of nature. But it depends still more upon culture and art. It does not lose its power with the loss of youth; on the contrary, it often increases with years. Men and women in extreme old age have been known to possess a sweet attractive grace, an actual power of fascination, which the young could by no means equal.

That which I recommend to you, is not to be won from the dancing master or the tailor. No one can be insensible to the claims of graceful posture, movement, and costume. But the charm of manner of which I have been speaking, lies deeper than these. It is no outside varnish. It springs from real goodness of heart, from a life hid with Christ in God. It is Christian charity clothing itself spontaneously in fitting external expression. It gives beauty to the plainest face, it teaches winning words and ways to the most ignorant.—*John S. Hart, LL.D.*

POVERTY OF THE LEARNED.

Of the heroes of modern literature the accounts are as copious as they are sorrowful.

Xylander sold his notes on Dion Cassius for a dinner. He tells us that at the age of eighteen he studied to acquire glory, but at twenty-five he studied to get bread.

Cervantes, the immortal genius of Spain, is supposed to have wanted food. Camoens, the solitary pride of Portugal, deprived of the necessaries of life, perished in a hospital at Lisbon, after having triumphed in the East Indies, and sailed five thousand five hundred leagues. The Portuguese after his death bestowed on the man of genius they had starved the appellation of "great."

Vondel, the Dutch Shakspeare, after composing a number of popular tragedies, lived in great poverty, and died at ninety years of age; then he had his coffin carried by fourteen poets, who without his genius probably partook of his wretchedness.

The great Tasso was reduced to such a dilemma that he was obliged to borrow a crown for a week's subsistence. He alludes to his distress, when entreating his cat to assist him during the night with the lustre of her eyes, having no candle to see to write his verses.

Cardinal Bentivoglio, the ornament of Italy and of literature, languished in his old age in the most distressful poverty; and having sold his palace to satisfy his creditors, left nothing behind him but his reputation.

Vugelas, the most polished writer of the French language, who devoted thirty years to his translation of Quintus Curtius, (a circumstance which modern translators can have no conception of,) died possessed of nothing valuable but his precious manuscripts. This ingenious scholar left his corpse to the surgeons for the benefit of his creditors.

Dryden, for less than three hundred pounds, sold Tonson ten thousand verses, as may be seen by the agreement.

Purchas, who in the reign of the first James of England spent his time in compiling his "Relation of the World," when he gave it to the public, for the reward of his labors was thrown into prison at the suit of his printer.

Louis the Fourteenth honored Racine and Boileau with a private monthly audience. One day the king asked what there was new in the literary world. Racine answered that he had seen a melancholy spectacle in the house of Corneille, whom he found dying, deprived even of a little broth. The king preserved a profound silence, and sent the dying poet a sum of money.

Spenser, the child of Fancy, languished out his life in misery. "Lord Burleigh," says Granger, who it is said prevented the queen giving him a hundred pounds, seems to have thought the lowest clerk in his office a more deserving person.

Le Sage resided in a little cottage while he supplied the world with their most agreeable novels, and appears to have derived the sources of his existence in his old age from the filial exertions of an excellent son, who was an actor of some genius.—*Curiosities of Literature.*

GO ON, SIR, GO ON!

Arago says in his autobiography, that his master in mathematics wrote a word or two of advice, which he found in the binding of one of his text-books. Puzzled and discouraged by the difficulties which he met with in his early studies, he was almost ready to give over the pursuit. Some words which he found on the waste leaf used to stiffen the cover of his paper bound text-book, caught his eye and interested him. "Impelled," he says, "by an indefinable curiosity, I dampened the cover of the book, and carefully unrolled the leaf to see what was on the other side. It proved to be a short letter from D' Alembert to a young person disheartened, like himself, by the difficulties of mathematical study, who had written to him for counsel. 'Go on, sir, go on,' was the counsel which D'Alembert gave him. "The difficulties you meet with resolve as you advance. Proceed, and light will dawn and shine with increased clearness on your path.' That maxim," says Arago, "was my greatest master in mathematics." Following out these simple words, "*Go on sir, go on,*" made him the first astronomical mathematician of his age. What Christians it would make of us! What heroes of faith, what sages of holy wisdom, would we become just by acting out that maxim, "*Go on, sir, go on!*"

ABOUT SANTO CLAUS.

BY MRS. L. M. CHILD.

SANTO CLAUS has an origin much less ancient than the festival which keeps him so busily employed; but his history goes far back into the ancient time, and is, like many others, a singular mixture of truth and fable. A child named Nicholas was born at Panthera, in Asia Minor, some four or five hundred years after the birth of Jesus. His parents, who were rich and of high rank, were converts to Christianity. This son was born to them many years after their marriage, and they received him as an answer to their many prayers. They wished to express their gratitude to God by educating him for the Christian priesthood, and the unusual sobriety and thoughtfulness of his boyhood confirmed them in that purpose. While he was yet a lad, both of his parents died of the plague, and he inherited their great wealth. But, partly from natural tenderness of heart and conscience and partly from the pious training he had received, he did not consider the riches as his own, but as a sacred trust placed in his hands by the Heavenly Father. He fed the hungry, clothed the naked, redeemed slaves, endowed poor maidens with marriage-portions, supported and educated destitute orphans, and performed all manner of charitable works, as secretly as possible. As a priest, he was greatly loved and reverenced by the poor; and when he became a bishop he continued to be as humble, self-denying, and benevolent as ever. After his death the church canonized him; his fame extended far and wide, and he became one of the greatest patron saints in Italy and in various Northern nations. He was everywhere reverenced as the helper of the poor and the protector of the weak against the strong; and he is so represented in a great variety of pictures in Catholic countries. St. George was a patron saint of knights and gentlemen; but St. Nicholas was the patron saint of the poor and weak, of serfs and prisoners, and especially of little children, who were always taught to believe that all their good gifts came from him. The story of his benevolent life received the addition of many miraculous incidents, which the untutored populace delighted to believe, and which artists loved to commemorate in pictures. It was said that on the first day of his life he stood up straight in the bath, folded his little hands, and audibly thanked God that he was born into the world. It was then the custom for members of the church to fast on Wednesdays and Fridays; and, so scrupulous was this baby saint, that he always refused to take his mother's milk more than once on those days. It is recorded that a word from his mouth stilled a raging tempest at sea and saved the lives of many sailors; that his prayers cured the sick, and restored three murdered boys to life. No saint had a more extensive popularity. The monks called him Santo Nicolaus. The natural tendency to clip familiar words changed this to Santo Nic'laus, and finally to Santo 'Claus. Under this latter name the good old bishop is still represented as coming down our chimneys in the night, with his arms full of Christmas presents for children. This is very kind of him considering that we are Protestants, and never dreamed of doing him reverence as a saint. But it seems he keeps on in his old habits of secret benevolence; and never had he such a charming variety of things wherewith to fill the mysterious stockings as he has this year. If you were to go into some of our book stores, you would say that they alone might furnish him with gifts enough for all the children in the country; they have such a variety of handsome juvenile books, by the best writers of England and America, abounding with pictures of all sorts of things on earth and sea and in the air. It is said that the meal with which St. Nicholas fed the poor was miraculously renewed; and it seems to be so with the Christmas gifts he brings to us.

A SCORE OF IMPOLITE THINGS,

IN WHICH YOUNG PERSONS RENDER THEMSELVES DISAGREEABLE.

1. Loud and boisterous laughter.
2. Reading when others are talking.
3. Reading aloud in company without being asked.
4. Talking when others are reading.
5. Spitting about the house, smoking or chewing.
6. Cutting finger nails in company.
7. Leaving a church before public worship is closed.
8. Whispering or laughing in the house of God.
9. Gazing rudely at strangers.
10. Leaving a stranger without a seat.
11. A want of respect and reverence for seniors.
12. Correcting older persons than yourself, especially parents.
13. Receiving a present without an expression of gratitude.
14. Making yourself the hero of your own story.
15. Laughing at the mistakes of others.
16. Joking of others in company.
17. Commencing talking before others have finished speaking.
18. Answering questions that have been put to others.
19. Commencing to eat as soon as you get to the table, and,
20. In not listening to what one is saying in company—unless you desire to show open contempt for the speaker. A well-bred person will not make an observation whilst another of the company is addressing himself to it.—*Educational Repository.*

THE CHRISTIAN'S BALANCE-SHEET.

"For I reckon that the sufferings of the present time are not worthy to be compared with the glory which shall be revealed in us."—Rom. viii. 18.

Dr.

"THE SUFFERINGS OF THE PRESENT TIME"

In labors more abundant.
In stripes above measure.
In prisons more frequent.
In deaths oft.
Five times received forty stripes, save one.
Thrice was I beaten with rods.
Once I was stoned.
Thrice I suffered shipwreck.
A night and day I have been in the deep.
In journeys often.
In perils of robbers.
In perils by my own countrymen.
In perils by the heathen.
In perils in the city.
In perils in the wilderness.
In perils in the sea.
In perils among false brethren.
In weariness and painfulness.
In watching often.
In hunger and thirst.
In fastings often.
In cold and nakedness.
Besides those things which are without, that which cometh upon me daily, the care of all the churches.

Total, . . "Light afflictions, but for a moment."

Cr.

"THE GLORY TO BE REVEALED IN US."

For we know that if our earthly house of this tabernacle were dissolved, we have a building of God, an house not made with hands, eternal in the heavens.

Eye hath not seen, nor ear heard, neither hath it entered into the heart of man, the things that God hath prepared for them that love him.

That he might make known the riches of his glory on the vessels of mercy which he hath before prepared unto glory.

Henceforth, there is laid up for me a crown of righteousness, which the Lord, the righteous Judge, shall give me at that day; and not to me only, but unto all them also that love his appearing.

When Christ who is our life shall appear, then shall ye also appear with him in glory.
And so shall we be ever with the Lord.

Total, ... "An eternal weight of glory."

The Apostle Paul having carefully examined the foregoing account, deliberately makes the following declaration: "I am persuaded that neither death, nor life, nor angels, nor principalities, nor powers, nor things present, nor things to come, nor height, nor depth, nor any other creature, shall be able to separate us from the love of God, which is in Christ Jesus our Lord."

THE VOYAGE DOWN THE DARK RIVER.

We know but little of the Heavenly state. Everything must be different from what we see here. All the outward means by which we are sustained even in doing our duty here, will be altered or gone. "Tongues, knowledge, prophecy," shall have "vanished away." There is no temple in that city; no church, no congregation, no liturgy, no directory, no priests, no elders, no ministers. "And that city has no need of the sun, neither of the moon to shine in it." Even all those lesser lights which are so cheering on earth; and even all good men, and all those dear familiar faces which had been our joy and stay on earth, will not be *needed* there. "They which are counted worthy to obtain that world, neither marry, nor are given in marriage; neither can they die any more: for they are equal unto the angels."

But is there then no certainty, no support, no light, in the great void of the other world? Not so. There are two Objects in that world, which include all others, and which make the darkness light, and fill the formless void. "The Lord God Almighty and the Lamb are the temple of it. The glory of God lightens it, and the Lamb is the light thereof." *God* and *Christ*. These are the two Ideas, these are the two Persons, rather this is the one Idea, this is the one Person, to see whom, to be with whom, is to the true believer the sufficient account of his hope in heaven. "In Thy light shall we see light," was the trust of the Psalmist. In the presence of God, all the difficulties of this world will be at last made clear. In the presence of God, all the goodness and justice and wisdom of this world will be at last made perfect. "To be with Christ." This was the one prayer of the apostle. If the world beyond the grave is dark, if the thought of God is too vast or wide for us to grasp, yet the promise of being with Christ is clear and definite to the humblest as well as to the wisest. We know what He was; we can figure to ourselves from the Gospels His truth, His love, His searching knowledge of every soul and character amongst us. What He was He is still. What He is, God is. What support we should have had from Him, had we known him on earth, we shall receive tenfold, without let or hindrance, from His everlasting arms, in that world of which He is at once the Temple and the Light. He is the Temple of heaven, for He is the end to which all earthly worship tends. Every ordinance, every prayer, every hymn, every psalm, every sacred day, every sacred memory, has or ought to have but one object—to bring us nearer to God by making us more like to Christ. When we have at last come into the presence of Christ, then the means will cease, for the end will be gained. "We shall be like him, for we shall see him as he is." He is the Light of heaven, for in Him are combined all the perfections which we see scattered amongst His faithful servants; all the beauty and glory which we see divided in the works of creation.

This last and best glimpse into the other world shall be explained by a tale, taken, from the dark hours of this world.

An old New Zealand chief, who, like King Edwin of Northumbria, had been converted in middle life to the Christian religion, and had lived a life of consistent Christian goodness, was at last brought to his deathbed. He gathered his friends and family round him—some pagans still, some Christians—and then he raised himself up and began to sing one of the ancient songs of his country, which he had learned in his youth, before his conversion. It told of a maiden who had a lover, a faithful lover; she had not seen him for years; he had gone off into the distant seas; and now she was determined to seek and to join him. And so the New Zealand chief sang of her voyage, in words well-known to those who stood around him, but with a meaning far deeper than they had ever before put on the words; for they saw that under the figure of the forlorn maiden he meant his own soul going forth on its last long voyage; and under the figure of the lover he meant that blessed Saviour whom he hoped now to join in that unknown sea. He sang how the maiden, in her frail canoe, went down the dark river; how she dashed down the foaming rapids; how the steep rocks closed in on either side; how through the black pass the river opened into the wide sea: how, in the wide sea, she still was not afraid, for she looked forward all the more to being with him whom she loved, forever.

So singing, and so transfiguring the old pagan song with the light of the Gospel, the Christian chieftain passed away. It is to that outer darkness, of which the Saxon chief spoke to the first missionary of our forefathers, through that dark river, and into that unknown sea—of which the New Zealand chief spoke to his newly-converted friends,—we must also go. Education, business, worship, life itself, will all take their proper color, and their proper proportions, then, and then only, when we remember that they are all means to one end, namely, to be like Christ and to be with Christ.—*Dean Stanley.*

KEEPING A DIARY.

If a man keeps no diary, the path crumbles away behind him as his feet leave it; and days gone by are but little more than a blank, broken by a few distorted shadows. His life is all confined within the limits of to-day. Who does not know how imperfect a thing memory is? It not merely forgets; it misleads. Things in memory do not merely fade away, preserving as they fade their own lineaments so long as they can be seen: they change their aspect, they change their place, they turn to something quite different from the fact. In the picture of the past, which memory unaided by any written record sets before us, the perspective is entirely wrong. How capriciously some events seem quite recent, which the diary shows are really far away; and how unaccountably many things look far away, which in truth, are not left many weeks behind us! A man might almost as well not have lived at all as entirely forget that he has lived, and entirely forget what he did on those departed days. But I think that almost every person would feel a great interest in looking back, day by day, upon what he did and thought upon that day twelve-months, that day three or five years. The trouble of writing the diary is very small. A few lines, a few words, written at the time, suffice, when you look at them, to bring all (what the Yankees call) the *surroundings* of that season before you. Many little things come up again, which you know quite well you never would have thought of again, but for your glance at those words, and still which you feel you would be sorry to have forgotten. There must be a richness about the life of a person who keeps a diary, unknown to other men. And a million more little links and ties must bind him to the members of his family circle, and to all among whom he lives. Life, to him looking back, is not a bare line, stringing together his personal identity; it is surrounded, intertwined, entangled with thousands and thousands of slight incidents, which give it beauty, kindliness, reality. Some folks' life is like an oak walking-stick, straight and varnished; useful, but hard and bare. Other men's lives (and such may yours and mine, kindly reader, ever be) are like that oak when it was not a stick, but a branch, and waved, leaf-enveloped, and with lots of little twigs growing out of it, upon the summer tree. And yet more precious than the power of the diary to call up again a host of little circumstances and facts, is its power to bring back the indescribable but keenly-felt atmosphere of those departed days. The old time comes over you. It is not merely a collection, an aggregate of facts, that comes back; it is something far more excellent than that—it is the soul of days long ago; it is the dear *Auld lang syne* itself! The perfume of hawthorn hedges is there; the breath of breezes that fanned our gray hair when it made sunny curls, often smoothed down by hands that are gone; the sunshine on the grass where these old fingers made daisy-chains; and snatches of music, compared, with which anything you hear at the opera is extremely poor. Therefore keep you a diary, my friend.

SCHOOL-CHILDREN.

THIS beautifully bright morning of March the 5th, the thermometer being near twelve of zero of Fahrenheit, at eight o'clock, found us taking the usual walk of a mile and a half along Fifth avenue, from dwelling to office, with our four responsibilities, who go to school near by. Alice, our eight year old, who was full of talk, said: "Father, I wish I was my teacher's pet, but I am not; her pets can do as they please, but she is so strict with the rest of us." "Who are her pets, my daughter?" "The ones that know their lessons best." "Are they larger or smaller than you?" "Oh; they are the tiniest girls in the school. My teacher says the smallest girls in the school are the smartest."

On another occasion, when told of a girl who was never absent, never missed a word in any of her lessons, I inquired if she was good-looking. The reply was: "She is so pale and thin; and there are sores on her hands and face."

Similar answers have been made in various other cases. The actual fact is that the good scholars study themselves to death, and are petted and favored in a great variety of ways; while those of less mental capacity are treated with an impatience and a sternness which soon gives them a dislike for school, for their teachers, and for learning in general, and Saturdays and Sundays are the only sunshiny days of the week to them. I frequently say to my children: "I don't want you to strive for 'head.' I don't want you to be promoted, for the oftener you are, the harder you will have to study. You have plenty of time, and I would rather see you eat heartily, and sleep soundly, and know but little, than that you should know a great deal, and grow pale, and thin, and weakly, and die before you are grown up."

Among the most important observances for school-children, and which every wise and affectionate parent will never lose sight of, are—

1. See that they have all the sleep they can take. Every

child under ten should be in bed by eight o'clock, summer and winter, so that they may have nearly eleven hours' sleep. Those older, should be in bed at nine, and be required to rise at six; thus they will have more time for study in the morning, when the brain is rested and acts sufficiently, and will also be prevented from injuring their eyes, as very many school-children do, by using artificial light.

2. See to it that every child goes to bed with warm, dry feet, and that they sleep warmly all night.

3. If you are human, and not a brute, never allow your child to go to bed with wounded or ruffled feelings, from any angry words, or harsh or hasty conduct on your part. Always send them off to school in a happy and affectionate state of mind; and when they return, let them be invariably received with a kindly greeting, and a loving, thankful gladness that they are once more returned to you in health and safety. These things are the more necessary, as their ambitions, their disappointments, their discouragements, and their troubles, in reference to their schools and their lessons, are as important to them as yours to you, in the mightier matters of life; and if they find not a balm for all these in the affection, and smiles, and sympathy of their mothers especially, it is to them a misfortune, and to such mothers a disgrace.

4. By all possible means arrange that your children shall reach school with dry feet and dry clothing; the neglect of this has sent many a sweet child to its early grave, the victim of a mother's carelessness or a teacher's stupidity.

5. School-children should eat with great regularity; thrice a day is all-sufficient for those above ten. Frequent eating, and tempting their appetites with sweetmeats and delicacies, has been the ground-work of early and life-long dyspepsia to multitudes.

6. Teach children perseveringly the importance of attending promptly to the calls of nature, and by any and every means bring it about that this shall be done before leaving for school in the morning. To this end, arrange that they shall be through with their breakfast an hour before it is necessary to start for school, even if they have to eat by candle-light. Cases of fatal inflammation of the bladder have often occurred in consequence of the ignorance or brutality of teachers in this connection.

7. Embrace every opportunity of impressing children's minds with the fact that teachers are laboring for their good, and therefore ought to be loved, respected, and obeyed, as their best friends.—*Hall's Journal.*

THE INTELLIGENCE OF IDIOTS.

IN Great Britain there are fifteen thousand imbeciles, the greater portion of whom are not only utterly valueless as helpers in performing the work of the world, but actually detract largely from the work of others, insomuch as they require to be watched and taken care of. It is evident that any attempt to make this unfortunate class even partially independent and self-supporting, should be watched with interest, not only on humanitarian, but on politico-economical grounds. Two such experiments have been tried in England, institutions for training imbeciles in manual labor of various kinds having been started—namely, Earlswood Asylum and Essex Hall.

It is estimated that in the former of these a little over one third (thirty-five per cent.)of imbeciles are capable of a certain degree of culture in some direction, and it is only those who are thought to belong to this class who are received at Earlswood. Thus the institution is a hospital, and not a mere receptacle for hopeless cases.

"The majority of the children reared here are simply specimens of what is termed 'arrested development.' At a very early age the functions of the brain—at least in regard to its intellectual operations—appear to have stopped; hence we see a school full of grown up boys and girls, sometimes of the age of eighteen or twenty, no more capable of taking care of themselves than children of three or four. They cannot use their hands in any ordinary operation; sometimes they don't know the way to eat with a knife and fork, and, as a rule, the newcomers are utterly incapable of dressing or undressing themselves. Their very actions are those of little children; their emotions and fears, their joys and sorrows remind us most forcibly of those we witness in a nursery of little ones. . . . The faculty of imitation, which is common to the monkey and to the child, is the great instrument by which these poor little ones are taught to exercise their senses, and to acquire the ordinary habits of civilized beings. They are grouped in classes, a few of those already instructed being mixed with those who have to learn. Finger lessons are the first that are taught. Most of the children, for instance, on first admission, cannot button a button, tie a string, nor do the commonest act which requires any adroit manipulation of the digits; hence all this has to be learned. It is certainly an odd sight to see a group of girls all actively engaged in buttoning and unbuttoning their clothes, in pinning them, and in tying and untying strings. In a short time, by watching those who are instructed in these simple arts, they become adepts, and are able to dress themselves with perfect ease. While witnessing the mechanical manner and the earnest expression with which these lessons were performed, we confess we were reminded of the performing monkey the Italian organ-grinder carries about with him, who sweeps with a broom, plays the drum, shoulders and lets off a musket, and does half a score of tricks with equal adroitness.

"Various handicrafts are taught here, and therefore many preliminary lessons of a similar character have to be acquired before the boys are entrusted with tools. All the tailoring is done by the inmates, a regular teacher presiding, and instructing the more advanced in cutting out, sewing, and fitting. The workmen give the spectator, however, the idea of being boys at play, for they come up to him and eagerly show their work, as the youngest children show their drawings on a slate, delighted at the smallest praise. Besides the handicrafts, the boys are taught agricultural pursuits; they cultivate the garden, and feed the stock—the favorite occupation; they milk the cows, and do it well too. . . . . The routine instruction of the asylum lifts all of these poor children, more or less, into the scale of rational beings, able to help themselves and others; but in some instances the most encouraging results are obtained. Thus, some of the lads are able to copy engravings in a surprising manner. It is done in a purely mechanical spirit, it is true, and this very fact affords a proof of the small intellectual merit of the merely copying capacity; but are there not many persons earning their bread in the world, and considered to be very clever, by means of the same limited powers?"

That great benefit arises from the enabling of idiots to perform any useful work, cannot be doubted. A similar enterprise has been started by Dr. Parrish, in Media, near Philadelphia, which has been quite as successful in its operations as those in England. The (London) *Daily News*, a short time since in noticing the annual *fete* at Earlswood Asylum, speaks as follows of the inmates:

"One idiot has a special power as a copyist of the finest engravings, and his imitations of Landseer and other well-known artists are plentifully hung about the walls. . . . One of the inmates we saw on Thursday—a smart, active man of thirty years, in nautical uniform—has constructed a model ship, and has developed mechanical genius of no mean order. He was wearing an ivory cravat ornament, manufactured by himself, which would have done credit to any West End shop, and appeared to be exercising an intelligent supervision over the pastimes of the day. Ask him a question, however, and he stares vacantly and in silence. Try to rouse him by your admiration of the vessel he has fashioned with such exquisite care and skill, and he gibbers unintelligibly, or tells you that 'Angels are good—devils bad—angels put top of masts, devils down below.' Boots are made by one idiot which have challenged comparison at the English and French Exhibitions for neatness and beauty; and in what is called the 'workshop-block.' . . . The inmates may be seen at work, except on such festivals as that of Thursday, upon a variety of trades. Household and laundry-work, mat-weaving, farming, gardening, carpentering, tailoring, shoemaking, plumbing, and basket making, are all carried on by idiots."

TESTIMONY IN FAVOR OF TEMPERANCE.

A LATE number of the *Turf, Field, and Farm* contains a letter from Edward P. Weston, the famous pedestrian, to Rev. T. L. Cuyler, of Brooklyn, from which we extract the following wholesome lesson:

"You ask for my 'experience as to the effect of alcholic stimulants on those who aim at athletic achievements.' In reply, I am constrained to say that, so far as my judgment and experience are concerned, the use of intoxicating liquors on the occasion of the performance of any task requiring strength and nerve, is not only unneccessary, but wholly injurious. The moment a man partakes of such stimulants at such a time, he ceases to work upon his own strength of manhood, and is simply using a false power built upon a medicine (for liquor is good for nothing else). It may help him for the moment, but the effect is of short duration, and then he is worse than before. It not only weakens his body, but his nerve, and takes away his will; and that is not all—it will take away his appetite for food. I know it is a custom prevalent among those who go into a regular course of instruction, or training, (as it is called,) for a feat of pedestrianism, to give them crackers soaked in wine at stated intervals. To my mind, this is not only folly and a loss of time, but morally wrong. The man should *always be in training*, (all that is necessary,) have his habits regular, and have a care of that which he eats and when he eats it. If he can not walk fifty miles a day without taking wine, he certainly will not walk long if he makes that his practice.

"Diet is an important consideration in a walk that places a stronger tax than usual upon the physical system. And if a man desires to excel in feats requiring endurance and strength, he must pay strict attention to a diet based upon the primitive laws of health. What I recommend has been proved valuable by personal experience. Of meats, beef is the best; and it should be cooked rare, and then eaten with cold wheat bread, and good sweet butter; potatoes boiled, mashed or stewed, and eggs soft boiled. Too much grease should be avoided. When you eat, drink hot tea or coffee. But, before eating at all, cease walking, and rest thirty minutes, at least. The stomach is heated, and it wants rest as well as the limbs; besides, food should not be taken into it when heated, for then mastication is unnatural; instead of seizing hold, as it were, of the food, the organs are in a state of excitement which induces exhaustion.

"As a beverage, when on the road, I generally use molasses and water, and with the best results. It keeps the stomach in a measure cool; and coolness internally is refreshing to the whole system. I first used molasses and water on the road to avoid the unpleasant tatse of the different qualities of water drawn from different wells and springs, and the experiment was so successful that now I never start on a journey trying to physical manhood, without it. When on the march, oatmeal gruel and beef-tea are good, as a change from molasses and water. Cold coffee and cold tea I also use as a beverage when walking; and the appetite craves either. If I am attacked with sudden pain when taking severe exercise, I lie down flat on my back, elevate my feet, and after a short rest, swallow two teaspoonfuls of peppermint and sugar with hot water. This does away with the use of alcoholic stimulants, since it is the only emergency in which they could be beneficial; and peppermint, even in this emergency, I find the best remedy."

A CHILD'S INFLUENCE.

Do not say you have no influence: all have some. A gentleman, lecturing in the neighborhood of London, said:

"Everybody has influence, even that child," pointing to a little girl in her father's arms.

"That's true!" cried the man.

At the close he said to the lecturer: "I beg your pardon, sir, but I could not help speaking. I was a drunkard, but as I did not like to go to the public house alone, I used to carry this child. As I approached the public house one night, hearing a great noise inside, she said:

"'Don't go, father.'

"'Hold your tongue, child.'

"'Please, father, don't go.'

"'Hold your tongue, I say.'

"Presently I felt a big tear fall on my cheek. I could not go a step further, sir. I turned round and went home, and have never been in a public house since, thank God for it! I am now a happy man, sir, and this little girl has done it all; and when you said that even she had influence, I could not help saying, 'That's true, sir.' All have influence."—*Rev. N. Hall.*

SEVEN REASONS FOR ABSTAINING FROM INTOXICATING DRINKS.

1. BECAUSE ale, porter, gin, rum, brandy, whisky, etc., all contain a spirit which is calculated to derange the human system.

2. Because none of these drinks, as a habitual beverage, are ever useful, but always injurious to persons in health, and many professing Christians, both young and old, have been ruined by them.

3. Because intemperance obstructs the progress of civilization, education, the religion of Jesus, and every useful reform.

4. Because abstinence is sure and safe, and drinking moderately is dangerous, and has led to all the drunkenness in the world.

5. Because I find I can not effectually warn the drunkard, or set him an example, unless I am myself an entire abstainer.

6. Because it is important to set a safe example of perfect sobriety to our children, friends, and associates.

7. Because I find myself by abstaining, healthier, wealthier, and happier, and better fitted to perform my duty to God and man.

NARROWNESS OF SPECIALTIES.

WE men are not fragments—we are wholes; we are not types of single qualities—we are realities of mixed, various, countless combinations. Therefore I say to each man: As far as you can—partly for excellence in your special mental calling, principally for completion of your end in existence—strive, while improving your one talent, to enrich your whole capital as a MAN. It is in this way that you escape from the wretched narrow-mindedness which is the characteristic of every one who cultivates his specialty alone. Take any specialty; dine with a distinguished member of Parliament—the other guests all members of Parliament except yourself—you go away shrugging your shoulders. All the talk has been that of men who seem to think that there is nothing in life worth talking about but the party squabbles and jealousies of the House of Commons. Go and dine next day with an eminent author—all the guests authors except yourself. As the wine circulates, the talk narrows to the last publications, with now and then, on the part of the least successful author present, a refining eulogium on some dead writer, in implied disparagement of some living rival. He wants to depreciate Dickens, and therefore he extols Fielding. If Fielding were alive and Dickens were dead, how he would extol Dickens! Go the third day; dine with a trader—all the other guests being gentlemen on the stock exchange. A new specialty is before you; all the world seems circumscribed to script and the budget. In fine, whatever the calling, let men only cultivate that calling, and they are as narrow-minded as the Chinese, when they place on the map of the world the Celestial Empire, with all its Tartaric villages in full detail, and out of that limit make dots and lines, with the superscription, "Deserts unknown—inhabited by barbarians!"—*Bulwer.*

YANKEE GIRLS.

THE paleness in the American girls, though often beautiful, is too universal. An eye from the old country begins to long for a rosy cheek. Lowell said that color was a thing of climate, and that I should find plenty of rosy cheeks among the mountains of Maine, where there is more moisture in the air. It may be so; I never got to the Maine mountains to see. But, as far as my observation went, I never saw any, either on mountain or valley, in any part of New England. My private impression is, making all allowance for the influence of dry air, that the peculiar paleness of the New England girls connects itself with too much metaphysics and pie!

I have strong convictions on the subject of pie. Not to speak of mere paleness, I don't see how the Americans can reconcile it with their notions of what is due to the laws of nature, to live to the age they do, considering the amount of pie they eat, and the rapidity with which they eat it. I don't remember that I ever sat down to a dinner in America, even in a poor man's house, without finding pie of some kind, often of several kinds, on the table, and without finding that everybody partook of it, down to the microscopic lady or gentleman whom we should call the baby. Pie is indispensable. Take anything away, but leave the pie. Americans can stand the prohibition of all intoxicating drinks, but attempt to prohibit pie, and you would plunge America into a revolution in a day.

Then metaphysics. In one family which I visited, in the Connecticut Valley, two of the girls were deep in the study of algebra and metaphysics, as a voluntary exercise, and shut themselves up, for three hours a day, with Colenso, and Sir William Hamilton, and Kant. This was, perhaps, exceptional; but the New England brain is very busy. It develops very soon and very fast, and begins at an exceedingly early age to exercise itself with the abstruser studies. Parents and teachers often told me that their difficulty, with the girls especially, was, not to get them urged on, but to get them held back. In one young ladies' seminary which I visited, they were held back with the following light studies, in addition to all the ordinary branches: Virgil and Horace, Latin prose composition, anatomy and hygiene, moral philosopy, mental philosophy, and quadratic equations. To this add pie and hot bread, and what could you expect but paleness, even among the mountains of Maine?

Paleness and pie notwithstanding, the American girls are very delightful; and, in one point, they fairly surpass the majority of English girls—they are well educated and well informed. . . . . . . Some girls are fascinating, whether they are educated or not; but to be left alone, as one sometimes is, with a girl who knows nothing, in a room with no piano, is exceedingly embarassing—after the weather has been exhausted. There is never the same difficulty with American girls. The admirable educational system of New England, covering the whole area of society, has given them education, whether they be poor or rich; has furnished them with a great deal of useful information, and has quickened their desire for more.

American girls will talk with you about anything, and feel (or, what has the same effect, seem to feel) interest in it. Their tendency is, perhaps, to talk too much, and to talk beyond their knowledge. With the cleverer (or, as they would say themselves, the "smarter") of them, it seemed to me sometimes to make no perceptible difference whether they knew anything of the subject they talked about or not. Mentioning this feature of American character to a Boston gentleman, he said: "It is true—I was struck in England with the silence of the people when they have nothing to say. One time, travelling in the carriage with a nobleman, I asked him his opinion of the ballot. He replied: 'I have not considered the subject yet.' You might travel all over America," said my friend, "and never hear a man say that." But the American girls generally know a little of everything, and their general intelligence and vivacity make them delightful companions.

I had an idea, before going over, that the New England ladies spent their time over intellectual pursuits, to the neglect of household duties. I did not find it so. Comparing class with class, they are quite as good housekeepers as I have seen anywhere. They had need be, for service at present is in a very wretched condition in America; so much so, that middle-class families in the country often dispense with servants altogether. The young ladies can make beds, as well as demonstrate propositions, and their mental philosophy, whatever it amounts to, never interferes with the perfection of the pies.—*Daniel M'Crea.*

DESPAIR EXPRESSED IN ART.

REV. F. W. ROBERTSON, A.M.

At Blenheim, the seat of the Duke of Marlborough, there is a Madonna, into which the old Catholic painter has tried to cast the religious conceptions of the Middle Ages, virgin purity and infinite repose. The look is upwards, the predominant color of the picture blue, which we know has in itself a strange power to lull and soothe. It is impossible to gaze on this picture without being conscious of a calming influence. During that period of the year in which the friends of the young men of Oxford come to visit their brothers and sons, and Blenheim becomes a place of favorite resort, I have stood aside near that picture, to watch its effect on the different gazers, and I have seen group after group of young undergraduates and ladies, full of life and noisy spirits, unconsciously stilled before it; the countenance relaxing into calmness, and the voice sinking to a whisper. The painter had spoken his message, and human beings, ages after, feel what he meant to say.

You may perhaps have seen in this town, some years ago, an engraving in the windows of the printsellers, called the "Camel of the Desert." I cannot say it was well executed. The engraving was coarse, and the drawing, in some points, false; yet it was full of Poetry. The story tells itself. A caravan has passed through the desert; one of the number has been seized with dangerous illness, and as time is precious, he has been left to die, but as there is a chance of his recovery, his camel has been left beside him, and in order that it may not escape, the knee of the animal has been forcibly bent, the upper and lower bones tied together, and the camel couched on the ground incapable of rising. The sequel is that the man has died, and the camel is left to its inevitable doom. There is nothing to break the deep deathfulness of the scene. The desert extends to the horizon, without interruption, the glowing heat being shown by the reflection of the sun from the sands in a broad band of light, just as it glows on the sea on a burning summer day.

Nothing, I said, breaks the deathfulness of the scene; there is only one thing that adds to it. A long line of vultures is seen in the distance, and one of these loathsome birds is hovering above the dead and the doomed; the camel bends back his neck to watch it, with an expression of terror and anguish almost human, and anticipates its doom. You cannot look at the print without a vivid sense and conception of Despair. You go through street after street before the impression ceases to haunt you. Had the plate been better executed, it is quite possible it might not have been so poetical. The very rudeness and vagueness of it leave much to the imagination. Had the plumage of the vulture, or the hair of the camel more accurately copied the living texture, or the face of the corpse been more deathlike, so as, instead of kindling the imagination with the leading idea, to have drawn away the attention to the fidelity with which the accessories had been painted, the Poetry would have been lessened. It is the effort to express a feeling, and the obstacles in the way of the expression, which together constitute the poetical.—*Rev. F. W. Robertson.*

CONSIDER THE LILIES OF THE FIELD.

Our Saviour was sitting on the side of one of the hills near the western shore of the Sea of Galilee. These hills were on the southern border of a broad and fertile meadow, stretching inland for more than a mile. The red and purple lilies were well known there, as Pliny has told us, and they readily suggested, by their colors, the robes which in those days were a part of the insignia of monarchs; whence the fitness of the allusion to the apparel of "Solomon in all his glory." There could have been no flower more appropriately "considered," none more forcibly associated with Solomon and the times of his "glory." It was at once a royal and a sacred flower. It had been wrought upon the molten sea, and carved upon the two noted pillars of the temple porch. It was the favorite in the flower imagery of the Song of Solomon, and now these lilies were blooming upon the plains and fields before them. Their grace and beauty were the more remarkable in that they grew so freely. They spring up from every field, shedding their fragrance upon every passing breeze, decorating the thorn as well as the olive, indebted to no one's care but God's, to his sunshine and his rains alone, for their existence and their beauty. They had survived the rending apart of the kingdom. They had remained upon the fields, and had been "clothed" and renewed in their weakness, while strong ones had been carried into captivity, or scourged by sword and by pestilence. "Consider the lilies of the field." In all this, every lily had its duty to perform—its place to fill in the cycles of the Creator's great and various purposes. Every lily-stalk was gifted with its minute channels, up which it drew the life-sap God had provided—it opened its petals in due season, and lavishly gave to the passing breeze its grateful incense of fragrance, or it smiled in its beauty under the warm rays of a spring-time sun. There it stood, quietly working out its duty and its history—"toiling not nor spinning"—a never-fading witness to God's condescending care and mysterious providence—a picture of a sublime truth enfolded in its petals, that God's eternal power may be felt and known in a leaf as in a world, and that the footprints of God's loving presence may be very near us, while to find them we are wandering far away.—*Rev. J. P. Newman.*

THE TALENT OF SUCCESS.

Every man must patiently abide his time. He must wait. Not in listless idleness, not in useless pastime, not in querulous defection; but in constant, steady, cheerful endeavor, always willing, fulfilling and accomplishing his task, "that when the occasion comes he may be equal to the occasion." The talent of success is nothing more than doing what you can do well, without a thought of fame. If it comes at all, it will come because it is deserved, not because it is sought after. It is a very indiscreet and troublesome ambition which cares so much about fame, about what the world says of us, as to be always looking in the face of others for approval, to be always anxious about the effect of what we do or say, to be always shouting to hear the echoes of our own voices.—*Longfellow.*

ON SICKNESS.

At the first address and presence of sickness, stand still and arrest thy spirit, that it may, without amazement or affright, consider that this was that thou lookedst for, and wert always certain should happen, and that now thou art to enter into the actions of a new religion, the agony of a strange constitution; but at no hand suffer thy spirits to be dispersed with fear or wildness of thought, but stay their looseness and dispersion by a serious consideration of the present and future employment. For so doth the Libyan lion,* spying the fierce huntsman; he first beats himself with the strokes of his tail, and curls up his spirits, making them strong with union and recollection; till, being struck with a Mauritanian spear, he rushes forth into his defence and noblest contention, and either scapes into the secrets of his own dwelling, or else dies the bravest of the forest.

In sickness, the soul begins to dress herself for immortality. And first, she unties the strings of vanity that made her upper garment cleave to the world and sit uneasy. Next she puts off the light and fantastic summer-robe of lust and wanton appetite. Next to this, the soul, by the help of sickness, knocks off the fetters of pride and vainer complacencies. Then she draws the curtains, and stops the light from coming in, and takes the pictures down—those fantastic images of self-love, and gay remembrances of vain opinion, and popular noises. Then the spirit stoops into the sobrieties of humble thoughts,

* See Theocritus, Idyll 25, line 230.

and feels corruption chiding the forwardness of fancy, and allaying the vapors of conceit and factious opinions. Next to these, as the soul is still undressing, she shakes off the roughness of her great and little angers and animosities, and receives the oil of mercies and smooth forgiveness, fair interpretations and gentle answers, designs of reconcilement and Christian atonement, in their places.

The temptations of this state—such, I mean, which are proper to it—are little and inconsiderable. The man is apt to chide a servant too bitterly, and to be discontented with his nurse, or not satisfied with his physician; and he rests uneasily, and (poor man!) nothing can please him; and, indeed, these little indecencies must be cured and stopped, lest they run into an inconvenience. But sickness is, in this particular, a little image of the state of blessed souls, or of Adam's early morning in paradise, free from the troubles of lust and violences of anger, and the intricacies of ambition or the restlessness of covetousness. For though a man may carry all these along with him into his sickness, yet there he will not find them; and in despite of all his own malice, his soul shall find some rest from laboring in the galleys and baser captivity of sin.—*Jeremy Taylor.*

THE SHINING CHURCH, AND THE SHINING LIFE.

STEPHEN OLIN, D.D., L.L.D.

The Church illuminates the world by the manifestation of its piety, but its manifested can never exceed its real piety. Its power to fulfil this, its most peculiar and essential function, may therefore be accurately measured by the faith, zeal, and holiness of its members. A Church may be what the world calls a strong Church in point of numbers and influence. A Church may be made up of men of wealth, men of intellect, men of power, high-born men, and men of rank and fashion; and, being so composed, may be, in a worldly sense, a very strong Church. There are many things that such a Church can do. It can launch ships, and endow seminaries. It can diffuse intelligence, can uphold the cause of benevolence, can maintain an imposing array of forms and religious activities. It can build splendid temples, can rear a magnificent pile, and adorn its front with sculptures, and lay stone upon stone, and heap ornament upon ornament, till the costliness of the ministrations at the altar shall keep any poor man from ever entering the portal. But, my brethren, I will tell you one thing that it cannot do—it cannot *shine.* It may glitter and blaze like an iceberg in the sun, but without inward holiness it cannot shine. Of all that is formal and material in Christianity it may make a splendid manifestation, but it cannot shine. It may turn almost everything into gold at its touch, but it cannot touch the heart. It may lift up its marble front, and pile tower upon tower, and mountain upon mountain; but it cannot touch the mountains, and they shall smoke; it cannot conquer souls for Christ; it cannot awaken the sympathies of faith and love; it cannot do Christ's work in man's conversion. It is dark in itself, and cannot diffuse light. It is cold at heart, and has no overflowing and subduing influences to pour out upon the lost. And with all its strength, that Church is weak, and, for Christ's peculiar work, worthless. And with all its glitter of gorgeous array, it is a dark Church—it cannot shine.

On the contrary, show me a Church poor, illiterate, obscure, unknown, but composed of praying people; they shall be men of neither power, nor wealth, nor influence; they shall be families that do not know one week where they are to get their bread for the next; but with them is the hiding of God's power, and their influence is felt for eternity, and their light shines and is watched, and wherever they go there is a fountain of light, and Christ in them is glorified, and his kingdom advanced. They are His chosen vessels of salvation, and His luminaries to reflect His light.

As the ability of the entire company of believers, or of any single Church, to perform its duty to God and the world, depends upon their piety, even so it is with the individual Christian. If his religion be merely decent, and formal, and ostensible, it will be utterly powerless. If, on the contrary, it is heartfelt, intense, and impulsive, it will be irresistible, and its speechless eloquence will reach hearts and habitations where the pastor and his preaching can get no access. In this view the purest, meekest, most child-like man is often the mightiest. He who wrestles most earnestly with God in his closet is most likely to go forth to his converse with men anointed for his mission. His garments smell of the spices of Paradise. His face shines as the face of an angel, and he unavoidably becomes in his sphere "the light of the world." The humble Christian, without suspecting that he is fulfilling such a ministry, is ever acting upon others. To some family or individual he appears from day to day the impersonation of all they know or heed of saving Christianity—the living epistle in which they read the character of the Gospel, its author, and his disciples. It is probably safe to affirm that every Christian holds a relation to some immortal soul, on which its final destiny is likely to turn. Father, brother, neighbor, superior or inferior, he is the man upon whose purity, or faith, or zeal, or consistency, or prayers, or faithful admonition, the salvation of another undying spirit is suspended. "Ye are the light of the world."

THE NOBLEST MONUMENT.

At the end of one of the suburbs of the town, on the right-hand side, stands a portico, supported by two columns, and furnished with iron gates. On the entablature of the portico is inscribed a verse from the Holy Scriptures. This is the entrance to the cemetery.

Whenever my heart is oppressed by sorrow, I go there, and, approaching a gray stone shaded by a weeping willow, give vent to my grief. The grave lying beneath is small, but a vacant space has been reserved beside it, (a place I am one day to occupy.) The epitaph is comprised in two lines, and contains only the name of the departed one who has gone before me, with three dates—that of her birth, of our marriage, and of our earthly separation. Up to within a short period it had been my intention to raise a more imposing monument; during many months I dreamed of the combined structure of bronze and marble to be erected beneath those waving branches. No longer able to exhibit, in this state of existence, any marks of devotion to her who reposes there, I indulged in the idea of proving thus, at least, my faithful remembrance of her. How many calculations were completed and recommenced with this object in view! what efforts were made to increase my savings month by month! what satisfaction I derived from wearing coarser garments, and the further saving effected by a more frugal table! At length the necessary sum was obtained. I went every day to the cemetery to measure our funeral couch, and erect in thought the cherished monument. One morning as I was there mentally realizing its form, two little girls passed me; they were carrying a half-filled watering-pot; beads of perspiration trickled down their heated foreheads, and both panted for breath.

"Where are you going so fast, my poor children? I asked."

"Down there," they replied, "to our father's grave, which we have planted with flowers."

"And you are carrying that water to refresh them?"

"Yes, sir, we are obliged to bring it from the well a long way off, at the end of the walk. In a short time the well will dry up, and then our flowers must die."

They said this so piteously that I strove to comfort them by pointing out the flower-beds which flourished amidst the graves around.

"Oh yes, sir!" they exclaimed; "the gravedigger is well paid to keep those flowers watered; they belong to rich people; but look yonder at the others!

They then showed me a corner of the cemetery which I had never visited, with long rows of graves already burnt up by the sun, where the flowers appeared to be nothing better than yellow and faded leaves.

"That is how our father's grave will look in a few days," said the elder of the two children, with emotion.

"So, then, without a supply of water, you must give up all idea of keeping it green and fresh?"

"Yes, indeed, sir. Poor people are very unfortunate not to be able to keep the flowers alive round the graves of their relations."

The elder, who said this, sighed, and then, beckoning to her sister, they both took up their watering-pot and went on. I followed them with my eyes for a long while.

"Dear and pious children, who crave only the means of ornamenting, with a few flowers, the grave of him whom they weep for! And how many others, doubtless, long for the same source of consolation! Whilst I am contemplating a stately monument to my departed wife, how many, less favored, would be satisfied with a shrub or a few roses at the foot of the wooden cross which surmounts their cherished dead! With the price of the costly materials I might cause enough moisture to flow from the soil to refresh every one of these faded graves. The sacrifice of my vain caprice would be a source of joy to all. Farewell, then, useless monument, which I had fondly dreamed of constructing in bronze and marble to the memory of my beloved Louise; in its place I will raise for her one of self-sacrifice and of true devotion. What these humble graves stand in need of, I will bestow in the name of her who was the better part of myself; the water which they all thirst for shall gush forth from the foot of her grave; though dead, she shall still be what she was when living—a source of material aid to those in want, and of consolation to those in sorrow."

God be praised for having afforded me the means of honoring her memory in a manner worthy of herself! To-day the spring has been found, and its waters murmur softly as they flow beside the trees of the cemetery, bedewing the graves of the poor equally with those of the more opulent.—*Emile Souvestre.*

TRUE COUNSELLORS.

Amid the duties and difficulties, the cares and perplexities of life, how many a pang and tear would it save us if we went with chastened and inquiring spirits to these "counselling" oracles? How many trials would be mitigated—how many sorrows soothed, and temptations avoided—if we preceded every step in life with the inquiry, "*What saith the Scripture?*" making the Bible a final court of appeal—an arbiter for the settlement of all the vexed questions in the consistory of the soul; with the docility of little children listening therein to their Father's counsel—recognizing every utterance as endorsed with the words, "*Thus saith the Lord.*" God keep us from that saddest phase and dogma of modern infidelity—the Sacred Volume regarded with only that misnamed "*veneration*" which the antiquary bestows on some piece of mediæval armor—a relic and memorial of bygone days, but unsuitable for an age which has superseded the cruder views of those old "chroniclers," and inaugurated a new era of religious development. Vain dreamers! "*For ever, O God, thy word is settled in heaven.*" "*The law of the Lord is perfect, converting the soul; the testimony of the Lord is sure, making wise the simple.*" "*The word of the Lord is tried.*" "*Thy word is very sure, therefore thy servant loveth it.*" What a crowd of witnesses could be summoned to give personal evidence of its preciousness and value! How many aching heads would raise themselves from their pillows and tell of their obligations to its soothing messages of love and power! How many deathbeds could send their occupants with pallid lips to tell of the staff which upheld them in the dark valley! How many, in the hour of bereavement, could lay their finger on the promise that first dried the tear from their eye, and brought back the smile to their saddened countenances! How many voyagers on life's tempestuous ocean, now landed on the heavenly shore, would be ready to hush their golden harps and descend to earth with the testimony, that this was the blessed beacon light which enabled them to avoid the treacherous reefs, and guided them to their desired haven!

Ah, *Philosophy!* thou hast never yet, as *this* Book, taught a man how to die! *Reason!* with thy flickering torch, thou hast never yet guided to such sublime mysteries, such comforting truths as these! *Science!* thou hast penetrated the arcana of nature, sunk thy shafts into earth's recesses, unburied its stores, counted its strata, measured the height of its massive pillars, down to the very pedestals of primeval granite. Thou hast tracked the lightning, traced the path of the tornado, uncurtained the distant planet, foretold the coming of the comet, and the return of the eclipse. But thou hast never been able to gauge the depth of man's soul; or to answer the question, "What must I do to be saved?"

No, no; this antiquated volume is still the "Book of books," the oracle of oracles, the beacon of beacons; the poor man's treasury; the child's companion; the sick man's health; the dying man's life; shallows for the infant to walk in; depths for giant intellect to explore and adore! Philosophy, if she would but own it, is indebted here for the noblest of her maxims—Poetry, for the loftiest of her themes. Painting has gathered here her noblest inspiration. Music has ransacked these golden stores for the grandest of her strains. And if there be life in the Church of Christ,—if her ministers and missionaries are carrying the torch of salvation through the world,—where is that torch lighted, but at these same undying altar-fires? When a philosophy "falsely so called" shall become dominant, and seek, with its proud dogmas, to supersede this *divine* philosophy—when the old Bible of David, and Timothy, and Paul, is clasped and closed—the only morality and philosophy worth speaking of will have perished from the earth. Dagon will have taken the place of God's ark—the world's funeral pile may be kindled!

Love your Bibles. As they are the *souvenirs* of your earliest childhood—the gift of a mother's love, or the pledge of a father's affection—so let them be your last and fondest treasures, the keepsakes and heirlooms which you are most desirous to transmit to your children's children.

In taking to you "the whole armor of God," forget not "*the sword of the Spirit.*" What noble words are these, addressed to a saintly hero more than three thousand years ago; may every youthful soldier girding himself for the great battle of life especially listen to them; they will prove to him, as they did to Joshua, the sure guarantee of "prosperity" in its nobler sense. "Only be thou strong and very courageous, that thou mayest observe to do according to all the law which Moses my servant commanded thee: turn not from it to the right hand or to the left, that thou mayest prosper whithersoever thou goest. This book of the law shall not depart out of thy mouth; but thou shalt meditate therein day and night, that thou mayest observe to do according to all that is written therein: *for then thou shalt make thy way prosperous, and then thou shalt have good success,*" (Joshua i. 7, 8.)

"Thy word have I hid in mine heart, that I might not sin against thee."—*Macduff.*

LOST ARTS.

And in regard to colors, we are far behind the ancients. None of the colors in the Egyptian painting of thousands of years ago are in the least faded, except the green. The Tyrian purple of the entombed city of Pompeii is as fresh to-day as it was three thousand years ago. Some of the stucco, painted centuries before the Christian era, broken up and mixed, revealed its original lustre. And yet we pity the ignorance of the dark-skinned children of the ancient Egypt. The colors upon the walls of Nero's Festal Vault are as fresh as if painted yesterday. So is the cheek of the Egyptian prince who was contemporaneous with Solomon, and Cleopatra, at whose feet Cæsar laid the riches of his empire.

And in regard to metals. The edges of the stones of the obelisks of Egypt, and of the ancient walls of Rome, are as sharp as if but hewn yesterday. And the stones still remain so closely fitted, that their seams, laid with mortar, cannot be penetrated with the edge of a pen-knife. And their surface is exceedingly hard—so that when the French artists engraved two lines upon an obelisk brought from Egypt, they destroyed in the tedious task, many sets of the best tools that could be manufactured. And yet these ancient monuments are traced all over with inscriptions placed upon them in olden time. This, with other facts of striking character, proved that they were far more skilled in metals than we are. Quite recently it is recorded that, when an American vessel was on the shores of Africa, a son of that benighted region made, from an iron hoop, a knife superior to any on board the vessel, and another made a sword of Damascus excellence from a piece of iron.

Fiction is very old. Scott has his counterparts two thousand years ago. A story is told of a warrior who had no time to wait for the proper forging of his weapon, but seizing it red-hot, rode forward, but found to his surprise that the cold air had tempered his iron into an excellent steel weapon. The tempering of steel, therefore, which was new to us a century since, was two thousand years ago.

Ventilation is deemed a very modern art. But this is not the fact, for apertures, unquestionably made for the purpose of ventilation, are found in the Pyramid Tomb of Egypt. Yes, thousands of years ago, the barbarous Pagans went so far as to ventilate their tombs, while we yet scarcely know how to ventilate our houses.—*Wendell Phillips.*

REMARKABLE PROVIDENTIAL OCCURRENCES.

LOST IN THE MOUNTAINS.

BY REV. J. B. FINLEY.

The following incident is one among many which have occurred in the history of my life, and which so strikingly illustrates the special providence of God, that I am induced to send it for publication in the Repository. Mrs. Boarer, the heroine and narrator of the story, was the wife of Mr. George Boarer, and was, by education and parentage, a Roman Catholic. Her parents were natives of Berkley county, Virginia, and, at the time, were residents of the country in the vicinity of Sleepy Creek. Early on the morning of the 7th of January, 1800, she left home on a borrowed horse, to cross the Capin Mountains. to visit her aged parents. She took with her an infant child, a daughter, seven months old. The snow upon the mountains was three feet deep, and the weather was exceedingly cold. For defense, and company's sake, she took with her the house-dog, a very large spaniel. Having gained the top of the mountain range, she concluded to leave the great road, and, by a short cut, arrive the same night at her father's house.

She had, however, not proceeded far, before she found herself bewildered; and, in consequence, becoming frightened. She dared not turn back, but wandered about through the mountain until night had settled its gloom over the world. She then dismounted; and having fastened her horse to a sapling, she prepared a place, as well as circumstances would admit, where to pass the night. The snow, as before remarked, was three feet deep; the darkness was profound, and the wind from the north-west broke in a hurricane above her. With no company but her child, and no protector but her dog, her condition was lonely beyond the imagination to conceive.

Fortunately, she had with her some extra clothing, in the shape of a cloak and a shawl. Removing, as well as she could, the snow from beneath a large tree, she took her apparel, and made the best disposition possible with it; and, with her child and her dog, she composed herself for the night.

Mrs. Boarer stated to me, that for a week previous to undertaking this journey, she was unusually exercised about her spiritual welfare, and very frequently took an old prayer-book, and read it.

Now, far from her home, desolate and distressed, she felt the need of close communion with God. The prayers which she had read the week before came fresh to her mind, which she offered fervently to her Maker. The night was long and dreary, and she spent it without sleep. Very shortly after fastening her horse, the animal became uneasy, and, breaking his bridle, started off at full speed. This greatly added to her misfortunes, for she had hoped by him to have reached some settlement the next day.

At length day dawned; and though, by the help of her clothing and her dog, she had kept herself and child from freezing, yet she was so benumbed by the cold as almost to be unable to walk and carry her infant daughter with her. This was Saturday morning. She now left part of her clothing, and made an effort to return to the point where she left the great road. After traveling until she was nearly exhausted, she concluded that, unless she reached the settlement, she must perish with the cold. Indulging the hope, however, that she might keep herself from freezing, or be found by some one, she thought it best to return to the spot where she passed the previous night. Accordingly, she started back, and, on her way, hung up her apron on a bush, and afterward a handkerchief, as signs of distress, in hope, though indeed but a faint hope, that some passing hunter might see one or the other, and come to her relief. Late in the afternoon of Saturday, and with great difficulty, she regained her lodging-place.

But feeling now the dread of passing another night in so desolate a place, and summoning that indomitable spirit of courage, peculiar to her sex when in difficulty and danger, and seeing the sun fast declining, she determined to change her course, and make one more desperate effort to gain some settlement. Throwing off part of her apparel, in order to be less encumbered, she began again to contend with the snow, rocks, and caverns of the mountains, and at length came to a deep, narrow gorge, down the sides of which she could not descend with her child.

She looked up and down, but could see no place that offered an easier passage than the one before her. She hesitated a moment, but having no other alternative, she threw her child over, and then followed herself. By taking hold of the laurel bushes on the opposite side of the ravine, she managed to crawl up to the place where her child lighted, which, to her great joy, she found uninjured, save by a slight scratch on its face, caused by its falling on the crust of the snow. Resuming her journey, she came upon a hog-path, which led to a cleft of shelving rocks where these animals were accustomed to sleep.

She had now traveled—as was afterward ascertained—one mile and a half. Here she might have remained sheltered for the night; but fearing the return of the half-starved hogs, and that herself, her child, and her dog, might all become a sudden prey to their voraciousness, and her family never learn their fate, she immediately resumed her march, and weary and faint, made her way about three hundred yards off, to the side of the mountain. Finding her stockings entirely cut up by the crust of the snow, and her limbs, and ankles, and feet all bleeding, she yielded the struggle, and, under some pine bushes hard by, she obtained a place to sit down; but the snow sinking beneath her, rendered her situation most critical and desperate.

She took care to wrap her clothes around her feet, and body, as well as she could; then clasping her babe warm to her bosom, she committed herself to God.

Her faithful dog had not left her, and this night would lie down just where she bade him; sometimes on her feet and limbs, and sometimes at her back, changing alternately, as if to keep her from freezing. During the night she fell asleep, being exhausted with labor and with want of food. This night it snowed and blew, until the new fall of snow was ten inches deep on the former. When she awoke, she heard the chickens crowing at the foot of the mountain, and the dogs barking, so near was she to a house; but the wind was blowing directly from them to her, which proved extremely unfavorable to her. About the same time she thought she heard the people feeding their cattle. She called as loud and as long as she could, but no one came to her relief. This morning she found that her feet and limbs were badly swelled, and the skin, in many places, broken.

This discovery went home to her heart, and she commenced to make her peace with God, and gave herself up to die. She thought if her infant child were dead, she, too, could die in peace; but, to leave it to perish with cold and hunger, was a thought more than a mother's heart could bear. She laid the little thing down to freeze to death before she should die herself, but when it wept, she would take it up, and clasp it to her bosom. Despairing at last to make herself heard, as the wind continued to blow violently in a contrary direction, she resorted to another expedient. It was this: She pinned her child's bonnet around the dog's neck, and sent him to solicit help. The poor animal, as if perfectly understanding her meaning, started off immediately, and was afterward tracked to the house nearest to his distressed mistress, and then to a mill; but, it being Sabbath day, and extremely cold, the dwellings were all shut up, and no one saw him, and in an hour or two he returned, and took up his station. When it was becoming about feeding time, she commenced calling again, and a man on the top of a stack of hay heard her, and told his wife that he heard something on the mountain making a noise like a person in distress; and he went to a neighbor and told him the same thing; to which the latter, however, only replied, "I suppose it must be a panther."

This night was likewise spent in making her peace with God, and she stated to me, that if she had perished that night, she had no doubt but that she would have gone to heaven. Part of the night was spent in great anxiety about her child. Her faithful dog, as he had done before, kept close to her, and would lay down precisely where told to. This circumstance, in connection with that of being covered with snow, kept her from freezing to death.

In the morning, which was Monday, she commenced calling, the third time, for help. Her clothes were frozen to the ground, and kept her from rising, and her exhaustion was complete. She called like one yielding to despair; but the wind being now favorable, a man who was feeding his flock heard her voice, as also did his wife in the house, who was intimately acquainted with the distressed heroine of our narrative, and who said to her husband, "If Polly Boarer was near, I should say it was her voice." James Smyth and John M'Intyre took their guns, and mounted their horses and started; but were deceived in their course by the echoes of Mrs. Boarer's voice. They hunted nearly all day, and returned home, and were about putting up their horses, when Mr. Smith heard the same plaint of distress. The sun was about an hour high, and the long, lingering beams, striking from the far horizon upon the snow-clad wilds, inspired feelings of the deepest gloom and solitude.

They started again, but the feeble cry of the perishing woman had ceased; and just as the men were taking a wrong direction, she said that she felt an indefinable, mysterious feeling come over her, which said that if she only would call again, help would come to her. She, therefore, called once more, and was heard, and found.

But a new difficulty now arose. She was frozen to the ground, and was almost lifeless, and her faithful dog refused to let the strangers approach. At length, however, he was pacified. She had not shed a tear until this moment of her rescue. But now, the tears fell, like rain-drops from her eyes. She was speedily conveyed to the nearest house, where she became insensible, and remained so for twenty-four hours. The flesh fell, or rather peeled off her limbs, and many of her toes came off; so that she was unable to walk until the following August—a period of over six months. Her husband supposed that his wife was safe at her father's, and her father never thought that she had started to visit his family. The horse, after becoming free, did not return home; so that there was no suspicion felt in regard to her safety.

I leave the reader to his and to her own reflections on this incident. I have heard the mother and the daughter tell in love-feast, what I have here imperfectly told you. How true, and how applicable in every condition of life—in poverty or in health, in prosperity or adversity, in sunshine or in storm, in plenty or in distress—that declaration of the merciful Keeper of our race, "My grace is sufficient for thee!"

THE WIDOW OF THE PINE COTTAGE.

It was Saturday night, and the widow of the Pine Cottage sat by her blazing fagots with her five tattered children at her side, endeavoring, by listening to the artlessness of their juvenile prattle, to dissipate the heavy gloom that pressed upon her mind. For a year her own feeble hands had provided for her helpless family, for she had no supporter; she thought of no friend in all the wide, unfriendly world around; but that mysterious Providence, the wisdom of whose ways are above human comprehension, had visited her with wasting sickness, and her little means had become exhausted. It was now, too, mid-winter, and the snow lay heavy and deep through all the surrounding forests, while storms still seemed gathering in the heavens, and the driving wind roared amidst the bending pines, and rocked her puny mansion.

The last herring smoked upon the coals before her; it was the only article of food she possessed, and no wonder her forlorn and desolate state brought up in her bosom all the anxieties of a mother when she looked upon her children; and no wonder, forlorn as she was, if she suffered the heart-swellings of despair to rise, even though she knew that He whose promise is to the widow and the orphan, cannot forget his word. Providence had many years before taken from her her eldest son, who went from his forest home to try his fortune on the high seas, since which she had heard no note or tidings of him; and in latter times, had, by the hand of death, deprived her of the companion and staff of her worldly pilgrimage, in the person of her husband. Yet to this hour she had been upborne—she had not only been able to provide for her little flock, but had never lost an opportunity of ministering to the wants of the poor and destitute.

The indolent may well bear with poverty, while the ability to gain sustenance remains. The individual who has but his own wants to supply, may suffer with fortitude the winter of want; his affections are not wounded, his heart not wrung. The most desolate in populous cities may hope, for charity has not quite closed her hand and heart, and shut her eyes on misery. But the industrious mother of helpless and depending children, far from the reach of human charity, has none of these to console her. And such an one was the widow of the Pine Cottage; but as she bent over the fire, and took up the last scanty remnant of food to spread before her children, her spirits seemed to brighten up, as by some sudden and mysterious impulse, and Cowper's beautiful lines came uncalled across her mind:

> Judge not the Lord by feeble sense,
> But trust him for his grace,
> Behind a frowning Providence
> He hides a smiling face.

The smoked herring was scarcely laid upon the table, when a gentle rap at the door, and the loud barking of a dog, attracted the attention of the family. The children flew to open it, and a weary traveler, in tattered garments, and apparently indifferent health, entered and begged a lodging, and a mouthful of food: said he, "it is now twenty-four hours since I tasted bread." The widow's heart bled anew, as under a fresh complication of distresses; for her sympathies lingered not round her fireside. She hesitated not even now; rest and share of all she had, she proffered to the stranger. "We shall not be forsaken," said she, "or suffer deeper for an act of charity."

The traveler drew near the board; but when he saw the scanty fare, he raised his eyes towards heaven with astonishment. "And is this all your store?" said he: "and a share of this do you offer to one you know not? Then never saw I charity before! But, madam," said he, continuing, "do you not wrong your children by giving a part of your last mouthful to a stranger?" "Ah!" said the poor widow, and the tears gushed to her eyes, "I have a boy, a darling son, somewhere on the face of this wide world, unless God has taken him away; and I only act towards you, as I would that others should act towards him. God who sent manna from heaven can provide for us as he did for Israel; and how should I this night offend him, if my son should be a wanderer, destitute as you, and he should have provided for him a home even poor as this, were I to turn you unrelieved away?"

The widow ended, and the stranger springing from his seat, clasped her in his arms. "God, indeed, has provided just such a home for your wandering son," said he, "and has given him wealth to reward the goodness of his benefactress—my mother! oh, my mother!"

It was her long lost son, returned from the Indies to her bosom. He had chosen that disguise, that he might the more completely surprise his family; and never was surprise more perfect, or followed by a sweeter cup of joy. That humble residence in the forest was exchanged for one comfortable, and indeed beautiful in the valley; and the widow lived long with her dutiful son in the enjoyment of worldly plenty, and in the delightful employments of virtue: and at this day the passer-by is pointed to the luxuriant willow that spreads its broad and green branches above her grave, while he listens to the recital of his simple and homely, but not altogether worthless tale.

THE PRESUMPTUOUS MURDERER.

A LITTLE more than fifty years ago, a man by the name of Henry Thomson called at the house of Mr. John Smith, a resident in a retired part of England, and requested a night's lodging. This request was readily granted and the stranger having taken some refreshment, retired early to bed, requesting that he might be awakened at an early hour the following morning.

When the servant appointed to call him entered the room for that purpose, he was found in his bed, perfectly dead.

On examining his body no marks of violence appeared, but his countenance looked extremely natural. The story of his death soon spread among the neighbors, and inquiries were made who he was, and by what means he came by his death.

Nothing certain, however, was known. He had arrived on horseback, and was seen passing through a neighboring village, about an hour before he reached the house where he came to his end. And then, as to the manner of his death, so little could be discovered, that the jury which was summoned to investigate the cause, returned a verdict that he died "by a visitation of God." When this was done, the stranger was buried.

Days and weeks passed on, and little further was known. The public mind, however, was not at rest. Suspicions existed that foul means had hastened the stranger's death. Whispers to that effect were expressed, and in the hearts of many, Smith was considered as the guilty man.

The former character of Smith had not been good. He had lived a loose and irregular life, involved himself in debt by his extravagances; and, at length, being suspected of having obtained money wrongfully, he suddenly fled from the town.

More than ten years, however, had now elapsed, since his return, during which he had lived at his present residence, apparently in good circumstances, and with an improved character. His former life, however, was now remembered, and suspicion, after all, fastened upon him.

At the expiration of two months, a gentleman one day stopped in the place for the purpose of making inquiry respecting the stranger, who had been found dead in his bed. He supposed himself to be a brother of the man. The horse and clothes of the unfortunate man still remained, and were immediately known as having belonged to his brother. The body also, itself was taken up, and though considerably changed, bore a strong resemblance to him.

He now felt authorized to ascertain, if possible, the manner of his death. He proceeded, therefore, to investigate the circumstances, as well as he was able. At length he made known to the magistrate of the district, the information he had collected, and upon the strength of this, Smith was taken to jail to be tried for the willful murder of Henry Thomson.

The celebrated Lord Mansfield was then on the bench. He charged the grand jury to be cautious as to finding a bill against the prisoner. The evidence of his guilt, if guilty, might be small. At a future time it might be greater; more information might be obtained. Should the jury now find a bill against him, and should he be acquitted, he could not be molested again, whatever testimony should rise up against him. The grand jury, however, did find a bill, but it was by a majority of only one.

At length, the time of trial arrived. Smith was brought into court, and placed at the bar. A great crowd thronged the room, eager and anxious to see the prisoner and to hear the trial. He himself appeared firm and collected. Nothing in his manner or appearance indicated guilt; and, when the question was put to him by the clerk, "Are you guilty, or not guilty?" he answered with an unfaltering tongue, and with a countenance perfectly unchanged, "Not guilty."

The counsel for the prosecution now opened the case. But it was apparent that he had little expectation of being able to prove the prisoner guilty. He stated to the jury, that the case was involved in great mystery. The prisoner was a man of respectability and of property. The deceased was supposed to have had about him, gold and jewels to a large amount; but the prisoner was not so much in want of funds, as to be under a strong temptation to commit murder. And, besides, if the prisoner had obtained the property he had effectually concealed it. Not a trace of it could be found.

Why, then, was the prisoner suspected? He would state the grounds of suspicion. The deceased, Henry Thomson, was a jeweler, residing in London, and a man of wealth. He had left London for the purpose of meeting a trader at Hull, of whom he expected to make a large purchase. That trader he did meet; and after the departure of the latter, Mr. Thomson was known to have had in his possession jewels and gold to a large amount.

With these in his possession, he left Hull on his return to London. It was not known that he stopped until he reached Smith's, and the next morning was discovered dead in his bed. He died, then, in Smith's house, and if it could be shown that he came to his death in an unnatural way, it would increase the suspicion, that the prisoner was in some way connected with the murder.

Now, then, continued the counsel, it will be proved beyond the possibility of a doubt, that the deceased died by *poison*. But what was that poison? It was a recent discovery of some German chemists, said to be produced from distilling the seed of the wild cherry tree. It was a poison more powerful than any other known, and deprived of life so immediately, as to leave no marks of suffering, and no contortions of the features.

But, then, the question was, by whom was it administered? One circumstance, a small one indeed, and yet upon it might hang a horrid tale, was, that the stopper of a small bottle of a very singular description had been found in the prisoner's house. That stopper had been examined, and said by medical men to have belonged to a German vial, containing the kind of poison which he had described. But, then, was that poison administered by Smith, or at his instigation? Who were the prisoner's family? It consisted only of himself, a housekeeper, and one man-servant. The man-servant slept in an out-house adjoining the stable, and did so on the night of Thomson's death. The prisoner slept at one end of the house, the housekeeper at the other, and the deceased had been put in a room adjoining the housekeeper's.

It would be proved, that about three hours after midnight, on the night of Thomson's death, a light had been seen, moving about the house, and that a figure holding the light was seen to go from the room in which the prisoner slept, to the housekeeper's room; the light now disappeared for a minute, when two persons were seen, but whether they went into Thomson's room, the witness could not swear; but shortly after they were observed passing quite through the entry to Smith's room, into which they entered, and in about five minutes the light was extinguished.

The witness would further state; that, after the person had returned with the light into Smith's room, and before it was extinguished, he had twice perceived some dark object to intervene between the light and the window, almost as large as the surface of the window itself, and which he described by saying, it appeared as if a door had been placed before the light. Now, in Smith's room, there was nothing which could account for this appearance; his bed was in a different part; and there was neither cupboard nor press in the room, which, but for the bed, was entirely empty, the room in which he dressed being at a distance beyond it.

The counsel for the prosecution here concluded what he had to say. During his address Smith appeared in no wise to be agitated or distressed; and equally unmoved was he while the witnesses testified in substance what the opening speech of the counsel led the court and the jury to expect.

Lord Mansfield now addressed the jury. He told them that, in his opinion, the evidence was not sufficient to condemn the prisoner; and that, if the jury agreed with him in opinion, the court would discharge him. Without leaving their seats, the jury agreed that the evidence was not sufficient.

At this moment, when they were about to render a verdict of acquittal, the prisoner rose and addressed the court. He said that he had been accused of a foul crime, and the jury had said that there was not sufficient evidence to convict him. Did the jury mean that there was *any evidence* against him? Was he to go out of court with suspicions resting upon him after all? This he was unwilling to do. He was an innocent man, and if the judge would grant him an opportunity, he would prove it. He would call his housekeeper, who would confirm a statement which he would now make.

The housekeeper had not appeared in court. She had concealed herself, or had been concealed by Smith. This was considered a dark sign against him. But he himself now offered to bring her forward, and stated as the reason, not that he was unwilling that she should testify, but knowing the excitement, he was fearful that she might be bribed to give testimony contrary to fact. But he was now ready to relate all the circumstances he knew; she might, then, be called, and be examined. If her testimony does not confirm my story, let me be condemned.

The request of the prisoner seemed reasonable, and Lord Mansfield, contrary to his usual practice, granted it.

The prisoner went on with his statement. He said he wished to go out of court relieved from the suspicions which were resting upon him. As to the poison, by means of which the stranger was said to have died, he knew neither the name of it, nor the effect of it, nor even of the existence of it, until made known by the counsel. He could call God to witness the truth of what he said.

And, then, as to Mr. Thomson, he was a perfect stranger to him. How should he know what articles of value he had with him! He did not know. If he had such articles at Hull, he might have lost them on the road; or, which was more probable, have otherwise disposed of them. And if he died by means of the fatal drug, he must have administered it himself.

He begged the jury to remember, that his premises had been repeatedly and minutely searched, and that not the most trifling article that belonged to the deceased, had been discovered in his possession. The stopper of a vial had been found—but of this he could only say, he had no knowledge, and had never seen it before it was produced in court.

One fact had been proved, and only one. That he would explain, and his housekeeper would confirm his statement. A witness had testified that some one had gone to the bedroom of the housekeeper, on the night in question. He was ready to admit that it was he himself. He had been subject for many years of his life to sudden fits of illness; he had been seized with one on that occasion, and had gone to her to procure her assistance in lighting a fire. She had returned with him to his room for that purpose, he having waited for a minute in the passage, while she put on her clothes. This would account for the momentary disappearance of the light. After remaining a few minutes in his room, finding himself better, he had dismissed her, and retired to bed, from which he had not risen when he was informed of the death of the guest.

Such was the prisoner's address, which produced a powerful effect. It was delivered in a very firm and impressive manner; and from the simple and artless manner of the man, perhaps not one present doubted his entire innocence.

The housekeeper was now introduced, and examined by counsel for the prisoner. She had not heard any part of the statement of Smith, nor a single word of the trial. Her story confirmed all that he had said.

To this succeeded her cross-examination by the counsel for the prosecution. One circumstance had made a deep impression on his mind; this was, that while the prisoner and the housekeeper were in the room of the former, something like a door had obstructed the light of the candle, so the witness testified to the fact, but could not see it. What was the obstruction? There was no door—nothing in the room which could account for this. Yet the witness was positive that something like a door did, for a moment, come between the window and the candle. This needed explanation. The housekeeper was the only person that could give it. Designing to probe this matter in the end to the bottom, but not wishing to excite her alarm, he began by asking her a few unimportant questions, and among others, where the candle stood, while she was in Mr. Smith's room.

"In the centre of the room," she replied.

"Well, and was the closet, or cupboard, or whatever you call it, opened once or twice, while it stood there?"

She made no reply.

"I will help your recollection," said the counsel; "after Mr. Smith had taken the medicine out of the closet, did he shut the door, or did it remain open?"

"He shut it."

"And, when he replaced the bottle in the closet, he opened it again, did he?"

"He did."

"And how long was it open the last time?"

"Not above a minute."

"Well, and when open, would the door be exactly between the light and the window?"

"It would."

"I forget," said the counsel, "whether you said the closet was on the right or the left hand side of the window?"

"On the left hand side."

"Would the door of the closet make any noise in opening?"

"None."

"Are you certain?"

"I am."

"Have you ever opened it yourself, or only seen Mr. Smith open it?"

"I never opened it myself."

"Did you ever keep the key?"

"Never."

"Who did?"

"Mr. Smith always."

At this moment the housekeeper chanced to cast her eye toward Smith, the prisoner. His countenance suddenly changed. A cold, damp sweat stood upon his brow, and his face had lost all its color: he appeared a living image of death. She no sooner saw him, than she shrieked and fainted. The consequence of her answers flashed across her mind. She had been so thoroughly deceived by the manner of the advocate, and by the little importance he had seemed to attach to her statements, that she had been led on by one question to another, till she had told him all he wanted to know.

She was obliged to be taken from the court, and a physician, who was present, was requested to attend her. At this time the solicitor for the prosecution (answering to our state's attorney,) left the court, but no one knew for what purpose. Presently the physician came into court, and stated that it would be impossible for the housekeeper to resume her seat in the box short of an hour or two.

It was about twelve in the day. Lord Mansfield, having directed that the jury should be accommodated with a room, where they could be kept by themselves, adjourned the court two hours. The prisoner in the mean time was remanded to jail.

It was between four and five o'clock, when the judge resumed his seat upon the bench. The prisoner was again placed at the bar, and the housekeeper brought in and led to the box. The court room was crowded to excess, and an awful silence pervaded the place.

The cross-examining counsel again addressed the housekeeper. "I have but a few more questions to ask you," said he; "take heed how you answer, for your own life hangs upon a thread."

"Do you know this stopper?"

"I do."

"To whom does it belong?"

"To Mr. Smith."

"When did you see it last?"

"On the night of Mr. Thomson's death."

At this moment the solicitor entered the court, bringing with him upon a tray, a watch, two money-bags, a jewel-case, a pocket-book, and a bottle of the same manufacture as the stopper, and having a cork in it. The tray was placed on the table in sight of the prisoner and the witness, and from that moment not a doubt remained in the mind of any man of the guilt of the prisoner.

A few words will bring this melancholy tale to its close. The house, where the murder had been committed, was between nine and ten miles distant. The solicitor, as soon as the cross-examination of the housekeeper had discovered the existence of the closet, and its situation, had set off on horseback, with two sheriff's officers, and, after pulling down a part of the wall of the house, had detected this important place of concealment. Their search was well rewarded: the whole of the property belonging to Mr. Thomson was found there, amounting in value to some thousand pounds; and to leave no room for doubt, a bottle was discovered, which the medical men instantly pronounced to contain the very identical poison which had caused the death of the unfortunate Thomson. The result was too obvious to need explanation.

It scarcely need be added that Smith was convicted and executed, and brought to this awful punishment by his own means. Had he said nothing—had he not persisted in calling a witness to prove his innocence, he might have escaped. But God had evidently left him to work out his own ruin, as a just reward of his awful crime.

THE HEADLESS NAIL.

THERE lived in England, some years since, a clergyman, by the name of Dr. Donne. In the earlier part of his ministerial life, he administered to a congregation out of London. One day, while taking a walk around his parish, he entered the churchyard, where he found the grave-digger employed in digging a grave. Advancing to the spot, he stood and watched, for a time, the movements of the man, at the same time holding such conversation with him, as would be likely to arise from the gloomy nature of the grave-digger's employment. In the midst of the work and the conversation, the latter came upon a skull, which he threw out.

The doctor observing it, picked it up for the purpose of examining it; in doing which, what was his surprise to notice a nail without a head, sticking in the bone of the temple. He said nothing to the grave-digger about the discovery, but drawing out the nail, he concealed it in the corner of his handkerchief. Having done this, without apparent design, he demanded of the man whether he knew whose skull that was.

The grave-digger replied that he believed he did. "In this spot," said he, "several years ago, there was buried a man who kept a brandy shop, at no great distance from this."

"And what character did he sustain?" inquired the doctor.

"Oh," said the grave-digger, "he was an honest man, for all that I know; but, then, he would drink too much, and one morning, after a night of intoxication, he was found dead in his bed."

"Had he a wife?" asked the doctor.

"Yes."

"And what sort of a woman was she?"

"Quite a clever woman," said the grave-digger; "only the neighbors used to reflect on her, because she married another man the day after her husband was buried."

"Is she still living?" asked the doctor.

"Yes," said the grave-digger; "she and her husband occupy the house which you observe yonder, down the hill."

The conversation here terminated, and the doctor continued his walk. There must have been, thought he to himself, as he left the churchyard, some foul work by which this man came to his death. After some reflection he determined to proceed to the house, and make such inquiries as circumstances might seem to justify.

On reaching the place, he introduced himself to the woman, with whom he entered into a conversation; and among other topics, alluded to her bereavement of a former husband. The woman was by no means backward to converse upon the subject, but affected great sorrow at her former loss. For a time the doctor listened to her with apparent sympathy; but, at length, suddenly opening his handkerchief, he demanded in a stern manner, "Woman, do you know this nail?"

Struck with horror, she instantly confessed her guilt.

From facts like this we may learn, that important results are often connected with apparently trifling circumstances; and that what God designs to disclose, no human foresight or cunning is able to conceal.

NARROW ESCAPE FROM EXECUTION.

Sir Evan Nepean, of the Home Department, relates the following respecting himself. One night during his office as under-secretary, he felt the most unaccountable wakefulness that could be imagined; he was in perfect health, had dined early, and had nothing whatever on his mind to keep him awake. Still he found all attempts to sleep impossible, and from eleven till two in the morning, he never closed an eye. At length, weary of this struggle, and as the twilight was breaking, (it was in summer,) he determined to try what would be the effect of a walk in the park. There he saw nothing but the sleepy sentinels. But in his walk, happening to pass the house-office several times, he thought of letting himself in with his key, though without any particular object. The book of entries of the day before, still lay on the table, and through sheer listlessness he opened it. The first thing he saw appalled him: "A reprieve to be sent to York for the coiners ordered for execution." The execution had been ordered for the next day. It struck him that he had received no return to his order to send the reprieve. He searched the "minutes." He could not find it there. In alarm he went to the house of the chief clerk, who lived in Downing-street, knocked him up, (it was then past three,) and asked him if he knew any thing of the reprieve being sent. In great alarm, the chief clerk could not remember. "You are scarcely awake," said Sir Evan, "recollect yourself; it must have been sent."

The clerk said that he now recollected he had sent it to the clerk of the crown, whose business it was to forward it to York.

"Good," said Sir Evan, "but have you his receipt and certificate that it is *gone?*"

"No."

"Then come with me to his house, we must find him, it is early?" It was now four, and the clerk of the crown lived in Chancery-Lane. There was no hackney coach to be seen and they almost ran. They were just in time. The clerk of the crown had a country house, and meaning to have a long holiday, he was at that moment stepping into his gig to go to his villa. Astonished at this visit of the under secretary of state at such an hour, he was still more so at his business.

"Heavens!" cried he, "the reprieve is locked up in my desk!" It was brought. Sir Evan sent to the post-office for the truest and fleetest express. The reprieve reached York next morning just at the moment the unhappy men were ascending the cart.

PRUDENTIAL TALENT.

To excel others is a proof of talent; but to know *when* to conceal that superiority is a greater proof of prudence. The celebrated orator Domitius Afer, when attacked in a set speech by Caligula, made no reply, affecting to be entirely overcome by the resistless eloquence of the tyrant. Had he replied, he would certainly have conquered, and as certainly have died; but he wisely preferred a defeat, that *saved* his life, to a victory that would have cost it.—*C. C. Colton.*

A TRAVELER SAVED FROM MURDER BY A DOG.

A TRAVELER in Cornwall, England, observed a strange dog following him on the road, which, notwithstanding every effort he used to drive him back, claimed acquaintance with him.

Being benighted in a lonely place, he called at the first inn he met with, and desired to be accommodated with a room. After supper the gentleman retired to rest. No sooner had he opened the door, than the before mentioned dog rushed in. After some fruitless efforts to drive the dog away, the gentleman permitted him to stay in the room, thinking he could do him no harm. When the gentleman began to prepare for bed, the dog ran to a closet door and then ran back to him, looking very wistfully at him. This the dog did several times, which so far excited the curiosity of the gentleman, that he opened the closet door, and to his great terror saw a person laid with his throat cut. Struck with horror, he began to think of his own state. To attempt to run away he supposed would be unsafe. He therefore began to barricade the door with the furniture of the room, and laid himself on the bed with his clothes on. About midnight two men came to the door and requested admittance, stating that the gentleman that slept there the preceding night had forgotten something, and was returned for it. He replied the room was his, and no one should enter it until morning. They went away, but soon returned with two or three other men, and demanded entrance; but the gentleman, with an austere voice, threatened if they did not desist he would defend himself. Awed apparently by this bold reply, they left him, and disturbed him no more.

In the morning he inquired for a barber; one was immediately sent for, when the gentleman took the opportunity of inquiring into the character of his host. The barber replied, he was a neighbor, and did not wish to say any thing to his disadvantage. The gentleman still urged his inquiry, assuring him that he had nothing to fear, till the barber said, "Sir, if I must tell the truth, they bear a very bad character; for it has been reported that persons have called here who have never been heard of afterward." Can you, said the gentleman, keep a secret? On his answering in the affirmative, the gentleman opened the closet door and showed him the person with his throat cut; he then directed the barber to procure a constable and proper assistance with all speed, which was done immediately, and the host and hostess were both taken into custody to take their trial at the next assize. Thy took their trial, were found guilty of the murder, condemned and executed. The dog was never seen by the gentleman afterward.

ESCAPE FROM BUFFALOES AND A PANTHER.

In one of my excursions, says Mr. Hunter, among the western Indians, while seated in the shade of a large tree, situated on a gentle declivity, with a view to procure some mitigation from the oppressive heat of the noonday sun, I was surprised by a tremendous rushing noise. I sprang up, and discovered a herd I believe of a thousand buffaloes, running at full speed directly toward me; as I supposed to beat off the flies, which at this season inconceivably trouble some of those animals.

I placed myself behind a tree, so as not to be seen, not apprehending any danger, because they ran with too great rapidity and too closely together to afford any one of them an opportunity of injuring me while protected in this manner. The buffaloes passed so near me on both sides that I could have touched several merely by extending my arm. In the rear of the herd, was one on which a huge panther had fixed, and was voraciously engaged in cutting off the muscles of its neck. I did not discover this circumstance till it had nearly passed beyond rifle-shot distance, when I discharged my piece and wounded the panther. It instantly left its hold on the buffalo, and bounded with great rapidity toward me. On witnessing the result of my shot, the apprehensions I suffered can hardly be imagined. I had, however, sufficient presence of mind to retreat, and secrete myself behind the trunk of the tree, opposite to its approaching direction. Here, solicitous for what possibly might be the result of my unfortunate shot, I prepared both my knife and tomakawk for what I supposed a dreadful conflict with this terrible animal. In a few moments, however, I had the satisfaction to hear it in the branches of the tree over my head. My rifle had just been discharged, and I entertained fears that I could not reload it without discovery, and yet exposing myself to the fury of its destructive rage. I looked into the tree with the utmost caution, but could not perceive it, though its groans and vengeance-breathing growls told me that it was not far off, and also what I had to expect, in case it should discover me. In this situation, with my eyes almost constantly upward to observe its motions, I silently loaded my rifle, and then creeping softly round the tree, saw my formidable enemy resting on a considerable branch about thirty feet from the ground, with his side fairly exposed. I was unobserved, took deliberate aim, and shot it through the heart. It made a single bound from the tree to the earth, and died in a moment afterward.

THE EAGLE AND CHILD.

A PEASANT, with his wife and three children, had taken up his summer quarters in a chalet, and was pasturing his flock on one of the rich Alps which overhang the Durance. The oldest boy was an idiot, about eight years of age; the second was five years old, and dumb; and the youngest was an infant. It so happened that the infant was left one morning in charge of his brothers, and the three had rambled to some distance from the chalet before they were missed.

When the mother went in search of the little wanderers, she found the two elder, but could discover no traces of the babe. The idiot boy seemed to be in a transport of joy, while the dumb child displayed every symptom of alarm and terror. In vain did the terrified parent endeavor to collect what had become of the lost infant. The antics of the one and the fright of the other explained nothing. The dumb boy was almost bereft of his senses, while the idiot appeared to have acquired an unusual degree of mirth and expression. He danced about, laughed, and made gesticulations as if he were imitating the action of one who had caught up something of which he was fond, and hugged it to his heart. This, however, was some slight comfort to the poor woman; for she imagined that some acquaintance had fallen in with the children, and had taken away the infant. But the day and night wore away, and no tidings came of the lost child. On the morrow, when the parents were pursuing their search, an eagle flew over their heads, at the sight of which the idiot renewed his antics, and the dumb boy clung to his father with shrieks of anguish and affright. The horrible truth then burst upon their minds, that their infant had been carried off in the talons of a bird of prey, and that the half-witted elder brother was delighted at his riddance of an object of whom he was jealous.

On the morning on which the accident happened, an Alpine yager had been watching near an eagle's seat, under the hope of shooting the bird on her return to her nest. The yager, waiting in all the anxious perseverance of a true sportsman, beheld the eagle slowly winging her way to the rock behind which he was concealed. Imagine his horror, when, upon her nearer approach, he heard the cries and distinguished the figure of an infant in her fatal grasp. In an instant his resolution was formed—to fire at the bird at all hazards the moment she should alight upon her nest, and rather to kill the child than leave it to be torn to pieces by the eagle. With a silent prayer, and with a steady aim, the mountaineer poised his rifle. The ball went directly through the eagle, and in a minute afterward the gallant hunter of the Alps had the unutterable delight of snatching the child from the nest and bearing it away in triumph. It was dreadfully wounded by the eagle in one of its arms and sides, but not mortally; and within twenty-four hours after it was first missed, he had the satisfaction of restoring it to its mother's arms.

A REMARKABLE CONFESSION.

A JEWELER, a man of good character and considerable wealth, having occasion, in the way of business, to travel some distance from his abode, took along with him a servant. He had with him some of his best jewels, and a large sum of money, to which his servant was likewise privy. The master having occasion to dismount on the road, the servant watched his opportunity, took a pistol from his master's saddle, and shot him dead on the spot; then, rifling him of his money and jewels, and hanging a large stone to his neck, he threw him into the nearest canal.

With the booty thus infamously secured, he made off to a distant part of the country, where he had reason to believe that neither he nor his master were known. There he began to trade, in a very low way at first, that his obscurity might screen him from observation; and in the course of many years seemed to rise up by the natural progress of business into wealth and consideration; so that his good fortune appeared at once the effect of industry and the reward of virtue. Of these he counterfeited the appearance so well, that he grew into great credit, married into a good family, and, by laying out his hidden stores discreetly, as he saw occasion, and joining to all a universal affability, he was at length admitted to a share of the government of the town, and rose from one post to another, till at last he was chosen chief magistrate.

In this office he maintained a fair character, and continued to fill it with no small applause, both as governor and judge; till one day, as he sat on the bench with some of his brethren, a criminal was brought before him who was accused of murdering his master. The evidence came out full, the jury brought in their verdict that the prisoner was guilty, and the whole assembly awaited the sentence of the president of the court (which happened to be himself,) in great suspense.

Meanwhile he appeared to be in unusual disorder and agitation of mind: his color changed often. At length he arose from his seat, and coming down from the bench, placed himself just by the unfortunate man at the bar, to the no small astonishment of all present. "You see before you," said he, addressing himself to those who had sat on the bench with him, "a striking instance of the just awards of Heaven; for this day, after thirty years' concealment, presents to you a greater criminal than the man just now found guilty." He then made an ample confession of his heinous offence, with all its peculiar aggravations. "Nor can I," continued he, "feel any relief from the agonies of an awakened conscience, but by requiring that justice be forthwith done against me in the most public and solemn manner."

We may easily imagine the amazement of all, especially his fellow-judges. They accordingly proceeded, upon his confession, to pass sentence upon him, and he died with all the symptoms of a penitent mind.

WESLEY'S PRESERVATION FROM FIRE.

Mr. Wesley, father of the Rev. John Wesley, was roused from sleep by the cry of fire from the street; but little imagining that the fire was in his own house, he opened his bed-room door and found the place full of smoke, and that the roof was already burned through. Directing his wife and two girls to rise and flee for their lives, he burst open the nursery-door, where the maid was sleeping with five children. She snatched up the youngest and bade the others follow her: the three eldest did so; but John, who was then six years old, was not awakened, and in the alarm was forgotten. The rest of them escaped—some through the windows, some through the garden-door; and Mrs. Wesley, to use her own expression, "waded through the fire." At this time John, who had not been remembered till that moment, was heard crying in the nursery. The father ran to the stairs, but they were so nearly consumed that they could not bear his weight; and being utterly in despair, he fell upon his knees in the hall, and in agony commended the soul of the child to God. John had been awakened by the light, and finding it impossible to escape by the door, climbed up a chest that stood near the window, and he was then seen from the yard. There was no time for procuring a ladder; but one man was hoisted on the shoulders of another, and thus he was taken out. A moment after the roof fell in.

When the child was rescued, the father cried out, "Come, neighbors, let us kneel down; let us give thanks to God! He has given me all my eight children: let the house go, I am rich enough."

Mr. Wesley remembered this providential deliverance through life with the deepest gratitude. Under one of the portraits published during his life, is a representation of a house on fire, with the scriptural inquiry, "Is not this a brand plucked out of the burning?"

PRESERVATION FROM ROBBERS.

In the year 1785, a widow woman and her family resided in the city of Diet, in a lonely situation. She had one son and two daughters, and was supported by some property which her husband had left her. One night a person dressed in uniform, with a musket and broadsword, came to the house and requested lodgings. "I let no lodgings, friend," said the widow, "and besides, I have no spare bed, unless you sleep with my son, which I think very improper on account of your being a perfect stranger to us all." The soldier showed a discharge from Diesbach's regiment, which gave him an excellent character, and a passport from Count Maillebois, governor of Breda. He was then hospitably entertained and withdrew to bed. Some hours after a knocking was heard at the door; and it was almost broken through by some robbers, when the soldier moved softly down stairs and stopped at the hall door, and the son, having seized a case of loaded pistols, joined him. Soon afterward the door was forced in, and two ruffians entered, who were instantly shot. Two associates of the dead men, however, returned the fire, but without effect. The intrepid stranger now rushed forward and killed one with his bayonet and the other with his gun, thus preserving the lives of his kind friends. This veteran's name was Adrian de Gries; he was a native of Middleburgh, and was upward of seventy years old at the time of this exploit.

ESCAPE OF GENERAL WASHINGTON.

Major Ferguson, who commanded a rifle corps in advance of the hussars under Kniphausen, during some skirmishing a day or two previous to the battle of Brandywine, was the hero of a very singular incident, which he thus relates in a letter to a friend. It illustrates, in a most forcible manner, the overruling hand of Providence in directing the operations of a man's mind in moments when he is least of all aware of it.

"We had not lain long when a rebel officer, remarkable by a hussar dress, pressed toward our army, within a hundred yards of my right flank, not perceiving us. He was followed by another, dressed in dark green and blue, mounted on a bay horse, with a remarkably high cocked hat. I ordered three good shots to steal near to them, and fire at them; but the idea disgusting me, I recalled the order. The hussar, in returning, made a circuit, but the other passed within a hundred yards of us, upon which I advanced from the wood toward him. Upon my calling, he stopped; but after looking at me, he proceeded. I again drew his attention, and made signs to him to stop, leveling my piece at him; but he slowly cantered away. As I was within that distance at which, in the quickest firing, I could have lodged half a dozen balls in or about him, before he was out of my reach, I had only to determine; but it was not pleasant to fire at the back of an unoffending individual, who was acquitting himself very coolly of his duty; so I let him alone.

The day after, I had been telling this story to some wounded officers who lay in the same room with me, when one of the surgeons, who had been dressing the wounded rebel officers, came in, and told us, that they had been informing him that General Washington was all the morning with the light troops, and only attended by a French officer in a hussar dress, he himself dressed and mounted in every point as above described. I am not sorry that I did not know at the time who it was."

THE MURDERED SON.

Two young men of Virginia, who served in the American army during the war, having regularly got their discharge, went home to their friends. One had only a mother living when he left home. When they had got near home, they fell into a conversation on the length of time they had been away, and concluded to try whether their parents would know them; and with this impression, each took the nearest path home.

The one who had only a mother came in; and, finding his mother did not know him, he asked for lodging, to whom she replied that she could not lodge him—that there was a tavern not far from the place, where he might get lodging, &c. He importuned, but she refused, till at last he told her he had a little money, and he was afraid to lodge in a tavern, lest some person should rob him. He took out his purse and offered it to her keeping. She, struck with the mammon, consented immediately to his staying. Accordingly he did, had supper, and still never discovered himself to his mother or any of the family. He was directed to a bed once more in the chamber of her who conceived him. How safe he must have thought himself then, compared to the field of battle. But she summoned a negro man, told him the scheme she had planned, hired him to aid her, where they murdered him in his bed.

Next day his fellow-soldier came to see his friend; but, on asking for the stranger, could hear nothing of him. He thought it was a trick to plague him that the old woman denied it, till hearing her affirm that no stranger had come there the last evening, nor any man, he asked her if she had not a son who went to the war. She said she had. "Well," said he, "I left him within a few miles of this house last evening, and he came here; and he told me he would not make himself known to you, to see if you had forgotten his looks. He must be here." The cruel mother fainted at the sentence, confessed her wickedness, and showed her murdered son, crammed in a closet of the house!

THE SERGEANT AND THE DRUMMER BOY.

JARVIS MUTCHAM was pay-sergeant in a regiment where he was so highly esteemed as a steady and accurate man, that he was permitted opportunity to embezzle a considerable part of the money lodged in his hands for the pay of the soldiers, bounty of recruits, (then a large sum,) and other charges, which fell within his duty. He was summoned to join his regiment from a town where he had been on the recruiting service; and this, perhaps, under some shade of suspicion. Mutcham perceived discovery was at hand, and would have deserted, had it not been for the presence of a little drummer lad, who was the only one of his party appointed to attend him. In the desperation of his crime, he resolved to murder the poor boy, and avail himself of some balance of money to make his escape. He meditated this wickedness the more readily, that the drummer, he thought, had been put as a spy on him.

He perpetrated his crime, and changing his dress after the deed was done, made a long walk across the country to an inn on the Portsmouth road, where he halted, and went to bed, desiring to be called when the first Portsmouth coach came. The waiter summoned him accordingly; but long afterward remembered that when he shook the guest by the shoulder, his first words as he awoke were, "I did not kill him."

Mutcham went to the seaport by the coach, and instantly entered as an able-bodied landsman or marine, I know not which. His sobriety and attention to duty gained him the same good opinion of the officers in his new service, which he had enjoyed in the army. He was afloat for several years, and behaved remarkably well in several actions. At length the vessel came into Plymouth, was paid off, and some of the crew, among whom was Jarvis Mutcham, were dismissed as too old for service. He and another seaman resolved to walk to town, and took the route by Salisbury. It was when within two or three miles of that celebrated city, that they were overtaken by a tempest, so sudden, and accompanied with such vivid lightning, and thunder so fearfully loud, that the obdurate conscience of the old sinner began to be awakened. He expressed more terror than seemed natural for one who was familiar with the war of elements, and began to look and talk so wildly, that his companion became aware that something more than usual was the matter. At length Mutcham complained to his companion that the stones rose from the road and flew after him. He desired the man to walk on the other side of the road, to see if they would follow him when he was alone. The sailor complied, and Jarvis Mutcham complained that the stones still flew after him, and did not pursue the other. "But what is worse," he added, coming up to his companion, and whispering with a tone of mystery and fear, "who is that little drummer boy, and what business as he to follow us so closely?" "I can see no one," answered the seaman. "What! not see that little boy with the bloody pantaloons!" exclaimed the secret murderer, so much to the terror of his comrade that he conjured him, if he had any thing on his mind to make a clear conscience, as far as confession could do it. The criminal fetched a deep groan, and declared he was unable longer to endure the life he had led for years. He then confessed the murder of the drummer; and added, that as a considerable reward had been offered, he wished his companion to deliver him up to the magistrates of Salisbury, as he would desire a shipmate to profit by his fate, which he was now convinced was inevitable. Having overcome his friend's objections to this mode of proceeding, Jarvis Mutcham was surrendered to justice accordingly, and made a full confession of his guilt. But before the trial, the love of life returned. The prisoner denied his confession, and pleaded not guilty. By this time full evidence had been procured from other quarters. Witnesses appeared from his former regiment to prove his identity with the murderer and deserter, and the waiter remembered the ominous words which he had spoken, when he awoke him to join the Portsmouth coach.

Jarvis Mutcham was found guilty, and executed. When his last chance of life was over, he returned to his confession, and with his dying breath averred, and truly, as he thought, the truth of the vision on Salisbury plain.

JOHN EYRE.

An anecdote is related of John Eyre, a man whose name is recorded in the annals of crime as possessing about one hundred and thirty thousand dollars, and yet being sentenced to transportation for stealing eleven quires of writing paper, which shows in a striking manner the depravity of the human heart, and may help to account for the meanness of the crime of which he stood convicted. An uncle of his, a gentleman of considerable property, made his will in favor of a clergyman who was his intimate friend, and committed it, unknown to the rest of the family, to the custody of the divine. However, not long before his death, having altered his mind with regard to the disposal of his wealth, he made another will, in which he left the clergyman only two thousand, two hundred dollars, bequeathing the bulk of his large property to his nephew and heir-at-law, Mr. Eyre. Soon after the old gentleman's death, Mr. Eyre, rummaging over his drawers, found his last will, and perceiving the legacy to the clergyman, without any hesitation or scruple of conscience put it into the fire, and took possession of the whole effects, in consequence of his uncle being supposed to die intestate.

The clergyman coming to town soon after, and inquiring into the circumstances of his old friend's death, asked if he had made a will before he died. On being answered by Mr. Eyre in the negative, the clergyman very coolly put his hand in his pocket and pulled out the former will, which had been committed to his care, in which Mr. Eyre had bequeathed him the whole of his fortune, amounting to several thousand dollars, excepting a legacy of about nine hundred dollars to his nephew.

A FAITHFUL AND AFFECTIONATE DOMESTIC.

A COMPLETE reverse having taken place in the circumstances of a gentleman, by his too great readiness to lend money to those who deceived him, he was obliged in his old age to dismiss all his domestics. It was, however, his happiness to have one among them, who, knowing the cause, said to him with tears, "I have now, sir, been your servant five-and-twenty years; I have always honored and respected you: you have treated me with the kindness of a master, a father, and a friend. I have saved some scores of pounds in your service, that I might be comfortable in my old age; but I cannot live in peace while I see you in distress. To you, under the good care of Providence, I owe my life; to you I am indebted for much good instruction, and for the salvation of my soul. I beg you will accept of my purse and all it contains. He that feedeth the ravens and letteth not a sparrow fall unheeded to the ground, will not forsake me! I am yet able for service: suffer me to attend your fortunes, and be your servant still. She drew tears from her old master by these and other affectionate expressions; he wept at her generosity, accepted her offer of service, and she remained with him.

Now, reader, mark the result, and be encouraged to every act of kindness to others within your power, especially to those from whom you have derived your enjoyments, and who may have seen better days. Not long after she had resumed her place, a relation of her master died and left him a good fortune. How must this have rejoiced the heart of a servant so attached! But one particular yet remains. When her master died he bequeathed this faithful servant a comfortable maintenance.

A MURDEROUS DAUGHTER.

A MAN and his wife were executed at Augsburg for a murder, the discovery of which, after a long lapse of time, strongly manifests the impossibility of eluding the all-seeing eye of Providence. The criminal, whose name was Wincze, was originally of Nuremberg, but removed to Augsburg in 1788, where he became a lawyer. In this city he became intimate in the family of M. Glegg, to whose daughter he paid his addresses; but the old gentleman not sanctioning his visits, he met the daughter privately, seduced her, and persuaded her, in order to remove the only obstacle to their union, to administer poison to her father. The horrid plan succeeded; no suspicions were entertained, and their union put him in possession of the old man's wealth. During a period of twenty-one years they lived externally happy, but in secret a prey to the greatest remorse. At length, unable to endure any longer the weight of guilt, the wife made confession of the particulars of the atrocious crime which she had been prevailed upon to commit. The husband was apprehended, and both of them received the award of justice in an ignominious death.

THE CRIMINAL DISCOVERED.

IN the beginning of 1815 a circumstance took place that excited much interest in Paris. A surgeon in the army, named Dautun, was arrested at a gambling-house in the Palais Royal, on the testimony of a scar on his wrist. Some time before the officers of the night had found, while passing their rounds in the different parts of the city, four parcels tied up. One contained the head, another the trunk, a third the thighs, and a fourth the legs and arms of a man. In the teeth, tightly compressed, was a piece of human flesh apparently torn out in the dying struggle. The parts were collected and put together in their regular order, and exhibited for a number of days at the Morgue. The mystery which enveloped this dark transaction excited considerable interest, and numbers went to view the corpse. The general conviction was that the deceased must have been murdered, but for a number of weeks no light was thrown upon the circumstance. When the body could not be kept any longer, a cast in plaster was taken, fully representing the murdered victim, which remained for some time exposed to the public.

Dautun happened to be engaged in gambling at the Palais Royal; he played high and lost; calling for liquor, and being angry because the waiter was somewhat tardy, Dautun emptied the glass and threw it at him. It was shivered into a thousand pieces, one of which entered into Dautun's wrist under the cuff of his coat. The spectators gathered round, and learning the accident wished to see the gash; he drew down his sleeve and firmly pressed it round his wrist; they insisted on seeing it, he obstinately refused. By this course the bystanders were led to suppose that something mysterious was involved in this conduct, and they determined at all events to see his wrist. By force they pushed up his sleeve, and a scar recently healed, as if made by tearing out the flesh, appeared. The landlord had been at the Morgue, had seen the murdered man with the flesh between the teeth, and it struck him in a moment that the flesh was torn from this man's wrist. Charging them to keep him safe, he hastened to call in the legal authorities and arrested him.

Dauton afterward confessed, that being quartered at Sedan, and without money, he came to Paris to try some adventure. Knowing that his brother had a large sum by him, directly on his arrival he went to his lodgings, in a retired part of the city, about eight in the evening. He entered the house unnoticed by the porter, and passing to his apartment, found his brother asleep. He immediately commenced his work of death: his brother waking up defended himself, but being in a feeble state of health he was speedily overpowered. In the struggle he tore out the flesh. Being killed, Dautun cut up the body, tied it up in four parcels as before mentioned, secured the money, and retired.

He also confessed that eleven months before this he had murdered an aunt (who was living with a second husband,) to obtain money. Her husband was arrested and imprisoned for a number of months, but as nothing appeared to criminate him, he had been discharged.

THE FATAL ELOPEMENT.

A YOUNG lady, named D'Aumont, was executed in the city of Lyons for the supposed murder of her uncle, the Chevalier de la Poulone, with whom she had lived in the most affectionate harmony from her infantile years. Having conceived a passion for a deserving young officer quartered in the town, and between whom and the young lady a mutual affection subsisted, she came to a determination of eloping with him unknown to her uncle, and only admitted one female servant to her confidence. It unfortunately happened that the servant was leagued with a private soldier, who meditated the plan of murdering the chevalier, with a view of plundering the house, on the night the intended elopement should take place, in order that the unhappy niece should be judged the perpetrator of the horrid deed, which was effected with every degree of barbarity. The young lady and the officer were immediately pursued, taken, and committed to prison. The former was tried and executed on the false evidence of the female servant, and the officer, her husband, was cashiered, and sent to the gallies for life.

Some time after, the servant being taken ill, threatened to divulge the whole matter before a magistrate; to prevent which the soldier, who had married her, put an end to his wife's existence; but at length, feeling sincere remorse for these repeated murders, he voluntarily surrendered himself up to justice, confessed the whole affair, and was publicly executed amidst the execrations of the enraged multitude.

What adds to the dreadful account is, that the young lady who was executed was not less remarkable for her beauty, than her unaffected piety and sweet simplicity of manners. A broken heart soon terminated the existence of the wretched officer, who died in six weeks after the execution of the most amiable sufferer, in the most excruciating tortures.

CONFESSION OF A MURDER IN A DREAM.

The following is translated from a respectable publication at Basle, Switzerland:

A person who worked in a brewery quareled with one of his fellow-workmen, and struck him in such a manner that he died on the spot. No other person was witness to the deed. He then took the dead body and threw it into a large fire under the boiling-vat, where it was in a short time so completely consumed, that no traces of its existence remained. On the following day, when the man was missed, the murderer observed, very coolly, that he had perceived his fellow-servant to have been intoxicated, and that he had probably fallen from a bridge which he had to cross in his way home, and been drowned. For the space of seven years after no one entertained any suspicion of the real state of the fact. At the end of this period the murderer was again employed in the same brewery. He was then induced to reflect on the singularity of the circumstance that his crime had remained so long concealed. Having retired one evening to rest, one of the other workmen, who slept with him, hearing him say in his sleep, "It is now fully seven years ago," asked him, "What was it you did seven years ago?" "I put him," he replied, still speaking in his sleep, "under the boiling-vat." As the affair was not entirely forgotten, it immediately occurred to the man that his bedfellow must allude to the person who was missing about that time, and he accordingly gave information of what he had heard to a magistrate. The murderer was apprehended; and though he at first denied that he knew any thing of the matter, a confession of his crime was at length obtained from him, for which he suffered condign punishment.

MURDERER DISCOVERED BY A JOKE.

THE Rev. H. G. Keene states, in his Persian Stories, that the following narrative was related by a person of authority and reputation, who was one of the party:

A vessel set sail from Bassorah to Bagdad, with several passengers on board. In the course of the voyage the sailors, by way of a joke, put a man in irons as he lay asleep, and he became an object of diversion to the whole party, till they drew near the capitol. But when the sailors wanted to let him loose, the key was nowhere to be found, and after a long and fruitless search they were compelled to send for a blacksmith to knock off the fetters. When, however, the blacksmith came, he refused to do what they wanted till he had the authority of the magistrate; for he thought the man might be some criminal whom the officers of justice had laid hold of, and that his friends wished to favor his escape. To the magistrates they accordingly went, who sent down an attendant to see into it. But the officer, when he had heard their story, and had taken the evidence of some of the most respectable among the passengers, shook his head, and with a look of solemnity, said it was much too serious a case for him to decide. So they repaired in a body to the magistrate, and carried the poor captive with them.

So strange a procession was sure to attract notice; and a crowd soon collected about them, each curious to know the prisoner's offense, and to catch a sight of him: till, at length one man, springing forward, seized the captive by the throat, and exclaimed, "Here is the villain I have been looking for these two years; ever since he murdered my poor brother." Nor would he quit his hold till they came before the magistrate; and the murder being clearly proved, the man, who had been confined in joke only, was given up to death, as a punishment for the blood that he had shed.

CHURCHILL AND THE TIGER.

THIS gentleman was a native of England, but resided about two miles from Vizagapatam, in India. One evening as he was reclining on a sofa, reflecting on the severe loss he had recently sustained in the death of his wife, and watching the slumbers of his two little ones who were near him on a bed, he was suddenly alarmed with the prospect of a terrible death, both for them and himself; but was as suddenly delivered both from the danger and the fear. A tiger walked into the house and entered the room; but instead of attacking its occupants, he beheld his own image in a large mirror: he rushed forward and broke it into a thousand pieces, and then immediately fled from the spot.

THE PEARL DIVER AND THE SHARK.

In diving for pearls, it is usual for the person so employed to carry a short stick, about nine inches long, and pointed at both ends. Armed with this, an experienced diver will often fight the shark in its own domain. He grasps the stick in the middle; and when attacked by the shark, he thrusts it into the monster's expanded jaws, in such a position that, in attempting to seize his victim, the jaws close upon the two sharp points. The following account of Don Pablo Ochon's adventure with a tinterero, is given by Mr. Hardy:

"The Placer de la Piedra Negada, which is near Loreto, was supposed to have quantities of very large pearl-oysters around it—a supposition which was at once confirmed by the great difficulty of finding this sunken rock. Don Pablo, however, succeeded in sounding it; and, in search of specimens of the largest and oldest shells, dived down in eleven fathoms water. The rock is not above a hundred and fifty or two hundred yards in circumference; and our adventurer swam round and examined it in all direction, but without meeting any inducement to prolong his stay. Accordingly, being satisfied that there were no oysters, he thought of ascending to the surface of the water; but first he cast a look upward, as all divers are obliged to do who hope to avoid the hungry jaws of a monster. If the coast is clear, they may rise without apprehension. Don Pablo, however, when he cast a hasty glance upward, found that a tinterero (the ground shark,) had taken a station three or four yards immediately above him, and most probably had been watching during the whole time that he had been down. A double-pointed stick was a useless weapon against such a tinterero, as its mouth was of such enormous dimensions, that both man and stick would be swallowed together. He therefore felt himself rather nervous, as his retreat was now completely intercepted. But under water time is too great an object to be spent in reflection, and therefore he swam round to another part of the rock, hoping by this means to avoid the vigilance of his persecutor. What was his dismay, when he again looked, to find the pertinacious tinterero still hovering over him, as a hawk would follow a bird! He described him as having large, round, and inflamed eyes, apparently just ready to dart from the sockets with eagerness, and a mouth (at the recollection of which he still shuddered,) that was continually opening and shutting, as if the monster was already, in imagination, devouring his victim, or at least that the contemplation of his prey imparted a foretaste of the gout!

Two alternatives now presented themselves to the mind of Don Pablo—one, to suffer himself to be drowned; the other, to be eaten. He had already been under water so considerable a time, that he found it impossible any longer to retain his breath, and was on the point of giving himself up for lost with as much philosophy as he possessed. But what is dearer than life? The invention of man is seldom at a loss to find expedients for its preservation in cases of great extremity. On a sudden he recollected that on one side of the rock he had observed a sandy spot, and to this he swam with all imaginable speed; his attentive friend still watching his movements, and keeping a measured pace with him. As soon as he reached the spot, he commenced stirring it with his pointed stick, in such a way that the fine particles rose and rendered the water perfectly turbid, so that he could not see the monster, nor the monster see him. Availing himself of the *cloud* by which himself and the tinterero were enveloped, he swam very far out in a transvertical direction, and reached the surface in safety, although completely exhausted. Fortunately he rose close to some of the boats, and those who were within seeing him in such a state, and knowing that an enemy must have been persecuting him, and that by some artifice he had saved his life, jumped overboard, as is their common practice in such cases, to frighten the creature away by splashing the water; and Don Pablo was taken into the boat more dead than alive."

SAVED FROM DROWNING.

On the 28th of January, 1838, the river Seine, which had been frozen for several days, was covered with skaters. It was in vain that they were told of the expected tide, which must certainly break the ice; neither the danger which they ran, nor the warning and efforts of the local authorities, succeeded in producing any effect upon them. Louis Brune, whose wife and aged mother were then ill, remained all day on the quay, in expectation of the disaster, which he knew to be inevitable. In vain pressing messages to return home came from his family; he firmly refused to leave the spot; and not even for his meals could he be induced to desert the post he had assigned to himself. Nor was it long before a rushing noise was heard; the ice was breaking in every direction; and the precipitate flight of the crowd increased the disaster. A gentleman and his lady who were enjoying the pleasures of skating, suddenly disappeared in a large opening which the breaking ice had formed beneath them. Brune, who was eagerly looking out, rushed over the ice that bent beneath his tread, plunged into the river, seized the gentleman and brought him safely to the shore. No sooner had he accomplished this, than he once more precipitated himself into the river, and was fortunate enough in seizing the lady, who had already disappeared under the ice; but, benumbed by the cold, and his strength failing him through this unwonted exertion, he in vain endeavored to rise to the surface: he laid hold of the masses of ice, but merely cut his hands in the attempt. Notwithstanding the most desperate efforts, he was on the point of perishing with her whom he endeavored to save, when a rope was thrown to him; he seized it, and, though not without difficulty, reached the shore with his burden amidst the applause of the assembled crowd.

REV. E. ERSKINE AND THE MURDERER.

The Rev. Ebenezer Erskine, after traveling at one time toward the end of the week, from Portmoak to the banks of the Forth, on his way to Edinburgh, was, with several others, prevented by a storm from crossing that frith. Thus obliged to remain in Fife during the Sabbath, he was employed to preach, it is believed, in Kinghorn. Conformably to his usual practice, he prayed earnestly in the morning for the Divine countenance and aid in the work of the day; but suddenly missing his note-book, he knew not what to do. His thoughts, however, were directed to the command, "Thou shalt not kill;" and having studied the subject with as much care as the time would permit, he delivered a short sermon on it in the forenoon. Having returned to his lodging, he gave strict injunctions to the servant that no one should be allowed to see him during the interval of worship.

A stranger, however, who was also one of the persons detained by the state of the weather, expressed an earnest desire to see the minister; and having with difficulty obtained admittance, appeared much agitated, and asked him, with great eagerness, whether he knew him, or had ever seen or heard of him. On receiving assurance that he was totally unacquainted with his face, character, and history, the gentleman proceeded to state, that his sermon on the sixth commandment had reached his conscience; that he was a murderer; that being the second son of a Highland laird, he had some time before from base and selfish motives, cruelly suffocated his elder brother, who slept in the same bed with him; and that now he had no peace of mind, and wished to surrender himself to justice to suffer the punishment due to his horrid and unnatural crime. Mr. Erskine asked him if any other person knew any thing of his guilt. His answer was, that so far as he was aware, not a single individual had the least suspicion of it; on which the good man exhorted him to be deeply affected with a sense of his atrocious sin, to make an immediate application to the blood of sprinkling, and to bring forth fruits meet for repentance; but at the same time, since his crime had hitherto remained a secret, not to disclose it, or to give himself up to public justice. The unhappy gentleman embraced this well intended counsel in all its parts, became truly pious, and maintained a friendly correspondence with Mr. Erskine in future life.

MURDERER DETECTED BY HIS OWN REMARK.

Eugene Aram, of Knaresborough, England, was descended from an ancient Yorkshire family, and had cultivated his talents with so much care, that he acquired a knowledge of Latin, Greek, Hebrew, and Chaldee, and was conversant with history, antiquity, botany, and poetry; but he associated with low and depraved company, and in conjunction with Daniel Clark, a shoemaker, and Richard Housman, a flax-dresser, it was agreed to make use of Clark's credit to borrow a quantity of silver plate and other valuables from their neighbors, and then to abscond. Having accomplished their object, they met on the evening of February 7th, 1744; and either to prevent detection, or to increase their own share of the plunder, Aram and Housman murdered Clark, and concealed his body in St. Robert's Cave.

No trace of the perpetrators of the deed occurred till fourteen years afterward, when a skeleton was discovered at Thistle Hill, near Knaresborough, which was at first supposed to be Clark's. Housman, who was then living, rejected the supposition, and taking up one of the bones, said, "This is no more one of Daniel Clark's bones than it is mine." Suspicion was immediately excited against Housman, who at length confessed his participation in the murder, but that Aram was the perpetrator. Aram, who at that time resided at Lynn, in Norfolk, was forthwith apprehended, tried, and executed. What an illustration of the text, "Be sure thy sin will find thee out."

THE MURDERER AND HIS SINGULAR WOUND.

A gentleman who was very ill, sending for Dr. Lake, of England, told him he found he must die, and gave him the following account of the cause of his death. He had, about a fortnight before, been riding over Hounslow-heath, where several boys were playing at cricket. One of them, striking the ball, hit him just on the toe with it, looked him in the face, and ran away. His toe pained him extremely. As soon as he came to Brentford, he sent for a surgeon, who was for cutting it off. But unwilling to suffer that, he went on to London. When he arrived there, he immediately called another surgeon to examine it, who told him his foot must be cut off. But neither would he hear of this; and so, before the next day, the mortification seized his leg, and in a day or two more struck up into his body. Dr. Lake asked him whether he knew the boy that struck the ball? He answered, "About ten years ago I was riding over Hounslow-heath, where an old man ran by my horse's side, begged me to relieve him, and said he was almost famished. I bade him begone. He kept up with me still; upon which I threatened to beat him. Finding that he took no notice of this, I drew my sword, and with one blow killed him. A boy, about four years old, who was with him, screamed out his father was killed! His face I perfectly remember. That boy it was who struck the ball against me, which is the cause of my death."

ESCAPE FROM THE INDIANS.

John Colter, a celebrated western hunter, "had occasion to match himself in a race of a somewhat serious nature with a party of Blackfeet Indians. The incident took place at the head waters of the Missouri, where he was trapping in company with a hunter named Potts. Aware of the hostility of the Blackfeet tribe, they proceeded with great caution, setting their beaver-traps at night, and taking them up in the morning, and remaining concealed during the day. Early one morning they were examining their traps in a creek about six miles from that branch of the Missouri now called Jefferson's Fork, and were ascending in a canoe, when they suddenly heard a great noise, resembling the tramping of animals; but they could not ascertain the fact, as the high perpendicular banks on each side of the river impeded their view. Colter immediately pronounced it to be occasioned by Indians, and advised an instant retreat; but was accused of cowardice by Potts, who insisted that the noise was caused by buffaloes, and they proceeded on.

In a few minutes afterward their doubts were removed by a party of Indians making their appearance on both sides of the creek, to the amount of five or six hundred, who beckoned them to come ashore. As retreat was now impossible, Colter turned the head of the canoe, and at the moment of its touching, an Indian seized the rifle belonging to Potts; but Colter, who was a remarkably strong man, retook it immediately, and handed it to Potts, who remained in the canoe, and, on receiving it, pushed off into the river. He had scarcely quitted the shore when an arrow was shot at him, and he cried out,

"Colter, I am wounded." Colter remonstrated with him on the folly of attempting to escape, and urged him to come ashore. Instead of complying, he instantly leveled his rifle at the Indian and shot him dead on the spot. This conduct, situated as he was, may appear to have been an act of madness; but it was doubtless the effect of sudden but sound reasoning; for if taken alive, he must have expected to be tortured to death, according to their custom. He was instantly pierced with arrows so numerous, that, to use Colter's words, "he was made a riddle of." They now seized Colter, stripped him entirely naked, and began to consult on the manner he should be put to death.

They were first inclined to set him up as a mark to shoot at; but the chief interfered, and seizing him by the shoulder, asked him if he could run fast. Colter, who had been some time among the Keekatso or Crow Indians, had in a considerable degree acquired the Blackfeet language, and was also well acquainted with Indian customs. He knew that he had now to run for his life, with the dreadful odds of five or six hundred against him, and those armed Indians: he therefore cunningly replied that he was a very bad runner, although he was considered by the hunters as remarkably swift. The chief now commanded the party to remain stationary, and he led Colter out on the prairie three or four hundred yards, and released him, bidding him save himself if he could.

At this instant the horrid war-whoop sounded in the ears of poor Colter, who, urged with the hope of preserving his life, ran with a speed at which himself was surprised. He proceeded toward the Jefferson Fork, having to traverse a plain six miles in breadth, abounding with prickly pear, on which he was every instant treading with his naked feet. He ran nearly half way across the plain before he ventured to look back over his shoulder, when he perceived that the Indians were very much scattered, and that he had gained ground to a considerable distance from the main body; but one Indian, who carried a spear, was much before all the rest, and not more than ninety or one hundred yards from him. A faint gleam of hope now cheered the heart of Colter: he derived confidence from the belief that escape was within the bounds of possibility; but that confidence was nearly fatal to him, for he exerted himself to such a degree, that the blood gushed from his nostrils, and soon almost covered the fore-part of his body.

He had now arrived within a mile of the river, when he distinctly heard the appalling sound of footsteps behind him, and every instant expected to feel the spear of the pursuer. Again he turned his head, and saw the Indian not twenty yards from him. Determined, if possible, to avoid the expected blow, he suddenly stopped, turned round, and spread out his arms. The Indian, surprised by the suddenness of the action, and perhaps by the bloody appearance of Colter, also attempted to stop. But, exhausted with running, he fell while endeavoring to throw his spear, which struck in the ground and broke. Colter instantly snatched up the pointed part, with which he pinned him to the earth, and then continued his flight. The foremost of the Indians, on arriving at the place, stopped till the others came up to join them, when they set up a hideous yell. Every moment of time was improved by Colter, who, although fainting and exhausted, succeeded in gaining the skirting of the cotton-wood trees, on the borders of the Fork; through this he pushed, and plunged into the river. Fortunately for him, a little below the place there was an island, against the upper end of which a raft of drift timber had lodged. He dived under the raft, and, after several efforts, got his head above water among the trunks of the trees, covered over with smaller wood to the depth of several feet. Scarcely had he secreted himself, when the Indians arrived at the river, screeching and yelling in a terrific manner. They were frequently on the raft during the day, and were seen through the chinks by Colter, who was congratulating himself on his escape, until the idea arose that they might set the raft on fire. In horrible suspense he remained until night; when hearing no more of the Indians, he dived a second time under the raft, and swam silently down the stream to a considerable distance, where he landed, and traveled all night.

Although happy in having escaped from the savages, his situation was still dreadful. He was completely naked; the soles of his feet were stuck full with spines of the prickly pear; he was hungry, and had no means of killing game, though tantalized with plenty around him; and he was at least seven days' journey from Lisa's Fort, on the Big Horn branch of the Rocke Jaune river. These were circumstances under which almost any man but an American hunter would have sunk in despair; yet he arrived at the fort in seven days, having subsisted on a root much esteemed by the Indians of the Missouri.

FIRE ON THE PRAIRIE.

George Catlin was one day riding across an Upper Missouri prairie, where the grass is seven or eight feet high, with three companions, one an Indian guide of the name of Pah-me-o-ne-qua, or the *red thunder*. Three of the party sat down to their mid-day meal, but the Indian stood aloof, sad and thoughtful. "This is the plain of *fire grass*," said he, "where the fleet-bounding wild horse mingles his bones with the red man, and the eagle's wing is melted as he darts over its surface." Notwithstanding these ominous words, after gazing long around, he gracefully sank down on the grass, and his relieved companions chatted cheerfully by his side. But on a sudden "Red Thunder was on his feet—his long arm was stretched over the grass. 'White man,' said he, 'see ye that small cloud lifting itself from the prairie?—he rises! the hoofs of our horses have waked him! 'The Fire Spirit is awake!—this wind is from his nostrils, and his face is this way.' No more; but his swift horse darted under him, and he gracefully slid over the waving grass as it was bent by the wind. Our viands were left, and we were swift on his trail. The extraordinary leaps of his wild horse occasionally raised his red shoulders to view, and he sank again in the waving billows of grass. The tremulous wind was hurrying by us fast, and on it was borne the agitated wing of the soaring eagle. His neck was stretched for the towering bluff, and the thrilling screams of his voice told the secret that was behind him. Our horses were swift, and we struggled hard; yet hope was feeble; for the bluff was yet blue, and nature nearly exhausted. The sunshine was dying, and a cool shadow advancing over the plain. Not daring to look back, we strained every nerve. The roar of a distant cataract seemed gradually advancing on us—the winds increased—the howling tempest was maddening behind us—and the swift-winged beetle and heath hens instinctively drew their straight lines over our heads. The fleet-bounding antelope passed us also; and the still swifter long-legged hare, which leaves but a shadow as he flies. Here was no time for thought; but I recollect the heavens were overcast—the distant thunder was heard—the lightning's glare was reddening the scene—and the smell that came on the winds struck terror to my soul. * *

The piercing yell of my savage guide at this moment came back upon the winds; his robe was seen waving in the air, and his foaming horse leaping up the towering bluff.

Our breath and our sinews, in this last struggle for life, were just enough to bring us to its summit. We had risen from a sea of fire!

'How sublime,' I exclaimed, 'to gaze into that valley, where the elements of nature are so strangely convulsed!' Ask not the poet or painter how it looked, for they can tell you not; but ask the naked savage, and watch the electric twinge of his manly nerves and muscles as he pronounces the lengthened 'Hush—sh—,' his hand on his mouth, and his glaring eyeballs looking you to the very soul.

I beheld beneath me an immense cloud of black smoke, which extended from one extremity of this vast plain to the other, and seemed majestically to roll over its surface in a bed of liquid fire; and above this mighty desolation, as it rolled along, the whitened smoke, pale with terror, was streaming and rising up in magnificent cliffs to heaven.

I stood secure, but tremblingly, and heard the maddening wind, which hurled this monster o'er the land—I heard the roaring thunder, and saw its thousand lightnings flash; and then I saw behind the black and smoking desolation of this storm of fire."

SKETCHES AND ANECDOTES ILLUSTRATIVE OF NATURAL HISTORY.

CAPTURE OF A WHALE.

BY J. F. COOPER.

THE cockswain cast a cool glance at the crests of foam that were breaking over the tops of the billows within a few yards of where their boat was riding, and called aloud to his men:

"Pull a stroke or two; away with her into dark water."

The drop of the oars resembled the movements of a nice machine, and the light boat skimmed along the water like a duck, that approaches to the very brink of some imminent danger, and then avoids it at the most critical moment, apparently without an effort. While this necessary movement was making, Barnstable arose, and surveyed the cliffs with keen eyes, and then, turning once more in disappointment from his search, he said:

"Pull more from the land, and let her run down at an easy stroke to the schooner. Keep a lookout at the cliffs, boys; it is possible that they are stowed in some of the holes in the rocks, for it's no daylight business they are on."

The order was promptly obeyed, and they had glided along for near a mile in this manner, in the most profound silence, when suddenly the stillness was broken by a heavy rush of air, and a dash of water, seemingly at no great distance from them.

"By heaven! Tom," cried Barnstable, starting, "there is the blow of a whale."

"Ay, ay, sir," returned the cockswain, with undisturbed composure; "here is his spout, not half a mile to seaward; the easterly gale has driven the creater to leeward, and he begins to find himself in shoal water. He's been sleeping, while he should have been working to windward!"

"The fellow takes it coolly, too! He's in no hurry to get an offing."

"I rather conclude," sir," said the cockswain, rolling over his tobacco in his mouth very composedly, while his little sunken eyes began to twinkle with pleasure at the sight, "the gentleman has lost his reckoning, and don't know which way to head, to take himself back into blue water."

"'Tis a fin-back!" exclaimed the lieutenant; "he will soon make head-way, and be off."

"No, sir, 'tis a right whale," answered Tom; "I saw his spout; he threw up a pair of as pretty rainbows as a Christian would wish to look at. He's a raal oil-butt, that fellow!"

Barnstable laughed, turned himself away from the tempting sight, and tried to look at the cliffs; and then unconsciously bent his eyes again on the sluggish animal, who was throwing his huge carcass at times for many feet from the water, in idle gambols. The temptation for sport, and the recollection of his early habits, at length prevailed over his anxiety in behalf of his friends, and the young officer inquired of his cockswain:

"Is there any whale-line in the boat to make fast to that harpoon which you bear about with you in fair weather or foul?"

"I never trust the boat from the schooner without part of a shot, sir," returned the cockswain; "there is something nateral in the sight of a tub to my old eyes."

Barnstable looked at his watch, and again at the cliffs, when he exclaimed in joyous tones:

"Give strong way, my hearties! There seems nothing better to be done; let us have a stroke of a harpoon at that impudent rascal."

The men shouted spontaneously, and the old cockswain suffered his solemn visage to relax into a small laugh, while the whale-boat sprang forward like a courser for the goal. During the few minutes they were pulling toward their game, long Tom arose from his crouching attitude in the stern sheets, and transferred his huge frame to the bow of the boat, where he made such preparation to strike the whale as the occasion required. The tub, containing about half of a whale-line, was placed at the feet of Barnstable, who had been preparing an oar to steer with, in place of the rudder, which was unshipped in order that, if necessary, the boat might be whirled round when not advancing.

Their approach was utterly unnoticed by the monster of the deep, who continued to amuse himself with throwing the water in two circular spouts high into the air, occasionally flourishing the broad flukes of his tail with graceful but terrific force, until the hardy seamen were within a few hundred feet of him, when he suddenly cast his head downwards, and, without an apparent effort, reared his immense body for many feet above the water, waiving his tail violently, and producing a whizzing noize, that sounded like the rushing of winds. The cockswain stood erect, poising his harpoon, ready for the blow; but, when he beheld the creature assume this formidable attitude, he waved his hand to his commander, who instantly signed to his men to cease rowing. In this situation the sportsmen rested a few moments, while the whale struck several blows on the water in rapid succession, the noise of which re-echoed along the cliffs, like the hollow reports of so many cannon. After this wanton exhibition of his terrible strength, the monster sunk again into his native element, and slowly disappeared from the eyes of his pursuers.

"Which way did he head, Tom?" cried Barnstable, the moment the whale was out of sight.

"Pretty much up and down, sir," returned the cockswain, whose eye was gradually brightening with the excitement of the sport; "he'll soon run his nose against the bottom, if he stands long on that course, and will be glad to get another snuff of pure air; send her a few fathoms to starboard, sir, and I promise we shall not be out of his track."

The conjecture of the experienced old seaman proved true, for in a few minutes the water broke near them, and another spout was cast into the air, when the huge animal rushed for half his length in the same direction, and fell on the sea with a turbulence and foam equal to that which is produced by the launching of a vessel, for the first time, into its proper element. After this evolution, the whale rolled heavily, and seemed to rest from further efforts.

His slightest movements were closely watched by Barnstable and his cockswain, and, when he was in a state of comparative rest, the former gave a signal to his crew to ply their oars once more. A few long and vigorous strokes sent the boat directly up to the broadside of the whale, with its bows pointing toward one of the fins, which was at times, as the animal yielded sluggishly to the action of the waves, exposed to view. The cockswain poised his harpoon with much precision, and then darted it from him with a violence that buried the iron in the body of their foe. The instant the blow was made, long Tom shouted with singular earnestness:

"Starn all!"

"Stern all!" echoed Barnstable; when the obedient seamen, by united efforts, forced the boat in a backward direction, beyond the reach of any blow from their formidable antagonist. The alarmed animal, however, meditated no such resistance; ignorant of his own power, and of the insignificance of his enemies, he sought refuge in flight. One moment of stupid surprise succeeded the entrance of the iron, when he cast his huge tail into the air with a violence that threw the sea around him into increased commotion, and then disappeared, with the quickness of lightning, amid the cloud of foam.

"Snub him!" shouted Barnstable; "hold on, Tom, he rises already."

"Ay, ay, sir," replied the composed cockswain, seizing the line which was running out of the boat with a velocity that rendered such a manœuvre rather hazardous, and causing it to yield more gradually round the large loggerhead, that was placed in the bows of the boat for that purpose. Presently the line stretched forward, and, rising to the surface with tremulous vibrations, it indicated the direction in which the animal might be expected to reappear. Barnstable had cast the bows of the boat toward that point, before the terrified and wounded victim rose once more to the surface, whose time was, however, no longer wasted in his sports, but who cast the waters aside as he forced his way, with prodigious velocity, along their surface. The boat was dragged violently in his wake, and cut through the billows with a terrific rapidity, that at moments appeared to bury the slight fabric in the ocean. When long Tom beheld his victim throwing his spouts on high again, he pointed with exultation to the jetting fluid, which was streaked with the deep red of blood, and cried :

"Ay, I've touched the fellow's life ! It must be more than two foot of blubber that stops my iron from reaching the life of any whale that ever sculled the ocean !"

"I believe you have saved yourself the trouble of using the bayonet you have rigged for a lance," said his commander, who entered into the sport with all the ardor of one whose youth had been chiefly passed in such pursuits; "feel your line, Master Coffin; can we haul alongside of our enemy ? I like not the course he is steering, as he tows us from the schooner."

"'Tis the creater's way, sir," said the cockswain; "you know they need the air in their nostrils when they run, the same as a man; but lay hold, boys, and let us haul up to him."

The seamen now seized their whale-line, and slowly drew their boat to within a few feet of the tail of the fish, whose progress became sensibly less rapid as he grew weak with the loss of blood. In a few minutes he stopped running, and appeared to roll uneasily on the water, as if suffering the agony of death.

"Shall we pull in and finish him, Tom ?" cried Barnstable; "a few sets from your bayonet would do it."

The cockswain stood examining his game with cool discretion, and replied to this interrogatory :

"No, sir, no—he's going into a flurry ; there's no occasion for disgracing ourselves by using a soldier's weapon in taking a whale. Starn off, sir, starn off ! the creater's in his flurry !"

The warning of the prudent cockswain was promptly obeyed, and the boat cautiously drew off to a distance, leaving to the animal a clear space while under its dying agonies. From a state of perfect rest, the terrible monster threw its tail on high as when in sport, but its blows were trebled in rapidity and violence, till all was hid from view by a pyramid of foam, that was deeply dyed with blood. The roarings of the fish were like the bellowings of a herd of bulls, and, to one who was ignorant of the fact, it would have appeared as if a thousand monsters were engaged in deadly combat behind the bloody mist that obstructed the view. Gradually these effects subsided, and when the discolored water again settled down to the long and regular swell of the ocean, the fish was soon exhausted, and yielding passively to its fate. As life departed, the enormous black mass rolled on one side, and when the white and glistening belly became apparent, the seamen well knew that their victory was achieved.

ANECDOTES OF SERPENTS.

JOCK HALL.

In the vicinity of the barracks assigned to European soldiers in India, there is usually a number of little solitary cells, where the disorderly members of the corps are confined for longer or shorter terms, by order of the commanding officer. In one of these, at Madras, on a certain occasion, was locked up poor Jock Hall, a Scotsman, belonging to Edinburgh or Leith. Jock had got intoxicated, and being found in that condition at the hour of drill, was sentenced to eight days' solitary imprisonment. Soldiers in India have ther bedding partly furnished by the Honorable Company, and find the remainder for themselves. About this part of house furnishing, however, Hall troubled himself very little, being one of those hardy and reckless beings on whom privation and suffering seem to make no impression. A hard floor was as good as a down bed to Jock, and therefore, as he never scrupled to sell what he got, it may be supposed that his sleeping furniture was none of the most abundant or select. Such as it was, he was stretched upon and under it one night in his cell, during his term of penance, and possibly was reflecting on the impropriety of in future putting "an enemy in his mouth to steal away his brains," when, lo! he thought he heard a rustling in the cell close by him. At this moment he recollected that he had not, as he ought to have done, stopped up an air-hole which entered the cell on a level with its floor, and also with the rock externally, on which the building was placed.

A strong suspicion of what had happened, or was about to happen, came over Hall's mind, but he knew it was probably too late to do any good, could he even find the hole in the darkness, and get it closed. He therefore lay still, and in a minute or two heard another rustle close to him, which was followed by the cold slimy touch of a snake upon his bare foot! Who in such a situation would not have started and bawled for help? Jock did neither; but lay stone still, and held his peace, knowing that his cries would most probably have been unheard by the distant guard. Had his bedclothes been more plentiful, he might have endeavored to protect himself by wrapping them closely around him; but this their scantiness forbade. Accordingly, being aware that, although a motion or touch will provoke snakes to bite, they will not generally do it without such incitement, Jock held himself as still as if he had been a log. Meanwhile his horrible bedfellow, which he at once felt to be of great size, crept over his feet, legs, and body, and lastly over his very face. Nothing but the most astonishing firmness of nerve, and the consciousness that the moving of a muscle would have signed his death-warrant, could have enabled the poor fellow to undergo this dreadful trial. For a whole hour did the reptile crawl backwards and forwards over Jock's body and face, as if satisfying itself, seemingly, that it had nothing to fear from the recumbent object on its own part. At length it took up a position somewhere about his head, and went to rest in apparent security. The poor soldier's trial, however, was not over. Till daylight he remained in the same posture, flat on his back, without daring to stir a limb, from the fear of disturbing his dangerous companion. Never, perhaps, was dawn so anxiously looked for by mortal man. When it did come, Jock cautiously looked about him, arose noiselessly, and moved over to the corner of his cell, where there lay a pretty large stone. This he seized, and looked for the intruder. Not seeing the snake, he became assured that it was under his pillow. He raised the end of this just sufficiently to get a peep of the creature's crest. Jock then pressed his knee firmly on the pillow, but allowed the snake to wriggle out its head, which he battered to pieces with the stone. This done, the courageous fellow breathed more freely.

When the hour for breakfast came, Jock, who thought little about the matter after it was fairly over, took the opportunity of the opening of the door to throw the snake out. When the officer whose duty it was to visit the cells for the day, was going his rounds, he perceived a crowd around the cell door examing the reptile, which was described by the natives as of the most venomous character, its bite being invariably and rapidly mortal. The officer, on being told that it had been killed by a man in the adjoining cell, went in and inquired into the matter. "When did you first know that there was a snake in the cell with you?" said he. "About nine o'clock last night," was Jock's reply. "Why didn't you call to the guard?" asked the officer. "I thought the guard wadna hear me, and I was feared I might tramp on't, so I just lay still." "But you might have been bit: did you know that you would have died instantly?" "I kent that very weel," said Hall; "but they say that snakes winna meddle with you if you dinna meddle with them; sae I just let it crawl as it likeit." "Well, my lad, I believe you did what was best after all, but it was what not one man in a thousand could have done." When the story was told, and the snake shown to the commanding officer, he thought the same, and Jock, for his extraordinary nerve and courage, got a remission of his punishment. For some time, at least, he took care how he again got into such a situation as to expose himself to the chance of passing another night with such a bedfellow.

A SNAKE HUNT.

Mr. Waterton, in his "Wanderings" in Demerara and the adjacent parts of South America, relates the following incident:

I was sitting, says he, with a Horace in my hand, when a negro and his little dog came down the hill in haste, and I was soon informed that a snake had been discovered; but it was a young one, called the bushmaster, a rare and poisonous snake. I instantly rose up, and laying hold of the eight-foot lance which was close by me, "Well, then, Daddy," said I, "we'll go and have a look at the snake." I was barefoot, with an old hat, check shirt, and trousers on, and a pair of braces to keep them up. The negro had his cutlass, and we ascended the hill; another negro, armed with a cutlass, joined us, judging from our pace that there was something to do. The little dog came along with us; and when he had got about half a mile in the forest, the negro stopped, and pointed to a fallen tree: all was still and silent. I told the negroes not to stir from the spot where they were, and keep the little dog in, and I would go and reconnoitre. I advanced up to the place slowly and cautiously. The snake was well concealed, but at last I made him out. It was a coulacanara, not poisonous, but large enough to have crushed any of us to death. On measuring him afterwards, he was something more than fourteen feet long. This species of snake is very rare, and much thicker, in proportion to his length, than any other snake in the forest. A coulacanara of fourteen feet in length is as thick as a common boa of twenty-four. After skinning this animal, I could easily get my head into its mouth, as the singular formation of the jaws admits of wonderful extension.

On ascertaining the size of game we had to encounter, I retired slowly the way I came, and promised four dollars to the negro who had shown it to me, and one to the other who had joined us. Aware that the day was on the decline, and that the approach of night would be detrimental to the dissection, a thought struck me that I could take him alive. I imagined that if I could strike him with the lance behind the head, and pin him to the ground, I might succeed in capturing him. When I told this to the negroes, they begged and intreated me to let them go for a gun, and bring more force, as they were sure the snake would kill some of us; but I had been in search of a large serpent for years, and now having come up with one, it did not become me to turn soft. So, taking a cutlass from one of the negroes, and then ranging both the sable slaves behind me, I told them to follow me, and that I would cut them down if they offered to fly. I smiled as I said this; but they shook their heads in silence, and seemed to have a bad heart of it. When we came to the place, the serpent had not stirred; but I could see nothing of his head, and I judged by the folds of his body that it must be at the farthest side of his den. A species of woodbine had formed a complete mantle over the branches of the fallen tree, almost impervious to the rain or the rays of the sun. Probably he had resorted to this sequestered place for a length of time, as it bore the marks of an ancient settlement. I now took my knife, determining to cut away the woodbine, and break the twigs in the gentlest manner possible, till I could get a view of his head. One negro stood guard close behind me with the lance, and near him the other with a cutlass. The cutlass which I had taken from the first negro was on the ground close by me, in case of need. After working in dead silence for a quarter of an hour, with one knee all the time on the ground, I had cleared away enough to see his head. It appeared coming out between the first and second coil of his body, and was flat on the ground. This was the very position I wished it to be in. I rose in silence, and retreated very slowly, making a sign to the negroes to do the same. We were at this time about twenty yards from the snake's den. I now ranged them behind me, and told him who stood next me to lay hold of the lance the moment I struck the snake, and that the other must attend my movements. It now only remained to take their cutlasses from them; for I was sure if I did not do this, they would be tempted to strike the snake in time of danger, and thus forever spoil his skin. On disarming them, if I might judge from their physiognomy, they seemed to consider it as a most intolerable act of tyranny in me. Probably nothing kept them from bolting but the consideration that I was to be between them and the snake. Indeed my own heart, in spite of all I could do, beat quicker than usual; and I felt those sensations which one has on board a merchant vessel in war time, when the captain orders all hands on deck to prepare for action, while a strange vessel is approaching under suspicious colors.

We went slowly on in silence, without moving our arms or heads, in order to prevent alarm as much as possible, lest the snake should glide off or attack us in self-defense. I carried the lance perpendicularly before me, with the point about a foot from the ground. The snake had not moved; and on getting up to him, I struck him with the lance on the near side, just behind the neck, and pinned him to the ground. That moment the negro next to me seized the weapon, and held it firm in its place, while I dashed head foremost into the den to grapple with the snake, and to get hold of his tail before he could do any mischief. On pinning him to the ground he gave a tremendous loud hiss, and the little dog ran away, howling as he went. We had a sharp fray in the den, the rotten sticks flying on all sides, and each party struggling for superiority. I called out to the second negro to throw himself upon me, as I found I was not heavy enough. He did so, and the additional weight was of great service. I had now got firm hold of his tail; and after a violent struggle or two he he gave in, feeling himself overpowered. This was the moment to secure him. So, while the first negro continued to hold the lance firm to the ground, and the other was helping me, I contrived to unloose my braces, and with them tied up the snake's mouth. The snake, now finding himself in an unpleasant situation, tried to better himself, and set resolutely to work; but we overpowered him. We contrived to make him twist himself round the shaft of the lance, and then prepared to convey him out of the forest. I stood at his head, and held it firm under my arm, one negro supporting the belly, and the other the tail. In this order we began to move slowly towards home, and reached it after resting ten times; for the snake was too heavy for us to support him without stopping to recruit our strength. As we proceeded onwards, he fought hard for freedom, but it was all in vain.

SOUTH AMERICAN ADVENTURE.

An English gentleman, who resided with a friend in British Guiana, employed himself chiefly in shooting and fishing in a neighboring river. One sultry day, tired with unsuccessful sport, he threw his lines, and drew his canoe to the river's edge, for the purpose of refreshing himself in the water. Having done so, he stretched himself, half-dressed, on the benches of his boat, with his gun at his head, loaded for a shot, if a chance should occur. In this position he fell asleep. "I know not how long I may have slept," he continues, "but I was roused from my slumber by a curious sensation, as if some animal were licking my foot. In that state of half-stupor felt after immediately waking from sleep, I cast my eyes downward, and never till my dying day shall I forget the thrill of horror that passed through my frame on perceiving the neck and head of a monstrous serpent covering my foot with saliva, preparatory, as immediately flashed upon my mind, to commencing the process of swallowing it. I had faced death in many shapes—on the ocean—on the battle-field—but never till that moment had I conceived he could approach me in a guise so terrible. For a moment, and but a moment, I was fascinated. But recollection of my state soon came to my aid, and I quickly withdrew my foot from the monster, which was all the while glaring upon me with its basilisk eyes, and at the same instant I instinctively grasped my gun, which was lying loaded beside me. The reptile, apparently disturbed by my motion, (I conceive it had previously, from my inertness, taken me for a dead carcase,) drew its head below the level of the canoe. I had just sufficient time to raise myself half up, pointing the muzzle of my piece in the direction of the serpent, when its neck and head again appeared moving backwards and forwards, as if in search of the object it had lost. The muzzle of my gun was within a yard or two of it; my finger was on the trigger; I fired, and it received the shot in its head. Rearing up part of its body into the air with a horrible hiss which made my blood run cold—and, by its contortions, displaying to my sight great part of its enormous bulk, which had hitherto escaped my notice—it seemed ready to throw itself upon me, and to embrace me in its monstrous coils. Dropping my gun, by a single stroke of the paddles I made the canoe shoot up the stream out of his reach. Just as I was escaping, I could observe that the shot had taken effect, for blood was beginning to drop from its head. But the wound appeared rather to have enraged than subdued him. Unfortunately, all my shot was expended, otherwise I would most certainly, at a respectable distance, have given him a salutation of the same kind as I had just bestowed. All that I have described passed in a much shorter time than I have taken up in recounting it.

"As I went up the stream with all the velocity I could impart to the canoe, I heard the reeds, among which the animal was apparently taking refuge, crashing under its weight. I never once thought of the lines I had left; but hurrying as fast as the canoe would go through the water, I was not long in reaching the landing-place below my friend's house. Hastily mooring the canoe, I jumped ashore, and hurried up to the house, where you may be certain I lost no time in communicating the almost miraculous escape I had made, and the wound I had inflicted on the animal. 'In that case,' said Mr. H., 'it cannot escape; we must immediately go in search of it;' and instantly summoning Cæsar, (a black servant,) he told him to get the guns ready, and to bring two of his fellows with him. 'If you choose to assist us in finishing the adventure you have begun, and to have a second encounter with your novel antagonist, we shall show you some of the best and most dangerous sport our country affords.' I protested that nothing was farther from my intention than staying behind, and added, that had not my shot been expended, we should not have parted on so easy terms. 'In general, said he, 'it is very dangerous to attack them at close quarters after being wounded, as they become extremely infuriated; and there are not wanting instances in which life has been sacrificed by doing so. But we now take such precaution in approaching them, that it is next to impossible that any accident can happen.' Just as he finished saying this, Cæsar reappeared, himself armed with a club, one of those who followed him carrying a weapon of the same kind, while the other was armed with a weapon similar to a billhook. This, Mr. H. told me, was to clear a road among the reeds, if the animal should have retreated among them; the club being reckoned the best instrument for a close encounter. We were soon seated in the canoes, and gliding down the stream as fast as a couple of pairs of brawny arms could urge us. In a short time we reached the spot where my adventure had happened. The small part of the bank not covered with reeds bore, from its sanguine hue, evident proof that the wound the animal had received could not have been slight. Exactly opposite this the reeds were crushed and broken, and a sort of passage was formed among them so wide, that a man could with little difficulty enter. My friend commanded a halt, to see that the arms were in proper order. All being right, we listened attentively, in order to hear if there was any noise which might direct us to our enemy. No sound, however, was heard. One of the negroes entered first, clearing with his billhook whatever obstructed our way. He was followed by Mr. H. and me with our guns; while Cæsar and his fellow-servant brought up the rear. The reeds were in general nearly double our hight, and at the same time pretty close. However, we easily made our way through them, partly assisted by the track which the serpent had evidently made.

"We had penetrated, I should suppose, about thirty yards, when the fellow who was in advance gave the alarm that we were close upon the animal. Mr. H. ordered him behind, and advancing along with me, we saw through the reeds part of the body of the monster coiled up, and part of it stretched out; but owing to their thickness, its head was invisible. Disturbed, and apparently irritated by our approach, it appeared, from its movements, about to turn and assail us. We had our guns ready, and just as we caught a glimpse of its head we fired, both of us almost at the same moment. From the obstruction of the reeds, all our shot could not have taken effect; but what did take effect seemed to be sufficient; for it fell, hissing, and rolling itself into a variety of contortions. Even yet it was dangerous to approach it. But Cæsar, who seemed to possess a great deal of coolness and audacity, motioning his master and me not to fire again in the direction of the animal, forced a way through the reeds at one side, and making a kind of circuit, came in before it, and succeeded in hitting it a violent blow, which completely stunned it; and a few repetitions of this gave us the victory. We could now examine the creature with safety. On measuring it, we found it to be nearly forty feet in length, and of proportional thickness. Mr. H. informed me that it was the largest he had seen killed, although he had often seen others under circumstances which convinced him that they must have been of a far greater size."

ANECDOTES OF THE ELEPHANT.

ELEPHANT HUNT.

The life of the Hottentot elephant hunter is indeed one of imminent peril, and few practice it for many years without being maimed or crushed to death by the infuriated animals. They are a brave, fearless set of men, encountering every species of risk, and enduring fatigue with a courage that is truly wonderful. Accompanied by a few such spirits, the European resident generally sets out on a hunting expedition—indeed it would be madness in him to enter the bush without such an escort. We have a spirited account of such an adventure in the following personal narrative of Lieutenant Moodie: "In the year 1821, I had joined the recently-formed semi-military settlement of Fredericksburg, on the picturesque banks of the Gualana, beyond the Great Fish River. At this place our party (consisting chiefly of the disbanded officers and soldiers of the Royal African Corps) had already shot many elephants, with which the country at that time abounded. The day previous to my adventure I had witnessed an elephant hunt for the first time. On this occasion a large female was killed, after some hundred shots had been fired at her. The balls seemed at first to produce little effect, but at length she received several shots in the trunk and eyes, which entirely disabled her from making resistance or escaping, and she fell an easy prey to her assailants.

"On the following day, one of our servants came to inform us that a large troop of elephants was in the neighborhood of the settlement, and that several of our people were already on their way to attack them. I instantly set off to join the hunters, but, from losing my way in the jungle through which I had to proceed, I could not overtake them until after they had driven the elephants from their first station. On getting out of the jungle, I was proceeding through an open meadow on the banks of the Gualana, to the spot where I heard the firing, when I was suddenly warned of approaching danger by loud cries of '*Passop!*—Look out!' coupled with my name in Dutch and English; and at the same moment heard the crackling of broken branches, produced by the elephants bursting through the wood, and the tremendous screams of their wrathful voices resounding among the precipitous banks. Immediately a large female, accompanied by three others of a smaller size, issued from the edge of the jungle which skirted the river margin. As they were not more than two hundred yards off, and were proceeding directly towards me, I had not much time to decide on my motions. Being alone, and in the middle of a little open plain, I saw that I must inevitably be caught, should I fire in this position and my shot not take effect. I therefore retreated hastily out of their direct path, thinking they would not observe me, until I should find a better opportunity to attack them. But in this I was mistaken, for on looking back, I perceived, to my dismay, that they had left their former course, and were rapidly pursuing and gaining ground on me. Under these circumstances, I determined to reserve my fire as a last resource; and turning off at right angles in the opposite direction, I made for the banks of the small river, with a view to take refuge among the rocks on the other side, where I should have been safe. But before I got within fifty paces of the river, the elephants were within twenty paces of me—the large female in the middle, and the other three on either side of her, apparently with the intention of making sure of me; all of them screaming so tremendously, that I was almost stunned with the noise. I immediately turned round, cocked my gun, and aimed at the head of the largest, the female. But the gun, unfortunately, from the powder being damp, hung fire till I was in the act of taking it from my shoulder, when it went off, and the ball merely grazed the side of her head. Halting only for an instant, the animal again rushed furiously forward. I fell—I cannot say whether struck down by her or not. She then caught me with her trunk by the middle, threw me beneath her fore feet, and knocked me about between them for a little space. I was scarcely in a condition to compute the number of minutes very accurately. Once she pressed her foot on my chest with such force, that I actually felt the bones, as it were, bending under the weight; and once she trod on the middle of my arm, which fortunately lay flat on the ground at the time. During this rough handling, however, I never entirely lost my recollection, else I have little doubt she would have settled my accounts with this world. But owing to the roundness of her foot, I generally managed, by twisting my body and limbs, to escape her direct tread. While I was still undergoing this buffeting, Lieutenant Chisholm, of the R. A. corps, and Diedrick, a Hottentot, had come up and fired several shots at her, one of which hit her in the shoulder; and at the same time her companions, or young ones, retiring, and screaming to her from the edge of the forest, she reluctantly left me, giving me a cuff or two with her hind feet in passing. I got up, picked up my gun, and staggered away as fast as my aching bones would allow; but observing that she turned round, and looked back toward me before entering the bush, I lay down in the long grass, by which means I escaped her observation.

"On reaching the top of the high bank of the river, I met my brother who had not been at this day's hunt, but had run out on being told by one of the men that he had seen me killed. He was not a little surprised at meeting me alone and in a whole skin, though plastered with mud from head to foot. While he, Mr. Knight, of the Cape regiment, and I, were yet talking of my adventure, an unlucky soldier of the R. A. corps, of the name of M'Clane, attracted the attention of a large male elephant, which had been driven towards the village. The ferocious animal gave chase, and caught him immediately under the hight where we were standing, carried him some distance in his trunk, then threw him down, and bringing his four feet together, trod and stamped upon him for a considerable time, till he was quite dead. Leaving the corpse for a little, he again returned, as if to make quite sure of his destruction, and kneeling down, crushed and kneaded the body with his fore-legs. Then seizing it again with his trunk, he carried it to the edge of the jungle, and threw it among the bushes. While this tragedy was going on, my brother and I scrambled down the bank as far as we could, and fired at the furious animal, but we were at too great a distance to be of any service to the unfortunate man, who was crushed almost to a jelly.

"Shortly after this catastrophe, a shot from one of the people broke this male elephant's left fore-leg, which completely disabled him from running. On this occasion we witnessed a touching instance of affection and sagacity in the elephant, which I cannot forbear to relate, as it so well illustrates the character of this noble animal. Seeing the distress and danger of her mate, the female before mentioned, (my personal antagonist,) regardless of her own danger, quitted her shelter in the bush, rushed out to his assistance, walked round and round him, chasing away the assailants, and still returning to his side and caressing him; and when he attempted to walk, she placed her flank under his wounded side and supported him. This scene continued nearly half an hour, until the female received a severe wound from Mr. C. Mackenzie of the R. A. corps, which drove her again to the bush, where she speedily sank from the loss of blood; and the male soon after received a mortal wound also from the same officer.

"Thus ended our elephant hunt; and I need hardly say that what we witnessed on this occasion of the intrepidity and ferocity of these powerful animals, rendered us more cautious in our dealings with them for the future."

DEXTERITY OF THE ELEPHANT.

Among the most interesting elephants kept in this country, without any reference to profit, was one which was lately at the Duke of Devonshire's villa, at Chiswick, the gift of a lady in India. This animal was a female, remarkable for the gentleness of its disposition; and from the kindness with which it was treated, and the free range that was allowed it, probably came nearer to an elephant in a state of nature than any other which ever appeared in this country. The house erected for her shelter was of large dimensions, and well ventilated; and she had, beside, the range of a paddock of considerable extent. At the call of her keeper she came out of her house, and immediately took up a broom, ready to perform his bidding in sweeping the grass or paths. She would follow him with a pail or watering-pot round the enclosure. Her reward was a carrot and some water; but previously to satisfying her thirst, she would exhibit her ingenuity by emptying the contents of a soda-water bottle which was tightly corked. This she did by pressing the bottle against the ground with her foot, so as to hold it securely at an angle of about forty-five degrees, and gradually twisting out the cork with her trunk, although it was very little above the edge of the neck; then, without altering the position, she turned her trunk round the bottle, so that she might reverse it, and thus empty the contents into the extremity of the proboscis. This she accomplished without spilling a drop, and she delivered the empty bottle to her keeper before she attempted to discharge the contents of the trunk into her mouth.

RESENTMENT AND REVENGE.

Every one must have read of the mishaps of the Delhi tailor. This individual was in the habit of giving some little delicacy, such as an apple, to an elephant that daily passed by his shop, and so accustomed had the animal become to this treatment, that it regularly put its trunk in at his window to receive the expected gift. One day, however, the tailor being out of humor, thrust his needle into the beast's proboscis, telling it to be gone, as he had nothing to give it. The creature passed on, apparently unmoved; but on coming to the next dirty pool of water, filled its trunk and returned to the shop-window, into which it discharged the whole contents, thoroughly drenching poor Snip and the wares by which he was surrounded. Again, a painter was desirous of drawing the elephant kept in the menagerie at Versailles in an uncommon attitude which was that of holding his trunk upraised in the air, with his mouth open. The painter's boy, in order to keep the animal in this posture, threw fruit into his mouth; but as he had frequently deceived him, and made him an offer only of throwing the fruit, he grew angry; and, as if he had known the painter's intention of drawing him was the cause of the affront that was offered him, instead of revenging himself on the lad, he turned his resentment on his master, and taking up a quantity of water in his trunk, threw it on the paper which the painter was drawing on, and spoiled it.

A sentinel belonging to the present menagerie at Paris was always very careful in requesting the spectators not to give the elephants any thing to eat. This conduct particularly displeased the female, who beheld him with a very unfavorable eye, and had several times endeavored to correct his interference by sprinkling his head with water from her trunk. One day, when several persons were collected to view these animals, a bystander offered the female a bit of bread. The sentinel perceived it; but the moment he opened his mouth to give the usual admonition, she, placing herself immediately before him, discharged in his face a violent stream of water. A general laugh ensued; but the sentinel having calmly wiped his face, stood a little to one side and continued as vigilant as before. Soon afterwards he found himself under the necessity of repeating his admonition to the spectators; but no sooner was this uttered, than the female laid hold of his musket, twirled it round with her trunk, trod it under her feet, and did not restore it till she had twisted it nearly into the form of a cork-screw.

Mr. Williamson tells an anecdote of an elephant which used to be called the Pangul, or fool, but which vindicated his claim to another character in a very singular manner. He had refused to bear a greater weight upon a march than was agreeable to him, by constantly pulling part of the load off his back; and a quarter-master of brigade, irritated at his obstinacy, threw a tent-pin at his head. In a few days after, as the animal was going from the camp to water, he overtook the quarter-master, and seizing him with his trunk, lifted him into a large tamarind tree which overhung the road, leaving him to cling to the boughs, and get down as well as he could. Lieutenant Shipp, to try this memory of injuries, gave an elephant a large quantity of Cayenne pepper between some bread. The animal was much irritated by the offense, and about six weeks after, when the unsuspecting joker went to fondle him, he endured the caresses very placidly, but finished the affair by drenching his persecutor with dirty water from head to foot.

MEMORY AND FORCE OF HABIT.

A FEMALE elephant that had escaped to the forest, and had enjoyed her liberty for more than ten years, was at length caught, along with a number of others, in a keddah. After the others had been secured, with the exception of seven or eight young ones, the hunters, who recognized this female, were ordered to call on her by name. She immediately came to the side of the ditch within the enclosure, on which some of the drivers were desired to carry in a plantain tree, the leaves of which she not only took from their hands with her trunk, but opened her mouth for them to put a leaf into it, which they did, stroking and caressing her, and calling to her by name. One of the trained elephants was now ordered to be brought to her, and the driver to take her by the ear, and order her to lie down. At first she did not like the koomkee to come near her, and retired to a distance, seeming angry ; but when the drivers, who were on foot, called to her, she came immediately, and allowed them to stroke and caress her as before ; and in a few minutes after, permitted the trained elephants to be familiar. A driver from one of these then fastened a rope round her body, and instantly jumped on her back, which at the moment she did not like, but was soon reconciled to it. A small cord was then put round her neck for the driver to put his feet in, who, seating himself on the neck in the usual manner, drove her about the enclosure in the same manner as any of the tame elephants. After this he ordered her to lie down, which she instantly did ; nor did she rise till she was desired. He fed her from his seat, gave her his stick to hold, which she took in her trunk and put into her mouth, kept, and then returned it as she was directed, and as she had formerly been accustomed to do. In short, she was so obedient, that had there been more wild elephants in the enclosure, she would have been useful in securing them.

In June, 1787, a male elephant, taken the year before, was traveling in company with some others, toward Chittigong, laden with baggage ; and having come upon a tiger's track, which elephants discover readily by the smell, he took fright and ran off to the woods in spite of all the efforts of his driver. On entering the wood, the driver saved himself by springing from the animal and clinging to the branch of a tree under which he was passing. When the elephant had got rid of his driver, he soon contrived to shake off his load. As soon as he ran away, a trained female was dispatched after him, but could not get up in time to prevent his escape.

Eighteen months after this, when a herd of elephants had been taken, and had remained several days in the enclosure, till they were enticed into the outlet, there tied, and led out in the usual manner, one of the drivers, viewing a male elephant very attentively, declared he resembled the one which had run away. This excited the curiosity of every one to go and look at him ; but when any person came near the animal struck at him with his trunk, and in every respect appeared as wild and outrageous as any of the other elephants. An old hunter at length coming up and examining him, declared that he was the very elephant that had made his escape.

Confident of this, he boldly rode up to him on a tame elephant, and ordered him to lie down, pulling him by the ear at the same time. The animal seemed taken by surprise, and instantly obeyed the word of command, uttering at the same time a peculiar shrill squeak through his trunk, as he had formerly been known to do, by which he was immediately recognized by every person who was acquainted with this peculiarity.

A female elephant belonging to a gentleman at Calcutta, being ordered from the upper country to Chotygone, by chance broke loose from her keeper, and was lost in the woods. The excuses which the keeper made were not admitted. It was supposed that he had sold the elephant; his wife and family, therefore, were sold for slaves, and he was himself condemned to work upon the roads. About twelve years afterward, this man was ordered up into the country to assist in catching the wild elephants. The keeper fancied he saw his long-lost elephant in a group that was before him. He was determined to go up to it; nor could the strongest representations of the great danger dissuade him from his purpose. When he approached the creature she knew him; and giving him three salutes by waving her trunk in the air, knelt down and received him on her back. She afterwards assisted in securing the other elephants, and likewise brought with her three young ones, which she had produced during her absence. The keeper recovered his character, and as a recompense for his sufferings and intrepidity, had an annuity settled on him for life. This elephant was afterwards in the possession of Governor Hastings.

SAGACITY OF THE ELEPHANT.

The following, given on the authority of the Rev. Robert Caunter, seems to be a purely deliberative act; and that, be it observed, by the animal when in a wild state, and perfectly unacquainted with the devices of human training:

"A small body of sepoys stationed at an outpost—Fort de Galle, in Ceylon—to protect a granary containing a large quantity of rice, was suddenly removed, in order to quiet some unruly villagers a few miles distant, who had set our authorities at defiance. Two of our party happened to be on the spot at the moment. No sooner had the sepoys withdrawn, than a herd of wild elephants, which had been long noticed in the neighborhood, made their appearance in front of the granary. They had been preceded by a scout, which returned to the herd, and having, no doubt, satisfied them, in a language which to them needed no interpreter, that the coast was clear, they advanced at a brisk pace towards the building. When they arrived within a few yards of it, quite in martial order, they made a sudden stand, and began deliberately to reconnoitre the object of their attack. Nothing could be more wary and methodical than their proceedings. The walls of the granary were of solid brickwork, very thick; and the only opening into the building was in the centre of a terraced roof, to which the ascent was by a ladder. On the approach of the elephants the two astonished spectators clambered into a lofty banyan tree, in order to escape mischief. The conduct of the four-footed besiegers was such as strongly to excite their curiosity, and they watched their proceedings with intent anxiety. The two spectators were so completely screened by the foliage of the tree to which they had resorted for safety, that they could not be perceived by the elephants, though they could see very well through the little vistas formed by the separate branches, what was going on below. Had there been a door to the granary, all difficulty of obtaining an entrance would have instantly vanished ; but four thick brick walls were obstacles which seemed at once to defy both the strength and sagacity of these dumb robbers. Nothing daunted by the magnitude of the difficulty which they had to surmount, they successively began their operations at the angles of the building. A large male elephant, with tusks of immense proportions, labored for some time to make an impression ; but after a while his strength was exhausted, and he retired. The next in size and strength then advanced, and exhausted his exertions with no better success. A third then came forward, and applying those tremendous levers with which his jaws were armed, and which he wielded with such prodigious might, he at length succeeded in dislodging a brick. An opening once made, other elephants advanced, when an entrance was soon obtained sufficiently large to admit the determined maurauders. As the whole herd could not be accommodated at once, they divided into small bodies of three or four. One of them entered, and when they had taken their fill, they retired, and their places were immediately supplied by the next in waiting, until the whole herd, upwards of twenty, had made a full meal. By this time a shrill sound was heard from one of the elephants, which was readily understood, when those that were still in the building immediately rushed out and joined their companions. One of the first division, after retiring from the granary, had acted as sentinel, while the rest were enjoying the fruits of their sagacity and perseverance. He had so stationed himself as to be enabled to observe the advance of an enemy from any quarter, and upon perceiving the troops as they returned from the village, he sounded the signal of retreat, when the whole herd, flourishing their trunks, moved rapidly into the jungle. The soldiers, on their return, found that the animals had devoured the greater part of their rice. A ball from a field-piece was discharged at them in their retreat; but they only wagged their tails as if in mockery, and soon disappeared in the recesses of their native forests."

THE PANTHERS' DEN.

THE occupants of a few log cabins in the vicinity of the Bayou Manlatte, a tributary of the noble Bay of Pensacola, situated in the western part of the then territory of Florida, had been for some weeks annoyed by the mysterious disappearance of the cattle and goats, which constituted almost the only wealth of these rude countrymen; and the belated herdsman was frequently startled by the terrible half-human cry of the dreaded panther, and the next morning, some one of the squatters would find himself minus of a number of cloven feet. About this time I happened into the settlement on a hunting excursion, in company with another son of Nimrod, and learning the state of affairs, resolved, if possible, to rid the "clearing" of its pest, and bind new laurels on our brows. The night before our arrival, a heifer had been killed within a few rods of the cabin, and the carcass dragged off toward the swamp, some two miles distant, leaving a broad trail to mark the destroyer's path; this being pointed out to us, Ned and myself resolved to execute our enterprise without delay—this was to "beard the lion in his den." Having carefully charged our rifles and pistols, and seen that our bowies were as keen as razors, we set out on the trail, which soon brought us to the edge of the Bayou Manlatte swamp—which covers a surface of some thousands of acres, being a dense, muddy hammock of teti, bay, magnolia, cane, grape-vines, etc. A perpetual twilight reigned beneath the dense foliage supported by the rank soil, and our hearts beat a few more pulsations to the minute, as we left the scorching glare of the noonday sun, and plunged into the gloomy fastnesses of the bear and alligator; to these latter gentlemen, whose clumsy forms were sprawling through the mud on every side, we gave no further heed other than to keep without the range of the deadly sweep of their powerful tails, with which they bring their unsuspecting prey within reach of their saw-like jaws; the bears we did not happen to meet, or we should most assuredly have given them some of the balls designed for the panthers.

Well, we followed the trail half a mile into the swamp, when on an elevated spot, we suddenly encountered the half-devoured body of the unfortunate heifer, apparently just deserted by the captors. We cautiously advanced a few paces further over a pavement of bones, "clean scraped and meatless," and entered an open space, when a sight met my eyes which certainly made me wish myself safe at home, or in fact, anywhere else but where I was. About twenty-five feet from us we saw, instead of one, an old she-panther and two cubs nearly grown, while directly over them, on the blasted and sloping trunk of an immense gum-tree, crouched the "old he one of all," lashing his sides fiercely with his tail, and snorting and spitting like an enraged cat, an example which was imitated by the three below. Here was a dilemma, on the particularly sharp horns of which we found ourselves most uncomfortably situated. To retreat would induce an immediate attack, the consequence of an advance would be ditto; so we stood *en tableaux*, for a brief second, our guns cocked and aimed, Ned drawing a bead on the dam, while I did the same on the sire. It seemed madness to fire. We were not long uncertain as to our course, for the old fellow suddenly bounded from the trunk upon me, with a deafening roar. I fired as he sprang, and the report of my piece was re-echoed by that of Ned's. I sprang aside, dropping my rifle and drawing my long and heavy knife; it was well I did so, for the mortally-wounded beast alighted on the very spot I had left. He turned and sprang upon me. I avoided the blow of its powerful paw, and grappling with him I rolled on the turf, winding my right arm tight around his neck, and hugging close to his body to avoid his teeth and claws, while I dealt rapid thrusts with my knife. I was very powerful; but never was in a situation where I felt more sensibly the need of exerting all my muscle. The contest was soon decided—my knife passing through the brute's heart—

"And panting from the dreadful close,
And breathless all, the champion rose."

And it was full time that I should do so, for Ned, having put a ball through the head of the dam, was now manfully battling with her two cubs; the poor fellow was sore pressed, streaming with blood from numberless scratches, and almost in a state of nature, for the sharp claws of the cubs had literally undressed him by piecemeal. His savage assailants, also, bore upon their bloody hides numerous tokens of his prowess in wielding his bowie.

Their system of attack seemed to be to spring suddenly upon him, striking with their paws, and as they did so, in most cases simultaneously, it was impossible for him to defend himself, strong and active as he was; and had no assistance been at hand, they would undoubtedly have gained the victory. It was a brave sight, though, to see the tall, strong hunter, meeting their attacks undauntedly, standing with his left arm raised to defend his head and throat, and darting his knife into their tough bodies as he threw them from him, but to meet the next moment their renewed efforts for his destruction.

All this I caught at one glance, as I rushed to his rescue. "Ned!" shouted I, mad and reckless with excitement, "take the one on your left!" And we threw ourselves upon them. I met my antagonist in his onward leap, and making a desperate blow at him, my wrist struck his paw, and the knife flew far from my hand. There was nothing else for me but to seize him by the loose skin of the neck with both hands, and hold on like "grim death," keeping him at arm's length, while his paws beat a tattoo to a double quick time on my breast and body, stripping my garments into ribbons in a most workmanlike manner, and ornamenting my sensitive skin with a variety of lines and characters, done in red—a process which I did not care to prolong, however, beyond a period when I could soonest put a stop to the operation.

As I was debating how to attain so desirable an end, the remembrance of the small rifle pistol, in my belt, and which, till now, in the hurry of the conflict I had forgotten, suddenly flashed upon my mind, and, disengaging one hand, I drew it forth, cocked it with my thumb, and the next moment the panther's brains were spattered in my face.

I turned to look for Ned, and found him trying to free himself from the dead body of the panther, whose teeth were fastened, in their death-grip, to the small remnant of his hunting coat which hung around his neck; I separated the strip of cloth with my recovered knife, and we sank panting to the ground, while our hearts went up in thankfulness for deliverance from so imminent danger to life and limb. After resting awhile, we washed the blood—our blood—from our bodies, and decorating them with "what was left," somewhat after the fashion of the Indian who wears only a "breech clout," we took the scalps of the four panthers, and started on our homeward march. Our success was speedily known in the clearing, and in the evening a barbacue was had in our honor, to furnish which a relation of the unfortunate heifer met with a fate scarcely less terrible. This exploit added not a little to our reputation among the hunter folk.

ANECDOTES OF THE DOG.

THE LOST CHILD AND THE DOG.

One of the most striking instances which we have heard of the sagacity and personal attachment in the shepherd's dog, occurred about half a century ago among the Grampian mountains. In one of his excursions to his distant flocks in these high pasturages, a shepherd happened to carry along with him one of his children, an infant about three years old. After traversing his pasture for some time, attended by his dog, the shepherd found himself under the necessity of ascending a summit at some distance, to have a more extensive view of his range. As the ascent was too fatiguing for the child, he left him on a small plain at the bottom, with strict injunctions not to stir from it till his return. Scarcely, however, had he gained the summit, when the horizon was suddenly darkened by one of those impenetrable mists which frequently descend so rapidly amidst these mountains, as, in the space of a few minutes, almost to turn day into night. The anxious father instantly hastened back to find his child; but owing to the unusual darkness, and his own trepidation, he unfortunately missed his way in the descent. After a fruitless search of many hours among the dangerous morasses and cataracts with which these mountains abound, he was at length overtaken by night. Still wandering on without knowing whither, he at length came to the verge of the mist, and by the light of the moon, discovered that he had reached the bottom of his valley, and was within a short distance of his cottage. To renew the search that night was equally fruitless and dangerous. He was therefore obliged to return to his cottage, having lost both his child and his dog, which had attended him faithfully for years.

Next morning by daybreak, the shepherd, accompanied by a band of his neighbors, set out in search of his child; but, after a day spent in fruitless fatigue, he was at length compelled by the approach of night, to descend from the mountain. On returning to his cottage, he found that the dog, which he had lost the day before, had been home, and, on receiving a piece of cake, had instantly gone off again. For several successive days the shepherd renewed the search for his child; and still, on returning at evening disappointed to his cottage, he found that the dog had been home, and, on receiving his usual allowance of cake, had instantly disappeared. Struck with this singular circumstance, he remained at home one day, and when the dog as usual departed with his piece of cake, he resolved to follow him, and find out the cause of his strange procedure. The dog led the way to a cataract, at some distance from the spot where the shepherd had left his child. The banks of the cataract, almost joined at the top, yet separated by an abyss of immense depth, presented that appearance which so often astonishes and appalls the travelers who frequent the Grampian mountains, and indicates that these stupendous chasms were not the silent work of time, but the sudden effect of some violent convulsion of the earth. Down one of these rugged and almost perpendicular descents the dog began without hesitation to make his way, and at last disappeared into a cave, the mouth of which was almost upon a level with the torrent. The shepherd with difficulty followed; but on entering the cave, what were his emotions when he beheld his infant eating with much satisfaction the cake which the dog had just brought him, while the faithful animal stood by, eyeing his young charge with the utmost complacence!

From the situation in which the child was found, it appears that he had wandered to the brink of the precipice, and then either fallen or scrambled down till he reached the cave, which the dread of the torrent had afterward prevented him from quitting. The dog, by means of his scent, had traced him to the spot, and afterward prevented him from starving, by giving up to him his own daily allowance. He appears never to have quitted the child by night or day, except when it was necessary to go for his food, and then he was always seen running at full speed to and from the cottage.

WONDERFUL SAGACITY OF A SHEPHERD'S DOG.

James Hogg, who possessed the best opportunities of studying the character of the shepherd's dog, mentions that he at one time had a dog, called Sirrah, an animal of a sullen disposition, and by no means favorable appearance, which was an extraordinary adept in managing a flock. One of his exploits was as follows: "About seven hundred lambs, which were once under his care at weaning-time, broke up at midnight, and scampered off in three divisions across the hills, in spite of all that the shepherd and an assistant lad could do to keep them together. 'Sirrah,' cried the shepherd in great affliction, 'my man, they're a' awa!' The night was so dark, that he did not see Sirrah; but the faithful animal had heard his master's words—words such as of all others were sure to set him most on the alert; and without more ado, he silently set off in quest of the recreant flock. Meanwhile the shepherd and his companion did not fail to do all that was in their own power to recover their lost charge; they spent the whole night in scouring the hills for miles around; but of neither the lambs nor Sirrah could they obtain the slightest trace. 'It was the most extraordinary circumstance,' says the shepherd, 'that had ever occurred in the annals of the pastoral life. We had nothing for it (day having dawned,) but to return to our master, and inform him that we had lost his whole flock of lambs, and knew not what was become of one of them. On our way home, however, we discovered a body of lambs at the bottom of a deep ravine, called the Flesh Cleuch, and the indefatigable Sirrah standing in front of them, looking all around for some relief, but still standing true to his charge. The sun was then up; and when we first came in view of them, we concluded that it was one of the divisions of the lambs which Sirrah had been unable to manage, until he came to that commanding situation. But what was our astonishment when we discovered by degrees that not one lamb of the whole flock was wanting! How he had got all the divisions collected in the dark, is beyond my comprehension. The charge was left entirely to himself from midnight until the rising of the sun; and if all the shepherds in the forest had been there to have assisted him, they could not have effected it with greater propriety. All that I can further say is, that I never felt so grateful to any creature below the sun, as I did to my honest Sirrah that morning.'"

EXTRAORDINARY CASE OF SHEEP-STEALING BY A DOG.

A YOUNG farmer in the neighborhood of Innerleithen, whose circumstances were supposed to be good, and who was connected with many of the best store-farming families in the county, had been tempted to commit some extensive depredations upon the flocks of his neighbors, in which he was assisted by his shepherd. The pastoral farms of Tweeddale, which generally consist each of a certain range of hilly ground, had in those days no enclosures: their boundaries were indicated only by the natural features of the country. The sheep were accordingly liable to wander, and to become intermixed with each other; and at every reckoning of a flock, a certain allowance had to be made for this, as for other contingencies. For some time Mr. William Gibson, tenant in Newby, an extensive farm stretching from the neighborhood of Peebles to the borders of

Selkirkshire, had remarked a surprising increase in the amount of his annual losses. He questioned his shepherds severely, taxed them with carelessness in picking up and bringing home the dead, and plainly intimated that he conceived some unfair dealing to be in progress. The men, finding themselves thus exposed to suspicions of a very painful kind, were as much chagrined as the worthy farmer himself, and kept their minds alive to every circumstance which might tend to afford any elucidation of the mystery. One day, while they were summering their lambs, the eye of a very acute old shepherd, named Hyslop, was caught by a black-faced ewe which they had formerly missed (for the shepherds generally know every particular member of their flocks,) and which was now suckling its own lamb as if it had never been absent. On inspecting it carefully, it was found to bear an additional *birn* upon its face. Every farmer, it must be mentioned, impresses with a hot iron a particular letter upon the faces of his sheep, as a means of distinguishing his own from those of his neighbors. Mr. Gibson's *birn* was the letter T, and this was found distinctly enough impressed on the face of the ewe. But above this mark there was an O, which was known to be the mark of the tenant of Wormiston, the individual already mentioned. It was immediately suspected that this and the other missing sheep had been abstracted by that person; a suspicion which derived strength from the reports of the neighboring shepherds, by whom, it appeared, the black-faced ewe had been tracked for a considerable way, in a direction leading from Wormiston to Newby. It was indeed ascertained that instinctive affection for her lamb had led this animal across the Tweed, and over the lofty hights between Cailzie and Newby; a route of very considerable difficulty, and probably quite different from that by which she had been led away, but the *most direct* that could have been taken. Mr. Gibson only stopped to obtain the concurrence of a neigboring farmer, whose losses had been equally great, before proceeding with some of the legal authorities to Wormiston, where Millar, the shepherd, and his master, were taken into custody, and conducted to the prison of Peebles. On a search of the farm, no fewer than thirty-three score of sheep belonging to various individuals were found, all bearing the condemnatory O above the original *birns;* and it was remarked that there was not a single ewe returned to Grieston, the farm on the opposite bank of the Tweed, which did not *minny* her lambs—that is, assume the character of mother toward the offspring from which she had been separated.

The magnitude of this crime, the rareness of such offences in the district, and the station in life of at least one of the offenders, produced a great sensation in Tweeddale, and caused the elicitation of every minute circumstance that could possibly be discovered respecting the means which had been employed for carrying on such an extensive system of depredation. The most surprising part of the tale is the extent to which it appears that the instinct of dumb animals had been instrumental both in the crime and in its detection. While the farmer seemed to have deputed the business chiefly to his shepherd, the shepherd seemed to have deputed it again, in many instances, to a dog of extraordinary sagacity, which served him in his customary and lawful business. This animal, which bore the name of *Yarrow,* would not only act under his immediate direction in cutting off a portion of a flock, and bringing it home to Wormiston, but is said to have been able to proceed solitarily, and by night, to a sheep-walk, and there detach certain individuals previously pointed out by its master, which it would drive home by secret ways, without allowing one to straggle. It is mentioned that, while returning home with their stolen droves, they avoided, even in the night, the roads along the banks of the river, or those that descend to the valley through the adjoining glens. They chose rather to come along the ridge of mountains that separate the small river Leithen from the Tweed. But even here there was sometimes danger; for the shepherds occasionally visit their flocks even before day; and often when Millar had driven his prey from a distance, and while he was yet miles from home, and the weather-gleam of the eastern hills began to be tinged with the brightening dawn, he has left them to the charge of his dog, and descended himself to the banks of the Leithen, off his way, that he might not be seen connected with their company. Yarrow, although between three and four miles from his master, would continue with care and silence, to bring the sheep onward to Wormiston, where his master's appearance could be neither a matter of question nor surprise.

Near to the thatched farmhouse was one of those old square towers, or peel-houses, whose picturesque ruins were then seen ornamenting the course of the Tweed, as they had been placed alternately along the north and south bank, generally from three to six hundred yards from it—sometimes on the shin, and sometimes in the hollow of a hill. In the vault of this tower, it was the practice of these men to conceal the sheep they had recently stolen; and while the rest of their people were absent on Sunday at the church, they used to employ themselves in canceling with their knives the ear-marks, and impressing with a hot iron a large O upon the face, that covered both sides of the animal's nose, for the purpose of obliterating the brand of the true owner. While his accomplices were so busied, Yarrow kept watch in the open air, and gave notice, without fail, by his barking, of the approach of strangers.

The farmer and his servant were tried at Edinburgh, in January, 1773, and the proceedings excited an extraordinary interest, not only in the audience, but among the legal officials. Hyslop, the principal witness, gave so many curious particulars respecting the instincts of sheep, and the modes of distinguishing them both by natural and artificial marks, that he was highly complimented by the bench. The evidence was so complete, that both culprits were found guilty, and, according to the barbarous policy of those times, they expiated their crimes on the scaffold.

The general tradition is, that Yarrow was also put to death, though in a less ceremonious manner; but this has probably no other foundation than a *jeu d'esprit*, which was cried through the streets of Edinburgh as his dying speech. We have been informed that the dog was in reality purchased, after the execution of Millar, by a sheep-farmer in the neighborhood, but did not take kindly to honest courses, and his new master having no work of a different kind in which to engage him, he was remarked to show rather less sagacity than the ordinary shepherd's dog.

FRENCH MERCHANT AND HIS DOG.

A French merchant having some money due from a correspondent, set out on horseback, accompanied by his dog, on purpose to receive it. Having settled the business to his satisfaction, he tied the bag of money before him, and began to return home. His faithful dog, as if he entered into his master's feelings, frisked round the horse, barked and jumped, and seemed to participate in his joy.

The merchant, after riding some miles, alighted to repose himself under an agreeable shade, and taking the bag of money in his hand, laid it down by his side under a hedge, and on remounting, forgot it. The dog perceived his lapse of recollection, and wishing to rectify it, ran to fetch the bag, but it was too heavy for him to drag along. He then ran to his master, and by crying, barking, and howling, seemed to remind him of his mistake. The merchant understood not his language; but the assiduous creature persevered in its efforts, and after trying to stop the horse in vain, at last began to bite his heels.

The merchant, absorbed in some reverie, wholly overlooked the real object of his affectionate attendant's importunity, but entertained the alarming apprehension that he was gone mad. Full of this suspicion, in crossing a brook, he turned back to look if the dog would drink. The animal was too intent on his master's business to think of itself; it continued to bark and bite with greater violence than before.

"Mercy!" cried the afflicted merchant: "it must be so; my poor dog is certainly mad: what must I do? I must kill him, lest some greater misfortune befall me; but with what regret! Oh, could I find any one to perform this cruel office for me! But there is no time to lose; I myself may become the victim if I spare him."

With these words he drew a pistol from his pocket, and with a trembling hand took aim at his faithful servant. He turned away in agony as he fired; but his aim was too sure. The poor animal fell wounded, and, weltering in his blood, still endeavored to crawl toward his master, as if to tax him with ingratitude. The merchant could not bear the sight; he spurred on his horse with a heart full of sorrow, and lamented he had taken a journey which had cost him so dear. Still, however, the money never entered his mind; he only thought of his poor dog, and tried to console himself with the reflection that he had prevented a greater evil by despatching a mad animal, than he had suffered a calamity by his loss. This opiate to his wounded spirit, however, was ineffectual: "I am most unfortunate," said he to himself: "I had almost rather have lost my money than my dog." Saying this, he stretched out his hand to grasp his treasure. It was missing; no bag was to be found. In an instant he opened his eyes to his rashness and folly. "Wretch that I am! I alone am to blame! I could not comprehend the admonition which my innocent and most faithful friend gave me, and I have sacrificed him for his zeal. He only wished to inform me of my mistake, and he has paid for his fidelity with his life."

Instantly he turned his horse, and went off at full gallop to the place where he had stopped. He saw with half-averted eyes the scene where the tragedy was acted; he perceived the traces of blood as he proceeded; he was oppressed and distracted; but in vain did he look for his dog; he was not to be seen on the road. At last he arrived at the spot where he had alighted. But what were his sensations! His heart was ready to bleed; he execrated himself in the madness of despair. The poor dog, unable to follow his dear but cruel master, had determined to consecrate his last moments to his service. He had crawled, all bloody as he was, to the forgotten bag, and, in the agonies of death, he lay watching beside it. When he saw his master, he still testified his joy by the wagging of his tail. He could do no more; he tried to rise, but his strength was gone. The vital tide was ebbing fast; even the caresses of his master could not prolong his fate for a few moments. He stretched out his tongue to lick the hand that was now fondling him in the agonies of regret, as if to seal forgiveness of the deed that had deprived him of life. He then cast a look of kindness on his master, and closed his eyes in death.

THE DOG AND THE SHILLING.

A GENTLEMAN of Suffolk, England, on an excursion with his friend, was attended by a Newfoundland dog, which soon became the subject of conversation. The master, after a warm eulogium upon the perfections of his canine favorite, assured his companion that he would, upon receiving the order, return and fetch any article he should leave behind, from any distance. To confirm this assertion, a marked shilling was put under a large square stone by the side of the road—being first shown to the dog. The gentlemen then rode for three miles, when the dog received his signal from the master to return for the shilling he had seen put under the stone. The dog turned back; the gentlemen rode on, and reached home;

but, to their surprise and disappointment, the hitherto faithful messenger did not return during the day. It afterward appeared that he had gone to the place where the shilling was deposited, but the stone being too large for his strength to remove, he had stayed howling at the place, till two horsemen riding by, and attracted by his seeming distress, stopped to look at him, when one of them alighting, removed the stone, and seeing the shilling, put it into his pocket, not at the time conceiving it to be the object of the dog's search. The dog followed their horses for twenty miles, remained undisturbed in the room where they supped, followed the chambermaid into the bedchamber, and secreted himself under one of the beds. The possessor of the shilling hung his trousers upon a nail by the bedside; but when the travelers were both asleep, the dog took them in his mouth, and leaping out of the window, which was left open on account of the sultry heat, reached the house of his master at four o'clock in the morning with the prize he had made free with, in the pocket of which were found a watch and money, that were returned upon being advertised, when the whole mystery was mutually unraveled, to the admiration of all the parties.

REMARKABLE PRESERVATION FROM MURDER BY A DOG.

Sir H. Lee, of Ditchley, Oxfordshire, ancestor of the late earls of Lichfield, had a mastiff which guarded the house and yard, but had never met with any particular attention from his master. In short, he was not a favorite dog, and was retained for his utility only, and not from any partial regard.

One night, as Sir Harry was retiring to his chamber, attended by his favorite valet, an Italian, the mastiff silently followed them up stairs, which he had never been known to do before, and to his master's astonishment, presented himself in the bedroom. Being deemed an intruder, he was instantly ordered to be turned out; which, being complied with, the poor animal began scratching violently at the door, and howling loudly for admission. The servant was sent to drive him away. Discouragement, however, could not check his intended labor of love; he returned again, and was more importunate to be let in than before. Sir Harry, weary of opposition, though surprised beyond measure at the dog's apparent fondness for the society of a master who had never shown him the least kindness, and wishing to retire to rest, bade the servant open the door that they might see what he wanted to do. This done, the mastiff, with a wag of the tail and a look of affection at his lord, deliberately walked up, and crawling under the bed, laid himself down, as if desirous to take up his night's lodging there.

To save further trouble, and not from any partiality for his company, this indulgence was allowed. The valet withdrew, and all was still. About the solemn hour of midnight the chamber door opened, and a person was heard stepping across the room. Sir

Harry started from sleep; the dog sprung from his covert, and seizing the unwelcome disturber, fixed him to the spot. All was dark: Sir Harry rang his bell in great trepidation, in order to procure a light. The person who was pinned to the floor roared for assistance. It was found to be the favorite valet, who little expected such a reception. He endeavored to apologise for his intrusion, and to make the reasons which induced him to take this step appear plausible; but the importunity of the dog, the time, the place, the manner of the valet, raised suspicions in Sir Harry's mind, and he determined to refer the investigation of the business to a magistrate. The terrified Italian, alternately terrified by the dread of punishment, and soothed by the hope of pardon, at length confessed that it was his intention to murder his master, and then rob the house. This diabolical design was frustrated solely by the unaccountable sagacity of the dog, and his devoted attachment to his master. A full-length picture of Sir Harry, with the mastiff by his side, and the words, "More faithful than favored," is still preserved among the family pictures.

HUNTING THE MOOSE.

THE habits of the moose, in his manner of defense and attack, are similar to those of the stag, and may be illustrated by the following anecdote from the "Random Sketches of a Kentuckian:"

"Who ever saw Bravo without loving him? His sloe-black eyes, his glossy skin, flecked here and there with blue; his wide-spread thighs, clean shoulders, broad back, and low-drooping chest, bespoke him the true stag-hound; and none, who ever saw his bounding form, or heard his deep-toned bay, as the swift-footed stag flew before him, would dispute his title. List, gentle reader, and I will tell you an adventure which will make you love him all the more.

"A bright, frosty morning in November, 1838, tempted me to visit the forest hunting-grounds. On this occasion, I was followed by a fine-looking hound, which had been presented to me a few days before by a fellow-sportsman. I was anxious to test his qualities, and, knowing that a mean dog will not often hunt well with a good one, I had tied up the eager Bravo, and was attended by the strange dog alone. A brisk canter of half an hour brought me to the wild forest hills. Slackening the rein, I slowly wound my way up a brushy slope some three hundred yards in length. I had ascended about half way, when the hound began to exhibit signs of uneasiness, and, at the same instant a stag sprang out from some underbrush near by, and rushed like a whirlwind up the slope. A word, and the hound was crouching at my feet, and my trained Cherokee, with ear erect, and flashing eye, watched the course of the affrighted animal.

"On the very summit of the ridge, full one hundred and fifty yards, every limb standing out in bold relief against the clear blue sky, the stag paused, and looked proudly down upon us. After a moment of indecision, I raised my rifle and sent the whizzing lead upon its errand. A single bound, and the antlered monarch was hidden from my view. Hastily running down a ball, I ascended the slope; my blood ran a little faster as I saw the 'gouts of blood' which stained the withered leaves where he had stood. One moment more, and the excited hound was leaping breast-high on his trail, and the gallant Cherokee bore his rider like lightning after them.

"Away—away! for hours we did thus hasten on, without once being at fault, or checking our headlong speed. The chase had led us far from the starting-point, and now appeared to be bearing up a creek, on one side of which rose a precipitous hill some two miles in length, which I knew the wounded animal would never ascend.

"Half a mile further on, another hill reared its bleak and barren head on the opposite side of the rivulet. Once fairly in the gorge, there was no exit save at the upper end of the ravine. Here, then, I must intercept my game, which I was able to do by taking a nearer cut over the ridge, that saved at least a mile.

"Giving one parting shout to cheer my dog, Cherokee bore me headlong to the pass. I had scarcely arrived, when black with sweat, the stag came laboring up the gorge, seemingly totally reckless of our presence. Again I poured forth the 'leaden messenger of death,' as meteor-like he flashed by us. One bound, and the noble animal lay prostrate within fifty feet of where I stood. Leaping from my horse, and placing one knee upon his shoulder, and a hand upon his antlers, I drew my hunting-knife; but scarcely had its keen point touched his neck, when, with a sudden bound, he threw me from his body, and my knife was hurled from my hand. In hunters' parlance, I had only 'creased him.' I at once saw my danger, but it was too late. With one bound he was upon me, wounding and almost disabling me with his sharp feet and horns. I seized him by his widespread antlers, and sought to regain possession of my knife, but in vain. Cherokee, frightened at the unusual scene, had madly fled to the top of the ridge, where he stood, looking down upon the combat, trembling and quivering in every limb.

"The ridge road I had taken placed us far in advance of the hound, whose bay I could not now hear. The struggles of the furious animal had now become dreadful, and every moment I could feel his sharp hoofs cutting deep into my flesh; my grasp upon his antlers became less and less firm, and yet I relinquished not my hold. The struggle had brought us near a deep ditch, washed by the fall rains, and into this I endeavored to force my adversary, but my strength was unequal to the effort; when we approached to the very brink, he leaped over the drain. I relinquished my hold and rolled in, hoping thus to escape him; but he returned to the attack, and throwing himself upon me, inflicted numerous severe cuts upon my face and breast before I could again seize him. Locking my arms around his antlers, I drew his head close to my breast, and was thus, by great effort, enabled to prevent his doing me any serious injury. But I felt that this could not last long; every muscle and fibre of my frame was called into action, and human nature could not long bear up under such exertion. Faltering a silent prayer to Heaven, I prepared to meet my fate.

"At this moment of despair, I heard the faint bayings of the hound; the stag, too, heard the sound, and springing from the ditch, drew me with him. His efforts were now redoubled, and I could scarcely cling to him. Yet that blessed sound came nearer and nearer! Oh, how wildly beat my heart, as I saw the hound emerge from the ravine, and spring forward with a short, quick bark, as his eye rested on his game. I released my hold of the stag, who turned upon the new enemy. Exhausted, and unable to rise, I still cheered the dog, that, dastard-like, fled before the infuriated animal, who, seemingly despising such an enemy, again threw himself upon me. Again did I succeed in throwing my arms around his antlers, but not until he had inflicted several deep and dangerous wounds upon my head and face, cutting to the very bone.

"Blinded by the flowing blood, exhausted and despairing, I urged the coward dog, who stood baying furiously, yet refusing to seize his game. Oh! how I prayed for Bravo! The thoughts of death were bitter. To die thus in the wild forest, alone, with none to help! Thoughts of home and friends, coursed like lightning through my brain. At that moment, when hope herself had fled, deep and clear over the neighboring hill, came the baying of my gallant Bravo! I should have known his voice among a thousand. I pealed forth in one faint shout, 'On, Bravo, on!' The next moment, with tiger-like bounds, the noble dog came leaping down the declivity, scattering the dried autumnal leaves like a whirlwind in his path. 'No pause he knew,' but, fixing his fangs into the stag's throat, he at once commenced the struggle.

"I fell back completely exhausted. Blinded with blood, I only knew that a terrible struggle was going on. In a few moments, all was still, and I felt the warm breath of my faithful dog, as he licked my wounds. Clearing my eyes from gore, I saw my late adversary dead at my feet, and Bravo, 'my own Bravo,' as the heroine of a modern novel would say, standing over me. He yet bore around his neck a fragment of the rope with which I had tied him. He had gnawed it in two, and following his master through all his windings, arrived in time to rescue him from a horrible death.

"I have recovered from my wounds. Bravo is lying at my feet. Who does not love Bravo? I am sure I do, and the rascal knows it—don't you Bravo? Come here, sir!"

A SKATER CHASED BY A WOLF.

A THRILLING incident in American country life is vividly sketched in "Evenings at Donaldson Manor." In the winter of 1844, the relater went out one evening to skate, on the Kennebec, in Maine, by moonlight, and having ascended that river nearly two miles, turned into a little stream to explore its course.

"Fir and hemlock of a century's growth," he says, "met overhead and formed an archway, radiant with frostwork. All was dark within; but I was young and fearless; and as I peered into an unbroken forest that reared itself on the borders of the stream, I laughed with very joyousness; my wild hurrah rang through the silent woods, and I stood listening to the echo that reverberated again and again, until all was hushed. Suddenly a sound arose—it seemed to me to come from beneath the ice; it sounded low and tremulous at first, until it ended in a low, wild yell. I was appalled. Never before had such a noise met my ears. I thought it more than mortal; so fierce, and amid such an unbroken solitude, it seemed as though from the tread of some brute animal, and the blood rushed back to my forehead with a bound that made my skin burn, and I felt relieved that I had to contend with things earthly and not spiritual; my energies returned, and I looked around me for some means of escape. As I turned my head to the shore, I could see two dark objects dashing through the underbrush, at a pace nearly double in speed to my own. By this rapidity, and the short yells they occasionally gave, I knew at once that these were the much-dreaded gray wolves.

I had never met with these animals, but from the description given of them, I had very little pleasure in making their acquaintance. Their untamable fierceness, and the enduring strength, which seems part of their nature, render them objects of dread to every benighted traveler.

There was no time for thought; so I bent my head and dashed madly forward. Nature turned me toward home. The light flakes of snow spun from the iron skates, and I was some distance from my pursuers, when their fierce howl told me I was their fugitive. I did not look back; I did not feel afraid, or sorry, or even glad; one thought of home, the bright faces waiting my return—of their tears if they should never see me again, and then every energy of body and mind were exerted for escape. I was perfectly at home on the ice. Many were the days that I had spent on my good skates, never thinking that at one time they would be my only means of safety. Every half minute, an alternate yelp from my ferocious followers, told me too certain that they were in close pursuit. Nearer and nearer they came; I heard their feet pattering on the ice nearer still, until I could feel their breath, and hear their sniffling scent.

Every nerve and muscle in my frame was stretched to the utmost tension. The trees along the shore seemed to dance in the uncertain light, and my brain turned with my own breathless speed, yet still they seemed to hiss forth their breath with a sound truly horrible, when an involuntary motion on my part, turned me out of my course. The wolves, close behind, unable to stop, and as unable to turn on the smooth ice, slipped and fell, still going on far ahead; their tongues were lolling out, their white tusks glaring from their bloody mouths, their dark, shaggy breasts were fleeced with foam, and, as they passed me, their eyes glared, and they howled with fury.

The thought flashed on my mind, that, by these means, I could avoid them, viz: by turning aside whenever they came too near; for they, by the formation of their feet, are unable to run on the ice except in a straight line.

At one time, by delaying my turning too long, my sanguinary antagonists came so near, that they threw the white foam over my dress as they sprang to seize me, and their teeth clashed together like the spring of a fox-trap!

Had my skates failed for one instant, had I tripped on a stick, or caught my foot in a fissure in the ice, the story I am now telling would never have been told.

I thought over all the chances; I knew where they would take hold of me if I fell; I thought how long it would be before I died; and then there would be a search for the body that would already have its tomb! for, oh! how fast man's mind traces out all the dread colors of death's picture, only those who have been so near the grim original can tell.

But I soon came opposite the house, and my hounds—I knew their deep voices—roused by the noise, bayed furiously from their kennels. I heard their chains rattle; how I wished they would break them! and then I would have protectors that would be peer to the fiercest denizens of the forest. The wolves, taking the hint conveyed by the dogs, stopped in their mad career, and after a moment's consideration, turned and fled. I watched them until their dusky forms disappeared over a neighboring hill; then taking off my skates, I wended my way to the house, with feelings much better imagined than described. But even yet, I never see a broad sheet of ice in the moonshine, without thinking of the sniffling breath, and those fearful things that followed me closely down the frozen Kennebec.

A SEA-FOWLING ADVENTURE.

One pleasant afternoon in summer, Frank Costello jumped into his little boat and pulling her out of the narrow creek where she lay moored, crept along the iron-bound shore until he reached the entrance of one of those deep sea-caves so common upon the western coast of Ireland. To the gloomy recesses of these natural caverns, millions of sea-fowl resort during the breeding season; and it was among these feathered tribes then congregated in the "Puffin Cave," that Frank meant, on that evening, to deal death and destruction. Gliding with lightly-dipping oars, into the yawning chasm, he stepped nimbly from his boat, and making the painter fast to a projecting rock, he lighted a torch, and, armed only with a stout cudgel, penetrated into the innermost recesses of the cavern. There he found a vast quantity of birds and eggs, and soon became so engrossed with his sport that he paid no attention to the lapse of time, until the hollow sound of rushing waters behind him, made him aware that the tide, which was ebbing when he entered the cave, had turned, and was now rising rapidly. His first impulse was to return to the spot where he had made his boat fast; but how was he horrified on perceiving that the rock to which it had been secured was now completely covered with water. He might, however, still have reached it by swimming; but, unfortunately, the painter, by which it was attached to the rock, not having sufficient scope, the boat, on the rising of the tide, was drawn, stern down, to a level with the water; and Frank, as he beheld her slowly fill and disappear beneath the waves, felt as if the last link between the living world and himself had been broken. To go forward was impossible; and he well knew that there was no way of retreating from the cave, which, in a few hours, would be filled by the advancing tide. His heart died within him, as the thought of the horrid fate which awaited him, flashed across his mind. He was not a man who feared to face death; by flood or field, on the stormy sea and the dizzy cliff, he had dared it a thousand times with perfect unconcern; but to meet the grim tyrant there, alone, to struggle hopelessly with him for life in that dreary tomb, was more than his fortitude could bear. He shrieked aloud in the agony of despair—the torch fell from his trembling hand into the dark waters that gurgled at his feet, and, flashing for a moment upon their inky surface, expired with a hissing sound that fell like a death-warning upon his ear. The wind, which had been scarcely felt during the day, began to rise with the flowing of the tide, and now drove the tumultuous waves with hoarse and hideous clamor into the cavern. Every moment increased the violence of the gale that howled and bellowed as it swept around the echoing roof of that rock-ribbed prison; while the hoarse dash of the approaching waves, and the shrill screams of the sea-birds that filled the cavern, formed a concert of terrible dissonance, well suited for the requiem of the hapless wretch who had been enclosed in that living grave! But the love of life, which makes us cling to it in the most hopeless extremity, was strong in Frank Costello's breast; his firmness and presence of mind gradually returned, and he resolved not to perish without a struggle. He remembered that at the farther extremity of the cavern, the rock rose like a flight of rude stairs, sloping from the floor to the roof; he had often clambered up those rugged steps, and he knew that, by means of them, he could place himself at an elevation above the reach of the highest tide.

But the hope thus suggested was quickly damped, when he reflected that a deep fissure, which ran perpendicularly through the rock, formed a chasm ten feet in width, in the floor of the cavern, between him and his place of refuge. The tide, however, which was now rising rapidly, compelled him to retire every instant, further into the cavern, and he felt that the only chance he had left him for life was to endeavor to cross the chasm. He was young, active, and possessed of uncommon courage, and he had frequently, by torch-light, leaped across the abyss, in the presence of his companions, few of whom dared to follow his example. But now, alone, and in utter darkness, how was he to attempt such a perilous feat? The conviction that death was inevitable if he remained where he was, decided him.

Collecting a handful of loose pebbles from one of the numerous channels in the floor, he proceeded cautiously over the slippery rocks, throwing at every step a pebble before him, to ascertain the security of his footing. At length he heard the stone, as it fell from his fingers, descend with a hollow, clattering noise, that continued for several seconds. He knew he was standing on the brink of the chasm. One quick and earnest prayer he offered to the invisible Power, whose hand could protect him in that dread moment—then, retiring a single pace, and screwing every nerve and muscle in his body to the utmost tension, he made a step in advance, and threw himself forward into the dark and fearful void. Who can tell the whirlwind of thought that rushed through his brain in the brief moment that he hung above that yawning gulf? Should he have miscalculated his distance, or chosen a place where the cleft was widest, should his footing fail, or his strength be unable to carry him over, what a death were his! Dashed down that horrible abyss—crashing from rock to rock, until he lay at the bottom a mutilated corpse. The agony of years was crowded into one moment—in the next, his feet struck against the firm rock on the opposite side of the chasm, and he was saved! At least, he felt that he had, for the moment, escaped the imminent peril in which he was placed, and, as he clambered joyfully up the rugged slope at the end of the cave, he thought little of the dangers he had still to encounter.

All through that long night he sat on the narrow ledge of a rock, while the angry waves thundered beneath, and cast their cold spray every instant over him. With the ebbing of the tide, the sea receded from the cavern; but Frank hesitated to attempt crossing the chasm again; his limbs had become stiff and benumbed, and his long abstinence had so weakened his powers that he shrank from the dangerous enterprise.

While giving way to the most desponding reflections, a stentorian hilloa! rang and echoed through the cavern, and never had the human voice sounded so sweetly in his ear. He replied to it with a thrilling shout of joy, and, in a few minutes, several persons with torches appeared advancing. A plank was speedily thrust across the fissure, and Frank Costello once more found himself amid a group of his friends, who were warmly congratulating him upon his miraculous escape. They told him that from his not having returned home the preceding night, it was generally concluded that he had been drowned, and a party of his neighbors proceeded in a boat, early in the morning in search of his body. On reaching "Puffin Hole," they discovered his boat fastened to a rock, and full of water, as she had remained on the ebbing of the tide. This circumstance induced them to examine the cavern narrowly, and the happy result of their search is already known.

THRILLING INCIDENT.

In mid-winter, about four years since, says Miss Martineau, in her Norway and the Norwegians, a young man named Hund, was sent by his master on an errand about twenty miles, to carry provisions to a village in the upper country. The village people asked him for charity, to carry three orphan children on his sledge a few miles on his way to Bergen, and to leave them at a house on the road, when they would be taken care of until they could be brought from Bergen. He took the little things, and saw that the two elder were well wrapped up from the cold. The third he took within his arms and on his knee, as he drove, clasping it warm against his breast—so those say that saw them set off, and it is confirmed by one who met the sledge on the road, and heard the children prattling to Hund, and Hund laughing merrily at their little talk. Before they got half way, however, a pack of hungry wolves burst out upon them from a hollow in the thicket to the right of the wood. The beasts followed close to the back of the sledge. Closer and closer the wolves pressed. Hund saw one about to spring at his throat. It was impossible for the horse to go faster than he did, for he went like the wind—so did the wolves. Hund, in his desperation, snatched up one of the children behind him, and threw it over the back of the sledge. This stopped the pack a little. On galloped the horse. But the wolves were soon crowded around again, with the blood freezing to their muzzles. It was easier to throw over the second child than the first, and Hund did it. But on came again the infuriated beasts, gaunt with hunger, and raging like fiends for the prey. It was harder to give up the third—the dumb infant that nestled in his breast, but Hund was in mortal terror. Again the hot breath of the wolves was upon him. He threw away the infant and saved himself. Away over the snow flew the sledge, the village was reached, and Hund just escaped after all the sacrifice he had made. But he was unsettled and wild, and his talk for some time, whenever he did speak, night or day, was of wolves—so fearful had been the effect upon his imagination.

ABOUT BIRDS.

Among my last letters from Peekskill, I told you of my birds. Their songs were over. Their life had become prosaic. There was no poetry of song—no signs of domestic bliss; but only a poor seed-picking affectation of business preparatory to their great flight southward. That many of them have gone to their damage, I know, as I have seen them in Fulton market. Rice-birds have been plenty. What are these but our famous bob-o'-links? How they disported themselves in all our fields! How did they set at naught all the rules of singing, and fill the air with strains that would have delighted Herr Wagner! But they went south; beguiled by luxurious living, they turned their coats, put off the sober black, and failing to reach a brilliant livery, they only hit a rusty brown. Is not this the fate reserved for turn-coats? Now they are in Fulton market, the desire of epicures! Alas for their gibberish!—sounding like a sweet song broken in pieces, and poured down through the air like the fragments of a shattered crystal vase—(whew! what a figure!);—alas for their freakish flight, their saucy balancing on little weeds, or spires of herdgrass!—has it all ended in lying here on their naked backs, with fat breasts, waiting for the gourmand's bite?

What did the gourmand ever do to deserve such fare? Did he hail their coming in spring? No, it was I that did it!—Did he watch their vagrant courses, their caprices of song, and their summer buffoonery? No, I was the gentleman that sat so many hours keeping them company! Did this ridiculous alderman put off the mowing for a week that they might get their young fledged and out of the nest, before Mr. Turner's relentless mower came along? No, that was my humanity! And now this all-devouring alderman gets all the birds, and I get nothing but the faint memories of the summer! But, perhaps *you* are an eater of rice birds. If so, I take all back that I have said. How do you have them cooked? I will inform you of a recipe which I heard yesterday from a gentleman who is often in foreign parts, and has learned some of the secrets of those who are knowing in luxuries. Here it is: Sweet potatoes are boiled, peeled, split in two lengthwise, a space scooped out large enough for a bird, and when it is snugly in, the other half returned, tied down, and the whole put into the oven and baked. That being done, no directions are needed for eating. The juice is retained, or if any escapes, it renders the potato all the more delicious. I suppose the method is as good for all small birds as for the rice bird. I am willing to have you let this be known to the readers of the *Ledger*—but to let it go no farther, as I mean to put it in my Millennial Cook Book, in which it will be shown that all moral and intellectual qualities have a definite relation to certain articles of food. Of course a world of trouble will be saved when a man can feed himself into virtue, and attain to grace by a wise bill-of-fare, rather than by the somewhat laborious way of self-denial and watchfulness. Should such a day come, chemistry would not content itself with a bare analysis of properties and contents. It would assume a moral function, and point out the bases of moral qualities in all physical substances. In that day old-fashioned tracts will be dóne with. We shall see impressive tracts entitled "Right Eating is Right Living." Ethical books will have chapters headed, "Lamb Chops and their relation to Meekness." "Beef-steak and Courage." "Coffee and Fortitude," "Black Tea and Tears."

Do not laugh. These things are quite as likely to happen, in that day of all perfection on earth, as a thousand and one other things which every one ascribes to the Millennium.

But I wander. Let us come back to birds, and all the rather because some truly English sparrows have just whirled chirping over the roof, and down into my back yard. Cheery and plucky little fellows they are. Brooklyn, as well as New York, is becoming full of them. Their sharp, short, jerking notes, do not count for much in summer, when all other birds are singing. But in late autumn and winter, when the very sunlight lies chilled along the ground as if frosted, and the trees and vines have no leaves to move, and there is no productive force in the air, then, in these November and December days, a flock of these chirping, fussy, quarrelling, nervous sparrows is exceedingly enlivening. There is, too, the mute bunting that hunts seeds along the fence, and on fence borders, plump and nimble, but dull-colored and, for all that we can hear, as taciturn as deacons at communion times. Yet it is welcome a as winter-bird, and I defend both the sparrow and the bunting from prowling cats, that lie and lurk about the contiguous yards below, with as little taste and conscience as if they were human, instead of being good and honest cats.

If our neighbors see flying from my window an empty Congress-water bottle, which striking the stone walk covers the amazed cat with glittering fragments, and sends her through the weeds like a flash, let it not be set down to the score of my hostility to cats. I am fond of cats. But there must be discipline in the family. These excursive battles are intended to rouse up the feline conscience, and to recall the cat to its duties as a member of society. Only men are allowed to slay and eat promiscuously.

But look! There are my flocks! See! far up in the blue, those dreamy gulls! They have come from the North, bringing snow on their wings! The cold has depopulated those hyperborean islands, and rugged crags, where all summer long millions of sea-fowl have brooded and bred their young. There is not a wing-beat there, not a single hoarse note. The key is turned, and the polar zone is locked up for the winter.

All the better for me! The broad bay before my windows is a very playground of gulls. I am never tired of watching them. But I can make nothing of their moods. That, when they fly low, skimming the water, or dipping down into it, they are feeding is plain enough. But what sends them on some days far up into the sky—mere specks, white feathers as it were, where they sail about in a quiet and gentle way, almost without moving their wings?

Why on other days do they seem in a solemn agitation, flying strangely about the harbor, going and returning, with some grave errand at heart, which they seem never to accomplish? On some days they do nothing but feed; on others they seem indifferent to food, and devote themselves to flying. They are shy or familiar by turns without any seeming reason—on some days driving so near to the crowded ferry-boats that a good staff could reach them, and on others keeping remote from all craft in the river. Well, there is no accounting for moods among men, and sea-gulls are not much better than human folk, and must be allowed their idiosyncrasies—with which long word we'll wind up this paper.—*Henry Ward Beecher.*

MOSQUITO MURDER.

THERE is something terrifying in killing a satiated mosquito. To kill a flea is a lively and cheerful operation. You talk to him ironically when caught, and crack him as you would a joke. The bug, even, you dismiss to limbo with one deep and not necessarily loud abjuration, wash your hands, and there is an end of the matter. You feel no more remorse for having played the part of Carnifex than does the head master at Eaton, after the victims of the "Bill" have been brought to the block. The monster, minute as he is bleeds; and it is your own blood which is expressed from his crushed carcass. You wonder as Gloster wondered over Henry's corpse, that he could have so much blood in him. The wall is absolutely bespattered, and that too from the body of an assassin no bigger than a pin's head. You are appalled, you shudder, for that great crimson stain on the wall is you. The wretch has robbed you of so much salt and iron, and, consequently, vitality. The blood is the life. From your sum of existence how many hours may not be deducted on account of the mosquito.—"*The Great Circumbendibus,*" *by George Augusta Sala.*

FISHING IN THE SARGOSSA SEA.

BY THE REV. J. T. GRACEY.

THE Sargossa Sea! why, where in the world, and what is that? Well, well, let me tell my story. Lieutenant Maury says: "There is a river in the midst of the sea." Such is the Gulf Stream, with its margin in many places so distinctly marked that you can readily discern that a ship floats half in the river and half in the sea. Ay, and there is a sea in the midst of the ocean, and in the sea a flower-garden. The sea is named Sargossa, and the flower-garden is of sea-weed, laid out in ever-varying form. But I must not anticipate. I always tell stories, however, by beginning in the middle and telling toward both ends, and must get through this after my own fashion.

There is a long scientific story about how the Gulf Stream is ridged like a house-roof, and about how the drift of spars and sea-weed, etc., show this, by floating on the different slopes, but never crossing the stream; and then they tell about this Gulf Stream curving across the Atlantic, till it meets a current that sets southward, along the coast of Africa, until it, in turn, meets another current that makes its way westward across the Atlantic, and joins yet another current setting northward, toward the Caribbean Sea, which completes the marvellous circuit of currents.

Stir the water in a tub round and round violently, and throw in bits of straw and small sticks, and you see them all whirl toward the middle of the water, and finally reach the centre. Thus spars, drift-wood, and sea-weed getting on the inner side of this circle of currents, must naturally be kept there, and everlastingly float in the centre of this gigantic belt of waters. The space enclosed by these currents covers many degrees of latitude and longitude, and is called the Sargossa Sea.

Now, all this may be a very unscientific way of telling what the Sargossa Sea is, and is quite as indefinite as to its whereabouts. I cannot locate it very precisely, because my own belief is that it varies at times in latitude, if not in longitude. These currents—as, for instance, the Gulf Stream itself—do not all the year flow in the same tract, but are a portion of the year much farther north than at other times. Of course, the Sargossa Sea must vary with its boundary belt of currents. But, substantially, this sea extends from the Cape de Verde Islands to the Bermudas, and lies in what are known as "the Horse Latitudes."

Gentle reader, if you do not know what the Horse Latitudes are, do not sing the Doxology, but be thankful that you have not experienced all that is gloomy, and depressing, and patience-trying in this world. They say these came to be named

"Horse Latitudes" because formerly, when men were used to carry horses to the West-Indies, so many of them died in this portion of the ocean. It is familiarly known at sea, too, as the Doldrums. A succession of squalls and calms (especially of the calms) makes you often seriously wonder if you will ever get away from that quarter of the globe, and to begin to inquire how many days' provision there is aboard your ship. Do you wonder, then, we went to fishing?

But the flower-garden! Well, nearly all over the surface of this Sargossa Sea floats a species of sea-weed. It is a coarse, vine-like thing, with a berry about the size of a huckleberry, but is of a dusky straw color. There were great, unbroken patches of this that were extensive enough, and looked firm enough for a game of base-ball; and then there were delicate strips in every variety of combination and form, in their varied shapes looking like a finely designed flower-garden. It was a panorama of artistic gardening, and many a new and neat form might have been learned here, for use in the lawns and gravel-walks of a more substantial kind of park and lawn culture.

This sea-weed, nay, this mistletoe of the sea, is a sensitive and delicate thing, though it does not look it. It will not live even in a tub of salt water, unless the water be renewed some three times a day. It is a living, rootless plant, or flower (or animal?) that must be fed with some sort of nourishment which it derives from its mother, the sea.

If, however, it be hermetically sealed in sea-water, it does not die, but may be kept for years. I have some now in bottles, which is as beautiful as the day I procured it. But other portions that I put even in salt water, not made air-tight, soon turned black, withered, and died.

Sometimes this sea-weed would be driven by the waves and wind into long, narrow strips; and it would always indicate a shift of the wind sooner than the dog-vane at the mast-head. We found this as far north as about two thousand miles from the coast of England, which was, we were informed, very unusual.

Well, but, you say, what about the fishing? For what and how did you fish? To say nothing about sharks and grampus, etc., I answer, we fished for sea-weed. At first, we tried great bunches of huge brass hooks, but these soon broke, and left us minus "bob, line and sinker." Then we did it after a less æsthetic mode. We got the log-lines and fastened to them the iron oar-locks from the life boats, and heaved these, harpoon-fashion, into a bed of weed, and dragged it on deck. Then we searched this for shrimps and infinitesimal fishes. Of these last we found many perfect fishes, not, perhaps, a quarter of an inch in length, that suggested many a reflection on the minute care of Divine Providence, which could watch over such tiny creatures all alone, out in that great sea. Yet, after all, what were we but other tiny beings compared to the vast, vast ocean on whose bosom we were rocked?

And then we fished for jelly-fish—not your great plebeian blubber, or bladder, or bubble, the mushroom-shaped nettle, that annoys you when bathing at Newport or Cape May; we had better taste than that. That for which we fished was a tube-like, gelatinous creature, with a single intestine, and which, by a peculiar contraction of its body, propelled itself, lying horizontally, through the water. They were of beautiful colors, for the most part being of deep purple in the centre, and shading off to pure white gelatine at the circumference. We frequently saw scores, or hundreds, of these joined together, and looking like a great sea-serpent as they rose and fell and propelled themselves through the water. What the object of thus being united was, we could not tell, unless it was that, by simultaneous contraction, they could propel themselves more steadily and swiftly through the water, and be less driven about by the violence of the waves.

And then we fished for the nautilus—the Portuguese man-of-war, the fairy of the jelly-fish tribe, the mimic sailor, who now furls sail, and drops anchor at every angry wind, and anon sets sails, which have more exquisite tints than rainbow hues, and rides gallantry over the waves. He is a good sailor, and knows even how to right ship if blown on beam ends. Thus, good reader, we fished, not for fabulous things in a fabulous sea, but whiled away many a dull hour, amid the depressing calms of the equatorial ocean, in studying some illustrated pages of God's wonder-book of the world, and ever taking our microscopes to see deeper and yet deeper into the mystery of being. I do not wish you in the Sargossa Sea, good readers, but can only hope, if ever you be there, you may be as jolly and as lucky fishermen as were we who fished there in March last.

WHAT A VOLCANO CAN DO.

COTOPAXI, in 1738, threw its fiery rockets three thousand feet above its crater, while in 1744 the blazing mass struggling for an outlet, roared so that its awful voice was heard a distance of more than six hundred miles. In 1797 the crater of Tunguragua, one of the peaks of the Andes, flung out torrents of mud which dammed up rivers, opened new lakes, and in valleys of a thousand feet wide made deposits of six hundred feet deep. The stream from Vesuvius, which in 1737 passed through Torre del Greco, contained 33,600,000 cubic feet of solid matter; and in 1794, when Torre del Greco was destroyed a second time, the mass of lava amounted to 45,000,000 cubic feet. In

1679 Etna poured forth a flood which covered eighty-four square miles of surface, which measured 100,000,000 cubic feet. On this occasion the scoriæ formed the Monte Rossi, near Nicolosi a cone two miles in circumference and 4000 feet high. The stream thrown out by Etna in 1810 was in motion at the rate of a yard per day for nine months after the eruption ; and it is on record that the lava of the same mountain after a terrible eruption, was not thoroughly cooled and consolidated ten years after the event. In the eruption of Vesuvius, A.D. 70, the scoriæ and ashes vomited forth far exceeded the entire bulk of the mountain ; while in 1660 Etna disgorged more than twenty times its own mass. Vesuvius has thrown its ashes as far as Constantinople, Syria, and Egypt ; it hurled stones eight pounds in weight to Pompeii, a distance of six miles, while similar masses were tossed 2000 feet above its summit. Cotopaxi has projected a block of 109 cubic yards in volume a distance of nine miles ; and Sambawa, in 1815, during the most terrific eruption on record, sent its ashes as far as Java, a distance of 300 miles surface, and out of a population of 12,000 souls only twenty escaped.—*Recreative Science.*

HUMOROUS SELECTIONS.

ANECDOTE OF DR. CHAUNCY.

Dr. Cooper, who was a man of accomplished manners, and fond of society, was able, by the aid of his fine talents, to dispense with some of the severe study that others engaged in. This, however, did not escape the envy and malice of the world, and it was said, in a kind of petulant and absurd exaggeration, that he used to walk to the south-end of a Saturday, and, if he saw a man riding into town in a black coat, would stop, and ask him to preach the next day. Dr. Chauncy was a close student, very absent, and very irritable. On these traits in the character of the two clergymen, a servant of Dr. Chauncy laid a scheme for obtaining a particular object from his master. Scipio went into his master's study one morning to receive some directions, which the doctor having given, resumed his writing, but the servant still remained. The master, looking up a few minutes afterward, and supposing he had just come in, said, "Scipio, what do you want?" "I want a new coat, massa." "Well, go to Mrs. Chauncy, and tell her to give you one of my old coats;" and was again absorbed in his studies. The servant remained fixed. After a while, the doctor, turning his eyes that way, saw him again, as if for the first time, and said, "What do you want, Scip?" "I want a new coat, massa." "Well, go to my wife, and ask her to give you one of my old coats;" and fell to writing once more. Scipio remained in the same posture. After a few moments, the doctor looked toward him, and repeated the former question, "Scipio, what do you want?" "I want a new coat, massa." It now flashed over the doctor's mind, that there was something of repetition in this dialogue. "Why, have I not told you before to ask Mrs. Chauncy to give you one? get away." "Yes, massa, but I no want a black coat." "Not want a black coat! why not?" "Why, massa,—I 'fraid to tell you,—but I don't want a black coat." "What's the reason you don't want a black coat? tell me directly." "O! massa, I don't want a black coat, but I 'fraid to tell the reason, you so passionate." "You rascal! will you tell me the reason?" "O! massa, I'm sure you be angry." "If I had my cane here, you villain, I'd break your bones: will you tell me what you mean?" "I 'fraid to tell you, massa; I know you be angry." The doctor's impatience was now highly irritated, and Scipio, perceiving, by his glance at the tongs, that he might find a substitute for the cane, and that he was sufficiently excited, said, "Well, massa, you make me tell, but I know you be angry—I 'fraid, massa, if I wear another black coat,

Dr. Cooper ask me to preach for him!" This unexpected termination realized the servant's calculation; his irritated master burst into a laugh,—"Go, you rascal, get my hat and cane, and tell Mrs. Chauncy she may give you a coat of any color; a red one if you choose." Away went the negro to his mistress, and the doctor to tell the story to his friend, Dr. Cooper.

HILL AND THE ANTINOMIAN.

Rowland Hill would have tried the critical sagacity of the most erudite. His eccentricities are of great notoriety. With many strong points of character, he combined notions prodigiously odd. One of those restless infesters of places of worship, commonly called Antinomians, one day called on Rowland Hill, to bring him to account for his too severe and legal gospel. "Do you, sir," asked Rowland, "hold the ten commandments to be a rule of life to Christians?" "Certainly not," replied the visitor. The minister rang the bell, and on the servant making his appearance, he quietly added, "John, show that man the door, and keep your eye on him until he is beyond the reach of every article of wearing apparel, or other property in the hall!"

THE SLANDEROUS PARROT.

We remember a parrot which belonged to a lady, which was the innocent means of getting his mistress into a very unfortunate scrape. A friend of hers having called one forenoon, the conversation of the two ladies took that turn toward petty scandal, to which we grieve to say, it is but too frequently bent. The friend mentioned the name of a lady of their acquaintance. "Mrs. ——!" exclaimed the owner of the parrot, "Mrs. —— drinks like a fish!" These words were hardly uttered, when the footman, in a loud voice, announced "Mrs. ——!" and as the new visitor, a portly, proud dame, came sailing into the room, "Mrs. ——!" exclaimed the parrot, "Mrs. —— drinks like a fish!" Mrs. —— wheeled around, with the celerity of a troop of heavy dragoons, furiously to confront her base and unknown maligner. "Mrs. ——!" cried the parrot again, "Mrs.—— drinks like a fish!" "Madam," exclaimed Mrs. —— to the lady of the house, "this is a piece of wickedness toward me which must have taken you no short time to prepare. It shows the blackness of your heart toward one for whom you have long pretended a friendship; but I shall be revenged." It was in vain that the mistress of the parrot rose and protested her innocence; Mrs. —— flounced out of the room in a storm of rage, much too loud to admit of the voice of reason being heard. The parrot, delighted with his new caught up words, did nothing for some days but shout

out, at the top of his most unmusical voice, "Mrs.——! Mrs. —— drinks like a fish!" Meanwhile, Mrs. ——'s lawyers having once taken up the scent, succeeded in ferreting out some information, that ultimately produced written proofs, furnished by some secret enemy, that the lady's imprudence in the propagation of this scandal had not been confined to the instance we have mentioned. An action at law was raised for defamation. The parrot was arrested and carried into court, to give oral testimony of the malignity of the plot which was supposed to have been laid against Mrs. ——'s good fame; and he was by no means niggardly of his testimony, for, to the great amusement of the bench, the bar, and all present, he was no sooner produced, than he began, and continued loudly to vociferate, "Mrs. ——! Mrs. —— drinks like a fish!" until judges and jury were alike satisfied of the merits of the case; and the result was, that the poor owner of the parrot was cast with immense damages.

EPITOME OF WAR.

The history of every war, says the Ettrick Shepherd, in his "Lay Sermons," is very like a scene I once saw in Nithsdale. Two boys from different schools met one fine day upon the ice. They eyed each other with rather jealous and indignant looks, and with defiance on each brow.

"What are ye glowrin at, Billy?"

"What's that to you? I'll look where I have a mind, an' hinder me if ye daur."

A hearty blow was the return to this, and there was such a battle begun! It being Saturday, all the boys of both schools were on the ice, and the fight instantly became general and desperate. At one time, they fought with missile weapons, such as stones, and snowballs; but, at length, they coped in a rage, and many bloody raps were liberally given and received. I went up to try if I could pacify them; for by this time a number of little girls had joined in the affray, and I was afraid they would be killed; so, addressing the one party, I asked what they were pelting the others for? what they had done to them?

"O, neathing at a' man; we just want to give them a good thrashin'!"

After fighting until they were quite exhausted, one of the principal heroes stepped forth between, covered with blood, and his clothes torn to tatters, and addressed the belligerent parties thus:

"Weel, I'll tell you what we'll do wi' ye: if ye'll let us alane, we'll let you alane."

There was no more of it; the war was at an end, and the boys scattered away to their play.

I thought at the time, and have often thought since, that that trivial affray was the best epitome of war in general, that I had ever seen. Kings and ministers of the state are just a set of grown-up children, exactly like the children I speak of, with only this material difference, that instead of fighting out the needless quarrels they have raised, they sit in safety and look on, while they send out their innocent but servile subjects to battle; and then, after a waste of blood and treasure, are glad to make the boy's conditions, "If ye'll let us alane, we'll let you alane."

COURTSHIP OF A BASHFUL CLERGYMAN.

The Rev. John Brown, of Haddington, the well known author of the self-interpreting Bible, was a man of singular bashfulness. In token of the truth of this statement, it need only be stated that his courtship lasted seven years. Six years and a half had passed away, and the reverend gentleman had got no further forward than he had been the first six days. This state of things became intolerable. A step in advance must be made, and Mr. Brown summoned all his courage for the deed.

"Janet," said he, as they sat in solemn silence, "we've been acquainted now for six years an' mair, and I've ne'er gottan a kiss yet. D'ye think I might take one, my bonnie girl?"

"Just as you like, John; only be becoming and proper wi' it."

"Surely, Janet, we'll ask a blessing."

The blessing was asked, the kiss was taken and the worthy divine most rapturously exclaimed:

"Oh, woman! but it's gude. We'll return thanks."

Six months after made this happy couple man and wife; and, added his descendant, who humorously told the tale; a happier couple never spent a long and useful life together.

THE NEW COAT AND OLD BLANKET.

An Indian and a white man, being at worship together, were both brought under conviction by the same sermon. The Indian was shortly after led to rejoice in the pardoning mercy. The white man, for a long time, was under distress of mind, and at times almost ready to despair, but at length he was brought to a comfortable experience of forgiving love. Some time after, meeting his *red* brother, he thus addressed him: "How is it, that I should be so long under conviction, when you found comfort so soon?" "Oh, brother," replied the Indian, "me tell you; there come along a rich prince, he propose to give you a *new coat;* you look at your coat, and say I don't know; my coat is pretty good; I believe it will do a little longer. He then offer me a new coat; I look on my *old blanket;* I say, this good for nothing; I fling it right away, and accept the new coat. Just so, brother, you try to keep your own righteousness for some time; you loth to give it up: but I, poor Indian, had none; therefore I glad at once to receive the righteousness of Lord Jesus Christ."

THE WISE COACHMAN.

An old gentleman in the county of Herts, having lost his coachman by death, who had served him many years, advertised for a successor. The first who applied, giving a satisfactory account of his character and capacity for such a place, was asked how near he could drive to the edge of a wood, where a sloping bank presented danger. He replied, "to an inch." The old gentleman ordered him to be supplied with suitable refreshment, and to leave his address, adding, that if he wished for his services, he should hear from him in a day or two. Shortly afterward, a second applied, who underwent the same examination as the former, and replied to the last question, that he could drive "to half an inch," and had often done it; he also received the same dismission with the same civilities as the former man. Soon afterward a third applied, and on being asked the same question, namely, how near he could drive to the edge of a sharp declivity, in case of necessity, coolly replied, "Really, I do not know, sir, having never tried: for it has always been my maxim to get as far as possible from such danger, and I have had my reward in my safety, and that of my employers."

With this reply the old gentleman expressed his entire satisfaction, and informed the man if he could procure a proper recommendation, wages should not part them, adding, "I am grown old and timid, and want a coachman on whose prudence and care I can rely, as well as his skill."

SHORT MEASURE.

The following incident in the life of William Dawson, a very humble, but a very excellent preacher, late of Barnbow, near Leeds, beautifully illustrates the power of the plainly preached word.

"He was preaching in the neighborhood of Leeds, on Daniel v: 27: "Thou art weighed in the balances, and art found wanting." A person who traveled the country in the character of a peddler, and who was exceedingly partial to him as a preacher, was one of Mr. Dawson's auditors. The person referred to, generally carried a stick with him, which answered the double purpose of a walking-stick and a "yard-wand;" and having been employed pretty freely in the former capacity, it was worn down beyond the point of justice, and procured for him an appellation of "Short Measure." He stood before Mr. Dawson, and being rather noisy in his religious professions, as well as ready with his responses, he manifested signs of approbation while the scales were being described and adjusted, and different classes of sinners were placed in them, and disposed of agreeably to the test of justice, truth and mercy,—uttering in a somewhat subdued tone, yet loud enough for those around to hear, at the close of each particular—"Light weight"—"short again," etc. After taking up the separate characters of the flagrant transgressor of the law of God, the hypocrite, the formalist, etc., Mr. Dawson at length came to such persons as possessed religious light, but little hallowed feeling, and the semblance of much zeal, but who employed false weights and measures. Here, without adverting in his mind to the case of his noisy auditor, he perceived the muscles of his face working, when the report of "short measure" occurred to him. Resolved, however, to soften no previous expression, and to proceed with an analysis and description of the question, he placed the delinquent, in his singularly striking way, in the scale, when, instead of the usual response, the man, stricken before him, took his stick—the favorite measure, from under his arm—raised one foot from the floor, doubled his knee, and, taking hold of the offending instrument by both ends, snapped it into two halves, exclaiming, while dashing it to the ground, "Thou shalt do it no more!" So true is it, to employ the language of an eminent minister, "that no man ever offended his own conscience, but first or last it was revenged upon him for it."

PERSEVERANCE OF THE SAINTS.

A PERSON, who suspected that a minister of his acquaintance was not sufficiently Calvinistic, went to him and said, "Sir, I am told that you are against the perseverance of the saints." "Not I, indeed," answered he, "it is the perseverance of *sinners* that I oppose." "But that is not a satisfactory answer, sir. Do you think that a child of God cannot fall very low, and yet be restored?" He replied, "I think it will be very dangerous to make the experiment."

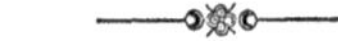

THE MOUNTAIN DOCTOR.

A WEALTHY farmer, much affected with hypochondria, came to Langenau, to consult Michael Scuppach, better known by the appellation of the *mountain doctor*. "I have seven devils in my body," said he, "no fewer than seven." "There are more than seven," replied the doctor, with the utmost gravity; "if you count them right you will find eight." After questioning the patient concerning his case, he promised to cure him in eight days, during which time, he would every morning rid him of one of his troublesome inmates, at the rate of one louisd'or each. "But," added he, "as the last will be more obstinate and difficult to expel than the others, I shall expect two louisd'ors for him. The farmer agreed to these terms: the bargain was struck, and the doctor, impressing upon all present the necessity of secrecy, promised to give the nine louisd'ors to the poor of the parish. Next morning, the imaginary demoniac was brought to him, and placed near a kind of machine, which he had never seen before, by which means he received an electric shock. The farmer roared out lustily. "There goes one!" said the doctor, with the utmost gravity. Next day the same operation was repeated: the farmer bellowed as before, and the doctor coolly remarked, "Another is off!" In this manner he proceeded to the seventh. When he was preparing to attack the last, Scuppach reminded his patient that he had need of all his courage, for this was the captain of the gang, who would make a more obstinate resistance than any of the others. The shock was at this time so strong, as to extend the demoniac on the floor. "Now they are all gone!" said the doctor, and ordered the farmer to be put to bed. On recovering himself, the latter declared he was completely cured; he paid the nine louisd'ors with abundance of thanks, and returned in the best spirits to the village.

Creditable witnesses attest this extraordinary cure, which proves the acuteness of the doctor, as well as the truth of Solomon's proverb, that with a fool we must sometimes talk like a fool.

ANECDOTE OF KING GEORGE III.

It is known that the king, after the close of the American revolutionary war, ordered a thanksgiving to be kept through the kingdom. A noble Scotch divine, in the presence of his majesty, inquired, "For what are we to give thanks?—that your majesty has lost thirteen of his best provinces?" The king answered, "No!" "Is it, then (the divine added), that your majesty has lost 100,000 lives of your subjects in the contest?" "No, no!" said the king. "Is it, then, that we have expended and lost a hundred millions of money, and for the defeat and tarnishing of your majesty's arms?" "No such thing!" said the king pleasantly. "What, then, is the object of the thanksgiving?" "Oh, to give thanks that it is no worse."

TWO PAILS OF WATER.

The Royal Society, on the day of its creation, was the whetstone of the wit of their patron, Charles II. With a peculiar gravity of countenance, he proposed to the assembly the following question, for their solution:—"Suppose two pails of water were fixed in two different scales, equally poised, and which weighed equally alike, and that two live bream, or small fish, were put into either of these pails, he wanted to know the reason why that pail, with such addition, should not weigh more than the other pail which stood against it." Every one was ready to set at quiet the royal curiosity; but it appeared that every one was giving a different opinion. One, at length, offered so ridiculous a solution that another of the members could not refrain from a loud laugh; when the king, turning to him, insisted that he should give his sentiments as well as the rest. This he did without hesitation, and told his majesty, in plain terms, that he denied the fact. On which the king, in high mirth, exclaimed, "Odds fish, brother, you are in the right!"

LOOK AT HOME.

The Rev. John Hurrion, a christian minister in Norfolk, England, had two daughters who were fond of dress, and on this account gave him great grief. He had often privately reproved them, but in vain; at length, while preaching one Lord's day, he took occasion to notice, among other things, pride in dress. After speaking for some time on the subject, he suddenly stopped and said with much feeling, "But you will say, look at home. My good friends, I do look at home, until my heart aches."

CUNNING DEVICE.

After the signal defeat of the French at this memorable action, Leipsic became full of a mixed medley of soldiers, of all arms and of all nations; of course, a great variety of coin was in circulation there; a British private, who was attached to the rocket-brigade, and who had picked up a little broken French and German, went to the largest hotel in Leipsic, and displaying an English shilling to the landlord, inquired if this piece of coin was current there. "Oh yes," replied he, "you may have whatever the house affords for that money: it passes current here at present." Our fortunate Bardolph, finding himself in such compliant quarters, called about him most lustily, and the most sumptuous dinner the house could afford, washed down by sundry bottles of the most expensive wines, was dispatched without ceremony. On going away, he tendered at the bar the identical shilling which the landlord had inadvertently led him to expect was to perform such wonders. The stare, the shrug, and the exclamation elicited from "*mine host of the garter,*" by such a tender, may be more easily conceived than expressed. An explanation, very much to the dissatisfaction of the landlord, took place, who quickly found not only that nothing more was likely to be got, but also that the laugh would be tremendously heavy against him.

This part of the profits he had a very christian wish to divide with his neighbor. Taking, therefore, his guest to the street-door of his hotel, he requested him to look over the way. "Do you see," said he, "that large hotel opposite? That fellow, the landlord of it, is my sworn rival, and nothing can keep this story from his ears, in which case I shall never hear the last of it. Now, my good fellow, you are not only welcome to your entertainment, but I will instantly give you a five-frank piece into the bargain, if you will promise, on the word of a soldier, to attempt the very same trick with him to-morrow that succeeded so well with me to-day." Our veteran took the money, and accepted the conditions; but having buttoned up the silver very securely in his pocket, he took his leave of the landlord with the following speech, and a bow that did no discredit to Leipsic. "Sir, I deem myself in honor bound to use my utmost endeavors to put your wishes in execution; I shall certainly do all I can, but must candidly inform you that I fear I shall not succeed, since I played the very same trick with that gentleman yesterday; and it is to his particular advice alone that you are indebted for the honor of my company to-day."

THE MISER OF MARSEILLES.

An old man, of the name of Guyot, lived and died in the town of Marseilles, in France. He amassed a large fortune by the most laborious industry, and the severest habits of abstinence and privation. His neighbors considered him a miser, and thought that he was hoarding up money from mean and avaricious motives. The populace pursued him, whenever he appeared, with hootings and execrations, and the boys sometimes threw stones at him. He at length died, and in his will were found the following words:—"Having observed from my infancy that the poor of Marseilles are ill supplied with water, which can only be purchased at a great price, I have cheerfully labored the whole of my life to procure for them this great blessing; and I direct that the whole of my property shall be laid out in building an aqueduct for their use."

HOW TO OVERCOME EVIL.

"I once had a neighbor," says Mr. White, "who, though a clever man, came to me one hay-day, and said: 'Esquire White, I want you to come and get your geese away.' 'Why,' said I, 'what are my geese doing?' 'They pick my pigs' ears when they are eating, and drive them away, and I will not have it.' 'What can I do?' said I. 'You must yoke them.' 'That I have not time to do now,' said I; 'I do not see but they must run.' 'If *you* do not take care of them I shall,' said the clever shoemaker, in anger. 'What do you say, Esquire White?' 'I cannot take care of them now; but I will pay you for all damages. 'Well,' said he, 'you will find that a hard thing, I guess.'

"So off he went, and I heard a terrible squalling among the geese. The next news from the geese was that three of them were missing. My children went and found them terribly mangled and dead, and thrown into the bushes.

"'Now,' said I, 'all keep still, and let me punish him.' In a few days the shoemaker's hogs broke into my corn. I saw them, but let them remain a long time. At last I drove them all out, and picked up the corn which they had torn down and fed them with it in the road. By this time the shoemaker came in great haste after them.

"'Have you seen any thing of my hogs?' said he. 'Yes, sir; you will find them yonder, eating some corn which they tore down in my field.' 'In your field?' 'Yes, sir,' said I; 'hogs love corn, you know—they were made to eat.' 'How much mischief have they done?' 'O, not much,' said I.

"Well, off he went to look, and estimated the damage to be equal to a bushel and a-half of corn.

"'Oh, no,' said I, 'it can't be.' 'Yes,' said the shoemaker; 'and I will pay you every cent of damage.' 'No,' said I, 'you shall pay me nothing. My geese have been a great trouble to you.'

"The shoemaker blushed and went home. The next winter, when we came to settle, the shoemaker determined to pay me for my corn. 'No,' said I; 'I shall take nothing.'

"After some talk we parted; but in a day or two I met him in the road, and fell into conversation in the most friendly manner. But when I started on he seemed loth to move, and I paused. For a moment both of us were silent. At last he said: 'I have something laboring on my mind.' 'Well, what is it?' 'Those geese. I killed three of your geese, and shall never rest until you know how I feel. I am sorry.' And the tears came in his eyes. 'Oh, well,' said I, 'never mind; I suppose my geese were very provoking.'

"I never took any thing of him for it; but whenever my cattle broke into his field after this, he seemed glad; because he could show how patient he could be.

"Now," said the narrator, "conquer yourself, and you can conquer with kindness where you can conquer in no other way."

DYSPEPSIA.

A WEALTHY manufacturer from the west of Scotland, while at Edinburgh on business, called upon Dr. Gregory for his advice. He was a man of middle stature, rather corpulent, with a rosy complexion, and whose exterior altogether spoke the comfortable liver. After seating himself, the following dialogue ensued:

GENTLEMAN.—Well, Dr. Gregory, I ha' come up to Edinbro' in the way o' business, and I just thought I would take your advice about my health.

DOCTOR.—Your health, sir! What's the matter with you?

"I'm no just sae weel i' the stomach as I'd like to be."

"The stomach! I suppose you are a drunkard or a glutton, then, sir."

"Na, na, Dr. Gregory, ye canna say that—ye canna say that; ye maun ken that I'm a sober mon and a temperate mon, and a deacon of the kirk, as my worthy father was afore me."

"Well, let us see. What do you eat and drink? What do you take for breakfast?"

"I take coffee or tea, wi' toast, and a fresh egg, or a bit o' salmon, though I have no' much appetite for breakfast."

"Yes; and then you take something by way of lunch between breakfast and dinner."

"I canna say I care ower much about the lunch; but can take a bit o' bread and cheese, and a glass o' ale, if it be there, but canna say I care ower much about it."

"Well, what do you eat for dinner?"

"O, I'm no very particular, though I maun say I like my dinner."

"I suppose you take soup first?"

"Yes, I canna say, I don't like my soup."

"And a glass of porter or brandy and water with it?"

"Yes, I like a glass o' something with the soup."

"And then you have fish, or beef and mutton, with vegetables?"

"Yes."

"And a glass of ale or porter with them?"

"Yes, I take a glass o' ale now and then, wi' my meat."

"And then you have boiled fowl and bacon, or something of that sort, I suppose?"

"I maun say I like a bit o' fowl and bacon now and then."

"And a glass of something with them?"

"Yes."

"And after the fowl you have pudding?"

"I'm na fond o' pudding, but I can take a bit, if it be there."

"And you must drink wine with the pudding?"

"I canna tak ower much o' the wine; but if I ha' a friend wi' me, I take a glass or so."

"And then you have cheese or nuts?"

"Yes, the gude wife is ower fond o' them; but I canna say I care much about them."

"But you take a glass of wine or two with your nuts?"

"Yes, a glass or two."

"Well, you do not finish your dinner without whisky punch?"

"I find my dinner sets better on my stomach with a little punch; so I tak a glass or so."

"And you have tea, I suppose?"

"Yes, I maun take my tea wi' the gude wife."

"And a glass of something with it?"

"Yes, I can take a bit o' something if it be there."

"But you do not go to bed without your supper?"

"Na, na, Gregory, I canna say I like to gang to bed without my wee bit supper."

"And what do you eat for supper?"

"O, a bit o' any thing—a bit o' salmon, or boiled tongue, or cold fowl."

"And a glass of something with it?"

"Yes."

"And can you go to bed without a night-cap of hot punch?"

"I maun say I sleep better for a glass o' hot punch, though I canna say I'm ower fond o' the habit."

"Well, sir, you're a fine fellow! You come to me with a lie in your mouth, and tell me you are a sober man, and a temperate man, and a deacon of the kirk, as your worthy father was before you; and you make yourself out, by your own statement, to be a glutton, and a wine-bibber, and a whisky-tippler, and a beer-swiller, and a drinker of that most abominable of all compositions, called punch. Go home, sir, and reform yourself, and become temperate in your eating and drinking, and you will have no need of my advice."

THE MISER IN THE WELL.

An old bachelor, possessed of a fortune of $50,000, meeting a friend one day began to harangue him very learnedly upon the detestable sin of avarice, and gave the following instance of it: "About three years ago," said he, "by a very odd accident I fell into a well, and was absolutely within a very few minutes of perishing before I could prevail upon an unconscious dog of a laborer, who happened to be within hearing of my cries, to help me out for a shilling. The fellow was so rapacious as to insist upon having twenty-five cents, for above a quarter of an hour, and I verily believe he would not have abated me a single farthing if he had not seen me at the last gasp; and I determined rather to die than submit to his extortion!"

HENRY VIII. AND THE ABBOT OF READING.

Henry the Eighth having been hunting in Windsor Forest, went down about dinner time to the Abbey of Reading, where, disguising himself as one of the king's guard, he was invited to the Abbot's table. Here, his tooth being whetted by the keen air of the forest,

he fed so lustily on a surloin of beef, that his vigorous appetite was noticed by the master of the ceremonies. "Well fare thy heart," quoth the abbot, "I would give a hundred pounds if I could feed so heartily on beef as thou dost. Alas! my weak and squeazie stomach will hardly digest the wing of a rabbit or chicken." The monarch having satisfied his palate, thanked the abbot for his good cheer, and departed undiscovered. Some weeks afterward, the abbot was arrested, conveyed to London, sent to the Tower, and allowed no food for several days, but bread and water. This treatment, together with his fears for the consequence of the king's displeasure, soon removed the effects of repletion; and at last, when a surloin was one day placed before him, he ate as freely as a famished plowman. When he had finished his meal, the king, who had been a hidden spectator, burst from his concealment. "My lord," said the laughing monarch, "presently deposit your hundred pieces of gold, or else no going hence all the days of your life. I have been the physician to cure your *squeazie stomach;* and now, as I deserve, demand my fee for so doing." The abbot knowing that argument was of no avail with the stern Henry, paid the money, and returned home; rejoicing that he had escaped so easily.

ANECDOTE OF A VENTRILOQUIST.

THOSE persons who speak without moving the lips, and who modify their voice so as to make it appear to proceed from different places or persons, while themselves seem unconnected with what is passing, are called ventriloquists. Bordeau, who was a learned critic of the sixteenth century, relates the following anecdote.

Louis Brabant was valet-de-chambre to Francis I, and accosted a widow, with whose daughter (a rich and handsome heiress,) he was in love, in a voice perfectly resembling that of her dead husband, exclaiming, "Give my daughter in marriage to Louis Brabant. I now endure the inexpressible torments of purgatory, for having refused her to him; you will thus provide a worthy husband for your daughter, and procure everlasting repose to the soul of your poor husband."

The widow could not, for a moment, resist so dreadful a summons, but immediately received Louis for her son-in-law; when the formalities of his marriage rendering it necessary for him to exhibit some show of riches, he contracted an intimate acquaintance with one Cornu, an old and rich banker at Lyons, and during an interval of silence, after a preparatory conversation on demons and specters, a voice was heard, which, to the astonished banker, seemed to be that of his deceased father.

It complained, as in the former case, of his dreadful situation in purgatory, and called upon his son, "to deliver him instantly, by putting into the hands of Louis Brabant, a sum for the redemption, from the Turks, of the Christians then in slavery; and threatened him with eternal damnation, if he did not take this method of expiating his own sins;" when the wary banker, demurring to the demand, made an appointment with the ghost's delegate for the next day; and, to render any design of imposing upon him utterly abortive, he took Louis into the open fields, where no confederate could possibly be concealed; but, wherever the banker conducted his associate, his ears were assaulted with the complaints and groans, not only of his father, but of all his deceased relations, imploring him, for the love of God, and in the name of every saint in the calendar, to have mercy on his own soul and theirs, by effectually seconding, with his purse, the intentions of his worthy companion; until Cornu, who could no longer resist the *voice of heaven*, carried his guest home, and gave him the sum of ten thousand crowns.

The secret, however, was made public some time afterward; and the usurer was so much affected by the loss of his money, and the mortifying railleries of his neighbors, that he took to his bed, and died.

THE ABBE OF CALVADOS.

In a village of Calvados, in the month of October, 1820, was buried an old man, who had retired from business, and owned some national property. Before his death, he was desirous of receiving the sacrament, and the priest gave him absolution, on condition that he would restore some acres to the church, which he promised to do; but death came before the notary. His property, therefore, wholly descended to his son, a simple youth. On the night after his father's funeral, the young man was awakened by a violent noise, accompanied with a vivid light, which in a moment disappeared. Being no stranger to fear, he shook as he lay in his bed, and tried to call out for help; but a cold and moist hand closed his lips, and completed his amazement. He fancied that he beheld a specter, covered with a long white mantle, pass before him, and in a sepulchral voice uttered these words: "*Badly obtained; the soul of P—— must go into torments, if his son makes not restitution.*" Another voice, weak and failing, continued: "*My son, restore the ill-gotten property, or else,*" the sepulchral voice added, "*I shall come night after night to drag you by your feet.*" These words were followed by total silence; the youth slept no mcre; and the next morning he went to relate to the priest and his family the vision of the night. The priest and some of the neighbors advised him to give up his property; but a young kinsman, just come from school, maintained that the dead do not come back again, and that the possessors of national property are no more likely to have their feet dragged by ghosts than their neighbors. Then taking the young heir aside, he offered to lie in the bed in his place, if he would keep it a secret, and would promise to wait one day more before he gave up the property. This proposal was accepted, and the young kinsman took possession of the other youth's bed for that night. Between twelve and one o'clock, he heard some person gently open the window, and at the same time beheld a phantom enter, who came up as if to speak to him with a threatening gesture. "So far so good;" said he, mentally, "as he mistakes me for another person, spirits are not omniscient." He then slipped out of bed as quietly as he could, seized the phantom with both his hands, and threw him in a moment into a little dark closet, which he shut and locked very carefully. The specter finding himself a prisoner, began to cry out for mercy; but the youth went to call in his neighbors, who soon recognized, in the semblance of a ghost, a young abbe, who, although as yet only in deacon's orders, had been desirous to give a proof of his zeal for the church of Rome.

OLD COOKE, THE MISER.

There was no greater pest to the medical tribe than old Cooke, the misér. Many are the anecdotes of the tricks this avaricious old man used to play, to cheat medical men and save his money: such as putting on ragged clothes, and going as a pauper to Mr. Saunders and other gentlemen, to have gratuitous advice for his eyes—getting a letter for the dispensary, and attending there as a decayed tradesman, for several weeks, until detected.

Having a wound in his leg, he employed a Mr. Pigeon, that lived nearly opposite to him, in White-lion-street, Pentonville, to cure it. "How long do you think it will be before you can cure it?" "A month." "And how much must I give you?" Pigeon, who saw the wound was not of any great importance, answered, "A guinea."

"Very well," replied Cooke; "but mark this — a guinea is an immense sum of money, and when I agree for sums of such magnitude, I go upon the system of *no cure, no pay;* so, if I am not cured by the expiration of the month, I pay you nothing." This was agreed to: after diligent attendance for several days, the wound was so near being healed, that Cooke expressed himself satisfied, and would not let Pigeon see it any more. However, within two or three days of the month being up, the old fellow got some sort of plaster with euphorbium in it, from a farrier, and made a new wound on the place, where the former had been, and, sending for Pigeon on the last day of the month, showed him that his leg was not well, and that, of course, the guinea he had agreed for was *forfeited.* This story the old fellow used to tell of himself with great satisfaction, and used to call it "plucking a Pigeon."

When on his death-bed, he sent for several medical men (some would not attend); among those who went to him, Mr. Aldridge, of Pentonville, was one. Him he permitted to send some medicine. At one of the interviews he earnestly entreated Mr. Aldridge to tell him candidly, how long he thought he might live. The anwer was, he might probably last six days. Cooke, collecting all his strength, and starting up in bed, exclaimed: "Are you not a dishonest man?—a rogue, a robber, to serve me so!" "As how?" asked Mr. Aldridge, with surprise. "Why, sir, you are no better than a pick-pocket; to go to rob me of my gold, by sending in two draughts a day to a man that all your physic will not keep alive above six days! Get out of my house and never come near me again!"

CONVERTING THE SCOLDS.

In an early period of the ministry of the Rev. John Wesley, he visited Epworth, in Lincolnshire, where his father had formerly been minister, but found the people greatly opposed to what they considered his new notions. He tells us in his journal, that many persons were convinced of the importance of the truths he delivered from the tombstone of his father, some of whom were conveyed in a wagon to a neighboring justice of the peace to answer for the heresy with which they were charged. Mr. Wesley rode over also. When the magistrate asked what these persons had done, there was a deep silence; for that was a point their conductors had forgotten. At length one of them said, "Why, they pretend to be better than other people; and beside, they pray from morning to night." He asked, "But have they done any thing beside?" "Yes," said an old man. "an't please your worship, they have *convarted* my wife. Till she went among them she had such a tongue; and now she is as quiet as a lamb." "Carry them back, carry them back," replied the justice, "and let them convert all the scolds in the town."

THE LAWYERS' PATRON.

St. Evona, a lawyer of Britain, went to Rome, to entreat the pope to give the lawyers of that country a *patron*, to which the pope replied, that he knew of no saint, but what was disposed of to other *professions*. At this Evona was very sad, and earnestly begged the pope to think of them. At last his holiness proposed to St. Evona, that he should go round the church of San Giovanni di Laterano *blindfold*, and after he should have said a certain number of Ave Marias, that the first saint he should lay hold of should be his patron. This the good old lawyer willingly undertook, and at the end of his Ave Marias, stopped at St. Michael's altar, where he laid hold of the *devil*, under St. Michael's feet, and cried out, "this is our *saint*, let him be our *patron*." Being unblinded, and seeing what a patron he had chosen, he went to his lodgings so dejected, that a few months after he died. His reputation for honesty was, however, so great, that a witty *Frenchman* wrote upon his tomb at Rome, "St. Evona un Breton avocat non larron, halleluiah."

WILLIAM LADD AND HIS NEIGHBOR.

"I HAD," the Apostle of Peace used to say, in relating the anecdote, "a fine field of grain, growing upon an out-farm at some distance from the homestead. Whenever I rode by I saw my neighbor Pulsifer's sheep in the lot, destroying my hopes of a harvest. These sheep were of the gaunt, long-legged kind, active as spaniels; they would spring over the highest fence, and no partition-wall could keep them out. I complained to neighbor Pulsifer about them, sent him frequent messages, but all without avail. Perhaps they would be kept out for a day or two; but the legs of his sheep were long, and my grain more tempting than the adjoining pasture. I rode by again—the sheep were still there; I became angry, and told my men to set the dogs on them; and if that would not do, I would pay them if they would shoot the sheep.

"I rode away much agitated; for I was not so much of a peace man then as I am now, and I felt literally full of fight. All at once a light flashed in upon me. I asked myself, 'Would it not be well for you to try in your own conduct the peace principle you are teaching to others?' I thought it all over, and settled down in my mind as to the best course to be pursued.

"The next day I rode over to see neighbor Pulsifer. I found him chopping wood at his door. 'Good morning, neighbor!' No answer. 'Good morning!' I repeated. He gave a kind of grunt without looking up. 'I came,' continued I, 'to see about the sheep.' At this, he threw down his ax and exclaimed, in an angry manner: 'Now are n't you a pretty neighbor, to tell your men to kill my sheep? I heard of it; a rich man, like you, to shoot a poor man's sheep!'

"'I was wrong, neighbor,' said I; 'but it won't do to let your sheep eat up all that grain; so I came over to say that I would take your sheep to my homestead pasture and put them in with mine; and in the fall you may take them back, and if any one is missing you may take your pick out of my whole flock.'

"Pulsifer looked confounded; he did not know how to take me. At last he stammered out: 'Now, 'Squire, are you in earnest?' 'Certainly I am,' I answered; 'it is better for me to feed your sheep in my pasture on grass, than to feed them here on grain; and I see the fence can't keep them out.'

"After a moment's silence, 'The sheep shan't trouble you any more,' exclaimed Pulsifer. 'I will fetter them all. But I'll let you know that, when any man talks of shooting, I can shoot, too; and when they are kind and neighborly, I can be kind, too.' The sheep never again trespassed on my lot. And, my friends," he would continue, addressing the audience, "remember that when you talk of injuring your neighbors, they will talk of injuring you. When nations threaten to fight, other nations will be ready, too. Love will beget love; a wish to be at peace will keep you in peace. You can overcome evil with good. There is no other way."

THE DUELIST OUTWITTED.

The Rev. J. Cooke, of Maidenhead, many years ago, published a very interesting pamphlet, containing the dying confession of a deist, under the title of, "Reason paying homage to Revelation." Soon after its publication, a great commotion was excited in Maidenhead and its neighborhood. The brother of the deceased gentleman conceived himself injured, and sent a message to Mr. Cooke, demanding the satisfaction of a gentleman. Mr. C. replied, "I am quite prepared to give Mr. —— the satisfaction of a Christian gentleman; and, according to the laws of honor, as he has sent the challenge, it rests with me to choose time, place, and weapons. I do not choose to fight with pistols; my weapon is a sword; and if he will meet me in this parlor to-morrow at noon, with any witnesses he may desire, I shall be prepared to meet him with 'the sword of the Spirit, which is the word of God.' My character, my principles, my office, forbid me using any other weapons." It need not be added that his opponent did not admire this method of meeting the challenge, and Mr. Cooke heard no more of him.

COBBETT'S RECOMMENDATION.

Cobbett, when challenged to fight, recommended the challenger to draw a Cobbett in chalk upon the floor, and if he succeeded in hitting it, to send him instant word, in order that he might have an opportunity of acknowledging that, had the true Cobbett been there, he, in all probability, would have been hit, too. But hit or no hit, the bullets could have no effect whatever, he maintained, on the original causes of the quarrel.

ANSWERING A CHALLENGE MATHEMATICALLY.

The eccentric mathematician, Professor Vince, of King's College, Cambridge, being once engaged in a conversation with a gentleman who advocated "dueling," is said to have thrown his adversary completely *hors du combat*, by the following 'cute and characteristic reply to his question: "But what could you do, sir, if a man told you to your face, 'You lie?'" "What could I do? why I wouldn't knock him down, but I'd tell him to prove it. Prove it, sir, *prove it*, I'd say. If he couldn't, he'd be the liar, and there I should have him; but, if he did prove that I lied, I must e'en pocket the affront; and there I expect the matter would end."

LORD TENTERDEN'S RETORT.

THE obscurity of Lord Tenterden's birth is well known, but he had too much good sense to feel any false shame on that account. We have heard it related of him, that when in an early period of his professional career, a brother barrister, with whom he happened to have a quarrel, had the bad taste to twit him on his origin, his manly and severe answer was, "Yes, sir, I am the son of a barber; if you had been the son of a barber, you would have been a barber yourself."

THE POPE AND THE AMBASSADORS.

IT is related of Pope Clement XIV (Ganganelli), that when he ascended the papal chair, the ambassadors of the several states represented at his court waited on him with their congratulations. When they were introduced and bowed, he returned the compliment by bowing also; on which the master of the ceremonies told his highness that he should not have returned their salute. "O, I beg your pardon," said the good pontiff, "I have not been pope long enough to forget good manners."

CICERO'S RETORT.

THIS Roman orator was one day sneered at by one of his opponents, a mean man of noble lineage, on account of his low parentage. "You are the *first* of your line," said the railer; "and you," rejoined Cicero, "are the *last* of yours."

I DO NOT MEAN THAT.

A GENTLEMAN who had been conspicuous in aiding a missionary collection, was met the following day by one of dissimilar habits, who chided him for the absurd eccentricity of which he deemed him guilty in giving to such an object and in such profusion. It was preposterous, he said, to be sending heaps of money abroad, to be spent, no one knew how, while there were so many unemployed and starving in ——. "I will give —— pounds to the poor of —— if you will give an equal sum;" said the Christian friend. "I did not mean that," replied the objector; "but," continued he, "if you must go from home, why so far? Think of the miserable poor of Ireland." "I will give —— pounds to the poor of Ireland, if you will give the same." "I do not mean that either," was the reply. No, it is neither *this* nor *that*, which this class of objectors exactly mean; but simply to vail their criminal parsimony by excepting against the proceedings of liberal men, whom, if they could not condemn, they must, for very shame, in some degree imitate.

KING HENRY AND THE POOR CITIZEN.

Henry IV, of France, was standing one day with some of his courtiers, at the entrance of a village, and a poor man passing by bowed down to the very ground; and the king, with great condescension, returned his salutation just in the same manner; at which one of his attendants ventured to express his surprise, when the monarch finely replied to him,—"Would you have your king exceeded in politeness by one of the lowest of his subjects?"

THE RECTOR AND THE POOR BOY.

An indigent boy applied for alms at the house of an avaricious rector, and received a dry mouldy crust. The rector inquired of the boy if he could say the Lord's Prayer, and was answered in the negative. "Then," said the rector, "I will teach you that." "Our Father!" "*Our* Father!" said the boy, "is he *my* Father as well as *yours?*" "Yes, certainly." "Then," replied the boy, "*how could you give your poor brother this mouldy crust of bread?*"

THE CAPTAIN'S REQUEST.

"My lads," said a captain, when about to take command of a ship, reading his orders to the crew on the quarter-deck, "there is one law I am determined to make, and I shall insist on its being kept. It is a favor, indeed, I will ask of you, and which, as a British officer, I expect will be granted by a crew of British seamen. What say you, my lads? are you willing to grant your new captain one favor?" "Ay, ay," cried all hands, "let's know what it is, sir."

"Well, my lads, it is this: that you must allow me to swear the first oath in this ship. No man on board must swear an oath before I do; I am determined to swear the first oath on board. What say you, my lads, will you grant me this favor?" The men stared, and stood for a moment quite at a loss what to say. "They were taken," one said, "all aback." "They were brought up," said another, "all standing." The appeal seemed so reasonable, and the manner of the captain so kind and prepossessing, that a general burst from the ship's company answered, "Ay, ay, sir," with their usual three cheers. Swearing was thus wholly abolished in the ship.

THE UNFASHIONABLE BOW.

WHEN Sir William Johnson returned the salute of a negro who had bowed to him, he was reminded that he had done what was very unfashionable. "Perhaps so," said Sir William, "but I would not be outdone in good manners by a negro."

FAITH OF THE COLLIER.

IMPLICIT faith has been sometimes styled *fides carbonaria*, from the story of one who, examining an ignorant collier on his religious principles, asked him what it was that he believed. He answered, "I believe what the church believes." The other rejoined, "What, then, does the church believe?" He replied, readily, "The church believes what I believe." The other, desirous, if possible, to bring him to particulars, once more resumed his inquiry. "Tell me, then, I pray you, what it is which you and the church *both* believe." The only answer the collier could give was, "Why, truly, sir, the church and I *both*—believe the same thing."

THE MONK AND THE MAGPIE.

ST. ANTHONY is thought to have had a great command over fire, and the power of destroying by that element those who incurred his displeasure. A certain monk of St. Anthony one day assembled his congregation under a tree where a magpie had built her nest, into which he had found means to convey a small box filled with gunpowder, and out of the box hung a long, thin match that was to burn slowly, and that was hidden among the leaves of the trees. As soon as the monk or his assistant had touched the match with a lighted coal, the friar began his sermon; in the meanwhile the magpie returned to her nest, and finding in it a strange body which she could not remove, she fell into a passion and scratched with her feet most vehemently. The friar affected to hear without emotion, and continued his sermon with great composure, only he would now and then lift up his eyes toward the top of the tree, as if he wanted to know what was the matter. At last, when he judged that the match was near reaching the gunpowder, he pretended to be out of patience; he cursed the magpie, wished St. Anthony's fire might consume her, and went on again with his sermon. But he had scarcely proceeded two or three periods, when the match on a sudden produced its effect, and blew up the magpie with its nest; which miracle wonderfully raised the character of the friar, and proved afterward very beneficial to him and his convent.

MIRACLE OF THE OMELET.

A PRIEST in extreme poverty resolved to get credit for a miracle. He put the yolks of several eggs in a hollow cane, and stopped the end with butter; then, walking into an alehouse, he begged to fry a single egg for his dinner. The smallness of his repast excited curiosity, and they gave him a morsel of lard. He stirred the lard with his cane, and, to the wonder of the surrounding peasants, produced a handsome omelet. This miracle established his fame; he sold omelets and got rich by his ingenuity.

SENIOR WRANGLER.

THE Senior Wrangler, of a certain year, piping hot from the Senate House at Cambridge, went to the play at Drury-Lane. It so happened, that a certain great personage entered at the same moment, on the other side of the house, but *unobserved* by the mathematician. The whole house testified their respect, by a general rising and clapping of hands. Our astonished academic instantly exclaimed, to the no small amusement of his London friends, "Well, well, this is more than I expected; how is it possible that these good people should so soon have discovered *that I am the Senior Wrangler.*"

THE BEDLAMITE.

IT proceeds rather from revenge than malice, when we hear a man affirm that all the world are knaves. For before a man draws this conclusion of the world, the world has usually anticipated him, and concluded all this of him who makes the observation. Such men may be compared to Brothers, the *prophet*, who, on being asked how he came to be clapped up into Bedlam, replied, I and the world happened to have a slight difference of opinion; the world said I was mad, and I said the world was mad; I was *outvoted*, and here I am.

SOME *reputed* saints that have been canonized, ought to have been cannonaded; and some *reputed* sinners that have been cannonaded, ought to have been canonized.

AN Irishman fights before he reasons, a Scotchman reasons before he fights, an Englishman is not particular as to the order of precedence, but will do either to accommodate his customers. A modern general has said, that the best troops would be as follows: an Irishman half drunk, a Scotchman half starved, and an Englishman with his belly full.

IF you cannot avoid a quarrel with a blackguard, let your lawyer manage it, rather than yourself. No man sweeps his own chimney, but employs a chimney-sweeper, who has no objection to dirty work, because it is his trade.

HE DOES NOT UNDERSTAND A JOKE.

THERE are many good-natured fellows, who have paid the forfeit of their lives to their love of bantering and raillery. No doubt they have had much diversion, but they have purchased it too dear. Although their wit and their brilliancy may have been often extolled, yet it has at last been extinguished forever; and by a foe, perhaps, who has neither the one nor the other, but who found it easier to point a sword than a repartee. I have heard of a man in the province of Bengal, who had been a long time very successful in hunting the tiger. His skill gained him great eclat, and insured him much diversion; at length he narrowly escaped with his life; he then relinquished the sport, with this observation: "Tiger hunting is very fine amusement, so long as we hunt the tiger; but it is rather awkward when the tiger takes it into his head to hunt us." Again, this skill in small wit, like skill in small arms, is very apt to beget a confidence which may prove fatal in the end. We may either mistake the proper moment, for even cowards have their fighting days, or we may mistake the proper man. A certain Savoyard got his livelihood by exhibiting a monkey and a bear; he gained so much applause from his tricks with the monkey, that he was encouraged to practice some of them on the bear; he was dreadfully lacerated, and on being rescued with great difficulty from the gripe of bruin, he exclaimed: "What a fool was I not to distinguish between a monkey and a bear! A bear, my friends, is a very grave kind of personage, and as you plainly see, does not understand a joke!"

AN INTERMITTENT.

It is better to have recourse to a quack, if he can cure our disorder, although he cannot explain it, than to a physician, if he can explain our disease, but cannot cure it. In a certain consultation of physicians, they all differed about the nature of an intermittent, and all of them were ready to define the disorder. The patient was a king. At length an empiric, who had been called in, thus interposed: "Gentlemen, you all seem to differ about the nature of an intermittent, permit me to explain it: an intermittent, gentlemen, is a disorder which I can cure, and which you cannot."

DID NOT HE SAY BEANS?

Two travelers put up for the night at a tavern. Early in the morning they absconded without reckoning with their host, also stealing from him a bag of beans. A few years after they passed that road in company again. Again they asked for lodgings at the same inn. The identical landlord was yet at his post. In the evening the landlord was busy in one corner of the bar-room, talking in a suppressed voice with one of his neighbors, about a swarm of bees. His two dishonest guests were seated in another part of the room, and indistinctly hearing the talk about bees, one says to the other, "Did he not say beans?" "I think he did," was the reply; and quickly they were missing.

WHITEFIELD AND ELECTIONS.

When Mr. Whitefield was in the zenith of his popularity, Lord Clare, who knew that his influence was considerable, applied to him, by letter, requesting his assistance at Bristol, at the ensuing general election. To this request Mr. Whitefield replied, that in general elections he never interfered; but he would earnestly exhort his lordship to use great diligence to make his own particular calling and election sure!

NEW USE FOR JACOB'S LADDER.

A Welsh clergyman, invited to assist in the ordination of a minister in some part of England, was appointed to deliver the address to the church and congregation; and having been informed that their previous minister had suffered much from pecuniary embarrassment, although the church was fully able to support him comfortably, he took the following singular method of administering reproof.

In his address to the church, he remarked: "You have been praying, no doubt, that God would send you a man after his own heart to be your pastor. You have done well. God, we hope, has heard your prayer, and given you such a minister as he approves, who will go in and out before you, and feed your souls with the bread of life. But now you have prayed for a minister, and God has given you one to your mind, you have something more to do; you must take care of him; and in order to his being happy among you, I have been thinking you have need to pray again. 'Pray again? Pray again? What should we pray again for?' Well, I think you have need to pray again. 'But for what?' Why, I'll tell you. Pray that God would put Jacob's ladder down to the earth again. 'Jacob's ladder! Jacob's ladder! What has Jacob's ladder to do with our minister?' Why, I think if God would put Jacob's ladder down, that your minister could go up into heaven on the Sabbath evening after preaching, and remain there all the week; then he could come down every Sabbath morning so spiritually minded and so full of heaven, that he would preach to you almost like an angel. 'Oh, yes, that may be all very well; and, if it were possible, we should like it; but then, we need our minister with us during the week, to attend prayer-meetings, visit the sick, hear experience, etc., etc., and therefore must have him always with us; we want the whole of his time and attention.' That may be, and I will admit the necessity of his daily attention to your concerns; but then, you will remember, that if he remains here he must have his bread and cheese; and I have been told that your former minister was often wanting the common necessaries of life, while many of you can enjoy its luxuries; and, therefore, I thought, if God would put Jacob's ladder down, your present minister might preach to you on the Sabbath, and by going up into heaven after the services of the day, save you the painful necessity of supporting him."

SENDING TO HEAVEN FOR A MINISTER.

The people of one of the out-parishes of Virginia, wrote to Dr. Rice, who was then at the head of the Theological Seminary in Prince Edward, for a minister. They said they wanted a man of first-rate *talents*, for they had run down considerably, and needed building up. They wanted one who could *write* well, for some of the young people were very nice about that matter. They wanted one who could *visit* a good deal, for their former minister had neglected that, and they wanted to bring that up. They wanted a man of very *gentlemanly deportment*, for some thought a great deal of that. And so they went on, describing a perfect minister. The last thing they mentioned was—they gave their last minister $350 ; but if the doctor would send them such a man as they had described, they would raise another $50, making it $400. The doctor sat right down and wrote them a reply, telling them they had better forthwith make out a call for old Dr. Dwight, in heaven ; for he did not know of any one in this world who answered this description. And as Dr. Dwight had been living so long on spiritual food, he might not need so much for the body, and possibly he might live on $400.

PREACHING ON THE TIMES.

In 1648, it was a question asked of the brethren, at the meetings of ministers, twice in the year, "If they preached the duties of the times?" And when it was found that Leighton did not, he was reproved for his omission ; but he replied, "If all the brethren have preached on the *times*, may not one poor brother be suffered to preach on *eternity?*"

HALL'S OPINION OF A SERMON.

A conceited minister having once delivered a sermon in the hearing of Mr. Hall, pressed him, with a disgusting union of self-complacency and indelicacy, to state what he thought of the sermon. Mr. Hall remained silent for some time, hoping that his silence would be rightly interpreted ; but this only caused the question to be pressed with greater earnestness. Mr. Hall at length said, "There was one very fine passage, sir." "I am rejoiced to hear you say so. "Pray, sir, which was it?" "Why, sir, it was the passage from the pulpit into the vestry."

BARROW AND ROCHESTER.

The celebrated Lord Rochester one day met Dr. Barrow in the Park, and being determined, as he said, to put down *the rusty piece of divinity*, accosted him by taking off his hat, and, with a profound bow, exclaimed, "Doctor, I am yours to my shoe-tie." The doctor perceiving his aim, returned the salute with equal ceremony: "My lord, I am yours to the ground." His lordship then made a deeper congee, and said, "Doctor, I am yours to the center." Barrow replied, with the same ceremony, "My lord, I am yours to the antipodes;" on which Rochester made another attempt, by exclaiming, "Doctor, I am yours to the lowest pit of hell." "There, my lord," said Barrow, "I leave you," and immediately walked away.

THE SPIRITUAL MONK.

A CERTAIN brother came to the convent of Mount Sinai, and finding all the monks at work, shook his head, and said to the abbot, "Labor not for the meat which perisheth," and, "Mary hath chosen that good part." "Very well," said the abbot, and ordered the good brother to a cell, and gave him a book to read. The monk retired, and sat hour after hour all day long alone; wondering much that nobody called him to dinner, or offered him any refreshment. Hungry, and wearied out, the night at length arrived: he left his solitary cell and repaired to the apartment of the abbot. "Father," says he, "do not the brethren eat to-day?"

"Oh, yes," replied the abbot, "they have eaten plentifully." "Then how is it, father," said the monk, "that you did not call me to partake with them?" "Because, brother," replied the abbot, "you are a *spiritual man*, and have no need of carnal food. For our part, we are obliged to eat, and on that account we work; but you, brother, who have chosen 'the good part,' you sit and read all the day long, and are above the want of the meat that perisheth." "Pardon me, father," said the monk, "I perceive my mistake."

No two things differ more than hurry and despatch. Hurry is the mark of a weak mind, despatch of a strong one. A weak man in office, like a squirrel in a cage, is laboring eternally, but to no purpose, and in constant motion without getting on a jot; like a turnstile, he is in everybody's way but stops nobody; he talks a great deal, but says very little; looks into everything, but sees into nothing; and has a hundred irons in the fire, but very few of them are hot, and with those few that are, he only burns his fingers.

KEEN RETORT.

COUNT STACKELBERG was sent on a particular embassy by Catharine of Russia, into Poland; on the same occasion, Thurgut was despatched by the emperor of Germany. Both these ambassadors were strangers to each other. When the morning appointed for an audience arrived, Thurgut was ushered into a magnificent saloon, where, seeing a dignified looking man seated and attended by a number of

Polish noblemen, who were standing most respectfully before him, the German ambassador (Thurgut,) concluded it was the king, and addressed him as such, with the accustomed formalities. This dignified looking creature turned out to be Stackelberg, who received the unexpected homage with pride and silence. Soon after the king entered the presence-chamber, and Thurgut, perceiving his mistake, retired, much mortified and ashamed. In the evening, it so happened that both these ambassadors were playing cards at the same table with his majesty. The German envoy threw down a card, saying, "The king of clubs!' "A mistake!" said the monarch; "it is the knave!" "Pardon me, sire," exclaimed Thurgut, casting a significant glance at Stackelberg; "this is the second time to-day I have mistaken a knave for a king!" Stackelberg, though very prompt at repartee, bit his lips, and was silent.

EARL OF BERKELY AND THE HIGHWAYMAN.

It is recorded of the late Earl of Berkely, that he was suddenly awakened at night in his carriage by a highwayman, who forcing a pistol through the window, and presenting it close to his breast, demanded his money, exclaiming at the same time, that he had heard his lordship had boasted that he never would be robbed by a *single* highwayman, but that he should now be taught the contrary. His lordship putting his hand into his pocket, replied: "Neither would I now be robbed, if it was not for that fellow who is looking over your shoulder." The highwayman turned round his head, when his lordship, who had drawn a pistol from his pocket, instead of a purse, shot him on the spot.

JESUITS.

It was observed of the Jesuits, that they constantly inculcated a thorough contempt of worldly things in their doctrines, but eagerly grasped at them in their lives. They were *"wise in their generation,"* for they cried down worldly things, because they wanted to obtain them, and cried up spiritual things, because they wanted to dispose of them.

RHEUMATISM.

"What keeps our friend farmer B. away from us?" was the anxious question proposed by our vigilant minister to his clerk. "I have not seen him amongst us," continued he, "these three weeks; I hope that it is not Socinianism that keeps him away." "No, your honor," replied the clerk, "it is something worse than that."

"Worse than Socinianism! God forbid it should be deism." "No, your honor, it is something worse than that." "Worse than deism! Astonishing! I trust it is not atheism!" "No, your honor, it is something worse than that." "Worse than atheism! impossible; nothing can be worse than atheism!" "Yes it is, your honor, it is *rheumatism!*"

A PENITENT ROGUE.

A Roman Catholic, who had filled up the measure of his iniquities, as far as he dared, went to the priest to confess and obtain absolution. He entered the apartment of the priest, and addressed him: "Holy father, I have sinned."

The priest bid him kneel before the penitential chair. The penitent was looking about, and he saw the priest's gold watch lying upon the table within his reach. He seized it and put it in his bosom. The priest approached him, and requested him to acknowledge the sins for which he wished absolution.

"Father," said the rogue, "I have stolen, and what shall I do?"

"Restore," said the priest, "the thing you have stolen to its rightful owner."

"Do you take it?" said the penitent.

"No, I shall not," said the priest; you must give it to the owner."

"But he has refused to take it."

"If this be the case you may keep it."

The priest granted him full absolution. The penitent knelt and kissed his hand, craved his benediction, crossed himself, and departed with a *clear* conscience, and a very valuable gold watch into the bargain.

THE CHEATER CHEATED.

There is no end to the dishonest tricks of professional gamblers. One of these gentry will often deal himself six or seven cards when he should have but five, and if he can make a good hand by laying out the two poorest in his lap, he will do so; or if he cannot make a good hand, he will take the two best to help him in his next hand. The following case, which occurred on a western steamboat, shows how men will play more than their number. A gambler was playing with a man whom he mistook for a green Hoosier that knew nothing of playing scientifically. But he was sadly deceived. The gambler, from the beginning, played somewhat carelessly, supposing it needed no science to beat the Hoosier; but the gambler lost, and commenced playing as scientifically as he could. He still lost, and finally lost nearly all he had, before he quit; and after quitting they went to the bar to drink. The gambler said to the Hoosier, "You beat any man for luck I ever played with; I've lost my money with you, and it makes no difference; I will be honest with you; you did not know it, but I played six cards all the time, and your luck beat it." "Well," said the Hoosier, "since you have been so frank, I will also be frank; I have played seven cards all the way through from the word go; besides stocking and palming occasionally for the sake of variety." The gambler was greatly surprised, and swore that he would not have supposed, that he much more than knew one card from another; but he was deceived in the man, and it would not have done for him to have shown any anger, as he first confessed having cheated the Hoosier, who was in fact a most expert gambler, and had purposely assumed that disguise.

MARLBORO' AND HIS SERVANT.

The Duke of Marlborough possessed great command of temper, and never permitted it to be ruffled by little things, in which even the greatest men have occasionally been found unguarded. As he was one day riding wtth Commissary Marriot, it began to rain, and he called to his servant for his cloak. The servant not bringing it immediately, he called for it again. The servant being embarrassed with the straps and buckles, did not come up to him. At last, it raining very hard, the duke called to him again, and asked him what he was about, that he did not bring his cloak. "You may stay, sir," grumbled the fellow, "if it rains cats and dogs, till I can get at it." The duke turned round to Marriot, and said, very coolly, "Now I would not be of that fellow's temper for all the world."

RELICS AT AIX LA CHAPELLE.

Doctor Raffles, in his tour through Europe, in 1817, visited the church of the Minorites in Aix La Chapelle. After describing sundry antiquities, among which were "the remains of one of the children whom Herod killed in the hope of destroying Christ," he proceeds:

"All this was interesting, but the cream of the antiquities yet remained. We were conducted to the vestry, or robing place of the priest, where a young man, whose province it is to expose these wonders to the gaze of the credulous, threw open the curiously painted doors of an immense recess, where in an instant we were dazzled with a profusion of gold and precious stones, wrought into various forms, to contain or emblazon the precious and sacred relics.

* * * * We were shown, 1. The girdle of Jesus Christ, brought from Jerusalem by Charlemagne, and with that monarch's seal annexed to it. 2. Girdle of the Virgin Mary, derived from the same quarter. 3. A bone of the Virgin Mary's father. 4. A bit of the cord with which Jesus was bound when he was scourged. 5. A

prickle from the crown of thorns. 6 A bit of the sponge with which they supplied the vinegar. 7. A bit of one of the nails by which he was fastened to the cross. 8. And lastly, some *sweat* which fell from him in the garden of Gethsemane. To this may be added a link of the chain with which Peter was chained at Rome! a bit of the bone of Simeon's arm, with which he embraced the infant Jesus! a rib of St. Stephen! and a tooth of St. Thomas!"

I thought of the sailor, who, after his messmates had told some wonderful stories of what had been found in the bellies of whales and sharks, and such monsters, determining to outstrip them all, said he had once been present at the catching of a fish, out of whose belly, when opened, there came a ship, with all its masts and rigging, and the whole of the crew.

DRAWING AN INFERENCE.

A young clergyman who had delivered a discourse in the place of an aged brother minister, requested the opinion of the latter respecting it.

"Oh," said he, plainly, "many of the words you used were beyond the comprehension of your hearers. Thus, for instance, the word 'inference,' perhaps not half of my parishioners understand its meaning." "Inference, inference!" exclaimed the other, "why, every one must understand that." "I think you will find it not so. There's my clerk, now; he prides himself upon his learning, and in truth, is very intelligent; we will try him. Zechariah, my brother here wishes you to draw an inference; can you do it?"

"Why, I am pretty strong, but Johanadab, the coachman, is stronger than I; I'll ask him." Zechariah went out a few moments, to look after the coachman, and returned. "Johanadab says he never has tried to draw an inference, sir; but he reckons his horses can draw any thing that the traces will hold!"

A NOBLEMAN REPROVED BY HIS SERVANT.

A nobleman seeing a large stone lying near his gate, ordered his servant, with an oath, to send it to hell. "If," said the servant, "I were to throw it to heaven, it would be more completely out of your lordship's way."

TARRYING AT JERICHO.

A very young clergyman who had just left college, presented a petition to the king of Prussia, requesting that his majesty would appoint him inspector in a certain place where a vacancy had just happened. As it was an office of much consequence, the king was offended at the presumption and importunity of so young a man, and instead of any answer to the petition, he wrote underneath, "2 book of Samuel, chap. x. ver. 5," and returned it. The young clergyman was eager to examine the quotation, but, to his great disappointment, found the words, "Tarry at Jericho until your beards be grown."

WHERE YOU OUGHT TO HAVE BEEN.

A CLERGYMAN who was in the habit of preaching in different parts of the country, was once at an inn, where he observed a horse-jockey trying to take in a simple gentleman, by imposing upon him a broken-winded horse for a sound one. The parson knew the bad character of the jockey, and taking the gentleman aside, told him to be cautious of the person he was dealing with. The gentleman finally declined the purchase, and the jockey, quite nettled, observed, "Parson, I would much rather hear you preach than see you privately interfere in bargains between man and man, in this way." "Well," replied the parson, "if you had been where you ought to have been last Sunday, you might have heard me preach." "Where was that?" inquired the jockey. "In the state prison," returned the clergyman.

LORENZO DOW AND THE THIEF.

THE celebrated itinerant preacher, Lorenzo Dow, while traveling one Sunday to the place where he had an appointment to preach, in passing a house, overheard a man who was standing at the door, swearing bitterly. Dow went up to him and inquired the cause. The man answered that he had an ax stolen the night before by some person. "Come along with me to meeting," said the preacher, "and I will find your ax." The man consented, and when they arrived near the church, Dow stopped and picked up a pretty large stone, which he carried with him into church, and laid upon the front of the pulpit. The subject of his sermon was very well fitted to his particular object, and when in the middle of it he stopped short, took the stone in his hand, and raising it with a threatening attitude, said, "A man in this neighborhood had an ax stolen last night, and if the person who stole it doesn't dodge, *I will hit him on the forehead with this stone*," at the same time making a violent effort to throw it, when a person present was observed to dodge his head violently, and it scarce need be added, proved to be the guilty person!

HANDSOMELY DECLINED.

THE late Bishop Doane of New Jersey, was strongly opposed to temperance, and his side-board and tables were loaded with brandy, wine, etc.

On one occasion, Rev. Mr. Perkins, of the Sons of Temperance, dined with the Bishop, who, pouring out a glass of wine, desired him to drink with him.

"Can't do it, Bishop! 'Wine is a mocker.'"

"Take a glass of brandy then."

"Can't do it Bishop! 'Strong drink is raging.'"

By this time the Bishop, becoming somewhat restive and excited, remarked to Mr. Perkins:

"You'll pass the decanter to the gentleman next to you?"

"No, Bishop, I can't do that! 'Wo unto him that putteth the bottle to his neighbor's lips.'"

ELECTRIC MARRIAGE.

THE telegraph between Paris and Havre lately concluded a marriage worthy of this fast age:

Lover.—"Saw your daughter last night. Party. What dowry?"

Father.—"Fifty thousand francs."

Lover.—"Not enough."

Father.—"How much?"

Lover.—"Hundred thousand."

Father.—"Can't come to it."

Lover.—"Sorry; love her; rich; say eighty thousand."

Father.—"All right."

Lover.—"Offer heart and hand."

Father.—"Accepted."

Lover.—"Leave by 2.40 train."

Father.—"Ordered wedding dress."

Lover.—"Eternal love to daughter."

Father.—"Of course."

HOW NOVELS ARE WRITTEN.

ALEXANDRE DUMAS published some time ago in a daily Paris paper, a novel, in which the heroine, prosperous and happy, is assailed by consumption. All the gradual symptoms were most touchingly described, and the greatest interest was felt for the heroine.

One day the Marquis de Dalomieu called on him. "Dumas," said he, "have you composed the end of the story now publishing in the——."

"Of course."

"Does the heroine die at the end?"

"Of course, dies of consumption. After such symptoms as I have described, how could she live?"

"You will have to make her live. You must change the catastrophe."

"I cannot."

"Yes, you must; for on your heroine's life depends my daughter's."

"Your daughter's!"

"Yes; she has all the various symptoms of consumption you have described, and watches mournfully for every new number of your novel, reading her own fate in your heroine's. Now, if you make your heroine live, my daughter, whose imagination has been deeply impressed, will live too. Come, a life to save is a temptation."

"Not to be resisted."

Dumas changed his last chapters. His heroine recovered and was happy.

About five years afterwards Dumas met the Marquis at a party.

"Ah! Dumas," he exclaimed, "let me introduce you to my daughter; she owes her life to you. There she is."

"That fine, handsome woman, who looks like Jeanne d'Arc?"

"Yes, she is married, and has had four children."

"And my novel four editions," said Dumas; "so we are quits."

BREAD AND BABIES.

We are constantly asked, if women vote, what will become of the bread and babies?

In view of the heavy bread, and badly cooked food we find on most tables, and the shocking mortality among infants, we contemplate with wonder and pity the blind faith of man, in the maternal and culinary intelligence of the "weak-minded," who have no aspirations beyond Hecker's flour, Mrs. Winslow's soothing syrup, and Wheeler and Wilson's sewing machine. Seeing that women have devoted themselves through the ages to domestic economy, and failed, as miserably as men have in the art of government, we have, after mature thought, come to the conclusion, that just as womans' enlightened interest in political questions will improve the state, so man's skill and science are necessary to redeem the home from its present disorder, disease and death. If there are two things we thoroughly understand they are babies and bread, and for our knowledge of both these divine arts we are indebted to philosophical, scientific gentlemen.

The only valuable work we ever saw on infancy was written by a man, Andrew Combe, of Scotland, a close observer, a sound thinker, and a learned physiologist. We shall never forget how tempest-tossed we were when we first found ourself the happy possessor of a male child, without the slightest knowledge of what to do for his comfort and protection. An ignorant nurse fidgeted round the room day and night, sang melancholy ditties, and rocked vehemently, while the child cried continually, with a loud voice, and we wept, prayed, and philosophized by turns. Reasoning on general principles, we at last came to the conclusion that inasmuch as the child was large and vigorous, there must be some mistake on the part of the nurse, that he was not quiet and comfortable, and we fortified ourself in that opinion by a faitnful reading of what Mr. Combe had to say on babies in general. The result of this consideration of his opinions, was a prompt revolution in the whole nursery department, and a transfer of pain from the baby to the nurse, who stood humbled and chagrined as she saw her time-honored system summarily set aside—the pins, paregoric, catmint, and cradle driven out—while pure air, sunlight, and common sense walked in. Oh! what sighs, what groans, what doubtful shakings of the head, what suppressed laughter and whisperings in the hall we heard, during the first few days after the inauguration of that dynasty of health, happiness, and rest to that new-born soul.

When the three hours' cry began that day, which ancient dames assured us was a custom that had been faithfully kept by all the sons of Adam, from time immemorial, we ordered the little sufferer to be promptly stripped to the skin, and put in a warm bath; that brought instant relief, after which he was dressed in a few light garments, hung on the shoulders, with no swaddling bands, no pressure on the lungs or bowels, and laid down to sleep. He was fed (according to Combe) every two hours by day, and but once during the night. After that we had peace, though eternal vigilance on our part was its price. The custom of pinning babies up as tight as a drum is both cruel and absurd. We asked the antiquarian who tortured our first-born in that way, why she did it? "The bones of young babies are so soft and their flesh so tender," said she, "that they are in constant danger of dissolution, unless tightly pinioned together." We soothed her fears by pointing to the fact that colts and calves, puppies and kittens, all lived and flourished without bandages, and for the benefit of the race we said we would make the experiment on one of the human family.

If babies are regularly fed, bathed, and comfortably dressed, and in a pure atmosphere, they will be quiet and healthy. The ignorance of women on these subjects is truly lamentable. We have seen children a year old that had never tasted water, when they should have it half a dozen times a day, from the hour of their birth. We have found fathers who worked hard all day, complain bitterly of being disturbed at night by crying children, hence the common use of Mrs. Winslow's soothing syrup, which only tends to increase the irritable condition of the nervous system, and permanently weaken the brain.

Young mothers no doubt imagine that this Mrs. Winslow is some experienced, humane, old lady, who loves little children, knows just how to soothe them to sleep, and pilot them through all the pitfalls of infancy, while, in fact, this abominable syrup is compounded by some ignorant man, in whiskers, broadcloth, and boots, who lives and fattens on his ill-gotten gains, while babies are sent by the hundreds to untimely graves, or made idiots and lunatics for life.—*Mrs. E. Cady Stanton.*

MUSTERED IN.

THE boys of the One Hundred and Seventeenth New York, tell a good joke in regard to the "muster in" of a darkey attached to that regiment, who became fearful he would be deprived of his pay unless he was joined to the service. A huge mustard plaster was applied to his back, about a foot below where the rear buttons of his coat were placed, and under the belief that all soldiers were served in the same manner, as a sort of military institution, he wore it until the pain became unendurable, at which time he was formerly declared "*Mustered in,*" according to the laws in such cases made and provided. If that darkey didn't get his wages it was not because he failed to suffer for his country as a patriot, duly put through by the One Hundred and Seventeenth.

GENERAL LANDER AND THE BIBLE.

THE beautiful illustration presented with such painstaking labor, and admirable taste, by Professor H. B. Hackett, of the value of religion to the soldier, are in keeping with his own high character as a Christian philanthropist. Everybody will read with pleasure the incident here narrated by the excellent author named.

One day, a staff officer caught General Lander with a Bible in his hand, and had the curiosity to inquire of him—" General, do you search the Scriptures ?" To this plain interrogatory, General Lander promptly replied: My mother gave me a Bible, which I have always carried with me. Once on the Rocky Mountains I had only fifteen pounds of flour. We used to collect grasshoppers at four o'clock in the day, to catch some fish for our supper at night. It was during the Mormon war, and my men desired to turn back. I was then searching for a route for the wagon road. "I will turn back if the Bible says so," said I, "and we will take it for an inspiration." I opened the book at the following passage: "Go on and search the mountain, and the gates of the city shall not be shut against you." All concurred in the definite statement of the passage, and the heroic explorer once more led his men into the wild country of the Indians. And yet Lander was not one to boast of his devotional practices. That he was "caught" by a staff officer was doubtless literally true, "with a Bible in his hand," for he was not one that read his Bible "to be seen of men."

Such 'Memorials of the war' as the above, constitute, at this era, the most interesting and profitable reading for the youth of our families and Sabbath schools.

THE LADY IN GRAY SILK.

A MOST amusing story is told of Judge B——, now occupying a high post in the Pennsylvania State government. Travelling some years since by rail to Harrisburg, on a blazing hot day, with some friends, the iron horse had stopped to water, when suddenly he drew his white handkerchief from his pocket and began vigorously waving it in the air, at the same time bobbing his head out of the window in a very energetic manner.

"What are you about, judge?" asked Mr. Q——, without rising from his seat.

"Why, don't you see yonder? There's a lady waving a white handkerchief, and I'm returning the salute."

"Who is she, judge?" asked Mr. Q——, as he lounged in one corner.

"Well, the fact is, I don't exactly know: I'm quite near-sighted, and I can't recognize her; but she is dressed in gray silk, and stands yonder, under a big maple tree, near my friend John B——'s house."

Mr. Q—— hobbled over to the judge's side and gazed in the direction indicated, but saw only that the judge had been exchanging salutes for ten minutes with an iron gray mare, whose long white tail, as it flapped away the flies, had been taken by him for a white handkerchief, waved by a lady in a gray silk dress.

The buttons that were subsequently picked up in that car are said to have been exceedingly numerous. The judge didn't swear, but he changed the subject to saw-mills, the only intelligible portion of which being the frequent repetition of the word "dam."

TEMPERANCE SELECTIONS.

THE PLEASURE BOAT.

THE course of the inebriate is fearfully rapid — when a young man in the prime of life lifts to his lips the poisoned chalice of death and destruction, and laughs and sneers at the admonitions of his friends, his course to ruin and blackness, to the vortex of misery and death, is like the speed of the devastating tornado. To more pathetically illustrate the rapid strides of the drunkard to an untimely grave, I will relate an affecting scene that transpired on the coast of Norway some twenty years ago, and has not to my knowledge ever appeared in print before. We have all heard of the awful whirlpool called the Maelstroom; it is but a few leagues from the west coast of the kingdom above mentioned. Its suction affects the water to many miles around it; and those who are so unfortunate as to come within the circle of its influence, can seldom make an effort so powerful as to escape — they are generally drawn into its funnel and perish. On the shore nearly opposite this whirlpool, one fine afternoon in the month of July, a party of young ladies and gentlemen agreed to take an excursion that evening in a pleasure boat. They were young and thoughtless, and not accustomed to the dangers of the sea — the young men could not ply the oars as effectually as those more accustomed to the water; but they supposed there could be no danger. All nature seemed to smile — the sunbeams briskly played upon the bosom of the ocean; calmness had thrown its oily wand upon the billow, and it slept. The water presented a smooth, unruffled surface — it seemed a sea of glass; the most timorous would scarcely have suspected that danger, in its most terrific form, was lurking just beneath the surface — but so it was, while the mirrored and glassy surface slept without a ripple. Just beneath, the circling current, formed by the suction of the whirlpool at that state of the tide, swept round and round at the distance of many miles with fearful velocity. The evening come — the young people assembled on the beach. The mellow moonbeam would tremble for a moment and then sleep on the calm, unagitated breast of the ocean. The pleasure boat was unmoored; the party gaily entered; the boat was moved from the shore; it was soon under way — it was rapidly propelled by those at the oars. But it was soon discovered that it would skim gently over the bosom of the deep when the motion produced by the oars had ceased. They allowed the boat to glide gently along — they felt no danger — all was thoughtless hilarity. The motion of the boat became gradually,

JOHN·ANDREW

but to them insensibly, more rapid; (mark the progress,) they were moved by the influence of the whirlpool. Their motion was rotary; they were insensibly drawn round in a huge circle with awful rapidity; they soon came round almost to the same spot from which they sailed. At this critical moment, the *only one* in which it was possible for them to be saved, a number of persons on shore who knew their danger, discovered them, and instantly gave the alarm; they entreated those in the boat to make one desperate effort and reach the shore, if possible. When they talked of danger, the party of pleasure laughed at their fears, and passed along without making one effort to deliver themselves from impending ruin. The boat moved on, the rapidity of its motions continually *increasing*, and the circle round which it was drawn by its rotary movement becoming smaller. It soon appeared a second time to those on the land. Again they manifested their anxiety for the safety of those whose danger they saw, but who, if delivered at all, must be delivered by their own exertions, for those on shore, even if they launched a boat and rushed into the very jaws of peril, could not save them while they were determined to remain inactive, and be carried by the accelerated velocity of the water round this mouth of the sea, ready at once to swallow both themselves and the boat. They still moved along in merriment; peals of laughter were often heard — sneers were the only thanks given to those who would with delight have saved them. For a time they continued to move round in all their thoughtlessness. But the tide began to ebb; presently they heard the far-off roar of the tremendous vortex below, like the wails and howlings of demons — it sounded like the hoarse, unsteady bellowings of an earthquake, or like a distant sea in a storm. By this time the boat ever and anon would quiver like an aspen leaf, and then shoot like lightning through the now troubled sea. The roar of the awful abyss was the knell of death — solemnity now began to banish mirth from the countenances of those in the devoted pleasure boat. They half suspected danger was near — soon they felt it. When they came again in sight of land, their cries would have pierced a heart of stone. O! help, for mercy's sake! were now the exclamations of despair; but alas! no human aid could reach them. A thick black cloud, as if to add horror to this scene of distress, at this moment shrouded the heavens in darkness, forked lightnings gleamed, and the hoarse, rebellious artillery of heaven boomed across the roaring and blackened waters. The oars were plied with every nerve; they snapped, and their fragments were hurried into the yawning abyss. The boat, now trembling, now tossed, now whirled suddenly round, now lashed by the spray, was presently thrown with violence into the jaws of death, opened wide to receive it and the immortals whom it carried. Oh! think of the feelings of those on shore, when, far away upon that awful ocean, by the vivid flashes of lightning, a party of their friends, young and in the morning of life, could be seen hurrying on to that fearful abyss — and at intervals, between the faint bellowings of far-off thunder, hear their cries of distress! Thus perished the pleasure boat and all that sailed in it. And thus perish thousands in the vortex of dissipation, who at first smoothly sail round the uttermost verge of it; who were scarcely, as they supposed, within the sphere of its influence, and who would laugh at those who were so faithful as to warn them of their danger, and still sail round and round, drawing nearer and more near to the awful precipice, their motion imperceptibly growing more rapid, till at last, when too late, they see their danger, but cannot reform, and they are plunged into the yawning chasm, which opens wide to receive them. I ask those who are young like myself, to lay this sketch up in the store-house of their memory — those who thoughtlessly tamper with the hydra monster. It may perhaps save some — may it save many — may it save all who read it, from a drunkard's untimely death, from filling a drunkard's grave.

THE REAL "TEMPERANCE CORDIAL."

"Well," said Andrew Furlong to James Lacey, "well! that ginger cordial, of all the things that I ever tasted, is the nicest and warmest. It's beautiful stuff and so cheap."

"What good does it do you, Andrew? And what want you of it?" inquired James Lacey.

"What good does it do me?" repeated Andrew, rubbing his forehead in a manner that showed he was perplexed by the question; "why no great good to be sure; and I can't say I've any want of it; for since I became a member of the Total Abstinence Society, I've lost the megrim in my head and the weakness I used to have about my heart. I'm as strong and hearty in myself as any one can be, God be praised! And sure, James, neither of us could turn out in such a coat as this, this time twelvemonth."

"And that's true," replied James, "but we must remember, that if leaving off whisky enables us to show a good habit, taking to 'ginger cordial,' or any thing of that kind, will soon wear a hole in it."

"You are always full of your fun," replied Andrew, "how can you prove that?"

"Easy enough," said James. "Intoxication was the worst part of a whisky-drinking habit; but it was not the only bad part. It spent TIME, and spent what well managed time always gives, money. Now, though they do say — mind I'm not quite sure about it, for they may put things in it they don't own to, and your eyes look brighter, and your cheek more flushed than if you had been drinking nothing stronger than milk or water — but they do say that ginger cordials, and all kinds of cordials, do not intoxicate. I will grant this, but you cannot deny that they waste both time and money."

"Oh, brother!" exclaimed Andrew, "I only went with two or three other boys to have a glass, and I don't think we spent more than half an hour, not three quarters, certainly; and there's no great harm in laying out a penny or two-pence that way now and again."

"Half an hour, even, breaks a day," said James, "and what is worse, it unsettles the mind for work; and we ought to be very careful of any return to the old habit, that has destroyed many of us, body and soul, and made the name of an Irishman a byword and a reproach, instead of a glory and an honor. A penny, Andrew, breaks the silver shilling into coppers; and two-pence will buy half a stone of potatoes—that's a consideration. If we don't manage to keep things comfortable at home, the women won't have the heart to mend the coat. Not," added James, with a sly smile, "that I can deny having taken to temperance cordials myself."

"You!" shouted Andrew, "you! a pretty fellow you are to be blaming me, and then forced to confess you have taken to them yourself. But I suppose they'll wear no hole in your coat? Oh, to be sure not, you are such a good manager!"

"Indeed," answered James, "I was any thing but a good manager eighteen months ago; as you well know, I was in rags, never at my work of a Monday, and seldom on Tuesday. My poor wife, my gentle Mary, often bore hard words; and although she will not own it, I fear still harder blows, when I had driven away my senses. My children were pale, half-starved, naked creatures, disputing a potatoe with the pig my wife tried to keep to pay the rent, well knowing I would never do it. Now ——"

"But the cordial?" interrupted Andrew, "the cordial! Sure, I believe every word of what you've been telling me is as true as the gospel; ain't there hundreds, ay, thousands, at this moment, on Ireland's blessed ground, that can tell the same story. But the cordial! and to think of your never owning it before; is it ginger, or anniseed, or peppermint?"

"None of these, and yet it's the rale thing, my boy."

"Well, then," persisted Andrew, "let's have a drop of it; you're not going, I'm sure, to drink by yourself; and as I've broke the afternoon ——"

A heavy shadow passed over James's face, for he saw that there must have been something hotter than even ginger, in the "temperance cordial," as it was falsely called, that Andrew had taken, or else he would have endeavored to save lost time, not to waste more; and he thought how much better the real temperance cordial was, that, instead of warming the brain, only warms the heart.

"No," he replied, after a pause; "I must go and finish what I was about; but this evening at seven o'clock, meet me at the end of our lane, and then I'll be very happy of your company."

Andrew was sorely puzzled to discover what James' cordial could be, and was forced to confess to himself that he hoped it would be different from what he had taken that afternoon, which certainly had made him feel confused and inactive.

At the appointed hour the friends met in the lane.

"Which way do we go?" inquired Andrew.

"Home," was James' brief reply.

"Oh, you take it at home?" said Andrew.

"I make it at home," answered James.

"Well," observed Andrew, "that's very good of the woman that owns ye. Now, mine takes on so about a drop of any thing, that she's as hard, almost, on the cordials, as she used to be on the whisky."

"My Mary helps to make mine," observed James.

"And do you bottle it, or keep it on draught?" inquired Andrew; very much interested in the "cordial" question.

James laughed very heartily at this, and answered:

"Oh, I keep mine on draught—always on draught; there's nothing like having a plenty of a good thing, so I keep mine always on draught;" and then James laughed again, and so heartily, that Andrew thought surely HIS real temperance cordial must contain something quite as strong as what he had blamed him for taking.

James's cottage door was open, and as they approached it, they saw a good deal of what was going forward within. A square table placed in the center of the little kitchen, was covered by a clean white cloth, and knives, forks, and plates for the whole family, were ranged upon it in excellent order; the hearth had been swept, the house was clean, the children rosy, well-dressed, and all doing something. Mary, whom her husband has characterized as "the patient," was busy and bustling in the very act of adding to the coffee, which was steaming on the table, the substantial accompaniment of fried eggs and bacon, with a large dish of potatoes.

When the children saw their father, they ran to meet him with a great shout, and clung around to tell him all they had done that day. The eldest girl declared she had achieved the heel of a stocking; one boy wanted his father to come and see how straight he had planted the cabbages; while another avowed his proficiency in addition, and volunteered to do a sum instanter upon a slate, which he had just cleaned. Happiness in a cottage seems more real than it does in a gorgeous palace. It is not wasted in large rooms; it is concentrated; a great deal of love in a small space; a great, great deal of joy within narrow walls, and compressed, as it were, by a low roof. Is it not a blessed thing that the most narrow means become enlarged by the affections? That all our best and purest affections will grow and expand in the poorest worldly soil; and that we need not be rich to be happy?

James felt all this and more when he entered his cottage, and was thankful to God, who had opened his eyes, and taught him what a number of this world's gifts that were within even his humble reach, might be enjoyed without sin. He stood, a poor, but happy father, within the sacred temple of his home: and Andrew had the warm heart of an Irishman, beating in his bosom and filling with joy.

"I told you," said James, "I had the true temperance cordial at home; do you see it in the simple prosperity by which, owing to the blessings of temperance, I am surrounded? Do you not see it in the rosy cheeks of my children, in the smiling eyes of my wife? Did I not tell truly that she helped to make it? Is not this true cordial," he continued, while his own eyes glistened with many tears, "is not the prosperity of this cottage a true temperance cordial? And is it not always on draught, flowing from an ever-filling fountain? Am I not right, Andrew; and will you not forthwith take my receipt, and make it for yourself? You will never wish any other; it is warmer than ginger, and sweeter than anniseed. I am sure that you will agree with me, that a loving wife, in the enjoyment of the humble comforts which an industrious, sober husband can bestow—smiling, healthy, well-clad children—and a clean cabin, where the fear of God banishes all other fears—make the true temperance cordial!"

EFFECTS OF INTEMPERANCE UPON NATIONAL INDUSTRY.

The results of national industry depend on the amount of well-directed intellectual and physical power. But intemperance paralyzes and prevents both these springs of human action.

In the inventory of national loss by intemperance, may be set down the labor prevented by indolence, by debility, by sickness, by quarrels and litigations, by gambling and idleness, by mistakes and misdirected efforts, by improvidence and wastefulness, and by the shortened date of human life and activity. Little wastes in great establishments constantly occurring, may defeat the energies of a mighty capital. But where the intellectual and muscular energies are raised to the working point daily by ardent spirits, until the agriculture, and commerce, and arts of a nation move on by the power of artificial stimulus, that moral power cannot be maintained which will guarantee fidelity, and that physical power cannot be preserved and well directed, which will insure national prosperity. The nation whose immense enterprise is thrust forward by the stimulus of ardent spirits, cannot ultimately escape debility and bankruptcy.

When we behold an individual cut off in youth or in middle age, or witness the waning energies, improvidence, and unfaithfulness of a neighbor, it is but a single instance, and we become accustomed to it; but such instances are multiplying in our land in every direction, and are to be found in every department of labor, and the amount of earnings prevented or squandered is incalculable: to all which must be added the accumulating and frightful expense incurred for the support of those and their families whom intemperance has made paupers. In every city and town the poor-tax, created chiefly by intemperance, is augmenting. The receptacles for the poor are becoming too strait for their accommodation. We must pull them down and build greater to provide accommodations for the votaries of inebriation; for the frequency of going upon the town has taken away the reluctance of pride, and destroyed the motives to providence which the fear of poverty and suffering once supplied. The prospect of a destitute old-age, or of a suffering family, no longer troubles the vicious portion of our community. They drink up their daily earnings, and bless God for the poor-house, and begin to look at it as, of right, the drunkard's home, and contrive to arrive thither as early as idleness and excess will give them a passport to this sinecure of vice. Thus is the insatiable destroyer of industry marching through the land, rearing poor-houses, and augmenting taxation: night and day, with sleepless activity, squandering property, cutting the sinews of industry, undermining vigor, engendering disease, paralyzing intellect, impairing moral principle, cutting short the date of life, and rolling up a national debt, invisible, but real and terrific as the debt of England; continually transferring larger and larger bodies of men from the class of contributors to the national income to the class of worthless consumers.

Add to the loss sustained by the substraction of labor and the shortened date of life, the expense of sustaining the poor created by intemperance, and the nation is now taxed annually more than the expense which would be requisite for the maintenance of government, and for the support of all our schools and colleges, and all the religious instruction of the nation. Already a portion of the entire capital of the nation is mortgaged for the support of drunkards. There seems to be no other fast property in the land, but this inheritance of the intemperate: all other riches may make to themselves wings and fly away. But until the nation is bankrupt, according to the laws of the state the drunkard and his family must have a home. Should the pauperism of crime augment in this country as it has done for a few years past, there is nothing to stop the frightful results which have come upon England, where property is abandoned in some parishes because the poor-tax exceeds the annual income. You who are husbandmen are accustomed to feel as if your houses and lands were wholly your own; but if you will ascertain the percentage of annual taxation levied on your property for the support of the intemperate, you will perceive how much of your capital is held by drunkards, by a tenure as sure as if held under mortgages or deeds of warranty. Your widows and children do not take by descent more certainly, than the most profligate and worthless part of the community. Every intemperate and idle man whom you behold tottering about the streets and steeping himself at the stores, regards your houses and lands as pledged to take care of him, annually puts his hands deep into your pockets, and eats his bread in the sweat of your brows, instead of his own: and with marvellous good-nature you bear it. If a robber should break loose on the highway to levy taxation, an armed force would be raised to hunt him from society. But the tippler may do it fearlessly in open day, and not a voice is raised, not a finger is lifted.—BEECHER.

A TEMPERANCE SHIP.

REV. T. HARRISON, at a temperance meeting, some time ago, in Cincinnati, related the following occurrence, which well deserves a place in this department of "GATHERED TREASURES:"

"When," said he, "I was about to leave England, two vessels were just ready for sailing; one was a "temperance ship," while the other allowed the use of ardent spirits. Of course I gave a decided preference to the former; and as 'the path of duty is the path of safety,' we nobly braved the thousand dangers of the sea, and, without the loss of one, arrived at

'The land of the free, and the home of the brave.'

Two or three weeks after our arrival, I saw it stated in a newspaper that the other vessel was lost, solely in consequence of improper directions being given by the mate when in a state of intoxication, and that nearly all the passengers perished. I have not words to express the feelings which rose in my breast, when I read of this occurrence—my soul was overpowered; and I scarcely need say, that my attachment to the cause of temperance became stronger and more intense than ever. O were I to remain silent on this delightful and inspiring theme, the ocean might lift its voice of storms against me, and boil with fury and indignation at my stupendous ingratitude!"

TRAFFIC IN ARDENT SPIRITS A GREAT NATIONAL EVIL.

IT employs a multitude of men, and a vast amount of capital, to no useful purpose. The medicinal use of ardent spirits is allowed; for this, however, the apothecary can furnish an adequate supply: but considered as an article of commerce for ordinary use, it adds nothing to animal or social enjoyment, to muscular power, to intellectual vigor, or moral feeling. It does, indeed, produce paroxyms of muscular effort, of intellectual vigor, and of exhilarated feeling; but this is done only by an improvident draught upon nature by anticipation, to be punished by a languor and debility proportioned to the excess. No man leaves behind him a more valuable product of labor, as the result of artificial stimulus, than the even industry of unstimulated nature would have produced; or blesses the world with better specimens of intellectual power; or instructs it by a better example; or drinks enjoyment from a fuller, sweeter cup, than that which nature provides. But if the premises are just, who can resist the conclusion? To what purpose is all this waste? Is it not the duty of every man to serve his generation in some useful employment? Is not idleness a sin? But in what respect does that occupation differ from idleness which adds nothing to national prosperity, or to individual or social enjoyment? Agriculture, commerce, and the arts are indispensable to the perfection of human character, and the formation of the happiest state of society; and if some evils are inseparable from their prosecution, there is a vast overbalancing amount of good. But where is the good produced by the traffic in ardent spirits, to balance the enormous evils inseparable from the trade? What drop of good does it pour into the ocean of misery which it creates? And is all this expense of capital, and time, and effort to be sustained for nothing? Look at the mighty system of useless operations—the fleet of vessels running to and fro—the sooty buildings throughout the land, darkening the heavens with their steam and smoke—the innumerable company of boats, and wagons, and horses, and men, a more numerous cavalry than ever shook the blood-stained plains of Europe, a larger convoy than ever bore on the waves the baggage of an army, and more men than were ever devoted at once to the work of desolation and blood. All these begin, continue, and end their days in the production and distribution of a liquid, the entire consumption of which is useless. Should all the capital thus employed, and all the gains acquired, be melted into one mass, and thrown into the sea, nothing would be substracted from national wealth or enjoyment. Had all the men and animals slept the whole time, no vacancy of good had been occasioned.—BEECHER.

A PATRIOT OF '76.

AN old gentleman, once the governor of the state in which he lives, who had long been afflicted with a disease for which ardent spirits had been prescribed as a remedy, at a temperance meeting said:

"Friends and neighbors: I am now more than seventy years of age—you all know my state of health. I have been trying an experiment for two months past in abstaining from the use of ardent spirits, which affords me much relief from the great distress I at times experience. My suffering has been great, but less than I feared. In the war of the revolution, I commanded a company of militia in this state. At the approach of the enemy to Bennington, I had just recovered from a fever that had confined me to my bed for many days—I had not then left my room. The alarm was given, the militia called out; and I, in opposition to the entreaties and expostulations of my friends, marched at the head of my company for Bennington. In our march we had to ford a river; a sturdy soldier shouldered and carried me over on his back. We met the enemy—fought—conquered—and returned in safety to our families. I thus put my life in jeopardy to aid in serving my country, and I am willing to do it again. An enemy more powerful and subtle than the British, is destroying firesides, and trampling with iron hoofs the fairest portions of our land. I present myself to join your ranks in this war of extermination, and enlist under your banner, bearing the motto, "Total Abstinence." This step will no doubt shorten my days. Be it so: I stand ready to sacrifice my life in the cause, and I freely subscribe your pledge, totally and forever to abstain from the use of ardent spirits."

FIRST AND LAST VISIT TO A DRAM SHOP.

Timothy Truesdell is the name we shall assign a very worthy, industrious, and thriving mechanic of New York, who became a burden to himself, a curse to his family, and a nuisance to society at large. A writer, in strong language, says of him, that during his devotion to strong drink, "he would have uncorked the bottle amid the quakings and thunders of Mount Sinai, and drained it by the crater of exploding Vesuvius." Yet this miserable and abandoned drunkard was cured—cured by a woman's love, mingled with a woman's independence.

Timothy Truesdell had a wife and five beautiful children; yet he neglected his work, squandered his earnings, which daily grew smaller, and spent his time at the pot-house, till the nigh prostration of all his faculties, or the distasteful words, "no more trust!" warned him to seek the shelter of his wife's care and protection. His children could not go to school, because learning was dear, and rum was cheap; the landlord dunned for his rent, and Mrs. Truesdell was obliged to keep at home, as she had no dress fit to appear abroad in, having pawned the last to pay a fine imposed upon her spouse by the police court. Misery, utter destitution, and famine, stared the unhappy family in the face. It is impossible to exaggerate the picture, even had we room or inclination. Mrs. Truesdell was a heroine, though not of romance. She loved her worthless husband, and had borne his neglect, the tears of her children, the gripe of famine, and the railing of the drunkard, without repining. Never had her exertions slackened—never had a harsh word passed her lips. At night, when she put her children to sleep, she wept and watched for his coming, and when he did come, drunk, as usual, she undressed and assisted him to bed, without a murmur of reproach. At length, her courage, well nigh exhausted, she resolved upon one last, desperate effort.

At night, having disposed of her three oldest children, she took the two youngest by the hand, and bent her steps to the groggery her husband was accustomed to frequent. She looked into the window, and there he sat, in the midst of his boon companions, with his pipe in his mouth, and his glass in his hand. He was evidently excited, though not yet drunk. Great was the astonishment of that bad company, and enormous Mr. Truesdell's dismay and confusion, when his wife, pale as marble, and leading two tattered and barefooted babes, stepped up to the bar, called for three glasses of brandy toddy, and then sat down by his side.

"What the devil brings you here, Mary?" said he, morosely.

"It is very lonesome at home, and your business seldom allows you to be there," replied the meek wife. "There is no company like yours, and as you cannot come to me, I must come to you. I have a right to share your pleasures as well as your sorrows."

"But to come to such a place as this!" expostulated Tim.

"No place can be improper where my husband is," said poor Mary. "Whom God hath joined together, let not man put asunder." She took up the glass of spirit.

"Surely, you are not going to drink that?" asked Tim, in huge astonishment.

"Why not? You say you drink to forget sorrow, and if brandy has that effect, I am sure no living creature has so good an excuse for drinking as I. Besides, I have not eaten a mouthful to-day, and I really need something to support my strength.

"Woman! woman! you are not going to give the children such stuff as that!" cried Tim, as she handed each of the children a glass of liquor.

"Why not? Can children have a better example than their father's? Is not what is good for him, good for them also? It will put them to sleep, and they will forget that they are cold and hungry. Drink, my children; this is fire, and bed, and food, and clothing. Drink—you can see how much good it does your father.

With seeming reluctance, Mary suffered her husband to conduct her home, and that night he prayed long and fervently, which he had not done before for years.

The next evening, as he returned homeward with a steady step, he saw his oldest boy run into the house, and heard him exclaim, "O, mother, here comes father, and he is not drunk!" Tears coursed down the parent's cheek, and from that hour he has not tasted strong drink. He had never been vicious or unfeeling, and as soon as his emancipation from the thraldom of a debasing appetite became known, friends, employment, and prosperity, returned to him. As for Mrs. Truesdell, she is the happiest of women; and never thinks, without joy and gratitude, of her first and last visit to the dram shop.

THE RUMSELLING DEACON.

DURING the last month, I called at the shop of a deacon in this city, and the following dialogue ensued between us.

"Pray, deacon," said I, "do you continue to sell rum?"

"Why, yes, sir;" he replied, "I sell a little."

"I looked over your bills last evening," I continued, "and I find I paid you more than four hundred dollars for grain last year, and I have paid you nearly that amount annually for several years. I must quit, deacon, unless you give up the sale of spirits."

"Really, Mr. Sargent, I don't sell much. I should be very sorry to lose your custom."

"It is of no importance, deacon, how much, or how little you sell. It is a scandal to the cause of religion to have deacons selling rum. I had rather ten common persons should sell it than one deacon. You have confessed to me that your clergyman disapproves of your conduct, and has talked with you on the subject."

"Why, Mr. Sargent, it would be a great loss to me, to give it up; my grain customers would go to other stores, and —"

"Deacon, I am astonished to hear you talk in this manner. I should have quitted you long ago, but for the hope of prevailing upon you to give up this ugly business. We have talked upon this subject frequently. I at one time supposed you would give it up, when poor Johnson died."

"Well, I don't know as 'twas ever proved he had his liquor at my shop."

"No, deacon, it was never *proved* except by his *dying declaration.* Johnson was not a very intemperate man; he had money laid up in the savings' bank; he was driving a load of manure into the country, and bought a bottle of gin at your shop. He drank till he was drunk, fell over the tongue of his wagon, in attempting to jump upon it, and was crushed beneath the wheels. This happened within a few rods of my own residence in Roxbury. This poor fellow was removed to the poor-house, and died there a few days after!"

"I really don't want to lose your custom, Mr. Sargent."

"Well, deacon, I will not drive you to a decision in this sudden manner. Think of it seriously, and I believe you will give it up. It is a horrible occupation for a deacon. I will call to learn your determination in a few days."

At the end of three days I called again. The deacon came readily to the side of my chaise, as I drew up before his door.

"Well, deacon," said I, "what is your decision?"

"Why, I've pretty much made up my mind to give that up."

"Really, deacon," said I, "I am rejoiced."

"Oh, sir," cried the deacon, hastily interrupting me, "not the traffic, but my office in the church!"

FATHER, HADN'T YOU BETTER TAKE A SHEEP, TOO?

A VALUED friend, and an able farmer, about the time the temperance reform was beginning to exert a healthful influence, said to his newly hired man, "Jonathan, I did not think to mention to you when I hired you, that I think of trying to do my work this year without rum. How much more must I give you to do without?"

"Oh," said Jonathan, I "don't care much about it, you may give me what you please." "Well," said the farmer, "I will give you a sheep in the fall, if you wish to do without."

"Agreed," said Jonathan.

The oldest son then said: "Father, will you give me a sheep if I do without rum?"

"Yes, Marshall, you shall have a sheep if you will do without."

The youngest son, a stripling, then said: "Father, will you give me a sheep, if I do without?"

"Yes, Chandler, you shall have a sheep also, if you do without rum."

Presently, Chandler speaks again: "Father, hadn't you better take a sheep, too?"

The farmer shook his head. He hardly thought that he could give up the "good creature" *yet*. But the appeal was from a source not to be easily disregarded; the result was, the demon rum was banished from the premises, to the great joy, and ultimate happiness of all concerned.

THE MYSTERIOUS WOMAN.

AT a certain town-meeting, the question came up whether any person should be licensed to sell rum. The clergyman, the deacon, and physician, strange as it may now appear, all favored it. One man spoke against it, because of the mischief it did. The question was about to be put, when all at once there arose from one corner of the room, a miserable female. She was thinly clad, and her appearance indicated the utmost wretchedness, and that her mortal career was almost closed. After a moment of silence, and all eyes being fixed upon her, she stretched her attenuated body to its utmost hight, and then her long arms to their greatest length, and raising her voice to a shrill pitch, she called upon all to look upon her. "Yes!" she said, "look upon me, and *then* hear me. All that the last speaker has said relative to temperate drinking, as being the father of drunkenness, is true. All practice, all experience, declare its truth. All drinking of alcoholic poison, as a beverage in health, is *excess*. Look upon *me*. You all know me, or once did. You all know I was once the mistress of the best farm in the town. You all know, too, I had one of the best, the most devoted of husbands. You all know I had fine, noble-hearted, industrious boys. Where are they now?

You all know. You all know they lie in a row, side by side in yonder churchyard; all, every one of them, filling the drunkard's grave! They were all taught to believe that temperate drinking was safe; *excess* alone ought to be avoided; *and they never acknowledged excess.* They quoted *you*, and *you*, and *you*," pointing with her shred of a finger to the priest, deacon, and doctor, "as authority. They thought themselves safe under such tender teachers. But I saw the gradual change coming over my family and prospects, with dismay and horror; I felt we were all to be overwhelmed in one common ruin; I tried to ward off the blow; I tried to break the spell, the delusive spell, in which the idea of the benefits of temperate drinking had involved my husband and sons; I begged, I prayed; but the odds were greatly against me.

"The priest said the poison that was destroying my husband and boys, was a good creature of God; the deacon (*who sits under the pulpit there*, and took our farm to pay his rum bills,) sold them the poison; the physician said a little was good, and *excess* ought to be avoided. My poor husband and my dear boys fell into the snare, and they could not escape, (there were no Washingtonians then,) and one after another was conveyed to the dishonored grave of the drunkard. Now look at me again; you probably see me for the last time; my sand has almost run. I have dragged my exhausted frame from my present abode—*your poor-house*—to warn you *all*—to warn you, deacon! to warn you, false teacher of God's word!" and with her arms high flung, and her tall form stretched to its utmost, and her voice raised to an unearthly pitch, she exclaimed: "I shall soon stand before the judgment-seat of God; I shall meet you there, you false guides, and be a witness against you all." The miserable female vanished—a dead silence pervaded the assembly—the priest, deacon, and physician hung their heads—the president of the meeting put the question: shall we have any more licenses to sell alcoholic poisons, to be sold as a beverage? The response was unanimous, no!

COLD WATER AND PROSPERITY.

We had the pleasure of hearing James Buchanan, Esq., deliver an address before the Howard Society, on which occasion he related the following circumstances:

Several years ago a gentleman dined with him, who had risen, by his own industry and integrity alone, from humble life to a proud elevation in society. On being invited to take a glass of wine, the following conversation ensued:

"Do you allow persons at your table to drink what they please?" asked the guest.

"Certainly," replied Mr. Buchanan.

"Then I'll take a glass of water."

"Ah, indeed! And how long have you drank cold water?"

"Ever since I was eleven years old."

"Is it possible! And pray, what induced you to adopt the principle of total abstinence?"

"Seeing a person intoxicated."

"Well," continued Mr. Buchanan, "if you have had the firmness of purpose to continue up to this time without taking intoxicating drinks, I do not wonder that you have reached your present position."

Mr. Buchanan afterwards learned that the person he saw intoxicated was his *father!*

CHILD'S PRAYER FOR A DRUNKEN FATHER.

A DRUNKARD who had run through his property, says Dr. Schnebly, returned one night to his unfurnished home. He entered his empty hall; anguish was gnawing at his heart-strings, and language is inadequate to express his agony as he entered his wife's apartment, and there beheld the victims of his appetite, his lovely wife and darling child. Morose and sullen, he seated himself without a word; he could not speak, he could not look upon them. The mother said to the little angel by her side, "Come, my child, it is time to go to bed;" and that little babe, as was her wont, knelt by her mother's lap, and gazing wistfully into the face of her suffering parent, like a piece of chiseled statuary, repeated her nightly orison; and when she had finished, the child (but four years of age,) said to her mother, "Dear ma, may I not offer up one more prayer?" "Yes, yes, my sweet pet, pray;" and she lifted her tiny hands, closed her eyes, and prayed, "Oh God! spare, oh, spare my dear papa!" That prayer was wafted with electric rapidity to the throne of God. It was heard on high—'twas heard on earth. The responsive "amen!" burst from that father's lips, and his heart of stone became a heart of flesh. Wife and child were both clasped to his bosom, and in penitence he said, "*My child, you have saved your father from the grave of a drunkard. I'll sign the pledge!*"

PRUDENT USE OF ARDENT SPIRITS.

INTEMPERANCE is a disease as well as a crime, and were any other disease as contagious, of as marked symptoms, and as mortal, to pervade the land, it would create universal consternation; for the plague is scarcely more contagious or deadly; and yet we mingle fearlessly with the diseased, and in spite of admonition we bring into our dwellings the contagion, apply it to the lip, and receive it into the system.

I know that much is said about the prudent use of ardent spirits, but we might as well speak of the prudent use of the plague—of fire handed prudently around among powder—of poison taken prudently every day—or of vipers and serpents introduced prudently into our dwellings, to glide about as a matter of courtesy to visitors and of amusement to our children.

First or last, in spite of your prudence, the contagion will take—the fatal spark will fall upon the train—the deleterious poison will tell upon the system—and the fang of the serpent will inflict death. There is no prudent use of ardent spirits, but when it is used as a medicine. All who receive it into the system are not destroyed by it: but if any vegetable were poisonous to as many, as the use of ardent spirits proves destructive, it would be banished from the table—it would not be prudent to use it at all. If in attempting to cross a river upon an elastic beam, as many should fall in and be drowned as attempt to use ardent spirits PRUDENTLY and fail, the attempt to cross in that way would be abandoned—there would be no prudent use of that mode of crossing. The effect of attempting to use ardent spirits prudently, is destructive to such multitudes, as precludes the possibility of prudence in the use of it. When we consider the deceitful nature of this sin, and its irresistible power when it has obtained an ascendency, no man can use it prudently, or without mocking God can pray while he uses it, "lead us not into temptation." There is no necessity for using it at all, and it is presumptuous to do so.—BEECHER.

DEATH'S PRIME MINISTER.

DEATH, the king of terrors, was determined to choose a prime minister, and his pale courtiers, the ghastly train of diseases, were all summoned to attend, when each preferred his claim to the honor of this illustrious office. Fever urged the numbers he had destroyed; cold Palsy set forth his pretensions by shaking all his limbs; Gout hobbled up, and alleged his great power in racking every joint; and Asthma's inability to speak was a strong though silent argument in favor of his claim. Stone and Colic plead their violence; Plague his rapid progress in destruction, and Consumption, though slow, insisted that he was sure.

In the midst of this contention, the court was disturbed with the noise of music, dancing, feasting, and revelry; when immediately entered a lady, with a bold, lascivious air, and flushed, jovial countenance. She was attended, on the one hand by a troop of bacchanals, and on the other, by a train of wanton youths and damsels, who danced half naked to the softest musical instruments. Her name was INTEMPERANCE. She waved her hand, and thus addressed the crowd of diseases: "Give way, ye sickly band of pretenders, nor dare to vie with my superior merits in the service of this monarch! Am I not your king? Do you not receive your power of shortening human life almost wholly from me? Who then so fit as myself for this important office?" The grisly monarch grinned a smile of approbation, placed her on his right-hand, and she immediately became his principal favorite and prime minister.—ADDISON.

THE MOUTH AND THE GOGGLES.

A LANDLORD, who gave to every customer an example of his moderate drinking, complained of the badness of his eyes, and asked a Quaker what he should do for them, removing his goggles and submitting his swollen, inflamed eyes to the examination of his customer. "My advice, friend," replied the Quaker, "is that thou shouldest put thy brandy on thy eyes, and tie thy goggles over thy mouth!"

RIGHT NAMES.

A BROTHER preacher, who happened to be lodging with Rev. Robert Hall, whispered to him that he was in the habit of taking a little refreshment after preaching. The refreshment called for was a glass of brandy and water. "You cannot have it by that name, my dear sir," replied Mr. Hall; "call it by its proper name and you shall have it." "And pray what is that?" "Not refreshment—but liquid poison and distilled damnation!"

SHINGLING A HOUSE.

JAMES A——, a reformed man, had fallen almost asleep, it being nearly midnight, when he heard the landlord's wife say, "I wish that man would go home, if he's got one to go to."

"Hush, hush!" said the landlord, "he'll call for something else directly."

"I wish he would make haste about it, then; for it's time every honest person was in bed," said the wife.

"He's taking the shingles off his house and putting them on ours," said the landlord.

At this time James began to come to his right senses, and commenced rubbing his eyes and stretching himself, as if just awoke, saying, "I believe I'll go."

"Don't be in a hurry, James," said the landlord.

"Oh, yes, I must go," said James, "good night!" and off he started.

After an absence of some time, the landlord met and accosted him.

"Hallo, Jim! why ain't you been down to see us?"

"Why," said James, "I had begun to take the shingles off my house, and it began to leak! so I thought it was time to stop the leak, and I have done it."

The tavern keeper was astonished, went home to tell his wife all about it, and James ever since has left rum alone, and attended to his own business. He is now a happy man, and his wife and children happier than ever.

SMITH, THE RAZOR STROP MAN.

Mr. Smith, the far-famed, "Razor Strop Man," was once endeavoring to get an inveterate grogseller to sign the pledge, but his arguments and entreaties were alike unavailing, and the grogseller, as quite a number of his peculiar friends and customers were standing around, determined, if he could, to pass the matter off as a joke at the expense of Smith.

"Look here, Smith," exclaimed the hero of toddy-sticks, "I understand that you get a dollar a-head for every man you get to sign the pledge."

"Who do you think pays it?" inquired Smith.

"Why, the temperance society, I 'spose; but I'll tell you what it is, Smith, you don't get a dollar on my head."

"Well," answered Smith, looking rather comical at the grogseller, "they would be fools to pay a dollar for such a head as yours, when they can get a sheep's head, pluck and all, for a shilling!"

The knight of the toddy-stick had nothing more to say.

RUM COLOR.

Not long since a religious society in Connecticut met to decide what color they should paint their meeting-house. Some proposed one color and some another. At last said one, "I move we paint it rum-color; for Deacon Smith has had his face painted that color for a number of years, and it grows brighter and brighter every year!"

"SOMETHING TO DRINK."

A good story was recently told at a temperance meeting in New Hampshire. A stranger came up to a Washingtonian with the inquiry:

"Can you tell me where I can get any thing to drink?"

"Oh, yes," said the other, "follow me."

The man followed him through two or three streets, till he began to be discouraged.

"How much further must I go?" said he.

"Only a few steps further," said the Washingtonian; "there is the pump!"

The man turned about and "moved his boots."

PLUCKING THE FRUITS.

Dr. Hewitt once related the following anecdote in a temperance lecture:

He said that a blacksmith in one of the villages which he had visited, had in possession, but under a mortgage, a house and piece of land, and, like too many others, he was fond of the social glass. But, in about three months after he had joined the temperance society, he observed one morning his wife busily employed setting out rose bushes and fruit trees. "My dear," said he, "I have owned this lot for five years, and yet I have never known you before to manifest any desire to improve and ornament it in this manner." "Indeed," was her reply, "I had no heart to do it, until you joined the temperance society. I had often thought of it before, but I was persuaded that should I do it, some stranger would pluck the roses and eat the fruit. Now, I know that, with the blessing of Providence, this lot will be ours; and that we and our children shall enjoy its products. *We* shall pluck the roses and eat the fruit."

PRODIGAL SON.

A young wife remonstrated with her husband, a dissipated spendthrift, on his conduct. "My love," said he, "I am only like the Prodigal Son; I shall reform by-and-by." "And I will be like the Prodigal Son, too," she replied, "for I will arise and go to my father!" And accordingly off she went.

A MATCH FOR A DISTILLER.

A distiller went to hear a reformed drunkard, thinking to browbeat him by his presence. The reformed man, with much eloquence, compared alcohol to Juggernaut, and said he had a temple in that place, pointing to the distillery, whose floor was strewed with human bones, and if he had a chance he should like to preach a sermon there. On coming out, the distiller said: "So, old fellow, you would like to preach in my temple, would you; when will you come?" "As soon as you get a congregation together," said the reformed man. "And what will be your text," was asked? "Out of the belly of hell cried I, and Thou heardst my voice!" The distiller was confounded.

THE VILEST OF MEN.

A GENTLEMAN stepped into a tavern, and saw a wretched drunkard, once a respectable man, waiting for his liquor. He thus accosted him:

"G——, why do you make yourself the vilest of men?"

"I aint the vilest," said the drunkard."

"Yes, you are," said the gentleman; "see how you look. Drink that glass, and you will be in the gutter."

"I deny your pozi-zi-tion," said the drunkard. Who—who is the vi-vilest, the temp-tempted, or the tempter? Who—who was wor-worst, Sa-Satan, or Eve?"

"Why Satan," said the gentleman.

"Well—well, be-behold the tempter!" said he, pointing to the bar. The argument was irresistible. The bar-keeper flew into a passion, and turned the poor fellow out of the house without his dram.

THE FOUR MILE WALK.

ONE of the best stories of the season is told by Sandy Welsh, of a man who was in the country on a visit, where they had no liquor. He got up two hours before breakfast, and wanted his bitters. None to be obtained, of course he felt bad. "How far is it to a tavern?" he asked. "Four miles." So off the thirsty soul started—walked the four miles in a pleasant frame of mind, arrived at the tavern, and found it was a temperance house!

A RUMSELLER NO GOOD CITIZEN.

THE Rev. John Chambers, of Philadelphia, in a speech before the American Union, said:

"A dealer in liquor was tried for some crime, convicted, and sentenced by Judge Parsons. The next day a lawyer waited upon the judge, and told him he could show a defect in the proceedings wherefore the man should be released. "O," said the judge, "that matter's settled." "But," said the lawyer, "he is a worthy man." "A worthy man!" said the judge, "and make drunkards?" "But," said the lawyer "he is a good citizen." "A good citizen," said the judge, "and fill up our jails and alms-houses, and cause our men to commit murder, and arson, and every iniquity? That question's settled, sir, and the man must abide by the law." The name of that judge was PARSONS, and may God send us more such *parsons* as this!"

THE FATHER AND HIS DAUGHTER.

DR. BEECHER, at a temperance meeting, related the following anecdote: "A gentleman walking the streets of London, saw a frightened horse with a cab running down the street with tremendous fury, and a little girl in the middle of the street, who might in an instant be killed. Forgetting his own safety, he instantly rushed to the child's rescue, snatched her in his arms, and bore her to the sidewalk, when the thought struck him, how would the parents of this child have felt, had she been killed. As he sat her down, he looked her in the face, and it was his own daughter. Little do parents," said he, "know, when they are rescuing children from the drunkard's path, how often the one saved, proves to be one of their own children."

THE MONKEY AND THE DRUNKARD.

MR. POLLARD states that in his drinking days, he was the companion of a man in Arundel county, Maryland, who had a monkey which he valued at a thousand dollars. "We always took him out on our chestnut parties. He shook off all our chestnuts for us, and when he could not shake them off, he would go to the very end of the limb and knock them off with his fist. One day we stopped at a tavern and drank freely. About half a glass of whisky was left, and Jack took the glass and drank it all up. Soon he was merry, skipped, hopped, and danced, and set us all in a roar of laughter. Jack was drunk.

"We all agreed, six of us, that we would come to the tavern next day, and get Jack drunk again, and have sport all day. I called at my friend's house next morning, and we went out for Jack. Instead of being as usual on his box, he was not to be seen. We looked in side, and he was crouched up in a heap. "Come out here," said his master. Jack came out on three legs; his fore-paw was upon his head. Jack had the headache; I knew what was the matter with him. He felt just as I felt many a morning. Jack was sick and couldn't go. So we waited three days. We then went, and while drinking, a glass was provided for Jack. But where was he? Skulking behind the chairs. "Come here, Jack, and drink." said his master, holding out the glass to him. Jack retreated, and as the door was opened, slipped out, and in a moment was on top of the house. His master went out to call him down, but he would not come. He got a cow-skin and shook it at him. Jack sat on the ridge-pole, and refused to obey. His master got a gun and pointed it at him. A monkey is much afraid of a gun. Jack slipped over the back side of the house. His master then got two guns, and had one pointed at each side of the house, when the monkey, seeing his predicament, at once whipped upon the chimney, and got down in one of the flues, holding on by his fore-paws! The master was beaten. The man kept that monkey twelve years, but could never persuade him to taste another drop of whisky. The beast had more sense than a man who has an immortal soul, and thinks himself the first and best of God's creatures on earth."

A PATRIOT'S RESOLUTION.

An old man of more than fourscore years, afflicted with a bodily infirmity, for which he had been advised by a physician to use ardent spirit as a medicine, was presented with the total abstinence pledge. After reading it he said:

"That is the thing that will save our country. I will sign it!"

"No," said one, "you must not sign it, because ardent spirit is necessary for you as a medicine."

"I know," said he, "I have used it, but if something is not done, our country will be ruined, and I will not be accessory to its ruin. I will sign it."

"Then," says another, "you will die."

"Well," said the old man, in the true spirit of '76, "for my country I *can* die;" and he signed the pledge, gave up his medicine, and his disease fled away.

It was the remedy that kept up the disease, and when he had renounced the one, he was relieved of the other. So it probably would be in nine cases out of ten where this poison is used as a medicine.

WESLEY AND THE DYSPEPTIC CLERGYMAN.

When stationed in the city of Bath, says Rev. Mr. Towle, I was introduced into the company of an aged man, whom I understood to have been intimate with Mr. Wesley, and once a useful local preacher. We entered into conversation about Mr. Wesley's times, when, among other things, he observed: "On one occasion, when Mr. Wesley dined with me, after dinner, as usual, I prepared a *little* brandy and water. On perceiving this, with an air of surprise, he cried: "What! my brother, what's that?" "It's brandy," says I; "my digestion is so bad, I am obliged to take a little after dinner." "How much do you take?" said he, "let me see." "Only about a table-spoonful." "Truly," said he, "that is not much; but one table-spoonful will soon lose its effect, and then you will take two, from two, you will get to a full glass; and that, in like manner, by habituating yourself to it, will lose its effect, and then you will take two glasses, and so on, till, in the end, perhaps, you will become a drunkard. Oh, my brother, take care what you do!"

Happy had it been for that man, if he had taken the timely warning of his good friend Wesley. But, alas! he trifled with his *little drops*, until he actually did become a drunkard, ruined his reputation, and at the very time I had an interview with him, he was a poor, old, miserable backslider, apparently within a few steps of the grave.

THE INTOXICATED HORSEMAN.

THE following event, says a correspondent of the Charleston Intelligencer, occurred in my native town: A young man, about twenty years of age, of the name of G——, on a public day, being somewhat intoxicated, rode down the main street with considerable rapidity, and meeting a friend, he reined in his horse, which was skittish, in order to converse with him. Not many words had passed, when the young man's friend requested him to turn about and go with him to the "North Woods." *"I'll go to hell first!"* was the reply. The words hardly escaped his lips, when his horse suddenly reared himself on his hind legs, and pitching backwards, fell on his rider, and crushed him to death! He was taken up a corpse, and carried into an adjoining house, where I saw him. He was taken at his word! Oh! where is his soul!

TIMING IT.

A MINISTER in the Highlands of Scotland, found one of his parishioners intoxicated. The next day he called to reprove him for it.

"It is very wrong to get drunk," said the parson.

"I ken that," said the guilty person, "but then I dinna drink as meikle as you do!"

"What, sir! how is that?"

"Why, gin it please ye, dinna ye aye take a glass o' whisky and water after dinner?"

"Why, yes, Jemmy, surely I take a little whisky after dinner merely to aid digestion."

"An dinna ye take a glass o' whisky toddy every night before ye gang to bed?

"Yes, to be sure, I just take a little toddy at night to help me sleep!"

"Weel," continued the parishioner, "that's jist fourteen glasses a week, an about sixty every month. I only get paid off once a month, an then if I'd take sixty glasses, it wad make me dead drunk for a week; now ye see the only difference is, ye *time* it better than I do!"

This is pretty much the view most people take of this matter; a moderate drinking clergyman may talk to his drunken parishioner till doomsday, but he will never make him a sober man so long as he drinks himself.

DEACON BARNES AND THE DRUNKARD.

A MAN once addicted to intemperance, but who for some months had entirely abstained, though he had not joined the temperance society, took occasion, not long since, to relate, in a temperance meeting, his experience in regard to the influence of temperate drinkers of respectable standing in society, upon the habits of the drunkard. "Many a time," said he, "have I gone to Captain Johnson's tavern and waited for half an hour, or an hour, for some respectable man to come in and go to the bar, and call for liquor. After a while, Deacon Barnes would come in and call for some spirit and water. Then I could get up to the bar and do as he did."

Deacon Barnes hearing of this, asked him if it was so.

"It is," said the man.

"Well," rejoined the deacon, "you shall hang on me no longer. I joined the temperance society yesterday."

"Did you?"

"Yes."

"Well, then, I will join to-day, for I can do without liquor as long as Deacon Barnes can."

He did join, and remained a consistent temperance man afterwards.

"THERE GOES A TETOTALER!"

A DRUNKARD assailed a Washingtonian, but could only say, "there goes a tetotaler!" The gentleman waited until the crowd had collected, and then turning upon the drunkard, said, "there stands a drunkard! Three years ago he had the sum of eight hundred pounds; now he cannot produce a penny. I know he cannot. I challenge him to do it, for if he had a penny he would be at a public house. There stands a drunkard, and here stands a tetotaler, with a purse full of money, honestly earned, and carefully kept. There stands a drunkard! Three years ago he had a watch, a coat, shoes, and decent clothes; now he has nothing but rags upon him, his watch is gone, and his shoes afford free passage to the water. There stands a drunkard; and here stands a tetotaler, with a good hat, good shoes, good clothes, and a good watch, all paid for. Yes, here stands a tetotaler! And now, my friends, which has the best of it?" The bystanders testified their approval of the tetotaler by loud shouts, while the crest-fallen drunkard slunk away, happy to escape further castigation.

HOW TO KEEP THE PLEDGE.

A REFORMED drunkard residing near Baltimore, Gen. J—— T———, stated, that at fourteen he joined the church; but when he became a voter, he formed, at political meetings, the habit of drinking, and gradually sunk into profaneness and excess until he made way with some *two quarts of brandy in a day*—and when his money failed, would keep himself drunk on *cider*, which was almost the only product of his neglected farm. As the *last hope* of relief from the intolerable sufferings thus brought upon himself and family, he signed the pledge of total abstinence; and knowing how strong might be the temptation to break it, he loaded a pistol with powder and ball, carried it with him, and resolved that if the cup should ever again approach his lips, he would at once put the pistol to his head and terminate his life.

He carried the pistol in his pocket seven months, when, riding alone one dark night, he reflected: "This cannot be the way to get strength to resist temptation—this cannot be pleasing to GOD." He continued to reflect, and at length stopped his horse, tied him, kneeled by the side of a fence, and prayed *to God* to give him strength to keep the pledge. He continued to pray till he could rest in the promise, "my grace is sufficient for thee." He rose from his knees, calmly trusting in the Lord Jesus Christ, to keep him from falling. He was again received as a member of the church, and now lives the life of a consistent Christian.

THE BAD LUMP.

THE following incident we relate on the authority of the old sailor, who delivered a temperance lecture on board a steamboat running between New York and New Haven.

Having found a man who was divested of all decent clothing, and in a wretched state of health in consequence of drinking, he induced him, amidst the discouragements of the tavern-keeper, at whose house he had found him, to sign the temperance pledge for one year. The landlord prophesied that he would not keep the pledge a year, or that if he did he would never renew it. As the year was coming to a close, the old sailor called upon the man, and secured his signature again. He signed it for 999 years, with the privilege of a life-lease afterward! When the day arrived upon which his first pledge expired, he roguishly went to visit his old friend the tavern-keeper. "There he comes," said the eager rumseller, "he will have a great spree now to pay for his long abstinence." When he arrived at the tavern, he complained of a bad feeling at his stomach, and of various evils, among which was a bad lump on one side, which had been growing for a number of months. "Ah," said the landlord, "did I not tell you it would kill you to break off drinking so suddenly? I wonder you have lived as long as you have. Come, what will you take?" and suiting the action to the word, he placed a decanter before him.

"But," said the visitor, "I have signed the pledge again for 999 years, with the privilege of a life-lease after it!"

"What a fool!" said the landlord; "if you go on as you have done, you will not live another year."

"Do you really think so, landlord?"

"Certainly. Come, what will you take?"

"Oh, no, landlord; I have signed the pledge again, and then this terrible lump on my side. I do not believe that drinking will make it any better."

"It is all," said the landlord, "because you left off drinking. You will have a bigger lump than that on the other side before long, if you continue another year as the last."

"Do you think I will? Well, then, so be it. I will not violate my pledge, for look here, landlord (pulling out a great purse, with a hundred dollars in silver shining through the interstices), that is my lump which has been growing for so many months, and, as you say, is all in consequence of signing the pledge. This is what you would have had, if I had not signed it; and if I have a bigger one than that for 999 years, I will not go to drinking again!"

THE DRUNKARD IN TEARS.

Last week, while absent from home, we were detained for an hour or two by the rain at a hotel in one of the villages of our state. While sitting by the fire in the bar-room, our attention was attracted to an individual who came in, and walking up to the bar called for something to drink. "Have you any money?" he was asked. "No," said he. "Then you can have nothing here." The poor fellow turned from the bar and walked to the door. There was something about him that won our sympathy, and we arose from our seat and followed him. We found him standing upon the porch, bathed in tears. "Friend," said we, "you seem to be greatly grieved that you cannot obtain liquor; surely you are better without it." "It is not that, sir, it is not that that grieves me, it is the remembrance of other days." Then, pointing to a fine farm that lay across the road, he said, "Do you see that farm? It was once mine—it now belongs to the keeper of this house; I have lost, and he has gained it by my intemperance. But that is not all—I had a wife who loved me dearer than her own life. My intemperance has killed her—she lies in yonder graveyard; and sometimes when I feel as I do now, I go there and weep: but what avail my tears! they will not bring her back—she is gone forever. And now, sir, as you have just seen, when I am almost dying for a dram, this man, who has robbed me of my lands, and assisted me to kill my wife, refuses to let me have it because I have not the money."

A RUMSELLER'S DREAM.

WELL, wife, this is too horrible! I cannot continue this business any longer.

Why dear, what's the matter now?

Oh, such a dream! Oh, I cannot endure it! Oh, if ever I sell rum again!

My dear, you are frightened.

Yes, indeed, I am; another such a night will I not pass for worlds.

My dear, perhaps ——

Oh, don't talk to me! I am determined to have nothing more to do with rum, any how. Do you think, Tom Wilson came to me with his throat cut from ear to ear, and such a horrid gash, and it was so hard for him to speak, and so much blood, and, said he, see here, Joe, the result of your rumselling. My blood chilled at the sight, and just then the house seemed to be turned bottom up, the earth opened, and a little imp took me by the hand, saying, follow me. As I went, grim devils held out to me cups of liquid fire, saying, drink this. I dared not refuse. Every draught set me in a rage. Serpents hissed on each side, and from above reached down their heads and whispered *rumseller!* On, and on, the imp led me through a narrow pass. All at once he paused and said, are you DRY? Yes, I replied. Then he struck a trap door with his foot, and down, down we went, and legions of fiery serpents rushed after us, whispering, *rumseller! rumseller!* At length we stopped again, and the imp asked me as before, are you DRY? Yes, I replied. He then touched a spring—a door flew open. What a sight! there were thousands, aye, millions of old, worn-out rum-drinkers, crying most piteously, rum, rum, give me more rum! When they saw me, they stopped a moment to see who I was—then the imp cried out, so as to make all shake again, *rumseller!* and hurling me in, shut the door. For a moment they fixed their ferocious eyes upon me, and then uttered a united yell, which filled me with such terror, I awoke. There wife, dream or no dream, I will never sell another drop.

HARVESTING WITHOUT LIQUOR.

IN the early stage of the temperance reformation a farmer, residing near "the gap" of the Blue Mountains, who had been for many years an intemperate man, was induced to sign the total abstinence pledge, and in a very short time afterward united himself with the Methodist church. The rumseller and his dependants were sorely dismayed at this extraordinary change, as they termed it, and set their wits to work to lure him back.

The time of harvesting having arrived, and the farmer having many acres of wheat to be cut, the anti-temperance men assembled with their cradles in their hands, and demanded their accustomed allowance of rum.

"Not a drop shall be given," firmly replied the farmer.

"We will not cut your wheat without it."

"Then it shall rot in the field."

The faithful followers of alcohol now returned to their respective homes, and left the "obstinate farmer" to his fate. His wheat had begun to "fall in the stubble," yet he placed his reliance on God, and commending himself to him, he retired to rest. Early in the morning he was awakened from his slumber by a shout which seemed to speak the very soul of joy. He looked out, and beheld a large number of men, with cradles in their hands, the foremost bearing a broad banner, with the words, "TOTAL ABSTINENCE," inscribed upon its ample folds.

"What can all this mean?" said the farmer, gazing with astonishment upon a scene which seemed rather the work of magic than reality.

"Isn't there a tetotaler somewhere about these parts, who has a field of grain to be cut?" inquired one of the crowd.

"Yes," replied the farmer, "I am he."

"Well, we've come to cut it," was the response.

The farmer hurried down to greet his kind-hearted visiters, who, having heard of his circumstances, had traveled many miles to give him a helping hand. He pointed to the field, the banner was erected in its midst, the men worked like good tetotalers, and in a few hours the farmer's crop was saved!

A TAVERN SIGN.

"MY dear," said an affectionate husband, "you are good at contriving things, I wish you would find some suitable design to paint on the sign for our new tavern."

"I'll do no such thing. I don't like your going to tavern-keeping. It's a dirty business, and the temperance men are making such a fuss about it, that it will soon come to nothing."

"There's no use talking, for my mind's made up. I've got a license, and paid for it, and I must use it. I want something neat and appropriate to paint on the sign."

"Well, I'll tell you what. Make a great big horn, and paint yourself crawling out of the *little end* of it!"

MORAL AND RELIGIOUS ANECDOTES.

THE WIDOW AND HER SHIPWRECKED SON.

In the north of England, in a small inland village, a lieutenant of the British navy, after serving his country for many years, took up his abode. He had a pious wife and six or seven children. She sent them to the village Sabbath school ; but the eldest, a boy of fourteen years, seemed determined to profit by neither maternal love, nor pious instructions at school. He played and mingled with a class of wicked idlers that infested the village, and would have been as bad as the worst of them, but for his father's rigid discipline. That, alone, restrained him from rushing into excesses of wickedness and riot. But that father died, and left his widow to combat the idleness of her boy alone. No, not alone; for she sought the help of her God.

The father being dead, the son grew worse. He was ungovernable ; and the afflicted widow wept, as with a broken heart, over her recreant child. Unable to restrain him, she adopted a very common mode in England of disposing of idle lads. She resolved to send him to sea. It was a painful alternative ; but he could not grow worse, she thought, and possibly the severe discipline of a ship might humble his proud spirit and lead him to reflection.

A ship was obtained for him. The bustle of preparation began and was over. Unknown to the youth, the mother placed a bible in his chest, with a secret hope that its light might lead him to his heavenly Father, when he should be far-off on the deep blue sea. Many were the prayers that mother offered for her son ; many the counsels she gave him from the fullness of her heart. The day of separation came. O, it was a day of trial to all but to him who was the occasion of all the sadness of that family. Warm were the tears she shed, as, pressing him to her bosom, she bade him adieu, and commended his wayward heart to God.

Many years had passed and the wanderer had not returned. The ship had perished at sea, and the widow mourned her son as dead ; and what was worse, she trembled for the safety of his undying soul. Could she have been assured of his safety in the better world, her pained heart would have been at rest. But she wept over him as doubly lost.

It was a stormy night in mid-winter. The wind howled, the rain

poured down in torrents, and deep darkness obscured the sky. The widow and her children sat beside the cheerful fire, and a chastened cheerfulness overspread the circle, though now and then a cloud of melancholy gathered over the mother's brow, as the driving storm reminded her of her lost son, when a slight tap was heard at the door. It was opened. A sailor stood there, way-worn and weather-beaten. He begged a shelter from the storm. It was not in that mother's heart to refuse a *sailor* on *such* a night, and she offered him her fireside and her food.

When he had refreshed himself, she modestly questioned him of his condition. His tale was soon told. He had been shipwrecked, and he was going home poor and penniless to his mother. He had been shipwrecked before. The widow asked him to tell the story of his sufferings.

He said that in a violent gale, the ship ran ashore and went to pieces. The crew were either drowned or dashed to death upon the rocks. Himself and another were the only persons who reached the shore. They were thrown high upon the beach by a powerful wave. His companion was senseless at first, but at last revived—alas! but to die. "He was a sweet youth," the sailor observed: "once he was the terror of the ship, for his excessive devotion to vice. But suddenly he had changed. He became a serious, praying man; as remarkable for piety now, as for vice before. When he revived a little on the beach," said the sailor, "he pulled a bible from his bosom and pressed it to his lips. It was this blessed book, he told me, that led him to change his way of life. Rummaging his chest one day, he found a bible; his first impression was to throw it away; but chancing to see his mother's writing, he paused to examine it. It was his name. It made him think of his mother; of her instructions, and the instructions of his teachers; and then he saw his sins, and felt he was a sinner. Overwhelmed, he sunk upon his knees, beside his chest, and wept and prayed, and vowed to change his way of life. And he did change it; for he became a decided Christian. After telling me about this change," continued the sailor, "he gave me his bible, and bade me keep it for his sake; and then falling back upon the sand, he expired with a half-offered prayer upon his lips."

As the sailor concluded, the widow, who had listened with deep interest and feeling, inquired:

"Have you got that bible, my friend?"

"Yes, madam," said he; and he took from his bosom what appeared to be a bunch of old canvass. Carefully removing several envelops, he at last produced a small pocket bible, and gave it into the hands of the lady.

Tremblingly and hastily she seized it. She turned to the blank page, when lo! her child's name in her own writing. A death-like paleness overspread her usually pale cheek, as she made the discovery, and exclaimed, "'tis his! 'tis his! my son! my son!"

Here, then, we see the idle Sunday scholar, at sea, away from the means of grace, suddenly profiting by the instructions of years past. His soul felt the inspiring leaven a teacher had placed within it, and grew ripe for paradise, when the teacher mourned his labor lost. How encouraging! How cheering! Labor on, dear teacher, in hope. Parents, despise not Sabbath school instruction, for your child may in like manner be saved.

ALL FOR THE BEST.

It was a frequent saying of the good Bernard Gilpin, when exposed to losses and troubles, "Ah! well; God's will be done; it is all for the best."

Towards the close of Queen Mary's reign, Bernard Gilpin was accused of heresy before the merciless Bishop Bonner; he was speedily apprehended, and he left his quiet home, "nothing doubting," as he said, "that it was all for the best," though he was well aware of what might await him; for we find him giving directions to his steward, "to provide him a long garment that he might go the more comely to the stake, at which he would be burnt."

While on his way to London, by some accident, he had a fall and broke his leg, which put a stop for some time to his journey. The persons in whose custody he was, took occasion thence maliciously to retort upon his habitual remark. "What," said they, "is this all for the best? You say, master, that nothing happens which is not for our good; think you your broken leg is so intended?"

"Sirs, I make no question but it is," was the meek reply, and so in truth it proved; for, before he was able to travel, Queen Mary died, the persecution ceased, and he was restored to his liberty and friends.

THE JEW AND HIS DAUGHTER.

An aged clergyman, in the western part of Virginia, as he was preaching to a large audience, observed a man in the congregation, who had in every respect the appearance of a Jew. He was well dressed, and appeared absorbed in deep and devout attention during the services; at the close of which, the clergyman went to him, and thus addressed him: "Sir, am I not correct in supposing that I am addressing one of the children of Abraham?" "You are, sir." "But how is it that I meet a Jew in a Christian assembly."

The substance of his narrative was as follows: He was a very respectable man, of superior education, who had lately come from London, with his books, his riches, and an only child, a daughter, in her seventeenth year. He had found a beautiful retreat on the fertile banks of the Ohio, had buried his wife before he left Europe, and now knew no pleasure, except in the society of his beloved child. She was, indeed, worthy of a parent's love—she was extremely beautiful in her person, but possessed the superior charms of a cultivated mind and amiable disposition; no pains had been spared on her education. She could read and speak with fluency several different languages, and her manners were most pleasing. No wonder, then, that a father, far advanced in age, should place his whole affection on this only child of his love; especially as he knew no source of happiness beyond the world. Being a strict Jew, he educated her in the strictest principles of his religion.

It was not long since that his daughter was taken ill; the rose faded from her cheek, her eye lost its fire, her strength decayed, and it soon became apparent that her disease was incurable and fatal. The father hung over the bed of his daughter, with a heart ready to burst with anguish. He often attempted to converse with her, but seldom spoke, except by the language of tears. He spared no trouble or expense in procuring medical assistance, but no human skill could turn aside the arrow of death.

The father was walking in a small grove near his house, weeping, when he was sent for by his dying daughter. With a heavy heart he entered the door of her chamber, soon, he feared, to be the chamber of death. He was now to take a last farewell of his child, and his religious views gave him but a feeble hope of meeting her hereafter. The child grasped the hand of her parent, and addressed him with all the energy which her expiring strength permitted.

"Father, do you love me?"

"My child, you know I love you—that you are more dear to me than all the world beside."

"But father, *do* you love me?"

"Why, my child, will you give me pain so exquisite? Have I, then, never given you any proofs of my love?"

"But, my dearest father, *do* you love me?" The father could not answer. The child added: "I know, my dear father, you have been the kindest of parents, and I *tenderly* love you. Will you grant me one request? O, my father, it is the dying request of your daughter, will you regard it?"

"My dearest child, ask what you will, though it take every shilling of my property; whatever it may be, it shall be granted—I will grant it."

"My dear father, *I beg you never again to speak against Jesus of Nazareth.*"

The father was dumb with astonishment. "I know," continued the dying girl, "I know but little about this Jesus, for I was never taught, but I know that he is the Savior, for he has manifested himself to me since I have been sick, even to the salvation of my soul; I believe he will save me, although I had never loved him before; I feel that I am going to him; that I shall be ever with him. And now, my father, do not deny me; I beg that you will never again speak against this Jesus of Nazareth. I entreat you to obtain a testament which tells of him, and I pray that you may know him; and when I am no more, that you may love and always serve him."

The exertion here overcame the weakness of her feeble body; she stopped, and her father's heart was too full even for tears. He left the room in great horror of mind; and before he could recover himself, the spirit of his beloved daughter had taken its flight, we may trust, to the Savior whom, though she scarcely knew, she yet loved and honored. The first thing the parent did, after committing to the dust this, his only and beloved child, was to procure a New Testament, which he read diligently; and taught by the Spirit from above, is now numbered among the meek and humble followers of his once despised Savior.

THE SUNDAY PARTY.

As I was walking one Lord's day to the house of God, I saw a party of young people on before me, whose volatile manners ill accorded with the sanctity of the day, and just as I was passing them, I heard one say:

"Indeed, I think we shall do wrong—my conscience condemns me—I must return."

"There can be no harm," replied another, "in taking an excursion on the water, especially as we have resolved to go to a place of worship this evening."

"I must return," rejoined a female voice; my conscience condemns me. What will my father say if he hears of it?"

By this time they had reached the bridge; and one of the party was busily engaged with a waterman, while the rest stood in close debate for a few minutes, when they all moved toward the water. Two of the gentlemen stepped into the boat, two more stood at the water's edge, and the females were handed one by one into the boat. It was a fine morning, though rather cold, and the tide was running at its usual rate; many were gazing on them, when a naval officer standing near, called to them through the ballustrades, and said:

"A pleasant morning to you."

One of the gentlemen suddenly arose to return the compliment, but from some cause which I could not perceive, he fell over into the water. This disaster threw the whole party into the utmost consternation, and each one, instead of remaining in his seat, rushed to the side of the boat over which their companion had fallen, which upset it, and all were instantaneously plunged into the deep. The shriek which the multitude of spectators gave, when they beheld this calamity, exceeded any similar noise I ever heard; several females fainted—boats immediately put off, and in a few minutes, the watermen rescued one, and another, and another, from a premature grave.

Having picked up all they could find, the different boats were rowed to the shore, where some medical gentlemen were in waiting; but when the party met together, no language can describe the horror which was depicted on every countenance, when they found that two were still missing.

"Where is my sister?" said the voice which had said, only a few minutes before, "there can be no harm in taking an excursion on the water, especially as we have resolved to go to church in the evening."

"Where's my Charles?" said a female, who had appeared the most gay and sprightly when I first saw them.

At length two boats, which had gone a considerable distance, were seen returning; on being asked, if they had picked up any, they replied, "Yes—two." This reply electrified the whole party; they wept for joy, and so did others who stood around them.

"Here's a gentleman," said the boatman; but I believe he's dead."

"Where's the lady," said the brother, "is she safe?"

"She is in the other boat, sir."

"Is she alive?—has she spoken?"

"No, sir; she has not spoken, I believe."

"Is she dead? oh, tell me."

"I fear she is, sir."

The bodies were immediately removed from the boats to a house in the vicinity, and every effort was employed to restore animation, and some faint hopes were entertained by the medical gentlemen that they should succeed. In the space of little more than ten minutes, they announced the joyful news, that the gentleman began to breathe; but they made no allusions to the lady. Her brother sat motionless, absorbed in the deepest melancholy, till the actual decease of his sister was announced, when he started up, and became almost frantic with grief. He exclaimed: "Oh, my sister! my sister! would to God I had died for thee!" They were all overwhelmed with trouble, and knew not what to do.

"Who will bear the heavy tidings to our father?" said the brother, as he paced the room backward and forward, like a maniac broke loose from the cell of misery. "Oh, who will bear the heavy tidings to our father?" He paused—a death-like silence pervaded the whole apartment; he again burst forth in the agony of despair: "I forced her to go against the dictates of her conscience; I am her murderer; I ought to have perished, and not my sister. Who will bear the heavy tidings to our father?"

"I will," said a gentleman, who had been unremitting in his attentions to the sufferers.

"Do you know him sir?"

"Yes, I know him."

"Oh! how can I ever appear in his presence? I enticed one of the best of children to an act of disobedience, which has destroyed her!"

THE DOCTRINE OF TRANSUBSTANTIATION.

A Roman Catholic gentleman in England being engaged to marry a Protestant lady, it was mutually agreed that there should be no contests on the subject of religion. For some years after their union, this agreement was scrupulously observed; but in the course of time, the priest, who had paid them frequent visits, expecting to find no difficulty in making a convert of the lady, began to talk upon the peculiarities of his religion. He particularly insisted upon the doctrine of transubstantiation, and grew troublesome by his importunity. To avoid being further teazed by him, she one day seemed to be overcome by his arguments, and agreed to attend at mass with her husband the following Sabbath, provided she might be allowed to prepare the wafer herself. The priest, not suspecting any thing, and glad on any terms to secure such a convert, gave his consent. The lady accordingly appeared at the chapel with her husband, and after the consecration of the wafers, which she had brought with her, she solemnly demanded of the priest, whether it was really converted into the body of Christ? To which question, he without hesitation replied, *that there was a conversion made of the whole substance of the bread into the body of Christ, and that there remained no more of its form or substance.*

"If this be really the case," said she, "you may eat the wafer without any danger; but as for *myself*, I should be afraid to touch it, as it is mixed with arsenic." The priest was overwhelmed by a discovery so unexpected, and was too wise to hazard his life upon a doctrine, for which he had, however, contended with all the earnestness of perfect assurance. The lady's husband was so struck by this practical confutation of a doctrine which he had before implicitly believed, that he never afterwards appeared at the mass.

OLD FATHER MORRIS.

The manner in which this aged New England clergyman illustrated some topics, is shown in the following extract from an article in the "Lady's Book," written by Mrs. H. B. Stowe.

Sometimes he would give the narration an exceedingly practical turn, as one example will illustrate:

He had noticed a falling off in his little circle, which met for social prayer, and took occasion, the first time he re-collected a tolerable audience, to tell concerning "the conference-meeting which the disciples attended," after the resurrection.

"But Thomas was not with them," said the old man, in a sorrowful voice. "Why! what could keep Thomas away?" "Perhaps," said he, glancing at some of the backward auditors, "Thomas had got cold-hearted, and was afraid they would ask him to make the first prayer, or, perhaps," said he, looking at some of the farmers, "Thomas was afraid the roads were bad; or, perhaps," added, after a pause, "Thomas had got proud, and thought he could not come in his old clothes." Thus he went on, significantly summing up with great simplicity and emotion, he added, "but only think what Thomas lost, for in the middle of the meeting, the Lord Jesus came, and stood among them! How sorry Thomas must have been!" This representation served to fill the vacant seats for some time to come.

Father Morris sometimes used his illustratic talent to a very good purpose in the way of rebuke. He had on his farm a fine orchard of peaches, from which some of the ten and twelve-year-old gentlemen helped themselves more liberally than the old gentleman thought expedient.

Accordingly he took occasion to introduce into his sermon one Sunday, in his little parish, an account of a journey he took, and how he saw a fine orchard of peaches, that made his mouth water to look at them.

"So," says he, "I came up to the fence, and looked all around, for I would not have touched one of them without leave, for all the world. At last I spied a man, and, says I:

"Mister, won't you give me some of your peaches?"

So the man came, and gave me nigh a handful. And while I stood there eating, I said:

"Mister, how do you manage to keep your peaches?"

"Keep them!" he said, and stared at me. "What do you mean?"

"Yes," said I, "don't the boys steal them?"

"Boys steal them?" said he, "no indeed!"

"Why, sir," said I, "I have a whole lot full of peaches, and I cannot get half of them (here the old man's voice grew tremulous,) because the boys in my parish steal them so."

"Why, sir," said he, "don't their parents teach them not to steal?"

"And I grew all over in a cold sweat, and told him I was afraid they didn't."

"Why, how you talk," says the man, "tell me where you live."

"Then," says Father Morris (the tears running over,) "I was obliged to tell him I lived in the town of G——."

After this, Father Morris kept his peaches.

A RASH FATHER.

In the neighborhood of Hitchin, in Hertfordshire, there lived a few years ago, a laboring man, who having a cross child, frequently wished, with an oath, that his next child might be both deaf and dumb. He afterward had three children, all of whom were deaf and dumb.

ADVANTAGES OF RELIGIOUS TRAINING.

REV. T. HARRISON, in preaching a sermon, some years ago, in Springfield, Ohio, on the advantages of parental instruction in connection with Sabbath school efforts, related the following striking circumstance:

"In childhood, I became acquainted with a little boy who attended the same Sabbath school as myself. He was a fine child, and promised to make an interesting youth. As life advanced, however, he forsook his Sabbath school, and became addicted to evil practices, commencing with Sabbath breaking, and then proceeding to intemperance, profanity, and other ruinous vices. His parents, though occasional attenders on public worship, neglected his spiritual interests; and as he ripened in years, he ripened in crime. At length, he attacked a man on the highway, took from him his money, and nearly deprived him of life. He was apprehended, brought to trial, and sentenced to be hung. On the other hand, I, after remaining for sometime a scholar in the Sabbath school, was appointed a teacher. My parents also endeavored to bring me up in the nurture and admonition of the Lord. Often has a pious father shed tears of holy sympathy and affection, while giving me religious advice. Their efforts were not in vain. By the blessing of God, my feet were restrained from the ways of wickedness, and I was led in the paths of righteousness and peace. It so happened that I witnessed the execution of my school-fellow; and the impression which was then made on my mind, will never, no never, be effaced. I saw him ascend the scaffold—I saw his arms pinioned, and his feet bound together—I saw his eyesight excluded forever from the glorious light of day, and the beautiful scenery of nature, by a dismal cap—I saw the rope tied around his neck—I saw his footing torn from under him—and there he was, a sad spectacle between heaven and earth, his pinioned body rapidly moving backward and forward. I looked and looked again; but the sight was more than I could bear: my eyes grew dim—my heart turned sick; and to the best of my ability, I retired from the horrifying scene. And never, in all my life, did virtue appear more beautiful, and religion more precious, than at that hour.

'Twill save us from a thousand snares
  To mind religion young:
Grace will improve our following years
  And make our virtue strong."

ANECDOTE OF GENERAL JACKSON.

THE Hon. —— ———, who as a Baptist preacher and lieutenant governor, had at one and the same time been in the service of the Lord, and of the state of Illinois, becoming dissatisfied with the honors or profits, or both, of the posts he held, determined to resign them, and devote his time and talents to the assistance of the administration in carrying on the general government of the country. Accordingly he went to Washington, and laid his case before the president. He stated his pretensions and his wishes, narrated at some length all the prominent events of his political life, dwelling especially upon his untiring devotion to the democratic party, the sacrifices he had submitted to, the exertions he had made in its behalf, and its consequent indebtedness to him; but said not a word of what he had done for the cause of religion. General Jackson heard the clerical aspirant through in silence, and after musing a moment, put the following question to him:

"Mr. K., are you not a minister of the gospel?"

"I am, sir," was the reply.

"Then, sir," said the general, with his usual quiet dignity, "you hold already a higher office than any in my gift—an office whose duties, properly performed, requires your whole attention; and really I think the best that I can do for you will be to leave you at liberty to devote your whole time to them; for, from what you tell me, I fear that hitherto they have been somewhat neglected."

CHRISTIAN FIRMNESS.

When the Rev. Mr. Baird was once pleading the cause of France, he related the following, which he received from the lips of one of the evangelists, employed by the Missionary Society of Paris. This evangelist was preaching in one of the towns of France, and a lady, the wife of one of its wealthiest citizens, attended at the chapel, and became deeply interested in the subject of her soul's salvation. Her husband, who was an infidel, opposed her violently; and, at length, when she became a decided Christian, told her that if she went to the chapel again, *he would take her life.* Knowing well the character of the man, and firmly believing that he would execute his threat, she called upon the minister to ask his advice. I know not, said he, what to give, but we will pray to God for wisdom. They kneeled, and prayed together. She arose from her knees, and without saying a word, returned home. The next Sabbath she was found at the house of God, listening, as if for the last time on this side of the eternal world. At the close of the service she returned, and upon entering her house, her husband met her, when the following conversation ensued: "Have you been to the chapel?" "Yes." "Did not I tell you that I would kill you if you went again? How dared you to go?" "Yes, but we must obey God rather than man." Perceiving that he hesitated, she embraced the opportunity of expostulating with him. "Why," said she, "do you intend to kill me? Have I been a worse wife to you, a worse mother to your children, since I became a Christian?" "No," replied he, letting his weapon fall from his hand, "no, and I promise never to oppose you any more. And now," continued he, "I wish you *to pray for me.*" They bowed before the mercy-seat, and she poured out her soul in prayer for him. He is now one of the most active members of the church.

THE FIRST STEP IN CRIME.

No man becomes a villain in a day. Congenial as sin is to the natural heart, and inclined as the wicked may be to the pursuits of vice, there is a first step in the path of every crime. At that point in the career of guilt the man would have shuddered at the *thought* of deeds which he afterwards performs without remorse. He never dreamed of the extremity to which one transgression will lead.

Several examples occur to mind just now.

A young lawyer, with connexions of the highest respectability, and talents to secure for him an elevated rank in his profession, married a lovely woman, and entered on life with the brightest prospects of success and happiness. The increasing expenses of a family demanded an increasing income, and as business did not advance as rapidly as he desired, in an evil hour he placed the names of some of his best friends to a note, and drew a sum of money from the bank. He promised himself that before it was due, he should be ready to meet it, and his crime would never be known. The note was renewed by forgery. It was an easy mode of raising money, and became easier the oftener he employed it. For a season he was successful, but when was dishonesty the best policy in the end ?

His guilt was discovered. He fled from justice, and was hunted through the woods in winter like a beast. His young wife woke almost in madness, to the consciousness that she was the wife of a felon. His retreat was at length cut off. He was arrested, but escaped again.

He flew to the chamber of his wife. The embrace was short and full of agony. He wept; and she wrung her hands, but uttered no reproach. She loved him too much even in his shame. He must fly again. He did fly, and was again arrested and brought to trial. The case was a plain one. There was no defense—there could be none. He was sentenced to the state prison for a term of years. His measure of iniquity was full. Now and then an old acquaintance looked in upon his cell where he pursued his solitary toil, but he never looked up. They said he was pining away, and they made an effort to procure his pardon and release. But death was before them, and he went from prison to judgment.

I went into the hospital of the prison at Sing Sing some years ago, and there lay, in the last struggles of life, a man of fine form and noble countenance. He was raving in delirium, and soon died mad. I asked his name and history, and found that he was a young lawyer from the city of New York, who had begun his course of crime by stealing paltry articles of clothing from his associates: soon he laid his hands on money; and by-and-by he was detected when far advanced in guilt. His end I have just mentioned. He was a child of luxury and had never known *want*. And when he lay dying in that prison hospital, cut off from the tenderness and sympathy that would have softened a death-bed in the house of parental love, I thought how truly, "the way of the transgressor is hard."

A clerk in a store, a teller in a bank, an agent in his office, constantly handling the money of others, is tempted to apply a little to his own use, with the promise *made to himself* that he will restore it, and speedily. But he finds it easier to borrow than to pay, when no one calls him to an account. The more he takes, the more he wants to take. He begins a course of extravagance, and falls into sins that require money to secure their indulgence. He speculates, in hopes of paying all back at once; every plunge increases his embarrassments; his guilt breaks out; he flies from justice, a lost, self-ruined man. What to him are the arrows that have pierced the fond hearts of too confiding friends. He planted those arrows, but can never draw them.

Now there was a time when that man was what the world calls virtuous. He would have trembled at the thought of crime; and he did tremble and turn pale when he committed his first offense. It disturbed his sleep that night, and when he met his employer the next morning, he thought he was suspected and trembled again. But that step taken, the next was easy.

THE BAG OF DUCATS.

A CAUSE was tried before a young cadi of Smyrna, the merits of which were as follows: A poor man claimed a house which a rich man usurped. The former held his deeds and documents to prove his right; but the latter had provided a number of witnesses to invalidate his title. In order to support their evidence effectually, he presented the cadi with a long bag containing five hundred ducats. When the day arrived for hearing the cause, the poor man told his story, and produced his writings, but could not support his case by witnesses; the other rested his whole case on his witnesses, and his adversary's defect in law, who could produce none: he urged the cadi, therefore, to give sentence in his favor. After the most pressing solicitations, the judge calmly drew out from under his sofa the bag of ducats which the rich man had given him as a bribe, saying to him very gravely, "You have been much mistaken in the suit, for if the poor man can produce no witnesses in confirmation of his right, I myself can produce at least five hundred." He then threw away the bag with reproach and indignation, and decreed the house to the poor plaintiff. Such was the noble decision of a Turkish judge, whose disinterested conduct was the reverse of that of the unjust, time-serving Felix.

ITALICS.

The late Mrs. Graham of New York regarded with particular esteem the works of Dr. Owen, the Rev. William Romaine, and the Rev. John Newton, and read them with pleasure and profit. One day she remarked to Mr. B. that she preferred the ancient writers on theology to the modern, because they dealt more in italics. "Dear mother," he replied, "what religion can there be in *italics?*" "You know," said she, "that old writers expected credit for the doctrines they taught, by proving them from the word of God to be correct; they inserted the *scripture* passages in italics, and their works have been sometimes one-half in italics. Modern writers on theology, on the contrary, give us a long train of reasoning to persuade us to their opinions, but very little in *italics!*"

THE BOY THAT WOULD NOT LET HIS SISTER WANT.

A French paper says that Lucille Romee, a pretty little girl with blue eyes and fair hair, poorly, but neatly clothed, was brought before the Sixth Court of Correction under a charge of vagrancy.

"Does any one claim you?" asked the magistrate.

"Ah! my good sir," said she, "I have no longer any friends; my father and mother are dead—I have only my brother James, but he is as young as I am. Oh, dear! what could he do for me!"

"The court must send you to the house of correction."

"Here I am, sister—here I am! do not fear!" cried a childish voice from the other end of the court. And at the same instant a little boy, with a sprightly countenance, started forth from amid the crowd, and stood before the judge.

"Who are you," said he.

"James Romee, the brother of this poor little girl."

"Your age?"

"Thirteen."

"And what do you want?"

"I come to claim Lucille?"

"But have you the means of providing for her?"

"Yesterday I had not, but now I have. Don't be afraid Lucille."

"Oh, how good you are, James!"

"But let us see, my boy," said the magistrate; "the court is disposed to do all it can for your sister. However, you must give us some explanation."

"About a fortnight ago, sir," continued the boy, "my poor mother died of a bad cough, for it was very cold at home. We were in great trouble. Then I said to myself, I will become an artizan, and when I know a good trade I will support my sister. I went apprentice to a brush-maker. Every day I used to carry her half my dinner, and at night I took her secretly to my room, and she slept on my bed, while I slept on the floor, wrapped in my blouse. But it appears the poor little thing had not enough to eat, for, unfortunately, one day she begged on the boulevard. When I heard she was taken up, I said to myself, 'come, my boy, things cannot last so; you must find something better.' I very much wished to become an artizan, but at last decided to look for a place. I have found a very good one, where I am lodged, fed, and clothed, and have twenty francs a month. I have also found a good woman, who, for these twenty francs, will take care of Lucille and teach her needle-work. I claim my sister."

"My boy," said the magistrate, "your conduct is very honorable. The court encourage you to persevere in this course and you will prosper."

The court then decided to render up Lucille to James, and she was going from the bar to join her brother, when the magistrate smilingly said, "You cannot be set at liberty until to-morrow."

"Never mind, Lucille, I will come and fetch you early to-morrow. (To the magistrate,) I may kiss her, may I not, sir?"

He then threw himself into the arms of his sister, and both wept warm tears of affection.

BENEFITS OF THE SABBATH.

In the year 1832, the British House of Commons appointed a committee to investigate the effects of laboring seven days in the week, compared with those of laboring only six, and resting one. That committee consisted of Sir Andrew Agnew, Sir Robert Peel, Sir Robert Inglis, Sir Thomas Baring, Sir George Murray, Fowell Buxton, Lord Morpeth, Lord Ashley, Lord Viscount Sandon, and twenty other members of parliament. They examined a great number of witnesses, of various professions and employments. Among them was John Richard Farre, M. D., of London, of whom they speak as "an acute and experienced physician." The following is the testimony:

"I have practised as a physician between thirty and forty years; and during the early part of my life, as the physician of a public medical institution. I had charge of the poor in one of the most populous districts of London. I have had occasion to observe the effect of the observance and non-observance of the seventh day of rest during this time. I have been in the habit, during a great many years, of considering the *uses* of the Sabbath, and of observing its *abuses*. The abuses are chiefly manifested in labor and dissipation. Its use, medically speaking, is that of a day of rest.

"As a day of rest, I view it as a day of compensation for the inadequate restorative power of the body under continued labor and excitement. A physician has always respect to the preservation of the restorative power; because, if once this be lost, his healing office is at an end. A physician is anxious to preserve the balance of circulation, as necessary to the restorative power of the body. The ordinary exertions of man *run down* the circulation every day of his life; and the first general law of nature, by which God prevents man from destroying himself, is the alternating of day and night, that repose may succeed action. But, although the night apparently equalizes the circulation, yet it does not sufficiently restore its balance for the attainment of a long life. Hence, one day in seven, by the bounty of Providence, is thrown in as a day of compensation, to perfect by its repose the animal system.

"I consider, therefore, that, in the bountiful provision of Providence for the preservation of human life, the sabbatical appointment is not, as it has sometimes been theologically viewed, simply a precept partaking of the nature of a political institution, but that it is to be numbered among the *natural* duties, if the preservation of life be admitted to be a duty, and the premature destruction of it a suicidal act."

PYTHEUS.

It is related of Pytheus of Lydia, that possessing valuable gold mines, he entirely neglected the cultivation of his lands, which naturally became so unprofitable as not to afford the common necessaries of life. His wife, who showed herself possessed of as much good sense as wit, at a banquet-supper, which Pytheus had ordered to be prepared, directed that all the dishes should be filled with gold, in different shapes and states, instead of viands. On the removal of the covers, this ingenious woman exclaimed to the guests, "I set before you what we have in greatest abundance, for we cannot reap what we do not sow."

MAKING BRIEFS ON SUNDAY.

The distinguished Dr. Wilson, pastor of the First Presbyterian Church in Philadelphia, for a number of years before he became a preacher of the gospel, was an eminent lawyer in the state of Delaware. He was accustomed, when pressed with business, to make out his briefs and prepare for his Monday's pleading on the Sabbath.

But he so uniformly failed during the week in carrying out his Sunday plans, that it arrested his attention. As a philosopher, he inquired into the cause of his uniform failure, and came to the conclusion that it might be, and probably was on account of his violation of the Sabbath by employing it in secular business. He, therefore, from that time, abandoned the practice of doing any thing for his clients on that day. The difficulty ceased. His efforts on Monday were as successful as on other days.

RETURNING GOOD FOR EVIL.

There was a Christian in New Jersey that had a neighbor of sucn a malevolent and savage character, as made him a plague and terror to those with whom he became offended. Forgiveness, or mercy, nobody expected from him.

One day he found the hogs of his good neighbor in his cornfield. He drove them out, and came to their owner in a storm of passion, making a great bluster about the damage done to his crop. "If I ever see them in my corn again," said he, "I'll kill them—that I will."

On he went, raving and scolding, his eyes flashing fire every word he spoke. But the good man kept calm as a summer's evening, and said nothing but what was kind and good-natured in reply.

Mr. Wrath, after he had spent all his fury, went off very much vexed to see that none of it took effect.

The good man shut up his swine at once. But, impatient for their favorite and new-found food, they soon made their escape, and got into the same cornfield again, without the knowledge of their owner.

Mr. Wrath discovered them, and at once attacked them with might and main; as much as to say, (like a duelist,) "Nothing but your blood will give me satisfaction!" He did, indeed, slaughter three or four of them before they could make their retreat. Then, to cap the climax, and aggravate his neighbor's feelings to the utmost, he put the dead bodies on a sled, or cart, and drew them over to his neighbor's house. He threw them down before the door, saying, with sarcastic bitterness, "Your hogs got into my corn again, and I thought I would bring them home!"

The owner of the swine kept perfectly cool, giving no look or word of resentment at the injury done to him. He might have gone to law with Mr. Wrath, and, perhaps, made him smart severely for destroying his property and insulting him as he did. But he thought it best to keep out of the law; and every man should think so, except when driven to it by a sense of duty.

The next year he himself had a cornfield situated in a similar way beside the road. Now it so happened that neighbor Wrath had somo unruly swine running in the street, which got into the good man's cornfield, and committed a depredation similar to that which his had done in Mr. Wrath's cornfield the year before. He went to Mr. Wrath, and told him what mischief his vagrant swine had done, and requested him to shut them up. But he paid no attention to the request.

Soon after they got into the same field again. The Christian discovered them; and he hit on a good-natured and witty expedient of contrasting his own temper and conduct with those of his neighbor under similar circumstances. Instead of killing them, and carrying them home dead, he caught them, tied their legs carefully, and drew them with his team to their owner's door. "Neighbor," said he, kindly, "*I found your hogs in my corn again, and I thought I would bring them home!*"

Never was a man more completely confounded! He saw the wide difference between his neighbor's conduct and his own: he looked on the *living* swine, but he thought of the *dead* ones! It was too much. He told his neighbor that he was very sorry, and that he would pay all damages the hogs had done. He offered to pay him, too, for the hogs he had killed the year before! "No," replied the other, "I shall make no account of the damages your hogs have done; and I shall take nothing for what you did to mine. I let that pass."

Mr. Wrath was completely overcome. He concluded at once to yield, and retreat from a contest where such unequal odds were against him. He was as kind and generous to his Christian neighbor afterwards, as he was mischievous and cruel before.

THE INFIDEL'S DEATH.

A society of infidels were in the practice of meeting together on Sabbath mornings to ridicule religion, and to encourage each other in all manner of wickedness. At length they proceeded so far as to meet, by previous agreement, to burn their bibles. They had lately initiated a young man into their awful mysteries, who had been brought up under great religious advantages, and seemed to promise well; but on that occasion, he proceeded the length of his companions, threw his bible into the flames, and promised, with them, never to go into a place of religious worship again. He was soon afterward taken ill. He was visited by a serious man, who found him in the agonies of a distressed mind. He spoke to him of his past ways. The poor creature said: "It all did well enough while in health, and while I could keep off the thoughts of death;" but when the Redeemer was mentioned to him, he hastily exclaimed: "What's the use of talking to me about mercy?" When urged to look to Christ, he said: "I tell you it's no use now; 'tis too late—'tis too late! Once I could pray, but now I can't." He frequently repeated, "I cannot pray—I will not pray." He shortly afterward expired, uttering some of the most dreadful imprecations against some of his companions in iniquity who came to see him, and now and then saying: "My bible! oh, the bible!"

THE PIOUS BOATSWAIN IN A STORM.

On board an East-Indiaman was a pious boatswain, whom, on this account, the crew looked upon as a strange man. The ship was overtaken with a storm so dreadful, that, after every effort to preserve life, the captain said: "All that could be done had been done —it was impossible the vessel could weather it." The ship seemed sinking—the captain withdrew into the cabin—the men were some on their knees, and others with horror hanging on parts of the rigging. All expected the vessel would founder. The boatswain had been very active, and apparently unalarmed during the whole of the gale. At this moment, when a heavy wave struck the ship, and seemed as if it would instantly sink her, looking up with a smile, he exclaimed: "Blessed be God, all is right!" and he began to sing. The storm afterwards abated, and the vessel was saved. Thus amid the storm of life, on the dark ocean of death, and amid the terrors of the judgment-day, the Christian may still smile, and exultingly exclaim: "Blessed be God, all is right!"

NAPOLEON'S OPINION OF CHRIST.

"I know men," said Napoleon at St. Helena, to Count de Montholon, "I know men, and I tell you that Jesus is not a man! The religion of Christ is a mystery, which subsists by its own force, and proceeds from a mind which is not a human mind. We find in it a marked individuality, which originated a train of words and actions unknown before. Jesus is not a philosopher, for his proofs are miracles, and from the first his disciples adored him.

"Alexander, Cæsar, Charlemagne, and myself, founded empires; but on what foundations did we rest the creations of our genius? Upon force. Jesus Christ founded an empire upon love; and at this hour millions of men would die for him!

"I die before my time, and my body will be given back to the earth, to become food for worms. Such is the fate of him who has been called the great Napoleon. What an abyss between my deep mystery and the eternal kingdom of Christ, which is proclaimed, loved, and adored, and is extending over the whole earth!"

Turning to Gen. Bertrand, the emperor added: "If you do not perceive that Jesus Christ is God, I did wrong to appoint you general!"

A SUCCESSFUL RETORT.

A CLERGYMAN was once accosted by a doctor, a professed deist, who asked him "if he followed preaching to save souls." "Yes." "Did you ever see a soul?" "No." "Did you ever hear a soul?" "No." "Did you ever taste a soul?" "No." "Did you ever smell a soul?" "No." "Did you ever feel a soul?" "Yes."

"Well," said the doctor, "there are four of the five senses against one upon the question, whether there be a soul."

The clergyman then asked, "if he were a doctor of medicine?" "Yes." "Did you ever see a pain?" "No." "Did you ever hear a pain?" "No." "Did you ever taste a pain?" "No." "Did you ever smell a pain?" "No." "Did you ever feel a pain?" "Yes."

"Well, then," said the clergyman, "there are also four senses against one, upon the question, whether there be a pain, and yet, sir, you know that there is a pain, and I know that there is a soul."

A NAME ABOVE EVERY NAME.

WHEN the pious Bishop Beveridge was on his deathbed, he did not know any of his friends or connexions. A minister with whom he had been well acquainted, visited him; and when conducted into his room he said: "Bishop Beveridge, do you know me?" "Who are you?" said the bishop. Being told who the minister was, he said that he did not know him. Another friend came, who had been equally well known, and accosted him in a similar manner. "Do you know *me*, Bishop Beveridge." "Who are you?" said he. Being told it was one of his intimate friends, he said he did not know him. His *wife* then came to his bedside and asked him if he knew *her*. "Who are you?" said he. Being told she was his wife, he said he did not know *her*. "Well," said one, "Bishop Beveridge, do you know the Lord Jesus Christ?" "JESUS CHRIST!" said he, reviving, as if the name had upon him the influence of a charm, "O! yes, I have known him these forty years. Precious SAVIOR! HE IS MY ONLY HOPE."

A GOOD REASON FOR NOT GOING TO WAR.

FREDERIC, Elector of Saxony, intending to war against the Archbishop of Magdeburg, sent a spy to inquire into his preparations; and being informed that he gave himself up to prayer and fasting, committed his cause to God alone. "Let him fight that will," said he; "I am not mad enough to fight with the man, who makes *God* his refuge and defense."

THE FARMER AND THE SOLDIERS.

Soon after the surrender of Copenhagen to the English, in the year 1807, detachments of soldiers were, for a time, stationed in the surrounding villages. It happened one day that three soldiers, belonging to a Highland regiment, were sent to forage among the neighboring farm-houses. They went to several, but found them stripped and deserted. At length they came to a large garden or orchard, full of apple trees, bending under the weight of fruit. They entered by a gate, and followed a path which brought them to a neat farm-house. Every thing without bespoke quietness and security; but as they entered by the front door, the mistress of the house and her children ran screaming out by the back. The interior of the house presented an appearance of order and comfort superior to what might be expected from people in that station, and from the habits of the country. A watch hung by the side of the fireplace, and a neat bookcase, well filled, attracted the attention of the elder soldier. He took down a book: it was written in a language unknown to him, but the name of Jesus Christ was legible on every page. At this moment, the master of the house entered by the door through which his wife and children had just fled.

One of the soldiers, by threatening signs, demanded provisions: the man stood firm and undaunted, but shook his head. The soldier who held the book, approached him, and pointing to the name of Jesus Christ, laid his hand upon his heart, and looked up to heaven. Instantly the farmer grasped his hand, shook it vehemently, and then ran out of the room. He soon returned with his wife and children laden with milk, eggs, bacon, etc., which were freely tendered; and when money was offered in return, it was at first refused. But as two of the soldiers were pious men, they, much to the chagrin of their companion, insisted upon paying for all they received. When taking leave, the pious soldiers intimated to the farmer that it would be well for him to secrete his watch: but, by the most significant signs, he gave them to understand that he feared no evil, for his trust was in God; and that though his neighbors, on the right hand and on the left, had fled from their habitations, and by foraging parties had lost what they could not remove, not a hair of his head had been injured, nor had he even lost an apple from his trees.

"The angel of the Lord encampeth round about them that fear him, and delivereth them."

ROWLAND HILL AND HIS GARDENER.

The Rev. Rowland Hill had great reason to rejoice in the consistent lives and zealous devotion to God, of many of his people at Wotton. There was among them a person of the name of Rugg, of a piety so deep, and of a life so useful and unblemished, that even his enemies admired and were awed by his character. Mr. Hill's gardener at Wotton, who had always passed for an honest, quiet sort of man, was at length discovered to have been the perpetrator of several burglaries, and other daring robberies in the neighborhood, though he had, till caught in the fact, never been even suspected. He was tried at Gloucester, condemned, and executed. It need scarcely be said that his master visited him in jail. During his interview with him there, he confessed the many crimes of which he had been guilty. "How was it, William," he inquired, "that you never robbed me, when you had such abundant opportunity?" "Sir," replied he, "do you recollect the juniper bush on the border against the dining-room? I have many times hid under it at night, intending, which I could easily have done, to get into the house and plunder it; but, sir, I was afraid: something said to me, he is a man of God: it is a house of prayer; if I break in I shall surely be found out: so I never could pluck up courage to attempt it." In another conversation, he told him: "Sir," I well know that old Mr. Rugg was in the habit of carrying a deal of money in his pocket: times and times have I hid behind the hedge of the lane leading to his house: he has passed within a yard of me, when going home from the prayer-meeting, again and again; I could not stir; I durst not touch so holy a man. I was afraid. I always began to tremble as soon as he came near me, and gave up the thought altogether, for I knew he was a holy man."

DYING CONFESSION OF BORGIA.

It is said of the celebrated Cæsar Borgia, that in his last moments he exclaimed: "I have provided, in the course of my life, for every thing except death; and now, alas! I am to die, although entirely unprepared."

I WON'T DIE NOW.

The following affecting account was written in 1775, by a Christian minister in London, to the Rev. Dr. Ryland, who then resided at Northampton: A young lady, who was educated at an academy at Bedford, but who afterward resided in town, became dangerously ill. Her father, a true Christian, procured for her a lodging in the neighborhood, to try the effects of a change of air. Finding her disorder prevail, he thought it high time for her to be concerned about her soul, and asked her what she thought of eternity. She replied: "Do not talk to me about eternity. You want me out of the way; but I shall live long enough to enjoy all that you have in the world." He left her. Next evening, the mistress of the house where she was, said, "Ma'am, I think you look a good deal worse." "Worse! I am much better. Why do you talk to me about death?" "You certainly are worse; do let the servant sit up with you to-night." "No, I am not about to die." They went to bed; at four in the morning she awoke her servant, who asked, "What is amiss, ma'am?" "Amiss! I'm dying, I'm dying!" The family was called up; the mistress, coming in to sée her, was thus addressed: "I won't die now; I am determined I won't die; I will live." Getting worse and worse, she said, "I feel I must die," and in an agony screamed out, "Lord! what must I do?" Her servant replied, "You must turn to the Savior." She fell back on the bed, and in a moment expired.

BUNYAN IN PRISON.

THE respectability of Bunyan's character and the propriety of his conduct while in prison at Bedford, appear to have operated very powerfully on the mind of the jailer, who showed him much kindness, in permitting him to go out and visit his friends occasionally, and once to take a journey to London.

The following anecdote is told respecting the jailer and Mr. Bunyan: It being known to some of his persecutors, in London, that he was often out of prison, they sent an officer to talk with the jailer on the subject: and, in order to discover the fact, he was to get there in the middle of the night. Bunyan was at home with his family, but so restless that he could not sleep; he therefore acquainted his wife, that, though the jailer had given him liberty to stay till the morning, yet, from his uneasiness, he must immediately return. He did so, and the jailer blamed him for coming in at such an unseasonable hour. Early in the morning the messenger came, and interrogating the jailer said, "Are all the prisoners safe?" "Yes." "Is John Bunyan safe?" "Yes." "Let me see him." He was called, and appeared, and all was well. After the messenger was gone, the jailer, addressing Mr. Bunyan, said: "Well, you may go in and out again just when you think proper, for you know when return better than I can tell you."

THE CZAR AND THE NOBLEMAN'S DINNER.

ALEXANDER MENZIKOFF, who rose to the highest offices of state in Russia, during the reign of Peter the Great, was born of parents so excessively poor, that they could not afford to have him taught to read and write. After their death, he went to Moscow to seek for employment, where he found an asylum with a pastry-cook. He had a very fine voice, and soon became known in that great city from the musical tone of his cry when vending his master's pastry in the street. His voice also gained him admission into the houses of many noblemen; and he was fortunate enough one day to be in the kitchen of a great lord with whom the emperor was to dine. While Menzikoff was there, the nobleman came into the kitchen and gave directions about a particular dish, to which he said the emperor was very partial; into this dish he dropped (as he thought unperceived,) a powder. Menzikoff observed it, but taking no notice, immediately left the house; and when he saw the emperor's carriage coming, he began to sing very loud. Peter, attracted by his voice, called him, and bought all the pies he had in his basket. He asked some questions of Menzikoff, and was so much pleased with his answers, that he commanded him to follow him to the nobleman's house, and wait behind his chair. The servants were surprised at this order, but it proved of the greatest importance to Peter; for when the nobleman pressed his royal guest to take of this favorite dish, his new servant gently pulled him by the sleeve, and begged he would not touch it till he had spoken to him. The emperor immediately withdrew with Menzikoff, who informed his imperial master of his suspicions. The czar returned to the company, and suddenly turning to his host pressed him to partake of the favorite dish. Terrified at this command, he said, "it did not become the servant to eat before his master." The emperor then offered it to a dog, who greedily devoured its contents, and shortly afterwards expired in the greatest torments!

TWO STRINGS TO OUR BOW.

"Well, Hodge," said a smart looking Londoner to a plain cottager, who was on his way home from church, "so you are trudging home, after taking the benefit of the fine balmy breezes in the country this morning." "Sir," said the man, "I have not been strolling about this sacred morning, wasting my time in idleness and neglect of religion; but I have been at the house of God, to worship him, and hear his preached word." "Ah! what then, you are one of those simpletons, that in these country places are weak enough to believe the bible? Believe me, my man, that book is a pack of nonsense, and none but weak and ignorant people now think it true." "Well, Mr. Stranger, but do you know, weak and ignorant as we are, *we* like to have *two strings to our bow?*" "Two strings to your bow! What do you mean by that?" "Why, sir, I mean that to believe the bible, and act up to it, is like having two strings to one's bow; for if it is *not* true, I shall be the better man for living according to it; and so it will be for my good in this life—that is one string; and if it *should* be true, it will be better for me in the next life—

that is another string, and a pretty strong one it is. But, sir, if you disbelieve the bible, and on that account do not live as it requires, you have not one string to your bow. *And oh! if its tremendous threats prove* TRUE, *oh, think! what then, sir, will become of* YOU ?" This plain appeal silenced the coxcomb, and made him feel, it is hoped, that he was not quite so wise as he supposed.

LOUIS XV.

WHEN a prince of the blood royal of France disgraced himself by committing robbery and murder in the streets of Paris, Louis XV. would not grant a pardon, though eagerly solicited to do so by a deputation from the parliament of Paris, who tried him, and suspended their sentence till the royal pleasure should be known. "My lords and counsellors," said the king, "return to your chambers of justice, and promulgate your decree." "Consider," said the first president, "that the unhappy prince has your majesty's blood in his veins." "Yes," said the king, "but the blood has become impure, and justice demands that it should be let out; nor would I spare my own son for a crime, for which I should be bound to condemn the meanest of my subjects." The prince was executed on the scaffold in the court of the grand Chatelet, on the 12th of August, 1729.

ANECDOTE OF WINFIELD (AFTERWARD GEN.) SCOTT.

THE following anecdote was related to a gentleman, during a night he spent in a farm-house in Virginia, some few years ago:

In December, 17—, toward the close of a dreary day, a woman with an infant child were discovered half buried in the snow, by a little Virginian, seven years old. The lad was returning from school, and hearing the moans of some one in distress, threw down his satchel of books, and repaired to the spot whence the sound proceeded, with a firmness becoming one of riper years. Raking the snow from the benumbed body of the mother, and using means to awaken her to a sense of her deplorable condition, the noble youth succeeded in getting her upon her feet; the infant nestling on its mother's breast, turned its eyes toward their youthful preserver and smiled, as it seemed, in gratitude for its preservation. With a countenance filled with hope, the gallant youth cheered the sufferer on, himself bearing within his tiny arms the infant child, while the mother leaned for support on the shoulder of her little conductor. "My home is hard by," would he exclaim, as oft as her spirits failed; and thus, for three miles, did he cheer onward to a happy haven, the mother and child, both of whom otherwise must have perished, had it not been for the humane feeling and perseverance of this noble youth.

A warm fire and kind attention soon relieved the sufferer, who, it appeared, was in search of her husband, an emigrant from New Hampshire, a recent purchaser of a farm in the neighborhood of ———, near this place. Diligent inquiry for several days found him, and in five months after, the identical house in which we are now sitting was erected, and received the happy family. The child grew up to manhood, entered the army, lost a limb at New Orleans, but returned to end his days, a solace to the declining years of his aged parents.

"Where are they now?" I asked the narrator.

"Here," exclaimed the son. "I am the rescued one—there is my mother, and here, imprinted on my naked arm, is the name of the noble youth, our preserver!"

I looked, and read, "*Winfield Scott.*"

THE KING AND THE SOLDIER.

A KING was riding alone in disguise, and seeing a soldier at a public-house door, stopped, and asked the soldier to drink with him; and while they were talking the king *swore.*

The soldier said, "Sir, I am sorry to hear a gentleman swear." His majesty took no notice, but soon swore again. The soldier said, "Sir, I'll pay part of the pot if you please, and go; for I so hate swearing, that if you were the king himself, I should tell you of it." "Should you indeed?" said the king. "I should," said the soldier. His majesty said no more, but left him. A while after, the king having invited some of his lords to dine with him, the soldier, was sent for; and while they were at dinner, he was ordered into the room, and to wait awhile. Presently the king uttered an oath; the soldier immediately, but with great modesty, said, "Should not my lord, the king, fear an oath?" The king, looking first at the lords, then at the soldier, said, "There, my lords, is an honest man: he can respectfully remind me of the *great sin* of swearing; but you can sit and let me send my soul to hell by swearing, and not so much as tell me of it."

A MERITED REBUKE.

MR. LOCKE, having been introduced by Lord Shaftesbury to the Duke of Buckingham and Lord Halifax, these three noblemen, instead of conversing with the philosopher, as might naturally have been expected, on literary subjects, in a very short time sat down to cards. Mr. Locke, after looking for some time, pulled out his pocket-book, and began to write with great attention. One of the company observing this, took the liberty of asking him what he was writing.

"My lord," said Locke, "I am endeavoring, as far as possible, to profit by my present situation; for having waited with impatience for the honor of being in company with the greatest geniuses of the age, I thought I could do nothing better than to write down your conversation; and, indeed, I have set down the substance of what you have said this hour or two." This well-timed ridicule had its desired effect, and these noblemen, fully sensible of its force, immediately quitted their play, and entered into a conversation more rational, and better suited to the dignity of their characters, and it may be added, better fitted to improve time, than so unprofitable a diversion.

TAMERLANE AND BAJAZET.

Tamerlane the Great, having made war on Bajazet, emperor of the Turks, overthrew him in battle and took him prisoner. The victor gave the captive monarch at first a very civil reception; and entering into familiar conversation with him, said, "Now, king, tell me freely and truly what thou wouldst have done with me had I fallen into thy power?" Bajazet, who was of a fierce and haughty spirit, is said to have thus replied: "Had the gods given unto me the victory, I would have enclosed thee in an iron cage, and carried thee about with me as a spectacle of derision to the world." Tamerlane wrathfully replied: "Then, proud man, as thou wouldst have done to me, even so shall I do unto thee." A strong iron cage was made, into which the fallen emperor was thrust; and thus exposed like a wild beast, he was carried along in the train of the conqueror. Nearly three years were passed by the once mighty Bajazet in this cruel state of durance; and at last being told that he must be carried into Tartary, despairing of then obtaining his freedom, he struck his head with such violence against the bars of his cage, as to put an end to his wretched life.

THE HONEST COTTAGER.

In a little town five miles from St. Petersburgh, lived a poor German woman. A small cottage was her only possession, and the visits of a few shipmasters, on their way to Petersburgh, her only livelihood. Several Dutch shipmasters having supped at her house one evening, she found, when they were gone, a sealed bag of money under the table. Some one of the company had no doubt forgotten it, but they had sailed over to Cronstadt, and the wind being fair, there was no chance of their putting back. The good woman put the bag in her cupboard, to keep it till it should be called for. Full seven years elapsed, however, and no one claimed it; and though often tempted by opportunity, and oftener tempted by want, to make use of the contents, the poor woman's good principles prevailed, and it remained untouched.

One evening some shipmasters again stopped at her house for refreshment. Three of them were English—the fourth a Dutchman. Conversing on various matters, one of them asked the Dutchman if he had ever been in that town before. "Indeed I have," replied he. "I know the place but too well: my being here cost me once seven hundred rubles." "How so?" "Why, in one of these wretched hovels, I once left behind me a bag of rubles." "Was the bag sealed?" asked the old woman, who was sitting in the corner of the room, and whose attention was roused by the subject. "Yes, yes, it was sealed, and with this very seal here at my watch chain." The woman knew the seal instantly. "Well, then, by that you may recover what you have lost." "Recover it, mother! no, no, I am rather too old to expect that; the world is not quite so honest—besides it is full seven years since I lost the money. Say no more about it—it always makes me melancholy."

Meanwhile the good woman slipped out, and presently returned with the bag. "See here," said she, "honesty is not so rare, perhaps, as you may imagine;" and she threw the bag on the table.

The guests were astonished, and the owner of the bag, as may be supposed, highly delighted. He seized the bag, counted out one hundred rubles and gave them to the old woman, who thus, at length, was handsomely rewarded for her honesty.

THE DROWNING LADY.

A GAY lady in New England once had occasion to go to a neighboring town, where she had often been before. In the immediate vicinity was a stream which she had to go near, and which at this period was high. With a view of showing her courage to a young person whom she had taken with her as a companion, she went into the stream with her horse, and in a very little time was thrown into the water—had already sunk once or twice to the bottom, and felt that she was within a few moments of an eternal world, without being prepared for so great a change.

It so happened that a young man in another neighboring town had felt a powerful impression on his mind that morning, that he should visit the same place. He had no business to transact; but, being forcibly impressed with the importance of going thither, he invited a young man to accompany him. Arriving at the side of the stream just as the young ladies were about to cross it, they saw it was improbable that they could ford it; yet, as the ladies went, they determined to follow.

By the time the young lady was thrown from her horse, the others had nearly reached the opposite shore; but, perceiving her danger, one of them immediately followed her on his horse, and in the last moment of life, as it then appeared, she caught hold of the horse's leg; he thus secured her, and snatching hold of the other drowning young lady, she was saved also. After the use of proper remedies, they recovered; and the young gentlemen, believing that the design of their coming from home was now answered, returned back.

The impression made on the mind of this young lady was permanent, and she was led to reflect on the sins she had committed against God, to pray for the pardon of her guilt, and to devote herself to the Divine service. She embraced the mercy of the Lord, believing in the Redeemer, who alone saves from the wrath to come.

In the same town with herself lived a young gentleman, who had often spent his hours in vain conversation with her. On her return home, he went to congratulate her on her escape, and, to his surprise, found she attributed her deliverance to the power of God, and urged him to seek that grace which they had both neglected. Her serious conversation was blest to his conversion, and he became a faithful minister of Jesus Christ.

FATHER HARRISON.

The following anecdote is given by Rev. T. Harrison, in reference to his father, Rev. R. Harrison, formerly of Yorkshire, England, and latterly of Springfield, Ohio.

One day he had a payment of five pounds, or about twenty-five dollars, to make by twelve o'clock at noon. Not having the money by him, and not wishing to trouble any one with the borrowing of it, he petitioned the God of all wealth, in his family devotions, that, if it was his will, a way might be opened by which he could meet his obligation and liquidate the debt. About two hours afterward, a gentleman, who lived in the country about four miles distant, and who had been converted by his instrumentality, rode up to his residence, and, after alighting, remarked: "Brother Harrison, it was impressed on my mind this morning that I was to come to town, and bring you five pounds. Please accept it from a Christian brother that loves you for your labors in the cause of Christ."

THE BULLET AND THE TEXT.

Dr. John Evans, the author of some excellent sermons on the Christian temper, introduced on one occasion, a sermon to young people, in the following manner:

"Shall I be allowed to preface this discourse with relating a passage concerning an acquaintance of mine, who has been many years dead, but which I remember to have received, when young, from himself? When he was an apprentice in this city, the civil war began; his inclination led him into the army, where he had a captain's commission. It was fashionable for all the men of that army to carry a bible along with them; which, therefore, he and many others did, who yet made little use of it, and hardly had any sense of serious religion. At length he was commanded, with his company, to storm a fort, where they were, for a short time, exposed to the thickest of the enemy's fire. When he had accomplished his enterprise, and the heat of the action was over, he found that a musket ball had lodged in his bible, which was in his pocket, upon such a part of his body that it must necessarily have proved mortal to him, had it not been for this seasonable and well-placed piece of armor. Upon a nearer observation, he found the ball had made its way so far in his bible as to rest directly upon that part of the first unbroken leaf where the words of my text are found. It was Eccles. xi. 9: "Rejoice, O young man, in thy youth; and let thy heart cheer thee in the days of thy youth, and walk in the ways of thine heart, and in the sight of thine eyes: but know thou, that for all these things God will bring thee into judgment."

"As the surprising deliverance, you may apprehend, much affected him, so a passage, which his conscience told him was very apposite to his case, and which Providence in so remarkable a way pointed to his observation, made the deepest and best impression on his mind; and, by the grace of God, he from that time attended to religion in earnest, and continued in the practice of it to a good old age—frequently making the remark with pleasure, that his bible had been the salvation of both of his body and his soul."

THE FUTURE.

A LADY had written on a card, and placed in her garden house on the top of an hour-glass, a beautiful and simple stanza from one of the fugitive pieces of John Clare, the rural poet; it was at the season of the year when the flowers were in their highest beauty:

"To think of summers yet to come,
  That I am not to see;
To think a weed is yet to bloom,
  From dust that *I shall be!*"

The next morning she found penciled on the back of the same card:

"To think when heaven and earth are fled,
  And times and seasons o'er,
When all that CAN die shall be dead,
  That I must die no more!
Ah! where will then my portion be?
  How shall I spend *eternity!*"

HOW TO CURE A HUSBAND.

A WOMAN, whom her husband used frequently to beat, went to a cunning man to inquire how she mignt cure him of his barbarity. The sagacious soothsayer heard her complaint; and after pronouncing some hard words, and using various gesticulation, while he filled a phial with a colored liquid, desired her, whenever her husband was in a passion, to take a mouthful of the liquor, and keep it in her mouth for five minutes. The woman, quite overjoyed at so simple a remedy, strictly followed the counsel which was given her, and, by her silence, escaped the usual chastisement. The contents of the bottle being at last expended, she returned to the cunning man, and anxiously begged to have another possessed of the same virtue. "Foolish woman!" said the man, "there was nothing in the bottle but brown sugar and water. When your husband is in a passion, hold your tongue, and, my life for it, he will not lay a finger upon you."

TRIAL OF FAITH.

WHEN Constantine was chosen emperor he found several Christians in office, and he issued an edict requiring them to renounce their faith, or quit their places. Most of them gave up their offices to preserve their consciences—but some cringed and renounced christianity. When the emperor had thus made full proof of their disposition and character, he removed all who thus basely complied with his supposed wishes, and retained the others, saying, "that those who would desert or deny their Divine Master, would desert him, and were not worthy of his confidence."

THE HONEST INSOLVENT.

A GENTLEMAN of Boston, says a religious journal, who was unfortunate in business thirty years ago, and consequently unable at that time to meet his engagements with his creditors, after more than twenty years of toil, succeeded in paying every creditor, (except one whose residence could not be ascertained,) the whole amount due them. He has in that twenty years brought up and educated a large family: but still he owed one of his former creditors. He was not satisfied to keep another's property. He made inquiry, and received information that the party had died some years since. He again pursued his inquiry respecting the administrator, and ascertained his name and residence, wrote to him, acknowledged the debt, and requested him to inform him of the manner he would receive the money. Afterward he remitted the whole amount, principal and interest.

OPINIONS OF EMINENT MEN ON THE BIBLE.

Among men of education and talents, those who have been known as enemies of the bible have, for the most part, unhesitatingly acknowledged their ignorance of its contents, or at least that they were not familiar with its pages; while the invariable testimony of all who have candidly studied it, has been in favor of its claims to divine authority, and to the sublimity, purity and wisdom of its precepts. The testimony following, will be very generally respected.

The venerable John Quincy Adams a short time before his death stated to a friend, that ever since he was thirty years old, he had been accustomed, among the first things, to read the bible every morning. With few interruptions, he followed the practice over half a century.

Dr. Samuel Johnson is distinguished as a writer on morals; his compositions have seldom been excelled in energy of thought and beauty of expression. To a young gentleman, who visited him on his deathbed, he said: "Young man, attend to the voice of one who has possessed a certain degree of fame in the world, and who will shortly appear before his Maker: read the bible every day of your life."

At the time when the celebrated Dr. Franklin lay upon his deathbed, he was visited by a young man who had a great respect for his judgment in all things; and having entertained doubts as to the truth of the scriptures, he thought that this awful period afforded a suitable opportunity of consulting the doctor on this important subject. Accordingly, he introduced it in a solemn and weighty manner, inquiring of Franklin what were his sentiments as to the truth of the scriptures. On the question being put, although he was in a very weak state, and near his decease, he replied: "Young man, my advice to you is, that you cultivate an acquaintance with, and a firm belief in, the holy scriptures: this is your certain interest."

When Sir Walter Scott returned, a trembling invalid from Italy, to die in his native land, the sight of his "sweet home," so invigorated his spirits, that some hope was cherished, that he might recover. But he soon relapsed. He found that he must die. Addressing his son-in-law, he said, "Bring me a *book*." "What book?" replied Lockhart. "Can you ask," said the expiring genius, whose fascinating novels have charmed the world, but have no balm for death, "can you ask *what* book? there is but *one*."

THE SCOTCH BAKER IN LONDON.

A rotund, full-priced baker, who was in the habit of bringing his miserable debtors into "Westminster Court of Requests," one day stepped into the plaintiffs' box with papers and ledger in hand, to make good his claim for twenty-five shillings, for bread supplied to a Mr. John Howard.

A tall young woman, wearing a handsome fur mantilla, and evidently careful to exhibit the externals of gentility, presented herself to answer the demand. Her age might be either eighteen or twenty-eight; the hollow cheek and spare form, produced by early sorrow or privation, or both, prevented a closer approximation to the truth.

A Commissioner.—Is the amount disputed?

Young Lady.—Certainly not. I have only to say, on the part of my father, that he sincerely regrets his inability to settle the amount at once.

Chairman.—How will you pay it?

Young Lady.—I have five shillings to offer now, and my father wishes to have the indulgence of paying the rest at half-a-crown a week.

Commissioner.—The bill is for bread, and it has been standing for some time. Judging from your appearance, I should think your father cannot be in such circumstances as to make it difficult to procure the few shillings left unpaid on this bill.

Young Lady.—Appearances are often deceitful. It is equally distressing to my father and myself to ask even for one day; but unexpected sickness in our family has totally exhausted our little means.

Baker (pocketing the money).—Twa and saxpence a-week is not enough. Ye gang about toon wi a grand boa, and a fine silk dress, while my wife maun wear a plaid shawl and a cotton goon, because the likes o' ye will eat an honest mon's bread wi'oot paying for't. That fine tippet ye hae gotten on maun hae cost, may be sax gowden guineas.

"It is true," said the young lady, coloring, "my dress may appear rather extravagant, and if I could with prudence dress at less cost, I would do so; but upon a respectable exterior, on my part, as a teacher of music, depends the subsistence of a sick father and two young sisters. (The baker shut his book abruptly, and thrust his papers into his pocket.) As for the boa you allude to, that was pledged this morning to raise a few shillings to pay you the five you have just received, and to provide food for those who have tasted little else beyond dry bread for the last week. The tippet I have on was kindly lent me by my landlady, as the day is wet and cold."

"Well, Mr. Baker," said the chairman, in a tone of compassion, "perhaps you will agree to the young lady's terms?"

"Oh, aye," said the baker, "twa and saxpence a month. Pit it down if you wull."

Chairman.—Two and sixpence a-week was offered.

"Mak it just what ye like," said the baker.

The order was made and handed to the young lady. As she was leaving the court, the baker stopped her. "Gie me haud o' that bit paper," said the baker. The request was complied with.

"Noo," said the baker, thrusting some silver into her hand, "tak bock your croon-piece, and dinna fash yoursel at a' wi' the weekly payment. Ye shall hae a four pund loaf ilka day at my shope, and ye may pay me just when ye're able, and if I niver git the siller, may be I'll niver miss it; but mind, young leddy," said he angrily, "gin ye deal wi' ony ither baker, I'se pit this order in force agin yere father."

The young lady looked her gratitude. The baker had vanished.

POOR JONATHAN.

In a large and populous village in Yorkshire, England, lived a poor but pious man called Jonathan. He was greatly paralyzed by disease; had a wife and two or three children chiefly depending on him for support; and was industrious and persevering in his efforts to provide for his family, all of whom were content with homely fare. At the time the writer of this account knew him, he might be from forty to fifty years of age. Among other occurrences of his life, he says, I distinctly recollect the following, which he related to me:

During the time of harvest, while employed in gathering the fruits of the earth, he accidentally slipped from the top of a barley-mow, and sprained his ankle, in consequence of which he was confined to his room and bed for some weeks. It is unnecessary to state that in the meantime his family must have felt the loss of his weekly labor and income. His wife, on one occasion, went up stairs into his room weeping. "What is the matter?" said Jonathan; "what is distressing thee?" "Why, the children are crying for something to eat, and I have nothing to give them," was the affecting reply. "Hast thou faith in God?" asked Jonathan. "Dost thou believe in Providence and in his word? Has he not said, 'bread shall be given thee, and thy water shall be sure?' Isa. 33: 16. Kneel down," he continued, "at the bedside, and pray to God. Tell him how thy children are circumstanced; that they have no bread; that thou hast nothing wherewith to buy them any; and I will also pray. Who can tell what God may do? He heareth prayer."

Jonathan and his wife prayed earnestly together; they pleaded the promises of God, and waited the result. Soon after a person came to the door with a loaf of bread. She came from a house in the immediate neighborhood of Jonathan, the occupier of which was one of several branches of a family who were proprietors of very extensive iron-works carried on in the village where Jonathan lived.

No sooner did the good woman receive the loaf of bread than she ran to Jonathan to tell him how God had answered their prayer. "Now," said Jonathan, "before any thing else be done, kneel down at the bedside and return thanks to God for having heard our prayer." She did so; they praised his name together; they then ate their food with gladness and singleness of heart. Not many hours elapsed before another kind interposition of Providence presented itself. A second visitor brought them a joint of meat. When this was told Jonathan, he replied to his wife, "Ay! see! God is better than his word! He promised bread, and he sends flesh in addition. Kneel down and thank him again."

I will add one more anecdote of pious Jonathan. He had a relative, in good circumstances, a few miles distant, whom he occasionally visited. He embraced an opportunity of paying a visit to that person on the same day on which he attended a quarterly religious meeting observed by the denomination of Christians to which he belonged. It so happened that a party of friends dined with his relative that day, who were sufficiently forward to taunt Jonathan with his religion and religious profession. Before he left the table, wine was brought, and Jonathan was urged and urged again to partake. They had their design in this, which Jonathan perceived. When pressed, he said, "Well, for once I will drink like a beast." He then took what he deemed sufficient and prepared to withdraw. "How so?" said one: "did you not say you would drink like a beast? Methodists, I see, will not swear, but they will lie." "I am not chargeable with that," said Jonathan; "how does a beast drink? Just as much as nature requires, and no more. I have done so. Beware you do not make yourselves worse than beasts." Jonathan left them to reflect upon the admonition. Reader, do not despise good men, though they are poor; and learn not to look upon the wine when it is red. "Who hath wo? Who hath sorrow? Who hath contention? They that tarry long at the wine?"

A YOUNG RECRUIT.

A young man in England whose manner indicated a well-cultivated mind, and commanded respect, went to a recruiting-officer requesting to be enlisted. Appearing to be greatly embarrassed, the officer asked him the cause of it. With tears he replied, "I tremble lest you should deny my request." "No," said the officer, "I accept your offer most heartily; but why should you fear a refusal?" "Because the bounty which I expect may perhaps be too high." "How much then do you demand?" said the officer. "It is no unworthy motive, but an urgent claim that compels me to ask ten guineas; and I shall be the most miserable of mankind if you refuse me." "Ten guineas!" said the officer; "that indeed is very high; but I am pleased with you: I trust to your honor for the discharge of your duty, and will strike the bargain at once. Here are ten guineas; to-morrow we depart." The young man, overwhelmed with joy, asked leave to return home, and promised to be back within an hour. The officer gave permission, and induced by curiosity, followed him at some distance. He went to the town-prison, where he knocked and was admitted. The officer, while standing at the door of the prison, overheard the young man say to the jailer, "Here is the money for which my father is imprisoned. I put it into your hands, and request you will conduct me to him immediately, that I may release him from his misery." The jailer did as he was requested. After the delay of a few minutes, the officer followed him. What a scene! He saw the son in the arms of a venerable and aged father, who, without uttering a word, pressed him to his heart and bedewed him with tears. The officer approached them, and said to the old man, "Compose yourself, I will not deprive you of so worthy a son. Permit me to restore him to you, that I may not regret the money which he has employed in so virtuous a manner." The father and son fell upon their knees at his feet. The young man refused at first to accept of this proffered freedom; but the generous officer insisted that he should remain with his father. He accompanied them both from the prison, and took his leave, with the pleasing reflection of having contributed to the happiness of a worthy son and an unfortunate father.

DISTRICTS IN PURGATORY.

A WOMAN and two children, says Doctor Brownlee, called on a lady in Broadway, New York, to ask alms. The woman was dressed in black, and said that she was left a widow, with the children she had accompanying her, in distressed circumstances, and she urged her request for alms with considerable earnestness. The lady informed her that she could give her no money, but offered her food and articles of clothing if she might need them. But these would not do; the widow wanted money, and she insisted so earnestly on the gift of money, that the lady asked her into the house, and entered into conversation with her, when she drew from the widow the following story:

"My husband," said she, "died a few weeks ago, and since that I've had no peace. Priest ——— called on me soon after, and reproved me for not paying over to him the sum of money necessary for his release from that place of torment. I asked him how much that would be? 'Oh,' said he, 'we have different prices for different souls. For saying mass for some we have one hundred dollars, for others fifty, and for others less. The least sum I can accept for praying the soul of your departed husband out of that place of torment is *twenty-four dollars*.' And now he gives me no peace, because, you know, I have not the money, and what can I do for the soul of my poor husband?"

The lady took a bible, and handing it to the afflicted widow, said to her: "Here, take this bible, and go to the priest you speak of, and request him to fold down a leaf on that place which teaches the doctrine of purgatory, and then you bring the bible back to me, and I will give you the whole amount you want to pay for the praying your husband out of that place of torment."

The poor Romanist was delighted with this proposal. She took the bible, and made off in great haste to the priest; but she was not gone a great while; she soon returned more sorrowful than before. She told the lady, in great distress, that she carried the bible to the priest, and informed him how he could put her in the way of obtaining the whole amount necessary to procure the release of her husband's soul from the torments of purgatory. But, alas! instead of turning down a leaf in her bible upon a place where it teaches the doctrine of purgatory, he flew into a violent rage, and ordered her from his presence, saying: "See that the twenty-four dollars are forthcoming, or I'll put you under penance for having in your presence that heretical book, and your husband shall never be released from purgatory till the money is paid down; and, mind you, no other priest but myself can pray him out, for he is *in my district!*"

I'LL TAKE BACK MY MONEY.

An Italian noble being at church one day, and finding a priest who begged for the souls in purgatory, gave him a piece of gold. "Ah! my lord," said the good father, "you have now delivered a soul." The count threw upon the plate another piece. "Here is another soul delivered," said the priest. "Are you positive of it?" replied the count. "Yes, my lord," replied the priest, "I am certain they are now in heaven." "Then," said the count, "I'll take back my money, for it signifies nothing to you now; seeing the souls are already got to heaven, there can be no danger of their returning to purgatory."

MADEMOISELLE SOMBRUIL.

During the French revolution, Mademoiselle Sombruil had been eight days with her father in prison, when the unhappy massacres of September commenced. After many prisoners had been murdered, and the sight of blood continually flowing, seemed only to increase the rage of the assassins, while the wretched inmates of the prison endeavored to hide themselves from the death that hovered over them, Mademoiselle Sombruil rushed into the presence of the murderers who had seized her father. "Barbarians!" she cried, "hold your hands, he is my father!" She threw herself at their feet. In one moment she seized the hand that was lifted against her father, and in the next she offered her own person to the sword, so placing herself that the parent could not be struck but through the body of his child. So much courage and filial affection in so young a girl, for a moment diverted the attention of the assassins. She perceived that they hesitated, and seized on the favorable opportunity. While she entreated for her father's life, one of the monsters proposed the following condition: "Drink," said he, "a glass of blood, and save your father." She shuddered, and retreated some paces; but filial affection gained the ascendancy, and she yielded to the horrible condition. "Innocent or guilty," said one of those who performed the office of judge, "it is unworthy of the people to bathe their hands in the blood of the old man, since they must first destroy this virtuous girl." A cry of "pardon!" was heard. The daughter, revived by this signal of safety, threw herself into her father's trembling arms, which scarcely had power to press her to his bosom, being overcome by such powerful affection and so providential a deliverance. Even the most outrageous assassins were unable to restrain their tears; and the father and daughter were triumphantly conducted to a place of comfort and safety.

THE INDIAN CONVERT.

"Do you remember," said an Indian convert to a missionary, "that a few years ago a party of warriors came to the vicinity of the tribe to whom you preach, and pretending friendship, invited the chief of the tribe to hold a talk with them?"

"Yes," replied the missionary, "I remember it very well."

"Do you remember," continued the Indian, "that the chief, fearing treachery, instead of going himself, sent one of his warriors to hold the talk?"

"Yes," was the reply.

"And do you remember," proceeded the Indian, "that warrior never returned, but that he was murdered by those who, with promises of friendship, had led him into their snare?"

"I remember it all very well," replied the missionary.

"Well," the Indian continued, weeping with emotion, "I was one of that band of warriors. As soon as our victim was in the midst of us, we fell upon him with our tomahawks and cut him to pieces."

This man became one of the most influential members of the christian church, and reflected with horror upon those scenes in which he formerly exulted. He gave his influence and his prayers, that there might be glory to God in the highest, peace on earth and good will to men.

FREDERICK AND HIS PAGE.

Frederick of Prussia, one day rung his bell, and nobody answering, he opened his door, and found his page fast asleep in an elbow-chair. He advanced toward, and was going to awaken him, when he perceived part of a letter hanging out of his pocket. His curiosity prompting him to know what it was, he took it out and read it. It was a letter from this young man's mother, in which she thanked him for having sent her a part of his wages to relieve her misery; and finished with telling him that God would reward him for his dutiful affection. The king, after reading it, went back softly into his chamber, took a bag full of ducats, and slipped it with the letter into the page's pocket. Returning to his chamber, he rang the bell so loudly that it awakened the page, who instantly made his appearance. "You have had a sound sleep," said the king. The page was at a loss how to excuse himself; and putting his hand into his pocket by chance, to his utter astonishment he there found a purse of ducats. He took it out, turned pale, and looking at the king, shed a torrent of tears without being able to utter a single word. "What is that?" said the king; "what is the matter?" "Ah! sire," said the young man, throwing himself on his knees, "somebody seeks my ruin! I know nothing of this money which I have found in my pocket!" "My young friend," replied Frederick, "God often does great things for us, even in our sleep. Send that to your mother; salute her on my part, and assure her that I will take care of both her and you."

PRESERVATION OF A FAMILY.

A CREDIBLE historian informs us, that about one hundred and fifty years ago, there was an earthquake in Switzerland, which precipitated part of a mountain upon a village that stood beneath it, and crushed every house and inhabitant to atoms, except the corner of one cottage, where the master of the house, with his poor family, were together praying to God.

EUCLID.

EUCLID, a disciple of Socrates, having offended his brother, the brother cried out in a rage, "Let me die if I am not revenged on you one time or other;" to whom Euclid replied, "And let me die if I do not soften you by my kindnesses, and make you love me as well as ever." What a reproof to unforgiving professors of Christianity!

SERGEANT FORBES.

MANY years ago, in a regiment of soldiers stationed at Edinburgh, there was a sergeant named Forbes, a very abandoned man, who got in debt for liquor wherever he could. His wife washed for the regiment, and thus obtained a little money. She was a pious woman, but all her attempts to reclaim him were long unsuccessful. During one of Mr. Whitefield's visit to that city, she offered her husband a sum of money if he would for once go and hear him. This was a strong inducement, and he engaged to go. The sermon was in a field, as no building could have contained the audience. The sergeant was rather early, and placed himself in the middle of the field, that he might file off when Mr. Whitefield ascended the pulpit; as he only wished to be able to say that he had seen him. The crowd however increased; and when Mr. Whitefield appeared they pressed forward, and he found it impossible to get away. The prayer produced some impression on his mind, but the sermon most deeply convinced him of his sinfulness and danger. He became an altered man, and proved the reality of his conversion by living for many years with the strictest economy, in order to liquidate the claims of every one of his creditors.

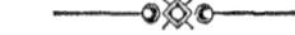

JUDGE BULLER.

Judge Buller, when in the company of a young gentleman of sixteen, cautioned him against being led astray, by the example or persuasion of others, and said: "If I had listened to the advice of some of those who called themselves my friends when I was young, instead of being a *judge* of the king's bench, I should have died long ago a *prisoner* in the king's bench."

SIR PHILIP SIDNEY.

This eminent man was governor of Flushing, (Neth.) and general of the horse under his uncle, the earl of Leicester. His valor, which was esteemed great, and not exceeded by any of his age, was at least equalled by his humanity. After he had received his death-wound at the battle of Zutphen, and was overcome with thirst from excessive bleeding, he called for drink, which was soon brought him. At the same time, a poor soldier, dangerously wounded, was carried along, who fixed his eager eyes upon the bottle just as Sir Philip was lifting it to his mouth. Sir Philip immediately presented it to him, with the remark: "Thy necessity is greater than mine."

THE BROTHERS AND THE SNOW-STORM.

In the year 1804, some young men of the Morayshire and Inverness-shire militia, being quartered at Edinburgh, obtained a short furlough. They were seven in number, two of them being brothers, named Forsythe. They had to walk, in the very depth of winter, one hundred and thirty miles. As they proceeded, they were overtaken by one of those sudden snow-storms which are usual in the mountains. And now the night began to close in around them, while the snow and the wind still grew thicker and stronger. At last, being bewildered by the shade of the evening, which was rendered yet more dismal by the incessant snow-drift, they strayed, as might be expected, from the right path, and exhausted their strength. They could just see one another; but the storm was so violent, they could not converse. Thus struggling onward, and scarcely knowing where they went, one of them sank in a hollow in the rock, and was buried. The others passed on, unconscious of his loss. Soon after, the younger Forsythe also dropped down, being quite spent. His body lay in the pathway of the rest, but being much weakened themselves, they, without helping him, stepped on; all did so but one. This one was the elder Forsythe, who knowing that he had a brother among the party, stooped when he came up to him, and felt his features. Having in this manner assured himself that it was his own brother, he, without hesitation, took him up, and placed him on his back. And now the number rapidly diminished; one after another perished, being frozen to death. Forsythe yet went on, bearing his burden, which neither his fatigue, nor the difficulties of the way, could induce him to cast off. As long as he had any strength, he persevered, holding his brother on his back, until at length, his powers giving way before his affection, he sank beneath the weight, and immediately expired. Before, however, he thus died, it appeared that he had succeeded in saving his brother, though he lost himself: for the younger Forsythe had been gradually reanimated by the warmth of his brother's body; and, when he dropped, was so thoroughly aroused, that he was enabled to reach his home, having escaped death by his brother's generous sacrifice of himself, and had the melancholy duty imposed upon him of attending his kind brother's funeral.

WASHINGTON'S REGARD FOR HIS MOTHER.

General George Washington when quite young, was about to go to sea as a midshipman; every thing was arranged, the vessel lay opposite his father's house, the little boat had come on shore to take him off, and his whole heart was bent on going. After his trunk had been carried down to the boat, he went to bid his mother farewell, and saw the tears bursting from her eyes. However, he said nothing to her; but he saw that his mother would be distressed if he went, and perhaps never be happy again. He just turned around to the servant and said, "Go and tell them to fetch my trunk back. I will not go away to break my mother's heart." His mother was struck with his decision, and she said to him: "George, God has promised to bless the children that honor their parents, and I believe he will bless you."

FREDERICK THE GREAT AND SERGEANT THOMAS.

It is well known that Frederick the Great took pride in having his soldiers well disciplined; and was therefore particularly attentive to the conduct of the subalterns. It is perhaps not so well known. that he sometimes manifested a real respect for religious people; for few men could more clearly discern the excellence of the conduct produced by holy principles. While, therefore, he sneered at Christianity, he sometimes promoted to offices of trust those who consistently maintained it.

A sergeant, of the name of Thomas, who was very successful in training his men, and whose whole deportment pleased the king, was often noticed by him. He inquired respecting the place of the sergeant's birth, his parents, his religious creed, and the place of worship which he frequented. On being informed that he was united with the Moravians, and attended their chapel in William-street, he exclaimed, "Oh! oh! you are a fanatic, are you? Well, well; only take care to do your duty, and improve your men."

The king's common salutation after this, was: "Well, how do you do? how are you going on in William-street?" His majesty at length, in conversation with Thomas's colonel, mentioned his intention of promoting the sergeant to an office in the commissariat department, upon the death of aged man who then filled it.

The colonel, in order to encourage Thomas, told him of the king's design. Unhappily this had an injurious effect upon the mind of the sergeant; for, alas! such is the depravity of the human heart, that few can endure the temptation of prosperity without sustaining spiritual loss. Thomas began to forsake the assemblies of his Christian brethren; and when reproved by his minister, he said, "his heart was with him, but he was afraid of offending the king." The minister told him to take good heed that his heart did not deceive him. Soon after the sergeant's religious declension, he was again accosted by the king, with, "Well, how do you do? how are your friends in William-street?" "I do not know, please your majesty," was the reply. "Not know! not know!" answered the king; "have you been ill?" "No, please your majesty," rejoined the sergeant; "but I do not see it necessary to attend there so often as I used to do." "Then you are not so great a fanatic as I thought you;" was the royal answer.

In a short time the aged officer died, and the colonel waited upon his majesty to inform him of the vacancy, and to remind him of his intention to raise Sergeant Thomas to the situation. "No, no!" said the king, "he shall not have it; he does not go so often to William-street as he used to do." Surprised with this peremptory refusal, the colonel withdrew, and on his return found his sergeant waiting for the confirmation of his appointment. "I do not know what is the matter with the king to-day," said the colonel, "but he will not give you the situation. He says you do not go so often to William-street as you used to do. I do not know what he means; but I suppose you do." Struck in a moment with the awful impropriety of his conduct, he bowed to the colonel, and departed to humble himself before God. He ever after adored the Divine mercy, which did not leave him fully to realize the scriptural threatening: "The prosperity of fools shall destroy them."

DOD'S SINGULAR VISIT.

It is recorded of Mr. Dod, one of the Puritan ministers, that being one evening late in his study, his mind was strongly inclined, though he could assign no reason for it, to visit a gentleman of his acquaintance, at a very unseasonable hour. Not knowing the design of Providence, he obeyed and went. When he came to the house, after knocking a few times at the door, the gentleman himself came, and inquired if he wanted him upon any particular business. Mr. Dod having answered in the negative, and signified that he could not rest until he had seen him, the gentleman replied: "O, sir, you are sent of God at this very hour, for I was just now going to destroy myself!" and immediately pulled the halter out of his pocket, by which he had intended to commit the horrid deed, which was thus prevented.

LOSING, BUT LIBERAL.

A wealthy merchant, having lost by one shipwreck, to the value of fifteen hundred pounds, ordered his clerk to distribute one hundred pounds among poor ministers and people; adding, that if his fortune was going by fifteen hundred pounds at a lump, it was high time to make sure of some part of it before it was gone.

SAVED FROM A ROBBER BY RAIN.

A merchant was one day returning from market. He was on horseback, and behind him was a valise filled with money. The rain fell with violence, and the good old man was wet to his skin. At this he was vexed, and murmured because God had given him such bad weather for his journey.

He soon reached the borders of a thick forest. What was his

terror on beholding on one side of the road a robber, with leveled gun, aiming at him and attempting to fire! But the powder being wet by the rain, the gun did not go off, and the merchant, giving spurs to his horse, fortunately had time to escape.

As soon as he found himself safe, he said to himself: "How wrong was I, not to endure the rain patiently as sent by Providence. If the weather had been dry and fair, I should not, probably, have been alive at this hour, and my little children would have expected my return in vain. The rain which caused me to murmur, came at a fortunate moment, to save my life and preserve my property." And thus it is with a multitude of our afflictions; by causing us slight and short sufferings, they preserve us from others far greater, and of longer duration.

WHY DO YOU PLANT TREES?

A VERY poor and aged man, busied in planting and grafting an apple tree, was rudely interrupted by the interrogation: "Why do you plant trees, who cannot hope to eat the fruit of them?" He raised himself up, and, leaning upon his spade, replied: "Some one planted trees before I was born, and I have eaten the fruit; I now plant for others, that the memorial of my gratitude may exist when I am dead and gone."

RESTITUTION.

THE following remarkable instance of the force of conscience occurred, in 1835, in the neighborhood of London. A lady, about thirty-eight years of age, elegantly dressed, entered the shop of Mr.——, a respectable pastry cook, in a state of great mental excitement, and inquired if Mr.—— were still alive. On being answered, in the most earnest manner begged to see him. Being engaged in superintending the making of some confectionary, he begged to be excused, and referred her to his daughter, who, he said, would wait upon her. The daughter immediately withdrew with her into the parlor; when, after sitting a few moments in silence, she burst into a flood of tears. When she became more composed, she stated, that upward of twenty years since, she was a boarder at a highly respectable boarding-school in that neighborhood, which school Mr.—— had for nearly forty years supplied with pastry, etc.; and while there, she was in the habit of abstracting small articles from his tray, unknown to the person who brought it. She had now been married some years, was the mother of six children, and in the possession of every comfort this world could afford; but still the remembrance of her youthful sin had so haunted her conscience, that she was never happy. Her husband perceiving her unhappiness, had, after many fruitless endeavors, at last got possession of the cause, when he advised her, for the easement of her conscience, to see if Mr.—— were alive, and to make him or his family a recompense; and as she was going to leave London on the following day, perhaps forever, she had then come for that purpose. Mr.——, on being informed of the object of her visit, told her not to make herself any longer unhappy, as she was not the only young lady who had acted in that manner. After begging his forgiveness, which he most readily granted, she insisted on his acceptance of a sum of money, which, she said, she believed was about the value of the articles she had stolen; and after remainining about an hour, she departed, evidently much happier.

CONTENTMENT.

A KING, walking out one morning, met a lad at the stable door, and asked him: "Well, boy, what do you do? what do they pay you?" "I help in the stable," replied the lad; "but I have nothing except victuals and clothes." "Be content," replied the king, "I have no more."

ANOTHER.

AN Italian bishop struggled through great difficulties, without repining or betraying the least impatience. One of his intimate friends, who highly admired the virtues which he thought it impossible to imitate, one day asked the prelate if he could communicate the secret of being always easy. "Yes," replied the old man; "I can teach you my secret with great facility; it consists in nothing more than making a right use of my eyes." His friend begged of him to explain himself. "Most willingly," returned the bishop. "In whatever state I am, I first of all look up to heaven, and remember that my principal business here is to get there; I then look down upon the earth, and call to mind how small a place I shall occupy in it, when I die and am buried; I then look abroad into the world, and observe what multitudes there are who are in all respects more unhappy than myself. Thus I learn where true happiness is placed; where all our cares must end; and what little reason I have to repine or to complain."

EXCOMMUNICATING A PRINCE.

WILLIAM IX, Duke of Aquitaine and Earl of Poitiers, was a violent and dissolute prince, and often indulged himself in improper behavior at the expense of religion. Though he had contracted a very suitable marriage, and one with which he was satisfied for some time, he parted from his wife without reason, to marry another, who pleased him better. The bishop of Poitiers, where he resided, was a holy prelate, named Peter. He could not brook so great a scandal;

and having employed all other means in vain, he thought it his duty to excommunicate the duke. As he began to pronounce the anathema, William furiously advanced, sword in hand, saying: "Thou art dead if thou proceedest." The bishop, as if afraid, required a few moments to consider what was most expedient. The duke granted it, and the bishop courageously finished the rest of the formula of excommunication. After which, extending his neck: "Now strike," said he, "I am quite ready." The astonishment which this intrepid conduct produced in the duke, disarmed his fury, and saying ironically: "I don't like you well enough to send you to heaven," he contented himself with banishing him.

THE SHEPHERD OF SALISBURY PLAIN.

MANY of our readers are acquainted with that beautiful tract, "The Shepherd of Salisbury Plain." The substance of this narrative is a correct account of David Saunders, of West Lavington, who died about the period of its publication. The conversation represented as passing between the shepherd and a Mr. Johnson, really took place with Dr. Stonehouse, a neighboring clergyman, who afterward befriended the shepherd on many occasions.

Dr. Stonehouse, who was on a journey, and somewhat fearful, from the appearance of the sky, that rain was at no great distance, accosted the shepherd with asking what sort of weather he thought it would be on the morrow. "It will be such weather as pleases me," answered the shepherd. Though the answer was delivered in the mildest and civilest tone that could be imagined, Dr. S. thought the words themselves rather rude and surly, and asked him how that could be. "Because," replied the shepherd, "it will be such weather as shall please God; and whatever pleases him always pleases me."

Dr. S. was quite satisfied with this reply, and entered into conversation with the shepherd in the following manner: "Yours is a troublesome life, honest friend." "To be sure, sir," replied the shepherd, "'tis not a very lazy life; but 'tis not near so toilsome as that which my great Master led for my sake, and he had every state and condition of life at his choice, and chose a hard one, while I only submit to the lot that is appointed me." "You are exposed to great cold and heat," said the gentleman. "True, sir," said the shepherd; "but then I am not exposed to great temptations; and so throwing one thing against another, God is pleased to contrive to make things more equal than we poor, ignorant, short-sighted creatures are apt to think. David was happier when he kept his father's sheep, on such a plain as this, and singing some of his own psalms, perhaps, than ever he was when he became king of Israel and Judah."

"You think, then," said the gentleman, "that a laborious life is a happy one?"

"I do, sir; and more especially so, as it exposes a man to fewer sins. If King Saul had continued a poor laborious man to the end of his days, he might have lived happy and honest, and died a natural death in his bed at last, which you know, sir, was more than he did."

God blessed Saunders with an excellent wife and numerous offspring: he had sixteen children, and twelve of them, at one time, were "like olive branches around his table." It is not to be supposed that a poor shepherd, with such a family, could be without difficulties, especially as his wife suffered much from sickness. His wages were but six shillings and threepence weekly, (about one dollar and forty cents,) out of which he was sometimes obliged to pay a boy for assistance; but when times of peculiar necessity occurred, God always raised him up a friend. Dr. (afterward Sir James) Stonehouse repeatedly assisted him; and sometimes his good neighbors, in humbler life, united to supply his wants. In one of his letters in his old age, he thus writes with much christian simplicity: "As for my part, I am but very poorly in body, having very sore legs, and cannot perform the business of my flock without help. As to the things of this world, I have but little share; having my little cot to pray and praise God in, and a bed to rest on: so I have just as much of this world as I desire. But my garment is worn out, and some of my christian friends think they must put their mites together and buy me one, or else I shall not be able to endure the cold in the winter; so I can say, Good is the Lord! He is still fulfilling his promise—'I will never leave thee, nor forsake thee!'"

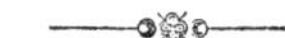

THE PARTITION FENCE.

Two neighbors, who were brothers by marriage, had a difficulty respecting their partition fence. Although they had mutually erected a substantial fence, four and one-half feet in hight on the line separating the sheep pasture of one from the grain field of the other, yet the lambs would creep through the crevices and destroy the grain.

Each asserted it to be the duty of the other to chink the fence. After the usual preliminaries of demands, refusals, threats, challenges, and mutual recriminations, they resolved to try the glorious uncertainty of the law. They were, however, persuaded by their friends to the more amicable mode of submitting the defense to the final determination of a very worthy and intelligent neighbor, who was forthwith conducted to the scene of trouble, and in full view of the premises. Each party in turn, and in a speech of some length, asserted his rights, and set forth the law and the facts; at the conclusion of which, the arbitrator very coolly remarked: "Gentlemen, the case involves questions of great nicety and importance, not only to the parties in interest, but to the community at large; and it is my desire to take suitable time for deliberation, and, also, for advisement with those who are learned in the law, and most experienced customs of good neighbors; in the meantime, however, I will just clap a billet or two of wood into the sheep holes." In ten minutes time, with his hands, he effectually closed every gap.

The parties silently retired, each evidently heartily ashamed of his own folly and obstinacy. The umpire has never been called upon to pronounce final judgment in the case; so the law remains unsettled unto this day.

BOLINGBROKE.

Bolingbroke left one of his publications to be published after his death by Mallet, a brother unbeliever. Dr. Johnson, when asked his opinion of the legacy, exclaimed: "A scoundrel! who spent his life in charging a pop-gun against christianity; and a coward, who, afraid of the report of his own gun, left half a crown to a hungry Scotchman to pull the trigger after his death."

THE SHIPWRECKED SAILOR AND THE BIBLE.

Fox, the martyrologist, informs us of an English sailor, who, being shipwrecked, lost all his property except his bible, which he was determined to save, and of which he took more care than of his money. Having clung to the wreck until all others on board perished, he committed himself to sea, with his bible tied round his neck with a handkerchief. After floating upon the water for a long time, supported by a piece of the mast, he was happily discovered by the crew of another vessel, sitting upon the broken fragment which preserved him from a watery grave; and when thus almost miraculously delivered from starvation and death, he was reading the bible!

WESLEY'S SIMPLICITY.

The greatness of Wesley consisted, to no small extent, in his simplicity. Yet this very simplicity he had to cultivate. When he first began his ministry, his style was so lofty that several hearers complained they could not understand him. Learning this, he resolved to change his course; and to the individual who informed him of the complaints, he observed: "I will make them understand me." How far he succeeded, may be seen from the following circumstance. In June, 1790, the year before he died, he preached at Lincoln, taking for his text, Luke x. 42: "One thing is needful." As the congregation was dispersing, a lady remarked, in a tone of great surprise, to a friend that accompanied her: "Is this the great Mr. Wesley, of whom we hear so much in the present day? Why, the poorest might have understood him." Her friend replied: "In this, madam, he displays his greatness; that while the poorest can understand him, the most learned are edified, and cannot be offended."

A PENITENT YOUTH.

A DRAPER in Yarmouth, England, discovered that a lad in his service had stolen his property. He was tried, found guilty, and sentenced to seven years' transportation; but, on account of some favorable traits in his character, application was made to the secretary of state, and the punishment was mitigated to five years' imprisonment in the Millbank penitentiary. At the expiration of three years his conduct induced the authorities to release him, when he went at once to Yarmouth, called on his former employer, and, in the spirit of a sincere penitent, expressed his sorrow for his dishonesty and ingratitude to so good a master, and said: "Sir, I have taken care of the money that I took away, and am now come to return your property." The gentleman was surprised at this announcement; and seeing him put his hand in his pocket, began to expect to receive a few pounds. Great was his astonishment when the lad handed to him one hundred and two pounds, sixteen shillings and sixpence—nearly five hundred dollars.

WASHINGTON AT THE COMMUNION.

WHILE the American army, under the command of Washington, lay encamped in the environs of Morristown, N. J., it occurred that the service of the communion, (there observed semi-annually only,) was to be administered in the Presbyterian church of that village. On a morning of a previous week, the general, after his accustomed inspection of the camp, visited the house of the Rev. Dr. Jones, then pastor of that church, and, after the usual preliminaries, thus accosted him: "Doctor, I understand that the Lord's supper is to be celebrated with you next Sunday; I would learn if it accords with the canons of your church to admit communicants of another denomination?" The doctor rejoined: "Most certainly; ours is not the Presbyterian table, general, but the Lord's table; and we hence give the Lord's invitation to all his followers of whatever name." The general replied: "I am glad of it; that is as it ought to be; but as I was not quite sure of the fact, I thought I would ascertain it from yourself, as I propose to join with you on that occasion. Though a member of the Church of England, I have no exclusive partialities." The doctor reassured him of a cordial welcome, and the general was found seated with the communicants the next Sabbath.

DEATH OF JULIAN.

THE Roman emperor, Julian, a determined enemy of Christianity, was mortally wounded in a war with the Persians. In this condition, we are told that he filled his hand with blood, and casting it into the air, said: "O Galilean! thou hast conquered!" During this expedition, one of Julian's followers asked a Christian of Antioch, "What the carpenter's son was doing?" "The Maker of the world," replied the Christian, "whom you call the carpenter's son, is employed in making a coffin for the emperor." In a few days after, news came to Antioch of Julian's death.

TRUST IN PROVIDENCE.

ON John's river, in the county of Burke, there lived a worthy old gentleman by the name of Copening. He was a man well at ease in point of worldly substance, and was known far and near for his charity and hospitality. There happened in the year——, a remarkable scarcity of provisions, especially grain. Money was also scarce, and times every way hard. Hunger—aching, maddening hunger—was felt by a few in every neighborhood; and, in some cases, we have heard of its proceeding to starvation; but to the honor of our country, and to the honor of human nature, be it said, these cases were extremely rare. In these difficult times, however, old Mr. Copening happened to have a large and well-filled corn crib, which for a long time he would not open. Grain became scarce, the prices rose higher, and still the old man held up his corn, as some supposed for a higher price. At length Mr. Copening began to let his corn go—but money could not buy it. To those who had money he would say: "You can get something to preserve life for your money; there are many who have no money, and being without food, they must perish, unless those who are blessed with the means shall feed them." Of course, the number who came without money and put up piteous tales was great. But this was foreseen, and before he had opened his crib, Copening had taken pains to find out who were really objects requiring his assistance.

A man, bringing a bag with him, came to Copening from a distant neighborhood, and told the usual story of wife and children being without bread, and being sorely wrought with hunger, etc., but no corn was to be had: and the disappointed man, with a heavy heart, turned his steps homeward, and for a time was no more thought of. In the course of the afternoon, however, word came to old Mr. Copening that a suspicious looking stranger, with a bag on his shoulder, was seen lurking about his premises. A few particulars more satisfied him that it was the applicant for charity who had visited him that morning, and that he had a design to rob his crib that night; accordingly, himself and another of his family secreted themselves and waited events. But they did not wait long before the stranger, with a bag on his shoulders, was seen making his way towards the crib; the crib was opened, not a dog was heard to bark, or the least difficulty opposed to his purpose. He entered, and with a deliberation, or rather hesitation, that surprised the observers, he proceeded to fill the bag. This being done, he tied it; and unlike such visitors generally, he continued on the spot with his hand still on the bag, apparently in great mental agony. At length he rose suddenly, untied the bag, poured out the corn, and said: "*I will trust to Providence one day longer.*" He departed in peace, but he did not trust in Providence in vain. Old Mr. Copening being satisfied from his own observation, that this man was indeed in a state of extreme suffering—moreover that he was of an honest heart—sent his son on the next morning with a full bag of corn, with a message that, when that was done, to let him know it, and he should have corn whenever he wished it.

STRETCHING IT.

A VERY respectable linen merchant in Coleraine, offered Dr. Clarke, when a youth, a situation in his warehouse, which was accepted by him, with the consent of his parents. Mr. B—— knew well that his clerk and overseer was a religious man, but he was not sensible of the extent of principle which actuated him. Some differences arose at times about the way of conducting the business, which were settled pretty amicably. But the time of the great Dublin market approached, and Mr. B. —— was busy preparing for it. The master and man were together in the folding-room, when one of the pieces was found short of the required number of yards. "Come," said Mr. B——, "it is but a trifle. We shall soon stretch it, and make out the yard. Come, Adam, take one end, and pull against me." Adam had neither ears nor heart for the proposal, and absolutely refused to do what he thought a dishonest thing. A long argument and expostulation followed, in which the usages of the trade were strongly and variously enforced; but all in vain. Adam kept to his purpose, resolving to suffer rather than sin. Mr. —— was therefore obliged to call for one of his men less scrupulous, and Adam retired quietly to his desk. Soon after Mr. B——, in the kindest manner, informed his "young friend," as he seemed always proud to call him, that he was not fit for worldly business, and wished him to look out for some employment more congenial to his own mind; adding, that he might depend on his friendship in any line of life into which he should enter.

These things may be counted little in the life of such a man, but not so in the sight of God.

THE BLOOD OF JESUS CHRIST CLEANSETH FROM ALL SIN.

A CERTAIN man on the Malabar coast had inquired of various devotees and priests how he might make atonement for his sin, and at last he was directed to drive iron spikes, sufficiently blunted, through his sandals, and on these spikes he was to place his naked feet and walk, if I mistake not, two hundred and fifty *coss*, that is about four hundred and eighty miles. If through loss of blood, or weakness of body, he was obliged to halt, he might wait for healing and strength. He undertook the journey, and while he halted under a large shady tree, where the Gospel was sometimes preached, one of the missionaries came and preached in his hearing, from these words: *The blood of Jesus Christ cleanseth from all sin.* While he was preaching, the man rose up, threw off his torturing sandals and cried aloud: *This is what I want!* and he became a lively witness that the blood of Jesus Christ does cleanse from all sin indeed.

TRUE HONOR.

"True honor is not derived from others, but originates only from ourselves."
CICERO.

A PORTUGUESE, who, from obscurity, had raised himself by the most distinguished merit to a peerage of the kingdom, being in company with several of the most ancient families in Lisbon, became the subject of their wit and raillery on account of his infant nobility. With a design, therefore, to pique him in the tenderest point, they turned their discourse alone on the honors derived from nobility of birth, each extolling the great achievements of his distinguished ancestors in the warmest terms of panegyric. At last it came to this nobleman, as is the custom of the country, to give his sentiments; when the rest of the company were scarcely able to contain themselves from laughter, expecting that he must leave the room in extreme disorder. But how great was their astonishment, and even their shame, when this truly illustrious personage with the greatest composure and good humor, addressed them thus: "My lords, I acknowledge that all of you have given a very flattering account of the immortal deeds of your ancestors; but from this I can only gather, that the honors you enjoy were thus simply delivered by hereditary succession in your hands; but, my lords, my plea is widely different: I have the virtuous satisfaction of saying more than you all—that I obtained all *my* honors by my own immediate actions, and shall, therefore, have the superior pleasure of transmitting them, unsullied to my successors, for *them* to boast of!"

THE HERMIT.

"One day a friend took me," says George Shadford, "to see a hermit in the woods. After some difficulty we found his hermitage, which was a little place like a hog-sty, built of several pieces of wood, covered with bark of trees; and his bed consisted of dry leaves. There was a narrow, beaten path, about twenty or thirty yards in length, by the side of it, where he frequently walked to meditate. If one offered him food, he would take it, but if money was offered him, he would be angry. If any thing was spoken to him which he did not like, he broke out into a violent passion. He had lived in this cell seven cold winters; and after all his prayers, counting his beads, and separating from the rest of mankind, still corrupt nature was all alive within him. Alas! alas! what will it avail us whether we are in England or Ireland, Scotland or America; whether we live amongst mankind, or retire into a hermitage, if we still carry with us our own hell—our corrupt, evil tempers!"

RELIEF IN DISTRESS.

The following simple and affecting narrative is related by Dr. Krummacher, of Elberfield, in Prussia, in his valuable work entitled, "Elisha the Tishbite:"

Who else was it but the God of Elijah, who, only a short time ago, in our neighborhood, so kindly delivered a poor man out of his distress; not, indeed by a raven, but a poor singing bird? You are acquainted with the circumstance. The man was sitting early in the morning at his house door; his eyes were red with weeping, and his heart cried to heaven, for he was expecting an officer to come and distrain him for a small debt. And whilst sitting thus with a heavy heart, a little bird flew through the street, fluttering up and down as if in distress, until at length, quick as an arrow, it flew over the good man's head into his cottage, and perched itself within an empty cupboard. The good man, who little imagined who had sent him the bird, closed the door, caught the bird and placed it in a cage, where it immediately began to sing very sweetly, and it seemed to the man as if it were in tune of a favorite hymn—"Fear thou not when darkness reigns;" and as he listened to it, he found it soothe and comfort his mind.

Suddenly some one knocked at the door. "Ah, it is the officer!" thought the man, and he was sore afraid. But no, it was the servant of a respectable lady, who said that the neighbors had seen a bird fly into his house, and she wished to know if he had caught it. "Oh, yes, answered the man, "and here it is;" and the bird was carried away. A few minutes after, the servant came again. "You have done my mistress a great service," said she; "she sets a high value upon the bird which had escaped from her. She is much obliged to you, and requests you to accept this trifle, with her thanks." The poor man received it thankfully, and it proved to be neither more nor less than the sum he owed! And when the officer came, he said: "Here is the amount of the debt; now leave me in peace, for God has sent it me."

REMARKABLE DETECTION OF AN IMPOSTER.

A JEWELER, who carried on an extensive trade, and supplied the deficiencies of one country by the superfluities of another, leaving his home with a valuable assortment of diamonds, for a distant region, took with him his son and a young slave, whom he had purchased in his infancy, and had brought up more like an adopted child than a servant. They performed their intended journey, and the merchant disposed of his commodities with great advantage; but while preparing to return, he was seized by a pestilential distemper, and died suddenly in the metropolis of a foreign country. This accident inspired the slave with a wish to possess his master's treasures, and relying on the total ignorance of strangers, and the kindness every where shown him by the jeweler, he declared himself the son of the jeweler, and took charge of the property. The true heir of course denied his pretensions, and solemnly declared himself to be the only son of the defunct, who had long before purchased his opponent as a slave. This contest produced various results. It happened that the slave was a young man of beautiful person, and of polished manners, while the jeweler's son was ill-favored by nature, and said to be injured in his education by the indulgence of his parents. This superiority operated in the minds of many to support the claims of the former; but since no certain evidence could be produced on either side, it became necessary to refer the dispute to a court of law. There, however, from a total want of proofs, nothing could be done. The magistrate declared his inability to decide on unsupported assertions, in which each party was equally positive. This caused a report of the case to be made to the prince, who, having heard the particulars, was also confounded, and at a loss how to decide the question. At length, a happy thought occurred to the chief of the judges, and he engaged to ascertain the real heir. The claimants being summoned before him, he ordered them to stand behind a curtain prepared for the occasion, and to project their heads through two openings, when, after hearing their several arguments, he would cut off the head of him who should prove to be the slave. This they readily assented to; the one from a reliance on his honesty, and the other from a confidence of the impossibility of detection. Accordingly, each taking his place as ordered, thrust his head through a hole in the curtain. An officer stood in front with a drawn cimeter in his hand, and the judge proceeded to the examination. After a short debate, the judge cried out, "Enough, enough! strike off the villain's head!" and the officer, who watched the moment, leaped toward the two youths; the imposter, startled at the brandished weapon, hastily drew back his head, while the jeweler's son, animated by conscious security, stood unmoved. The judge immediately decided for the latter, and ordered the slave to be taken into custody to receive the punishment due to his diabolical ingratitude.

MONSIEUR DE SALLO AND THE ROBBER.

In the year 1662, when Paris was afflicted with a long and severe famine, Monsieur de Sallo, returning from an evening's walk, accompanied with only a page, was accosted by a man who presented his pistol, and in a manner far from hardened resolution, asked him for his money. M. de Sallo, observing that he came to the wrong person, and that he could obtain but little from him, added: "I have but three pistoles, which are not worth a scuffle, so, much good may it do you with them; but, like a friend, let me tell you, you are going on in a very bad way." The robber took them, and without asking him for more, walked away with an air of dejection and terror.

The fellow was no sooner gone than M. de Sallo ordered his page to follow the robber, to observe where he went, and to bring him an account of all he should discover. The boy obeyed, pursued him through several obscure streets, and at length saw him enter a baker's shop, where he observed him change one of the pistoles and buy a large brown loaf; with this salutary purchase, the robber went a few doors further, and entering an alley, ascended several flights of stairs. The boy crept up after him to the topmost story, where he saw him go into a room which was not otherwise illuminated than by the friendly light of the moon; and peeping through a crevice, he perceived the wretched man cast the loaf upon the floor, and, bursting into tears, cry out: "There, eat your fill; this is the dearest loaf I ever bought; I have robbed a gentleman of three pistoles; let us husband them well, and let me hear no more teazings; for, soon or late, these things must bring me to ruin." His wife, having calmed the agony of his mind, took up the loaf, and cutting it, gave four pieces to four poor starving children.

The page, having performed his commission, returned home and gave his master an account of all he had seen and heard. De Sallo, who was much moved, (what *christian* breast can be unmoved at distress like this!) commanded the boy to call him at five the next morning. He rose accordingly, and took his boy to show him the way: he inquired of his neighbors the character of a man who lived in such a garret, with a wife and four children; by whom he was informed that he was a very industrious man, a tender husband, and a quiet neighbor; that his occupation was that of a shoemaker, and that he was a neat workman; but was overburdened with a family, and struggled hard to live in such dear times. Satisfied with this account, M. de Sallo ascended to the shoemaker's, and knocking at the door, it was opened by the unhappy man himself; who, knowing him at first sight to be the gentleman whom he had robbed, prostrated himself at his feet. M. de Sallo desired him to make no noise, assuring him he had not the least intention to hurt him. "You have a good character," said he, "among your neighbors, but you must expect your life will be cut short if you are so wicked as to continue the freedom you took with me. Hold your hand; here are thirty pistoles to buy leather; husband it well, and set your children a laudable example. To put you out of further temptations to commit such ruinous and fatal crimes, I will encourage your industry. I hear you are a neat workman; you shall therefore now take measure of me and my lad for two pairs of shoes each, and he shall call upon you for them." The whole family seemed absorbed in joy; amazement and gratitude in some measure deprived them of speech. M. de Sallo departed, greatly moved, and with a mind replete with satisfaction at having saved a man from the commission of guilt, from an ignominious death, and perhaps from everlasting misery.

Never was a day much better begun; the consciousness of having performed such an action, whenever it recurs to the mind, must be attended with pleasure, and that self-complacency which is more desirable than gold, will be ever the attendant on such truly christian character.

THE GRATEFUL SOLDIER.

The Rev. John Craig, a distinguished minister and colleague of Knox, having gone to reside in Bologna, in a convent of Dominicans, found a copy of "Calvin's Institutes," which God made the means of his conversion to the reformed faith. He was seized as a heretic, soon after, and carried to Rome, where he was condemned to be burnt; but on the evening preceding the day of execution the reigning pontiff died, and according to custom, the doors of all the prisons were thrown open. All others were released; but heretics, after being permitted to go outside the walls, were re-conducted to their cells. That night, however, a tumult was excited, and Craig and his companions escaped. They had entered a small inn at some distance from Rome, when they were overtaken by a party of soldiers sent to apprehend them. On entering the house, the captain looked Craig steadfastly in the face, and asked him if he remembered having once relieved a poor wounded soldier in the neighborhood of Bologna? Craig had forgotten it. "But," said the captain, "I am the man; I shall requite your kindness; you are at liberty; your companions I must take with me; but for your sake I shall treat them with all possible lenity." He gave him all the money he had, and Craig escaped. But his money soon failed him; yet God, who feeds the ravens, did not. Lying at the side of a wood, full of gloomy apprehensions, a dog came running up to him with a purse in his teeth. Suspecting some evil, he attempted to drive the animal away, but in vain. He at length took the purse, and found in it a sum of money which carried him to Vienna.

FRIENDSHIP TO A ROBBER.

A young man was stopped in a little street in one of the cities of France; his purse or his life was demanded. A courageous and sensible heart soon distinguishes between the voice of the unfortunate wretch, whom misery drags to crime, and that of the villain whose wickedness prompts him to it. The young man thought it was an unfortunate person whom he ought to save.

"What do you ask, miserable creature, what do you ask?" said he, in an imposing tone to his agressor.

"Nothing, sir," answered a sobbing voice; "I ask nothing of you."

"Who are you? what do you do?"

"I am a poor journeyman shoemaker, without the means of supporting my wife and four children."

"I do not know whether you speak the truth. Where do you live?"

"In such a street, at a baker's house."

"We shall see, lead the way."

The shoemaker, awed by his firmness, led him to his abode as he would have led him to the bottom of a dungeon. They arrived at the baker's. There was none but a woman in the shop.

"Madam, do you know this man?"

"Yes sir, he is a poor journeyman shoemaker who lives in the fifth story, and who has much difficulty in supporting his numerous family."

"How can you let him want bread?"

"Sir, we are young people, newly established; we cannot give much; my husband does not wish me to give more than twenty-four cents credit to this man."

"Give him two loaves of bread. Take these two loaves, and mount to your room."

The shoemaker obeys, as much agitated as if he were about to commit some crime, but in a very different kind of trouble. They enter. The wife and children eagerly take the food which is offered them. The young man has seen too much. He goes out, after giving two louis to the baker's wife, with orders to supply the family with bread according to their wants. Some days after he returns to see the children, to whom he has given a second life, and he tells their father to follow him. He conducts his poor protege into a shop, well built and well furnished with tools, and all the necessary materials for working at his trade. "Would you be contented and happy if this shop were yours?"

"Ah, sir, but alas!"

"What?"

"I have not the freeman's right, and it costs"—

"Take me to the syndic jury."

The license was bought, and the shoemaker placed in the shop.

The author of so fine an act of humanity, was a young man about twenty-seven years old. It is calculated that the establishment of this workman cost him from three to four thousand livres. He is not known, and useless researches have been made to discover him.

MR. SCOTT AND THE DUELIST.

THE preaching of the Rev. J. Scott, who had been a captain in the army, having been instrumental in the conversion of a young lady, the daughter of a country gentleman, her father was greatly offended, because she would not join in the usual amusements of their circle. Looking upon Mr. Scott as the sole cause of what he regarded as the melancholy of his daughter, he lay in wait to shoot him. Mr. Scott, being providentially apprised of it, was enabled to escape the danger. The diabolical design of the gentleman being thus defeated, he sent Mr. Scott a challenge. Mr. Scott might have availed himself of the law, and prosecuted him; but he took another method. He waited upon him at his house, was introduced to him in his parlor, and, with his characteristic boldness and intrepidity, thus addressed him: "Sir, I hear that you have designed to shoot me, by which you would have been guilty of murder; failing in this, you have sent me a challenge. And what a coward must you be, sir, to wish to engage with a blind man!" (alluding to his being short-sighted). "As you have given me the challenge, it is now my right to choose the time, the place, and the weapon; I therefore, sir, appoint the present moment, the place where we now are, and the sword for the weapon, to which I have been the most accustomed." The gentleman was evidently greatly terrified; when Mr. Scott, having attained his end, produced a pocket bible, and exclaimed: "This is my sword, sir; the only weapon I wish to engage with." "Never," said Mr. Scott to a friend, to whom he related this anecdote, "never was a poor, careless sinner so delighted with the sight of a bible before!"

Mr. Scott reasoned with the gentleman on the impropriety of his conduct, in treating him as he had done, for no other reason but because he had preached the truth. The result was, the gentleman took him by the hand, begged his pardon, expressed his sorrow for his conduct, and became afterward very friendly to him.

DYING FOR HIS MASTER.

A GENTLEMAN was traveling, with his valet de chambre, in a sledge, through one of the extensive forests of Poland, when they were suddenly attacked by a number of wolves, which leaped furiously at the carriage. The servant, who instantly perceived that either he or his master must fall a victim to their fury, exclaimed: "Protect my wife and children;" and instantly rushing into the midst of them, perished in a moment, and by this generous act saved his master, who fled from the danger, by driving forward with the greatest rapidity.

THE INFIDEL'S DYING DAUGHTER.

COLONEL ALLEN, of Vermont, was an avowed deist, and the author of several works against the christian religion. But how little faith he possessed in the hour of danger and of death is evinced by the following fact: While reading some of his own writings to a friend who was on a visit to his house, he received information that his daughter was at the point of death. His wife was a pious woman, who had instructed the daughter in the principles of Christianity. When the father appeared at the bed-side, his daughter said to him, "I am about to die; shall I believe in the principles you have taught me, or shall I believe in what my mother has taught me?" On hearing this question, he became much agitated, and after waiting a few minutes, replied: "Believe in what your mother has taught you."

INCONSIDERATE REQUEST.

IT is of great importance that we should entreat the Spirit of God to enable us to pray as we ought. It is quite possible to ask for what may appear to us good things, but which, if we had them, would prove evil. Rachel, indulging a petulant disposition said:

"Give me children, or I die:" her desire was granted, and, as the result, she died.

The late Mr. Kilpin, of Exeter, writes: "I knew a case, in which the minister, praying over a child apparently dying, said: 'If it be thy will, spare—.' The poor mother's soul yearning for her beloved, exclaimed: 'It must be his will! I cannot bear *ifs*.' The minister stopped. To the surprise of many the child recovered; and the mother, after almost suffering martyrdom by him while a stripling, lived to see him hanged before he was two-and-twenty! Oh! it is good to say, 'Not my will, but thine be done.'"

DISCARDED LOVER.

Eliza Embert, a young Parisian lady, resolutely discarded a gentleman to whom she was to have been married the next day, because he ridiculed religion. Having given him a gentle reproof for some impropriety, he replied "that a man of the world would not be so old-fashioned as to regard God and religion." Eliza immediately started; but soon recovering herself, said: "From this moment, as I discover you do not respect religion, I cease to be yours."

A SUBMISSIVE WIFE.

A married woman was effectually called by Divine grace, and became an exemplary Christian, but her husband was a lover of sinful pleasure. When spending an evening as usual with his jovial companions at a tavern, the conversation happened to turn on the excellencies and faults of their wives; the husband just mentioned pronounced the highest encomiums on his wife, saying she was all that was excellent, only she was religious. "Notwithstanding which," said he, "such is the command she has of her temper, that were I to take you, gentlemen, home with me at midnight and order her to rise and get you a supper, she would be all submission and cheerfulness!" The company regarded this merely as a vain boast, and dared him to make the experiment by a considerable wager. The bargain was made, and about midnight the company adjourned as proposed. Being admitted: "Where is your mistress?" said the husband to the maid servant who sat up for him. "She is gone to bed, sir." "Call her up," said he. "Tell her I have brought some friends home with me, and desire she would get up and prepare them a supper." The good woman obeyed the unreasonable summons, dressed, came down, and received the company with perfect civility; told them she happened to have some chickens ready for the spit, and that supper should be got as soon as possible. It was accordingly served up, when she performed the honors of the table with as much cheerfulness as if she had expected company at a proper season.

After supper the guests could not refrain from expressing their astonishment. One of them particularly, more sober than the rest, thus addressed himself to the lady: "Madam," said he, "your civility fills us all with surprise. Our unreasonable visit is in consequence of a wager, which we have certainly lost. As you are a very religious person, and cannot therefore approve of our conduct, give me leave to ask what can possibly induce you to behave with so much kindness to us?" "Sir," replied she, "when I married, my husband and myself were both unconverted. It has pleased God to call me out of that dangerous condition. My husband continues in it. I tremble for his future state. Were he to die as he is, he must be miserable forever; I think it therefore my duty to render his present existence as comfortable as possible."

This wise and faithful reply affected the whole company. It left a deep impression on the husband's mind. "Do you, my dear," said he, "really think I should be eternally miserable? I thank you for the warning. By the grace of God I will change my conduct." From that time he became another man, a serious Christian, and consequently a good husband.

ADMIRAL WILLIAMS.

The late Admiral Williams, when a young man, was gay and so addicted to expensive pleasures that no remonstrances could reclaim him. When his father died, he met the rest of the family to hear the will read. His name did not occur among the other children, and he supposed the omission was a mark of his father's resentment against him. At the close of it, however, he found that he was mentioned as residuary legatee, in these words: "All the rest of my estate and effects I leave to my son Peere Williams, knowing that he will spend it all."

On hearing this he burst into tears. "My father," said he, "has touched the right string, and his reproach shall not be thrown away." His conduct from that time was altered, and he became an honor to the christian profession.

REMORSE AND SUICIDE.

In the year 1832, died in Essex, England, under very painful circumstances, a young man who had once promised to be happy and useful. He was apprenticed to a respectable shopkeeper, who insisted on his always being at home by a certain hour in the evening. For some time he appeared very attentive to his business, and was useful to his master; but he unhappily acquired the habit of walking about the streets in an evening, and soon after formed very improper connections at a public house. He was seriously admonished, and at times appeared to feel the impropriety of his conduct; but the sins he cherished hardened his heart, and his irregularities became confirmed. At length, his master, on returning from a journey, heard complaints of his conduct, which led him to threaten that unless his conduct was altered, he would cancel his indentures. He now felt that his sins were hastening him to the ruin against which he had often been warned; he had lost alike the confidence of his master and his parents. Stung by the convictions of his guilt, he repaired to his room, when he knew that he would be expected at dinner, and committed suicide; thus rushing into the presence of his Judge uncalled, and every way unprepared. Who can conceive the acuteness of his anguish, when he found himself in the presence of that God whose laws he had trampled under his feet, but from whose wrath he found it impossible to escape?

SIR EARDLEY WILMOT.

IN the evening of the day that Sir Eardley Wilmot was appointed chief justice of England, one of his sons, a youth of seventeen, attended him to his bedside. "Now," said he, "my son, I will tell you a secret worth your knowing and remembering. The elevation I have met with in life, particularly this last instance of it, has not been owing to any superior merits or abilities, but to my humility; to my not having set up myself above others, and to a uniform endeavor to pass through life void of offense toward God and man."

REWARDING GOOD FOR EVIL.

A SLAVE in one of the West India Islands, originally from Africa, having been brought under the influence of religious instruction, became so valuable to his owner on account of his integrity and general good conduct, that his master employed him to assist in the management of his plantation. On one occasion, his owner wishing to purchase twenty additional slaves, employed him to make the selection from those who were offered for sale. Soon after commencing his examination of those who were in the market, he fixed his eye intently on an old decrepit slave, and told his master he must take him for one. The master was greatly surprised, and objected, but the slave entreated so earnestly for this indulgence, that the offer of the seller to add the old man to the twenty, without increasing the price, was accepted. The newly purchased slaves were conducted to the plantation and placed under the charge of the slave who had made the selection. On the poor old decrepid African he bestowed uncommon care. He took him to his own habitation, and laid him on his own bed; he fed him at his own table, and gave him drink out of his own cup; when he was cold he carried him into the sunshine; and when he was hot, he placed him in the shade of the cocoa-nut trees. The master, astonished at the careful attention bestowed by him upon his fellow slave, interrogated him on the subject. "Is that old man," said he, "your father, that you take so much interest in him?" "No, massa," answered the poor fellow, "he no my fader." "Perhaps, then, he is your elder brother?" "No, massa, he no my broder." "Then he must be your uncle, or some other relation." "No, massa, he be no of my kindred at all; he be no my friend."

"Why, then, do you bestow upon him so much care and attention?" "Oh, massa," replied the slave, "he be my old enemy; he sold me to the slave-dealer, and my bible tell me to love my enemy; when he hunger, feed him, when he thirst, give him drink, and so me only do what my bible tell me."

ARCHBISHOP SHARP AND THE HIGHWAYMAN.

It was his lordship's custom to have a saddle horse attend his carriage, that, in case of fatigue from sitting, he might refresh himself with a ride. As he was thus going to his episcopal residence, a decent, well-looking young man came up to him, and with a trembling hand and faltering tongue, presenting a pistol to his breast, demanded his money. The archbishop, with great composure, turned about, and looking steadfastly at him, desired him to remove that dangerous weapon, and tell him fairly his condition. "Sir! sir!" with great agitation, cried the youth, "your money instantly!" "Hear me, young man," said the archbishop, "you see I am a very old man, and my life is of very little consequence; yours is far otherwise. I am named Sharp, and am archbishop of York; my carriage and servants are behind; tell me what money you want, and who you are, and I'll not injure you, but prove a friend. Here, take this, and now ingenuously tell me how much you want to make you independent of so destructive a business as you are engaged in?" "O, sir," replied the man, "I detest the business as much as you. I am—but at home there are creditors who will not stay. Fifty pounds, my lord, indeed would do what no tongue can tell." "Well sir, I take your word; and upon my honor, if you will, in a day or two, call on me at ———, with what I have now given shall be made up that sum." The highwayman looked at him, was silent, and went off; and at the time appointed actually waited on the archbishop, and assured his lordship that his words had left impressions, which nothing could ever destroy.

Nothing more transpired for a year and a half, or more; when one morning a person knocked at his grace's gate, and with peculiar earnestness, desired to see him. He entered the room where his lordship was, but had scarce advanced a few steps before his countenance changed, his knees tottered, and sank almost breathless on the floor. On recovering, he requested an audience in private. The apartment being cleared, "My lord," said he, "you cannot have forgotten the circumstance at such a time and place; gratitude will never suffer them to be obliterated from my mind. In me, my lord, you now behold that once most wretched of mankind: but now, by your inexpressible humanity, rendered equal, perhaps superior, in happiness, to millions. Oh, my lord, (tears for a while prevented his utterance,) 'tis you, 'tis you that has saved me, body and soul; 'tis you that has saved me a dear and much loved wife, and a brood of children whom I hold dearer than my life. Here are fifty pounds; but never shall I find language to testify what I feel. Your God is your witness; your deed itself is your glory; and may heaven and all its blessings be your present and everlasting reward. I was the younger son of a wealthy man; your lordship knows him—my marriage alienated his affections, and my brother withdrew his love, and left me to sorrow and penury. A month since, my brother died a bachelor and intestate. What was his became mine; and by your astonishing goodness, I am now at once the most penitent, the most grateful and happiest of my species."

THE ARGYLESHIRE FISHERMAN.

Two fishermen, a few years ago, were mending their nets on board their vessel on one of the lakes in the interior of Argyleshire, at a considerable distance from the shore, when a sudden squall upset their boat. One of them could not swim, and the only oar which floated was caught by him that could swim. His sinking companion cried: "Ah, my poor wife and children, they must starve now!" "Save yourself, I will risk my life for their sakes!" said the other, thrusting the oar under the arm of the drowning man. He committed himself instantly to the deep, expecting to perish for the safety of his companion. That moment the boat struck the bottom, and started the other oar by their side, and thus both were enabled to keep afloat till they were picked up.

BENEFICENCE OF LUTHER.

Disinterestedness was a leading feature in the character of Luther: superior to all selfish considerations, he left the honors and emoluments of this world to those who delighted in them. The poverty of this great man did not arise from wanting the means of acquiring riches; for few men have had it in their power more easily to obtain them. The Elector of Saxony offered him the produce of a mine at Sneberg; but he nobly refused it; "lest," said he, "I should tempt the devil, who is lord of these subterraneous treasures, to tempt me." The enemies of Luther were no strangers to his contempt for gold. When one of the popes asked a certain cardinal, why they did not stop that man's mouth with silver and gold; his eminence replied: "That German beast regards not money!" It may easily be supposed that the liberality of such a man would often exceed his means. A poor student once telling him of his poverty, he desired his wife to give him a sum of money; and when she informed him they had none left, he immediately seized a cup of some value, which accidentally stood within his reach, and giving it to the poor man, bade him go and sell it, and keep the money to supply his wants. In one of his epistles Luther says: "I have received one hundred guilders from Taubereim; and Schartts has given me fifty; so that I begin to fear lest God should reward me in this life. But I will not be satisfied with it. What have I to do with so much money? I gave half of it to P. Priorus, and made the man glad."

THE HEROIC PEASANT.

The following generous instance of heroism in a peasant, has somewhat even of the sublime in it. A great inundation having taken place in the north of Italy, owing to an excessive fall of snow in the Alps, followed by a speedy thaw, the river Adige carried off a bridge near Verona, except the middle part, on which was the house of the toll-gatherer, who, with his whole family, thus remained imprisoned by the waves, and in momentary expectation of certain destruction. They were discovered from the banks, stretching forth their hands, screaming, and imploring succor, while fragments of this only remaining arch were continually dropping into the impetuous torrent. In this extreme danger, the Count of Pulverini, who was a spectator, held out a purse of one hundred sequins, as a reward to any adventurer who would take a boat and save this unhappy family. But the risk of being borne down by the rapidity of the stream, and being dashed against the fragment of the bridge, and of being crushed by the falling of the heavy stones, was so great that not one of the vast number of lookers-on had courage enough to attempt such an exploit. A peasant passing along, was informed of the promised reward. Immediately jumping into a boat, he, by amazing strength of oars, gained the middle of the river, and brought the boat under the pile, when the whole terrified family safely descended into it by means of a rope. "Courage," cried he, "now you are safe!" By a still more strenuous effort, and great strength of arm, he brought the boat and family to shore. "Brave fellow!" exclaimed the count, handing the purse to him; "here is your promised recompense." "I shall never expose my life *for money,*" answered the peasant; "my labor affords a sufficient livelihood for myself, my wife and my children; give the purse to this poor family who has lost its all!"

SERIOUS REPARTEE.

A lady traveling in the stage, in company with Mr. James Hervey (author of Meditations), expatiated largely on the pleasure derived from theatrical amusements: "They afford me," says she, "three sources of pleasure. The pleasure of anticipation, before I attend—the pleasure I enjoy while present—and the pleasure of reflecting on the subject, the next day." Mr. Hervey observed: "Madam, there is one source of pleasure you have omitted." She asked with surprise what that could be? He replied: "The pleasure it will afford you on a *dying bed.*" This struck her with force, and was instrumental of making her hopefully pious.

THE SADDLE-BAG IN THE WRONG BOAT.

The Rev. T. Charles, who was well known as a holy and useful minister in Wales, had once a remarkable escape from death. In one of his journeys to Liverpool, his saddle-bag was, by mistake, put into a boat different from that in which he intended to go, which made it necessary to change his boat, even after he had taken his seat. By this change, so contrary to his intentions, he was graciously preserved; for the boat in which he meant to sail was lost, and all its passengers were drowned.

A THRILLING EXORDIUM.

In a seaport town, on the west coast of England, some years ago, there was notice given of a sermon to be preached one Sunday evening, in a dissenting chapel. The preacher was a man of great celebrity in his calling; and that circumstance, together with the pious object of the discourse—to enforce the duty of the strict observance of the Sabbath—attracted an overflowing audience. After the usual prefatory prayer and hymn of praise, the preacher gave out the text, and was about to proceed with his sermon, when he suddenly paused, leaned his head on the pulpit, and remained silent for a few moments. It was imagined that he had become indisposed; but he soon recovered himself, and addressing the congregation, said, that before entering upon his discourse, he begged to narrate to them a short anecdote. "It is now exactly fifteen years," said he, "since I was last in this place of worship; and the occasion was, as many here may probably remember, the very same which has now brought us together. Among those who came thither that evening were three dissolute young men, who came not only with the intent of insulting and mocking the venerable pastor, but even with stones in their pockets to throw at him, as he stood in his pulpit. Accordingly they had not listened long to the discourse, when one of them said impatiently: 'Why need we listen any longer to the blockhead? throw!' but the second stopped him, saying, 'Let us first see what he makes of this point.' The curiosity of the latter was no sooner satisfied, than he said: 'Ay, its only as I expected, throw, now!' But here the third interposed, and said: 'It would be better altogether to give up the design which had brought them there.' At this remark, his two associates took offense, and left the church, while he himself remained to the end. Now, mark, my brethren, continued the preacher, with much emotion, what were afterward the several fates of these young men? The first was hanged many years ago at Tyburn, for the crime of forgery; the second is now lying under sentence of death, for murder, in the jail of this city. The third, my brethren,"—and the speaker's agitation here became excessive while he paused, and wiped the large drops from his brow—"the third, my brethren, is *he who is now about to address you. Listen to him.*"

POWER OF RELIGION.

Lord —— was a man of the world. His pleasures were drawn from his riches, his honors, and his friends. His daughter was the idol of his heart. Much had been expended for her education; and well did she repay, in her intellectual endowments, the solicitude of her parents. She was highly accomplished, amiable in her disposition, and winning in her manners. They were both strangers to God.

At length Miss —— attended a Dissenters' meeting in London; was deeply awakened, and was soon happily converted. Now she was delighted in the service of the sanctuary, and in social meetings. To her the charms of christianity were overflowing. She frequented those places, where she met with congenial minds, animated with similar hopes.

The change was marked by the fond father, with painful solicitude. To see his lovely daughter, thus infatuated, was to him an occasion of deep grief; and he resolved to correct her erroneous notions on the subject of the real pleasure and business of life. He placed at her disposal large sums of money, hoping she would be induced to go into the fashions and extravagances of others of her birth, and leave the meetings. But she maintained her integrity. He took her long journeys, and conducted in the most engaging manner, in order to direct her mind from religion; but she still delighted in the Savior.

After failing in many projects, which he fondly anticipated would be effectual, he introduced her into company, under circumstances that she must either join in the recreation of the party, or give offense. Hope lighted up in the countenance of this affectionate, but misguided father, as he saw his snare about to entangle the object of his solicitude. It had been arranged among his friends, that several young ladies on the approaching festive occasion, should give a song, accompanied by the pianoforte!

The hour arrived; the party assembled. Several had performed their parts, to the great delight of the party, which was in high spirits. Miss —— was now called on for a song, and many hearts beat high in hopes of victory. Should she decline, she was disgraced. Should she comply, their triumph was complete. This was the moment to seal her fate. With perfect self-possession she took her seat at the pianoforte, ran her fingers over its keys, and commenced playing and singing in a sweet air the following words:

No room for mirth or trifling here,
For worldly hope or worldly fear,
  If life so soon is gone;
If now the Judge is at the door,
And all mankind must stand before
  The inexorable throne;

No matter which my thoughts employ,
A moment's misery or joy;
  But oh! when both shall end!
Where shall I find my destined place?
Shall I, my everlasting days,
  With fiends or angels spend?

She arose from her seat. The whole party was subdued. Not a word was spoken. Her father wept aloud. One by one they left the house. Lord —— never rested until he became a Christian. He lived an example of christian benevolence—having given to benevolent christian enterprises, at the time of his death, nearly half a million of dollars.

THE KING'S LAST LOAF.

Alfred the Great, who died in the year 900, was of a most amiable disposition, and, we would hope, of genuine piety. During his retreat at Athelney, in Somersetshire, after his defeat by the Danes, a beggar came to his little castle, and requested alms. His queen informed Alfred that they had but one small loaf remaining, which was insufficient for themselves and their friends, who were gone in search of food, though with little hope of success. The king replied: "Give the poor Christian one-half of the loaf. He that could feed five thousand men with five loaves and two fishes, can certainly make the half loaf suffice for more than our necessity." The poor man was accordingly relieved, and Alfred's people shortly after *returned with a store of fresh provisions!*

BLAIR'S EXTREMES.

Mr. Robert Blair, in a memoir of his life, written by himself, says: "That year (1615), having, upon an evening, been engaged in company with some irreligious persons, when I returned to my chamber, and went to my ordinary devotion, the Lord did show so much displeasure and wrath, that I was driven from prayer, and heavily threatened to be deserted of God. For this I had a restless night, and resolved to spend the next day in extraordinary humiliation, fasting, and prayer; and toward the evening of that day, I found access to God, with sweet peace, through Jesus Christ, and learned to beware of such company; but then I did run into another extreme of rudeness and incivility toward such as were profane and irreligious, so hard a thing is it for short-sighted sinners to hold the right and the straight way."

THE STUDENT'S TRICK.

A young man of eighteen or twenty, a student in a university, took a walk one day with a professor, who was commonly called the student's friend, such was his kindness to the young men whom it was his office to instruct.

While they were walking together, and the professor was seeking to lead the conversation to grave subjects, they saw a pair of old shoes lying in their path, which they supposed to belong to a poor man who was at work close by, and who had nearly finished his day's work.

The young student turned to the professor, saying: "Let us play the man a trick; we will hide his shoes, and conceal ourselves behind those bushes, and watch to see his perplexity when he cannot find them."

"My dear friend," answered the professor, "we must never amuse ourselves at the expense of the poor. But you are rich, and you may give yourself a much greater pleasure. Put a dollar into each shoe, and then we will hide ourselves."

The student did so, and then placed himself with the professor behind the bushes close by, through which they could easily watch the laborer, and see whatever wonder or joy he might express.

32

The poor man soon finished his work, and came across the field to the path, where he had left his coat and shoes. While he put on the coat, he slipped one foot into one of his shoes; but feeling something hard, he stooped down and found the dollar. Astonishment and wonder were seen upon his countenance; he gazed upon the dollar, turned around, and looked again and again; then he looked around him on all sides, but could see no one. Now he put the money in his pocket and proceeded to put on the other shoe, but how great was his astonishment when he found the other dollar! His feelings overcame him; he fell upon his knees, looked up to heaven and uttered aloud a fervent thanksgiving, in which he spoke of his wife, sick and helpless, and his children without bread, whom this timely bounty, from some unknown hand, would save from perishing.

The young man stood there deeply affected, and tears filled his eyes.

"Now," said the professor, "are you not much better pleased than if you had played your intended trick?"

"O, dearest sir," answered the youth, "you have taught me a lesson now that I will never forget. I feel now the truth of the words which I never before understood: 'it is better to give than to receive.'"

THE BANKRUPT QUAKER.

A PERSON of the Quaker profession, says a London paper, having through misfortune become insolvent, and not being able to pay more than eleven shillings to the pound, formed a resolution, if Providence smiled on his future endeavors, to pay the whole amount, and in case of death he ordered his sons to liquidate his debts by their joint proportions. It pleased God, however, to spare his life, and after struggling with a variety of difficulties (for his livelihood chiefly depended on his own labor), he at length saved sufficient to satisfy every demand. One day the old man went with a considerable sum to the surviving son of one of his creditors, who had been dead thirty years, and insisted on paying him the money he owed his father, which he accordingly did with heart-felt satisfaction.

ONE JOURNEY THROUGH THE WORLD.

WHEN I was a young man, there lived in our neighborhood a Christian who was universally reported to be a very liberal man, and uncommonly upright in his dealings. When he had any of the produce of his farm to dispose of, he made it an invariable rule to give good measure—over good, rather more than could be required of him. One of his friends observing him frequently doing so, questioned him why he did, told him he gave too much, and said it would not be to his advantage. Now, my friends, mark the answer of this good man: "God Almighty has permitted me but one journey through the world, and when gone I cannot return to rectify mistakes." Think of this, friends, "but one journey through the world!"

RESCUING A DROWNING BOY.

THE Rev. Mr. Kelly, of the town of Ayr, once preached an excellent sermon from the parable of the man who fell among thieves. He was particularly severe on the conduct of the priest, who saw him, and ministered not unto him, but passed by on the other side; and, in an animated and pathetic flow of eloquence, he exclaimed: "What! not even the servant of the Almighty! he whose tongue was engaged in the work of charity, whose bosom was appointed the seat of brotherly love, whose heart the emblem of pity; did he refuse to stretch forth his hand, and to take the mantle from his shoulders to cover the nakedness of woe? If he refused, if the shepherd himself went astray, was it to be wondered at that the flock followed?" Such were the precepts of the preacher, and he practiced what he preached. The next day, when the river was much increased, a boy was swept overboard from a small boat by the force of the current. A great concourse of people were assembled, but none of them attempted to save the boy; when Mr. Kelly threw himself from his chamber window into the current, and at the hazard of his own life saved that of the boy.

THE QUAKER AND THE PRIVATEER.

A QUAKER, unknown to his family and friends, had joined with some others in fitting out a privateer to act against the French, who had allied themselves to the American states while in arms against Great Britain. The privateer was successful, and when peace was concluded, there was a considerable dividend for the proprietors. The Quaker received his share among the rest; but his conscience reproached him for what he had done. He considered himself guilty of robbery. About this time he was brought by affliction to the gates of death, which greatly increased his distress. He frequently exclaimed: "Oh, that ill-gotten money!" Neither his wife nor friends knew what he meant. At length he resolved, that should the Lord raise him up, he would make restitution to the injured parties, if they could be found. The Lord did raise him up, and he sent his son to Paris with the sum, directing him to advertise in the sum, directing him to advertise in the Paris Gazette, that any person who had suffered by such a privateer, upon coming and proving his losses, would be refunded in proportion to his share in the prizes. This was accordingly done, to the astonishment of all France.

AN APT REJOINDER.

An American minster, who was earnestly exhorted to take a decided stand on a great moral question, excused himself by saying: "You know ministers must *live!*" "No," said his friend, "I was not aware of that; I thought they might *die* for the truth's sake!"

I DON'T WANT TO GO TO HEAVEN.

There was a clergyman, who was of nervous temperament, and often became quite vexed, by finding his little grandchildren in his study. One day, one of these little children was standing by his mother's side, and she was speaking to him of heaven.

"Ma," said he, "I don't want to go to heaven."

"Do not want to go heaven, my son?"

"No, ma, I'm sure I don't."

"Why not, my son?"

"Why, grandpa will be there, won't he?"

"Why, yes, I hope he will."

"Well, as soon as he sees us, he will come scolding along, and say: 'Whew, whew! what are these boys here for?' I don't want to go to heaven if grandpa is going there."

THE TWO GARDENERS.

Two gardeners, who were neighbors, had their crops of early peas killed by frost; one of them came to condole with the other on this misfortune. "Ah!" cried he, "how unfortunate we have been, neighbor! do you know I have done nothing but fret ever since. But you seem to have a fine healthy crop coming up already; what are these?" "These!" cried the other gardener, "why these are what I sowed immediately after my loss." "What! coming up already?" cried the fretter. "Yes; while you were fretting, I was working." "What! don't you fret when you have a loss?" "Yes; but I always put it off until after I have repaired the mischief." "Why, then you have no need to fret at all." "True," replied the industrious gardener; "and that's the very reason."

BUFFON AND EARLY RISING.

Buffon, the celebrated naturalist, rose always with the sun, and he used often to tell by what means he accustomed himself to get out of bed so early. "In my youth," he said, "I was very fond of sleep; it robbed me of a great deal of my time; but my servant Joseph was of great service in enabling me to overcome it. I promised to give Joseph a crown every time that he could make me get up at six. The next morning he did not fail to awake and torment me; but he received only abuse. The day after he did the same with no better success; and I was obliged at noon to confess that I had lost my time. I told him that he did not know how to manage his business; that he ought to think of my promise, and not mind my threats. The day following he employed force; I begged for indulgence; I bid him begone; I stormed; but Joseph persisted. I was therefore obliged to comply, and he was rewarded every day for the abuse which he suffered at the moment when I awoke, by thanks, accompanied by a crown, which he received about an hour after. Yes, I am indebted to poor Joseph for ten or a dozen of the volumes of my work."

CYRUS.

Cyrus, when quite a youth, at the court of his grandfather, Astyages, undertook one day to perform the office of cup-bearer. He delivered the cup very gracefully, but omitted the usual custom of first tasting it himself. The king reminded him of it, supposing he had forgotten the practice. "No, sir," replied Cyrus; "but I was afraid there might be poison in it; for I have observed that the lords of your court, after drinking, become noisy, quarrelsome, and frantic; and that even you, sir, seem to have forgotten that you are a king." "Does not the same thing," replied Astyages, "happen to your father?" "Never," answered Cyrus. "How so?" "Why when he has taken what he sees proper, he is no longer thirsty, that is all."

THE GOD WAS WITHIN.

While Mr. Kirkland was a missionary to the Oneidas, being unwell, he was unable to preach on the afternoon of a certain Sabbath, and told Peter, one of the head men of the Oneidas, that he must address the congregation. Peter modestly and reluctantly consented. After a few words of introduction, he began a discourse on the character of the Savior. "What, my brethren," said he, "are the views which you form of the character of Jesus? You will answer, perhaps, that he was a man of singular benevolence. You will tell me that he proved this to be his character, by the nature of the miracles which he wrought. All these, you will say, were kind in the extreme. He created bread to feed thousands who were ready to perish. He raised to life the son of a poor woman, who was a widow, and to whom his labors were necessary for her support in old age. Are these, then, your only views of the Savior? I will tell you, they are lame. When Jesus came into the world, he threw his blanket around him, but the God was within."

THE DYING COAL-MINER.

Stephen Karkeet, twenty-five years old, whilst employed under ground in a mine, in the parish of Newlyn, was buried alive, by the falling together of the shaft in which he was, at the depth of five fathoms from the surface. The first person who arrived at the spot was a man named George Trevarrow, who called to know if any living being was beneath, when Karkeet answered, in a firm voice: "I feel the cold hand of death upon me; if there is any hope of my being rescued from this untimely grave, tell me; and if not, tell me." Trevarrow at once informed him that there was not a shadow of hope left, as upwards of four tons of rubbish had fallen round and upon him, and that suffocation must inevitably take place before human aid could afford relief. On hearing which, Karkeet exclaimed: "All's well; it is the Lord! let him do what seemeth him good. Tell my dear father and mother not to be sorry as those without hope for me; 'tis now only that I am happy—'tis now that I feel the advantages of a religious life; now I feel the Lord is my stronghold; and now I feel I am going to heaven." Here his voice failed him; he never spoke again.

GUSTAVUS AND THE PEASANT GIRL.

Gustavus III., king of Sweden, passing one morning on horseback through a village in the neighborhood of his capital, observed a young peasant girl, of interesting appearance, drawing water at a fountain by the wayside. He went up to her and asked her for a draught. Without delay she lifted up her pitcher, and with artless simplicity put it to the lips of the monarch. Having satisfied his thirst, and courteously thanked his benefactress, he said:

"My girl, if you would accompany me to Stockholm, I would endeavor to fix you in a more agreeable situation."

"Ah, sir," replied the girl, "I cannot accept your proposal. I am not anxious to rise above the state of life in which the providence of God has placed me; but, even if I were, I could not for an instant hesitate."

"And why?" rejoined the king, somewhat surprised.

"Because," answered the girl, somewhat coloring, "my mother is poor and sickly, and has no one but me to assist and comfort her under her many afflictions: and no earthly bribe could induce me to leave her, or to neglect the duties which affection requires from me."

"Where is your mother?" asked the monarch.

"In that little cabin," replied the girl, pointing to a wretched hovel beside her.

The king, whose feelings were interested in favor of his companion, went in, and beheld stretched on a bedstead, whose only covering was a little straw, an aged female, weighed down with years, and sinking under infirmities. Moved at the sight, the monarch addressed her: "I am sorry, my poor woman, to find you in so destitute and afflicted a condition."

"Alas, sir," answered the venerable sufferer, "I should be indeed to be pitied, had I not that kind and attentive girl, who labors to support me, and omits nothing she thinks can afford me relief. May a gracious God remember it to her for good," she added, wiping away a tear.

Never, perhaps, was Gustavus more sensible, than at that moment, of the pleasure of occupying an exalted station. The gratification arising from the consciousness of having it in his power to assist a suffering fellow-creature, almost overpowered him; and putting a purse into the hand of the young villager, he could only say: "Continue to take care of your mother; I shall soon enable you to do so more effectually. Good-bye, my amiable girl, you may depend on the promise of your king."

On his return to Stockholm, Gustavus settled a pension for life on the mother, with the reversion to her daughter at her death.

EARL RODEN.

The following anecdote is related by the Rev. Dr. Sprague in his letters giving an account of his journey to Europe, as being well authenticated:

When George IV. was in Ireland, he told lord Roden that on a particular morning he was coming to breakfast with him. He accordingly came, and bringing with him two or three of the nobility, happened to arrive just as his lordship and family assembled for domestic worship. Lord Roden being told his guest had arrived, went to the door and met him with every expression of respect, and seated him and the gentlemen that accompanied him in his parlor. He then turned to the king, and said: "Your majesty will not doubt that I feel highly honored by this visit; but there is a duty which I have not yet discharged this morning, which I owe to the King of kings—that of performing domestic worship; and your majesty will be kind enough to excuse me while I retire with my household and attend to it." "Certainly," replied the king, "but I am going with you;" and he immediately rose and followed him into the hall where the family were assembled; and taking his station in an old arm-chair, remained during the family devotions.

This anecdote certainly reflects honor upon his lordship and the king; while it exhibits in the one the dignity of unyielding christian principles, it displays in the other the courtesy of a gentleman, and the regard felt for a consistent religious character.

AN HONEST PEASANT.

A Russian was traveling from Tobolsk to Beresow. On the road he stopped one night at the hut of an Ostiak. In the morning, on continuing his journey, he discovered that he had lost his purse, containing about one hundred roubles.

The son of the Ostiak found the purse while out hunting, but instead of taking it up, went and told his father, who was equally unwilling to touch it, and ordered his son to cover it with bushes.

A few months after this the Russian returned and stopped at the same hut, but the Ostiak did not recognize him. He related the loss he had met with.

The Ostiak listened very attentively, and when he had finished, "You are welcome," said he; "here is my son who will show you the spot where it lies; no hand has touched it but the one which covered it over, that you might recover what you have lost."

HE WILL NEVER MAKE A MERCHANT.

A country gentleman not long since, placed a son with a merchant in —— street. And for a season all went on well. But, at length, the young man sold a dress to a lady; and as he was folding it up, he observed a flaw in the silk, and remarked: "Madam, I deem it my duty to tell you there is a fracture in the silk."

This spoiled the bargain. But the merchant overheard the remark; and had he reflected a moment, he might have thus reasoned with himself: "Now I am safe, while my affairs are committed to the care of an *honest* clerk."

But he was not pleased; so he wrote immediately to the father to come and take him home; "for," said he, "*he will never make a merchant!*"

The father, who had brought up his son with the strictest care, was not a little surprised and grieved, and hastened to the city to ascertain wherein his son had been deficient. Said the anxious father, "And why will he not make a merchant?"

Merchant. Because he has no *tact.* Only a day or two since, he *voluntarily* told a lady, who was buying silk, that the goods were damaged, and so I lost the bargain. Purchasers must look out for themselves. If they cannot discover flaws, it will be foolishness in me to tell them of their existence.

Father. And is this all the fault?

Merchant. Yes: he is very well in other respects.

Father. Then I love my son better than ever; and I *thank you* for telling me of the matter; I would not have him in YOUR STORE another day for the world.

A HEROIC SERVANT.

THE servant of a lady, sojourning at Ramsgate for the benefit of her health, in the summer of 1833, happened to be walking under the cliffs at the flowing of the tide. He heard the voice of some one crying for assistance, which he discovered to have proceeded from a woman, with her two children in her arms, embayed by the sea, and up to her waist in the water. He immediately rushed to her assistance, and rescued her and her two children from her perilous situation. On hearing the mother exclaim that there was another, he again dashed into the water, when he found a male child struggling to clamber up a rock, and an old woman, the latter having been twice washed away by the waves; both of whom he also succeeded in rescuing from a watery grave. On reaching his mistress' house, the excitement and exhaustion produced by his efforts were such, that it was with difficulty he was restored from a long fainting fit. It is worthy of remark, that the man was unable to swim.

TESTIMONY OF SEVERAL CHRISTIANS.

Two aged disciples, one eighty-seven years old, one day met. Well, inquired the younger of his fellow-pilgrim, how long have you been interested in religion? "Fifty years," was the old man's reply. Well, have you ever regretted that you began so young to devote yourself to religion? "O no," said he, and the tears trickled down his furrowed cheeks; "I weep when I think of the sins of my youth. It is this which makes me weep now."

Another man of eighty, who had been a Christian fifty or sixty years, was asked if he was grieved that he had become a disciple of

Christ. "O no," said he; "if I grieve for any thing, it is that I did not become a Christian before."

A christian friend visited a woman of ninety, as she lay on her last bed of sickness. She had been hoping in Christ for half a century. In the course of conversation she said: "Tell all the children that an old woman, who is just on the borders of eternity, is very much grieved that she did not begin to love the Savior when a child. Tell them youth is the time to serve the Lord."

Said an old man of seventy-six: "I did not become interested in religion till I was forty-five; and I often have to tell God, I have nothing to bring him but the dregs of old age."

Said another man, between sixty and seventy years of age: "I hope I became a disciple of the Lord Jesus when I was seventeen;" and he burst into tears as he added, "and there is nothing which causes me so much distress as to think of those seventeen years—some of the very best portion of my life—which I devoted to sin and the world."

PRINCESS CHARLOTTE.

When this amiable princess was quite young, a noble and pious lady devoted much of her time in teaching her the principles of virtue and piety. The princess was anxious to give some testimony of her esteem for the character of this peeress, and one day presented her with a gold pencil-case. According to the established etiquette in such cases, her ladyship was kneeling to receive it, when the princess threw her arms around her neck and, weeping, requested her to rise. "What!" said she, shall the venerable Lady E—— kneel before a child? No, that I can never permit. It is I who ought to kneel, and who feel myself honored by your acceptance of a trifle, as a mark of my reverence for your worth, and of my gratitude for your valuable instructions, which I can never either forget or repay."

THE DEACON'S TWO CENTS.

A minister who was urged by his people to go out on a begging excursion, to solicit money to liquidate a debt on their meeting-house, put up on Saturday night with the deacon of a church to which he was to present the subject on the ensuing Sabbath. He seemed to be quite wealthy, and as he treated his guest with great cordiality and kindness, the preacher cherished glowing expectations of a very generous contribution from his purse. On the Sabbath, after setting forth the claims of his object in as forcible and eloquent a manner as possible, the plates were passed around for money. As the deacon sat near the pulpit, the preacher could not resist the temptation of rising up a little and peering over the pulpit to witness the expression of the good man's liberality. As the plate approaches the deacon, he leisurely puts his hand into his pocket. The preacher's heart palpitates with anxiety. But, alas! the deacon just drops from his thumb and fingers two red cents upon the plate and lets it pass! The preacher suddenly sank back into his seat, and hope and faith died within him. The collection, it seems, was small, and the preacher, mortified and indignant, went straight back to his people, told them the story of the two cents, and assured them they must raise the funds needed themselves or send some one else forth to beg besides him. The people caught his spirit—they determined to solicit no further—increased their subscriptions, and paid their debts themselves.

DR. WILSON.

THE benevolent Dr. Wilson once discovered a clergyman at Bath, who, he was informed, was sick, poor, and had a numerous family. In the evening he gave a friend fifty pounds, requesting him to deliver it in the most delicate manner, and as from an unknown person. The friend said: "I will wait upon him early in the morning." "You will oblige me, sir, by calling directly. Think of what importance a good night's rest may be to that poor man."

A GRATEFUL WOMAN.

A PERSON applied to a pious woman, requesting her husband to become bound for an amount which, if ever demanded, would sweep away all his property. On her replying: "My husband will attend, sir, whenever you may appoint;" a bystander asked her: "Do you know what you are engaging to do, and that perhaps this may be the means of leaving you destitute?" She replied: "Yes, I do; but that gentleman found us in the greatest distress, and by his kindness we are surrounded with comforts; now, should such an event take place he will only leave us where he found us."

LINKS AND THE MURDERER.

PETER LINKS, a Namacqua, was the brother of Jacob Links, who was murdered when on a journey into the country with Mr. Threlfall, the Wesleyan missionary. After we heard of his brother Jacob's murder, Peter, when speaking on the subject, said: "Oh that I could find the murderer that took away my brother's life! I would not care what distance I might have to travel; I would not mind any exposure, fatigue, or danger; I would not care what expense I might incur, if I could only lay hold of that man." Being aware that men in their savage state cherish an indomitable spirit of revenge, but believing Peter to be a decidedly pious character, I was a little astonished at his language, and rather hastily inquired: "Well, supposing you could find the man, what would you do to him?" "Do to him?" said Peter; "Mynheer, I would bring him to this station, that he might hear the gospel, and that his soul might be converted to God."

THE REWARD OF WAR.

THE Duke of Marlborough observing a soldier leaning pensively on the butt end of his musket, just after victory had declared itself in favor of the British arms at the battle of Blenheim, accosted him thus: "Why so pensive, my friend, after so glorious a victory?" "It may be glorious," replied the brave fellow, "but I am thinking that all the human blood I have spilled this day *has only earned me fourpence.*"

FRIENDSHIP OF DAMON AND PYTHIAS.

WHEN Damon was sentenced, by Dionysius of Syracuse, to die on a certain day, he begged permission, in the interim, to retire to his own country, to set the affairs of his disconsolate family in order. This the tyrant intended peremptorily to refuse, by granting it, as he conceived, on the impossible conditions of his procuring some one to remain as hostage for his return, under equal forfeiture of life. Pythias heard the conditions, and did not wait for an application upon the part of Damon: he instantly offered himself as security for his friend; which being accepted, Damon was immediately set at liberty. The king and all the courtiers were astonished at this action; and therefore, when the day of execution drew near, his majesty had the curiosity to visit Pythias in his confinement. After some conversation on the subject of friendship, in which the tyrant delivered it as his opinion, that self-interest was the sole mover of human actions; as for virtue, friendship, benevolence, love of one's country, and the like, he looked upon them as terms invented by the wise to keep in awe and impose upon the weak: "My lord," said Pythias, with a firm voice and noble aspect, "I would it were possible that I might suffer a thousand deaths, rather than my friend should fail in any article of his honor. He cannot fail therein, my lord: I am as confident of his virtue, as I am of my own existence. But I pray, I beseech the gods, to preserve the life and integrity of my Damon together: oppose him, ye winds, prevent the eagerness and impatience of his honorable endeavors, and suffer him not to arrive, till by death I have redeemed a life a thousand times of more consequence, of more value, than my own; more estimable to his lovely wife, to his precious little children, to his friends, to his country. Oh, leave me not to die the worst of deaths in my Damon." Dionysius was awed and confounded by the dignity of these sentiments, and by the manner in which they were uttered: he felt his heart struck by a slight sense of invading truth: but it served rather to perplex than undeceive him. The fatal day arrived. Pythias was brought forth, and walked amid the guards with a serious but satisfied air, to the place of execution. Dionysius was already there; he was exalted on a moving throne, which was drawn by six white horses, and sat pensive and attentive to the prisoner. Pythias came, he vaulted lightly on the scaffold, and beholding for some time the apparatus of his death, he turned with a placid countenance, and addressed the spectators: "My prayers are heard," he cried, "the gods are propitious; you know, my friends, that the winds have been contrary till yesterday. Damon could not come, he could not conquer impossibilities; he will be here to-morrow, and the blood which is shed to-day shall have ransomed the life of my friend. Oh, could I erase from your bosoms every doubt, every mean suspicion of the honor of the man for whom I am about to suffer, I should go to my death, even as I would to my bridal. Be it sufficient in the meantime, that my friend will be found noble; that his truth is unimpeachable; that he will speedily prove it; that he is now on his way, hurrying on, accusing himself, the adverse elements, and the gods: but I haste to prevent his speed; executioner do your office." As he pronounced the last words, a buzz began to rise among the remotest of the people; a distant voice was heard, the crowd caught the words, and "Stop, stop the execution!" was repeated by the whole assembly: a man came at full speed: the throng gave way to his approach: he was mounted on a steed of foam; in an instant he was off his horse, on the scaffold, and clasped Pythias in his arms. "You are safe," he cried, "you are safe, my friend, my beloved friend: the gods be praised, you are safe, I now have nothing but death to suffer, and am delivered from the anguish of those reproaches which I gave myself for having endangered a life so much dearer than my own." Pale, cold, and half speechless in the arms of his Damon, Pythias replied in broken accents: "Fatal haste! Cruel impatience! What envious powers have wrought impossibilities in your favor! But I will not be wholly disappointed. Since I cannot die to save, I will not survive you." Dionysius heard, beheld, and considered all with astonishment. His heart was touched, he wept, and leaving his throne, he ascended the scaffold: "Live, live, ye incomparable pair!" cried he: "ye have borne unquestionable testimony to the existence of virtue; and that virtue equally evinces the existence of a God to reward it. Live happily, and with renown: and, oh! form me by your precepts, as ye have invited me by your example, to be worthy of the participation of so sacred a friendship."

ERSKINE'S DELIVERANCES.

Rev. Henry Erskine was often in great straits and difficulties. Once when he and his family had supped at night, there remained neither bread, meal, flesh, nor money in the house. In the morning the young children cried for their breakfast, and their father endeavored to divert them, and did what he could at the same time to encourage himself and wife to depend upon that Providence that hears the young ravens when they cry. While thus engaged, a countryman knocked hard at the door, and called for some one to help him off with his load. Being asked whence he came, and what he would have, he told them he came from Lady Reburn with some provisions for Mr. Erskine. They told him he must be mistaken, and that it was more likely to be for another Mr. Erskine in the same town. He replied, no, he knew what he said, he was sent to Mr. Henry Erskine, and cried, "Come, help me off with my load, or else I will throw it down at the door." Whereupon they took the sack from him, and on opening it, found it well stored with fish and meat.

At another time, being at Edinburgh, he was so reduced that he had but three half-pence in his pocket. When he was walking about the streets, not knowing what course to steer, one came to him in a countryman's habit, presented him with a letter in which were inclosed several Scotch ducatoons, with these words written: "Sir, receive this from a sympathizing friend. Farewell." Mr. Erskine never could find out whence the money came.

At another time, being on a journey on foot, his money fell short and he was in danger of being reduced to distress. Having occasion to fix his walking-stick in some marshy ground, among the rushes, he heard something tinkle at the end of it; it proved to be two half-crowns, which greatly assisted in bearing his charges home. In days of persecution and poverty God wonderfully interposes for his people.

SERGEANT GLANVILLE.

The father of that eminent lawyer, Mr. Sergeant Glanville, who lived in the days of Charles II. had a good estate, which he intended to settle on his eldest son; but he proving vicious, and affording no no hope of reformation, he devolved it upon the sergeant, who was his second son. Upon his father's death the eldest son, finding that what he had hitherto considered as the mere threat of his father was really true, became greatly dejected, and in a short period his character underwent an entire change. His brother observing this, invited him with a party of his friends to a feast; and after several other dishes had been removed, he ordered one, covered up, to be set before his brother, which on being examined was found to contain the writings of the estate. The sergeant then told him that he had now done what he was sure their father would have done had he lived to witness the happy change they all saw, and that he therefore freely conveyed to him the whole property.

A TURKISH FEMALE MARTYR.

THE following fact, while it shows the intolerance of the mildest nation of the Turkish empire, at the same time illustrates the powerful influence of the Gospel and the holy fortitude with which it blesses its possessor:

A Turkish woman being divorced from her husband, lived with a Greek for two years. She avowed herself a Christian, and having offended one of her servants, he went to her father, a man of some consequence, to state the fact. Some soldiers were sent to take her into custody; on examination she confessed herself to be a Christian, and was sentenced to be drowned in the Nile. Seated on an ass, she was conducted amid the maledictions of the multitude to the Boulac; they took her in a small boat on the stream, stripped her of her dress and ornaments, in which they were hastened by her declaration: "I shall die a Christian;" bound her arms behind her back and cast her into the Nile, where she expired.

Happy, indeed, are those who like us can enjoy their christian privileges unmolested; but awful is their condition who have these privileges and do not improve them.

FRANKLIN AND HIS PAPER.

SOON after his establishment in Philadelphia, Franklin was offered a piece for publication in his newspaper. Being very busy, he begged the gentleman would leave it for consideration. The next day the author called and asked his opinion of it. "Why, sir," replied Franklin, "I am sorry to say I think it highly scurrilous and defamatory. But being at a loss on account of my poverty, whether to reject it or not, I thought I would put it to this issue,—at night, when my work was done, I bought a two-penny loaf, on which I supped heartily, and then wrapping myself in my great coat, slept very soundly on the floor till morning; when another loaf and mug of water afforded a pleasant breakfast. Now, sir, since I can live very comfortably in this manner, why should I prostitute my press to personal hatred or party passion for a more luxurious living?"

One cannot read this anecdote of our American sage, without thinking of Socrates' reply to king Archelaus, who had pressed him to give up preaching in the dirty streets of Athens, and come and live with him in his splendid courts: "*Meal, please your majesty, is a half-penny a peck at Athens, and water I get for nothing!*"

THE POOR ARTIST.

Mr. H ——, an ingenious artist, being destitute of employment, and reduced to great distress, had no other resource than to solicit the aid of an elder brother who was in good circumstances. To him therefore he applied, and begged some little hovel to live in, and some provision for his support. The brother was melted into tears, and said: "You, my dear brother! you live in a hovel! you are a man; you are an honor to the family. I am nothing. You shall take this house and the estate, and I will be your guest if you please." The brothers thus affectionately lived together, as if it were common property, till the death of the elder put the artist in possession of the whole.

BROTHER OF ÆSCHYLUS.

Æschylus, one of the most celebrated poets of Greece, lived about four hundred years before Christ. With his two brothers, Cynegirus and Aminius, he distinguished himself in the battles of Marathon, Platæa and Salamis. But his countrymen forgot their obligations both to his valor and his genius, and in compliance to the voice of popular clamor, he was unjustly sentenced to death, and would have been immediately executed had not his brother Aminius, who had lost a hand in the service of his country, at the battle of Salamis, promptly throwing off his cloak, presented his maimed arm to the view of his brother's judges. The appeal, though silent, was powerful, and Æschylus was in consequence pardoned.

VESSEL SAVED BY A DOLPHIN.

Mr. Colstone, an eminent merchant of Bristol, who lived a century ago, was remarkable for his liberality to the poor, and equally distinguished for his success in commerce. The providence of God seemed to smile, in a peculiar manner, on the concerns of one who made so good a use of his affluence. It has been said that he never insured, nor ever lost a ship. Once, indeed, a vessel belonging to him on her voyage home, struck on a rock, and immediately sprang a leak, by which so much water was admitted as to threaten speedy destruction. Means were instantly adopted to save the vessel, but all seemed ineffectual, as the water rose rapidly. In a short time, however, the leak stopped without any apparent cause, and the vessel reached Bristol in safety. On examining her bottom, a fish, said to be a dolphin, was found fast wedged in the fracture made by the rock when she struck; which had prevented any water from entering during the remainder of the voyage. As a memorial of this singular event, the figure of a dolphin is carved on the staves which are carried in procession, on public occasions, by the children who are educated at the charity schools founded by Mr. Colstone.

SUICIDE PREVENTED.

A Piedmontese nobleman, into whose company I fell at Turin, (says Mr. Rages, of Italy,) told me his story without reserve, as follows:

"I was weary of life, and after a day such as few have known, and none would wish to remember, was lounging along the street to the river, when I felt a sudden check: I turned, and beheld a little boy, who caught the skirt of my coat in his anxiety to solicit my notice, whose look and manner were irresistible. Not less was the lesson he had learned: "There are six of us, and we are dying for food." Why should not I, said I to myself, relieve this wretched family? I have the means, and it will not delay me many minutes. But what if it does? The scene of misery he conducted me to, I cannot describe; I threw them my purse, and their burst of gratitude overcame me. It filled my eyes, it went as cordial to my heart. I will call again to-morrow, I said. Fool that I was, to think of leaving a world where so much pleasure was to be had, and so cheaply."

WORK FOR THE DAY BEFORE DEATH.

Rabbi Eliezer said: "Turn to God *one* day before your death." His disciples said: "How can a man know the day of his death?" He answered them: "Therefore you should turn to God TO-DAY. Perhaps you may die *to-morrow;* thus, every day will be employed in returning."

RESIGNATION.

A lady who had lost a beloved child, was so oppressed with grief that she even excluded herself from the society of her own family, and kept herself locked in her chamber; but was at length prevailed on by her husband to come down stairs and to take a walk in the garden. While there, she stooped to pick a flower, but her husband appeared as though he would hinder her. She plaintively said: "What! deny a flower!" He replied: "You have denied God your flower, and surely you ought not to think it hard in me to deny you mine."

It is said the lady suitably felt the gentle reproof, and had reason to say: "A word spoken in season, how good is it!"

ANOTHER.

Ebenezer Adams, an eminent member of the society of Friends, on visiting a lady of rank, whom he found, six months after the death of her husband, on a sofa covered with black cloth, and in all the dignity of wo, approached her with great solemnity, and gently taking her by the hand, thus addressed her: "So, friend, I see then thou hast not yet forgiven God Almighty." This reproof had so great an effect on the lady that she immediately laid aside the symbols of grief, and again entered on the important duties of life.

LOSING A SEAT IN CONGRESS.

"Sir, bring me a good plain dinner," said a melancholy looking individual to a waiter at one of our principal hotels.

The dinner was brought and devoured, and the eater called the landlord aside and thus addressed him:

"You are the landlord?"

"Yes."

"You do a good business here?"

"Yes!" (in astonishment.)

"You make, probably, ten dollars a day clear?"

"Yes."

"Then I am safe. I cannot pay for what I have consumed; I have been out of employment seven months; but have engaged to go to work to-morrow. I had been without food four-and-twenty hours when I entered your place. I will pay you in a week."

"I cannot pay my bills with such promises," blustered the landlord, and "I do not keep a poor-house. You should address the proper authorities. Leave me something for security."

"I have nothing."

"I will take your coat."

"If I go into the streets without that such weather as it is, I may get my death."

"You should have thought of that before you came here."

"Are you serious? Well, I solemnly aver that in one week from now I will pay you."

"I will take the coat."

The coat was left, and a week afterwards redeemed. Seven years after that a wealthy man entered the political arena, and was presented at a caucus as an applicant for a congressional nomination. The principal of the caucus held his peace; he heard the name and the history of the applicant, who was a member of the church, and one of the most respectable citizens. He was chairman. The vote was a tie, and he cast a negative, thereby defeating the wealthy applicant, whom he met an hour afterwards, and to whom he said:

"You don't remember me?"

"No."

"I once ate a dinner at your hotel; and, although I told you I was famishing, and pledged my word and honor to pay you in a week, you took my coat, and saw me go out into the inclement air at the risk of my life, without it."

"Well, sir, what then?"

"*Not much. You called yourself a Christian. To-night you were a candidate for nomination, and but for me you would have been elected to Congress!*"

Three years after, the christian hotel keeper became bankrupt, and sought a home in Bellevue. The poor dinnerless wretch that was, afterwards became a high functionary in Albany.

PAINFUL EFFECTS OF A JOKE.

A GENTLEMAN in ——— attended the preaching of Dr. Clarke, and was deeply convinced of sin. With strong prayer and tears he sought pardon, but found it not. Being confined by sickness soon after, he sent for Dr. Clarke, who came; but learning how long he had mourned, and with what earnestness he had sought salvation, he secretly wondered at God's so long withholding freedom from such deep repentance; and finding the lamp of life burning low, and mental agony hurrying on its extinction, with tender but firm language he said: "It is not often, Mr. ——, that God thus deals with a soul so deeply humbled as yours, and in his own appointed way seeking redemption. Sir, there must be a cause. You have left something undone which it is your duty and interest to have done. God judge between you and it."

Fixing his eyes intently on Dr. Clarke, the gentleman gave the following narration: "In the year ——, I was at ——, and took my passage in the ship —— for England. Before sailing, some merchants put on board a small bag of dollars, which were given in charge to the captain for such and such parties. I saw the transaction, and noticed the captain's carelessness, who left the bag day after day rolling upon the locker. For the simple purpose of frightening him I hid it. He made no inquiries, and we arrived at ——. I still retained it till it should be missed. Months passed, and still no inquiry was made. The parties to whom it had been consigned came to the captain for it. He remembered receiving it in charge, but no more. It must have been left behind. Search was made, letters written, but it could not be found. All this occupied some months. I had now become alarmed and ashamed to confess, lest I should implicate my character.

"The captain was sued, and, having nothing to pay, was cast into prison. He maintained his innocence as to the theft, but confessed his carelessness. He languished two years in prison, and died. Guilt by this time had hardened my mind. I strove to be happy in the amusements of the world, but all in vain. Under your preaching the voice of God broke in upon my conscience. I have agonized at the throne of mercy for the sake of Christ for pardon; but God is deaf to my prayer. I must go down to the grave unsaved."

Dr. Clarke suggested to the dying penitent that God claimed from him not only *repentance,* but *restitution.* The widow and fatherless children still lived. The gentleman readily consented. The sum, with interest and compound interest, was made up and given to the widow, to whom the circumstances were made known. The dying man's mind was calmed, and soon, in firm hope of pardon, he died.

A PRAYER WITHOUT SUBMISSION.

Dr. Edmund Calamy relates, in his life, that some persons of the name of Mart, in whose family he resided for some time, had a son who discovered the most wicked and impious disposition. When confined in prison he wrote letters professing penitence; but as soon as he had an opportunity he returned to his former sin.

This young man had been the darling both of his father and mother; and the latter had set her affections upon him to so great a degree, that when she saw him a monster of wickedness, she became deranged and attempted to destroy herself, which she at length effected. So far from being suitably impressed with this awful event, her son now proceeded to greater lengths in wickedness. At length he professed to be sorry for his depraved course, and applied to the Rev. Samuel Pomfret to intercede for him with his father. He was made ready for sea, but unhappily became connected with a gang of villains, and on the very night before he was to set sail he robbed Mr. Pomfret, was pursued, tried, and condemned to die.

On the Sabbath preceding the Wednesday on which he was condemned to die, his father entreated Dr. Calamy to accompany him that evening to his cell in Newgate, to converse with his unhappy son, and to give his opinion as to the propriety of seeking to obtain his pardon. The doctor went, and found him in a very awful state of mind, resenting different things which he conceived his father had done wrong, and saying that he might obtain a pardon for him if he would but part with some of his money. In vain did the doctor expostulate with him on the improper feelings he manifested, and entreat him to humble himself before God on account of his sins, not only as his solemn duty, and the way to secure the salvation of his soul, but as the only way of engaging his friends to obtain for him a reprieve. His reply was: "Sir, I scorn any thing of that nature, and would rather die with my company." The doctor reasoned with him on the existence of an hereafter, charged him with the death of his mother, taxed him with the murder of some persons abroad whose blood he had actually shed, and showed him the heavy punishment he must endure in an eternal world unless he turned to God, repented of his sins, and sought and obtained pardon through the atonement of the Lord Jesus. He admitted the truth of all these things, but was full of trifling unconcern. He frankly said that he had no hope of being better in his character, and that, on the contrary, he was satisfied he should grow worse. The next morning he was visited by Dr. Jekyl, who asked him whether, during the whole time he had been confined in Newgate, he had once bowed his knees to the great God, making it his earnest request to him to give him a sense of his sins, and to create in him a tender heart. He admitted that he had not, nor did he think it of any use. He was promised that if he would relent and pray morning and evening for the grace of God, an effort should be made, with every probability of success, for a reprieve, and subsequently a pardon. But he would make no engagement, and was hung on the day appointed.

On the day of his execution the father of this unhappy young man told Dr. Calamy, that when the culprit was a very young child, and their only child, he was exceedingly ill with a fever, and that both his wife and himself, thinking their lives were bound up in the life of the child, were exceedingly importunate with God in prayer that his life might be spared. A pious woman expostulated with him on the vehemence he manifested, and said she dreaded the consequence of his praying in such a way, and that it became him to leave the matter to an infinitely wise God. At length the father said: "Let him prove what he will, so he is but spared I shall be satisfied." The old man added: "This I now see to have been my folly. For, through the just hand of God I have lived to see this wretched son of mine a heart-breaking cross to them that loved him with the greatest tenderness, a disgrace to my whole family, and likely to bring down my gray hairs with sorrow to the grave. I read my sin very distinctly in my punishment; but must own that God is righteous in all his ways and holy in all his works."

GEMS OF THOUGHT.

THE WORLD WAS MADE WITH A BENEVOLENT DESIGN.

It is a happy world after all. The air, the earth, the water, teem with delighted existence. In a spring-noon, or a summer-evening, on whichever side I turn my eyes, myriads of happy beings crowd upon my view. "The insect youth are on the wing." Swarms of new-born flies are trying their pinions in the air. Their sportive motion, their wanton mazes, their gratuitous activity, their continual change of place without use or purpose, testify their joy and the exultation they feel in their lately discovered faculties. A bee among the flowers in spring is one of the most cheerful objects that can be looked upon. Its life appears to be all enjoyment; so busy and so pleased: yet it is only a specimen of insect life, with which, by reason of the animal being half domesticated, we happen to be better acquainted than we are with that of others. The whole winged insect tribe it is probable, are equally intent upon their proper employments, and under every variety of constitution, gratified, and perhaps equally gratified, by the offices which the Author of their nature has assigned to them. But the atmosphere is not the only scene of enjoyment for the insect race. Plants are covered with aphides, greedily sucking their juices, and constantly, as it should seem, in the act of sucking. It cannot be doubted but this is a state of gratification; what else should fix them so close to the operation, and so long? Other species are running about with an alacrity in their motions which carries with it every mark of pleasure. Large patches of ground are sometimes half covered with these brisk and sprightly natures. If we look to what the waters produce, shoals of fish frequent the margins of rivers, of lakes, and of the sea itself. These are so happy that they know not what to do with themselves. Their attitudes, their vivacity, their leaps out of the water, their frolics in it (which I have noticed a thousand times with equal attention and amusement,) all conduce to show their excess of spirits, and are simply the effects of that excess. Walking by the sea-side on a calm evening upon a sandy shore, and with an ebbing tide, I have frequently remarked the appearance of a dark cloud, or rather very thick mist, hanging over the edge of the water to the hight, perhaps of half a yard, and of the breadth of two or three yards, stretching along the coast as far as the eye could reach, and always retiring with the water. When this cloud came to be examined, it proved to be nothing else than so much space filled with young shrimps in the act of bounding into the air from the shallow margin of the water, or from the wet sand. If any motion of a mute animal could express delight, it was this; if they had meant to make signs of their happiness, they could not have done it more intelligibly. Suppose, then, what I have no doubt of, each individual of this number to be in a state of positive enjoyment, what a sum, collectively of gratification and pleasure, have we here before our view!

The young of all animals appear to me to receive pleasure simply from the exercise of their limbs and bodily faculties, without reference to any end to be attained, or any use to be answered by the exertion. A child, without knowing any thing of the use of language, is in a high degree delighted with being able to speak. Its incessant repetition of a few articulate sounds, or perhaps of the single word which it has learned to pronounce, proves this point clearly. Nor is it less pleased with its first successful endeavors to walk, or rather to run (which precedes walking,) although entirely ignorant of the importance of the attainment to its future life, and even without applying it to any present purpose. A child is delighted with speaking, wthout having any thing to say; and with walking, without knowing where to go. And, prior to both these, I am disposed to believe that the waking hours of infancy are agreeably taken up with the exercise of vision, or perhaps, more properly speaking, with learning to see.

But it is not for youth alone that the great Parent of creation hath provided. Happiness is found with the purring cat no less than with the playful kitten; in the arm-chair of dozing age, as well as in either the sprightliness of the dance or the animation of the chase. To novelty, to acuteness of sensation, to hope, to ardor of pursuit, succeeds what is, in no inconsiderable degree, an equivalent for them all, "perception of ease." Herein is the exact difference between the young and the old. The young are not happy but when enjoying pleasure; the old are happy when free from pain. And this constitution suits with the degrees of animal power which they respectively possess. The vigor of youth was to be stimulated to action by impatience of rest; whilst to the imbecility of age, quietness and repose become positive gratifications. In one important step the advantage is with the old. A state of ease is, generally speaking, more attainable than a state of pleasure. A constitution, therefore, which can enjoy ease, is preferable to that which can taste only pleasure. This same perception of ease oftentimes renders old age a condition of great comfort, especially while riding at its anchor after a busy or tempestuous life. It is well described by Rosseau to be the interval of repose and enjoyment between the hurry and end of life. How far the same cause extends to other animal natures, cannot be judged of with certainty. The appearance of satisfaction with which most animals, as their activity subsides, seek and enjoy rest, affords reason to believe that this source of gratification is appointed to advanced life under all or most of its various forms. In the species with which we are best acquainted, namely, our own, I am far, even as an observer of human life, from thinking that youth is its happiest season, much less the only happy one.—PALEY.

THE STAR OF BETHLEHEM.

LATE one night, when all was still around a rude hostelry in Judea, save, perchance, the rippling of the wind through the tree-tops, a young mother gave birth to a son. She was one of a company of poor travelers, who had taken up their night lodgings in a stable. Such a birth was no uncommon thing among the poorer classes ; and yet Heaven never bent over a universe just rolled into being with such intense, absorbing interest, as it did over that unconscious babe, as it lay with feeble, fluttering breath upon its mother's bosom. The heavens were quiet above—the inmates of the low inn slumbered peacefully — the shepherds were dreaming, free from care, amid their flocks on the fresh hill-sides, and all nature was at rest when the birth-throes of that fair young mother brought troops of angels from the throne of God.

But suddenly a change seemed to pass over nature, mysterious influences were in the air, the slumberers on the hill-side and in the valley felt a strange unrest, and arose and came forth into the open air. Whisperings were about them, and sounds like the passage of swift wings, all sweeping onward to one place, and then on the darkness of night a new star arose, bathing the landscape in mellow splendor, and flooding that rude inn and ruder stable with light that dazzled the beholder. There it stood, beautiful and bright, pointing with its steady beam to that slumbering babe. Encompassed in the still glory, the wondering shepherds turned in alarm one to another, but saw in the shining countenance of each only cause of greater fear. While they thus stood hesitating what to do, an angel hovered above them, saying: "Fear not, for behold I bring you good tidings of great joy, which shall be to all people: for unto you is born this day, in the city of David, a Savior, which is Christ the Lord." Suddenly, crowds on crowds of radiant beings swept around them, singing, "Glory to God in the highest, and on earth peace, good-will to men." Oh, how that glorious anthem arose and fell along the Judea mountains. "Glory to God in the highest!" from voices tuned in heaven for ages to melody, and sent up in one exultant shout from that excited host, burst again and again on the ear. The heavens trembled with the song, and far away, beyond the reach of watching shepherds, or listening men, were louder shouts, and more entrancing melody.

With that shout and that song on their lips, the host of glad angels wheeled away to heaven, and all was still again. But still that star kept shining on, and lo! the shepherds from the hill-tops, and wise men from afar, guided by its finger of light, came to where its beam fell on the infant in the manger, and worshipped him there. Strange occupants were in that stable. The wise and proud were there kneeling. Angels had been there adoring. The Son of God was there sleeping in a human mother's arms. That stable was greater than the palace of a king, for its manger cradled the "KING of kings, Emmanuel, The Wonderful, Counsellor, Prince of Peace, Redeemer, Savior of men," were all embraced in that helpless infant. There it lay, calm, and fair, and lovely, the companion of cattle, and yet the Maker of the earth, and the adored of heaven—the son of a carpenter, and the "Son of God." The feeble arm could scarcely lift itself to its mother's neck, yet on it the universe stood balanced. Its voice was faint, low, and infantile, and yet, at its slightest cry, myriads on myriads of angelic beings would crowd to its relief. A few hours measured its existence, and yet it lived before the stars of God. Born to die, and yet the conqueror of death. No wonder that star beamed on its face, for it did more than declare its heavenly birth, or direct the wise men to where it was cradled. It was pointing to the great solution of the problem of life, and of the profoundest mystery of heaven. For four thousand years the world had summoned its thought and energies, and exhausted its wisdom on the single question, "How shall man be just with God!" The smoke of the first altar-fire kindled on the yet unpeopled earth, as it curled slowly heavenward, was burdened with this question. From the borders of deserted Eden, from the top of Mount Ararat, from the Bethel of Abraham, and from the tents of Jacob, had the sacrificial flame burned skyward in vain. The priests of Aaron had stood before the altar, and struggled for ages with the mighty problem, and lo! the "Star of Bethlehem" pointed to that babe as its solution. The long wanderings of the Hebrews, the miracles that preserved them, the imposing ceremonies of their religion, the "ark of God," the "mercy-seat," the pomp of temple worship, what did they all mean? That silent star pointed to the reply. Altars and sacrifices, prayers and prophecies, all were to end here. For four thousand years the earth had been rolling on its axis to bring about one event, and lo! it was accomplished. To the thousand inquiries of the human heart, to its painful questionings, to all its hopes and fears for so long a period, this was the answer and the end. Like a shadow for ever fleeing, had the mystery of justification baffled both the thoughtful and inspired. The Hebrew with his temple worship and his offerings; the pagan with his heathen rites and his gods; the philosopher with his reason and his conscience, and the poet with his imagination, had pondered for ages over it. Watchings and fastings, self-humiliation, long pilgrimages, self-immolation, and death, had been cheerfully, nay, joyfully endured, to solve it. Too high for the rapt prophet, too deep for the sage, it still remained to sadden and excite the heart of man, till the "Star of Bethlehem" arose on the plains of Judea. Then the problem was solved and the mystery explained, but by One greater than all.

The long line of David, unbroken through so many centuries, was maintained solely to secure the birth of that child. Rapt in holy enthusiasm, Isaiah and Jeremiah, and all the prophets of God, had spoken of a King of Israel yet to come, whose throne should excel all the thrones of earth, and in the sublimest strains of eloquence spoken of the glory of his kingdom and the splendor of his reign. Through ages of oppression, through long years of captivity, from the depths of suffering, had prophets and people looked forward to the coming of the "Redeemer of Israel," and now, as if to mock their hopes, that silent star pointed to the babe of a carpenter's wife as the fulfillment of all.

Oh what a bitter disappointment, to be told that the King of Glory, the Prince of Peace, the Redeemer of Israel, the hope of the human heart, were in that infant, coarsely clad and laid in a manger.

Yet that star said more than all this. To the longings after *immortality*—to the dim hopes—the painful bitter cry of the human soul after a *life to come*, it still cast its dazzling rays on that rude manger. The sad soul may question on and struggle on; but the sleeper there alone can satisfy its desires. It may range the fields of thought—exhaust all learning and all philosophy—dive into its own unfathomed depths; yet there alone is unfolded the mystery. "*Life and immortality*" are in that manger—so speaks the ever-beaming star. Kneel there with thy soul, which has fallen back exhausted from the fearful hights it has endeavored to climb unaided; fling thy philosophy, thy pride, as well as thy fears away, and let the light of that wondrous star fall on thy countenance, and its ray subdue and gladden thy spirit. Painful doubts and appalling fears, lest the sinful heart could never be accounted pure—unsatisfied longings and shadowy visions of a life to come, are all over. Oh, with what thrilling eloquence that silent star spoke to the bewildered, melancholy race of men!

Not only did it point to the only way of justification, and reveal the life of the soul, when its earthly clog is cast away, but it shed light on the *grave of the body*—cast the first ray that ever fell within its dark and voiceless chambers. It said, as it shone, "Behold the resurrection and the life:" "There is the first-fruits of them that sleep." Wondrous beam, penetrating to the caverned dead, casting unearthly splendor on the charnel-house, and flooding with light and glory the mutilated fragments which the worm and corruption have left. To the "whole creation, travailing in pain and groaning," waiting for the redemption of the body, it said, in accents sweeter than ever yet fell on mortal ears, "Be still—that babe shall open the portals of death, and lead captivity captive."

To the heavens above it also spoke a language. It solved the mystery of redemption—showed how mercy and justice could be united; and revealed the length, and breadth, and depth, and hight of the love of God—a length that reaches from everlasting to everlasting, "a breadth that encompasses every intelligence and every interest; a depth that reaches the lowest state of human degradation and misery, and a hight that throws floods of glory on the throne and crown of Jehovah."

Two great events mark the long history of the earth. One is the coming of Christ in a human form as the "Babe of Bethlehem," to save and redeem—the other is to be his coming in the plenitude of his divinity to judge the world. A single star arose and beamed on his birth: at his second appearance, the stars of heaven shall all be quenched, the sun "be turned into darkness, and the moon into blood."—Headley.

GRANDEUR OF ASTRONOMICAL DISCOVERIES

It was a pleasant evening in the month of May; and my sweet child, my Rosalie, and I had sauntered up to the castle's top to enjoy the breeze that played around it, and to admire the unclouded firmament that glowed and sparkled with unusual lustre from pole to pole. The atmosphere was in its purest and finest state for vision; the milky way was distinctly developed throughout its whole extent; every planet and every star above the horizon, however near and brilliant, or distant and faint, lent its lambent light or twinkling ray to give variety and beauty to the hemisphere; while the round, bright moon (so distinctly defined were the lines of her figure, and so closely visible even the rotundity of her form,) seemed to hang off from the azure vault, suspended in midway air; or stooping forward from the firmament her fair and radiant face, as if to court and return our gaze.

We amused ourselves for some time, in observing through a telescope the planet Jupiter, sailing in silent majesty with his squadron of satellites along the vast ocean of space between us and the fixed stars; and admired the felicity of that design, by which those distant bodies had been parcelled out and arranged into constellations; so as to have served not only for beacons to the ancient navigator, but, as it were, for landmarks to astronomers at this day; enabling them, though in different countries, to indicate to each other with ease the place and motion of those planets, comets, and magnificent meteors, which inhabit, revolve, and play in the intermediate space.

We recalled and dwelt with delight on the rise and progress of the science of astronomy; on that series of astonishing discoveries through successive ages, which display in so strong a light, the force and reach of the human mind; and on those bold conjectures and sublime reveries, which seem to tower even to the confines of divinity, and denote the high destiny to which mortals tend: that thought, for instance, which is said to have been first started by Pythagoras, and which modern astronomers approve; that the stars which we call fixed, although they appear to us to be nothing more than large spangles of various sizes, glittering on the same concave surface, are, nevertheless, bodies as large as our sun, shining like him, with original and not reflected light, placed at incalculable distances asunder, and each star the solar centre of a system of planets, which revolve around it as the planets belonging to our system do around the sun; that this is not only the case with all the stars which our eyes discern in the firmament, or which the telescope has brought within the sphere of our vision, but, according to the modern improvements of this thought, that there are probably other stars, whose light has not yet reached us, although light moves with a velocity of a million times greater than that of a cannon ball; that those luminous appearances, which we observe in the firmament, like flakes of thin, white cloud, are windows, as it were, which open to other firmaments, far, far beyond the ken of human eye, or the power of optical instruments, lighted up like ours, with hosts of stars or suns; that this scheme goes on through infinite space, which is filled with thousands upon thousands of these suns, attended by ten thousand times ten thousand worlds, all in rapid motion, yet calm, regular, and harmonious, invariably keeping the paths prescribed to them; and these worlds peopled with myriads of intelligent beings.

One would think that this conception, thus extended, would be bold enough to satisfy the whole enterprise of the human imagination. But what an accession of glory and magnificence does Doctor Herschell superadd to it, when, instead of supposing all those suns fixed, and the motion confined to their respective planets, he loosens those multitudinous suns themselves from their stations, sets them all into motion with their splendid retinue of planets and satellites, and imagines them, thus attended, to perform a stupendous revolution, system above system, around some grander, unknown centre, somewhere in the boundless abyss of space!—and when, carrying on the process, you suppose even that centre itself not stationary, but also counterpoised by other masses in the immensity of spaces, with which, attended by their accustomed trains of

> "Planets, suns, and adamantine spheres
> Wheeling unshaken through the void immense,"

it maintains harmonious concert, surrounding in its vast career, some other centre still more remote and stupendous, which in its turn——

"You overwhelm me," cried Rosalie, as I was laboring to pursue the immense concatenation; "my mind is bewildered and lost in the effort to follow you, and finds no point on which to rest its weary wing." "Yet there *is* a point, my dear Rosalie—the throne of the Most High. Imagine *that* the ultimate centre to which this vast and inconceivably magnificent and august apparatus is attached, and around which it is continually revolving. Oh! what a spectacle for the cherubim and seraphim, and the spirits of the just made perfect, who dwell on the right hand of that throne, if, as may be, and probably is, the case, their eyes are permitted to pierce through the whole, and take in, at one glance, all its order, beauty, sublimity, and glory, and their ears to distinguish that celestial harmony, unheard by us, in which those vast globes, as they roll on in their respective orbits, continually hymn their great Creator's praise."—WIRT.

GOODNESS OF DEITY DISPLAYED IN THE BEAUTY OF CREATION.

WERE all the interesting diversities of color and form to disappear, how unsightly, dull, and wearisome would be the aspect of the world! The pleasures conveyed to us by the endless varieties with which these sources of beauty are presented to the eye, are so much things of course, and exist so much without intermission, that we scarcely think either of their nature, their number, or the great proportion which they constitute in the whole mass of our enjoyment. But, were an inhabitant of this country to be removed from its delightful scenery to the midst of an Arabian desert, a boundless expanse of sand, a waste, spread with uniform desolation, enlivened by the murmur of no stream, and cheered by the beauty of no verdure; although he might live in a palace, and riot in splendor and luxury, he would, I think, find life a dull, wearisome, melancholy round of existence; and amid all his gratifications would sigh for the hills and valleys of his native land, the brooks, and rivers, the living lustre of the spring, and the rich glories of autumn. The ever-varying brilliancy and grandeur of the landscape, and the magnificence of the sky, sun, moon, and stars, enter more extensively into the enjoyment of mankind, than we perhaps ever think, or can possibly comprehend, without frequent and extensive investigation. This beauty and splendor of the objects around us, it is ever to be remembered, is not necessary to their existence, nor to what we commonly intend by their usefulness. It is, therefore, to be regarded as a source of pleasure, gratuitously superinduced upon the general nature of the objects themselves, and, in this light, as a testimony of the Divine goodness peculiarly affecting.—DWIGHT.

SCENERY OF THE ALPS.

NOTHING can be finer or more exact than Mr. Pope's description of a traveler straining up the Alps. Every mountain he comes to he thinks will be the last: he finds, however, an unexpected hill rise before him; and that being scaled, he finds the highest summit almost at as great a distance as before. Upon quitting the plain, he might have left a green and fertile soil, and a climate warm and pleasing. As he ascends, the ground assumes a more russet color, the grass becomes more mossy, and the weather more moderate. When he is still higher, the weather becomes more cold, and the earth more barren. In this dreary passage he is often entertained with a little valley of surprising verdure, caused by the reflected heat of the sun, collected into a narrow spot on the surrounding hights. But it much more frequently happens that he sees only frightful precipices beneath, and lakes of amazing depth, from whence rivers are formed, and fountains derive their original. On those places next the highest summits vegetation is scarcely carried on; here and there a few plants of the most hardy kind appear. The air is intolerably cold—either continually refrigerated with frosts, or disturbed with tempests. All the ground here wears an eternal covering of frost and snow, that seem continually accumulating. Upon emerging from this war of the elements, he ascends into a purer and serener region, where vegetation is entirely ceased—where the precipices, composed entirely of rocks, rise perpendicularly above him: while he views beneath him all the combat of the elements, clouds at his feet, and thunders darting upwards from their bosoms below. A thousand meteors, which are never seen on the plain, present themselves. Circular rainbows, mock suns, the shadow of the mountain, projected upon the body of the air, and the traveler's own image reflected as in a looking-glass upon the opposite cloud.—Goldsmith.

FACULTIES OF THE HUMAN SOUL.

Consider, in the first place, the many excellent faculties of the human soul; the imagination, memory, reason, judgment, will; the power it has of receiving such a multitude of ideas from external objects; of depositing them in the storehouse of the memory for many years; of drawing them out again for use whenever it thinks fit; of comparing, arranging, combining, and diversifying them in such an infinite number of ways; of reflecting, meditating, and reasoning upon them; of comprehending such a prodigious number of different arts and sciences; of creating the exquisite beauties and refined delights of music, painting, and poetry; of carrying on, through a long train of dependent propositions, the most abstruse and intricate speculations; of extracting, from a few plain, self-evident axioms, a demonstration of the most sublime and astonishing truths; of penetrating into every part of the material, the vegetable, the animal, the intellectual world; of conceiving and executing so many wise and beneficial designs; of turning its eye inward upon itself; of observing and regulating its own movements; of refining, purifying, and exalting its affections; of bringing itself, by a proper course of discipline and self-government, to bear with patience the acutest pains and the heaviest afflictions; to face with intrepidity the greatest dangers; to restrain its strongest passions; to resist the most inviting temptations; to exert, upon occasion, the most heroic fortitude; to renounce, for the sake of conscience and of duty, all that the world has to give; to abstract itself from all earthly enjoyments; to live as it were out of the body; to carry its views and hopes to the remotest futurity, and raise itself to the contemplation and the love of divine and spiritual things. Consider, now, whether it be probable, that a being possessed of such astonishing powers as these, should be designed for this life only; should be sent so richly furnished into the world merely to live a few years in anxiety and misery, and then to perish forever? Is it credible, is it possible, that the mighty soul of a Newton should share exactly the same fate, with the vilest insect that crawls upon the ground; that, after having laid open the mysteries of nature, and pushed its discoveries almost to the very boundaries of the universe, it should on a sudden have all its lights at once extinguished, and sink into everlasting darkness and insensibility? To what purpose all this waste and profusion of talents, if their operation is to be limited to this short period of existence? Why are we made so like immortal beings if mortality is to be our lot? What need was there that this little vessel of ours should be fitted out and provided with stores sufficient to carry it through the vast ocean of eternity, if, at the same time, its voyage was meant to be confined within the narrow straits of the present life? Instinct would have served for this purpose as well as reason; would have conducted us through the world with as much safety, and with less pain, than all our boasted intellectual endowments.—PORTEUS.

PERPETUAL PROGRESS OF THE SOUL TO PERFECTION.

ANOTHER presumption in favor of a future state, is *the perpetual progress of the soul toward perfection,* and its endless capacity of further improvements and larger acquisitions. This argument has been set in so strong and beautiful a light, by one of our finest writers, (Mr. ADDISON,) that it is hardly possible to do justice to it in any other words than his own. "A brute," says he, "arrives at a point of perfection which he can never pass. In a few years he has all the endowments he is capable of, and were he to live ten thousand more he would be the same thing that he is at present. Were a human soul thus at a stand in her accomplishments, were her faculties full blown and incapable of further enlargement, I could imagine she might fall away insensibly, and then drop at once into a state of annihilation. But who can believe that a thinking being, which is in a perpetual progress of improvements, and traveling on from perfection to perfection, must perish at her first setting out, and be stopped short in the very beginning of her inquiries? Death overtakes her while there is yet an unbounded prospect of knowledge open to her view, whilst the conquest over her passions is still incomplete, and much is still wanted of that perfect standard of virtue, which she is always aiming at but can never reach. Would an infinitely wise Being create such glorious creatures for so mean a purpose; or can he delight in the production of such abortive intelligences? Would he give us talents which are never to be fully exerted, and capacities which are never to be filled? Is it not far more reasonable to suppose, that man is not sent into the world merely to propagate his kind; to provide himself with a successor, and then to quit his post: but, that those short-lived generations of rational creatures, which rise up and disappear in such quick succession, are only to receive their first rudiments of existence here, and then to be translated into some more friendly climate, where they may spread and flourish; where they may go on from strength to strength; where they may shine forever with new accessions of glory, and brighten to all eternity?—PORTEUS.

WHERE SHOULD THE SCHOLAR LIVE?

WHERE should the scholar live? In solitude or in society? In the green stillness of the country, where he can hear the heart of nature beat, or in the dark gray city, where he can hear and feel the throbbing heart of man? I will make answer for him, and say, in the dark, gray city. Oh, they do greatly err who think, that the stars are all the poetry which cities have; and therefore, that the poet's only dwelling should be in sylvan solitudes, under the green roof of trees. Beautiful, no doubt, are all the forms of nature, when transfigured by the miraculous power of poetry: hamlets and harvest-fields, and nut-brown waters, flowing ever under the forest, vast and shadowy, with all the sights and sounds of rural life. But after all, what are these but the decorations and painted scenery in the great theatre of human life? What are they but the coarse materials of the poet's song? Glorious, indeed, is the world of God around us, but more glorious the world of God within us. There lies the land of song; there lies the poet's native land. The river of life, that flows through streets tumultuous, bearing along so many gallant hearts, so many wrecks of humanity; the many homes and households, each a little world in itself, revolving round its fireside, as a central sun; all forms of human joy and suffering brought into that narrow compass; and to be in this, and be a part of this; acting, thinking, rejoicing, sorrowing, with his fellow-men; such, such should be the poet's life. If he would describe the world, he should live in the world. The mind of the scholar, also, if you would have it large and liberal, should come in contact with other minds. It is better that his armor should be somewhat bruised even by rude encounters, than hang for ever rusting on the wall. Nor will his themes be few or trivial, because apparently shut in between the walls of houses, and having merely the decorations of street scenery. A ruined character is as picturesque as a ruined castle. There are dark abysses and yawning gulfs in the human heart, which can be rendered passable only by bridging them over with iron nerves and sinews, as Challey bridged the Savine in Switzerland, and Telford the sea between Anglesea and England, with chain bridges. These are the great themes of human thought; not green grass, and flowers, and moonshine. Besides, the mere external forms of nature we make our own and carry with us into the city, by the power of memory.—LONGFELLOW.

GLORY.

THE crumbling tombstone and the gorgeous mausoleum, the sculptured marble and the venerable cathedral, all bear witness to the instinctive desire within us to be remembered by coming generations. But how short-lived is the immortality which the works of our hands can confer! The noblest monuments of art that the world has ever seen are covered with the soil of twenty centuries. The works of the age of Pericles lie at the foot of the Acropolis in indiscriminate ruin. The plowshare turns up the marble which the hand of Phidias had chiselled into beauty, and the Mussulman has folded his flock beneath the falling columns of the temple of Minerva. But even the works of our hands too frequently survive the memory of those who have created them. And were it otherwise, could we thus carry down to distant ages the recollection of our existence, it were surely childish to waste the energies of an immortal spirit in the effort to make it known to other times, that a being whose name was written with certain letters of the alphabet once lived, and flourished, and died. Neither sculptured marble, nor stately column can reveal to other ages the lineaments of the spirit; and these alone can embalm our memory in the hearts of a grateful posterity.

As the stranger stands beneath the dome of St. Paul's, or treads, with religious awe, the silent aisles of Westminster Abbey, the sentiment which is breathed from every object around him is, the utter emptiness of sublunary glory...... The fine arts, obedient to private affection, or public gratitude, have here embodied, in every form, the finest conceptions of which their age was capable. Each one of these monuments has been watered by the tears of the widow, the orphan, or the patriot. But generations have passed away, and mourners and mourned have sunk together into forgetfulness. The aged crone, or the smooth-tongued beadle, as now he hurries you through aisles and chapel, utters, with measured cadence and unmeaning tone, for the thousandth time, the name and lineage of the once honored dead; and then gladly dismisses you, to repeat again his well-conned lesson to another group of idle passers-by. Such, in its most august form, is all the immortality that matter can confer. It is by what we ourselves have done, and not by what others have done for us, that we shall be remembered by after ages. It is by thought that has aroused my intellect from its slumbers, which has "given lustre to virtue, and dignity to truth," or by those examples which have inflamed my soul with the love of goodness, and not by means of sculptured marble, that I hold communion with Shakspeare and Milton, with Johnson and Burke, with Howard and Wilberforce.—WAYLAND.

CHRISTIANITY THE TRUE SOURCE OF REFORM.

THE great element of reform is not born of human wisdom; it does not draw its life from human organizations. I find it only in CHRISTIANITY. "Thy kingdom come!" There is a sublime and pregnant burden in this prayer. It is the aspiration of every soul that goes forth in the spirit of reform. For what is the significance of this prayer? It is a petition that all holy influences would penetrate, and subdue, and dwell in the heart of man, until he shall think, and speak, and do good, from the very necessity of his being. So would the institutions of error and wrong crumble and pass away. So would sin die out from the earth. And the human soul, living in harmony with the Divine Will, this earth would beccome like heaven.

It is too late for the reformers to sneer at Christianity—it is foolishness for them to reject it. In it are enshrined our faith in human progress—our confidence in reform. It is indissolubly connected with all that is hopeful, spiritual, capable in man. That men have misunderstood it, and perverted it, is true. But it is also true that the noblest efforts for human melioration have come out of it—have been based upon it. Is it not so? Come, ye remembered ones, who sleep the sleep of the just, who took your conduct from the line of christian philosophy—come from your tombs and answer!

Come, Howard, from the gloom of the prison and the taint of the lazar-house, and show us what philanthropy can do when imbued with the spirit of Jesus. Come, Eliot, from the thick forest, where the red-man listens to the word of life: come, Penn, from thy sweet counsel and weaponless victory; and show what christian zeal and love can accomplish with the rudest barbarians or the fiercest hearts. Come, Raikes, from thy labors with the ignorant and the poor, and show us with what an eye this faith regards the lowest and least of our race, and how diligently it labors, not for the body, not for the rank, but for the plastic soul, that is to course the ages of immortality.

And ye, who are a great number—ye nameless ones—who have

done good in your narrower spheres, content to forego renown on earth, and seeking your reward in the record on high, come and tell us how kindly a spirit, how lofty a purpose, or how strong a courage, the religion ye professed can breathe into the poor, the humble, and the weak.

Go forth, then, Spirit of Christianity, to thy great work of REFORM! The Past bears witness to thee in the blood of thy martyrs, and the ashes of thy saints and heroes. The Present is hopeful because of thee. The Future shall acknowledge thy omnipotence.—CHAPIN.

A CITY NIGHT PIECE.

THE clock has just struck two; the expiring taper rises and sinks in the socket; the watchman forgets the hour in slumber; the laborious and the happy are at rest; and nothing wakes but meditation, guilt, revelry, and despair. The drunkard once more fills the destroying bowl; the robber walks his midnight round; and the suicide lifts his guilty arm against his own sacred person.

Let me no longer waste the night over the page of antiquity or the sallies of contemporary genius, but pursue the solitary walk, where vanity, ever changing, but a few hours past walked before me—where she kept up the pageant, and now, like a froward child, seems hushed with her own importunities.

What a gloom hangs all around! The dying lamp feebly emits a yellow gleam; no sound is heard but of the chiming clock or the distant watch-dog; all the bustle of human pride is forgotten. An hour like this may well display the emptiness of human vanity.

There will come a time when this temporary solitude will be made continual, and the city itself, like its inhabitants, fade away, and leave a desert in its room.

What cities, great as this, have once triumphed in existence, had their victories as great, joy as just and as unbounded, and, with short-sighted presumption, promised themselves immortality! Posterity can hardly trace the situation of some; the sorrowful traveler wanders over the awful ruins of others; and, as he beholds, he learns wisdom, and feels the transcience of every sublunary possession.

Here, he cries, stood their citadel, now grown over with weeds; there their senate house, but now the haunt of every noxious reptile. Temples and theatres stood here, now only an undistinguished heap of ruin. They are fallen, for luxury and avarice first made them feeble. The rewards of state were conferred on amusing, and not on useful members of society. Their riches and opulence invited the invaders, who, though at first repulsed, returned again, conquered by perseverence, and at last swept the defendants into undistinguished destruction.

How few appear in those streets, which but some few hours ago were crowded! And those who appear now no longer, wear their daily mask, nor attempt to hide their lewdness or their misery.

But who are those who make the street their couch, and find a short repose from wretchedness at the doors of the opulent? These are strangers, wanderers, and orphans, whose circumstances are too humble to expect redress, and whose distresses are too great even for pity. Their wretchedness excites rather horror than pity. Some are without the covering even of rags, and others emaciated with disease. The world has disclaimed them: society turns its back upon their distress, and has given them up to nakedness and hunger. These poor shivering females have once seen happier days, and been flattered into beauty.

Why, why was I born a man, and yet see the sufferings of wretches I cannot relieve? Poor houseless creatures! the world will give you reproaches, but will not give you relief. The slightest misfortunes of the great, the most imaginary uneasiness of the rich, are aggravated with all the power of eloquence, and held up to engage our attention and sympathetic sorrow. The poor weep unheeded, persecuted by every subordinate species of tyranny; and every law which gives others security, becomes an enemy to them.

Why was this heart of mine formed with so much sensibility? or why was not my fortune adapted to its impulses? Tenderness without the capacity of relieving, only makes the man more wretched than the object which sues for assistance.—Goldsmith.

LIFE—AN ALLEGORY.

It is now morning. Still and glassy lies the lake, within its green and dewsprent shores. Light mist hangs around like a skiey veil; and only reveals the uncertain outlines of woods and hills. The warm, vernal air is just stirring in the valleys, but has not yet ruffled the water's mirror. Turns the eye upward, the misty vault opens into the calm, clear heavens, over which there seems suffused a genial spirit's breath. Far distant on the horizon flash out the gilded and reddening peaks, and from yonder crown of snow, a sudden radiance announces the risen sun. Now in the east stream the golden rays through the soft blue vapor. The breeze freshens, and comes loaded with fragrance from the woods. A faint, dark curl sweeps over the water; the mist rolls up, lifts itself above meadow and hill, and in gathered folds hangs light around the mountains. Away on the level lake till it meets the sky, silvery gleams the sheeted wave, sprinkled with changeful stars, as the ever-rising breeze breaks it in ripples. Now the pennon, that hung loose around the mast, rises and fitfully floats. We spread the sail, and casting off from the shore glide out with cheerful hearts on our voyage. Before us widens the lake; rock after rock receding back on either hand, and opening between still bays, hung round with sparkling woods, or leading through green meadow vistas to blue sunny hills.

It is now noon. In the middle lake speeds the bark over light glancing waves. Dark opens down the clear depth. White toss the crests of foam, and as the sail stoops to the steady wind, swift flies the parted water round the prow, and rushing pours behind the stern. The distant shores glow bright in the sun, that alone in the heaven looks unveiled with vivifying goodness over the earth. How high and broad swells the sky! The agitated lake tosses like a wide field of snowy blossoms. Sweep after sweep of the long-retiring shores; hill gleaming over hill, up to the shadowy mountains; and over these, Alpine needles, shooting pearly white into the boundless azure—all lie still and happy under the ever-smiling sun.

And now it is evening. The sun is sinking behind the dark mountains, and clouds, scattered far in the east, float soft in rosy light. The sun is now hidden, and strong and wide sweeps up its golden flame, like the holy blaze of a funeral pile. The breeze slackens, the waves subside in slumber, and slowly the bark steers into its sheltering bay. Long shadows stretch from hill to valley, fall like dark curtains on the lake, and a solemn, subdued serenity broods, like a protecting spirit, over the hushed and quiet earth. Only the far summits yet retain their brightness. Faint blushes stain the eternal snows, recalling the first dawning roses, like the memory of early joys in the tranquil moments of departing age. These, too, fade; but the evening star looks bright from the blue infinite, and like the herald of a better world, leads us softly to our haven.—PERCIVAL.

BEAUTY.

THE presence of a higher, namely, of the spiritual element, is essential to its perfection. The high and divine beauty which can be loved without effeminacy, is that which is found in combination with the human will, and never separate. Beauty is the mark God sets upon virtue. Every natural action is graceful. Every heroic act is also decent, and causes the place and the bystanders to shine. We are taught by great actions that the universe is the property of every individual in it. Every rational creature has all nature for his dowry and estate. It is his, if he will. He may divest himself of it; he may creep into a corner, and abdicate his kingdom, as most men do; but he is entitled to the world by his constitution. In proportion to the energy of his thought and will, he takes up the world into himself. "All those things for which men plow, build, or sail, obey virtue," said an ancient historian. "The winds and waves," said Gibbon, "are always on the side of the ablest navigators." So are the sun and moon, and all the stars of heaven. When a noble act is done—perchance in a scene of great natural beauty; when Leonidas and his three hundred martyrs consume one day in dying, and the sun and moon come each and look at them once in the steep defile of Thermopylæ; when Arnold Winkelried, in the high Alps, under the shadow of the avalanche, gathers in his side a sheaf of Austrian spears to break the line of his comrades; are not these heroes entitled to add the beauty of the scene to the beauty of the deed? When the bark of Columbus nears the shores of America; before it, the beach lined with savages, fleeing out of all their huts of cane; the sea behind; and the purple mountains of the Indian Archipelago around, can we separate the man from the living picture? Does not the New World clothe his form with her palm-groves and savannahs as fit drapery? Ever does natural beauty steal in like air, and envelope great actions. When Sir Harry Vane was dragged up the Tower-hill, sitting on a sled, to suffer death, as the champion of the English laws, one of the multitude cried out to him: "You never sat on so glorious a seat."

Charles II., to intimidate the citizens of London, caused the patriot Lord Russel to be drawn in an open coach, through the principal streets of the city on his way to the scaffold. "But," to use the simple narrative of his biographer, "the multitude imagined they saw liberty and virtue sitting by his side." In private places, among sordid objects, an act of truth or heroism seems at once to draw to itself the sky as its temple, the sun as its cradle. Nature stretcheth out her arms to embrace man, only let his thoughts be of equal greatness. Willingly does she follow his steps with the rose and the violet, and bend her lines of grandeur and grace to the decoration of her darling child. Only let his thoughts be of equal scope, and the frame will suit the picture. A virtuous man is in unison with her works, and makes the central figure of the visible sphere.—EMERSON.

PUBLIC VIRTUE.

I HOPE, that in all that relates to personal firmness, all that concerns a just appreciation of the insignificance of human life—whatever may be attempted to threaten or alarm a soul not easily swayed by opposition, or awed or intimidated by menace—a stout heart and a steady eye, that can survey, unmoved and undaunted, any mere personal perils that assail this poor, transient, perishing frame, I may, without disparagement, compare with other men. But there is a sort of courage, which, I frankly confess it, I do not possess, a boldness to which I dare not aspire, a valor which I cannot covet. I cannot lay myself down in the way of the welfare and happiness of my country. That I cannot, I have not the courage to do. I cannot interpose the power with which I may be invested, a power conferred, not for my personal benefit, nor for my aggrandizement, but for my country's good, to check her onward march to greatness and glory. I have not courage enough. I am too cowardly for that. I would not, I dare not, in the exercise of such a trust, lie down, and place my body across the path that leads my country to prosperity and happiness. This is a sort of courage widely different from that which a man may display in his private conduct and personal relations. Personal or private courage is totally distinct from that higher and nobler courage which prompts the patriot to offer himself a voluntary sacrifice to his country's good.

Apprehensions of the imputations of the want of firmness sometimes impel us to perform rash and inconsiderate acts. It is the greatest courage to be able to bear the imputation of the want of courage. But pride, vanity, egotism, so unamiable and offensive in private life, are vices which partake of the character of crimes, in the conduct of public affairs. The unfortunate victim of these passions cannot see beyond the little, petty, contemptible circle of his own personal interests. All his thoughts are withdrawn from his country, and concentrated on his consistency, his firmness, himself. The high, the exalted, the sublime emotions of a patriotism, which, soaring towards heaven, rises far above all mean, low, or selfish things, and is absorbed by one soul-transporting thought of the good and the glory of one's country, are never felt in his impenetrable bosom. That patriotism, which, catching its inspirations from the immortal God, and leaving, at an immeasurable distance below all groveling, personal interests and feelings, animates and prompts to deeds of self-sacrifice, of valor, of devotion, and of death itself—that is public virtue; that is the noblest, the sublimest of all public virtues.—CLAY.

THE COLOR OF SOUNDS.

EVERY one who has attentively listened to sounds, must have noticed that, besides their acuteness and gravity, loudness or softness, shape and figure, there is another quality which musicians have agreed to denominate color. The answer of the blind man, who, on being asked what idea he had of scarlet, replied that it was like the sound of a trumpet, is less absurd than may at first be apprehended. If, as Sir Isaac Newton supposed, the impulse upon the nerves of the eye produced by color, is similar in kind or degree, to that produced upon the ear by sounds, the impression upon the sensorium, or seat of sensation, in the brain, will probably be the same, or so nearly so, that the ideas of the respective external objects will be associated in the mind. According to this theory, the different musical instruments may be characterized by corresponding colors, so as to be fancifully classed in the following manner:

WIND INSTRUMENTS.

Trombone	Deep red.
Trumpet	Scarlet.
Clarionette	Orange.
Oboe	Yellow.
Bassoon Alto	Deep yellow.
Flute	Sky blue.
Diapason	Deeper blue.
Double diapason	Purple.
Horn	Violet.

STRINGED INSTRUMENTS.

Violin	Pink.
Viola	Rose.
Violincello	Red.
Double bass	Deep crimson.

In addition to what the preceding scale expresses, let it be understood that the lowest notes of each instrument, partake of the darkest shades of its color, and as they ascend they become of a lighter hue. The symphony in the Creation, which represents the rising-sun, is an exemplification of this theory. In the commencement of this piece our attention is attracted by a soft-streaming note from the violins, which is scarcely discernible till the rays of sound, which issue from the second violin, diverge into the chord of the first, to which is gradually imparted a greater fullness of color, as the viols and violincellos steal in with expanding harmony. At the fifth bar, the oboes begin to shed their yellow lustre, while the flute silvers the mounting rays of the violins as the notes continue ascending to the highest point of lightness; the orange, the scarlet, and the purple unite in the increasing splendor, and the glorious orb at length appears refulgent with the brightest beams of harmony.

In the human voice, the shades of color are still more perceptible. The lowest tones are formed in the chest, partake of the most sombre hues, and forcibly express our inmost feelings ; as they ascend, they become more bright and cheerful, expressing the more lively sensation of mirth and joy. It is in the utterance of these tones that we disclose where the soul of music lies concealed.—GARDINER.

THE PRIMITIVE CHRISTIANS.*

THEY are not distinguished from other men by their place of residence, their language, or manners. Though they live in the cities of the Greeks and barbarians, each where his lot is cast; and in clothing, food, and manner of life, follow the customs of their country, yet they are distinguished by a wonderful and universally

* From an epistle to Diognetus written early in the second century.

astonishing walk and conversation. They dwell in their own native land, but as foreigners; they take part in every thing as citizens, they endure every thing as foreigners. Every foreign land is to them as their native country; and their native country as a foreign land. They live in the flesh, but not after the flesh. They dwell on the earth, but they live in heaven; they obey the existing laws, but by their life elevate themselves above the laws. They love all men, and are persecuted, misunderstood, and condemned by all. They are slain and made alive; they are poor, and make many rich; they suffer want in every thing, and possess abundance in every thing. They are cursed, and they bless. In one word, what the soul is in the body, that Christians are in the world. As the soul is diffused through all the members of the body, so the Christians are spread through all the cities of the world. The soul, indeed, dwells in the body, but is not of the body: so Christians dwell in the world, but they are not of the world. The invisible soul is shut up in the visible body, and so men know Christians as inhabitants of the world, but their life is hid with Christ in God. The flesh hates and fights the soul, though the soul does no injury to the flesh, but only prevents its giving itself up to its lusts; so also the world hates Christians; they do it no harm, but only set themselves against its lusts. The soul loves its hating flesh, and so Christians love those by whom they are hated. The soul is shut up in the body, and yet it is that by which it is held together; and Christians are held to their post in the world, and it is they who hold the world together. The immortal soul dwells in the mortal body, and Christians dwell as strangers in the corruptible world, and await the unchangeable life in heaven.—Augusti.

CENSORIOUSNESS.

There is an uncommon beauty, force, and propriety in that caution which our Savior gives us: "And why beholdest thou the mote that is in thy brother's eye, but considerest not the beam that is in thine own eye; or how wilt thou say to thy brother, Let me pull out the mote out of thine eye, and behold a beam is in thine own eye? Thou hypocrite! first cast the beam out of thine own eye, and then shalt thou see clearly to cast out the mote out of thy brother's eye." In which words these four things are plainly intimated: first, that some are much more quick-sighted to discern the faults and blemishes of others than their own; can spy a mote in another's eye, sooner than a beam in their own. Second, that they are often the most forward to correct and cure the foibles of others, who are most unqualified for that office. The beam in their own eye makes them altogether unfit to pull out the mote from their brother's. A man half blind himself should never set up for an oculist. Third, they who are inclined to deal in censure, should always begin at home. Fourth, great censoriousness is great hypocrisy.

This common failing of human nature the heathen were very sensible of, and imaged it in the following manner: Every man (say they,) carries a wallet, or two bags with him; the one hanging before him, and the other behind him; into that before he puts the faults of others; into that behind his own, by which means he never sees his own failings, while he has those of others always before his eyes.—JOHN MASON.

TENDENCY OF THE HUMAN MIND TO FUTURITY.

THERE is, in the human mind, *a constant and natural tendency toward futurity.* Our thoughts are perpetually wandering from the present moment, and looking forward to something that is to take place hereafter. Be our happiness ever so great, yet it is not sufficient to gratify and content the soul. There is always a void left in it, which can never be filled up without calling in the aid of futurity, without the anticipation of something more than we at present possess. Whatever may chance to be our ruling passion, whether it be the love of wealth, of power, of honor, of pleasure, we are scarce ever satisfied with that share of it which we enjoy; but are always thirsting and reaching after more, are perpetually forming projects from which we promise ourselves greater satisfaction than any we have yet experienced. There is constantly some favorite object in view, some point to be obtained; and "we are continually hurrying over some period of our existence, in order to arrive at certain imaginary stations or resting places," where we hope to find that quiet and content which has hitherto eluded our search. We reach those wished-for stations, but "we find no rest for the sole of our feet."—Gen. viii. 9. The imaginary horizon of our project flies before us as we advance; no sooner do we gain one eminence, than another instantly appears beyond it; and when that is passed, still others present themselves in endless succession to our view. Thus are we continually drawn on through life with the same delusive expectations. We live upon the future, though the future constantly deceives us; we continue grasping at distant happiness, though it always escapes out of our hands, and go on to the very end, pressing forward toward some imagined good, with the same eagerness and alacrity as if we had never suffered the least disappointment in our pursuit.—PORTEUS.

STRENGTH OF MIND.—Strength of mind is an attaching, as well as a ruling power; all human creatures, women especially, become attached to those who have power over their own minds.—MISS EDGEWORTH.

CONTENTMENT.

Every misery that I miss is a new mercy, and therefore let us be thankful. There have been, since we met, others that have met disasters of broken limbs, some have been blasted, others thunder-stricken, and we have been freed from these, and all those many miseries that threaten human nature; let us therefore rejoice and be thankful. Nay, which is a far greater mercy, we are free from the insupportable burthen of an accusing conscience, a misery that none can bear; and therefore let us praise Him for His preventing grace, and say every misery that I miss is a new mercy.

Let me tell you, scholar, I have a rich neighbor that is always so busy that he has no leisure to laugh; the whole business of his life is to get money, and more money that he may still get more and more money; he is still drudging on, and says that Solomon says, "the hand of the diligent maketh rich;" and it is true indeed, but he considers not that it is not in the power of riches to make a man happy; for it was wisely said by a man of great observation: "that there be as many miseries beyond riches as on this side of them," and yet God deliver us from pinching poverty, and grant that, having a competency, we may be content and thankful. Let us not repine, or so much as think the gifts of God unequally dealt if we see another abound with riches; when, as God knows, the cares, which are the keys that keep those riches, hang often so heavily at the rich man's girdle, that they clog him with weary days and restless nights, even when others sleep quietly. We see but the outside of the rich man's happiness; few consider him to be like the silk-worm, that when she seems to play is at the very same time spinning her own bowels, and consuming herself.

I have heard of a man who was angry with himself because he was no taller, and of a woman that broke her looking-glass because it would not show her face to be as young and handsome as her next door neighbor's was. And I knew another to whom God had given health and plenty, but a wife that nature had made peevish, and her husband's riches had made purse-proud, and must, because she was rich, and for no other virtue, sit in the highest pew in the church, which being denied her, she engaged her husband into a contention for it, and at last into a law-suit with a dogged neighbor who was as rich as he, and had a wife as peevish and purse-proud as the other; and this law-suit begot higher oppositions and actionable words, and more vexations and law-suits, for you must remember that both were rich, and must therefore have their wills. Well, this willful, purse-proud law-suit lasted during the life of the first husband, after which his wife vexed and chid, and chid and vexed till she also vexed and chid herself into her grave; and so the wealth of these poor rich people was curst into a punishment, because they wanted meek and thankful hearts, for they only can make us happy. I know a man that had health and riches, and several houses, all beautiful and ready furnished, and would often trouble himself and family to be removing from one house to another, and being asked by a friend why he removed so often from one house to another, replied, "it was to find content in some of them." But his friend, knowing his temper, told him that if he would find content in any of his houses, he must leave himself behind him, for content will never dwell but in a meek and quiet soul.

And this may appear if we read and consider what our Savior says in St. Matthew's gospel, for he there says, "Blessed are the merciful, for they shall obtain mercy. Blessed be the pure in heart, for they shall see God. Blessed be the pure in spirit, for theirs is the kingdom of heaven: and blessed be the meek, for they shall inherit the earth." Not that the meek shall not also obtain mercy, and see God, and be comforted, and at last come to the kingdom of heaven, but in the mean time he, and he only, possesses the earth as he goes towards that kingdom, by being humble and cheerful, and content with what his good God has allotted him; he has no turbulent, repining, vexatious thoughts that he deserves better, nor is vexed when he sees others possessed of more honor or more riches than his wise God has allotted for his share; but he possesses what he has with a meek and contented quietness—such a quietness as makes his very dreams pleasing both to God and himself.—Izaak Walton.

CURIOUS EXTRACT, DEPICTING OLD ENGLISH MANNERS.*

Monday morning. Rose at four o'clock and helped Katherine to milk the cows; Rachel the dairy-maid, having scalded her hand in so bad a manner the day before. Gave a penny to Robin to get something comfortable from the apothecary's. Six o'clock.—The buttock of beef a little too much boiled, and the beer a little of the stalest. Seven o'clock.—Went to walk with the lady, my mother, in the court-yard; fed five-and-twenty poor men and women; chid Robin for expressing some ill-will at attending with broken meat. Ten o'clock.—Went to dinner. John Gray a most comely youth, but what is that to me? A virtuous maiden should be entirely under the direction of her parents. John ate but little, and stole many tender looks at me. Said women could never be handsome who were not good-tempered. I think my temper is not intolerable. John likes white teeth: my teeth are of a pretty good color. Rose at eleven from the table, the company being desirous of a walk in the fields John Gray would lift me over every stile, and twice pressed my hand. I cannot say I have any objection to John Gray; he plays at prison-bars as well as any country gentleman, and is remarkably dutiful to my lord and lady, his parents: he never

* From Lady Elizabeth Woodville's Journal, 1450.

misses church. Three o'clock.—Poor James Robinson's house burnt down by accident. John Gray proposed a subscription among the company for the relief of the farmer, and gave as much as four pounds himself with this benevolent intent; never saw him look so comely as at this moment. Four o'clock.—Went to prayers. Six.—Fed the hogs and poultry. Seven.—Supper on table, delayed to that late hour on account of Farmer Robinson's misfortune. The goose-pie too much baked, pork roasted to rags. I must talk to the cook about this fault. Nine o'clock.—All in bed. These late hours very disagreeable: said my prayers a second time, John Gray having disturbed my thoughts too much the first.

[She was married to this Sir John Gray, who in the prime of life fell at the battle of St. Albans, 1460. He being a zealous Lancasterian, his estates were confiscated, and the widow returned to the family-house at Grafton. Hearing that Edward the Fourth was hunting in Wittlebury Forest, she sought the monarch for the purpose of petitioning the restoration of her husband's lands to her, and her impoverished children. Ignorant of the king's person, she inquired of a young stranger if he could direct her to him, when he told her he himself was the object of her search. She threw herself at his feet, and implored his compassion. He raised her from the ground, with assurances of favor; and, captivated with her person and manners, privately married her at Grafton House, on the 1st of May, 1464. On the Michaelmas following she was declared queen, and received the compliments of the nobility in the abbey at Reading. She was the mother of Edward the Fifth and Richard Duke of York, who were smothered in the Tower by order of their uncle, Richard the Third, which barbarous deed Tyrrel, the governor, confessed he had perpetrated, when executed in the following reign.]—*Baker's History of Northampton.*

SORROW FOR THE DEAD.

THE sorrow for the dead is the only sorrow from which we refuse to be divorced. Every other wound we seek to heal, every other affliction to forget; but this wound we consider it a duty to keep open, this affliction we cherish and brood over in secret. Where is the mother who would willingly forget the infant that perished like a blossom from her arms, though every recollection is a pang? Where is the child that would willingly forget the most tender of parents, though to remember be but to lament? Who, even in the hour of agony, would forget the friend over whom he mourns? No: the the love which survives the tomb is one of the noblest attributes of the soul. If it has its woes, it has likewise its delights; and when the overwhelming burst of grief is calmed into the gentle tear of recollection; when the sudden anguish and the convulsive agony over the present ruins of all that we most loved, is softened away into pensive meditation on all that it was in the days of its loveliness—who would root out such a sorrow from the heart? Though it may sometimes throw a passing cloud over the bright hour of gaiety, or spread a deeper sadness over the hour of gloom, yet who would exchange it, even for a song of pleasure, or the burst of revelry? No: there is a voice from the tomb sweeter than song. There is a remembrance of the dead to which we turn even from the charms of the living! Oh! the grave! the grave! It buries every error—covers every defect—extinguishes every resentment. From its peaceful bosom spring none but fond regrets and tender recollections. Who can look down upon the grave even of an enemy, and not feel a compunctious throb, that he should ever have warred with the poor handful of earth that lies mouldering before him?—Irving.

LIBERTY.

Till men have been some time free, they know not how to use their freedom. The nations of wine-countries are always sober. In climates where wine is a rarity, intemperance abounds. A newly-liberated people may be compared to a northern army encamped on the Rhine or Xeres. It is said that when soldiers in such a situation first find themselves able to indulge without restraint in such a rare and expensive luxury, nothing is to be seen but intoxication. Soon, however, plenty teaches discretion, and after wine has been for a few months their daily fare, they become more temperate than they had ever been in their own country. In the same manner the final and permanent fruits of liberty are wisdom, moderation, and mercy. Its immediate effects are often atrocious crimes, conflicting errors, scepticism on points the most clear, dogmatism on points the most mysterious. It is just at this crisis that its enemies love to exhibit it. They pull down the scaffolding from the half-finished edifice; they point to the flying dust, the falling bricks, the comfortless rooms, the frightful irregularity of the whole appearance, and then ask in scorn where the promised splendor and comfort are to be found? If such miserable sophisms were to prevail, there would never be a good house, or a good government in the world.

Ariosto tells a pretty story of a fairy, who, by some mysterious law of her nature, was condemned to appear at certain seasons in the form of a foul and poisonous snake. Those who injured her during the period of her disguise, were forever excluded from participation in the blessings which she bestowed. But to those who, in spite of her loathsome aspect, pitied and protected her, she afterwards revealed herself in the beautiful and celestial form that was natural to her, accompanied their steps, granted all their wishes, filled their houses with wealth, made them happy in love, and victorious in war. Such a spirit is Liberty! At times she takes the form of a hateful reptile. She grovels, she hisses, she stings. But wo to those who in disgust shall crush her. And happy are those who, having dared to receive her in her degraded and frightful shape, shall at length be rewarded by her in the time of her beauty and her glory.

There is only one cure for the evils which newly-acquired freedom produces, and that cure is *freedom!* When a prisoner leaves his cell he cannot bear the light of day; he is unable to discriminate colors, or recognize faces. But the remedy is not to remand him to his dungeon, but to accustom him to the rays of the sun. The blaze of truth and liberty may at first dazzle and bewilder nations which have become half blind in the house of bondage. But let them gaze on, and they will soon be able to bear it. In a few years men learn reason. The extreme violence of opinions subsides. Hostile theories correct each other. The scattered elements of truth cease to conflict, and begin to coalesce; and, at length, a system of consistence and order is educed out of the chaos.

Many politicians of our time are in the habit of laying it down as a self-evident proposition, that no people ought to be free till they are fit to use their freedom. The maxim is worthy of the fool in the story, who resolved not to go into the water till he had learnt how to swim. If men are to wait for liberty till they become wise and good in slavery, they may indeed wait for ever.—MACAULAY.

DEMOCRACY.

THAT is the best government which desires to make its people happy, and knows how to make them happy. Neither the inclination nor the knowledge will suffice alone, and it is difficult to find them together. Pure democracy, and pure democracy alone, satisfies the former condition of this great problem. That the governors may be solicitous only for the interests of the governed, it is necessary that the interests of the governors and the governed should be the same. This cannot often be the case where power is intrusted to one or to few. The privileged part of the community will doubtless derive a certain degree of advantage from the general prosperity of the state, but they will derive a greater from oppression and exaction. The king will desire a useless war for his glory, or a *pare aux cerfs* for his pleasure. The nobles will demand monopolies and *lettres-de-catchet.* In proportion as the number of governors is increased, the evil is diminished. There are fewer to contribute and more to receive. The dividend which each can obtain of the public plunder becomes less and less tempting. But the interests of the subjects and the rulers never absolutely coincide till the subjects themselves become the rulers, that is, till the government be either immediately or mediately democratic.—MACAULAY.

THE CHRISTIAN'S LIFE NOT ALL SORROW.

"MAN is born to trouble," says Job. Many are the afflictions of the righteous; bitter the cup which the children of God have placed to their lips; dark the clouds that lower above their pathway; and gloomy the wilderness through which they travel to Mount Zion, the city of God. Yet, O Christian! the cup is not all bitter, the clouds not all darkness, nor the wilderness all gloom. The Savior's kind love sweetens the bitterness of the cup, fringes the clouds with rays of mercy, and throws a beam of heavenly light across the dark gloom of the wilderness waste. How sweet to have a resting-place when the soul is weary—to find a secure haven when the tempest is gathering, when the professed friends in whom we have trusted, leave us to contend alone with the surging elements. When afflictions surround our path—when the head reclines weariedly on its languid pillow—when all the beautiful scenes of earth recede from the vision, and the tendrils of holy affection, woven in the deep recesses of the heart, begin to break by the iron hand of death: sweet is it to realize that the poor tempest-tost soul can find that resting-place in the bosom of her God.—J. BROOKWELLL PEAT.

SYMPATHY.

SYMPATHY we consider one of the primal principles of efficient genius. It is this truth of feeling which enabled Shakspeare to depict so strongly the various stages of passion, and the depth, growth, and gradations of sentiment. In whom does this primitive readiness to sympathize—to enter into all the moods of the soul—continue beyond early life, so often as in men devoted to imaginative objects? How frequently are we struck with the childlike character of artists and poets! It sometimes seems as if, along with childhood's ready sympathy, many of the other characteristics of that epoch were projected into the more mature stages of being.

It is by their sympathy, their sincere and universal interest in humanity, that the sweetest poets, and the most renowned dramatists, are enabled to write in a manner corresponding with the heaven-attuned, unwritten music of the human heart.—TUCKERMAN.

PRUDENCE.—There is a prudence that coexists with morality. This is a holy prudence; the steward, faithful and discreet, the eldest servant in the family of faith, born in the house, and made the ruler over his lord's household. In general, morality may be compared to the consonant; prudence to the vowel. The former cannot be uttered (reduced to practice) but by means of the latter.—COLERIDGE.

BOOKS.

Books are of incalculably immense advantage. They furnish us with the choice thoughts and choice sayings of the wisest and best men that have adorned our world. We esteem it a high privilege to be admitted into the society of an individual of brilliant intellect and vast stores of knowledge; but the privilege is not one-thousandth part so great as that of being permitted to peruse standard books. They introduce us into the society of illustrious men that lived centuries ago; and through their agency, these illustrious men hold converse with us on topics that engaged their attention the most of their lives. By books the laws of Moses, Solon, and Lycurgus, are still extant: by books the strains of David, Homer, Virgil, and Milton, are still sung: by books the orations of Demosthenes, Cicero, Burke, and Patrick Henry, are still thundered forth: by books, the wise sayings of Solomon, Socrates, Plato, Confucius, and Bacon, are still heard: by books, in short, all that is splendid in history, all that is grand in legislation, all that is profound in philosophy, all that is valuable in science, all that is useful in art, all that is rich in eloquence, all that is beautiful in poetry, all that is sublime in music, and all that is divine in theology, still exists. O, how great and glorious are the advantages of the present age of the world! By the simple means alluded to, the wisdom of six thousand years is placed within the reach of all. Every man can converse with earth's most celebrated philosophers over his own fireside. Thanks be to God for the grand invention of books!—T. Harrison.

POLITENESS.

The tolerance with which we receive the opinions of others is a part, and an indispensable part, of that general refinement of manners to which we give the name of politeness. But politeness itself, in all its most important respects, indeed, in every respect in which it is to be separated from the more fluctuating and arbitrary forms and ceremonies of the month and year, is nothing more than knowledge of the human mind directing general benevolence. It is the art of producing the greatest happiness, which in the more external courtesies of life can be produced, by raising such ideas or other feelings in the minds of those with whom we are conversant, as will afford the most pleasure, and averting, as much as possible, every idea which may lead to pain. It implies, therefore, when perfect, a fine knowledge of the natural series of thoughts, so as to distinguish not merely the thought which will be the immediate or near effect of what is said or done, but those which may arise still more remotely; and he is the most successful in this art of giving happiness, who sees the future at the greatest distance. It is this foresight, acquired by attentive observation of the various characters of mankind in a long intercourse with society, which is the true knowledge of the world; for the knowledge of the mere *forms* and *ceremonies* of the world, which is of far easier acquisition, is scarcely worthy of being called a part of it. The essential and the only valuable part of politeness, then, is as truly the result of study of the human mind, as if its minutest rules had formed a regular part of our system of intellectual and moral philosophy.—Dr. Brown.

MAY YOU DIE AMONG YOUR KINDRED.

It is a sad thing to feel that we must die away from our home. Tell not the invalid who is yearning after his distant country, that the atmosphere around him is soft; that the gales are filled with balm, and the flowers are springing from the green earth: he knows that the softest air to his heart would be the air which hangs over his native land; that more grateful than all the gales of the south, would breathe the low whispers of anxious affection; that the very icicles clinging to his own eaves, and the snow beating against his own windows, would be far more pleasant to his eyes, than the bloom and verdure which only more forcibly remind him how far he is from that one spot which is dearer to him than the world beside. He may, indeed, find estimable friends, who will do all in their power to promote his comfort and assuage his pains; but they cannot supply the place of the long known and long loved; they cannot read as in a book the mute language of his face; they have not learned to wait upon his habits, and anticipate his wants; and as he has not learned to communicate, without hesitation, all his wishes, impressions, and thoughts, to them, he feels that he is a stranger; and a more desolate feeling than that could not visit his soul. How much is expressed by that form of Oriental benediction, *May you die among your kindred.*—Greenwood.

Hope.—True hope is based on energy of character. A strong mind always hopes, and has always cause to hope, because it knows the mutability of human affairs, and how slight a circumstance may change the whole course of events. Such a spirit, too, rests upon itself; it is not confined to partial views, or to one particular object. And if at last all should be lost, it has saved itself, its own integrity and worth. Hope awakens courage, while despondency is the last of all evils; it is the abandonment of good, the giving up of the battle of life with dead nothingness. He who can plant courage in the human soul is the best physician.—Von Knebel.

WORK.

THE only happiness a brave man ever troubled himself with asking much about, was happiness enough to get his work done. Not, I can't *eat*, but I can't *work*, that was the burden of all wise complaining among men. It is after all, the one unhappiness of a man that he cannot work, that he cannot get his destiny, as a man, fulfilled. Behold the day is passing swiftly over, our life is passing swiftly over, and the night cometh, when no man can work. The night once come, our happiness, our unhappiness, it is all abolished, vanished, clean gone, a thing that has been. But our work, behold that is not abolished, that has not vanished; our work, behold it remains, or the want of it remains; for endless time and eternity remains, and that is the sole question with us forever more! Brief, brawling day, with its noisy phantasms, its poor, paper crowns, tinsel guilt, is gone! and divine, everlasting night, with her star diadems, with her silences, and her veracities, is come! *What* hast thou done, and *how?* Happiness, unhappiness, all that was but the wages thou hadst; thou hast spent all that in sustaining thyself hitherward, not a coin of it remains with thee, it is all spent, eaten; and now thy work, where is thy *work?* Swift, out with thy work!—CARLYLE.

EFFECT OF A BRIGHT DISTANCE OVER A DARK HORIZON.

WHATEVER beauty there may result from effects of light on foreground objects, from the dew of the grass, the flash of the cascade, the glitter of the birch trunk, or the fair daylight hues of darker things, (and joyfulness there is in all of them,) there is yet a light which the eye invariably seeks with a deeper feeling of the beautiful, the light of the declining or breaking day, and the flakes of scarlet cloud burning like watch-fires in the green sky of the horizon; a deeper feeling, not perhaps more acute, but having more of spiritual hope and longing, less of animal and present life; more manifest invariably in those of more serious and determined mind, (I use the word serious, not as being opposed to cheerful, but to trivial and volatile,) but, I think, marked and unfailing even in those of the least thoughtful dispositions. I am willing to let it rest on the determination of every reader, whether the pleasure he has received from these effects of calm and luminous distance be not the most singular and memorable of which he has been conscious; whether all that is dazzling in color, perfect in form, gladdening in expression, be not of evanescent and shallow appearing, when compared with the still small voice of the level twilight behind purple hills, or the scarlet arch of dawn over the dark, troublous-edged sea.

It is not then by a nobler form, it is not by positiveness of hue, it is not by intensity of light, (for the sun itself at noonday is effectless upon the feelings,) that this strange distant space possesses its attractive power. But there is one thing that it has, or suggests, which no other object of sight suggests in equal degree, and that is INFINITY. It is of all visible things the least material, the least finite, the farthest withdrawn from the earth prison-house, the most typical of the nature of God, the most suggestive of the glory of his dwelling-place. For the sky of night, though we may know it boundless, is dark, it is a studded vault, a roof that seems to shut us in and down, but the bright distance has no limit, we feel its infinity as we rejoice in its purity of light.—RUSKIN.

ACCOMPLISHMENTS.

NOT a few of the evils of the present day arise from a new and perverted application of terms; among these, perhaps, there is not one more absurd, misunderstood, or misapplied, than the term *accomplishments*. This word, in its original meaning, signifies *completeness, perfection*. But I may safely appeal to the observation of mankind, whether they do not meet with swarms of youthful females, issuing from our boarding schools, as well as emerging from the more private scenes of domestic education, who are introduced into the world under the broad and universal title of accomplished young ladies, of *all* of whom it cannot very truly and correctly be pronounced that they illustrate the definition, by a completeness which leaves nothing to be added, and a perfection which leaves nothing to be desired.—HANNAH MORE.

ATHEISM.

I HAD rather believe all the tables in the Legend, and the Talmud, and the Alcoran, than that this universal frame is without mind. And therefore God never wrought miracle to convince Atheism, because his ordinary works convince it. It is true that a little philosophy bringeth men's minds about to religion. For while the mind of man looketh upon second causes scattered, it may sometimes rest in them, and go no further; but when it beholdeth the chain of them confederate and linked together, it must needs flee to Providence and Deity. Nay, even that school, which is most accused of Atheism, doth most demonstrate religion: that is, the school of Leucippus, and Democritus, and Epicurus. For it is a thousand times more credible that four immutable elements, and one immutable fifth essence, duly and eternally placed, need no God, than that an army of infinite small portions, or seeds unplaced, should have produced this order and beauty without a Divine Marshal. The scripture saith: "*The fool hath said in his heart, there is no God:*" it is not said, *The fool hath thought in his heart.* So as he rather saith it by rote to himself, as that he would have, than that he can thoroughly believe it, or be persuaded of it. For none deny there is a God, but those for whom it maketh that there were no God. It appeareth in nothing more, that Atheism is rather in the lip, than the heart of man, than by this—that atheists will ever be talking of that their opinion, as if they fainted in it within themselves, and would be glad to be strengthened by the consent of others.—Lord Bacon.

METHOD.

Method, in the administration of minute things, is what perseverance is in the fixedness of the principal idea. Man being unable to obtain any thing from nothing, and having the power only to collect, his creations are mere combinations, which are more learned in proportion as they are complex and composed of various elements. Order, then, is the first merit of his works. As it alone constitutes their beauty, so it alone warrants their solidity and usefulness; for it determines the relations of parts to each other, and the relation of the whole to the end. Order draws the general plan, estimates advantages, decides conditions, foresees difficulties, and marks favorable occasions. Method establishes the preliminaries, and prepares the materials of the edifice. The elements upon which we are to work are offered to us scattered, and in heterogeneous medleys; method draws them out, compares, classes, and puts them at our disposal, furnishing us with the means of judging, at a glance, of the relative fitness of each, and of the place it should occupy in the structure. Method creates means of execution, adjusts the parts, and regulates the course of successive operations, so that each may profit by those which precede, and prepare for those which are to follow. It does not suffer an instant of time, a single effort, or any portion of matter to be lost; it prevents lassitude or disgust, because at every step it allows us to measure our progress; it keeps up strength and gives encouragement, by the secret influences of the harmony which breathes from it. Method judges of the advantages, the use, and the seasonableness of what has been executed; it furnishes means of preservation, and puts them within reach; it alone can render wealth profitable, and prevent that confusion through which nothing is properly used. It simplifies what is complicated, and diffuses universal light. It serves as an aid to the memory, as inspiration to imagination, and as light to the judgment. It calms and gives energy to the will, and produces facility and security in action. Even to see order reign around us, enables us to do every thing better, and feel a certain degree of inward serenity. The order which is diffused without penetrates us by a secret sympathy, and puts us involuntarily in unison with itself. And method supposes beforehand the power of governing at once, both our minds and the movements of our souls. It is a privilege of internal liberty. It is an expression of law, that is of enlightened authority. It is the very genius of reason, ruling all the faculties of our being.—DEGERANDO.

THE ATONEMENT.

WHATEVER difficulty there may be in the conception of vicarious punishments, it is an opinion which has had possession of mankind in all ages. There is no nation that has not used the practice of sacrifices. Whoever therefore denies the propriety of vicarious punishments, holds an opinion which the sentiments and practice of mankind have contradicted from the beginning of the world. The great sacrifice for the sins of mankind was offered at the death of the Messiah, who is called in scripture, "The Lamb of God that taketh away the sins of the world." To judge of the reasonableness of the scheme of redemption, it must be considered as necessary to the government of the universe, that God should make known his perpetual and irreconcilable detestation of moral evil. He might indeed punish, and punish only the offenders; but as the end of punishment is not revenge of crimes, but propagation of virtue, it was more becoming the Divine clemency to find another manner of proceeding, less destructive to man, and at least equally powerful to promote goodness. The end of punishment is to reclaim and warn. That punishment will both reclaim and warn, which shows evidently such abhorrence of sin in God as may deter us from it, or strike us with vengeance when we have committed it? This is effected by vicarious punishment. Nothing could more testify the opposition between God and moral evil, or more amply display his justice to men and angels, to all orders and succession of beings, than that it was necessary for the highest and purest nature, even for Divinity itself, to pacify demands of vengeance by a painful death, of which the natural effect will be, that when justice is appeased, there is a proper place for the exercise of mercy. The peculiar doctrine of Christianity is, that of a universal sacrifice and perpetual propitiation. Other prophets only proclaimed the will and the threatenings of God; Christ satisfied his justice.—DR. JOHNSON.

A TRUE FRIEND is not born every day; it is best to be courteous to all—intimate with few; for though perhaps we may have less cause for joy, I am sure we shall have less occasion for sorrow.

EFFECTS OF LOVE AND HAPPINESS ON THE MIND.

There needs no other proof that happiness is the most wholesome atmosphere, and that in which the immortality of man is destined ultimately to thrive, than the elevation of soul, the religious aspiration, which attends the first assurance, the first sober certainty of true love. There is much of this religious aspiration amidst all warmth of virtuous affections. There is a vivid love of God in the child that lays its cheek against the cheek of its mother, and clasps its arms about her neck. God is thanked (perhaps unconsciously) for the brightness of his earth, on summer evenings, when a brother and sister, who have long been parted, pour out their heart-stores to each other, and feel their course of thought brightening as it runs. When the aged parent hears of the honors his children have won, or looks round upon their innocent faces as the glory of his decline, his mind reverts to Him who in them prescribed the purpose of his life, and bestowed its grace. But religious as is the mood of every good affection, none is so devotional as that of love, especially so called. The soul is then the very temple of adoration, of faith, of holy purity, of heroism, of charity. At such a moment the human creature shoots up into the angel; there is nothing on earth too defiled for its charity—nothing in hell too appalling for its heroism—nothing in heaven too glorious for its sympathy. Strengthened, sustained, vivified by that most mysterious power, union with another spirit, it feels itself set well forth on the way of victory over evil, sent out conquering and to conquer. There is no other such crisis in human life. The philosopher may experience uncontrollable agitation in verifying his principle of balancing systems of worlds, feeling, perhaps, as if he actually saw the creative hand in the act of sending the planets forth on their everlasting way; but this philosopher, solitary seraph as he may be regarded amidst a myriad of men, knows at such a moment no emotions so divine as those of the spirit becoming conscious that it is beloved—be it the peasant girl in the meadow, or the daughter of the sage reposing in her father's confidence, or the artisan beside his loom, or the man of letters musing by his fireside. The warrior about to strike the decisive blow for the liberties of a nation, however impressed with the solemnity of the hour, is not in a state of such lofty resolution as those who, by joining hearts, are laying their joint hands on the whole wide realm of futurity for their own. The statesman who, in the moment of success, feels that an entire class of social sins and woes is annihilated by his hand, is not conscious of so holy and so intimate a thankfulness as they who are aware that their redemption is come in the presence of a new and sovereign affection. And these are many—they are in all corners of every land. The statesman is the leader of a nation, the warrior is the grace of the age, the philosopher is the birth of a thousand years; but the lover, where is he not? Wherever parents look round upon their children, there he has been—wherever children are at play together, there he will soon be—wherever there are roofs under which men dwell, wherever there is an atmosphere vibrating with human voices, there is the lover, and there is his lofty worship going on, unspeakable, but revealed in the brightness of the eye, the majesty of the presence, and the high temper of the discourse.—Harriet Martineau.

FAME.

Among the variety of principles by which mankind are actuated, there is one, my dear Asem, which I scarcely know whether to consider as springing from grandeur and nobility of mind, or from a refined species of vanity and egotism. It is that singular, although almost universal desire, of living in the memory of posterity, of occupying a share of the world's attention when we shall long since have ceased to be susceptible either of its praise or censure. Most of the passions of the mind are bounded by the grave; sometimes, indeed, an anxious hope or trembling fear will venture beyond the clouds and darkness that rest upon our mortal horizon, and expatiate in boundless futurity; but it is only this active love of fame which steadily contemplates its fruition in the applause or gratitude of future ages. Indignant at the narrow limits which circumscribe existence, ambition is for ever struggling to soar beyond them: to triumph over space and time, and to bear a name at least above the inevitable oblivion in which every thing else that concerns us must be involved.—Washington Irving.

THE ROSE.

I saw a rose perfect in beauty; it rested gracefully upon its stalk, and its perfume filled the air. Many stopped to gaze upon it, many bowed to taste its fragrance, and its owner hung over it with delight. I passed it again, and behold it was gone—its stem was leafless—its root had withered; the enclosure which surrounded it was broken down. The spoiler had been there; he saw that many had admired it; he knew it was dear to him who planted it, and beside it he had no other plant to love. Yet he snatched it secretly from the hand that cherished it; he wore it on his bosom till it hung its head and faded, and, when he saw that its glory had departed, he flung it rudely away. But it left a thorn in his bosom, and vainly did he seek to extract it; for now it pierces the spoiler, even in his hour of mirth. And when I saw that no man, who had loved the beauty of the rose, gathered again its scattered leaves, or bound up the stalk which the hands of violence had broken, I looked earnestly at the spot where it grew, and my soul received instruction. And I said, Let her who is full of beauty and admiration, sitting like the queen of flowers in majesty among the daughters of women, let her watch lest vanity enter her heart, beguiling her to rest proudly upon her own strength; let her remember that she standeth upon slippery places, "and be not high-minded, but fear."—Mrs. Sigourney.

THE IVY AND THE OAK.

An interesting volume, entitled "Algic Researches," contains the following allegory:

A vine was growing beside a thrifty oak, and had just reached that hight at which it requires support. "Oak," said the ivy vine, "bend your trunk so that you may be a support to me." "My support," replied the oak, "is naturally yours, and you may rely on my strength to bear you up, but I am too large and too solid to bend. Put your arms around me, my pretty vine, and I will manfully support and cherish you, if you have an ambition to climb, even as high as the clouds. While I thus hold you up, you will ornament my trunk with your pretty green leaves and shining scarlet berries. They will be as frontlets to my head, and I shall stand in the forest like a glorious warrior, with all his plumes. We were made by the Master of life to grow together, that by our union the weak should be made strong, and the strong render aid to the weak."

"But I wish to grow *independently*," said the vine; "why cannot you twine around me, and let me, grow up straight, and not be a mere dependent upon you?" "Nature," answered the oak, "did not design it. It is impossible that you should grow to any hight alone; and if you try it, the winds and rain, if not your own weight, will bring you to the ground. Neither is it proper for you to run your arms hither and yon, among the trees. The trees will begin to say it is not my vine—it is a stranger—get thee gone, I will not cherish thee. By this time thou wilt be be so entangled among the different branches, that thou canst not get back to the oak; and nobody will then admire thee, or pity thee."

"Ah me!" said the vine, "let me escape from such a destiny," and with this, she twined herself around the oak, and they both grew and flourished together."

Earthly Joys.—As Jonah's gourd—having done him no service in the night when he needed it not—withered in the *morning*, when he hoped for most benefit by it against the ensuing heat of the day: so the blessings of this world frequently wither at such times as we looked to find the most freshness in the refreshment from them.—Arrowsmith.

INCONSISTENCY OF HUMAN DESIRES.

Every thing is marked at a settled price. Our time, our labor, our ingenuity, is so much ready money, which we are to lay out to the best advantage. Examine, compare, choose, reject; but stand to your own judgment, and do not, like children, when you have purchased one thing, repine that you do not possess another, which you would not purchase. Would you be rich? Do you think that the single point worth sacrificing every thing else to? You may then be rich. Thousands have become so from the lowest beginnings, by toil, and diligence, and attention to the minutest articles of expense and profit. But you must give up the pleasures of leisure, of an unembarrassed mind, and of a free, unsuspicious temper. You must learn to do hard, if not unjust things; and as for the embarrassment of a delicate and ingenuous spirit, it is necessary for you to get rid of it as fast as possible. You must not stop to enlarge your mind, polish your taste, or refine your sentiments; but must keep on in one beaten track, without turning aside to the right hand or the left. "But," you say, "I cannot submit to drudgery like this; I feel a spirit above it." 'Tis well, be above it then; only do not repine because you are not rich. Is knowledge the pearl of price in your estimation? That, too, may be purchased by steady application, and long, solitary hours of study and reflection. "But," says the man of letters, "what a hardship is it that many an illiterate fellow, who cannot construe the motto on his coach, shall raise a fortune, while I possess merely the common conveniencies of life." Was it for fortune, then, that you grew pale over the midnight lamp, and gave the sprightly years of youth to study and reflection? You have then mistaken your path, and ill-employed your industry. "What reward have I then for all my labor?" What reward? A large, comprehensive soul, purged from vulgar fear and prejudices, able to interpret the works of man and God. A perpetual spring of fresh ideas, and the conscious dignity of superior intelligence. The most characteristic mark of a great mind is to choose some one object which it considers important, and pursue that object through life. If we expect the purchase, we must pay the price.—Mrs. Barbauld.

The Glory of Christ.—The glory of Christ is not like the airy phantom which men call glory, but hath everlasting weight and solidity; it not only sends forth light, but is light; and all that can be conceived of splendor, excellence, durability, and bliss, meets in this glory, as its sole and substantial essence. The believer, therefore, is said to enjoy in Christ an exceeding, eternal weight of glory; exceeding all conception and comparison; eternal in its enjoyment and duration.—Ambrose Serle.

THE HIGH CALLING OF GOD IN CHRIST JESUS.

The high calling of God in Christ Jesus! I have no fear of displeasing God, or of dishonoring his institutions, by repeating this proclamation. I have no apology to make to men or angels, for inviting attention to this theme. This calling! this *high* calling! this *high calling of God!* this high calling of *God in Christ Jesus!* Rather—I ask audience—I claim audience; with a sublime confidence, with a Divine assurance that it will be well rewarded. I claim the audience of both sexes; of manhood in all its strength; and of womanhood in all its beauty. I claim the audience of all ages; of childhood in its bloom; of youth in its radiance; of maturity in its activity; and of decrepitude in its stillness and tears. I claim the audience of all classes: of the hunter, the fisherman, and factor; of the shepherd, the herdsman, and drover; of the slave, the overseer, and planter; of the laborer and farmer; of the miner and coiner; of the diver and jeweler; of the operative and manufacturer; of the mechanic and merchant; of the sailor and soldier; of the artist and scholar; of the lawyer, physician, and pastor; of the legislator, the judge, and magistrate; and of all others that intervene among these gradations. I claim the audience of all conditions: of the richest and poorest; of the fairest and roughest; of the wisest and dullest; of the noblest and meanest; of the mightiest and weakest: I challenge, in particular, the blind, that they may see; and the deaf, that they may hear; and the dumb, that they may speak; and the lame, that they may leap; and the sick, that they may revive; and the leprous, that they may be clean; and the paralytic, that they may be composed; and the maimed, that they may be whole; and the lunatic, that they may be calm; and the demoniac, that they may be dispossessed; and the imprisoned, that they may be free; and the dead, that they may rise; and all, to give audience. I claim the audience of all schools, in art and science; in philosophy and literature: of all parties, in patriotism and philanthropy, in politics and social reform: and of all sects—in theology, ecclesiasticism, and ritualism. I claim the audience of all these, and of all other divisions of humanity, let them belong to what race, to what nation, to what tribe, or to what family, they may. I claim the audience of mankind, in whole. Nay, more: I claim the audience of the whole heavenly host; to whom it is given, as occasion requires, to descend from their bowers of bliss, and minister to mankind. Nay, more: I claim the audience of all the inhabitants, of all the worlds, of all the systems, in all the universe. I claim the audience of all, with no apology to make to any: the audience of all sages and saints; of all angels and archangels; of all cherubim and seraphim; of all thrones, and dominions, and principalities, and powers; of all the morning stars, that fill immensity with the light of joy; and of all the sons of God, that fill eternity with the music of praise: but with no apology, for any sage or saint; for any angel or archangel; for any cherub or seraph; for any throne, or dominion, or principality, or power; for any morning star, in all immensity, or any son of God, to all eternity. Rather, I honor them, by this claim: and they will prize the compliment as an augmentation of their felicity. I hail them, from afar, by the silver trumpet of Isaiah: "Hear, O heavens! and give ear, O earth! for the Lord hath spoken!" and lo! all the hum of all their interests, and all the roar of all their motions, are succeeded by the hallowed silence that thrills at the opening of the mind of God. I hail the earth alone, by the silver trumpet of Jeremiah: "O earth! earth! earth! hear the word of the Lord!" I extend the cry, to every moon; to every planet; to every comet; and to every sun: to every star in the milky way; and to every star in every misty nebula—to every star of every form, of every hue, in every region, of the whole creation, saying: "O star! star! star! hear the word of the Lord!" And if any moon, or any planet, or any comet, or any sun, or any star: if any sage on earth, or any saint in heaven; or any angel, or any archangel, or any cherub, or any seraph, or any throne, or any dominion, or any principality, or any power, or any morning star, or any son of God, demand of me, in this universal stillness, why it is that I have thus stopped their movement and hushed their harmony? what it is that the Lord hath spoken? and what is the nature of the word that I wish them to hear? I reply to them, one and all, with a sublimity of style which is still but a poor expression of the infinitely greater sublimity of spirit: "I have no apology to make for this interruption. You will rejoice in my message. I come with the humility of a child in my heart, and with the simplicity of a child upon my lips, to repeat the divinest of all the utterances of our common Father: I come to recite in your hearing, the high calling of God in Christ Jesus!" And lo! is it not as I said? They do prize the compliment! They do rejoice in the message! The stars are brighter and stiller than ever. The immortal intelligencies that dignify their spheres, have but one feeling—the radiance of the truth, and the rapture of the love, evolved by the essential inspiration of—*The high calling of God in Christ Jesus!*—Stockton.

THE VOICE OF CREATION.—The works of Creation, as they unfold themselves in all their variegated loveliness and splendor, I cannot but love. I love the mighty and majestic ocean, the loud anthem of the cataract, the onward-flowing river, and the sweet murmuring of pleasant streams; the rich drapery of old and venerable forests, the green fields, the beauty and incense of flowers, and the music of the birds; the wondrous orbs that shine in the far-off blue of heaven, illuminating the wide canopy with beams of holy light, worlds upon worlds, performing their onward march to the grand music of time! All these I love, and love fervently. There is a voice here, that if listened to and obeyed, will teach man to be holier and happier, and will lead him higher than their created beauty, even to the footstool of the eternal.—J. Brookwell Peat.

PREACHING OF IMMORTALITY TO THE INDIANS.

Thomas Story and his companion went to a town of the Chickahomine Indians, and spake to them concerning the immortality of the soul, and told them that God had placed a witness in the heart of every man, which approves that which is good, and reproves that which is evil.

The Sagmore then pointed to his head, and said, that was treacherous; but pointing to his breast, said it was true and sweet there. And then he sent forth his breath, as if he had poured out his soul unto death; and signing up toward heaven with his hand, raised a bold, cheerful, and loud *Hey*, as if the soul ascended thither in a triumphant manner; and then pointing to his body, from thence put his hand toward the earth, to demonstrate his opinion that the body remains there when the soul is departed and ascended.

Luther and the Friars.—God, in the beginning, made but only one human creature, which was a wise council: afterwards he created also a woman; then came the mischief. The friars follow God's first council, for they live alone, without marrying; wherefore, according to their rule and judgment, it had been good, nay better, that God had remained by his first determination and council, namely, that one man alone had lived.—Luther.

Resignation to the Path appointed us in life.—It pleases Heaven to give us no more light in our way, than will leave virtue in possession of its recompense.

—— Grant me, gracious God! to go cheerfully on the road which thou hast marked out; I wish it neither more wide or more smooth; continue the light of this dim taper thou hast put into my hands: I will kneel upon the ground seven times a day to seek the best track I can with it, and having done that, I will trust myself and the issue of my journey to thee, who art the fountain of joy, and will sing songs of comfort as I go along.—Sterne.

Morality.—Morality is the body, of which faith in Christ is the soul; so far indeed its earthly body, as it is adapted to its state of warfare on earth, and the appointed form and instrument of its communion with the present world; yet not *terrestrial*, nor of the world, but a celestial body, capable of being transfigured from glory to glory, in accordance with the varying circumstances and outward relations of its moving and informing spirit.—Coleridge.

MAN.

Man is so great, that his greatness appears even in the consciousness of his misery. A tree does not know itself to be miserable. It is true, there is misery in knowing one's self miserable; but there is greatness also. Thus all man's miseries prove his greatness. They are the miseries of a mighty potentate, of a dethroned monarch. Man is but the weakest reed in the universe, but he is a reed that thinks; it does not need the universe to crush him—a breath of air, a drop of water is enough to kill him. But even if the material universe should overwhelm him, man would be more noble than that which destroys him; because he knows that he dies, while the universe knows nothing of its advantage over him. Our true dignity, then, consists in thought—thence we must derive our elevation.

Live for something.—Thousands of men breathe, move and live—pass off the stage of life, and are heard of no more. Why? None were blessed by them; none could point to them as the means of their redemption; not a line they wrote, not a word they spoke, could be recalled, and so they perished: their light went out in darkness, and they were not remembered more than insects of yesterday. Will you thus live and die, O man immortal? Live for something. Do good, and leave behind you a monument of virtue, that the storms of time can never forget. Write your name in kindness, love, and mercy, on the hearts of those you come in contact with, and you will never be forgotten. Good deeds will shine as brightly on the earth, as the stars of heaven.—Chalmers.

Influence.—Influence is to be measured, not by the extent of surface it covers, but by its kind. A man may spread his mind, his feelings, and opinions, through a great extent, but, if his mind be a low one, he manifests no greatness. A wretched artist may fill a city with daubs, and, by a false, showy style, achieve a reputation; but the man of genius, who leaves behind him one grand picture, in which immortal beauty is embodied, and which is silently to spread a true taste in his art, exerts an incomparably higher influence.

No Wisdom without Thought.—He that never thinks never can be wise. Perpetual levity must end in ignorance: and intemperance, though it may fire the spirits for an hour, will make life short or miserable. Let us consider that youth is of no long duration, and that in maturer age, when the enchantments of fancy shall cease, and phantoms of delight dance no more about us, we shall have no comforts but the esteem of wise men, and the means of doing good.—Dr. Johnson.

THE VANITY OF EARTHLY THINGS.

When I look upon the tombs of the great, every emotion of envy dies in me; when I read the epitaphs of the beautiful, every inordinate desire goes out; when I meet with the grief of parents upon a tombstone, my heart melts with compassion; when I see the tomb of the parents themselves, I consider the vanity of grieving for those whom we must quickly follow; when I see kings lying by those who deposed them, when I consider rival wits placed side by side, or the holy men that divided the world with their contests and disputes, I reflect, with sorrow and astonishment, on the little competitions, factions, and debates of mankind. When I read the several dates of the tombs, of some that died yesterday, and some six hundred years ago, I consider that great day when we shall all of us be contemporaries, and make our appearance together.—Addison.

REFORM THYSELF.

The present is generally styled the age of reform. This we do not feel disposed to controvert. It cannot, however, be denied, that mankind are wofully deficient in the greatest of all reforms—individual reform. Societies for the reformation of others are multiplied almost *ad infinitum;* but efforts for personal reformation are much neglected. Editors universally complain of the corrupt state of the press, and yet most of them aid in the perpetuation of that corruption. Infidels, as well as Christians, mourn, or profess to mourn, over the evils of society; while those evils are augmented by their own wrong doings. Reformers must take an entirely different course—first reform themselves, and then their influence will be felt with a hundred-fold more force on others.

"Man know thyself: all wisdom centres there."

So said the profound, though poetical writer, Young. And until this wisdom is acquired, and likewise exhibited in the life, no thorough reform can take place in the world.—T. Harrison.

Influence of Woman.—The influence of woman, in giving sweetness and purity to the character of the other sex, is acknowledged by the most candid infidel writers, as well as by all Christians. Lord Byron, whose principles and habits were far below the proper standard, once remarked, that when in the society of a virtuous and intelligent female, he invariably felt a desire to be a better man. If such is the power of woman, it becomes her well to reflect on her responsible station, and to aim most sacredly at the preservation of her own uprightness and dignity.—T. Harrison.

RESOLUTION.

Resolution is omnipotent; and if we will but solemnly determine to make the most and best of our powers and capacities, and if, to this end, with Wilberforce, we will but seize and improve even the shortest intervals of possible action and effort, we shall find that there is no limit to our advancement. Without this resolute and earnest purpose, the best aid and means are of little worth, but with it, even the weakest are mighty. Without it, we shall accomplish nothing, with it, every thing. A man who is deeply in earnest acts upon the motto of the pickaxe on the old seal: "Either I will find a way or make one." He has somewhat the spirit of Buonaparte, who, when told on the eve of battle that circumstances were against him, replied: "Circumstances! I make and control circumstances, —not bow to them!" In self-cultivation, as in every thing else, to think we are able is almost to be so; to resolve to attain is often almost attainment. Everywhere are the means of progress, if we have but the fixed purpose to use them. And if, like the old philosopher, we will but take as our motto, "Higher—for ever higher," we may rise by them all. He that resolves upon any great end, by that very resolution has scaled the chief barrier to it. And he who seizes the grand idea of self-cultivation, and solemnly resolves upon it, will find that idea, that resolution, burning like a living fire within, and ever putting him upon his own improvement. He will find it removing difficulties, searching out or making means, giving courage for despondency, and strength for weakness; and, like the star in the east to the wise men of old, guiding him nearer and still nearer to the sun of all perfection. If we are but fixed and resolute on self-improvement, we shall find means to it on every side, at every moment, and even obstacles and oppositions will but make us like the fabled specter-ships, which "sail the fastest in the very teeth of the wind."—Rev. Tryon Edwards.

ON PROVIDENCE.

If God should manage his ways according to our prescriptions, what satisfaction would God have? or what satisfaction would the world have? He might be unjust to himself and unjust to others. Your own complaints would not be stilled when you should feel the smart of your own counsels; yet if they were, what satisfaction could there be to the complaints of others, whose interests, and therefore judgments and desires lie cross to yours? Murmur not, therefore; whatsoever is done in the world is the work of a wise agent, who acts for the perfection of the whole universe; and why should I murmur at that which promotes the common happiness and perfections of any one particular person? Must a lutinist break all his strings because one is out of tune?—Charnock.

THE PILGRIMS OF THE MAYFLOWER

METHINKS I see it now, that one solitary, adventurous vessel, the Mayflower of a forlorn hope, freighted with the prospects of a future state, and bound across the unknown sea. I behold it pursuing, with a thousand misgivings, the uncertain, the tedious voyage. Suns rise and set, and weeks and months pass, the winter surprises them in the deep, but brings them not the sight of the wished-for shore. I see them now scantily supplied with provisions, crowded almost to suffocation in their ill-stored prison, delayed by calms, pursuing a circuitous route; and now driven in fury before the raging tempest, on the high and giddy waves. The awful voice of the storm howls through the rigging. The laboring masts seem straining from their base; the dismal sound of the pumps is heard; the ship leaps, as it were, madly from billow to billow; the ocean breaks, and settles with engulfing floods over the deck, and beats with deadening weight against the staggered vessel. I see them, escaped from these perils, pursuing their all but desperate undertaking, and landed at last, after a five months' voyage, on the ice-clad rocks of Plymouth; weak and weary from the voyage, poorly armed, scantily provisioned, depending on the charity of their shipmaster for a draught of beer on board, drinking nothing but water on shore, without shelter, without means, surrounded by hostile tribes. Shut now the volume of history, and tell me, on any principle of human probability, what shall be the fate of this handful of adventurers. Tell me, man of military science, in how many months were they all swept off by the thirty savage tribes, enumerated within the early limits of New England? Tell me, politician, how long did this shadow of a colony, on which your conventions and treaties had not smiled, languish on the distant coast? Student of history, compare for me the baffled projects, the deserted settlements, the abandoned adventures of other times, and find the parallel of this! Was it the winter's storm, beating upon the houseless heads of women and children; was it hard labor and spare meals; was it disease; was it the tomahawk; was it the deep malady of a blighted hope, a ruined enterprise, and a broken heart, aching in its last moments at the recollection of the loved and left, beyond the sea; was it some, or all of these united, that hurried this forsaken company to their melancholy fate? And is it possible that neither of these causes, that not all combined, were able to blast this bud of hope? Is it possible that from a beginning so feeble, so frail, so worthy—not so much of admiration as of pity—there has gone forth a progress so steady, a growth so wonderful, a reality so important, a promise, yet to be fulfilled, so glorious?—EDWARD EVERETT.

DEATH.—Death is the liberator of him whom freedom cannot re lease, the physician of him whom medicines cannot cure, and the comforter of him whom time cannot console.

36

THE PASSING OF THE RUBICON.

A GENTLEMAN, speaking of Cæsar's benevolent disposition, and of the reluctance with which he entered into the civil war, observes: "How long did he pause upon the brink of the Rubicon!" How came he to the brink of that river! How dared he cross it! Shall private men respect the boundaries of private property, and shall a man pay no respect to the boundaries of his country's rights? How dared he cross that river! O! but he paused upon the brink! He should have perished upon the brink ere he had crossed it! Why did he pause? Why does a man's heart palpitate when he is on the point of committing an unlawful deed? Why does the very murderer, his victim sleeping before him, and his glaring eye, taking the measure of the blow, strike wide of the mortal part? Because of conscience! 'Twas that made Cæsar pause on the bank of the Rubicon. Compassion! What compassion! The compassion of an assassin, that feels a momentary shudder, as his weapon begins to cut! Cæsar paused upon the brink of the Rubicon! What was the Rubicon? The boundary of Cæsar's province. From what did it separate his province? From his country. Was his country a desert? No; it was cultivated and fertile; rich and populous. Its sons were men of genius, spirit, and generosity! Its daughters were lovely, susceptible, and chaste! Friendship was its inhabitant! Love was its inhabitant! Domestic affection was its inhabitant! Liberty was its inhabitant! All bounded by the stream of the Rubicon! What was Cæsar, that stood upon the bank of that stream? A traitor, bringing war and pestilence into the heart of that country! No wonder that he paused—no wonder if, his imagination wrought upon by his conscience, he had beheld blood instead of water; and heard groans instead of murmurs! No wonder if some gorgon horror had turned him into stone upon the spot! But, no! he cried: "The die is cast!" He plunged! he crossed!—and Rome was free no more!—KNOWLES.

COMPENSATION.—There is a touching anecdote of one, endowed with rank and fortune, chancing to enter a poor cottage, where some six or eight healthy, ruddy children were waiting with longing looks, the final distribution of the last morsel of an exhausted loaf. "Here are the mouths, but where is the meat?" exclaimed the child of luxury in the house of want. Some time after, the cottage mother having an errand to the noble mansion of her visiter, found the doors and windows closed; silence and sorrow reigned through the splendid hall; the lady had that day lost her only child. The remark in the cottage came into her thoughts. "Here is the meat, but where are the mouths?" said the child of poverty in the mansion of wealth and splendor.—CAROLINE MAY.

HIGHER MANIFESTATIONS OF CHRISTIANITY.

Already the Gospel, in its expansive diffusion, is every where received as the solar light of the philosophical world, and the mount of vision from which we survey the living landscape of mind and morals outspreading before and about us. And as such, by an exhibition of its lofty motives and grand results, and borrowing impulse alike from the interests of time and the awards of eternity, it has curbed the lawlessness of genius in the instance of the loftiest minds, has directed and purified its flame, and sent it kindling to the throne of God! It has pressed the phenomena of nature—extending throughout the infinitely little and the infinitely great, comprehending all the gradations of earthly littleness and heavenly grandeur—into its own service. Guided by the Gospel, the field of nature and the tablet of the human mind become a book which all can read, and reading, none dispute.

But for Christianity, large portions of the world's history would have been lost, and its most eventful fortunes unknown. It is in her keeping, we are to look for the most valuable treasures of human lore. She has rescued from the grasp of oblivion, and the withering scorn of pagan hate and infidel meanness, spoils that belong to eternity! It is under her guidance we see the bark of knowledge, where all beside was wreck, booming in safety over the rolling seas of time! When nations without number, for ages uncounted, trod a moral waste and wandered on, without stumbling upon the landmarks of the desolation, the star of Bethlehem cast its radiance over the travel of earth, and lit the wanderer home to God! She did more. Not only did she eclipse, by the splendor of her revelations, the wisdom of paganism, and give its mythology to the ridicule of childhood, but in wrath she led the Gaul and the Goth, and the gods of Greece and of Rome crumbled upon their altars—the startled East shrank back, and the nations of the West waxed pale before her deeds!

This work of mental regeneration is going on. Whether we look at individual or social man, the fireside or the map of nations, the familes and kingdoms of earth, are submitting, one after another, to her gently subduing scepter, and soon the uttermost parts of the earth shall share the heavenly illumination, and pagan lands of every lip and every name become the resting-place of Heaven's light.—Bascom.

Despise no One.—The Jews would not willingly tread upon the smallest piece of paper in their way, but took it up; "for possibly," said they, "the name of God may be on it." Trample not on any: there may be some work of grace there thou knowest not of. The name of God may be written on that soul thou treadest on: it may be a soul that Christ thought so much of, as to give his precious blood for it; therefore despise it not.—Leighton.

THE HAND OF GOD SEEN IN THE DISCOVERIES OF THE AGE.

WHATEVER evils arrest, or pervert the growth of civilization, we believe Christianity is competent to remove. It does not indeed act directly upon physical nature. But it puts man in such a position as that he can overcome its obstacles to improvement, and employ its vast powers in the furtherance of divine designs. It points him to the treasures of the Universe, and bids him seek them. We are not authorized to think that God has had no agency in those important inventions and discoveries, which have so signally promoted the welfare of humanity. Who can tell how many ways he may have of operating upon mind? The idea of unlimited intelligence and power, opens a boundless field for contemplation; though we cannot trace the footsteps of Jehovah in it, nor hear his voice, nor behold his radiance, yet may we be assured that he is there in the plenitude of his might, and magnificence of his glory. If the veil that hides him were lifted, we should see him nearer to the scenes amid which we dwell, than in the happiest moments of faith we imagine him to be, leading man to ascertain facts, and apply means, that may place him on vantage-ground, and give him a firmer hold upon his natural birthright. The silence of Christianity with regard to such subjects is admitted. Let us not however misunderstand it. Let us not take advantage of it, to indulge the spirit of carnal pride. The voice of Christianity is silent, after it has made known the close relation, subsisting between God and his material works, and declared his presence to be constantly diffused throughout every portion of the vast universe. The illustrations of his Providence, that it employs, are drawn from the most insignificant objects surrounding us; while the favorite images that adorn and exemplify the operations of mediatorial grace, are derived from those departments of physical nature, which are visibly the most dependent upon his ever-active energy. Such is the preparation for its silence! If this impressive reservedness had preceded the anouncements above mentioned, our faith in the temporal welfare of society had realized no consoling refuge of this kind; but as it is, we feel warranted in believing, that in the introduction of those mighty instrumentalities, which anticipate the ordinary labor of years, and augment individual power so wonderfully, God has exerted no unimportant agency.—LIPSCOMB.

ORIGIN OF THE WORD BRITON.—Our primitive ancestors distinguished themselves, in pride or simplicity, as Brith and Brithon; Brith signifying *stained*, and Brithon a *stained man*. The predilection for coloring their bodies, induced the civilized Romans to designate the people who were driven to the Caledonian forests as *Picts*, or a painted people.—D'ISRAELI.

HAPPINESS OF THE CHILD OF GOD.

THAT soul whose zeal is regulated by an enlightened understanding, nourished by a calm, dispassionate love of truth, and founded upon a firm adherence to the moral attributes of God, is a plant of our heavenly Father's right-hand planting, and shall be useful and happy here, and inherit eternal life hereafter. Being delivered from the dark shades of ignorance, the contradicting influence of partiality, and the tyrannical ascendancy of appetite, the mind is free to think, and judge, and exercise its pious affections without obstruction, in which consists "the glorious liberty of the children of God." Free from the pitiful shackles of bigotry, such a soul enjoys a most pleasant and reviving range through all the wonders of redeeming love. The attributes, and works, and providence, and grace of God, afford abundant matter for his pious meditations. His active mind travels through the beauties of creation, and adores that beneficent hand which sends us rain from heaven, and fills our hearts with food and gladness. He turns to the pages of revelation, explores the opening beauties of the moral law, surveys the wonderful goodness of God manifested in the flesh, then rising on the wings of contemplation, with ecstacy of thought, to those salubrious regions of ineffable tranquility, "where momentary ages are no more." His soul adheres to God, as to the centre of all its desires. He finds no pleasure in existence equal to that of doing good. He looks over the face of the earth, with conscious friendship for every living creature. He mourns over the ignorance and wickedness of men, and melts into sympathetic tears for the misery of Adam's children. His enlarged and generous mind embraces the different nations of the earth with affection, and beseeches Heaven to bless all his brethren of the human race.—SHINN.

STANDING UPON PEDIGREE.

CRANTZ, in his Saxon History, tells us of an Earl of Alsatia, surnamed *Iron* on account of his great strength, who was a great favorite with Edward the Third, of England, and much envied, as favorites are always sure to be, by the rest of the courtiers. On one occasion, when the king was absent, some noblemen maliciously instigated the queen to make trial of the noble blood of the favorite, by causing a lion to be let loose upon him, saying, according to the popular belief, that, if "the earl was truly noble, the lion would not touch him." It being customary with the earl to rise at break of day, before any other person in the palace was stirring, a lion was let loose during the night, and turned into the lower court. When the earl came down in the morning, with no more than a night-gown cast over his shirt, he was met by the lion, bristling his hair, and growling destruction between his teeth. The earl, not in the least daunted, called out, with a stout voice, "Stand, you dog." At these words, the lion crouched at his feet, to the great amazement of the courtiers, who were peeping out at every window to see the issue of their ungenerous project. The earl laid hold of the lion by the mane, turned him into his cage, and placing his night-cap upon the lion's back, came forth without ever casting a look behind. "Now," said the earl, calling out to the courtiers, whose presence at the windows instantly convinced him of the share they had in this trial of his courage, "let him amongst you all, that standest most upon his pedigree, go and fetch my night-cap."

A DISPOSITION TO DEGRADE OTHERS.

Too much, even in later life, I have perceived in men that pass for good men, a disposition to degrade (and if possible to degrade through self-degradation,) those in whom unwillingly they feel any weight of oppression to themselves, by commanding qualities of intellect or character. They respect you: they are compelled to do so, and they hate to do so. Next, therefore, they seek to throw off the sense of this oppression, and to take vengeance for it, by co-operating with any unhappy accidents in your life to inflict a sense of humiliation upon you, and, if possible, to force you into becoming a consenting party to that humiliation. Oh! wherefore is it that those who presume to call themselves the "friends" of this or that woman, are so often those, above all others, whom in the hour of death that man or woman is most likely to salute with the valediction: Would God I had never seen your face!—De Quincey.

Religion and Science.—Religion and science are more powerfully at work at present than in any former period of time, in removing the physical and moral evils of the world, and in elevating man to his highest state of earthly existence. In some periods, the work has been scarcely perceptible, but now it is visible to the most ordinary observer. Changes are taking place, and improvements are being effected, which are the wonder of all minds. Glorious will be the consummation.—T. Harrison.

The Mind never stationary.—The human mind is never stationary; when it is not progressive, it is necessarily retrograde. He who imagines at any period of his life, that he can advance no further in moral or intellectual improvement, is as little acquainted with the extent of his own powers as the voyager was with that of the terrestrial globe—who supposed he had erected pillars at the end of the world, when he had only left a monument how much further he might have proceeded.—Cicero.

PRAYER WITH DEVOTION.

The Pharisee is said to pray with himself; God and the Pharisee were not together, there was only the Pharisee and himself. Paul knew not what to pray for without the Holy Ghost joined himself with him, and helped him with groans unutterable; but the Pharisee had no need of that; 'twas enough that *he* and *himself* were together at this work, for he thought, without doubting, that *he* and *himself* together could do. How many times have I heard ancient men, and ancient women, at it, with themselves, when all alone in some private room, or in some solitary path; and in their chat, they have, been sometimes reasoning, sometimes chiding, sometimes pleading, sometimes praying, and sometimes singing; but yet all has been done by themselves when all alone; but yet so done, as one that had not seen them must needs have concluded that they were talking, singing, and praying with company; when all that they had said, they did it with themselves, and had neither auditor nor regarder.

So the Pharisee was at it with himself; he and himself performed, at this time, the duty of prayer.—Bunyan.

A firm and Religious Belief. — I envy no quality of the mind or intellect of others,—not genius, wit, nor fancy; but if I could choose what would be the most delightful, and, I believe, most useful to me, I prefer a firm religious belief to any other blessing; for it makes discipline of good, creates new hopes when earthly hopes vanish, and throws over the decay, the destruction of existence, the most gorgeous of all lights; awakens life in death, and from corruption and decay, calls up beauty and divinity; makes an instrument of misfortune and of shame the ladder of ascent to paradise; and far above all combinations of earthly hopes, calls up the most delightful visions of palms and amaranths,—the gardens of the blest, and the security of everlasting joys, where the sensualist and the skeptic view only gloom, decay, annihilation, and despair.—Sir H. Davy.

Kindness to the Dead.—Certainly it is the noblest thing in the world to do an act of kindness to him, whom we shall never see, but yet hath deserved it of us, and to whom we would do it if he were present; and unless we do so our charity is mercenary, and our friendships are direct merchandise, and our gifts are brocage; but what we do for the dead, or to the living for their sakes, is gratitude and virtue, for virtue's sake, and the noblest portion of humanity.—Bishop Taylor.

ALL BEAUTY IS OF GOD.

THE Golden Gates of Day opening on the palmy East: the Night's pale Regent, and the countless stars; the fruits of the earth, the flowers of the field; the valley, the mountain, the streamlet and the ocean! Love and truth are of God, for they are beautiful in their purity and immutability! Music is of God, for to its sacred voice sang the Morning Stars when they hymned his glory and his praise! Wisdom is of God, for it is Beauty intellectual; and Virtue, for it is Beauty moral. Penitence is of God, for it is the portal of heaven! Conscience, the soul's monitor; Sorrow, its chastener; Hope, its comforter, and Peace, its reward, are of God, for they are beautiful in their fidelity, patience, constancy, and celestial quietude! Justice and Mercy are of God, for they are the Beauty of Holiness, and Holiness is God Himself in his Beatitude and Beauty.—*Uncle Timothy.*

VOCATION OF THE SCHOLAR ETERNAL.

WHEN we contemplate the idea unfolded, even without reference to ourselves, we see around us a community in which no one can labor for himself without at the same time laboring for his fellow-men, or can labor for others without also laboring for himself; where the success of one member is the success of all, and the loss of one a loss to all:—a picture which, by the harmony it reveals in the manifold diversity of being, introduces a cordial feeling of satisfaction to the mind, and powerfully raises the soul above the things of time.

But the interest is heightened when we turn our thoughts to ourselves, and contemplate ourselves as members of this great spiritual community. The feeling of our dignity and our power is increased when we say—what each of us may say—"My existence is not in vain and aimless: I am a necessary link in the great chain of being which reaches from the awakening of the first man to perfect consciousness of his existence, onward through eternity; all the great and wise and noble that have ever appeared among men—those benefactors of the human race, whose names I find recorded in the world's history, and the many others whose benefits have outlived their names—all have labored for me; I have entered into their labors; I follow their footsteps on this earth where they dwelt, where they scattered blessings as they went along. I may, as soon as I will, assume the sublime task which they have resigned, of making our common brotherhood ever wiser and happier; I may continue to build where they had to cease their labors; I may bring nearer to its completion the glorious temple which they had to leave unfinished."

"But"—some one may say—"I too, like them, must rest from my labors." Oh! this is the sublimest thought of all! If I assume this noble task, I can never reach its end; and so surely as it is my vocation to assume it, I can never cease *to act*, and hence can never cease *to be*. That which men call Death cannot interrupt my activity; for my work must go on to its completion, and it cannot be completed in Time;—hence my existence is limited by no Time, and I am Eternal:—with the assumption of this great task, I have also laid hold of Eternity. I raise my head boldly towards the threatening rock, the raging flood, or the fiery tempest, and say—"I am Eternal, and I defy your might! Break all upon me!—and thou Earth, and thou Heaven, mingle in the wild tumult, and all ye elements, foam and fret yourselves, and crush in your conflict the last atom of the body which I call mine!—my WILL, secure in its own firm purpose, shall soar undisturbed and bold over the wreck of the universe:—for I have entered upon my vocation, and it is more enduring than ye are: it is ETERNAL, and I am ETERNAL like it."—*Johann Gottlieb Fichte.*

DEATH OF ARTHUR HENRY HALLAM.

IT is needless to tell what was the promise of his son Arthur, whose qualities and honors were the joy and pride of his life. The young man was advanced in his professional studies, was engaged to a sister of Alfred Tennyson, and had the prospect of the brightest of lives, when he went on the Continent with his father, for a tour of recreation. At a German town he was slightly unwell with a cold; and Mr. Hallam went alone for his afternoon walk, leaving Authur on the sofa. Finding him sleeping on his return, he took a book and read for an hour; and then he became impressed with the extreme stillness of the sleeper. The sleeper was cold, and must have been dead from almost the moment when he had last spoken. In like manner died the eldest daughter; and in like manner the cherished wife—an admirable woman. * * * There was still a son, Henry, but he died too in opening manhood; and then there was but one daughter, and she married, to cheer his old age. Yet he seemed always cheerful. His social disposition, and his love of literature, and his generosity of spirit, and his kindly sympathies, kept him fresh and bright for many a long year after the sunshine of his life seemed to be gone.—*Harriet Martineau.*

GRANDFATHER'S REVERIE.

BY THEODORE PARKER. (FROM HIS SERMON ON "OLD AGE.")

GRANDFATHER is old. His back is bent. In the street he sees crowds of men looking dreadfully young, and walking fearfully swift. He wonders where all the *old* folks are. Once when a boy, he could not find people young enough for him, and sidled up to any young stranger he met on Sundays, wondering why God made the world so old. Now he goes to Commencement to see his grandson take his degree, and is astonished at the youth, of the audience. "This is new," he says; "it did not use to be so fifty years ago." At meeting, the minister seems surprisingly young, and the audience young. He looks round, and is astonished that there are so few venerable heads. The audience seem not decorous. They come in late, and hurry off early, clapping the doors after them with irreverent bang. But grandfather is decorous, well mannered, early in his seat; if jostled, he jostles not again; elbowed, he returns it not; crowded, he thinks no evil. He is gentlemanly to the rude, obliging to the insolent and vulgar; for grandfather is a gentleman; not puffed up with mere money, but edified with well-grown manliness. Time has dignified his good manners.

It is night. The family are all abed. Grandfather sits by his old-fashioned fire. He draws his old-fashioned chair nearer to the hearth. On the stand which his mother gave him are the candlesticks, also of old time. The candles are three quarters burnt down; the fire on the hearth also is low. He has been thoughtful all day, talking half to himself, chanting a bit of verse, humming a snatch of an old tune. He kissed his pet granddaughters more tenderly than common, before she went to bed. He takes out of his bosom a little locket; nobody ever sees it. Therein are two little twists of hair. As Grandfather looks at them, the outer twist of hair becomes a whole head of ambrosial curls. He remembers stolen interviews, meetings by moonlight. He remembers how sweet the evening star looked, and how he laid his hand on another's shoulder, and said, "*You* are my evening star."

The church-clock strikes the midnight hour. He looks in his locket again. The other twist is the hair of his first-born son. At this same hour of midnight, once, many years ago, he knelt and prayed, when the long agony was over—"My God, I thank thee that, though I am a father, I am still a husband, too! What am I, that unto me a life should be given and another spared!" Now he has children, and children's children, the joy of his old age. But for many a year his wife has looked to him from beyond the evening star. She is still the evening star herself, yet more beautiful; a star that never sets; not mortal wife now, but angel.

The last stick on his andirons snaps asunder, and falls outward. Two faintly-smoking brands stand there. Grandfather lays them together, and they flame up; the two smokes are united in one flame. "Even so let it be in heaven," says Grandfather.

INTERPRETATION OF SCRIPTURE.

Put the matter thus. For more than a thousand years the Bible, collectively taken, has gone hand in hand with civilization, science, law—in short, with the moral and intellectual cultivation of the species, always supporting, and often leading the way. Its very presence, as a believed Book, has rendered the nations emphatically a chosen race, and this too in exact proportion as it is more or less generally known and studied. Of those nations, which in the highest degree enjoy its influences, it is not too much to affirm, that the differences public and private, physical, moral and intellectual, are only less than what might be expected from a diversity in species. Good and holy men, and the best and wisest of mankind, the kingly spirits of history, enthroned in the hearts of mighty nations, have borne witness to its influences, have declared it to be beyond compare the most perfect instrument, the only adequate organ of Humanity;—the organ and instrument of all the gifts, powers, and tendencies, by which the individual is privileged to rise above himself—to leave behind, and lose his dividual phantom self, in order to find his true Self in that Distinctness where no division can be—in the Eternal I Am, the Ever-living Word, of whom all the elect, from the archangel before the throne to the poor wrestler with the Spirit *until the breaking of day*, are but the fainter and still fainter echoes. And are all these testimonies and lights of experience to lose their value and efficiency, because I feel no warrant of history, or Holy Writ, or of my own heart for denying, that in the framework and outward case of this instrument a few parts may be discovered of less costly materials and of meaner workmanship? Is it not a fact that the Books of the New Testament were tried by their consonance with the rule, and according to the analogy of Faith? Does not the universally admitted canon—that each part of Scripture must be interpreted by the spirit of the whole—lead to the same practical conclusion as that for which I am now contending;—namely, that it is the spirit of the Bible, and not the detached words and sentences, that is infallible and absolute? Practical, I say, and spiritual too;—and what knowledge not practical or spiritual are we entitled to seek in our Bibles? Is the grace of God so confined—are the evidences of the present and actuating Spirit so dim and doubtful—that to be assured of the same we must first take for granted that all the life and co-agency of our humanity is miraculously suspended?

Whatever is spiritual, is *eo nomine* supernatural; but must it be always and of necessity miraculous? Miracles could open the eyes of the body; and he that was born blind beheld his Redeemer. But miracles, even those of the Redeemer himself, could not open the eyes of the self-blinded, of the Sadducean sensualist, or the self-righteous Pharisee;—while to have said, I *saw thee under the fig tree,* sufficed to make a Nathanael believe.—*S. T. Coleridge.*

WOMEN AND CHARITY WORK.

We cannot look around us without seeing that a demand has not only been created, but becomes every day increasingly urgent, for a supply of working women at once more efficient and more effective. I use the words advisedly as distinct in meaning; women and men too are *efficient* through energy and experience, and *effective* through higher gifts and sympathies—higher aims and motives; *materially* efficient, *morally* effective. Meantime, with no want of zeal or aptitude, there is such a lamentable deficiency in training, in knowledge, in the means or opportunity of acquiring either, that I should despair—if I were not too old to despair—if I had not so often counted up the price we have to pay for truth, and the penance we must pay for falsehood too. If, among the hapless women I see struggling to bring their external existence into harmony with their inner life—or what is harder still, to bring their inner life into subjection to harsh and deteriorating circumstance—one half should go distracted, and the other half turn Roman Catholics, I might "even die with pity;" but certainly not yield up one inch of the ground I have taken, nor one iota of the faith that is in me.

I remember that, when speaking on these subjects to a very benevolent and accomplished man—a clergyman—he said, thoughtfully: "I have little doubt that you are right; and yet, if there be such a Divine law involving all human well-being and progress in its recognition, how is it that it has not been more distinctly revealed to us? how is it that it comes to us now like a novelty to be subjected to the examination of the sceptical and the carping of the foolish?"

I did not answer.

We know that there has existed from the commencement of the creation a law of God, binding the whole universe into one harmonious whole, guiding the planets in their orbits, connecting our own world with far-off worlds of light and life, and at the same time so regulating our least movements on this earth, that we cannot put one foot before the other, but in subjection to it. Yet of the existence of this law we knew nothing, till, one hundred and fifty years ago, the fall of an apple revealed it to Newton; and to what revelations most important to our well-being has it not since led! And may there not be a law of moral and physical life as universal, as essential, as eternal, which in its agency has always been felt, and yet in its relation to happiness and progress, is only just beginning to be understood, and not yet fully applied? I do not say it *is* so; but may it not possibly be so?—*Mrs. Jameson.*

DIFFICULTY THE CONDITION OF LITERARY SUCCESS.

It is a vulgar error that Literature is incompatible with less intellectual pursuits. "Prior," writes Swift in his Journal to Stella, "hates his Commission of the Customs because it spoils his wit. He says he dreams of nothing but cockets, and dockets, and drawbacks, and other jargon words of the Custom-House." This is affectation. Prior's was an easy and and gentleman-like employment, with a very liberal remuneration. What a contrast to the ill-paid drudgery that broke the heart of Burns! "Let poetry be your staff, not your crutch," said Sir Walter Scott. As the sole means of providing for the day that is passing, Literature is indeed a painful calling! its success depending more on public caprice than desert; the popular idol being too often as worthless as he is ephemeral. Literature, without the healthful excitement of active employment, produces bodily lassitude and mental depression. Was Cowley contented at his classic retirement at Chertsey? Was Shenston happy at his lovely Leasowes? Coleridge regretted that he had no pursuit but poetry and philosophy. The bustle of the world (not its turmoil and selfishness!) braces the mind after an interval of study, as the quiet of the closet strengthens it for renewed exertion. However men may *effect* to hold cheap the intellectual world, it is *there* only that the truly noble can enjoy communion with kindred spirits. But this high privilege demands some grosser sacrifices. To postpone a sensual pleasure is the first step toward its abandonment. We sow resignation, and we reap content. Difficulty is the condition of success. We must learn "to scorn delights, and live laborous days."—*Democritus in London.*

OBLIGATION OF PARENTS TO EDUCATE THEIR CHILDREN.

I HAVE already observed that, owing to the absence of any recognized general principles, liberty is often granted where it should be withheld, as well as withheld where it should be granted; and one of the cases in which, in the modern European world, the sentiment of liberty is the strongest, is a case where, in my view, it is altogether misplaced. A person should be free to do as he likes in his own concerns; but he ought not to be free to do as he likes in acting for another under the pretext that the affairs of another are his own affairs. The State, while it respects the liberty of each in what specially regards himself, is bound to maintain a vigilant control over his exercise of any power which it allows him to possess over others. This obligation is almost entirely disregarded in the case of the family relations, a case, in its direct influence on human happiness, more important than all others taken together. The almost despotic power of husbands over wives needs not to be enlarged upon here, because nothing more is needed for the complete removal of the evil, than that wives should have the same rights, and should receive the protection of law in the same manner, as all other persons; and because, on this subject, the defenders of established injustice do not avail themselves of the plea of liberty, but stand forth openly as the champions of power. It is in the case of children, that misapplied notions of liberty are a real obstacle to the fulfilment by the State of its duties. One would almost think that a man's children were supposed to be literally, and not metaphorically, a part of himself, so jealous is opinion of the smallest interference of law with his absolute and exclusive control over them; more jealous than of almost any interference with his own freedom of action: so much less do the generality of mankind value liberty than power. Consider, for example, the case of education. Is it not almost a self-evident axiom, that the State should require and compel the education, up to a certain standard, of every human being who is born its citizen? Yet who is there that is not afraid to recognize and assert this truth? Hardly any one, indeed, will deny that it is one of the most sacred duties of the parents (or, as law and usage now stand, the father), after summoning a human being into the world, to give to that being an education fitting him to perform his part well in life, towards others and towards himself. But while this is unanimously declared to be the father's duty, scarcely anybody, in this country, will bear to hear of obliging him to perform it. Instead of his being required to make any exertion or sacrifice for securing education to the child, it is left to his choice to accept it or not when it is provided gratis!

It still remains unrecognized, that to bring a child into existence without a fair prospect of being able, not only to provide food for its body, but instruction and training for its mind, is a moral crime, both against the unfortunate offspring and against society; and that if the parent does not fulfil this obligation, the State ought to see it fulfilled at the charge, as far as possible, of the parent.—*John Stewart Mill.*

UNNATURAL PUNISHMENT OF CHILDREN.

In the first place, observe that, in states of rapid transition like ours, which witness a long-drawn battle between old and new theories and old and new practices, the educational methods in use are apt to be considerably out of harmony with the times. In deference to dogmas fit only for the ages that uttered them, many parents inflict punishments that do violence to their own feelings, and so visit on their children *un*natural reactions; while other parents, enthusiastic in their hopes of immediate perfection, rush to the opposite extreme. And then observe, in the second place, that the discipline on which we are insisting is not so much the experience of parental approbation or disapprobation, which, in most cases, is only a secondary consequence of a child's conduct; but it is the experience of those results which would naturally flow from the conduct in the absence of parental opinion or interference. The truly instructive and salutary consequences are not those inflicted by parents when they take upon themselves to be Nature's proxies; but they are those inflicted by Nature herself. We will endeavor to make this distinction clear by a few illustrations, which, while they show what we mean by natural reactions as contrasted with artificial ones, will afford some directly practical suggestions.

In every family where there are young children there almost daily occur cases of what mothers and servants call "making a litter." A child has had out its box of toys, and leaves them scattered about the floor. Or a handful of flowers, brought in from a morning walk, is presently seen dispersed over tables and chairs. Or a little girl, making doll's-clothes, disfigures the room with shreds. In most cases the trouble of rectifying this disorder falls anywhere but in the right place: if in the nursery, the nurse herself, with many grumblings about "tiresome little things," etc., undertakes the task; if below stairs, the task usually devolves either on one of the elder children or on the housemaid; the transgressor being visited with nothing more than a scolding. In this very simple case, however, there are many parents wise enough to follow out, more or less consistently, the normal course—that of making the child itself collect the toys or shreds. The labor of putting the things in order is the true consequence of having put them in disorder. Every trader in his office, every wife in her household, has daily experience of this fact. And if education be a preparation for the business of life, then every child should also, from the beginning, have daily experience of this fact. If the natural penalty be met by any refractory behavior (which it may perhaps be where the general system of moral discipline previously pursued has been bad), then the proper course is to let the child feel the ulterior reaction consequent on its disobedience. Having refused or neglected to pick up and put away the things it has scattered about, and having thereby entailed the trouble of doing this on some one else, the child should, on subsequent occasions, be denied the means of giving this trouble. When next it petitions for its toy-box, the reply of its mamma should be—"The last time you had your toys you left them lying on the floor, and Jane had to pick them up. Jane is too busy to pick up every day the things you leave about; and I cannot do it myself. So that, as you will not put away your toys when you have done with them, I cannot let you have them." This is obviously a natural consequence, neither increased nor lessened; and must be so recognized by a child. The penalty comes, too, at the moment when it is most keenly felt. A new-born desire is balked at the moment of anticipated gratification; and the strong impression so produced can scarcely fail to have an effect on the future conduct: an effect which, by consistent repetition, will do whatever can be done in curing the fault. Add to which, that, by this method, a child is early taught the lesson which cannot be learnt too soon, that in this world of ours pleasures are rightly to be obtained only by labor.

Take another case. Not long since we had frequently to listen to the reprimands visited on a little girl who was scarcely ever ready in time for the daily walk. Of eager disposition, and apt to become thoroughly absorbed in the occupation of the moment, Constance never thought of putting on her things until the rest were ready. The governess and the other children had almost invariably to wait; and from the mamma there almost invariably came the same scolding. Utterly as this system failed it never occurred to the mamma to let Constance experience the natural penalty. Nor, indeed, would she try it when it was suggested to her. In the world the penalty of being behind time is the loss of some advantage that would else have been gained: the train is gone; or the steamboat is just leaving its moorings; or the best things in the market are sold; or all the good seats in the concert-room are filled. And every one, in cases perpetually occurring, may see that it is the prospective deprivations entailed bv being too late which prevent people from being too late. Is not the inference obvious? Should not these prospective deprivations control the child's conduct also? If Constance is not ready at the appointed time, the natural result is that of being left behind, and losing her walk. And no one can, we think, doubt that after having once or twice remained at home while the rest were enjoying themselves in the fields, and after having felt that this loss of a much-prized gratification was solely due to want of promptitude, some amendment would take place. At any rate, the measure would be more effective than that perpetual scolding which ends only in producing callousness.

Again, when children, with more than usual carelessness, break or lose the things given to them, the natural penalty—the penalty which makes grown-up persons more careful—is the consequent inconvenience. The want of the lost or damaged article, and the cost of supplying its place, are the experiences by which men and women are disciplined in these matters; and the experience of children should be as much as possible assimilated to theirs. We do not refer to that early period at which toys are pulled to pieces in the process of learning their physical properties, and at which the results of carelessness cannot be understood; but to a later period, when the meaning and advantages of property are perceived. When a boy, old enough to possess a penknife, uses it so roughly as to snap the blade, or leaves it in the grass by some hedge-side, where he was cutting a stick, a thoughtless parent, or some indulgent relative, will commonly forthwith buy him another; not seeing that, by doing this, a valuable lesson is lost. In such a case, a father may properly explain that penknives cost money, and that to get money requires labor; that he cannot afford to purchase new penknives for one who loses or breaks them; and that until he sees evidence of greater carefulness he must decline to make good the loss. A parallel discipline may be used as a means of checking extravagance.

These few familiar instances, here chosen because of the simplicity with which they illustrate our point, will make clear to every one the distinction between those natural penalties which we contend are the truly efficient ones, and those artificial penalties which parents commonly substitute for them.—*Herbert Spencer.*

WORK AND PLAY.

Let us go directly to nature for our first lesson in the meaning and mission of work and play. The boy is born into the world a delicate organism—a soft bundle of brains and nerves, and bones and muscles, and vessels and limbs, without will, and without the power of self-support and self-direction. The first months of his life are passed in a kind of unconscious consciousness, and nothing higher is expected of him than that he pull the whiskers of his father, and smile appreciatingly when his mother talks nonsense to him. Soon he begins to grasp, or to reach after, the things he sees—a pearl-button, a coffee-pot, a chandelier, or a church-steeple; and we feel that great progress has been made when he can shake his rattle-box three times and repeat, even if the performance be slightly spasmodic and irregular. The months pass away, and he stands upon his feet; and after a brief and delightful tutelage, he waddles about wherever his impulses lead him. He takes trips of ten feet upon his father's cane, which not unfrequently proves refractory and throws him. He frolics with the kittens, or hugs them to death. He builds block-houses, and knocks them down. He excavates convenient sand-banks. He delights, above all things, in the open air, and runs because he loves to run; but whether within doors or without, he is always in mischief. From morning to night his little muscles are in motion; and when compelled, at last, to go to bed, he relinquishes his play with tears. Year by year, as he grows up through boyhood, the range of his play is widened. He drives other boys four-in-hand, or plays at ball, or slides down hill, or runs races, or wrestles, or goes hunting and fishing.

Now, what makes this boy play? And what does this play do for him?

He plays because he cannot help it—because in the central, motive forces of his nature God has written the command to play. He has no end beyond the gratification of his momentary and shifting impulses. He plays because the life within him exults in action, and delights in expenditure. Tired in one direction of amusing or pleasant effort, he turns toward another; and thus, one by one, or group by group, he calls into activity all the faculties of his mind and all the functions of his body. He has no object, I repeat, in this constant action and constant change; but God has. This play is for the symmetrical development of the boy, of all the powers of which he is the possessor; and no boy without play was ever well-developed, or ever can be. A boy who does not play, and does not love to play, is not a healthy boy, mentally, morally, or physically, no matter how many precious hymns he can repeat, nor how well he can say his catechism. Play is the Creator's ordained means for the development of the child. I am aware that it drives weak-headed mothers crazy, and aggravates the aggregate of the shoe-bill, and makes terrific work with trousers; but it makes men, and, as a general rule, the boy that plays the best, makes the best man.

There is a sad amount of fighting against Heaven in the attempts made by irritable and impatient parents to repress the playful manifestations of their children. Carefully and reverently I declare that God impels, nay, compels, the child to play, and that those who strive to crush the spirit of play in children for the security of their own ease and comfort, or from mistaken notions of the nature and the mission of play, oppose Him as really as when they set themselves against any movement or policy in His moral universe.

Play is a sacred thing, a divine ordinance, for developing in the child a harmonious and healthy organism, and preparing that organism for the commencement of the work of life. I insist upon this. I insist that play is not only an innocent thing in itself, but that it is an essential portion of the divinely appointed means for the development of the race into its highest earthly estate.—*J. G. Holland.*

TEMPTATIONS OF THE INTELLECTUAL.

Every gift of God has its own special temptations, and intellect has temptations, more like those of Satan than of mankind. Others forget God, ignore God, steal away from Him, rob Him of their hearts, and give them to the world. But they do not come face to face with Him. The temptation of intellect is to measure itself against God, to criticise God, to dispute His Being, to dethrone Him in His creation, to set up His laws against Himself, to question His Providence, to doubt his Wisdom, to pull to pieces His revelation, to mend it for Him, to make conditions with Him, on what terms it will acknowledge Him, to require Him to abdicate His absolute sovereignty, to set up an idol in His room; to re-create their Creator, instead of being "re-created by Him in Christ Jesus." And yet withal they often mean, poor things, nothing less. They have got loose from the old beliefs in God; they have lost all knowledge of things supernatural, nay, even of their own eternal existence. Yet some of them have gifts, which might be used to the great glory of God, if they would but cease to measure by their own created Intelligence the Mind of the Uncreated, which conceived their's, and of which their's is a little spark. These, and especially at the Universities, where intellect has often not yet taken its side,—either to be willingly beneath God or to be against Him,—would be a special subject of prayer, that they might find their wisdom in the Uncreated Wisdom and their knowledge from the Omniscient.—*Dr. Pusey.*

ANGELS OF THE HOUSE.

I know a man. He is not a Christian, His daily life is not in accordance with even principles of morality. He has three beautiful, well-behaved children. The other day he told me this incident of one of them, his little girl, three or four years old.

Said he—" Perhaps some people would think it sacrilege, but I don't; but for some time back I have been in the habit of reading the Bible and of having prayers every night before the children go to bed. I have done it because it has a good influence on the children, and because I hope it may have a good influence on myself. Last night I went to 'Lodge' (he is a Mason), and did not get home till after 11 o'clock. The children, of course, were all abed, and I supposed asleep. Before going to bed I knelt down by my bed to pray, and had been there but a moment when I heard Nobie get up from her bed in the next room, and her little feet came pattering across the floor toward me. I kept perfectly still, and she came and knelt down beside me without saying a word. I did not notice her, and in a moment, speaking just above her breath, she said, '*Pa, pray 'oud.*' I prayed. I kissed her, and she went back to bed; and I tell you, G—, I have had nothing affect me so for the last ten years. I have thought of nothing else all day long but just that little—'*Pa, pray 'oud,*' "—*Dr. Haven.*

WORK AND ACHIEVEMENT

It is in achievement that work throws off all its repulsive features, and assumes the form and functions of an angel. Before her, like a dissolving scene, the forest fades, with its wild beasts and its wild men, and under her hand smiling villages rise among the hills and on the plains, and yellow harvests spread the fields with gold. The city, with its docks and warehouses, and churches and palaces, springs at her bidding into being. The trackless ocean mirrors her tireless pinions as she ransacks the climes for the food of commerce, or flames with the torches of her steamsped messengers. She binds states and marts and capitals together with bars of iron, that thunder with the ceaseless rush of life and trade. She pictures all scenes of beauty on canvas, and carves all forms of excellence in marble. Into huge libraries she pours the wealth of countless precious lives She erects beautiful and convenient homes for men and women to dwell in, and weaves the fibres which nature prepares into fabrics for their covering and comfort. She rears great civilizations that run like mountain-ranges through the level centuries, their summits sleeping among the clouds, or still flaming with the fire that fills them, or looming grandly in the purple haze of history. Nature furnishes material, and work fashions it. By the hand of art, work selects, and moulds, and modifies, and re-combines that which it finds, and gives utterance and being to those compositions of matter and of thought which build for man a new world, with special adaptation to his desires, tastes, and necessities. Man's record upon this wild world is the record of work, and of work alone.

Work explores the secrets of the universe, and brings back those contributions which make up the sum of human knowledge. It counts the ribs of the mountains and feels the pulses of the sea, and traces the foot-paths of the stars, and calls the animals of the forest and the birds of the air and the flowers of the field by name. It summons horses of fire and chariots of fire from heaven, and makes them the bearers of its thought. It plunders the tombs of dead nationalities, and weaves living histories from the shreds it finds. It seeks out and sets in order the secrets of the soil, and divides to every plant its food. It builds and binds into unity great philosophies, along which run the life and thought of ages. It embalms the life of nations in literatures, in whose crypts are scattered seeds of thought that only need the light to spread into harvests of bread for living generations.

How wonderful a being is man, when viewed in the light of his achievements! It is in the record of these that we find the evidence of his power and the credentials of his glory. Into the results of work each generation pours its life; and as these results grow in excellence, with broader forms and richer tints and nobler meanings, they become the indexes of the world's progress. We estimate the life of a generation by what it does; and the results of its work stand out in advance of its successor, to show it what it can do, and to show it what it must do, to reach a finer consummation. Thus the results of work become the most powerful stimulus of the worker. They inspire emulation; they instruct in mode and style; they feed perennially the springs of ambition.—*J. G. Holland.*

CLEANLINESS RECOMMENDED.

Cleanliness may be recommended under the three following heads: as it is a mark of politeness; as it produces affection; and as it bears analogy to purity of mind.

First. It is a mark of *politeness;* for it is universally agreed upon, that no one unadorned with this virtue can go into company without giving a manifest offence. The different nations of the world are as much distinguished by their cleanliness, as by their arts and sciences. The more advanced in civilization, the more they consult this part of politeness.

Secondly. Cleanliness may be said to be the foster-mother of *affection*. Beauty commonly produces love, but cleanliness preserves it. Age itself is not unamiable while it is preserved clean, and unsullied; like a piece of metal constantly kept smooth and bright, we look on it with more pleasure than on a new vessel that is cankered with rest.

I might further observe, that as cleanliness renders us agreeable to others, so it makes us easy to ourselves; that it is an excellent preservative of health; and that several vices destructive both to body and mind, are inconsistent with the habit of it.

In the third place, it bears a great analogy with *purity of mind*, and naturally inspires refined sentiments and passions. We find from experience, that through the prevalence of custom the most vicious actions lose their horror, by being made familiar to us. On the contrary, those who live in the neighborhood of good examples, fly from the first appearance of what is shocking; and thus pure and unsullied thoughts are naturally suggested to the mind by those objects that perpetually encompass us, when they are beautiful and elegant in their kind.

In the East, where the warmth of the climate makes cleanliness more immediately necessary than in colder countries, it is a part of religion; the Jewish law (as well as the Mahometan, which in some things copies after it) is filled with bathings, purifications, and other rites of the like nature; and we read several injunctions of this kind in the book of Deuteronomy.—*Addison.*

INDEX.

K

L

M

N

O

P

INDEX OF AUTHORS.

www.ingramcontent.com/pod-product-compliance
Lightning Source LLC
LaVergne TN
LVHW021106110826
845150LV00001B/188

* 9 7 8 1 4 2 5 5 6 4 9 3 3 *